WHAT OTHERS ARE SAYING ABOUT NANDA LWIN AND TOP 40 HITS: THE ESSENTIAL CHART GUIDE

If you want to be on top of the music, *Top 40 Hits: The Essential Chart Guide* is the bible. It's chock full of fascinating facts.

Rob Christie
Host of *The Canadian Hot 20*
Morning personality, Mix 99.9 Toronto

Nanda Lwin's books are essential to anyone looking for chart information. From Anne Murray to the Beastie Boys, Nanda's books have it all.

Doug Spence
General Manager,
SoundScan/BDS
Entertainment Information Group

Thousands of CANOE readers read Nanda Lwin's Chart Talk column every week for its in-depth analysis and context. I have Nanda's books on my shelf. They're an invaluable research tool.

John Sakamoto
Executive Producer
Jam! Showbiz
www.canoe.ca

Every Monday morning one of the first things I do is go on-line and read Nanda Lwin's Chart Talk column. As Director of Publicity and Artist Relations for BMG Music Canada I am always being asked about chart numbers and records and I find most of my information on Chart Talk. *Top 40 Hits: The Essential Chart Guide* will serve as a daily reference guide.

Cameron Carpenter
Director, Publicity & Artist Relations
BMG Music Canada

Other books by Nanda Lwin:

The Record 1994 Chart Almanac

The Canadian Singles Chart Book

Canada's Top Hits of the Year

Canada's Top 1000 Singles

The 1996 Country Chart Yearbook

Nanda Lwin's ChartTalk column:

www.canoe.ca/JamMusicCharts/home.html

Top 40 Hits
The Essential Chart Guide

Nanda Lwin

Dedicated to my parents for their love and support.

Copyright © 2000 by Nanda Lwin
The Record chart data used and contained in this work is copyright © 1983-1999 by *The Record*. All BDS charts are copyright © 1997-1999 by Broadcast Data Systems. The SoundScan chart data used and contained in this work is copyright © 1996-1999 by SoundScan Inc.

All rights reserved.
No part of this publication may be reproduced, stored in a retrieval system, or transmitted, in any form or by any means, electronic, mechanical, photocopying, recording, or otherwise, without the prior written permission of the author.

Canadian Cataloguing in Publication Data

Lwin, Nanda, 1971-
   Top 40 Hits: The Essential Chart Guide

ISBN 1-896594-13-1

1. Popular music - Discography. 2. Popular music - Canada - Discography.
I. Title. II. Title: Top forty hits.

ML156.4.P6L98 1999   016.78164'0266   C99-931166-2

Warning!
This publication is designed to provide accurate and authoritative information on the subject matter presented. Every attempt has been made to eliminate errors. However, the author and publisher expressly disclaim any responsibility for any liability, loss, or risk, personal or otherwise, which is incurred as a consequence, directly or indirectly, of the use and application of any of the contents of this book.

Edited by Catherine Lipa
Cover design by Patricia Heeney
Printed and bound in Canada by AGMV Marquis

Music Data Canada
P.O. Box 52626
Turtle Creek Postal Station
Mississauga, Ontario
L5J 4S6

TABLE OF CONTENTS

About The Author 6

Introduction 7

The Charts 11

Synopsis of the Charts 13

THE ARTISTS 15
An alphabetical listing, by artist, of every record that hit the
national singles chart from 1975 to the present.

THE HITS 313
An alphabetical listing, by song title, of every record that hit the
national singles chart from 1975 to the present.

FACTS & FIGURES 365
A collection of chart achievements and records.
    Top 100 Singles 366
    Singles With Most Weeks In The Top 40 368
    Top 100 Artists 369
    Artist Achievements 370
        Most Weeks At Number One 370
        Most Discs At Number One 370
        Top Artists Without A #1 Single 370
        Top Groups And Duos 370
        Most Weeks In The Top 40 371
        Most Top 40 Hits 371
    The Number One Singles 372

ABOUT THE AUTHOR

Nanda Lwin is an author, journalist, entrepreneur, and engineer. He was born in 1971 in London, Ontario the same week "Sweet Hitch Hiker" by Creedence Clearwater Revival was number one.

His interest in music charts began at the age of twelve when he first listened to a top 40 countdown show on the radio. An avid chart hobbyist, Lwin continues to keep tabs on the national listings of countries around the world and has developed a large library of music charts. Over the years, his knowledge of the charts has been used in articles in both *The Record* and *Billboard*.

In 1995, Lwin turned his hobby into a business by founding Music Data Canada, a company dedicated to researching and publishing chart data. He is the author of six books on charted music including *The Canadian Singles Chart Book*, *Canada's Top Hits of the Year*, and *Canada's Top 1000 Singles*, and is a contributor to the Canadian edition of *Top 10 of Everything*, published by Reader's Digest. He is also the weekly ChartTalk columnist on the CANOE website.

In his leisure time, Lwin likes to cycle, read, and play the piano.

A graduate of the Civil Engineering program at the University of Toronto in 1993, Lwin has held positions as a Structural Engineer and a Transportation Engineer.

INTRODUCTION

Somewhere in the corner of my mind I have vague recollections watching the television show *America's Top 10* in the early-1980's. I watched host Casey Kasem rhyme off the top 10 of the week on the pop, R&B, country, and album charts. I was in my pre-teens at the time and didn't have a devoted interest in popular music so the show didn't really capture my interest. However, it was probably the first time I was aware that a ranking system of the most popular songs existed.

It was a few weeks after my twelfth birthday that my longtime chart passion really began. On the evening of September 25, 1983 I tuned into radio station CKOC in nearby Hamilton for the radio countdown program *American Top 40* for the first time. Little did I realize and appreciate at the time the impact that evening and *AT40* would have on my career and my life. What started as a few casual listens soon blossomed into a serious hobby and a Sunday evening tradition. The thought of listening and keeping a continuous record of the top records each week appealed to me instantly.

However, one of my most important chart discoveries didn't stem from listening to the radio but from shopping. During a shopping trip in downtown Toronto in October 1984, I finally had a chance to buy and to read *The Record*. It was a much different publication from what it is now: an industry tipsheet with 50 or so pages stapled in the left-hand corner. Of course, there was the usual round of charts and industry news but what caught my eye was the retail singles chart near the back of the magazine. "I Just Called To Say I Love You" by Stevie Wonder had just gone to number one, a position it went on to hold for eleven weeks straight.

It is that chart - *The Record*'s retail singles - which is the source of the data for 13 of the 24 years covered in this book. Because of a slump in single sales in the mid-1990's, the trade publication finally abandonned its singles chart in March 1996 in favour of the "Hit Parade" listing. Unlike its predecessor, it was based entirely on radio airplay on stations playing Top 40, Adult Contemporary, and Rock music. Nevertheless, "Hit Parade's" reign as the nation's "official" chart was short-lived and by the end of 1996, the national charts were ushered into the computer age with the emergence of new tallying technologies.

SoundScan, the retail music research firm that provides data for the U.S. trade magazine, *Billboard*, started its operations in Canada in 1996. The SoundScan method of using barcode scanning technology to measure record sales revolutionized the way the charts were compiled. Whereas *The Record*'s in-house chart department used rough estimates from the stores, the SoundScan charts were now compiled using scientific methods giving more precise figures than ever before. Seemingly overnight, the charts became a science and uprooted the "human" element which had become commonplace in the compilation of charts.

The radio airplay charts were also revamped. In April 1995, Broadcast Data Systems (BDS) started to monitor radio stations across the country. The monitoring system, which is also used to compile the *Billboard* airplay charts in the U.S., counts the actual number of times a record is played on the radio. This is accomplished by using computer tracking technology which listens to the stations in a market 24 hours a day, seven days a week.

Over the past decade or so, changes have occured not only in chart compilation methodologies but also in the business practices of the music industry. Before the 1990's, it was taken for granted that any song on the radio could be purchased as a single in the local music store. Today that fundamental truth is no longer valid. Instead, many hit songs are available exclusively as album tracks.

As a result, many hit songs in the 1990's failed to hit the upper reaches of the singles chart if the songs charted at all. To make sure these non-singles are represented, peak positions on *The Record*'s Contemporary Hit Radio chart starting in January 1990 appear in this book alongside their retail counterparts.

Writing *Top 40 Hits: The Essential Chart Guide* was truly a labour of love for me. However, it was the people I worked with that made this book even more special for me.

There were many individuals in the music business from whom I benefitted when I first set out to research and write this book. Thanks especially to Doug Spence of SoundScan who is one of the most generous, supportive, and helpful people I have ever met in the music business. His advice to target the average music fan instead of primarily focusing on the recording and radio industries resulted in the publication of this book. Paul Tuch of Broadcast Data Systems (BDS) deserves a special mention for sending me the advance copies of the charts almost every week for the past ten years or so. He took on this task not only in his current capacity at BDS but also in his previous position as *The Record*'s chart editor. The charts have changed over the past decade as have the technological means by which Paul sent them: at first, it was by phone, then by fax, and currently, by e-mail.

I am always grateful to Derek Steede, former editor of the *Steede Report*, Brian Robertson of the Canadian Recording Industry Association (CRIA), and Barbara Brown of the CBC for the use of the charts of their respective organizations. Because of them I was able to capture chart data for the years leading up to the inception of *The Record* charts.

I'm also indebted to the staff of *The Record*, past and present, who have extended their support. It is because of them the magazine remains a must-read to those with an interest in music, both professionally and personally. Special thanks go to Pat McSweeney, Marketing & Advertising Manager, for her advice on the publishing business, and David Farrell and Patricia Dunn-Farrell, Publishers of *The Record*, for letting me use the charts in the first place. I am proud and honoured to be associated with one of my all-time favourite magazines.

I also appreciate the authors and journalists who wrote the different reference books available to me: *The Rolling Stone New Encyclopedia Of Rock & Roll*, *Q Encyclopedia of Rock Stars* by Dafydd Rees and Luke Crampton, *MusicHound Rock: The Essential Album Guide* (edited by Gary Graff and Daniel Durchholz), *MusicHound R&B: The Essential Album Guide* (edited by Gary Graff, Josh Freedom du Lac and Jim McFarlin), *The Virgin Encyclopedia of Dance Music* by Colin Larkin, Joel Whitburn's collection of American chart books (especially *Top Pop Singles* and *Rock Tracks*), *The Billboard Book Of Number One Hits* by Fred Bronson, *The Billboard Book Of Number One Adult*

Contemporary Hits by Hyatt Wesley, *Encyclopedia of Canadian Rock, Pop & Folk Music* by Rick Jackson, *Heart of Gold* by Martin Melhuish, *Electro Shock! Groundbreakers of Synth Music* by Greg Rule, and *The Guinness Book Of Number One Hits* by Paul Gambaccini, Tim Rice, and Jonathan Rice.

    Many websites also proved to be crucial in getting the latest information on the newest acts. In writing *Top 40 Hits*, I discovered the incredible depth and breadth of CANOE's online resources (www.canoe.ca), especially its "Canadian Pop Encyclopedia". They were instrumental in the research of this book, as were other websites such as the Internet Movie Database (www.IMDb.com), All Music Guide (www.allmusic.com), the Ultimate Band List (www.ubl.com), Artist Information (www.artistinformation.com). I also turned my queries over to various record company media relations representatives. I extend my appreciation to those reps for providing me with hard-to-find biographical information. Thanks also to Jaimie Vernon, the author of the above-mentioned "Canadian Pop Encyclopedia". Jaimie came to the rescue during the final stages of this book with badly-needed information on Canadian acts.

    My team of legal experts explained the intricacies of contracts and were available whenever I needed an expert opinion. Thanks to my attorney Michael Garvey, who currently advises me in legal matters, and my former lawyer Brian Madigan, who recently left the profession to pursue other endeavours. Brian served me well for the past few years and his valuable advice will be sorely missed. Kudos also to my brother Teza Lwin whose law degree and legal knowledge proved to be useful in this project.

    The support and love of friends and family is always comforting when taking on life's ventures and challenges. Besides my aforementioned brother, a message of gratitude goes out to my parents, Sann and Avelina Lwin for being a constant source of love and support. There were also friends of mine who know little about music but gave me their encouragement. Thanks to Elizabeth Gonzalez, a friend from engineering school, and Cheryl Barton, one of my best friends from high school, for their e-mail messages which inadvertently gave me a much-needed boost. Simon Galton, a friend of mine for the past 22 years, helped out in technical matters.

    There were also the three "wisewomen" - one relative and two friends of mine - in this project whose guidance and skills made this book a reality. My cousin Aye Nyein San took the photograph that appears at the back of this book. (Thanks also to Meghyn Garner who lent Aye Nyein the proper lighting when she needed it.) Patricia Heeney designed the front and back covers and accompanied me to dinner a few times. When I first met her in Mr. Luxton's Grade 6 class, little did I know that her artistic abilities would one day prove to be beneficial to me, if not essential. Catherine Lipa, whom I met in my final year of high school, edited the front matter by correspondence at the University of Western Ontario in London. It is fitting that Catherine is involved: we both have a deep love of modern music and writing.

    I should also acknowledge my co-workers at Moon-Matz Ltd. and A&M Engineering who provided me with an escape via engineering when things got frustrating. There's no doubt that structural design is one of the farthest removed careers from writing about music.

    One of the greatest jobs I ever had is writing the weekly ChartTalk column on the CANOE website. ChartTalk has allowed me to reach thousands of readers around the globe every week. Thanks to all ChartTalk readers for their insight, questions, and comments. Similar kind words go out to the entire staff of Jam! Showbiz, CANOE's entertainment section, including Richard John, Adrian Bromley, and Sung-Tae Han. A special thanks to John Sakamoto, Jam!'s Executive Producer, who gave me the work in the first place. His vision and direction has made Jam! one of the world's leading entertainment news websites.

Finally, thanks to those who created and brought us the music of the past 24 years. To the thousands of recording artists, producers, composers, and writers, who provided us with a soundtrack to our lives, I salute you.

Nanda Lwin
lwin@canoe.ca
Mississauga, Ontario
August 1999

THE CHARTS

In *Top 40 Hits: The Essential Chart Guide*, the national charts of five different sources over a span of twenty-four years beginning in 1975 were consulted. The charts used in this book are generally the most widely accepted charts in the business and media at the time of their publication.

Steede Report (1975-77): The charts used in this book from 1975 to 1977 are from the *Steede Report*, which was published from 1975 to 1979. A radio business magazine, the *Steede Report* featured industry news and airplay charts. The magazine's main pop singles chart configured from Contemporary Hit Radio station playlists was used in writing this book.

CRIA (1977-80): The Canadian Recording Industry Association (CRIA) top fifty singles is the source for the charts from 1977 to 1980. The chart was based on retail sales information and was published in music trade magazines. Originally a biweekly service of the CRIA, it became a weekly chart in 1980, shortly before its demise.

CBC (1980-83): The Canadian Broadcasting Corporation (CBC) singles chart was compiled for the CBC Radio program *90 Minutes With A Bullet* (later renamed *60 Minutes With A Bullet*) from 1976 to 1981. From 1981 to 1983, the CBC's "Beaver Bin" chart service prepared the chart. The CBC charts published in *Billboard* from 1980 to 1983 were used in this book.

The Record (1983-present): From 1983 to present, various singles charts of *The Record* were used. Based on sales reports from a national sample of retailers and rack jobbers, the retail singles chart began in 1983 and was quoted in various media sources. It was discontinued on April 1, 1996.

Hit Parade, the chart that replaced the retail singles chart, was based on radio airplay on Top 40, Adult Contemporary, and Rock radio stations. Songs were ranked by the total number of plays as provided by radio station personnel. Included in this book are the singles that appeared for at least one week on that chart from April 8 to October 14, 1996. For the sake of completion, complete Hit Parade chart data is included even if a record appeared on that chart before or after that time period. "Hit Parade" was discontinued in January 1997.

From January 1990 to the present, peak positions of each record which charted on *The Record*'s Contemporary Hit Radio chart were also cited. The chart is based on airplay on Top 40 radio. In January 1997, *The Record* started publishing charts from Broadcast Data Systems, the radio tracking firm that electronically monitors radio play via encoded audio "fingerprints".

SoundScan (1996-present): The SoundScan singles chart was used from October 20, 1996 onward. Based solely on sales, the chart is compiled using barcode scanning data gathered from 800 retail outlets across the country. The SoundScan singles chart is published on CANOE and in *Billboard*.

Unpublished charts: Occasionally, a week or two went by without a chart being published (usually this would occur during the Christmas holidays or *The Record*'s annual summer vacation). In these cases, the chart published immediately prior to the vacation period is used for each week a new chart was not published. In two occasions in 1991, a chart was compiled by *The Record* but not published. These two unpublished charts are used in this research.

Multiple charts: Besides *The Record*'s Contemporary Hit Radio list, three charts were consulted for the year 1996: *The Record*'s retail singles, *The Record*'s Hit Parade, and the SoundScan singles chart. If a single hits more than one of these charts, the chart data to the left of the title (peak date, peak position, weeks on the chart) in the "Artists" section is taken from the chart on which it achieved its highest position. Data from the other chart(s) is shown below the title.

Longevity on the charts: When perusing the numbers, one may notice that records which charted between 1994 and 1999 generally stayed on the charts longer than titles from any other period in the history of the charts. This phenomenon can be attributed to the fact that sales were slow and sluggish in this period, and that competition was reduced by an industry which opted not to release a number of hit records in the single configuration. The fact that SoundScan was introduced in the marketplace in this time period also contributed to longer stays on the chart. Since the company produces unprecedentedly accurate charts through point of sale (POS) data, a more precise picture emerges in which singles sell over a long period of time.

Chart errors: From time to time, albums mistakenly entered the SoundScan singles chart due to errors in configuration data provided by the record companies to SoundScan. These albums have been excluded from this book, however, no attempt was made to change the chart numbers of the singles which ranked lower than those albums. For instance, a single ranked at #3 behind an album ranked at #2 would still be considered to occupy the #3 spot.

Multiple versions: SoundScan chart policy states that different versions (CD, maxi-CD, import) of the same song will chart as separate entries. If a song hits the chart with more than one version, the chart data to the left of the title (peak date, peak position, weeks on the chart) in the "Artists" section is taken from the version which ranked the highest on the chart. Data from the other version(s) is shown below the title.

SYNOPSIS OF THE SINGLES CHART

June 14, 1975
Steede Report begins compiling the "Top 20", a chart based on Contemporary Hit Radio airplay. "Most Played records on Canadian Radio Stations this week according to the SR Research Department."

August 9, 1975
Steede Report begins publishing a top 30 chart.

March 13, 1976
Steede Report begins publishing a top 40 chart.

March 19, 1977
Steede Report "Top 40 Airplay National Chart" becomes a biweekly listing.

May 28, 1977
"Top 40 Airplay National Chart" becomes "The Top 40 National Singles" based "exclusively on airplay charts from reporting stations and not necessarily meant as a sales indicator". The chart is suspended for the following two weeks.

June 18, 1977
Steede Report "Top 40 National Singles" resumes as a weekly chart.

August 24, 1977
The first **Canadian Recording Industry Association (CRIA)** "National Best Selling Record Chart" used in this research. The biweekly chart is "compiled from sales reports supplied by selected retailers across Canada" and audited by an accounting firm.

April 23, 1980
The **CRIA** chart becomes a weekly listing.

July 23, 1980
The **CRIA** discontinues compilation and publication of its chart due to financial constraints.

September 13, 1980
The first **Canadian Broadcasting Corporation (CBC)** chart used in this research. The chart is based on a combination of sales and airplay and is featured on the radio show *90 Minutes With A Bullet*.

April 25, 1981
The **CBC** discontinues *90 Minutes With A Bullet*. The **CBC** "Beaver Bin" chart is used. The chart is discontinued in April 1983.

January 17, 1983
The Record begins publishing a top 30 singles sales chart. The issue date is actually January 10, 1983, but the charts were published for the week ending

January 17, 1983.

October 31, 1983
The Record begins publishing a top 40 singles sales chart "compiled from national rack and retail accounts".

February 11, 1985
The Record begins publishing a top 50 singles sales chart.

January 22, 1990
The Record begins publishing a top 40 singles sales chart.
The first Contemporary Hit Radio airplay chart used in this research; the chart first appeared in ***The Record*** in 1982.

April 8, 1996
The Record discontinues the top 40 singles sales chart. The first Hit Parade chart from ***The Record*** used in this research. The chart is based on radio airplay using precise numbers of plays as supplied by reporting radio stations. The chart is discontinued in January 1997.

October 20, 1996
SoundScan begins compiling a top 200 singles chart. The chart is based on a piece count using point of sale data via barcode scanning.

January 27, 1997
The **Broadcast Data Systems (BDS)** charts debut in ***The Record***. The chart is based on radio airplay using precise numbers of plays as detected by **BDS'** computerized tracking system.

THE ARTISTS
An alphabetical listing, by artist, of every record that hit the national singles chart from 1975 to the present.

HOW TO USE THIS SECTION

The Artists section lists the records that charted in the top 40 on the national singles charts from June 14, 1975 to July 25, 1999 (CANOE publication date of August 2, 1999) and/or *The Record*'s airplay chart from January 22, 1990 to August 9, 1999. The information is presented in alphabetical order by artist. Each artist's singles are listed in chronological order.

Explanation of Headings

DATE: The date the record attained its highest position.
PK: The highest position the record attained on the chart.
WK: The total number of weeks the record charted in the top 40.
LABEL: Record label.
RA: The highest position the record attained on the radio airplay chart (*The Record*'s Contemporary Hit Radio).

Explanation of Symbols

h   The letter "h" indicates the chart data to the left of the title is taken from the airplay-based Hit Parade, as opposed to the retail charts of the day.

(1)   A number in brackets to the right of a number one, number two, or number three peak position indicates the number of weeks the record held its peak position.

+   A plus sign "+" indicates that the single was on the last charts used in this book. A plus sign in the weeks on the chart (WK) column indicates the single was still on the SoundScan singles chart as of July 25, 1999 (CANOE publication date of August 2, 1999). A plus sign in the radio airplay (RA) column indicates the single was still on *The Record*'s Contemporary Hit Radio chart as of August 9, 1999.

RA   The letters "RA" in the WK column indicate that the record hit the radio airplay chart exclusively. A line "---" appears in the peak position (PK) column.

DATE	PK	WK	TITLE	LABEL	RA

A

AALIYAH
American R&B female singer born Aaliyah Haughton on 01/16/79 in Brooklyn, New York. Married R. Kelly on 08/31/94.

DATE	PK	WK	TITLE	LABEL	RA
08/15/94	---	RA	Back And Forth	Jive	25
04/17/95	22	9	Age Ain't Nothin' But A Number	Jive	
11/03/96	40	1	If Your Girl Only Knew	Atlantic	
09/13/98	11	11	Are You That Somebody?	Atlantic	7

AARON, Lee
Canadian female rock singer born Karen Greening in 1962 in Belleville, Ontario. Toronto-based backup band also named Lee Aaron: John Albani (guitar), Greg Doyle (guitar), Kimio Oki (drums), and Chas Rotunda (bass).

DATE	PK	WK	TITLE	LABEL	RA
12/11/89	25	9	Whatcha Do To My Body	Attic	
03/19/90	35	7	Hands On	Attic	37
11/25/91	21	11	Sex With Love	Attic	

ABBA
Swedish disco-pop band formed in 1971 in Sweden: Benny Andersson (keyboards, synthesizer, vocals, b. 12/16/46 in Stockholm, Sweden), Bjorn Ulvaeus (guitar, vocals, b. 04/25/45 in Gothenburg, Sweden), Agnetha "Anna" Faltskog (previously Ulvaeus) (vocals, b. 04/05/50 in Jönköping, Sweden), Anni-Frid "Frida" Synni-Lyngstad-Fredriksson-Andersson (vocals, b. 11/15/45 in Narvik, Norway). Benny and Anni-Frid were married 1978-1981. Bjorn and Agnetha were married 1973-1979. Name "ABBA" is the acronym of the members' first initials. Disbanded in 1982.

DATE	PK	WK	TITLE	LABEL	RA
12/13/75	9	12	S.O.S.	Atlantic	
05/15/76	12	6	I Do I Do I Do I Do	Atlantic	
08/14/76	20	8	Mamma Mia	Atlantic	
11/27/76	2(1)	16	Fernando	Atlantic	
02/26/77	2(5)	21	Dancing Queen	Atlantic	
08/06/77	2(1)	17	Knowing Me, Knowing You	Atlantic	
04/19/78	15	10	Name Of The Game	Atlantic	
07/26/78	7	14	Take A Chance On Me	Atlantic	
02/21/79	34	2	Summer Night City	Atlantic	
08/08/79	8	14	Does Your Mother Know	Atlantic	
02/06/80	17	8	Chiquitita	Atlantic	
02/20/80	39	2	Angel Eyes	Atlantic	
02/07/81	10	8	Winner Takes It All	Atlantic	

ABBOTT, Gregory
American male R&B-pop singer/songwriter from New York City. Psychology graduate from Boston University; studied literature at Stanford University. Taught English at University of California Berkeley.

DATE	PK	WK	TITLE	LABEL	RA
02/16/87	4	14	Shake You Down	Columbia	

ABC
British electric rock group formed in 1980 in Sheffield, England. Led by vocalist Martin Fry (b. 03/09/58 in Manchester, England). Original line-up: Mark White (guitar/keyboards, b. 04/01/61 in Sheffield, Eng-

DATE	PK	WK	TITLE	LABEL	RA

land), Mark Lickley (bass), David Robinson (drums), Stephen Singleton (saxophone, b. 04/17/59 in Sheffield, England).

11/20/82	1(1)	17	The Look Of Love	Mercury	
01/31/83	8	7	All Of My Heart	Mercury	
04/18/83	29	1	Poison Arrow	Mercury	
01/23/84	32	2	That Was Then But This Is Now	Mercury	
11/11/85	25	8	Be Near Me	Mercury	
10/05/87	2(2)	18	When Smokey Sings	Mercury	

ABDUL, Paula
American female pop singer/choreographer born on 06/19/62 in Los Angeles. Captain and member of Los Angeles Lakers cheerleaders while attending college. Choreographed videos for Janet Jackson, the Jacksons, Z.Z. Top, Pointer Sisters, and Duran Duran. Married actor Emilio Estevez on 04/29/92, split up on 05/10/94.

03/27/89	1(5)	21	Straight Up	Virgin	
06/19/89	1(3)	16	Forever Your Girl	Virgin	
10/16/89	1(2)	18	Cold Hearted	Virgin	
12/11/89	9	16	(It's Just) The Way That You Love Me	Virgin	
02/26/90	1(6)	20	Opposites Attract	Virgin	1
07/30/90	---	RA	Knocked Out	Virgin	18
07/01/91	1(4)	14	Rush Rush	Virgin	1
10/07/91	8	18	The Promise Of A New Day	Virgin	1
01/20/92	6	13	Blowing Kisses In The Wind	Virgin	5
03/23/92	7	7	Vibeology	Virgin	4
05/25/92	---	RA	Will You Marry Me?	Virgin	4
07/24/95	23	11	My Love Is For Real	Virgin	8
10/16/95	---	RA	Crazy Cool	Virgin	13

ABRAMSON, Ronney
Canadian female folk singer from Toronto. Born in Paris, France, raised in Montreal.

08/06/77	26	7	Your Love Gets Me Around	True North	

AC/DC
Australian heavy metal group formed in Sydney in 1973: Angus Young (guitar), Malcolm Young (guitar), Bon Scott (vocals), Phillip Rudd (drums), Mark Evans (bass). Cliff Williams replaced Evans in 1977. Scott died of alcohol abuse on 02/19/80 at age of 33, replaced by Brian Johnson. Simon Wright replaced Rudd in 1983. Chris Slade replaced Wright in 1989.

12/03/90	---	RA	Thunderstruck	Atlantic	39
02/11/91	13	9	Money Talks	Atlantic	15
07/26/93	5	25	Big Gun	Columbia	

ACE
British pub-rock group formed in London in 1972: Paul Carrack (vocals, keyboards, b. 04/22/51 in Sheffield, England). Disbanded in 1977. Carrack later joined Roxy Music, Squeeze, Mike + The Mechanics and went solo.

06/07/75	3(1)	2	How Long	Anchor	

ACE OF BASE

DATE	PK	WK	TITLE	LABEL	RA

Swedish pop/dance group formed in 1990 in Gothenburg, Sweden: Jenny Berggren (vocals, b. 05/19/72 in Gothenberg), Malin "Linn" Berggren (vocals, b. 10/31/70 in Gothenberg), Jonas "Joker" Berggren (keyboards, b. 03/21/67 in Gothenberg), Ulf "Buddha" Ekberg (keyboards, b. 12/06/70 in Gothenberg). Jonas is the the brother of Jenny and Linn.

DATE	PK	WK	TITLE	LABEL	RA
11/08/93	4	45	All That She Wants	Arista	2
07/04/94	24	16	The Sign	Arista	1
06/20/94	---	RA	Don't Turn Around	Arista	1
11/07/94	---	RA	Living In Danger	Arista	4
01/15/96	4	19	Beautiful Life	Arista	1
04/29/96	11	10	Lucky Love	Arista	2
08/16/98	5	13	Cruel Summer	Arista	6

ACOSTA RUSSELL
Canadian pop duo based in Scarborough, Ontario: John Acosta, James Russell. Acosta was born in Uruguay.

DATE	PK	WK	TITLE	LABEL	RA
04/22/91	36	8	Never Change My Mind	Eureka	19
08/19/91	37	3	Call Me	Eureka	39
07/27/92	---	RA	Deep In My Soul	Eureka	29
09/28/92	---	RA	You're So Tempting	Eureka	36

ACTION
Canadian ensemble of fourteen recording artists formed in 1985 by Loverboy's Doug Johnson to raise funds for food banks.

DATE	PK	WK	TITLE	LABEL	RA
02/03/86	35	2	Action Speaks Louder Than Words	WEA	

A.D.A.M.

DATE	PK	WK	TITLE	LABEL	RA
12/04/95	11	19	Zombie	Quality	

ADAMS, Bryan
Canadian male rock singer/songwriter/musician born on 11/05/59 in Kingston, Ontario. Joined Sweeney Todd as lead singer in 1976. Began songwriting with partner Jim Vallance (formerly of the rock band, Prism) in 1977. His *Reckless* album was the first Canadian album to receive a Diamond award by the CRIA for sales of one million copies. Winner of 17 Juno Awards including Best Male Vocalist in 1983, 1984, 1985, 1986, 1987, and 1997.

DATE	PK	WK	TITLE	LABEL	RA
05/02/83	9	11	Cuts Like A Knife	A&M	
06/20/83	10	12	Straight From The Heart	A&M	
09/05/83	28	3	This Time	A&M	
12/24/84	12	15	Run To You	A&M	
03/25/85	13	15	Somebody	A&M	
07/08/85	6	15	Heaven	A&M	
10/07/85	12	14	Summer Of '69	A&M	
12/16/85	12	11	It's Only Love *	A&M	
12/23/85	39	4	Christmas Time	A&M	
04/20/87	4	12	Heat Of The Night	A&M	
07/06/87	37	3	Hearts On Fire	A&M	
07/29/91	1(12)	22	(Everything I Do) I Do It For You	A&M	1
10/28/91	2(7)	21	Can't Stop This Thing We Started	A&M	1
02/17/92	13	16	There Will Never Be Another Tonight	A&M	3

DATE	PK	WK	TITLE	LABEL	RA
04/27/92	5	16	Thought I'd Died And Gone To Heaven	A&M	1
10/12/92	6	15	Do I Have To Say The Words?	A&M	2
02/01/93	---	RA	Is Your Mama Gonna	A&M	36
11/22/93	1(4)	29	Please Forgive Me	A&M	1
12/27/93	6	32	All For Love **	A&M	1
05/01/95	1(10)	38	Have You Ever Really Loved A Woman?	A&M	1
08/21/95	---	RA	Low Life	A&M	23
07/22/96	1(1)	14 h	The Only Thing That Looks Good On Me Is You	A&M	7
09/30/96	32	5 h	18 Til I Die	A&M	
10/14/96	6	21 h	Let's Make A Night To Remember	A&M	9
12/15/96	5	9	I Finally Found Someone ***	Columbia	27
12/30/96	---	RA	Do To You	A&M	37
03/09/98	---	RA	Back To You	A&M	4
05/17/98	32	8	I'm Ready	A&M	13
09/27/98	14	8	On A Day Like Today	A&M	4
01/25/99	---	RA	When You're Gone ****	A&M	4
07/05/99	---	RA	Cloud #9	A&M	8+

* Bryan Adams/Tina Turner
** Bryan Adams/Rod Stewart/Sting
*** Barbra Streisand & Bryan Adams
**** Bryan Adams featuring Melanie C

ADAMS, Oleta
American female R&B singer born on 05/04/62 in Seattle. Backup vocalist for Tears For Fears on tour and on *Seeds Of Love* album.

06/10/91	23	7	Get Here	Fontana	38

ADDRISI BROTHERS
American pop duo: Dick (b. 07/04/41) and Don (b. 12/14/38, d. 11/13/84) Addrisi from Winthrop, Massachusetts.

07/09/77	19	11	Slow Dancin' Don't Turn Me On	Buddha	

AEROSMITH
American hard rock band formed in Sunapee, New Hampshire in 1970: Steven Tyler (vocals, b. Steve Tallarico, 03/26/48 in New York City), Joe Perry (guitar, b. 09/10/50 in Lawrence, Massachusetts), Brad Whitford (guitar, b. 02/23/52 in Winchester, Massachusetts), Tom Hamilton (bass, b. 12/31/51 in Colorado Springs, Colorado), Joey Kramer (drums, b. 06/21/50 in New York City). Perry left in 1979 for Joe Perry Project, replaced by Jimmy Crespo. Whitford left in 1981, replaced by Rick Dufay. Original lineup reunited in 1984. Actress/model Liv Tyler is Steven Tyler's daughter.

04/10/76	10	10	Dream On	Columbia	
02/19/77	17	12	Walk This Way	Columbia	
10/18/78	17	8	Come Together	Columbia	
02/20/80	20	4	Remember	Columbia	
02/15/88	16	12	Dude (Looks Like A Lady)	Geffen	
06/13/88	15	15	Angel	Geffen	
10/10/88	11	13	Rag Doll	Geffen	
11/20/89	4	11	Love In An Elevator	Geffen	
02/12/90	3(1)	8	Janie's Got A Gun	Geffen	
04/30/90	23	6	What It Takes	Geffen	7

DATE	PK	WK	TITLE	LABEL	RA
08/13/90	35	4	The Other Side	Geffen	31
02/03/92	35	6	Sweet Emotion	Columbia	
06/07/93	---	RA	Livin' On The Edge	Geffen	8
10/11/93	---	RA	Cryin'	Geffen	6
02/14/94	---	RA	Amazing	Geffen	3
05/02/94	---	RA	Dueces Are Wild	Geffen	27
08/15/94	---	RA	Crazy	Geffen	2
01/16/95	---	RA	Blind Man	Geffen	8
03/23/97	40	1	Falling In Love (Is Hard On The Knees)	Columbia	17
06/30/97	---	RA	Hole In My Soul	Columbia	19
09/20/98	15	8	I Don't Want To Miss A Thing	Columbia	2

Two other versions peaked at #33 on 08/30/98 and #36 on 09/20/98.

AFTER 7
American R&B trio from Indianapolis, Indiana: Keith Mitchell, Kevon Edmonds, Melvin Edmonds. Mitchell is a cousin of producer/songwriter L.A. Reid. Kevon and Melvin are the brothers of Babyface.

DATE	PK	WK	TITLE	LABEL	RA
07/30/90	16	6	Ready Or Not	Virgin	23
11/05/90	---	RA	Can't Stop	Virgin	34

AFTER THE FIRE
British rock band consisting of Andy Piercy, Peter Banks, Tim Haywell, and Nick Battle.

DATE	PK	WK	TITLE	LABEL	RA
01/17/83	21	5	Der Kommisar	Epic	

AGLUKARK, Susan
Canadian female folk singer born on 01/27/67 in Churchill, Manitoba. Won the 1995 Juno Award for Best New Solo Artist.

DATE	PK	WK	TITLE	LABEL	RA
04/24/95	---	RA	O Siem	EMI	12

AGUILERA, Christina
American female pop singer born Christina Maria Aguilera on 12/18/80 in Staten Island, New York. Currently lives in Wexford, Pennsylvania. Cast member of *The New Mickey Mouse Club* at age 12.

DATE	PK	WK	TITLE	LABEL	RA
07/11/99	3(1)	4 +	Genie In A Bottle	RCA	7+

A-HA
Norwegian pop trio formed in Oslo, Norway in 1982: Morten Harket (vocals, b. 09/14/59 in Kongsberg, Norway), Pal Waaktaar (guitar, b. 09/06/61 in Oslo), and Magne "Mags" Furuholmen (keyboards, b. 11/01/62 in Oslo).

DATE	PK	WK	TITLE	LABEL	RA
11/18/85	6	20	Take On Me	Warner	
02/24/86	7	11	The Sun Always Shines On TV	Warner	
09/07/87	35	3	Living Daylights	Warner	

AIR SUPPLY
Australian pop vocal group formed in Melbourne in 1976: Graham Russell (vocals, guitar, b. 06/01/50 in Melbourne), Russell Hitchcock (vocals, b. 06/15/49 in Melbourne), Ralph Cooper (drums, b. 04/06/51 in Coffs Harbour, Australia), David Moyse (guitar, b. 11/05/57 in Adelaide, Australia), David Green (bass, b. 10/30/49 in Melbourne), Rex Goh (guitar, b. 05/05/51 in Singapore), Frank Esler-Smith (keyboards, b. 06/05/48 in London, England). Disbanded in 1988, reunited in 1991.

DATE	PK	WK	TITLE	LABEL	RA
04/23/80	5	11	Lost In Love	Arista	
09/20/80	1(4)	8	All Out Of Love	Arista	
02/07/81	6	12	Every Woman In The World	Arista	
07/25/81	1(2)	12	The One That You Love	Arista	
11/28/81	7	10	Here I Am	Arista	
03/06/82	10	6	Sweet Dreams	Arista	
08/07/82	7	10	Even The Nights Are Better	Arista	
11/28/83	3(1)	17	Making Love Out Of Nothing At All	Arista	
09/02/85	19	12	Just As I Am	Arista	

ALANIS - see MORISSETTE, Alanis

ALBERT, Morris
Brazilian singer/songwriter, Morris Albert Kaisermann.

DATE	PK	WK	TITLE	LABEL	RA
11/08/75	2(1)	16	Feelings	RCA	

ALEXIA
Italian female dance singer born Alessia Aquilani on 05/19/67 in La Spezia, Italy.

DATE	PK	WK	TITLE	LABEL	RA
03/09/97	19	10	Number One	NuMuzik	
11/26/97	---	RA	Uh La La La	NuMuzik	38

ALI, Tatyana
American female pop singer/actress born Tatyana Marisol Ali on 01/24/79 in Brooklyn, New York. Raised in Long Island, New York; currently lives in Los Angeles. Played Ashley Banks in the television series *The Fresh Prince of Bel-Air*.

DATE	PK	WK	TITLE	LABEL	RA
08/30/98	5	14	Daydreamin'	MJJ	34

ALIAS
Canadian/American rock band formed in Los Angeles: Freddy Curci (vocals) and Steve De Marchi (guitar), both formerly of Sheriff, and Roger Fisher of Heart.

DATE	PK	WK	TITLE	LABEL	RA
09/03/90	28	8	Haunted Heart	Capitol	
12/03/90	3(1)	13	More Than Words Can Say	Capitol	1
02/04/91	19	11	Waiting For Love	Capitol	4
01/20/92	---	RA	Into The Fire	Capitol	38

ALICE IN CHAINS
American alternative rock group formed in 1987 in Seattle: Jerry Cantrell (guitar, b. 03/18/66 in Tacoma, Washington), Layne Staley (vocals, b. 08/22/67 in Bellevue, Washington), Sean Kinney (drums, b. 05/27/66 in Seattle), Mike Inez (bass, b. 05/14/66 in San Fernando, California).

DATE	PK	WK	TITLE	LABEL	RA
05/09/94	---	RA	No Excuses	Columbia	20
10/14/96	38	1	Over Now	Columbia	

ALL-4-ONE
American R&B-pop vocal quartet formed in 1993 in Los Angeles: Jamie Jones, Tony Borowiak, Alfred Nevarez, Delious Kennedy.

DATE	PK	WK	TITLE	LABEL	RA
05/09/94	---	RA	So Much In Love	Atlantic	19
07/04/94	---	RA	I Swear	Atlantic	2
11/27/95	19	23	I Can Love You Like That	Atlantic	7

ALL SAINTS
British female pop vocal quartet: Natalie Jane Appleton (b. 05/14/73 in Mississauga, Ontario), Nicole Marie Appleton (b. 12/07/74 in Hamilton, Ontario), Melanie Blatt (b. 03/25/75 in London, England), Shaznay T. Lewis (b. 10/14/75 in London, England). The Appletons are sisters.

DATE	PK	WK	TITLE	LABEL	RA
02/22/98	2(1)	14	I Know Where It's At	London	2
06/14/98	4	15	Never Ever	London	7
10/18/98	11	22	Lady Marmalade	London	30

ALLURE
American R&B female vocal group based in New York City: Linnie Belcher, Alia Davis, Akissa Mendez, Lalisha McLean. Signed to Mariah Carey's Crave label.

DATE	PK	WK	TITLE	LABEL	RA
04/13/97	26	6	Head Over Heels	Crave	
10/26/97	34	2	All Cried Out	Crave	37

ALPERT, Herb
American trumpeter/bandleader/producer/composer born on 03/31/35 in Los Angeles. Wrote Sam Cooke's "Wonderful World", produced Jan and Dean in the late-1950's. Founded A&M Records with Jerry Moss in 1962, former Chairman of A&M. Sold A&M to PolyGram in 1990, formed new label, Almo Sounds with Moss in 1994.

DATE	PK	WK	TITLE	LABEL	RA
10/31/79	5	20	Rise	A&M	
07/20/87	10	13	Diamonds	A&M	

A.L.T. AND THE LOST CIVILIZATION
American male rapper born Al Trivette in Rosemonte, California. A.L.T. is his initials and also stands for "Another Latin Timebomb".

DATE	PK	WK	TITLE	LABEL	RA
09/21/92	23	12	Tequila	Eastwest	

AMAZING RHYTHM ACES
American country-rock band formed in 1974 in Knoxville, Tennessee: Russell Smith (guitars, vocals), Butch McDade (drums, vocals), Jeff Davis (bass), Billy Earhart III (keyboards), James Hooker (keyboards, vocals), Barry "Byrd" Burton (mandolin, guitar, vocals). Disbanded in 1980.

DATE	PK	WK	TITLE	LABEL	RA
11/04/75	11	8	Third Rate Romance	ABC	

AMAZULU
British reggae group from London consisting of Annie Ruddock (lead vocals, b. Ann-Marie Teresa Antoinette Ruddock, 07/02/61), Claire Kenny (bass), Lesley Beach (saxophone, b.09/30/54), Sharon Bailey (percussion, b. 11/22/57), Margo Sagov (guitar).

DATE	PK	WK	TITLE	LABEL	RA
04/06/87	7	19	Montego Bay	Island	

AMBER
Dutch female dance singer.

DATE	PK	WK	TITLE	LABEL	RA
12/30/96	13	20	This Is Your Night	Tommy Boy	27

DATE	PK	WK	TITLE	LABEL	RA

03/16/97   23   3   Color Of Love .... Tommy Boy

AMBROSIA
American pop quartet formed in Los Angeles in 1971: David Pack (guitar, vocals, b. 1952), Joe Puerta (bass, vocals, b. 1952), Burleigh Drummond (drums, vocals, b. 1952), Christopher North (keyboards, vocals, b. 1952).

08/23/75	25	2	Holdin' On To Yesterday .... 20th Century
01/10/79	20	10	How Much I Feel... Warner
09/13/80	11	3	You're The Only Woman (You & I) .... Warner

AMERICA
American/British pop band formed in 1969 in London: Dewey Bunnell (guitar, vocals, drums, b. 01/19/52 in Yorkshire, England), Dan Peek (guitar, vocals, b. 11/01/50 in Panama City, Florida), Gerry Beckley (guitar, vocals, b. 09/12/52 in Fort Worth, Texas).

06/14/75	1(2)	6	Sister Golden Hair .... Warner
07/10/76	17	7	Today's The Day... Warner
10/16/82	19	1	You Can Do Magic....................................... Warner

AMOS, Tori
American female rock singer/pianist born Myra Ellen Amos on 08/22/63 in Newton, North Carolina. Studied classical piano at John Hopkins University in Baltimore. Moved to Los Angeles in 1984. Her hard rock band Y Kant Tori Read released an album in 1988. Moved to London in the early-1990's.

04/04/94	---	RA	Cornflake Girl ....EastWest	32
12/08/96	38	1	Professional Widow ....EastWest	
06/07/98	25	4	Spark (Pt. 2) ....EastWest	
01/24/99	20	1	Raspberry Swirl ....EastWest	
03/21/99	12	12	Jackie's Strength......................................EastWest	

ANIMOTION
American/British pop group originally led by Astrid Plane and Bill Wadhams. Plane and Wadhams replaced in 1988 by Paul Engemann (formerly of Device) and actress/dancer Cynthia Rhodes. Rhodes appeared in the films *Staying Alive* and *Dirty Dancing*, married singer Richard Marx on 01/08/89.

| 05/20/85 | 7 | 16 | Obsession .... Mercury |
| 05/01/89 | 21 | 9 | Room To Move .... Polydor |

ANDREONE, Leah
American female singer born on 05/24/73 in San Diego.

04/14/97   ---   RA   It's Alright, It's OK... RCA   30

ANGELINA
American female dance singer born Angelina Camarillo in Union City, California.

11/10/96   18   8   I Don't Need Your Love .... Upstairs

ANKA, Paul
Canadian male pop singer/songwriter born on 07/30/41 in Ottawa. Late-1950's teen idol. Wrote "My Way" by Frank Sinatra, "She's A Lady" by Tom Jones, and "It Don't Matter Anymore" by Buddy Holly.

DATE	PK	WK	TITLE	LABEL	RA

Wrote *The Tonight Show* theme. Appeared in film, *The Longest Day*. Host of television programs *Hullabaloo* and *The Midnight Special*. Received Juno Hall of Fame Award in 1980.

08/23/75	6	8	(I Believe) There's Nothing Stronger Than Our Love	United Artists	
01/31/76	16	5	Times Of Your Life	United Artists	
01/15/77	27	8	Happier	United Artists	
06/18/77	23	8	My Best Friend's Wife	United Artists	

ANOTHER BAD CREATION
American R&B/rap group from Atlanta consisting of pre-teens, Chris Sellers, Dave Shelton, Romell Chapman, Marliss and Demetrius Pugh.

| 04/29/91 | 15 | 12 | Iesha | Motown | |
| 03/23/92 | 36 | 4 | My World | Motown | |

ANT, Adam
British male punk singer born Stuart Leslie Goddard on 11/03/54 in London, England.

03/07/83	2(1)	14	Goody Two Shoes	Epic	
05/28/90	---	RA	Room At The Top	MCA	15
06/19/95	---	RA	Wonderful	EMI	18

ANTHRAX
American heavy metal band formed in New York City in 1981 led by John Bush.

| 09/06/93 | 28 | 5 | Only | Elektra | |

APACHE
American male rapper born Anthony Teaks in Jersey City, New Jersey.

| 03/29/93 | 36 | 1 | Gangsta Bitch | Isba | |

APACHE INDIAN
British male reggae/dance singer.

| 04/12/93 | 14 | 11 | Arranged Marriage | Island | |
| 06/14/93 | 30 | 5 | Chok There | Island | |

APPLE, Fiona
American female rock singer/songwriter born Fiona Apple Maggart on 09/13/77 in New York City.

| 12/08/97 | --- | RA | Criminal | Work | 27 |

APRIL WINE
Canadian hard rock band formed in Halifax, Nova Scotia in 1969: David Henman (guitar), Ritchie Henman (drums), Jimmy Henman (bass), Myles Goodwyn (piano, guitar, vocals, b. 06/23/48 in Woodstock, Ontario). Jimmy left in 1970, replaced by Jimmy Clench (bass); David and Ritchie left in 1971, replaced by Gary Moffet (guitar), Jerry Mercer (drums); Clench left in 1975, replaced by Steve Lang (bass). Brian Greenway (guitar, vocals, keyboards) joined in 1977. Disbanded in 1985, reunited in 1991.

| 11/29/75 | 5 | 12 | Tonight Is A Wonderful Time | Aquarius | |

DATE	PK	WK	TITLE	LABEL	RA
05/08/76	15	11	The Whole World's Goin' .... Aquarius		
06/18/77	6	19	You Won't Dance With Me .... Aquarius		
03/08/78	27	8	Rock And Roll Is A Vicious Game .... Aquarius		
01/09/80	34	4	Say Hello .... Aquarius		
04/04/81	6	10	Just Between You And Me .... Aquarius		
08/14/82	8	9	Enough Is Enough .... Aquarius		
06/07/93	---	RA	If Y ou Believe In Me .... Aquarius		32

AQUA
Danish pop group formed in 1994: Lene Grawford Nystrom (b. 10/10/73 in Tonsberg, Norway), Rene Dif (b. 10/17/67 in Frederiksberg, Denmark), Claus Norreen (b. 06/05/70 in Charlottenlund, Denmark), Soren Rasted (b. 06/13/69 in Blovstrod, Denmark).

11/02/97	7	6	Barbie Girl .... MCA		4
			Above is import edition. The domestic version peaked at #29 on 11/02/97.		
01/05/98	---	RA	Lollipop (Candyman)...................................... MCA		37
03/30/98	---	RA	Turn Back Time .... MCA		27

ARCADIA
British pop group consisting of Duran Duran members, Simon LeBon (vocals, b. 10/27/58 in Bushey, England), Nick Rhodes (keyboards, b. Nicholas James Bates on 06/08/62 in Birmingham, England), and Roger Taylor (drums, b. 04/26/60 in Birmingham).

12/02/85	7	12	Election Day .... Capitol		

ARCHER, Tasmin
British female singer from Bradford, England.

06/21/93	4	21	Sleeping Satellite .... Capitol		4

ARDEN, Jann
Canadian female pop/MOR singer/songwriter born Jann Arden Richards on 03/27/62 in Calgary. Started career as a songwriter in 1982. Received Juno Award for Best Female Vocalist in 1995.

05/24/93	---	RA	Will You Remember Me? .... A&M		34
11/22/93	---	RA	I'm Not Your Lover... A&M		39
09/26/94	---	RA	Could I Be Your Girl....................................... A&M		5
02/06/95	9	26	Insensitive .... A&M		2
05/22/95	---	RA	Wonderdrug.. A&M		12
08/28/95	---	RA	Unloved .... A&M		34
12/25/95	---	RA	Good Mother... A&M		23
07/22/96	16	12 h	Looking For It .... A&M		37
11/24/97	---	RA	The Sound Of... A&M		12
03/02/98	---	RA	Wishing That .... A&M		27
07/20/98	---	RA	I Know You... A&M		27

ARENA, Tina
Australian female pop singer/actress born in 1968. Starred in the Australian television show *Young Talent Team* in the 1970's. Appeared in several theatrical productions.

05/27/96	15	10	Chains... Epic		11

DATE	PK	WK	TITLE	LABEL	RA

ARENDS, Carolyn
Canadian female pop singer/songwriter from Vancouver.

| 04/01/96 | 17 | 15 h | This Is The Stuff | RCA | 24 |
| 09/23/96 | 20 | 12 | I Can Hear You | RCA | 21 |

ARMSTRONG, Louis
American male R&B singer born on 08/04/01 near Henderson, Tennessee. Popular in the 1920's to the 1960's.

| 05/09/88 | 13 | 12 | What A Wonderful World | A&M | |

ARRESTED DEVELOPMENT
American R&B-hip-hop band formed in 1988 in Atlanta: Speech (vocals, b. Todd Thomas on 10/25/68 in Milwaukee, Wisconsin), Headliner (DJ, b. Tim Barnwell on 07/26/67 in New Jersey), Rasa Don (vocals, drums, b. Donald Jones on 11/22/68 in New Jersey), Aerle Taree (vocals, dancer, stylist, b. Taree Jones on 01/10/73 in Milwaukee), Montsho Eshe (dancer, choreographer, b. Temelca Gaither on 12/23/74 in Georgia), Bab Oje (spiritual adviser, b. 05/15/32 in Laurie, Mississippi). Taree left in 1994. Dionne Farris is the featured vocalist on "Tennessee".

08/24/92	7	15	Tennessee	Chrysalis	
10/19/92	4	23	Everyday People	Chrysalis	35
12/21/92	28	1	Revolution	SBK	
02/22/93	4	30	Mr. Wendal	Chrysalis	16
08/08/94	6	27	Ease My Mind	Chrysalis	

ARROW
Montserrat, West Indies-born male R&B-calypso singer born on 11/16/54.

| 08/27/84 | 34 | 2 | Hot Hot Hot | Chrysalis | |

ARROWS, The
Canadian rock band from Toronto: Dean McTaggart (vocals), Douglas Macaskill (guitar), Earl Seymour (saxophone), Rob Gusevs (keyboards), Bobby Economou (drums), Glenn Olive (bass).

| 07/16/84 | 30 | 3 | Meet Me In The Middle | A&M | |

ART OF NOISE
British techno-pop band formed in 1983 in London: Anne Dudley (keyboards, b. 05/07/56 in London), Jonathan "J.J." Jeczalik (keyboards, b. 05/11/55), Gary Langan (various instruments). Disbanded in 1990.

07/21/86	14	14	Peter Gunn	Chrysalis	
10/27/86	35	3	Paranoimia	Chrysalis	
02/27/89	27	7	Kiss *	Polydor	

* Art Of Noise/Tom Jones

ARTISTS UNITED AGAINST APARTHEID
International benefit group organized to protest the apartheid policies of South Africa. Consisted of 49 stars including Pat Benatar, Bono (of U2), Jackson Browne, Jimmy Cliff, Bob Dylan, Peter Gabriel, Bonnie Raitt, Lou Reed, Bruce Springsteen. Proceeds to South African political prisioners.

DATE	PK	WK	TITLE	LABEL	RA
01/27/86	6	14	Sun City...Capitol		

ASHFORD & SIMPSON
American husband-and-wife R&B-pop singing/songwriting duo: Nickolas Ashford (b. 05/04/43 in Fairfield, South Carolina) and Valerie Simpson (b. 08/26/48 in Bronx, New York).

| 03/18/85 | 7 | 15 | Solid..Capitol | | |

ASIA
British rock supergroup consisting of popular musicians: drummer Carl Palmer (of Emerson, Lake and Palmer, b. 03/20/47 in Birmingham), bassist/vocalist John Wetton (of King Crimson, Roxy Music; b. 07/12/49 in Derby, England), guitarist Steve Howe (of Yes, b. 04/08/47 in London), keyboardist Geoffrey Downes (Yes). Wetton replaced in 1983 by Greg Lake (Emerson, Lake, and Palmer) in 1983. Howe replaced by Mandy Meyer in 1985. Lake replaced by Wetton in 1985. Disbanded in 1985, re-formed in 1990.

06/05/82	3(4)	13	Heat Of The Moment .... Geffen		
09/25/82	5	9	Only Time Will Tell .... Geffen		
10/03/83	12	10	Don't Cry .... Geffen		

ASTLEY, Rick
British male pop singer born on 02/06/66 in Warington, England, and raised in Manchester.

03/21/88	1(4)	17	Never Gonna Give You Up............................ RCA		
07/11/88	1(3)	16	Together Forever .... RCA		
10/17/88	2(1)	14	It Would Take A Strong Strong Man............... RCA		
02/27/89	1(3)	14	She Wants To Dance With Me .... RCA		
06/12/89	29	10	Giving Up On Love .... RCA		
05/13/91	3(1)	14	Cry For Help .... RCA	3	
10/18/93	---	RA	Hopelessly... RCA	23	

ATLANTA RHYTHM SECTION
American group formed in Doraville, Georgia in 1971: Barry Bailey (guitar), Rodney Justo (vocals), Paul Goddard (bass), Robert Nix (drums), J.R. Cobb (guitar), Dean Daughtry (keyboards). Justo left in 1972, replaced by Ronnie Hammond. Disbanded in 1981, re-forms as ARS in 1989.

05/28/77	5	12	So Into You..Polydor		
05/31/78	12	10	Imaginary Lover...Polydor		
09/05/79	27	8	Do It Or Die ....Polydor		

ATLANTIC STARR
American R&B band formed in 1976 in White Plains, New York. Led by vocalists, brothers David Lewis (b. 09/08/58 in White Plains) and Wayne Lewis (b. 04/13/57 in White Plains), and Sharon Bryant (b. 08/14/56 in Westchester County, New York). Bryant replaced in 1984 by Barbara Weathers (b. 12/07/63 in Greensboro, North Carolina). Weathers replaced in 1989 by Porscha Martin. Martin replaced in 1992 by Rachel Oliver. Oliver replaced in 1994 by Aisha Tanner (b. 07/27/73 in Oakland, California).

04/07/86	18	12	Secret Lovers... A&M		
07/20/87	9	16	Always .... Warner		
05/25/92	12	14	Masterpiece .... Atlantic	19	

AUSTIN, Patti

DATE	PK	WK	TITLE	LABEL	RA

American female R&B singer/backup vocalist born on 08/10/48 in New York City.

| 02/21/83 | 2(1) | 12 | Baby, Come To Me * | Qwest | |

* Patti Austin with James Ingram

AZ
American male rapper born Anthony Cruz in Brooklyn.

| 10/16/95 | 25 | 5 | Sugarhill | EMI | |

AZ YET
American R&B group from Philadelphia: Dion Allen, Darryl Anthony, Marc Nelson, Shawn Rivera, Kenny Terry.

| 11/03/96 | 36 | 2 | Last Night | LaFace | |
| 06/08/97 | 11 | 15 | Hard To Say I'm Sorry * | LaFace | 28 |

* AZ Yet featuring Peter Cetera

B

BABY TALK

| 05/17/98 | 14 | 6 | Dancing Baby | Peter Pan | |

BABYFACE
American male R&B vocalist/songwriter/producer born Kenneth Edmonds on 04/10/59 in Indianapolis, Indiana. Songwriting/producing partnership with L.A. Reid.

11/13/89	40	2	It's No Crime	Solar	
09/14/92	---	RA	Give U My Heart	LaFace	29
10/10/94	---	RA	When Can I See You	Epic	11
07/24/95	25	12	Someone To Love *	Epic	
01/12/97	10	18	This Is For The Lover In You	Epic	
04/28/97	---	RA	Everytime I Close My Eyes	Epic	33

* Jon B./Babyface

BABYLON ZOO
British singer/songwriter/producer Jas Mann born circa 1971 in England, raised in India and the United States. Part-Asian, Native American.

| 04/01/96 | 17 | 2 | Spaceman | EMI | |

BABYS, The
British rock band formed in London in 1976 featuring vocalist John Waite (b. 07/04/55 in Lancashire, England). Disbanded in 1981. Waite later pursued solo career and fronted the band, Bad English.

| 12/14/77 | 24 | 10 | Isn't It Time | Chrysalis | |

DATE	PK	WK	TITLE	LABEL	RA

BACHMAN, Tal
Canadian male rock singer from Vancouver, born circa 1969. Son of Bachman-Turner Overdrive and Guess Who vocalist and guitarist Randy Bachman.

| 07/05/99 | --- | RA | She's So High .... Columbia | 4+ |

BACHMAN-TURNER OVERDRIVE
Canadian rock band formed in Winnipeg in 1972: Randy Bachman (vocals, guitar, b. 09/27/43 in Winnipeg), Tim Bachman (guitar, b. in Winnipeg), Robbie Bachman (drums, b. 02/18/53 in Winnipeg), C.F. (Fred) Turner (bass, vocals, b. 10/16/43 in Winnipeg). Tim replaced by Blair Thornton (guitar, b. 07/23/50) in 1973. Randy replaced by Jim Clench (bass, vocals) in 1977. Winner of seven Juno Awards including Most Promising Group of the Year in 1974 and Group of the Year in 1975 and 1976.

06/21/75	5	8	Hey You.. Mercury
02/21/76	33	4	Take It Like A Man................................. Mercury
05/22/76	29	7	Looking Out For #1 .... Mercury
10/09/76	27	4	Give Me Your Money .... Mercury
09/20/75	9	9	Quick Change Artist................................ Mercury
05/28/77	25	6	My Wheels Won't Turn............................ Mercury

BACKSTREET BOYS
American pop vocal quintet from Orlando, Florida: Nicholas Gene Carter (b. 01/28/80 in Jamestown, New York), Howard Dwaine "Howie" Dorough (b. 08/22/73 in Orlando), Brian Thomas Littrell (b. 02/20/75 in Lexington, Kentucky), Alexander James "A.J." McLean (b. 01/09/78 in Boynton Beach, Florida), Kevin Richardson (b. 10/03/72 in Lexington). Littrell and Richardson are cousins.

10/20/96	2(2)	53	Get Down (You're The One For Me) ....Jive	12
01/17/97	11	31	We've Got It Goin' On.......................................Jive	
			Another version peaked at #15 on 02/09/97.	
04/06/97	6	23	Anywhere For You ....Jive	
			Above is "P1" version. "P2" version peaked at #15 on 02/09/97.	
04/20/97	32	2	I'll Never Break Your Heart................................Jive	
05/11/97	3(2)	85	Quit Playing Games (With My Heart) ....Jive	18
07/20/97	2(5)	36	Everybody (Backstreet's Back)..........................Jive	6
			"Remixes" version peaked at #6 on 08/03/97.	
12/07/97	2(2)	29	As Long As You Love Me...................................Jive	1
04/19/98	3(2)	33	All I Have To Give...Jive	16
			"Pt. 1" version peaked at #16 on 03/01/98. "Pt.2" version peaked at #33 on 03/01/98.	
04/19/98	24	5	Nick Shape CD .... NuMuzik	
08/17/98	---	RA	That's The Way I Like It ....Jive	24
05/02/99	1(3)	13+	I Want It That Way ....Jive	1+

BAD COMPANY
British rock group formed in England in 1973: Paul Rodgers (vocals, b. 12/17/49 in Middlesbrough, England) and Simon Kirke (drums, b. 07/28/49 in Shrewsbury, England) of the rock band Free, Mick Ralphs (guitar, b. 03/31/44 in Hereford, England) of Mott the Hoople, Boz Burrell (bass, b. Raymond Burrell, on 08/01/46 in Lincoln, England) of King Crimson.

10/11/75	21	3	Feel Like Makin' Love............................ Swan Song	
06/12/76	24	6	Young Blood... Swan Song	
07/11/79	26	4	Rock N' Roll Fantasy .... Swan Song	
03/11/91	---	RA	If You Needed Somebody ....Atco	34

DATE	PK	WK	TITLE	LABEL	RA

BAD ENGLISH
British rock band formed circa 1988, consisting of former members of The Babys, John Waite (vocals, b. 07/04/55 in Lancashire, England), Jonathan Cain (keyboards), Ricky Phillips (bass), and ex-Journey member, Neal Schon (guitar), and drummer Deen Castronovo.

Date	PK	WK	Title	Label	RA
12/18/89	4	17	When I See You Smile	Epic	
03/26/90	11	11	Price Of Love	Epic	8
08/20/90	---	RA	Posession	Epic	34
11/25/91	36	4	Straight To Your Heart	Epic	

BADLEES, The
American rock band from Philadelphia: Pete Palladino (vocals), Bret Alexander (guitar), Jeff Feltenberger (guitar), Paul Smith (bass), Ron Simasek (drums).

Date	PK	WK	Title	Label	RA
09/09/96	---	RA	Angeline Is Coming Home	Polydor	33

BADU, Erykah
American female R&B vocalist born Erykah Wright on 02/26/71 in Dallas.

Date	PK	WK	Title	Label	RA
03/16/97	35	1	On & On	Universal	
04/19/99	---	RA	You Got Me *	MCA	40

* The Roots featuring Erykah Badu

BAHA MEN
Bahamian seven-member pop band led by Isaiah Taylor. The Junjanoo sound of the band's music blends dance music and West African rhythms.

Date	PK	WK	Title	Label	RA
08/01/94	---	RA	Dancing In The Moonlight	Atlantic	32

BAILEY, Phillip
American male R&B vocalist born on 05/08/51 in Denver, Colorado. Percussionist/vocalist in R&B group, Earth, Wind and Fire.

Date	PK	WK	Title	Label	RA
02/11/85	1(6)	20	Easy Lover *	Columbia	

* Phillip Bailey & Phil Collins

BAINBRIDGE, Merril
Australian female pop singer born on 06/02/68 in Melbourne.

Date	PK	WK	Title	Label	RA
11/25/96	2(4)	14 h	Mouth	Universal	1
			SoundScan: #26 (12/08/96) / 10 wks.		

BAIRD, Dan
American male rock singer born on 12/12/53 in San Diego. Vocalist and guitarist for the George Satellites.

Date	PK	WK	Title	Label	RA
02/08/93	---	RA	I Love You Period	American	27

BAKER, Anita
American female R&B singer born on 12/20/57 in Detroit. Lead singer of the Detroit band Chapter 8.

DATE	PK	WK	TITLE	LABEL	RA

12/15/86   33   2   Sweet Love .... Elektra

BAKER, George, Selection
Dutch vocal/instrumental group. George Baker is Johannes Bouwens (vocals, guitar, keyboards, b. 12/09/44).

02/14/76   6   14   Paloma Blanca .... Warner

BALDRY, Long John
British/Canadian male blues vocalist born 01/12/41 in East Maddon, England. Became Canadian citizen in 1980.

09/19/79   36   2   Come And Get Your Love .... Capitol

---

BALIN, Marty
American male vocalist born on 01/30/43 in Cincinnati, Ohio. Vocalist in Jefferson Airplane.

08/01/81   3(1)   9   Hearts .... EMI

BALTIMORA
Irish male pop vocalist, Jimmy McShane, born on 05/23/57 in Londonderry, Northern Ireland.

01/20/86   5   19   Tarzan Boy .... Manhattan

BANANARAMA
British pop-dance vocalist trio formed in London in 1981: Sarah Dallin (b. 12/17/60 in Bristol, England), Keren Woodward (b. 04/02/61 in Bristol), Siobhan Fahey (b. 09/10/60 in Ireland). Fahey married Dave Stewart of the Eurythmics in 1987 and left in 1988, replaced by Jacqui O' Sullivan. Name combines 1960's children's show, "The Banana Splits" and Roxy Music's "Pyjamarama". Fahey later formed Shakespear's Sister.

04/18/83   7   12   Shy Boy (Don't It Make You Feel Good) ..... London
10/29/84   17   7   Cruel Summer .... London
10/06/86   1(2)   22   Venus .... London
10/19/87   2(3)   15   I Heard A Rumour .... London
09/25/95   35   5   Every Shade Of Blue .... Quality

---

BAND, The
Canadian/American rock band formed in 1967 in Woodstock, New York: James Robbie Robertson (guitar, b. 07/05/44 in Toronto), Richard Manuel (piano, vocals, b. 04/03/45 in Stratford, Ontario), Garth Hudson (organ, saxophone, b. 08/02/43 in London, Ontario), Rick Danko (bass, viola, vocals, b. 12/09/43 in Simcoe, Ontario), Levon Helm (drums, vocals, mandolin, b. 05/26/40 in Marvell, Arkansas). Manuel committed suicide on 03/04/86 in Winter Park, Florida. Robertson pursued solo career in 1980's. Received Juno Hall of Fame Award in 1989.

04/17/76   25   5   Ophelia .... Capitol

BAND AID
British ensemble of recording artists organized in 1984 by Boomtown Rats lead singer Bob Geldof to raise funds to fight famine in Ethiopia: U2 (Adam Clayton, Bono), Phil Collins, Boomtown Rats (Geldof, Johnny Fingers, Simon Crowe, Peter Briquette), David Bowie, Paul McCartney, Holly Johnson (of Frankie Goes To Hollywood), Ultravox (Midge Ure, Chris Cross), Duran Duran (Simon LeBon, Nick

DATE	PK	WK	TITLE	LABEL	RA

Rhodes, John Taylor, Andy Taylor, Roger Taylor), Paul Young, Spandau Ballet (Tony Hadley, Martin Kemp, John Keeble, Gary Kemp, Steve Norman), Heaven 17 (Glenn Gregory, Martyn Ware), Status Quo (Francis Rossi, Rick Parfitt), Sting, Culture Club (Jon Moss, Boy George), Marilyn, Bananarama (Siobhan Fahey, Sarah Dallin), Jody Watley, Paul Weller (of Style Council), Kool & The Gang (Robert "Kool" Bell, James Taylor, Dennis Thomas), George Michael.

| 01/14/85 | 1(1) | 9 | Do They Know It's Christmas? | Columbia | |

BAND AID II

British ensemble of recording artists organized in 1989: Bananarama, Big Fun, Bros, Cathy Dennis, D Mob, Jason Donovan, Kevin Godley, Glen Goldsmith, Kylie Minogue, the Pasadenas, Chris Rea, Cliff Richard, Jimmy Sommerville, Sonia, Lisa Stansfield, Technotronic, Wet Wet Wet.

| 01/22/90 | 38 | 1 | Do They Know It's Christmas? | PolyGram | |

BANGLES

American pop/rock female band formed in 1981 in Los Angeles: Susanna Hoffs (vocals, guitar, b. 01/17/57 in Newport Beach, California), Debbi Peterson (drums, vocals, b. 08/22/61 in Los Angeles), Vicki Peterson (guitar, vocals, b. 01/11/58 in Los Angeles), Annette Zilinskas (bass, vocals, b. 11/06/64 in Van Nuys, California). Michael Steele (vocals, bass, b. 06/02/54) replaced Zilinskas in 1984. Disbanded in 1989. Hoffs later pursued a solo career.

05/12/86	11	19	Manic Monday	Columbia	
07/07/86	40	2	If She Knew What She Wants	Columbia	
02/09/87	1(3)	22	Walk Like An Egyptian	Columbia	
05/18/87	32	4	Walking Down Your Street	Columbia	
03/07/88	9	17	Hazy Shade Of Winter	Columbia	
01/16/89	14	12	In Your Room	Columbia	
05/08/89	11	18	Eternal Flame	Columbia	

BANNED IN THE UK

| 07/26/93 | 19 | 17 | The Truth | A&M | 30 |

BARDEUX

American dance duo from Los Angeles: Stacy "Acacia" Smith and Jazz. Jazz replaced by Melanie Taylor in 1989.

| 07/25/88 | 30 | 8 | When We Kiss | Enigma | |

BARENAKED LADIES

Canadian pop/rock band formed in 1988 in Scarborough, Ontario: Steven Page (vocals, guitar, b. 06/22/70 in Scarborough), Ed Robertson (vocals, guitar, b. 10/25/70 in Scarborough), Andy Creegan (congas, piano), Jim Creegan (bass), Tyler Stewart (drums). Won the Juno Award for Group of the Year in 1993 and 1999.

10/05/92	4	16	Enid	Sire	8
11/16/92	---	RA	Grade Nine	Sire	22
02/08/93	---	RA	If I Had A $1,000,000	Sire	15
05/03/93	15	8	Brian Wilson	Sire	21
10/24/94	---	RA	Jane	Sire	3
01/31/95	---	RA	Alternative Girlfriend	Sire	10
04/10/95	---	RA	Life In A Nutshell	Sire	36

DATE	PK	WK	TITLE	LABEL	RA
04/15/96	13	8 h	Shoebox	Reprise	15
07/15/96	36	5 h	The Old Apartment	Reprise	24
10/11/98	5	16	One Week	Reprise	5
12/21/98	---	RA	It's All Been Done	Reprise	4
07/05/99	---	RA	Call And Answer	Reprise	27

BARRA MACNEILS
Canadian family Celtic/traditional group from Sydney Mines, Nova Scotia: Sheumas MacNeil (piano, keyboard, vocals, b. 10/26/61), Kyle MacNeil (violin, acoustic & electric guitar, mandolin, vocals, b. 04/21/63), Stewart MacNeil (vocals, accordian, keyboards, whistle, flute, electric guitar, b. 10/20/64), Lucy MacNeil (vocals, bodhrn, celtic harp, backing vocals, viola, violin, b. 10/24/68), Ryan MacNeil (uillean pipes), Boyd MacNeil (violin). The prefix Barra is added in honour of the family's ancestral homeland, the Scottish Isle of Barra.

02/21/94	---	RA	Darling Be Home Soon	Polydor	38

BARRY, Claudja
Jamaican/Canadian female disco singer raised in Toronto. Won the 1979 Juno Award for Most Promising Female Vocalist.

02/21/79	5	20	(Boogie Woogie) Dancin' Shoes	Chrysalis	

BASIA
Polish female singer born Basia Trzetrzelewska on 09/30/54 in Jaworzno, Poland.

06/11/90	---	RA	Cruising For Bruising	Epic	35

BASEMENT JAXX
British electronica dance disc jockey from Brixton, London, England.

07/18/99	27	3 +	Red Alert	XL	

BASIL, Toni
American female pop singer/actress/choreographer/video director. Born in 1950.

01/24/83	1(5)	21	Mickey	Virgin	

BASS IS BASE
Canadian R&B-funk trio formed in 1993 in Toronto: Chin Injeti (bass, vocals, b. 1969 in India), Ivana Santilli (keyboards, vocals, b. 1971; of Italian ancestry), Roger "MC Mystic" Mooking (rap vocals, b. 1974 in Trinidad).

12/04/95	---	RA	Diamond Dreams	A&M	16
05/13/96	15	15 h	I Cry	A&M	13
09/30/96	---	RA	Why	A&M	28

BASS LINE SYNDICATE
Canadian dance group produced by Chris Sheppard of BKS.

12/01/96	28	5	Could Be Good	Quality	

BAY CITY ROLLERS

DATE	PK	WK	TITLE	LABEL	RA

Scottish pop band formed in Edinburgh, Scotland in 1970: Alan Longmuir (bass, b. 06/20/53 in Edinburgh), Eric Faulkner (guitar, b. 10/21/55 in Edinburgh), Derek Longmuir (drums, b. 03/19/55 in Edinburgh), Leslie McKeown (vocals, b. 11/12/55 in Edinburgh), Stuart "Woody" Wood (guitar, b. 02/25/57 in Edinburgh). Alan replaced by Ian Mitchell (guitar), Mitchell replaced by Pat McGlynn (guitar) in 1976. Several personnel changes took place in late-1970's.

01/17/76	1(1)	14	Saturday Night	Arista
04/10/76	4	12	Money Honey	Arista
05/29/76	13	10	Rock N' Roll Love Letter	Arista
09/04/76	10	11	Don't Stop The Music	Arista
10/30/76	3(2)	16	I Only Want To Be With You	Arista
02/19/77	22	8	Yesterday's Hero	Arista
08/13/77	2(1)	16	You Made Me Believe In Magic	Arista
02/22/78	23	14	The Way I Feel Tonight	Arista

BAZUKA

American instrumental/vocal studio group assembled by producer Tony Camillo. "Dynomite-Part 1" inspired by expression used by actor J.J. Walker on the television series, *Good Times*.

08/30/75	5	9	Dynomite-Part 1 *	A&M

* Tony Camillo's Bazuka

BB JEROME & THE BANG GANG

Belgian dance-rock quartet: B.B. Jerome, Mike, Serge G., Littlemilk.

10/14/91	33	8	Shock Rock	EMI

BEACH BOYS

American pop group formed in 1961 in Hawthorne, California. Credited with introducing California rock music in the 1960's. Original line-up: Brian Wilson (vocals, bass, piano, b. 06/20/42 in Hawthorne), Dennis Wilson (vocals, drums, b. 12/04/44 in Hawthorne), Carl Wilson (b. 12/21/46 in Hawthorne, d. of cancer on 02/06/98), Mike Love (vocals, percussion, b. 03/15/41 in Los Angeles), Alan Jardine (vocals, guitar, b. 09/03/42 in Lima, Ohio). Country singer Glen Campbell joined briefly, 1964-65, until replaced by Bruce Johnston. Dennis drowned on 12/28/83 in Marina del Rey, California. Carnie and Wendy Wilson, daughters of Brian Wilson are members of Wilson Phillips. Brian, Carl, and Dennis all pursued solo careers. Inducted into the Rock and Roll Hall of Fame in 1988. Line-up as of 1988: Carl and Brian Wilson, Love, Jardine, Johnston.

08/07/76	8	12	Rock & Roll Music	Reprise
10/16/76	24	5	It's OK	Reprise
10/03/81	20	3	The Beach Boys Medley	Capitol
07/22/85	23	8	Getcha Back	Brother
12/12/88	3(6)	21	Kokomo	Elektra
10/30/89	32	2	Still Cruisin'	Capitol
09/21/92	39	1	Hot Fun In The Summertime	Attic

BEASTIE BOYS

American rap trio formed in 1981 in New York City: MCA (vocals, bass, b. Adam Yauch on 08/05/65 in New York City), Mike D (vocals, drums, b. Michael Diamond on 11/20/66 in New York City), King Ad-Rock (bass, vocals, b. Adam Horovitz on 10/31/67 in New York City).

04/13/87	11	13	(You Gotta) Fight For Your Right (To Party!)	Def Jam

DATE	PK	WK	TITLE	LABEL	RA
08/23/98	9	24	Intergalactic	Capitol	35
01/24/99	31	3	Body Movin' (Part 1)	Pedd	

BEATLES, The

British pop/rock group formed in 1959 in Liverpool. The most successful rock group of all-time. Original line-up: John Lennon (vocals, harmonica, guitar, b. John Winston Lennon on 10/09/40 in Liverpool), Paul McCartney (bass, vocals, guitar, keyboards, b. James Paul McCartney on 06/18/42 in Liverpool), George Harrison (guitar, vocals, b. 02/25/43 in Liverpool), Stu Sutcliffe (bass, b. Stuart Fergusson Victor Sutcliffe on 06/23/40 in Edinburgh, Scotland), Pete Best (drums, b. 1941 in England). Sutcliffe left the group in April 1961 and died from a brain hemorrhage on 04/10/62 in Hamburg, Germany. Ringo Starr (drums, percussion, vocals, b. Richard Starkey Jr. on 07/07/40 in Liverpool) replaced Best in 1962. Appeared in several films including A Hard Day's Night (1964), Help (1965), Magical Mystery Tour (1967), and Let It Be (1970). Manager Brian Epstein died from an overdose of sleeping pills on 08/27/67 in London. Formed own record label, Apple, in 1968. McCartney announced on 04/10/70 group was splitting up. McCartney, Lennon, Starr, and Harrison later had successful solo careers. Lennon murdered on 12/08/80 in New York City. Inducted into the Rock and Roll Hall of Fame in 1988. "Free As A Bird", released in 1995, was the first new Beatle single since 1970.

DATE	PK	WK	TITLE	LABEL	RA
08/07/76	5	12	Got To Get You Into My Life	Capitol	
12/18/76	32	4	Ob La Di Ob La Da	Capitol	
05/08/82	19	1	The Beatles' Movie Medley	Capitol	
10/06/86	24	12	Twist And Shout	Capitol	
02/05/96	18	9	Free As A Bird	Apple	13
04/08/96	16	7 h	Real Love	Apple	

BECK

American male alternative rock singer born Beck Hansen on 07/08/70 in Los Angeles.

DATE	PK	WK	TITLE	LABEL	RA
04/18/94	---	RA	Loser	DGC	10

BEE GEES

British pop trio of brothers from Manchester, England: Barry Gibb (vocals, guitar, b. 09/01/47 in Manchester) and twins Robin (vocals, b. 12/22/49 in Isle of Man, England) and Maurice Gibb (vocals, bass, keyboards, b. 12/22/49 in Isle of Man). Sons of English bandleader Hugh Gibb. Started performing in 1955 under various names. Moved to Brisbane, Australia in 1958. Recorded under Festival Records starting in 1962. Hosted a weekly Australian TV show in the 1960's. Relocated to England in 1967; expanded to a quintet with the addition of drummer Colin Peterson and bassist Vince Melouney. Melouney left in 1968; Robin left to record solo. When Peterson left in 1969, Barry and Maurice recorded solo. The brothers reunited in 1970. Composed the soundtrack for the movie Saturday Night Fever, the best-selling film soundtrack album of all time. Appeared in the movie Sgt. Pepper's Lonely Hearts Club Band. Youngest brother, singer Andy Gibb died on 03/10/88.

DATE	PK	WK	TITLE	LABEL
08/23/75	1(4)	14	Jive Talkin'	RSO
11/29/75	3(4)	11	Nights On Broadway	RSO
03/13/76	9	11	Fanny (Be Tender)	RSO
09/04/76	3(1)	14	You Should Be Dancing	RSO
11/27/76	8	16	Love So Right	RSO
03/19/77	17	11	Boogie Child	RSO
10/19/77	28	4	Edge Of The Universe	RSO
11/30/77	3(2)	32	How Deep Is Your Love	RSO
02/22/78	1(10)	26	Stayin' Alive	RSO
05/03/78	1(4)	24	Night Fever	RSO
01/24/79	3(2)	18	Too Much Heaven	RSO
04/04/79	2(2)	16	Tragedy	RSO

DATE	PK	WK	TITLE	LABEL	RA
05/30/79	11	12	Love You Inside Out	RSO	
10/16/89	18	10	One	Warner	
12/27/93	29	8	Paying The Price Of Love	Polydor	
06/29/97	9	12	Alone	Polydor	12

BEENIE MAN
Jamaican reggae singer/DJ born Anthony Moses David in 1972 in Kingston, Jamaica. Got his stage name because of his diminutive size.

DATE	PK	WK	TITLE	LABEL	RA
09/14/97	27	8	Dancehall Queen	Island	
06/14/98	10	41	Who Am I	VP	

BELL BIV DEVOE
American R&B trio of former members of New Edition, formed in Boston in 1988: Michael Bivins (vocals, b. 08/10/68 in Boston), Ricky Bell (vocals, b. 09/18/67 in Boston), Ronnie DeVoe (vocals, b. 11/17/67 in Boston).

DATE	PK	WK	TITLE	LABEL	RA
07/02/90	8	11	Poison	MCA	5
10/22/90	---	RA	Do Me!	MCA	19
01/18/93	4	19	Gansta	MCA	

BELL, William
American male R&B singer born William Yarborough on 07/16/39 in Memphis, Tennessee.

DATE	PK	WK	TITLE	LABEL	RA
05/28/77	20	9	Tryin' To Love Two	Mercury	

BELLAMY BROTHERS
American country duo from Darby, Florida: brothers Howard (guitar, b. 02/02/46) and David (guitar, keyboards, b. 09/16/50) Bellamy.

DATE	PK	WK	TITLE	LABEL	RA
04/24/76	2(1)	14	Let Your Love Flow	Warner	

BELLE STARS
British pop band formed as The Bodysnatchers in 1981 led by vocalist Jennie McKeown. Name changed in 1983.

DATE	PK	WK	TITLE	LABEL	RA
06/12/89	17	11	Iko Iko	Capitol	

BELLE, Regina
American female R&B singer born Regina Edna Belle on 07/15/63 in Englewood, New Jersey. Backup vocalist for the Manhattans beginning in 1985.

DATE	PK	WK	TITLE	LABEL	RA
03/08/93	2(1)	25	A Whole New World *	Columbia	4
05/17/93	23	6	If I Could	Columbia	

* Peabo Bryson and Regina Belle

BEN FOLDS FIVE
American rock trio from Chapel Hill, North Carolina: Ben Folds (lead vocals, piano), Robert Sledge (backing vocals, bass), Darren Jessee (backing vocals, drums).

DATE	PK	WK	TITLE	LABEL	RA
04/06/98	---	RA	Brick	550 Music/Epic	22

DATE	PK	WK	TITLE	LABEL	RA

BENATAR, Pat
American female rock singer/songwriter born Patricia Andrzejewski on 01/10/53 in Brooklyn, New York. Married her guitarist/musical director, Neil Giraldo in 1982.

DATE	PK	WK	TITLE	LABEL
04/23/80	7	8	Heartbreaker	Chrysalis
06/11/80	11	8	We Live For Love	Chrysalis
11/29/80	3(1)	12	Hit Me With Your Best Shot	Chrysalis
03/14/81	10	6	Treat Me Right	Chrysalis
09/12/81	6	9	Fire And Ice	Chrysalis
12/18/82	13	6	Shadows Of The Night	Chrysalis
12/26/83	6	16	Love Is A Battlefield	Chrysalis
01/28/85	4	17	We Belong	Chrysalis
09/02/85	7	9	Invincible	Chrysalis
01/27/86	23	9	Sex As A Weapon	Chrysalis
09/26/88	14	15	All Fired Up	Chrysalis

BENSON, George
American male R&B-pop vocalist/jazz guitarist born on 03/22/43 in Pittsburgh.

DATE	PK	WK	TITLE	LABEL
09/11/76	11	8	This Masquerade	Warner
09/20/80	12	3	Give Me The Night	Warner
02/20/82	20	1	Turn Your Love Around	Warner

BENTALL, Barney, & The Legendary Hearts
Canadian rock band based in Vancouver formed in 1978 under the name, Brandon Wolf: Barney Bentall (vocals, guitar), Will Froese (keyboards), Doug McFetridge (guitar), Barry Muir (bass), Jack Guppy (drums). Froese later replaced by Cam Bowman. McFetridge replaced by Colin Nairn.

DATE	PK	WK	TITLE	LABEL	RA
09/12/88	31	5	Something To Live For	Epic	
12/03/90	22	5	Crime Against Love *	Epic	24
07/10/95	---	RA	Do Ya *	Epic	19
10/30/95	---	RA	I'm Shattered *	Epic	33
02/26/96	---	RA	Oh Shelly *	Epic	31
07/01/96	27	9 h	Gin Palace *	Epic	40

* Barney Bentall

BERLIN
American rock trio formed in Los Angeles in 1979: Terry Nunn (vocals, b. 06/26/59 in Baldwin Hills, California), John Crawford (bass, vocals, b. 01/17/57 in Palo Alto, California), Rob Brill (drums, b. 01/21/56 in Babylon, New York). Nunn was a teenager when she acted on TV's *Lou Grant*.

DATE	PK	WK	TITLE	LABEL
04/25/83	20	5	Sex (I'm A...)	Geffen
10/20/86	1(3)	22	Take My Breath Away	Columbia

BETTER THAN EZRA
American alternative band from Louisiana: Kevin Griffin (guitar, lead vocals), Tom Drummond (bass), Cary Bonnecaze (drums). Bonnecaze was later replaced by Travis McNabb.

DATE	PK	WK	TITLE	LABEL	RA
08/14/95	---	RA	Good	Epic	19
10/21/96	18	8 h	King Of New Orleans	Elektra	

DATE	PK	WK	TITLE	LABEL	RA

B-52s, The
American rock band formed in 1976 in Athens, Georgia: Cindy Wilson (vocals, percussion, guitar, b. 02/28/57 in Athens), Keith Strickland (drums, b. 10/26/53), Fred Schneider III (vocals, b. 07/01/56 in Newark, New Jersey), Ricky Wilson (guitar, b.03/19/53 in Athens), Kate Pierson (vocals, b. 04/27/48 in Weehawken, New Jersey). Ricky died of AIDS on 10/12/85. Cindy left in 1990. Appeared in the 1994 film *The Flintstones* as the BC-52s.

04/30/80	10	8	Rock Lobster	Warner	
11/27/89	23	9	Love Shack	Reprise	
04/23/90	8	8	Roam	Reprise	3
07/09/90	39	2	Deadbeat Club	Reprise	18
08/24/92	15	13	Good Stuff	Reprise	6
07/04/94	---	RA	(Meet) The Flintstones *	MCA	6

* The BC-52's

BIF
Canadian female alternative-hard rock singer/songwriter born Beth Torbert in 1971 in New Delhi, India. Studied theatre at the University of Winnipeg. Bif is short for her stage name, Bif Naked. Based in Winnipeg.

| 06/28/98 | 2(1) | 26 | Spaceman | Aquarius | |

BIG COUNTRY
Scottish rock band formed in Dunfermline, Scotland in 1982: Stuart Adamson (vocals, guitar), Mark Brzezicki (drums), Tony Butler (bass), Bruce Watson (guitar).

| 11/21/83 | 6 | 17 | In A Big Country | Mercury | |

BIG HOUSE
Canadian rock band from Edmonton: Jan Ek (vocals), Kevin Broc (rhythm guitar), Sjor Throndson (percussion, drums), Craig Beakhouse (bass). Beakhouse later replaced by Jay Scott King.

| 05/18/92 | 20 | 14 | Baby Doll | Boomtown | 14 |

BIG MOUNTAIN
American reggae band from San Diego: Quino (vocals, rhythm guitar), Jerome Cruz, Manfred Reinke, Gregory Blakney, Lance Rhodes, Lynn Copeland.

08/01/94	28	28	Baby I Love Your Way	RCA	1
09/19/94	29	12	Sweet Sensual Love	Giant	
02/05/96	---	RA	Get Together	Giant	6

BIG PIG
Australian rock group consisting of seven members.

| 07/11/88 | 14 | 10 | Breakaway | A&M | |

BIG PUNISHER
American male rapper from New York City.

| 02/01/98 | 40 | 1 | I'm Not A Player | Loud | |

DATE	PK	WK	TITLE	LABEL	RA

BIG SUGAR
Canadian rock group formed in 1991 in Toronto: Gordie Johnson (vocals, guitar), Al Cross (drums), Terry Wilkins (bass), Kelly Hoppe (harmonica, melodica, steel guitar), Gary Lowe (bass), Patrick Ballantyne (acoustic guitar). Stych Wilson replaced Cross in 1995; Paul Brennan replaced Wilson in 1996; Gavin Brown replaced Brennan 1997.

11/04/96	20	11 h	Diggin' A Hole	A&M	
01/12/97	25	13	Dear M.F.	A&M	
07/19/99	---	RA	Turn The Lights On	A&M	17+

BILLIE
British female pop singer born Billie Piper on 09/09/82 in Swindon, England.

| 08/30/98 | 14 | 12 | Because We Want To | Virgin | 38 |

BIM
Canadian male singer/songwriter Roy Forbes from Vancouver. Born in 1953 in Dawson Creek, British Columbia. Bim is a nickname used by his father.

| 04/10/76 | 35 | 2 | Can't Catch Me | Casino | |

BINGOBOYS featuring Princessa
Austrian dance trio of disc jockeys from Vienna: Klaus Biedermann, Paul Pfab, Helmut Wolfgruber. Princessa is an American female rapper from New York.

| 04/29/91 | 14 | 10 | How To Dance | Atlantic | |

BISCUIT
American male rapper Steve Walker from Oakland, California. Former bodyguard for New Kids On The Block.

| 01/21/91 | 36 | 2 | Biscuit's In The House | Columbia | |

BISHOP, Elvin
American male guitarist born on 10/21/42 in Tulsa, Oklahoma.

| 05/22/76 | 5 | 11 | Fooled Around And Fell In Love... | Capricorn | |

BISHOP, Stephen
American pop singer/songwriter born on 11/14/51 in San Diego, California.

| 10/05/77 | 8 | 12 | On And On | GRT | |
| 05/23/83 | 15 | 7 | It Might Be You | Warner | |

BIZARRE INC. featuring Angie Brown
British techno-dance trio of disc jockeys: Andrew Meecham (b. circa 1968), Dean Meredith (b. circa 1969), Carl Turner (b. circa 1969). Angie Brown is a female session singer.

| 04/19/93 | 16 | 20 | I'm Gonna Get You | Columbia | |

BKS

DATE	PK	WK	TITLE	LABEL	RA

Canadian techno-dance trio from Toronto: Hennie Bekker, Greg Kavanagh, Chris Sheppard. Bekker, a native of Africa, is a jazz musician/band leader; Sheppard is a club and radio disc jockey and host of a weekly syndicated dance radio program.

04/26/93	33	2	Talkin' About Love	Quality	
05/29/95	5	28	Square Dance Song (I Wanna Go Higher) *	A&M	33
10/09/95	11	6	Take Control	Quality	
08/19/96	---	RA	Astroplane	Quality	19

* BKS featuring Ashley MacIsaac

BLACK BOX
Italian dance group: producer Daniele Dovoli, and musicians Valerio Semplici and Mirko Limoni. Lead vocalist Martha Wash is uncredited. French model Katrin Quinol appears in videos as lead singer. Based in the Regio D'Emillia region of Northern Italy.

11/19/90	---	RA	Everybody Everybody	RCA	11
02/25/91	---	RA	I Don't Know Anbody Else	RCA	24
06/24/91	---	RA	Strike It Up	RCA	19

BLACK CROWES
American rock band formed in 1988 in Atlanta: Chris Robinson (vocals, b. 12/20/66 in Atlanta), Rich Robinson (guitar, b. 05/24/69 in Atlanta), Jeff Cease (guitar, b. 06/24/67), Johnny Colt (bass, b. 05/01/68 in Cherry Point, North Carolina), Steve Gorman (drums, b. 08/17/65 in Hopkinsville, Kentucky). Cease left in 1990, replaced by Marc Ford (b. 04/13/66 in Los Angeles). Eddie Harsch (keyboards, b. 05/27/57 in Toronto) joined in 1994. Originally named the Mr. Crowe's Garden after a childhood fairy tale.

05/27/91	---	RA	She Talks To Angels	American	23
08/19/91	---	RA	Hard To Handle	American	38
07/13/92	---	RA	Remedy	American	36
09/16/96	17	10 h	Good Friday	American	

BLACKBYRDS
American R&B group formed in 1973 by Donald Byrd while teaching jazz at Howard University in Washington, D.C.

| 06/14/75 | 9 | 2 | Walking In Rhythm | Fantasy | |

BLACKOUT ALL STARS
American all-star Latin dance group: Shiela E., Grover Washington Jr., Ray Barretto, Paquito D'Rivera, Tito Puente, Tito Nieves, Dave Valentin.

| 04/13/97 | 21 | 4 | I Like It | Sony Import | 29 |

BLACKSTREET
American R&B vocal quartet formed in 1993 in Virginia Beach, Virginia: Teddy "Street" Riley (lead vocals), Chauncey "Black" Hannibal, Eric Williams, Mark Middleton.

10/27/96	2(1)	14	No Diggity	Interscope	19
06/09/97	---	RA	Don't Leave Me	Interscope	30
08/17/97	3(1)	16	Fix	Interscope	
02/28/99	35	1	Take Me There *	Interscope	15

DATE	PK	WK	TITLE	LABEL	RA

04/19/99 --- RA Girlfriend/Boyfriend **............................Interscope 29

* Blackstreet & Mya
** Blackstreet featuring Janet

BLACK, Jully
Canadian dance vocalist from Toronto.

06/20/99 14 7 + Rally 'N' ....I.L.L. Vibe 39

BLAHZAY BLAHZAY
American rap duo formed in Brooklyn: rapper Out Loud, producer DJ P.F. Cuttlin.

03/18/96 2(3) 12 Danger ....Polydor

BLAIR
British male pop singer/songwriter/multi-instrumentalist Blair McKichan. Born circa 1970 in London to a Scottish father and a Canadian mother.

06/08/98 --- RA Have Fun, Go Mad!... MCA 38

BLAQUE
American R&B vocal trio Blaque: Shamari, Natina, Brandi. "Blaque" is an acronym for Believe, Life, Achieving, Quest, Unity, Everything. Discovered by TLC's Lisa "Left Eye" Lopes.

07/11/99 39 2 808..Columbia

BLESSID UNION OF SOULS
American pop vocal group from Cincinnati: Eliot Sloan, Jeff Pence, C.P. Roth, Eddie Hedges.

06/12/95 --- RA I Believe..SBK 3
09/25/95 --- RA Let Me Be The One...SBK 9
04/08/96 38 1 h Oh Virginia ....SBK 19
06/16/97 --- RA I Wanna Be There...SBK 21
08/02/99 --- RA Hey Leonardo (She Likes Me For Me) .... V2 10+

BLIGE, Mary J.
American female R&B singer born Mary Jane Blige on 01/11/71 in Atlanta.

12/14/92 --- RA Real Love .... MCA 10
04/05/93 --- RA Sweet Thing... MCA 22
09/25/95 1(5) 37 I'll Be There For You/You're All I Need
              (To Get By) * ....Def Jam
              Re-entered and peaked at #40 on 08/17/97.

* Method Man featuring Mary J. Blige

BLIND MELON
American rock band formed in 1990 in Los Angeles: Shannon Hoon (vocals, b. 09/26/67 in Laffayette, Indiana), Roger Stevens (guitar, b. 10/31/70 in West Point, Mississippi), Christopher Thorn (guitar, b. 12/16/68 in Dover, Pennsylvania), Brad Smith (bass, b. 09/29/68 in West Point), Glen Graham (drums, b. 12/05/68 in Columbus, Mississippi). Hoon died of a drug overdose on 10/21/95.

DATE	PK	WK	TITLE	LABEL	RA

| 11/01/93 | --- | RA | No Rain .... Capitol | 1 |

BLONDIE
American pop band formed in New York City in 1975: Deborah Harry (vocals, b. 07/01/45 in Miami), Chris Stein (guitar, vocals, b. 01/05/50 in Brooklyn, New York), Clem Burke (drums, b. 11/24/55 in New York City), Jimmy Destri (keyboards, b. 04/13/54 in Brooklyn, New York), Frank Infante (bass), Nigel Harrison (bass, b. 04/24/51 in Stockport, England). Disbanded in 1982. Harry pursued solo career.

05/02/79	1(6)	28	Heart Of Glass... Chrysalis
08/23/79	14	10	One Way Or Another .... Chrysalis
11/14/79	6	16	Dreaming.. Chrysalis
04/23/80	1(6)	19	Call Me .... Chrysalis
01/31/81	1(4)	16	The Tide Is High .... Chrysalis
04/04/81	1(3)	12	Rapture .... Chrysalis

BLOW MONKEYS
British pop band consisting of Dr. Robert (lead vocals, b. Bruce Robert Howard, 05/02/61 in Norfolk, England), Tony Kiley (b. 02/16/62), Mick Anger (b. 07/02/57).

| 08/25/86 | 18 | 4 | Digging Your Scene .... RCA |
| 06/01/87 | 38 | 2 | It Doesn't Have To Be This Way..................... RCA |

BLUE OYSTER CULT
American hard rock band formed in Long Island, New York in 1970 led by vocalist Eric Bloom.

| 11/27/76 | 14 | 12 | (Don't Fear) The Reaper .... Columbia |

BLUE RODEO
Canadian band from Toronto: Jim Cuddy (vocals, guitar), Cleave Anderson (drums), Bazil Donovan (bass), Greg Keelor (vocals, guitar), Bobby Wiseman (piano). Andersen replaced by Mark French in 1989. Wiseman replaced by Kim Deschamps in 1992. French replaced by Glenn Milchem in 1992. Cuddy recorded solo in 1998. Won the Juno Award for Group of the Year in 1989, 1990, and 1991. Cuddy won the 1999 Juno Award for Best Male Vocalist.

12/28/87	7	17	Try... Risque Disque	
03/28/88	36	3	Day After Day .... Risque Disque	
06/12/89	26	10	Diamond Mine .... Risque Disque	
02/18/91	29	7	Til I Am Myself Again......................................WEA	23
05/06/91	---	RA	Trust Yourself ....WEA	25
09/21/92	---	RA	Lost Together ....WEA	11
12/28/92	---	RA	Rain Down On Me..WEA	29
01/24/94	---	RA	Five Days In May ....WEA	33
04/18/94	---	RA	Hasn't Hit Me Yet...WEA	33
02/26/96	---	RA	Better Off As We Are ....WEA	29
09/22/97	---	RA	It Could Happen To You..................................WEA	30

BLUES BROTHERS
American/Canadian comedy act: Joliet "Jake" (comedian/actor John Belushi b. 01/24/49 in Wheaton, Illinois, d. 03/05/82 of drug overdose) and Elwood Blues (comedian/actor Dan Aykroyd, b. 07/01/52 in Ottawa). Blues Brothers are characters on television's *Saturday Night Live*.

| 02/21/79 | 20 | 2 | Soul Man .... Atlantic |

DATE	PK	WK	TITLE	LABEL	RA
07/16/80	19	1	Gimme Some Lovin' .... Atlantic		

BLUES TRAVELER
American rock group formed in 1985 in Princeton, New Jersey: John Popper (vocals, harmonica, guitar, b. 03/29/67 in Cleveland), Chandler Kinchla (guitar, b. 05/29/69 in Hamilton, Ontario), Bobby Sheehan (bass, b. 06/12/68 in Summit, New Jersey), Brendan Hill (drums, percussion, b. 03/27/70 in London).

06/19/95	---	RA	Run Around .... A&M	17
04/22/96	---	RA	Hook.. A&M	19

BLUR
British alternative group formed in 1989 in Colchester, England: Damon Albarn (vocals, keyboards, b. 03/23/68 in London, England), Graham Coxon (guitar, saxophone, b. 03/12/69 in Rintein, West Germany), Alex James (bass, b. 11/21/68 in Boscombe, England), Dave Rowntree (drums, b. 05/08/64 in Colchester).

09/12/94	---	RA	Girls & Boys .... Parlophone	13
02/02/97	35	1	Beetlebum .... MCA	
			Above is "Pt.2" version. "Pt.1" version peaked at #37 on 01/26/97.	
02/28/99	29	2	Tender (Part 1) ....Lightning	
			Above is "Part 1" version. "Part 2" version peaked at #31 on 02/28/99.	

BoDEANS
American rock duo from Waukesha, Wisconsin: Sam Llanas and Kurt Neumann.

05/20/96	7	15 h	Closer To Free.. Slash	4

BOLLAND, C.J.
British male techno-dance remixer born Christian Jay Bolland in Tyneside, England.

02/09/97	20	8	Sugar Is Sweeter .... London	

BOLTON, Michael
American male pop-MOR singer/songwriter born Michael Bolotin on 02/26/53 in New Haven, Connecticut. Former lead singer of the hard rock band Blackjack. Wrote Laura Branigan's "How Am I Supposed To Live Without You" and songs for Kiss, Kenny Rogers, Barbra Streisand. In 1994, a federal jury found "Love Is A Wonderful Thing" borrowed from the Isley Brothers' composition of the same title, and ordered that the Isleys receive 66 percent of the royalties of the song.

01/18/88	39	1	That's What Love Is All About .... Columbia	
04/04/88	13	12	(Sittin' On) The Dock Of The Bay .... Columbia	
03/26/90	10	14	How Am I Supposed To Live Without YouColumbia	14
05/28/90	4	11	How Can We Be Lovers .... Columbia	3
08/13/90	---	RA	When I'm Back On My Feet Again .... Columbia	7
10/22/90	32	6	Georgia On My Mind............................... Columbia	
07/01/91	7	18	Love Is A Wonderful Thing....................... Columbia	3
10/07/91	12	14	Time, Love And Tenderness.................... Columbia	2
12/09/91	20	6	When A Man Loves A Woman .... Columbia	3
03/02/92	15	13	Missing You Now .... Columbia	6
07/06/92	---	RA	Steel Bars... Columbia	10
01/18/93	5	22	To Love Somebody.................................. Columbia	2

DATE	PK	WK	TITLE	LABEL	RA
12/20/93	1(12)	47	Said I Loved You...But I Lied	Columbia	7
05/16/94	9	24	Completely	Columbia	
08/01/94	---	RA	Ain't Got Nothin' If You Ain't Got Love	Columbia	25
11/27/95	6	28	Can I Touch You...There?	Columbia	18

BON JOVI
American hard rock quintet formed in 1983 in New Jersey: Jon Bon Jovi (vocals, b. John Francis Bongiovi on 03/02/62 in Sayreville, New Jersey), Richie Sambora (guitar, b. 07/11/59 in Woodbridge, New Jersey), David Bryan (keyboards, b. David Bryan Rashbaum on 02/07/62 in New York City), Alec John Such (bass, b. 11/14/56 in Yonkers, New York), Tico Torres (drums, b. Hector Torres on 10/07/53 in New York City).

DATE	PK	WK	TITLE	LABEL	RA
01/19/87	3(1)	19	You Give Love A Bad Name	Mercury	
03/02/87	3(1)	19	Livin' On A Prayer	Mercury	
06/22/87	15	11	Wanted Dead Or Alive	Mercury	
12/19/88	5	17	Bad Medicine	Mercury	
02/20/89	7	13	Born To Be My Baby	Mercury	
06/12/89	16	10	I'll Be There For You	Mercury	
09/04/89	26	9	Lay Your Hands On Me	Mercury	
01/25/93	5	18	Keep The Faith	Mercury	5
03/08/93	3(4)	22	Bed Of Roses	Mercury	3
06/14/93	10	24	In These Arms	Mercury	6
08/23/93	20	13	I'll Sleep When I'm Dead	Mercury	
11/29/93	10	14	I Believe	Mercury	
01/16/95	1(7)	49	Always	Mercury	1
04/17/95	7	40	Someday I'll Be Saturday Night	Mercury	12
06/26/95	4	21	This Ain't A Love Song	Mercury	2
09/25/95	32	20	Something For The Pain	Mercury	18
01/29/96	---	RA	Lie To Me	Mercury	18

BON JOVI, Jon
American male rock singer born John Francis Bongiovi on 03/02/62 in Sayreville, New Jersey. Lead singer of Bon Jovi.

DATE	PK	WK	TITLE	LABEL	RA
08/13/90	2(1)	9	Blaze Of Glory	Mercury	1
12/24/90	---	RA	Miracle	Mercury	10
06/01/97	3(1)	14	Midnight In Chelsea	Mercury	5
09/22/97	---	RA	Janie Don't Take Your Love To Town	Mercury	28

BONDS, Gary "U.S."
American singer born Gary Anderson on 06/06/39 in Jacksonville, Florida.

DATE	PK	WK	TITLE	LABEL	RA
06/27/81	5	10	This Little Girl	EMI	

BONE THUGS-N-HARMONY
American R&B formed in 1993 in Cleveland. Consists of Steven Howse ("Layzie Bone"), Byron McCane ("Bizzy Bone"), Anthony Henderson ("Krayzie Bone"), Curtis Scruggs ("Wish Bone") and Stanley Howse ("Flesh-N-Bone"). Discovered by Eazy E, rapper and founder of Ruthless Records.

DATE	PK	WK	TITLE	LABEL	RA
11/17/96	9	16	Tha Crossroads	Sony	21

BONEY M

DATE	PK	WK	TITLE	LABEL	RA

West Indian disco vocal group formed and based in Germany: Marcia Barrett (b. 10/14/48 in St. Catherine's, Jamaica), Maizie Williams (b. 03/25/51 in Montserrat), Liz Mitchell (b. 07/12/52 in Clarendon, Jamaica), Bobby Farrell (b. 10/06/49 in Aruba).

01/25/78	38	2	Ma Baker	Atlantic	
09/06/78	8	28	Rivers Of Babylon	Atlantic	
01/10/79	37	2	Mary's Boy Child	Atlantic	
02/21/79	6	20	Rasputin	Atlantic	
10/17/79	11	6	Gotta Go Home	Atlantic	

BOO, Betty
British female rapper, Allison Clarkson from Kensington, London.

| 12/10/90 | 6 | 18 | Doing The Do | Sire | |

BOOMERS
Canadian pop/rock group formed in 1991: Ian Thomas (vocals), Peter Cardinali (bass), Bill Dillon (guitar), Rick Gratton (drums). Originally formed as a back-up band for Thomas.

| 09/20/93 | --- | RA | You've Gotta Know | Warner | 36 |

BOOMTANG BOYS
Canadian pop/dance production team from Toronto. Consists of Bob DeBoer and brothers Tony and Paul Grace.

04/04/99	1(4)	11	Squeeze Toy	Virgin	16
			Features vocals by Kim Esty.		
08/09/99	---	RA	Pictures	Virgin	34+

BOOMTOWN RATS
Irish rock group formed in 1975 in Dun Laoghaire, Ireland: Bob Geldof (vocals, b. 10/05/54 in Dublin), Johnnie Fingers (keyboards, vocals, b. John Moylett on 09/10/56 in Eire), Pete Briquette (bass, vocals, b. Patrick Cusack on 07/02/54 in Eire), Gerry Roberts (guitar, vocals, b. 06/16/54), Simon Crowe (drums, vocals). Fingers and Briquette are cousins. Geldof organized Band Aid in 1984 to raise funds for African famine relief.

| 12/12/79 | 6 | 24 | I Don't Like Mondays | Mercury | |

BOONE, Debby
American female pop singer born on 09/22/56 in Hackensack, New Jersey. One of four daughters of 1950's teen idol, Pat Boone. Married Gabriel Ferrer, son of actor Jose Ferrer and singer Rosemary Clooney. Later became contemporary Christian artist.

| 11/16/77 | 1(12) | 36 | You Light Up My Life | Warner | |

BOOTSAUCE
Canadian rock group: Drew Ling (vocals), Alan Baculis (bass), Pere Fume (guitar), Sonny Greenwich, Jr. (guitar), Marc Villeneuve (drums).

04/29/91	11	17	Everyone's A Winner	Vertigo	9
04/27/92	22	7	Love Monkey #9	Vertigo	
07/06/92	40	1	Whatcha Need	Vertigo	36
05/02/94	---	RA	Moanie	Vertigo	20

DATE	PK	WK	TITLE	LABEL	RA

BORELLY, Jean-Claude

| 04/10/76 | 31 | 5 | Dolannes Melodie | Able | |

BOSTON
American rock group formed in Boston in 1975: Tom Scholz (guitar, keyboards, b. 03/10/47 in Toledo, Ohio), Brad Delp (vocals, guitar, b. 06/12/51 in Boston), Barry Goudreau (guitar, b. 11/29/51 in Boston), Fran Sheehan (bass, b. 03/26/49 in Boston), Sib Hashian (drums, b. 08/17/49 in Boston). Goudreau, Sheehan, Hashian left in the early-1980's. Disbanded in 1986, re-formed in 1994 with Scholz, the only original member.

11/06/76	5	12	More Than A Feeling	Epic	
04/02/77	19	8	Long Time	Epic	
06/25/77	37	2	Peace Of Mind	Epic	
09/20/78	13	12	Don't Look Back	Epic	
12/01/86	1(1)	21	Amanda	MCA	

BOTTOMLEY, John
Canadian male pop singer.

| 05/22/95 | --- | RA | You Lose And You Gain | RCA | 20 |

BLVD
Canadian pop group formed in Calgary in 1983: David Forbes (lead vocals), Randy Burgess (bass), Randy Gould (guitar), Mark Holden (saxophone, vocals), Andrew Johns (keyboards), Randal Stohl (drums).

| 05/30/88 | 25 | 9 | Never Give Up | MCA | |
| 05/21/90 | --- | RA | Lead Me On | MCA | 26 |

BOURGEOIS, Brent
American male pop singer born in New Orleans. Former member of Bourgeois Tagg.

| 07/02/90 | --- | RA | Dare To Fall In Love * | Capitol | 24 |

* Brent Bourgeois

BOURGEOIS TAGG
American rock group formed in 1984. Led by New Orleans-born Brent Bourgeois and Larry Tagg.

| 01/18/88 | 31 | 5 | I Don't Mind At All | MCA | |

BOWIE, David
British male rock singer/songwriter born David Robert Jones on 01/08/47 in London. First recorded with three different bands in the 1960's. Started mime troupe, Feathers, in 1968. Worked on and acted in theatrical production, *Ziggy Stardust*. Lived in Berlin in mid-1970's in semi-seclusion recording with Brian Eno. Narrated Philadelphia Orchestra's recording of *Peter and the Wolf* in 1977. Starred in films *Absolute Beginners* (1986) and *Labyrinth* (1986). Formed Tin Machine in 1989. Married Somalian supermodel Iman in 1992. Inducted into the Rock and Roll Hall of Fame in 1996.

| 10/18/75 | 1(1) | 12 | Fame | RCA | |
| 04/03/76 | 8 | 10 | Golden Years | RCA | |

DATE	PK	WK	TITLE	LABEL	RA
12/06/80	17	6	Ashes To Ashes	RCA	
01/16/82	7	12	Under Pressure *	Elektra	
05/09/83	2(2)	18	Let's Dance	Capitol	
08/08/83	10	12	China Girl	Capitol	
10/31/83	5	14	Modern Love	Capitol	
10/22/84	12	12	Blue Jean	Capitol	
01/14/85	21	9	Tonight	Capitol	
06/01/87	16	11	Day-In Day-Out	Capitol	
04/01/85	27	6	This Is Not America **	Capitol	
11/04/85	5	18	Dancing In The Street ***	Capitol	
05/31/93	---	RA	Jump They Say	Savage	26
10/09/95	---	RA	Hearts Filthy Lesson	Virgin	37
12/01/96	11	6	Peace On Earth/Little Drummer Boy ****	Oglio	
03/09/97	21	3	Little Wonder	Virgin	
10/26/97	15	20	I'm Afraid Of Americans	Virgin	
12/13/98	8	7	Peace On Earth/Little Drummer Boy ****	Oglio	

Above is a re-entry.

* Queen & David Bowie
** David Bowie & Pat Metheny
*** David Bowie/Mick Jagger
**** Bing Crosby/David Bowie

BOX, The
Canadian pop/rock band from Montreal: Jean-Marc Pisapia (vocals), Phillipe Bernard (drums), Jean-Pierre Brie (bass), Guy Pisapia (keyboards), and Claude Thibeault (guitar). Bernard and Guy Pisapia left in 1992.

DATE	PK	WK	TITLE	LABEL	RA
02/10/86	21	8	L'Affaire Dumoutier (Say To Me)	Alert	
06/22/87	10	14	Closer Together	Alert	
09/28/87	10	12	Ordinary People	Alert	
04/16/90	33	8	Carry On	Alert	18
08/06/90	---	RA	Temptation	Alert	32
11/05/90	---	RA	Inside My Heart	Alert	37

BOY GEORGE
British male vocalist born George O'Dowd on 06/14/61 in Eltham, Kent, England. Former lead vocalist in Culture Club.

DATE	PK	WK	TITLE	LABEL	RA
06/01/87	11	13	Everything I Own	Virgin	
05/17/93	---	RA	The Crying Game	Virgin	2

BOY KRAZY
American female pop quartet formed in New York City: Kimberly Blake, Johnna Lee Cummings, Josselyne Jones, Ruth Ann Roberts.

DATE	PK	WK	TITLE	LABEL	RA
05/03/93	3(2)	19	That's What Love Can Do	Next Plateau	2
07/12/93	---	RA	Good Times With Bad Boys	Next Plateau	14

BOY MEETS GIRL

DATE	PK	WK	TITLE	LABEL	RA

American recording/songwriting duo from Seattle: Shannon Rubicam (b. 10/11/51 in Seattle), George Merrill (b. 01/10/56 in Renton, Washington). Wrote Whitney Houston's "How Will I Know" and "I Wanna Dance With Somebody (Who Loves Me)". Married in 1988.

| 02/06/89 | 1(1) | 18 | Waiting For A Star To Fall | RCA | |

BOYS BRIGADE
Canadian band from Toronto: Tony Lester (guitar), Malcolm Burn (keyboards), Wayne Lorenz (bass), Billie Brock (drums), David Porter (percussion), Jeff Packer (percussion). Founded in 1981 as Arson by Brock.

| 02/27/84 | 32 | 5 | Melody | Capitol | |

BOYS CLUB
American R&B duo from Minneapolis consisting of Joe Pasquale and Gene Hunt. Hunt's real name is Eugene Wolfgramm, former member of The Jets.

| 02/13/89 | 30 | 4 | I Remember Holding You | MCA | |

BOYS DON'T CRY
British quintet led by vocalist Nick Richards.

| 06/09/86 | 15 | 14 | I Wanna Be A Cowboy | Mercury | |

BOYZ II MEN
American R&B vocal quartet formed in Philadelphia in 1988: Wanya "Squirt" Morris (b. 07/29/73), Michael "Bass" McCary (b. 12/16/72), Shawn "Slim" Stockman (b. 09/26/72), Nathan "Alex Vanderpool" Morris (b. 06/18/71). All four members were born in Philadelphia.

09/02/91	38	2	Motownphilly	Motown	34
01/20/92	5	21	It's So Hard To Say Goodbye To Yesterday	Motown	17
03/02/92	8	11	Uhh Ahh	Motown	
04/27/92	31	4	Please Don't Go	Motown	
10/12/92	1(11)	23	End Of The Road	Motown	1
03/01/93	6	22	In The Still Of The Nite (I'll Remember)	Motown	3
10/03/94	1(6)	30	I'll Make Love To You	Motown	1
03/06/95	2(1)	33	On Bended Knee	Motown	1
05/29/95	31	13	Thank You	Motown	17
08/14/95	33	4	Water Runs Dry	Motown	2
02/05/96	2(5)	16	One Sweet Day *	Columbia	1
			Hit Parade: #3(4) (01/22/96) / 18 wks.		
09/14/97	5	14	4 Seasons Of Loneliness	Motown	10
02/15/98	25		Song For Mama	Motown	
06/21/98	25	1	Can't Let Her Go	Motown	

* Mariah Carey/Boyz II Men

BOYZONE
Irish male pop vocal group formed in 1993: Ronan Keating, Stephen Gately, Keith Duffy, Mikey Graham, Shane Lynch. Shane's twin sisters Edele and Keavy are members of B*Witched.

| 09/21/97 | 27 | 4 | Picture Of You | PolyGram | 26 |

DATE	PK	WK	TITLE	LABEL	RA

BRAIDS, The
American female R&B vocal duo based in Oakland, California: Caitlin Cornwell and Zoe Ellis.

| 12/01/96 | 12 | 16 | Bohemian Rhapsody.................................... | Atlantic | 37 |

BRAM TCHAIKOVSKY
British rock trio formed in Licolnshire, England: Peter Bramall (vocals, guitars), Micky Broadbent (bass), and Keith Boyce (drums). Bramall is a former member of The Motors.

| 09/05/79 | 21 | 4 | Girl Of My Dreams....................................... | Polydor | |

BRAN VAN 3000
Canadian alternative rock group formed in 1996 in Montreal: James "Bran Man" DiSilvio (songwriter, rapper, multi-instrumentalist), "Electronic-Pierre" Bergen (DJ, keyboards), Jayne Hill (vocals), Sara Johnston (vocals), Stephanie Moraille (vocals), Steve "Liquid" Hawley (rapper), Gary McKenzie (bass), Nick Hynes (guitar), Rob Joanisse (drums).

| 07/21/97 | --- | RA | Drinking In L.A...................................... | Audiogram | 28 |
| 05/18/98 | --- | RA | Everywhere.. | Audiogram | 10 |

BRAND NEW HEAVIES
British funk quartet formed in 1986 in London: N'Dea Davenport (vocals), Andrew Levy, Simon Bartholomew, Jan Kincaid. Davenport was replaced by Siedah Garrett in 1996.

| 05/16/94 | --- | RA | Dream On Dreamer .... | EastWest | 29 |

BRANDY
American female R&B singer/actress born Brandy Rayana Norwood on 02/11/79 in McComb, Mississippi. Acted in the television sitcoms *Thea* and *Moesha*. Starred in the movie *I Still Know What You Did Last Summer*.

04/24/95	15	13	Baby...	Atlantic	40
10/16/95	22	3	Brokenhearted	Atlantic	
05/06/96	39	1 h	Sittin' Up In My Room	Arista	9
11/03/96	35	2	Missing You *	Elektra	
05/24/98	1(15)	47	The Boy Is Mine **	Atlantic	1
09/27/98	21	4	Top Of The World ***	Atlantic	27
02/14/99	20	5	Have You Ever?...	Atlantic	6
06/07/99	---	RA	Almost Doesn't Count	Atlantic	27

* Brandy, Tamia, Gladys Knight & Chaka Khan
** Brandy & Monica
*** Brandy featuring Mase

BRANIGAN, Laura
American female pop singer born on 07/03/57 in Brewster, New York. Toured Europe with Leonard Cohen as a backup singer.

01/17/83	2(4)	24	Gloria	Atlantic	
05/23/83	8	8	Solitaire	Atlantic	
07/23/84	1(3)	17	Self Control...	Atlantic	
01/14/85	5	11	Ti Amo..	Atlantic	

DATE	PK	WK	TITLE	LABEL	RA
09/16/85	34	3	Spanish Eddie .... Atlantic		

BRAXTON, Toni
American female R&B singer born Toni Michelle Braxton on 10/07/68 in Severn, Maryland. Recorded with her sisters as The Braxtons up to 1992.

10/04/93	---	RA	Another Sad Love Song .... Arista		11
01/31/94	---	RA	Breathe Again .... Arista		2
07/04/94	---	RA	You Mean The World To Me .... Arista		7
07/22/96	27	8 h	Let It Flow .... Arista		
11/03/96	6	37	You're Making Me High .... Arista		3
			Hit Parade: #17 (09/30/96) / 10 wks.		
02/02/97	2(3)	36	Un-Break My Heart .... Arista		2
			"P1" version peaked at #29 on 02/16/97.		
07/06/97	13	15	I Don't Want To .... Arista		

BREAD
American pop/MOR group formed in 1969 in Los Angeles. Line-up in 1977: David Gates (vocals, guitar, keyboards, b. 12/11/40 in Tulsa, Oklahoma), James Griffin (vocals, guitar, b. Memphis, Tennessee), Mike Botts (drums, b. Sacramento, California), Larry Knechtel (keyboards, b. in Bell, California).

03/05/77	11	14	Lost Without Your Love .... Elektra		

BREAKFAST CLUB
American pop/dance quartet from New York City featuring producer Steve Bray. Madonna was a member in the early-1980's.

07/06/87	15	13	Right On Track .... MCA		

BREATHE
British pop group from London: David Glasper (vocals), Ian "Spike" Spice, Marcus Lillington, Michael Delahunty (who left in 1988).

09/19/88	2(3)	18	Hands To Heaven .... Virgin		
01/16/89	6	16	How Can I Fall .... Virgin		
04/10/89	35	5	Don't Tell Me Lies .... Virgin		
11/12/90	19	8	Say A Prayer .... Virgin		9

BREEN, Michael
Canadian male pop singer/songwriter from Montreal. Native of Nicolet, Quebec.

11/02/87	33	5	Rain .... Alert		

BRICK
American jazz-disco group formed in Atlanta in 1972 featuring vocalist Jimmy Brown.

02/05/77	18	8	Dazz .... RCA		

BRICKELL, Edie, & The New Bohemians
American band formed in Dallas in 1985: Edie Brickell (vocals, guitar, b. 03/10/66 in Oak Cliff, Texas), Kenny Withrow (guitar, b. 04/13/65), Brad Houser (bass, b. 09/07/60), Wes Burt-Martin (guitar, b. 05/28/64), Matt Chamberlain (drums, b. 04/17/67), John Bush (percussion). Brickell married singer/songwriter Paul Simon in June 1992.

DATE	PK	WK	TITLE	LABEL	RA

| 03/20/89 | 6 | 13 | What I Am .... Geffen | | |
| 10/17/94 | --- | RA | Good Times * .... Geffen | 39 | |

* Edie Brickell

BRIDGES, Alicia
American disco singer/songwriter from Atlanta. Native of Lawndale, North Carolina; born on 07/15/53.

| 12/27/78 | 7 | 12 | I Love The Night Life .... Polydor | | |

BRIGHTON ROCK
Canadian rock band from Hamilton-Niagara region of Ontario: Gerald McGhee (vocals), Greg Fraser (lead guitar), Mark Cavarzan (drums), Stevie Skreebs (bass), and Martin Victor (keyboards). Disbanded in 1992.

| 05/15/89 | 37 | 1 | One More Try .... WEA | C |

BRONSKI BEAT
British techno-pop trio consisting of Jimmy Somerville (vocals), Steve Bronski, Larry Steinbachek.

| 01/14/85 | 11 | 17 | Smalltown Boy... London |

BROOKS & DUNN
American country duo: Kix Brooks (b. 05/12/55 in Shreveport, Louisiana), Ronnie Dunn (b. 06/01/53 in Tulsa, Oklahoma). Dunn raised in Texas.

| 09/28/92 | 31 | 9 | Boot Scootin' Boogie....................................Arista |

BROOKS, Alma Faye
Canadian female disco vocalist.

| 08/13/77 | 20 | 6 | Stop I Don't Need No Symphony .... RCA |

BROOKS, Garth
American male country singer born Troyal Garth Brooks on 02/07/62 in Tulsa, Oklahoma.

| 09/05/94 | --- | RA | Hard Luck Woman..................................... Mercury | 28 |

BROOKS, Meredith
American female rock singer/guitarist born on 06/12/66 near Eugene, Oregon.

| 07/13/97 | 33 | 1 | Bitch .... Capitol | 1 |
| 02/02/98 | --- | RA | What Would Happen .... Capitol | 22 |

BROS
British pop trio: Matt and Luke Goss, Craig Logan (b. 04/22/69 in Kirkcaldy, Scotland). Goss are twin brothers born on 09/29/68 in London.

| 02/12/90 | 18 | 10 | Too Much .... Epic | |
| 04/16/90 | 20 | 7 | Chocolate Box .... Columbia | 32 |

DATE	PK	WK	TITLE	LABEL	RA

BROTHERHOOD CREED
American R&B-rap duo of Tyrone Ward and Sean McDuffie.

| 05/25/92 | 28 | 11 | Helluva | Gasoline Alley | |

BROTHERHOOD OF MAN
British studio group featuring Tony Burrows, Johnny Goddison, and Sunny.

| 07/10/76 | 28 | 4 | Save Your Kisses For Me | Pye | |

BROTHERS JOHNSON
American R&B duo of brothers, George (b. 05/17/53) and Louis Johnson (b. 04/13/55).

| 08/28/76 | 20 | 11 | I'll Be Good To You | A&M | |
| 11/02/77 | 14 | 8 | Strawberry Letter 23 | A&M | |

BROWN, Bobby
American R&B-pop singer born Robert Baresford Brown on 02/05/69 in Boston. Former member of New Edition. Married Whitney Houston on 07/18/92.

02/13/89	3(1)	18	My Prerogative	MCA	
04/17/89	15	11	Roni	MCA	
06/26/89	22	10	Every Little Step	MCA	
09/04/89	1(4)	16	On Our Own	MCA	
11/06/89	28	3	Rock Wit'cha	MCA	
08/27/90	---	RA	She Ain't Worth It *	MCA	3
09/28/92	1(2)	13	Humpin' Around	MCA	1
12/14/92	---	RA	Good Enough	MCA	4
02/22/93	---	RA	Get Away	MCA	14
12/27/93	---	RA	Something In Common **	MCA	19

* Glenn Medeiros featuring Bobby Brown
** Bobby Brown/Whitney Houston

BROWN, Charity
Canadian female singer based in Kitchener, Ontario. Real name is Phyllis Boltz.

06/07/75	18	2	Take Me In Your Arms	A&M	
01/24/76	30	2	Saving All My Love	A&M	
04/17/76	21	10	Anyway You Want	A&M	
08/13/77	40	1	Hold On Baby	A&M	

BROWN, Foxy
American female rapper born Inga Marchand on 09/06/79 in Brooklyn, New York.

| 06/13/99 | 26 | 5 | I Can't | Def Jam | |

BROWN, James
American male R&B singer born on 05/03/33 in Barnwell, South Carolina. Commonly billed as "The Godfather of Soul" and "Soul Brother Number One". Most successful black artist of the 1960's. On 12/15/88, received a six-year prison term after leading police on an interstate car chase; released from prison on 02/27/91.

DATE	PK	WK	TITLE	LABEL	RA
02/24/86	2(1)	13	Living In America	Scotti Brothers	

BROWN, Peter
American male R&B singer/keyboardist/producer born on 07/11/53 in Blue Island, Illinois.

07/26/78	16	12	Dance With Me	TK	

BROWN, Sam
British female singer/songwriter. Backup singer for several recording artists such as Spandau Ballet and Mark Knopfler.

04/03/89	8	16	Stop	A&M	

BROWN, Troy

05/09/99	22	8	Feel Alright	Page	

BROWNE, Jackson
American male rock singer/songwriter born on 10/09/48 in Heidelberg, Germany. Wrote songs for Bonnie Raitt, Tom Rush, Linda Ronstadt, and the Byrds. First wife, Phyllis committed suicide in 1976.

DATE	PK	WK	TITLE	LABEL	RA
05/03/78	17	12	Running On Empty	Asylum	
09/06/78	28	6	Stay	Asylum	
09/13/80	3(2)	6	Boulevard	Asylum	
10/09/82	4	10	Somebody's Baby	Asylum	
09/26/83	24	7	Lawyers In Love	Asylum	
01/20/86	37	2	You're A Friend Of Mine *	Capitol	

* Clarence Clemons/Jackson Browne

BROWNSTONE
American R&B trio consisting of New Orleans-born Monica "Mimi" Doby, Detroit-born Nichole "Nicci" Gilbert, Guyana-born Charmayne "Maxee" Maxwell. Doby left in 1995, replaced by Kina Cosper.

05/22/95	12	19	If You Love Me	Epic	

BRYSON, Peabo
American male R&B singer born on 04/13/51 in Greenville, South Carolina.

DATE	PK	WK	TITLE	LABEL	RA
12/05/83	4	16	Tonight, I Celebrate My Love *	Capitol	
10/01/84	7	10	If Ever You're In My Arms Again	Elektra	
03/16/92	2(1)	34	Beauty And The Beast **	Columbia	
03/08/93	2(1)	25	A Whole New World ***	Columbia	4
07/19/93	---	RA	By The Time This Night Is Over ****	Arista	23

* Peabo Bryson/Roberta Flack
** Celine Dion & Peabo Bryson
*** Peabo Bryson and Regina Belle
**** Kenny G with Peabo Bryson

DATE	PK	WK	TITLE	LABEL	RA

BUCKINGHAM, Lindsey
American male rock guitarist/singer/songwriter born on 10/03/47 in Palo Alto, California. Member of Fleetwood Mac (1974-1987).

| 12/26/81 | 4 | 12 | Trouble | Asylum | |

BUFFETT, Jimmy
American male singer/songwriter born on 12/25/46 in Pascagoula, Mississippi. Former *Billboard Magazine* reporter. To Key West, Florida in 1972, built "Margaritaville" empire. Own record label in 1990's. Wrote two best-selling books as well as two children's books.

| 08/06/77 | 15 | 12 | Margaritaville | ABC | |

BUGGLES
British pop duo: Trevor Horn (bass, vocals, b. 07/15/49 in Hertfordshire, England), Geoffrey Downes (keyboards). Horn is the producer for Frankie Goes To Hollywood, ABC as well as "Do They Know It's Christmas" by Band Aid.

| 03/05/80 | 2(2) | 18 | Video Killed The Radio Star | WEA | |

BURNETTE, Rocky
American male rock-country singer born on 06/12/53 in Memphis, Tennessee. Son of early-1960's rock singer Johnny Burnette.

| 07/16/80 | 12 | 4 | Tired Of Toein' The Line | Capitol | |

BURNS, George
American male comedian/actor born Nathan Birnbaum on 01/20/1896 in New York City. Starred with wife, Gracie, in vaudeville, and television's *George Burns and Gracie Allen Show*. Appeared in several movies including *Oh, God!* and *Oh, God, You Devil!* Died on 03/09/96 in Beverly Hills, California.

| 04/16/80 | 19 | 1 | I Wish I Was 18 Again | Mercury | |

BUSH
British rock group formed in 1992 in London: Gavin Rossdale (vocals, guitar, b. 10/30/67 in London), Nigel Pulsford (guitar, b. 04/11/63), Dave Parsons (bass, b. 07/02/64), Robbie Goodridge (drums, b. 09/10/66). Originally named "Bush X" in Canada due to another band owning the Canadian rights to the name "Bush".

| 02/17/97 | --- | RA | Swallowed * | Interscope | 39 |

* Bush X

BUSH, Kate
British female singer/songwriter born on 07/30/58 in Bexleyheath, England.

12/02/85	27	12	Running Up That Hill	Capitol	
06/22/87	40	1	Don't Give Up *	Geffen	
11/15/93	15	25	Rubberband Girl	Capitol	14

* Peter Gabriel/Kate Bush

DATE	PK	WK	TITLE	LABEL	RA

BUSTA RHYMES
American male rapper born circa 1971 in Brooklyn, New York.

05/31/98	3(1)	29	Turn It Up/Fire It Up .... Elektra		

Above is domestic version. An import version peaked at #8 on 04/19/98.

04/18/99	21	5	What's It Gonna Be?! * .... Elektra	27

* Busta Rhymes featuring Janet

B*WITCHED
Irish female pop vocal group from Dublin: Edele Lynch (b. Edele Claire Christina Edwina Lynch, 12/15/79 in Dublin), Sinead O'Carroll (b. Sinead Maria O'Carroll, b. 05/14/78 in Dublin), Lindsay Armaou (b. Lindsay Gael Christina Armaou, b. 12/18/80 in Greece), Keavy Lynch (b. Keavy-Jane, Elizabeth, Annie Lynch, b. 12/15/79 in Dublin). Edele and Keavy are twin sisters; their brother Shane is a member of Boyzone.

03/21/99	23	9	C'est La Vie .... Epic	31

C

CADELL, Meryn
Canadian female alternative music singer/songwriter/actress from Toronto.

07/13/92	---	RA	The Sweater .... Intrepid	24

CAFFERTY, John, & The Beaver Brown Band
American rock group from Narrangansett, Rhode Island: John Cafferty (vocals, guitar), Bob Cotoia, Gary Gramolini, Kenny Jo Silva, Pat Lupo, Michael Antunes.

11/19/84	14	8	On The Dark Side .... Scotti Brothers	
07/29/85	30	4	Tough All Over .... Scotti Brothers	
10/14/85	38	2	C-I-T-Y .... Scotti Brothers	

CALLOWAY
American R&B duo of brothers Reggie and Vincent Calloway from Cincinnati.

06/11/90	4	15	I Wanna Be Rich .... Solar	15

CAMEO
American R&B-funk group formed in 1974 in New York City: Larry Blackmon (drums, bass, vocals, b. 05/29/56 in New York City), Tomi Jenkins (vocals), Nathan Leftenant (trumpet, vocals). Blackmon produced Bobby Brown's debut, was Vice-President A&R at Warner-Reprise Records in early-1990's.

01/19/87	2(1)	18	Word Up .... Mercury	

CAMERON, Doug
Canadian male pop-rock singer.

10/07/85	36	4	Mona With The Children .... True North	

DATE	PK	WK	TITLE	LABEL	RA

CAMILLE
Canadian female dance singer.

05/29/95	---	RA	A Deeper Shade Of Love	Epic	26
11/04/96	---	RA	Do Ya Own Thing	Epic	14

CAMPBELL, Glen
American male country-pop singer born on 04/22/36 in Billstown, Arkansas. Session work with Frank Sinatra, Rick Nelson, Johnny Cash, Dean Martin in 1960's. Played guitar/bass with Beach Boys for a short time in 1965. Hosted own *The Glen Campbell Goodtime Hour* (1969-1972), *The Glen Campbell Music Show* (1982-1983). Acted in movies such as *True Grit*, *Norwood*.

09/13/75	1(2)	12	Rhinestone Cowboy	Capitol
01/24/76	22	2	Thank God I'm A Country Boy	Capitol
05/14/77	2(2)	14	Southern Nights	Capitol
10/05/77	27	4	Sunflowers	Capitol

CAMPBELL, Tevin
American male R&B vocalist born on 11/12/78 in Waxahachie, Texas. Appeared in the movie, *Graffiti Bridge*.

03/02/92	---	RA	Tell Me What You Want Me To Do	Warner	38
02/21/94	19	12	Can We Talk?	Warner	28

C+C MUSIC FACTORY
American dance group featuring the production/songwriting duo of Robert Clivilles (drums, percussion, bass, b. 08/30/64 in New York City) and David Cole (keyboards, bass, vocals, b. 06/03/62 in Johnson City, Tennessee). Cole died on 01/24/95 in New York City of complications from spinal meningitis. Featured vocalists included Zelma Davis (b. 08/02/70 in Liberia) and Freedom Williams (b. 02/13/66 in Brooklyn), Martha Wash (b. San Francisco), Deborah Cooper.

02/04/91	1(6)	12	Gonna Make You Sweat *	Columbia	4
05/13/91	2(3)	19	Here We Go	Columbia	7
09/16/91	3(2)	17	Things That Make You Go Hmmmm	Columbia	8
02/24/92	13	17	Just A Touch Of Love	Columbia	
03/23/92	6	19	Pride (In The Name Of Love) **	Columbia	
09/28/92	16	10	Keep It Coming	Columbia	
10/31/94	4	47	Do You Wanna Get Funky	Columbia	29

* C&C Music Factory Featuring Freedom Williams
** Clivilles & Cole

CANDI
Canadian dance-pop group from Toronto: Candy Pennella (vocals), Nino Milazzo, Rick Imbrogno, Paul Russo.

11/21/88	16	9	Dancing Under A Latin Moon	I.R.S.	
02/20/89	5	19	Under Your Spell	I.R.S.	
05/08/89	10	13	Love Makes No Promises	I.R.S.	
12/24/90	7	16	The World Just Keeps On Turning *	I.R.S.	11
04/08/91	15	11	Good Together *	I.R.S.	15
06/10/91	---	RA	Friends Forever *	I.R.S.	33

DATE	PK	WK	TITLE	LABEL	RA

* Candi & The Backbeat

CANDYMAN
American male rapper born on 06/25/68 in Los Angeles. Backup rapper for Tone Loc.

| 01/28/91 | 13 | 11 | Knockin' Boots | Epic |
| 03/11/91 | 21 | 5 | Melt In Your Mouth | Epic |

CANIBUS
Jamaican/American male rapper born Germaine Williams in Jamaica. Moved to the Bronx at age 13. Raised in Miami, Washington, D.C., London and Atlanta. Holds a degree in computer science.

| 04/19/98 | 9 | 19 | Second Round K.O. | Universal |

CAPALDI, Jim
British male rock vocalist/drummer born on 08/24/44 in Evesham, England. Member of Traffic.

| 03/20/76 | 26 | 6 | Love Hurts | Island |

CAPITOL SOUND

| 05/04/97 | 31 | 3 | Higher Love | Unit |

CAPPRICHO FEATURING CHILLI

| 07/13/97 | 13 | 10 | Tic Tic Tac | BMGA |

CAPTAIN & TENNILLE
American husband-and-wife pop duo: Daryl "The Captain" Dragon (keyboards, b. 08/27/42 in Los Angeles), Toni Tennille (vocals, b. as Catheryn Antoinette Tennille, 05/08/43 in Montgomery, Alabama). Dragon worked with Beach Boys in 1960's. Hosted own prime time television series in 1976-77. Tennille had own television talk show in 1980's.

06/28/75	1(4)	13	Love Will Keep Us Together	A&M
12/13/75	4	11	The Way I Want To Touch You	A&M
03/27/76	2(3)	13	Lonely Night	A&M
06/19/76	5	12	Shop Around	A&M
12/04/76	4	14	Muskrat Love	A&M
05/14/77	22	9	Can't Stop Dancing	A&M
11/29/78	8	10	You Never Done It Like That	A&M
03/05/80	8	16	Do That To Me One More Time	Casablanca

CAPTAIN HOLLYWOOD PROJECT
American dance group led by Tony Harrison, born in Newark, New Jersey; raised in Detroit.

| 07/19/93 | --- | RA | More And More | Imago | 5 |

CARA, Irene
American female pop singer/actress/dancer born on 03/18/59 in New York City. Appeared on TV's *Electric Company*, *Roots 2*. In the movies *Fame* and *The Cotton Club*.

| 05/30/83 | 1(6) | 22 | Flashdance...What A Feelin' | Casablanca |

DATE	PK	WK	TITLE	LABEL	RA
12/26/83	22	7	Why Me?	Geffen	
06/04/84	6	13	Breakdance	Geffen	

CARDIGANS, The
Swedish pop band formed in October 1992 in Jonkoping, Sweden: Nina Persson (vocals), Peter Svensson (guitar), Magnus Sveningsson (bass), Bengt Lagerberg (drums), Lasse Johansson (guitar, keyboards).

DATE	PK	WK	TITLE	LABEL	RA
02/24/97	---	RA	Lovefool	Mercury	1
10/18/98	19	16	My Favourite Game	TRM	

CAREY, Mariah
American female pop singer born on 03/27/70 in Long Island, New York. To New York City in 1987. Background vocals for dance singer Brenda K. Starr, who introduced her to Tony Mottola, Sony Music Entertainment President, who in turn signed her to Columbia in 1990. Married Mottola on 06/05/93; divorced in 1997.

DATE	PK	WK	TITLE	LABEL	RA
09/03/90	1(2)	21	Vision Of Love	Columbia	1
12/17/90	1(1)	24	Love Takes Time	Columbia	2
03/11/91	5	15	Someday	Columbia	1
05/20/91	7	14	I Don't Wanna Cry	Columbia	2
11/11/91	3(2)	21	Emotions	Columbia	1
01/20/92	7	14	Can't Let Go	Columbia	2
04/27/92	16	13	Make It Happen	Columbia	1
07/06/92	1(2)	13	I'll Be There	Columbia	1
10/18/93	1(3)	41	Dreamlover	Columbia	1
01/31/94	10	36	Hero	Columbia	5
03/28/94	2(5)	37	Without You	Columbia	3
07/11/94	---	RA	Anytime You Need A Friend	Columbia	7
04/17/95	14	40	Endless Love *	Epic	8
10/30/95	1(12)	28	Fantasy	Columbia	1
02/05/96	2(5)	16	One Sweet Day **	Columbia	1
			Hit Parade: #3(4) (01/22/96) / 18 wks.		
05/20/96	2(1)	20 h	Always Be My Baby	Columbia	1
			Retail Singles: #16 (04/01/96) / 2 wks.		
09/09/96	13	12 h	Forever	Columbia	11
08/31/97	2(2)	14	Honey	Columbia	2
			Above is domestic version. An import version peaked at #29 on 11/30/97.		
12/08/97	---	RA	Butterfly	Columbia	16
08/30/98	12	28	My All	Columbia	31
01/31/99	26	5	When You Believe ***	Columbia	
			Another version peaked at #29 on 01/03/99.		
02/21/99	9	17	I Still Believe	Columbia	30

* Luther Vandross/Mariah Carey
** Mariah Carey & Boyz II Men
*** Mariah Carey & Whitney Houston

CAREY, Tony
American male rock singer/keyboardist born on 10/16/53 in Fresno, California.

DATE	PK	WK	TITLE	LABEL	RA
06/25/84	23	7	A Fine Fine Day	MCA	

DATE	PK	WK	TITLE	LABEL	RA

CARLISLE, Belinda
American female pop vocalist born on 08/17/58 in Hollywood, California. Lead singer of the Go-Go's, 1978-1984.

DATE	PK	WK	TITLE	LABEL	RA
09/15/86	5	15	Mad About You	I.R.S.	
12/28/87	6	18	Heaven Is A Place On Earth	MCA	
03/28/88	6	14	I Get Weak	MCA	
07/04/88	4	14	Circle In The Sand	MCA	
12/18/89	11	12	Leave A Light On	MCA	
03/19/90	31	4	Summer Rain	MCA	38
12/09/91	27	2	Do You Feel Like I Feel	MCA	

CARLISLE, Bob
American male Christian singer/songwriter born on 09/29/56 in Santa Anna, California.

DATE	PK	WK	TITLE	LABEL	RA
07/14/97	---	RA	Butterfly Kisses	DMG	31

CARMEN, Eric
American male pop singer born on 08/11/49 in Cleveland. Lead singer/bassist/guitarist of The Raspberries. Wrote "That's Rock N' Roll" by Shaun Cassidy and "Almost Paradise" by Mike Reno and Ann Wilson.

DATE	PK	WK	TITLE	LABEL	RA
03/13/76	1(3)	13	All By Myself	Arista	
07/03/76	12	8	Never Gonna Fall In Love Again	Arista	
11/30/77	11	12	She Did It	Arista	
03/14/88	6	13	Hungry Eyes	RCA	
09/19/88	3(1)	16	Make Me Lose Control	Arista	

CARNES, Kim
American female pop singer/songwriter born on 07/20/45 in Los Angeles. Along with husband/backup band member Dave Ellingson, wrote songs for Anne Murray, Frank Sinatra, Rita Coolidge, Barbra Streisand, Kenny Rogers.

DATE	PK	WK	TITLE	LABEL	RA
05/28/80	7	11	Don't Fall In Love With A Dreamer *	United Artists	
05/30/81	1(5)	13	Bette Davis Eyes	Capitol	
10/16/82	8	5	Voyeur	Capitol	
12/26/83	29	4	Invisible Hands	Capitol	
12/03/84	18	8	What About Me? **	RCA	
08/26/85	25	12	Crazy In The Night (Barking At Airplanes)	Capitol	

* Kenny Rogers/Kim Carnes
** Kenny Rogers/Kim Carnes/James Ingram

CARPENTERS
American brother/sister pop-MOR duo: Richard Carpenter (vocals, keyboards, b. 10/15/46 in New Haven, Connecticut), Karen Carpenter (vocals, drum, b. 03/02/50 in New Haven, Connecticut). Formed jazz-pop instrumental trio in 1965 consisting of Richard, Karen, and friend bassist Wes Jacobs, who later joined the Detroit Symphony. Performed in sextet, Spectrum in late-1960's. Signed as Carpenters to A&M in 1969. Three-time Grammy winner. Hosted variety series on NBC, *Make Your Own Kind Of Music* in 1971. Karen died on 02/04/83 of cardiac arrest, resulting from anorexia nervosa. 1988 television movie *The Karen Carpenter Story* told of Karen's life and battle with anorexia nervosa. Tribute album performed by fourteen artists was released in 1994.

DATE	PK	WK	TITLE	LABEL RA
06/07/75	8	2	Only Yesterday	A&M
10/04/75	23	2	Solitaire	A&M
04/24/76	11	9	(There's A) Kind Of Hush	A&M
07/24/76	31	3	I Need To Be In Love	A&M
12/14/77	9	16	Calling Occupants	A&M
04/19/78	33	4	Sweet Sweet Smile	A&M

CARRA, Raffaella

11/16/77	40	2	Fiesta	CBS

CARRACK, Paul
British male pop singer born on 04/22/51 in Sheffield, England. Lead singer of Ace, Squeeze, and Mike + The Mechanics.

01/25/88	36	2	Don't Shed A Tear	Chrysalis

CARS, The
American pop-rock group formed in 1976 in Boston: Ric Ocasek (vocals, guitar, b. Richard Otcasek on 03/23/49 in Baltimore), Ben Orr (bass, vocals, b. Benjamin Orzechowski on 08/09/55 in Cleveland), Elliot Easton (guitar, b. Elliot Steinberg on 12/18/53 in Brooklyn, New York), Greg Hawkes (keyboards), David Robinson (drums, b. 04/02/53).

09/19/79	12	12	Let's Go	Elektra
11/01/80	18	2	Touch And Go	Elektra
02/20/82	6	12	Shake It Up	Elektra
05/07/84	10	14	You Might Think	Elektra
08/27/84	21	9	Magic	Elektra
10/29/84	5	18	Drive	Elektra
02/03/86	39	2	Tonight She Comes	Elektra

CARTER, Clarence
American male R&B-pop singer/songwriter born on 01/14/36 in Montgomery, Alabama. Blind since age one. Briefly married to R&B singer Candi Staton.

10/15/90	33	17	Strokin'	MCA

CARTOUCHE
Belgian dance duo: Myrelle Tholen (vocals), Jean-Paul Visser (vocals).

09/25/95	24	3	Miracles	NuMuzik

CASSIDY, David
American male pop singer/actor born on 04/12/50 in New York City. Son of actor Jack Cassidy and actress Evelyn Ward. On television's *Marcus Welby, M.D.* and *Bonanza*. Played Keith Partridge, lead singer of TV's *Partridge Family*. Later pursued career in television and theatre.

12/10/90	29	7	Lyin' To Myself	Enigma	22

CASSIDY, Shaun

DATE	PK	WK	TITLE	LABEL	RA

American male pop singer/actor born on 09/27/59 in Hollywood. Half brother of David Cassidy, son of actor Jack Cassidy and actress Shirley Jones. Starred in *The Hardy Boys Mysteries* television series, 1977-1979. Later pursued acting career in television and theatre.

08/13/77	1(3)	24	Da Doo Ron Ron	Warner	
11/30/77	2(2)	24	That's Rock N' Roll	Warner	
02/08/78	5	20	Hey Deanie	Warner	

CATS CAN FLY
Canadian pop group based in Toronto formed in 1982: Eddie Zeeman (drums), David Ashley (bass), Peter Alexandre (keyboards), Mitchell James (guitar).

04/14/86	29	7	Flippin' To The "A" Side	Epic	

CETERA, Peter
American male pop singer born on 09/13/44 in Chicago. Former vocalist/bassist of Chicago.

09/29/86	1(1)	19	Glory Of Love	Full Moon	
10/17/88	25	10	One Good Woman	Full Moon	
01/19/87	4	19	The Next Time I Fall *	Full Moon	
05/29/89	6	17	After All **	Geffen	
08/17/92	---	RA	Restless Heart	Warner	26

* Peter Cetera/Amy Grant
** Cher/Peter Cetera

CHALK CIRCLE
Canadian rock group from Newcastle, Ontario formed in 1983 consisting of Chris Tait (vocals, guitar), Brad Hopkins (bass), Derrick Murphy (drums), and Tad Winklarz (keyboards).

07/21/86	27	5	April Fool	WEA	
07/13/87	31	5	This Mourning	Duke Street	
10/19/87	39	2	20th Century Boy	MCA	

CHANDLER, Gene
American male R&B singer/producer born Eugene Dixon on 07/06/37 in Chicago.

01/24/79	33	4	Get Down	Chi-Sound	

CHANGING FACES
American R&B duo from New York City: Bronx-born Charisse Rose and Manhattan-born Cassandra Lucas.

04/17/95	21	22	Stroke You Up	Atlantic	

CHAPMAN, Tracy
American female folk-rock singer/songwriter born on 03/20/64 in Cleveland. Winner of four Grammy awards in 1988.

09/26/88	5	19	Fast Car	Elektra	
07/15/96	1(1)	20 h	Give Me One Reason	Elektra	3

DATE	PK	WK	TITLE	LABEL	RA

CHARLENE
American female pop singer Charlene Duncan (nee: D'Angelo), born on 06/01/50 in Hollywood.

| 06/12/82 | 5 | 11 | I've Never Been To Me | Motown | |

CHARLES & EDDIE
American R&B vocal duo of Charles Pettigrew and Eddie Chacon. Pettigrew is from Philadelphia, Chacon is from Oakland, California.

| 12/07/92 | 4 | 15 | Would I Lie To You | Capitol | 4 |
| 02/08/93 | 35 | 4 | N.Y.C. | Capitol | |

CHARLES, Tina
British female dance singer. Former vocalist for the group 5000 Volts.

| 09/11/76 | 14 | 18 | I Love To Love | Columbia | |
| 02/12/77 | 26 | 8 | Dance Little Lady Dance | Columbia | |

CHEAP TRICK
American rock group formed in Rockford, Illinois in 1974: Robin Zander (vocals, b. 01/23/53), Tom Petersson (bass, b. Tom Peterson on 05/09/50), Rick Nielsen (guitar, b. 12/22/46), Bun E. Carlos (drums, b. Brad Carlson on 06/12/51). All four members were born in Rockford. Petersson left in 1980, replaced by Pete Comita, returned in 1986. Zander, Nielsen, and Carlos played on John Lennon and Yoko Ono's *Double Fantasy* album.

07/11/79	6	18	I Want You To Want Me (live)	Epic	
10/03/79	14	8	Ain't That A Shame	Epic	
01/09/80	24	16	Dream Police	Epic	
02/20/80	17	6	Voices	Epic	
08/15/88	3(1)	19	The Flame	Epic	
11/07/88	8	18	Don't Be Cruel	Epic	
02/13/89	31	7	Ghost Town	Epic	
10/08/90	12	13	Can't Stop Fallin' Into Love	Epic	6
10/05/92	---	RA	All Shook Up	Epic	33

CHEMICAL BROTHERS
British techno-dance duo formed as the Dust Brothers in 1992 in Manchester. Consists of Ed Simons and Tom Rowlands.

| 09/28/97 | 28 | 1 | Electro Bank | Interscope | |
| 06/06/99 | 3(1) | 8 + | Hey Boy Hey Girl | Virgin | |

CHER
American female rock singer/songwriter/actor born Cherilyn Sarkasian LaPier on 05/20/46 in El Centro, California. Recorded with Sonny Bono; married to Bono, 1963-1975. Hosted own variety show in 1975. Married to guitarist Gregg Allman, 1975-1979. Made Broadway debut in 1982. Appeared in films like *Moonstruck*, *Mermaids*, *The Witches of Eastwick*, *Silkwood*, and *Mask*. Won Oscar for best actress for role in *Moonstruck* in 1987. Reunited with Sonny Bono for a performance on *Late Night with David Letterman* in February 1988. Released exercise videos, diet guides, perfume, line of skin-care products in the 1990's.

| 03/28/88 | 12 | 10 | I Found Someone | Geffen | |
| 05/29/89 | 6 | 17 | After All * | Geffen | |

DATE	PK	WK	TITLE	LABEL	RA
10/16/89	7	15	If I Could Turn Back Time .... Geffen		
05/07/90	26	5	Heart Of Stone... Geffen		36
02/18/91	38	1	The Shoop Shoop Song (It's In His Kiss)..... Geffen		35
08/05/91	16	10	Love And Understanding............................. Geffen		8
07/29/96	20	9 h	One By One..EastWest		
01/24/99	2(7)	27 +	Believe...WEA		1
			Three other versions peaked at #8 on 01/03/99, #37 on 01/17/99, #24 on 02/21/99.		
05/30/99	16	6	Strong Enough...WEA		24
			Another version peaked at #21 on 05/30/99.		

* Cher/Peter Cetera

CHERRY POPPIN' DADDIES
American swing band formed in 1988 in Eugene, Oregon: Steve Perry (vocals, guitar), Jason Moss (guitar), Dana Heitman (trumpet, trombone), Dan Schmid (bass), Sean Flannery (saxophone), Ian Early (saxophone), Dustin Lanker (keyboards), Tim Donahue (drums).

06/29/98	---	RA	Zoot Suit Riot.. Mojo	24

CHERRY, Eagle Eye
Swedish male pop/rock singer born on 05/07/69 in Stockholm. Son of jazz trumpeter Don Cherry and younger brother of Neneh Cherry. Moved to New York City at age 14. Named "Eagle Eye" after he looked at his father with only one eye open at birth.

12/07/98	---	RA	Save Tonight .... Work	2

CHERRY, Neneh
American/Swedish female pop/dance singer born Neneh Mariann Karlsson on 03/10/64 in Stockholm, Sweden. Her stepfather is jazz trumpeter Don Cherry; her younger brother is Eagle Eye Cherry.

07/10/89	1(5)	15	Buffalo Stance ....Virgin	
10/02/89	20	7	Kisses On The Wind ....Virgin	
05/10/93	---	RA	Buddy X...Virgin	20

CHIC
American disco-pop band formed in Bronx, New York in 1976 consisting of Bernard Edwards (bass, b. 10/31/52 in Greenville, North Carolina), Nile Rodgers (guitar, b. 09/12/52), Luci Martin (vocals, b. 01/10/55), Tony Thompson (drums, b. 11/15/54), Alfa Anderson (vocals, b. 09/07/46). Disbanded in 1983, reunited in 1992 with different lead singers. Thompson became a member of Power Station in 1985. Edwards produced Power Station, Rod Stewart, and Robert Palmer; Rodgers produced 50 records from 1981 to 1993 including Madonna's *Like A Virgin* CD. Edwards died of pneumonia on 04/18/96 in Tokyo.

03/08/78	14	18	Dance Dance Dance .... Atlantic
12/27/78	1(8)	24	Le Freak .... Atlantic
05/16/79	12	6	I Want Your Love.. Atlantic
08/22/79	5	12	Good Times.. Atlantic

CHICAGO
American pop-MOR group formed in Chicago in 1967 consisting of Peter Cetera (bass, vocals, b. 09/13/44 in Chicago), Terry Kath (guitar, vocals, b. 01/31/46 in Chicago), Robert Lamm (keyboards, vocals, b. 10/13/44 in Brooklyn, New York), Walter Parazaider (saxophone, clarinet, b. 03/14/45 in Chi-

DATE	PK	WK	TITLE	LABEL	RA

cago), Danny Seraphine (drums, b. 08/28/48 in Chicago), James Pankow (trombone, b. 08/20/47 in Chicago), and Lee Loughnane (trumpet, b. 10/21/46 in Chicago). Various personnel changes followed. Kath died of gun accident on 01/28/78 in Los Angeles. Cetera left in 1984 to pursue solo career; replaced by Jason Scheff, son of Elvis Presley bassist Jerry Scheff.

DATE	PK	WK	TITLE	LABEL	RA
06/14/75	2(2)	6	Old Days	Columbia	
07/31/76	23	5	Another Rainy Day In New York City	Columbia	
11/06/76	1(3)	21	If You Leave Me Now	Columbia	
11/30/77	8	14	Baby What A Big Surprise	Columbia	
12/13/78	23	6	Alive Again	Columbia	
09/04/82	3(6)	14	Hard To Say I'm Sorry	Full Moon	
11/27/82	17	4	Love Me Tomorrow	Full Moon	
11/12/84	11	15	Hard Habit To Break	Warner	
03/11/85	7	16	You're The Inspiration	Warner	
05/20/85	20	6	Along Comes A Woman	Warner	
10/06/86	36	2	25 Or 6 To 4	Warner	
03/23/87	8	12	Will You Still Love Me?	Warner	
10/10/88	21	13	I Don't Wanna Live Without Your Love	Reprise	
02/13/89	21	12	Look Away	Reprise	
02/12/90	---	RA	What Kind Of Man Would I Be	Reprise	13

CHILD, Desmond
American male producer/songwriter born John Charles Barrett Jr. on 10/28/53 in Miami. Wrote "Livin' On A Prayer" (Bon Jovi), "We All Sleep Alone" (Cher), "Dude (Looks Like A Lady)" (Aerosmith).

DATE	PK	WK	TITLE	LABEL	RA
08/12/91	---	RA	Love On A Rooftop	Elektra	38

CHILD, Jane
Canadian female singer from Toronto. Attended Royal Conservatory Of Music in Toronto.

DATE	PK	WK	TITLE	LABEL	RA
05/14/90	17	9	Don't Wanna Fall In Love	Warner	5
08/20/90	25	6	Welcome To The Real World	Warner	
07/04/94	---	RA	All I Do	Warner	35

CHILL ROB G
American male rapper Robert Frazier (b. Queens, New York).

DATE	PK	WK	TITLE	LABEL	RA
09/24/90	27	6	Power Jam	Somersault	

CHILLIWACK
Canadian rock group based in Vancouver. Formed in 1964. Original line-up included Bill Henderson (guitar, vocals), Claire Lawrence (keyboards, saxophone), Ross Turney (drums), Howie Vickers (vocals), Glenn Miller (bass guitar). Vickers and Miller left group in late-1960's. Changed name to Chilliwack in 1969-1970. Brian Macleod (keyboards, saxophone) and Howard Froese (guitar) joined in 1977. Macleod died 04/25/92 of cancer.

DATE	PK	WK	TITLE	LABEL	RA
01/15/77	19	10	California Girl	Mushroom	
06/25/77	15	8	Fly At Night	Mushroom	
08/23/78	32	2	Arms Of Mary	Mushroom	
11/21/81	1(3)	14	My Girl (Gone, Gone, Gone)	Solid Gold	
02/27/82	7	7	I Believe	Solid Gold	
11/20/82	9	11	Whatcha Gonna Do (When I'm Gone)	Solid Gold	

DATE	PK	WK	TITLE	LABEL	RA

CHRISTIANS, The
British R&B vocal group formed in 1984 in Liverpool: Henry Priestman (b. 07/21/58 in Liverpool), and brothers Garry (b. 02/27/55 in Liverpool), Russell (b. 07/08/56 in Liverpool), Roger (b. 02/13/50 in Liverpool).

01/24/94	---	RA	The Bottle	Island	27

CHRISTOPHER, Gavin
American male R&B singer/composer/producer. Brother of female R&B singer/Lil' Louis lead singer Shawn Christopher.

08/25/86	19	4	One Step Closer To You	Manhattan	

CHUMBAWAMBA
British alternative band formed in 1982 in Leeds: Jude Abbott, Dunstan Bruce, Neil Ferguson, Paul Greco, Harry Hamer, Danbert Nubacon, Alice Nutter, Lou Watts.

10/19/97	13	4	Tubthumping	Universal	1
05/04/98	---	RA	Amnesia	Universal	16

CINDERELLA
American heavy metal band formed in Philadelphia in 1983: Eric Brittingham (bass), Tom Keifer (guitar, vocals, keyboards), Jeff LeBar (guitar), Tony Destra (drums). Discovered by Jon Bon Jovi in 1985.

03/09/87	22	7	Nobody's Fool	Mercury	
12/26/88	21	12	Don't Know What You Got	Mercury	
02/11/91	9	15	Shelter Me	Mercury	23

CIRRUS
American hip-hop/rock trio formed in 1995 in Los Angeles: Aaron Carter, Stephen James Barry (b. England), René Padilla.

07/04/99	19	4 +	Stop & Panic	Moonshine	

CLAPTON, Eric
British male blues-rock vocalist/guitarist born Eric Patrick Clapp on 03/30/45 in Ripley, England. In 1960's, performed with British R&B/blues bands including the Yardbirds and the Bluesbreakers. Co-founded Cream with bassist Jack Bruce and drummer Ginger Baker. Formed Blind Faith in 1968. Performed with John Lennon's Plastic Ono Band in 1969. Formed Derek and the Dominos. Married to George Harrison's ex-wife, Patti Boyd Harrison, 1979-1989. "Tears In Heaven" inspired by Clapton's only son, four year-old Conor, who fell to his death from a New York City apartment on 03/20/91. Honoured with Member of the British Empire (M.B.E.) on 01/01/95.

04/05/78	8	20	Lay Down Sally	RSO	
07/12/78	22	4	Wonderful Tonight	RSO	
02/07/79	21	6	Promises	RSO	
07/23/80	18	1	Cocaine	RSO	
05/02/81	6	6	I Can't Stand It	RSO	
04/11/83	17	5	I've Got A Rock N' Roll Heart	Duck	
01/29/90	---	RA	Pretending	Reprise	38
05/18/92	1(1)	14	Tears In Heaven	Reprise	7
07/27/92	11	12	It's Probably Me *	A&M	33
01/18/93	6	14	Layla	Reprise	9

DATE	PK	WK	TITLE	LABEL	RA

08/19/96	1(3)	23 h	Change The World .... Reprise	4
			SoundScan: #8 (11/03/96) / 30 wks.	
05/11/98	---	RA	My Father's Eyes .... Reprise	13

* Sting & Eric Clapton

CLARK, Terri
Canadian female country singer/guitarist born on 08/05/68 in Montreal. Raised in Medicine Hat, Alberta. Won the 1997 Juno Award for the Best New Solo Artist.

| 05/17/98 | 30 | 2 | Now That I Found You .... Mercury | |

CLASH, The
British punk band formed in 1976 in London: Mick Jones (guitar, vocals, b. Michael Jones on 06/26/53 in Brixton, England), Paul Simonon (bass, b. 12/15/55 in Brixton), Tory Crimes (drums, b. Terry Chimes in London), Joe Strummer (vocals, guitar, b. John Graham Mellors on 08/21/52 in Ankara, Turkey). Drummer Nicky "Topper" Headon (b. 05/30/55 in Bromley, England) was a member, 1977-82. Lyrics contain political messages of anit-Thatcherism, racial harmony. Jones left band in 1984 to form Big Audio Dynamite. Clash disbanded in 1986.

| 05/21/80 | 9 | 1 | Train In Vain .... Epic | |
| 02/07/83 | 26 | 2 | Rock The Casbah .... Epic | |

CLAYTON, Adam/Larry Mullen
Irish rock musicians from the group U2: bassist Adam Clayton (b. 03/13/60 in Oxford, England), drummer Larry Mullen Jr. (b. 10/31/61 in Dublin).

| 07/01/96 | 17 | 7 h | Theme From Mission: Impossible .... Island | 7 |

CLEGG, Johnny, & Savuka
South African world music band of formed in Johannesburg in 1986 led by anti-Apartheid activist Johnny Clegg (vocals, guitars b. 10/31/53 in Rochdale, England) and consisting of Zulu tribe members. Vocalist/percussionist Dudu Zulu was murdered on 05/04/92 in South Africa during factional warfare between different Zulu tribes.

| 03/19/90 | 34 | 2 | Cruel Crazy Beautiful World .... EMI | |

CLEMONS, Clarence
American male singer/saxophonist born on 01/11/42 in Norfolk, Virginia. Played saxophone in Bruce Springsteen's E Street Band, 1973-1989.

| 01/20/86 | 37 | 2 | You're A Friend Of Mine * .... Capitol | |

* Clarence Clemons/Jackson Browne

CLIFF, Jimmy
Jamaican male reggae singer born James Chamber on 04/01/48 in St. Catherine, Jamaica

| 01/17/94 | --- | RA | I Can See Clearly Now .... Cahos | 13 |

CLIMAX BLUES BAND
British rock-blues band formed in Stafford, England in 1968. Original line-up: Colin Richard Francis Cooper, Peter John Haycock, Arthur Wood, Derek Holt, George Newsome.

DATE	PK	WK	TITLE	LABEL	RA
06/18/77	3(1)	13	Couldn't Get It Right	Sire	
06/06/81	16	8	I Love You	Warner	

CLIMIE FISHER
British pop-rock duo consisting of Simon Climie (vocals) and Rob Fisher (keyboards). Fisher was a member of Naked Eyes. Climie is a songwriter, wrote "I Knew You Were Waiting (For Me)" by Aretha Franklin & George Michael, "Invincible" by Pat Benatar.

DATE	PK	WK	TITLE	LABEL	RA
08/22/88	16	10	Love Changes (Everything)	Capitol	

CLIVILLES & COLE - see C+C MUSIC FACTORY

CLUB NOUVEAU
American R&B-dance group formed in 1986 in Sacramento, California: Jay King, Denzil Foster, Thomas McElroy, Valerie Watson, Samuelle Prater. King formed Timex Social Club in 1985. Disbanded in 1990.

DATE	PK	WK	TITLE	LABEL	RA
05/18/87	1(3)	18	Lean On Me	Warner	

CLUELESS
American dance-pop group led by vocalist Gina Pincosy.

DATE	PK	WK	TITLE	LABEL	RA
05/11/97	36	1	Don't Speak	Quality	

COATES, Odia
American female pop singer from Berkeley, California. Sang with Paul Anka in 1974-75. Died of breast cancer on 05/19/91.

DATE	PK	WK	TITLE	LABEL	RA
12/18/76	38	2	Make It Up To Me In Love	Epic	

COCHRANE, Tom, & Red Rider
Canadian rock group formed in 1976 in Toronto: Tom Cochrane (vocals, guitar, b. 05/14/53 in Lynn Lake, Manitoba), Rob Baker (drums), Peter Boynton (vocals, keyboards), Jeff Jones (bass), Ken Greer (vocals, guitar). Won the 1987 Juno Award for Group of the Year; Cochrane won the 1992 Juno Award for Male Vocalist of the Year.

DATE	PK	WK	TITLE	LABEL	RA
05/28/80	16	2	White Hot *	Capitol	
05/02/83	27	2	Human Race *	Capitol	
07/23/84	34	3	Young Thing, Wild Dreams (Rock Me)	Capitol	
08/25/86	27	6	Boy Inside The Man	Capitol	
01/16/89	8	14	Big League	Capitol	
04/24/89	22	8	Good Times	Capitol	
01/29/90	28	5	White Hot	Capitol	37
11/04/91	1(6)	16	Life Is A Highway **	Capitol	1
01/27/92	12	14	No Regrets **	Capitol	1
05/18/92	---	RA	Sinking Like A Sunset **	Capitol	3
08/24/92	---	RA	Mad Mad World **	Capitol	19
11/16/92	---	RA	Washed Away **	Capitol	12
10/16/95	---	RA	I Wish You Well **	EMI	5
02/05/96	---	RA	Your Wildest Dreams	EMI	9
05/20/96	8	15 h	Dreamer's Dream **	EMI	23

DATE	PK	WK	TITLE	LABEL	RA
10/07/96	16	11 h	Crawl **	EMI	16
12/07/98	---	RA	I Wonder	EMI	28

* Red Rider
** Tom Cochrane

COCKBURN, Bruce
Canadian male rock vocalist/songwriter born on 05/27/45 in Ottawa. Winner of eight Juno Awards including Male Vocalist of the Year in 1981 and 1982.

DATE	PK	WK	TITLE	LABEL	RA
07/30/84	24	8	Lovers In A Dangerous Time	True North	
04/24/89	39	1	If A Tree Falls	True North	
12/02/91	---	RA	A Dream Like Mine	True North	38
05/02/94	---	RA	Listen For The Laugh	True North	38

COCKER, Joe
American male rock singer born John Robert Cocker on 05/20/44 in Sheffield, England. Started recording career with the Cavaliers in 1959, renamed Vance Arnold and the Avengers. Toured with the Rolling Stones as member of that group. Toured with Mad Dogs & Englishmen in 1970.

DATE	PK	WK	TITLE	LABEL
11/27/82	1(2)	15	Up Where We Belong *	Island
01/14/85	30	6	Edge Of A Dream	Capitol
02/05/90	22	8	When The Night Comes	Capitol

* Joe Cocker and Jennifer Warnes

COHN, Marc
American male singer/keyboardist born on 07/05/59 in Cleveland.

DATE	PK	WK	TITLE	LABEL	RA
07/08/91	---	RA	Walking In Memphis	Atlantic	8

COLE, Holly, Trio
Canadian jazz trio led by Holly Cole (b. Holly Jean Cole on 11/25/63 in Halifax).

DATE	PK	WK	TITLE	LABEL	RA
12/08/97	---	RA	I've Just Seen A Face *	Alert	15
12/22/96	14	6	Christmas Blues	Attic	
12/21/97	20	6	Christmas Blues (re-entry)	Attic	

* Holly Cole

COLE, Jude
American male rock singer/guitarist, native of East Moline, Illinois.

DATE	PK	WK	TITLE	LABEL	RA
07/02/90	24	5	Baby, It's Tonight	Reprise	13
10/08/90	---	RA	Time For Letting Go	Reprise	25

COLE, Natalie
American female R&B-pop singer born on 02/06/50 in Los Angeles. Daughter of Nat "King" Cole, legendary R&B singer. Married briefly to songwriter Marvin Yancy, later to producer Andre Fischer, an ex-member of Rufus. In TV's *I'll Fly Away* series in 1993.

DATE	PK	WK	TITLE	LABEL
11/29/75	28	4	This Will Be	Capitol

DATE	PK	WK	TITLE	LABEL	RA
05/28/77	7	10	I've Got Love On My Mind	Capitol	
05/17/78	13	10	Our Love	Capitol	
07/11/88	4	16	Pink Cadillac	EMI-Manhattan	
08/21/89	35	3	Miss You Like Crazy	EMI	
09/30/91	4	16	Unforgettable	Elektra	26
12/30/91	28	4	The Christmas Song	Elektra	

COLE, Paula
American female pop singer/songwriter born on 04/05/68 in Rockport, Massachusetts.

DATE	PK	WK	TITLE	LABEL	RA
01/16/95	---	RA	I Am So Ordinary	Imago	37
04/20/97	29	9	Where Have All The Cowboys Gone	Imago	5
11/10/97	---	RA	I Don't Want To Wait	Imago	18

COLLECTIVE SOUL
American rock group from Stockbridge, Georgia: brothers Ed (vocals, guitar) and Dean Roland (guitar), Ross Childress (guitar), Shane Evans (drums), Will Turpin (bass).

DATE	PK	WK	TITLE	LABEL	RA
08/01/94	---	RA	Shine	Atlantic	6
04/03/95	---	RA	Gel	Atlantic	8
07/10/95	---	RA	December	Atlantic	4
02/19/96	5	18 h	The World I Know	Atlantic	6
06/03/96	22	6 h	Where The River Flows	Atlantic	
03/31/97	---	RA	Precious Declaration	Atlantic	27
04/05/99	---	RA	Run	Atlantic	15

COLLINS, Edwin
Scottish male rock singer/songwriter born on 08/23/59 in Glasgow.

DATE	PK	WK	TITLE	LABEL	RA
10/30/95	---	RA	A Girl Like You	Koch	9

COLLINS, Judy
American female folk singer/songwriter born on 05/01/39 in Seattle. Began classical piano training at age five. Public debut at age 13 with the Denver Symphony. Became political activist involved in variety of subjects: ecology, endangered species, civil rights, and abortion rights. Co-directed documentary *Antonia: A Portrait of the Woman*, about a music teacher and conductor; nominated for Academy Award in 1974.

DATE	PK	WK	TITLE	LABEL	RA
12/14/77	16	10	Send In The Clowns	Elektra	

COLLINS, Phil
British male pop-rock singer/songwriter born on 01/31/51 in London. Member of Genesis, joined as drummer in 1970, lead singer since 1975. Performed in both London and Philadelphia in Live Aid, 07/13/85. Professional child actor at young age. Starred in the 1988 movie *Buster*.

DATE	PK	WK	TITLE	LABEL	RA
05/16/81	10	9	I Missed Again	Atlantic	
08/22/81	4	10	In The Air Tonight	Atlantic	
01/24/83	4	15	You Can't Hurry Love	Atlantic	
05/14/84	1(3)	23	Against All Odds (Take A Look At Me Now)	Atlantic	
02/11/85	1(6)	20	Easy Lover *	Columbia	
04/15/85	2(2)	15	One More Night	Atlantic	
06/24/85	1(2)	13	Sussudio	Atlantic	

DATE	PK	WK	TITLE	LABEL	RA
09/09/85	16	12	Don't Lose My Number................................	Atlantic	
12/16/85	1(2)	21	Separate Lives **	Atlantic	
11/21/88	1(5)	23	Groovy Kind Of Love	Atlantic	
02/13/89	1(2)	13	Two Hearts	Atlantic	
12/25/89	4	14	Another Day In Paradise	Atlantic	
04/16/90	3(6)	12	I Wish It Would Rain Down	Atlantic	1
07/09/90	11	14	Do You Remember?	Atlantic	2
10/08/90	9	9	Something Happened On The Way To Heaven	Atlantic	1
01/28/91	---	RA	Hang In Long Enough	Atlantic	13
12/13/93	---	RA	Both Sides Of The Story	Atlantic	2
03/14/94	---	RA	Everyday	Atlantic	9
06/06/94	---	RA	We Wait And We Wonder.........................	Atlantic	36
12/02/96	7	14 h	Dance Into The Light................................	Atlantic	11
03/03/97	---	RA	It's In Your Eyes	Atlantic	18

* Phillip Bailey & Phil Collins
** Phil Collins/Marilyn Martin

COLOR ME BADD
American pop-R&B group consisting of four vocalists, formed in Oklahoma City in 1987: Bryan Abrams (b. 11/16/69 in Oklahoma City), Mark Calderon (b. 09/27/70 in Oklahoma City), Sam Watters (b. 07/23/70 in Oklahoma City), Kevin "KT" Thornton (b. 06/17/69 in Oklahoma City). Discovered by Robert Bell of Kool & The Gang.

DATE	PK	WK	TITLE	LABEL	RA
07/08/91	20	7	I Wanna Sex You Up	Giant	11
10/21/91	13	7	I Adore Mi Amor..	Giant	4
01/27/92	3(1)	16	All 4 Love	Giant	4
04/13/92	---	RA	Thinkin' Back	Giant	36
06/29/92	---	RA	Slow Motion	Giant	14
11/02/92	5	14	Forever Love...	Giant	9
12/27/93	4	19	Time And Chance	Giant	
02/14/94	16	28	Choose..	Giant	9
07/01/96	24	9 h	The Earth, The Sun, The Rain.....................	Giant	8

COLTER, Jessi
American female country singer/songwriter born Miriam Johnson on 05/25/47 in Phoenix, Arizona. Married to guitarist Duane Eddy at age of 16. Divorced in 1968; married country star Waylon Jennings in 1969.

DATE	PK	WK	TITLE	LABEL	RA
07/26/75	7	7	I'm Not Lisa	Capitol	

COLVIN, Shawn
American female folk singer born Shanna Colvin on 01/10/58 in Vermillion, South Dakota. Raised in London, Ontario and Carbondale, Illinois.

DATE	PK	WK	TITLE	LABEL	RA
07/14/97	---	RA	Sunny Came Home..................................	Columbia	5

COMMODORES
American R&B group formed in 1967 in Tuskegee, Alabama: Lionel Richie (vocals, piano, b. 06/20/49 in Tuskegee), Milan Williams (keyboards, trombone, guitar, drums, b. 03/28/48 in Mississippi), Ronald LaPread (bass, trumpet, b. 09/04/46 in Alabama), Walter "Clyde" Orange (vocals, drums, b. 12/10/47 in

DATE	PK	WK	TITLE	LABEL	RA

Florida), William King Jr. (horns, b. 01/30/49 in Alabama), Thomas McClary (guitar, b. 10/06/50). Richie left in 1982 to pursue solo career.

DATE	PK	WK	TITLE	LABEL
04/17/76	22	7	Sweet Love	Motown
01/08/77	24	12	Just To Be Close To You	Motown
09/21/77	6	10	Easy	Motown
11/30/77	35	4	Brick House	Motown
09/06/78	1(4)	24	Three Times A Lady	Motown
10/31/79	8	12	Sail On	Motown
12/12/79	7	18	Still	Motown
09/26/81	9	7	Lady (You Bring Me Up)	Motown
12/19/81	7	9	Oh No	Motown
05/06/85	6	13	Nightshift	Motown

CONCRETE BLONDE

American rock band formed in Los Angeles in 1981: Johnette Napolitano (vocal, bass, b. 09/22/57 in Hollywood), Jim Mankey (guitar, b. 05/23/55 in Pennsylvania), Harry Rushakoff (drums, b. 11/17/59 in Chicago).

DATE	PK	WK	TITLE	LABEL	RA
08/20/90	12	8	Joey	I.R.S.	9
02/25/91	35	4	Caroline	I.R.S.	25
07/20/92	---	RA	Someday	I.R.S.	28

CONTI, Bill

American male composer/conductor born on 04/13/42 in Providence, Rhode Island. Composed for first three Rocky movies, *For Your Eyes Only*, *The Karate Kid*, and *The Right Stuff*.

DATE	PK	WK	TITLE	LABEL
06/25/77	7	12	Theme From "Rocky" - Gonna Fly Now	United Artists

CONTOURS

American R&B group formed in Detroit in 1958: Billy Gordon (vocals), Billy Hoggs (vocals), Joe Billingslea (vocals), Sylvester Potts (vocals), Hubert Johnson (vocals), Huey Davis (vocals, guitar). Johnson committed suicide on 07/11/81. "Do You Love Me?" re-released after being featured in the 1987 movie *Dirty Dancing*.

DATE	PK	WK	TITLE	LABEL
08/15/88	19	13	Do You Love Me?	Motown

COOLIDGE, Rita

American female pop singer born on 05/01/44 in Lafayette, Tennessee. Married to country singer Kris Kristofferson, 1971-1980. Backup vocals for Joe Cocker, Eric Clapton, and Boz Scaggs. Inspiration of "Delta Lady" by Joe Cocker. Made cameo appearance in movies like *A Star Is Born* and *Convoy*. One of the original video jockeys on the video music channel VH-1.

DATE	PK	WK	TITLE	LABEL
09/07/77	7	19	(Your Love Has Lifted Me) Higher And Higher	A&M
12/14/77	15	14	We're All Alone	A&M
03/22/78	16	8	The Way You Do The Things You Do	A&M
09/20/78	36	6	You	A&M

COOLIO

American male rapper born Artis Ivey on 08/01/63 in Los Angeles. Based in Compton, California. Member of WC and the MAAD Circle.

DATE	PK	WK	TITLE	LABEL
08/22/94	16	32	Fantastic Voyage	Denon

DATE	PK	WK	TITLE	LABEL	RA
09/25/95	2(2)	30	Gansta's Paradise *.................................	Denon	8
06/17/96	---	RA	1,2,3,4 (Sumpin' New)	Tommy Boy	30
11/03/96	17	10	All The Way Live..................................	Tommy Boy	
07/27/97	5	17	C U When You Get There	Tommy Boy	

* Coolio featuring LV

COOPER BROTHERS
Canadian rock band formed in Ottawa in 1971: brothers Brian (vocals, bass) and Richard (vocals, guitar) Cooper, Glenn Bell (drums), Darryl Alguire (guitar), Terry King (vocals, steel guitar), Charles Robertson (vocals, reeds), Al Serwa (keyboards).

DATE	PK	WK	TITLE	LABEL	RA
09/06/78	34	2	Rock And Roll Cowboys.............................	Polydor	

COOPER, Alice
American male hard rock singer born on 02/04/48 in Detroit. First band formed in Phoenix in the late-1960's. In 1968, to Los Angeles, where Frank Zappa released band's first two albums. Appeared on TV's *Hollywood Squares*, *Alice Cooper - The Nightmare*. In several films including *Freddy's Dead: The Final Nightmare* (1991) and *Wayne's World* (1992).

DATE	PK	WK	TITLE	LABEL	RA
06/28/75	2(3)	10	Only Women	Atlantic	
01/08/77	3(1)	14	I Never Cry	Warner	
09/07/77	6	13	You And Me..	Warner	
02/07/79	27	4	How You Gonna See Me Now	Warner	
07/16/80	15	2	Clones	Warner	
01/29/90	10	17	Poison	Epic	
03/19/90	27	4	House Of Fire	Epic	
08/19/91	12	11	Hey Stoopid...	Epic	

COPPOLA, Imani
American female singer from Long Island, New York.

DATE	PK	WK	TITLE	LABEL	RA
11/24/97	---	RA	Legend Of A Cowgirl..............................	Coumbia	8

CORINA
American female dance singer born and raised in New York City.

DATE	PK	WK	TITLE	LABEL	RA
09/09/91	9	11	Temptation	Atco	17

CORNERSHOP
British pop group formed in 1992 in London: Tjinder Singh (vocals, guitar), Ben Ayres (guitar), Avtar Singh (guitar), Anthony Saffery (sitar, keyboards), Nick Simms (drums), Pete Hall (percussion).

DATE	PK	WK	TITLE	LABEL	RA
04/27/98	---	RA	Brimful of Asha...	Warner	37

CORONA
Italian dance singer Olga Maria de Souza.

DATE	PK	WK	TITLE	LABEL	RA
08/21/95	21	5	Baby Baby	NuMuzik	

CORRS, The

DATE	PK	WK	TITLE	LABEL	RA

Irish pop group formed in Dundalk, Ireland consisting of one brother and three sisters: Jim (keyboards, guitar, vocals, b. James Stephen Ignatius Corr on 07/31/64), Andrea (lead vocals, tin whistle, b. Andrea Jane Corr on 05/17/74), Caroline (drums, bodhran, vocals, b. 03/17/73), Sharon (violin, vocals, b. 03/23/70) Corr.

| 11/13/95 | --- | RA | Runaway | Lava | 37 |
| 05/13/96 | --- | RA | The Right Time | Lava | 39 |

COSTELLO, Elvis
British male rock singer/guitarist born Delcan Patrick McManus on 08/25/54 in London. Costello is his mother's maiden name. Founded backing band, The Attractions, in 1977. Married Cait O'Riordan, ex-bassist of The Pogues on 05/16/86.

| 11/14/83 | 29 | 3 | Everyday I Write The Book * | Columbia | |

* Elvis Costello & The Attractions

COUNTING CROWS
American rock group formed in 1993 in San Francisco: Adam Duritz (vocals, piano, b. 08/01/64 in Baltimore), David Bryson (rhythm guitar, b. 11/05/61 in San Francisco), Matt Malley (bass, b. 07/04/63), Charlie Gillingham (keyboards, b. 01/12/60 in Torrance, California), Steve Bowman (drums, b. 01/14/67). Dan Vickrey (lead guitar, b. 08/26/66 in Walnut Creek, California) joined in 1994. Bowman left in 1994; replaced by Ben Mize (b. 02/02/71).

04/11/94	---	RA	Mr. Jones	DGC	1
08/22/94	---	RA	Round Here	DGC	3
11/07/94	---	RA	Rain King	DGC	31
03/10/97	---	RA	A Long December	DGC	8

COVER GIRLS
American female dance trio: Louise "Angel" Sabater, Caroline Jackson, Sunshine Wright (replaced by Margo Urban in 1989). By 1992, Sabater, Urban left, replaced by Evelyn Escalera and Michelle Valentine.

| 03/19/90 | 9 | 8 | We Can't Go Wrong | Capitol | 21 |
| 09/14/92 | 25 | 7 | Wishing On A Star | Epic | 15 |

COWBOY JUNKIES
Canadian blues-rock band formed in 1985 in Toronto: Margo Timmins (vocals, b. 01/27/61 in Montreal), Michael Timmins (guitar, b. 04/21/59 in Montreal), Alan Anton (bass, b. Alan Alizojvodic on 06/22/59 in Montreal), Peter Timmins (drums, b. 10/29/65 in Montreal).

04/16/90	31	4	Sun Comes Up, It's Tuesday Morning	RCA	
05/09/94	---	RA	Anniversary Song	RCA	22
04/29/96	3(2)	14 h	A Common Disaster	RCA	16

COX, Deborah
Canadian female R&B singer/songwriter born on 07/13/74 in Toronto. Started singing at age 12. To Los Angeles in 1994, where she signed to Arista.

11/20/95	31	4	Sentimental	Arista	16
06/10/96	15	12 h	Who Do U Love	Arista	6
09/02/96	37	6 h	Where Do We Go From Here	Arista	35

DATE	PK	WK	TITLE	LABEL	RA
09/21/97	29	5	Things Just Ain't The Same	Arista	
02/07/99	8	21	Nobody's Supposed To Be Here	Arista	20

CRANBERRIES, The
Irish alternative band formed in 1989 in Limerick, Ireland: Dolores Mary Eileen O'Riordan (vocals, b. 09/06/71 in Ballybricken, Ireland), Noel Hogan (guitar, b. 12/25/71 in Moycross, Ireland), Mike Hogan (bass, b. 04/29/73 in Moycross), Fergal Lawler (drums, b. 03/04/71 in Parteen, Ireland).

DATE	PK	WK	TITLE	LABEL	RA
02/21/94	---	RA	Linger	Island	2
04/25/94	12	21	Dreams	Island	27
12/12/94	---	RA	Zombie	Island	14
06/05/95	13	22	Ode To My Family	Island	16
07/17/95	---	RA	Ridiculous Thoughts	Island	36
06/24/96	27	6 h	Salvation	Island	
09/02/96	8	15 h	Free To Decide	Island	6
12/22/96	7	23	When You're Gone	Island	13
03/28/99	6	12	Promises	Island	

CRASH TEST DUMMIES
Canadian rock band from Winnipeg: Brad Roberts (vocals, b. Bradley Kenneth Roberts, on 01/10/64 in Winnipeg), Benjamin Darvill (harmonica, mandolin, b. 01/04/67), Mitch Dorge (drums, accordion, b. Michel Dorge, on 09/15/60 in Winnipeg), Ellen Reid (keyboards, vocals, b. 07/14/66 in Selkirk, Manitoba), Dan Roberts (bass, b. 05/22/67 in Winnipeg). The Roberts are brothers. Won the 1992 Juno Award for Group of the Year.

DATE	PK	WK	TITLE	LABEL	RA
08/12/91	---	RA	Superman's Song	Arista	7
12/30/91	38	3	The First Noel	Arista	
12/27/93	---	RA	Mmm Mmm Mmm Mmm	Arista	28
05/02/94	---	RA	Swimming In Your Ocean	Arista	14
08/29/94	---	RA	Afternoons & Coffeespoons	Arista	9
12/26/94	---	RA	God Shuffled His Feet	Arista	16
04/17/95	---	RA	Ballad of Peter Pumpkinhead	Arista	2
10/28/96	6	15 h	He Liked To Feel It	Arista	10
02/21/99	13	12	Keep A Lid On Things	Vik.	6

CRASH VEGAS
Canadian rock band from Toronto, formed in the mid-1980's: Michelle McAdorey (vocals), Colin Cripps (guitar), Jocelyne Lanois (bass), Ambrose Pottie (drums). McAdorey was the vocalist of Martha & The Muffins and Cripps was guitarist for The Spoons.

DATE	PK	WK	TITLE	LABEL	RA
03/12/90	---	RA	Inside Out	Risque Disque	28
01/17/94	38	1	Land *	Cargo	
06/05/95	---	RA	On And On	Epic	33

* Crash Vegas/Hothouse Flowers/Daniel Lanois/Midnight Oil/Tragically Hip

CREWZ CONTROL
Canadian female dance trio: Julie, Melanie, Tina.

DATE	PK	WK	TITLE	LABEL	RA
10/21/96	---	RA	I Need Your Love Tonight	Quality	37

CROSBY, Bing - see BOWIE, David

DATE	PK	WK	TITLE	LABEL	RA

CROSBY, STILLS, NASH & YOUNG

American/British/Canadian quartet formed in Los Angeles in 1968: David Crosby (guitar, vocals, b. David Van Cortland on 08/14/41 in Los Angeles), Stephen Stills (guitar, keyboards, bass, vocals, b. 01/03/45 in Dallas), Graham Nash (guitar, keyboards, vocals, b. 02/02/41 in Blackpool, England), Neil Young (guitar, vocals, b. 11/12/45 in Toronto). Young, formerly of Buffalo Springfield, left in 1974, rejoined in 1988. Crosby was a member of the Byrds, Stills a member of Buffalo Springfield, Nash a member of the Hollies.

DATE	PK	WK	TITLE	LABEL	RA
09/21/77	21	10	Just A Song Before I Go *	Atlantic	
09/04/82	17	5	Wasted On The Way *	Atlantic	
02/06/89	9	11	American Dream	Atlantic	
06/21/93	---	RA	Hero **	Atlantic	19

* Crosby, Stills & Nash
** David Crosby

CROSS, Christopher

American male pop-MOR singer/songwriter born Christopher Geppert on 05/03/51 in San Antonio, Texas.

DATE	PK	WK	TITLE	LABEL	RA
05/21/80	4	7	Ride Like The Wind	Warner	
09/13/80	4	6	Sailing	Warner	
12/13/80	12	7	Never Be The Same	Warner	
10/24/81	2(2)	11	Arthur's Theme (The Best That You Can Do)	Warner	
02/21/83	17	6	All Right	Warner	
02/27/84	9	11	Think Of Laura	Warner	

CROW, Sheryl

American female pop/rock singer born on 02/11/62 in Kennett, Missouri. Received degree in classical piano from University of Missouri. Former elementary school music teacher in St. Louis. To Los Angeles in 1986 where sang backup on Michael Jackson's 1987-88 Bad Tour. Backup vocalist for Don Henley, George Harrison, Rod Stewart, Stevie Wonder, Joe Cocker. Won the 1994 Grammy Award for Record of the Year for "All I Wanna Do".

DATE	PK	WK	TITLE	LABEL	RA
06/06/94	---	RA	Leaving Las Vegas	A&M	14
03/13/95	---	RA	Strong Enough	A&M	1
04/17/95	15	14	All I Wanna Do	A&M	1

"All I Wanna Do" was released before "Strong Enough" and actually became an airplay hit first. "All I Wanna Do" peaked at #1 on 09/19/94.

DATE	PK	WK	TITLE	LABEL	RA
08/28/95	---	RA	Can't Cry Anymore	A&M	4
11/04/96	1(3)	18 h	If It Makes You Happy	A&M	3
03/24/97	---	RA	Everyday Is A Winding Road	A&M	2
06/30/97	---	RA	A Change Would Do You Good	A&M	2
09/20/98	6	25	My Favorite Mistake	A&M	3
05/31/99	---	RA	Anything But Down	A&M	24
08/09/99	---	RA	Sweet Child O' Mine	C2	32+

CROWDED HOUSE

Australian rock-pop band formed in 1985 in Melbourne: songwriter Neil Finn (vocals, guitar, b. 05/27/56 in Te Awamutu, New Zealand), Paul Hester (drums, b. 01/08/59 in Melbourne), Nick Seymour (bass, b. 12/09/58 in Benalla, Australia). Disbanded in 1996.

DATE	PK	WK	TITLE	LABEL	RA
05/18/87	5	16	Don't Dream It's Over	Capitol	
08/03/87	15	12	Something So Strong	Capitol	
10/10/88	1(2)	20	Better Be Home Soon	Capitol	
08/19/91	20	11	Chocolate Cake	Capitol	15
03/14/94	---	RA	Distant Sun	EMI	3

CRUSH
British female vocal duo: Donna Air, Jayni Hoy.

01/20/97	---	RA	Jellyhead	Isba	29

CRYSTAL, Billy
American actor/comedian born on 03/14/47 in New York City. Played roles in TV's *Soap*, 1977-81 and *Saturday Night Live*, 1984-85. Appeared in several movies; hosted the Academy Awards.

09/23/85	25	10	You Look Marvelous	A&M	

CULT, The
British alternative rock band formed in Brixton, London, England in 1983: Ian Astbury (vocals, b. Ian Lindsay on 05/14/62 in Heswell, Merseyside, England), Billy Duffy (guitar, b. William H. Duffy on 05/12/61 in Manchester), Jamie Stewart (bass), Les Warner (drums, b. 02/13/61).

04/14/86	12	14	She Sells Sanctuary	Vertigo	
07/13/87	35	5	Love Removal Machine	Vertigo	
07/24/89	38	1	Fire Woman	Beggar's Banquet	

CULTURE BEAT
German/British/American dance group formed in 1989 by Torsten Fenslau (DJ/producer, b. circa 1964 in Germany). Consists of rapper Jay Supreme (from New Jersey) and singer Tania Evans (from London). Fenslau died in a car accident on 11/06/93 in Darmstadt, Germany; replaced by Alex Abraham, with Peter Zweier (composer/engineer) and Juergen "Nosie" Katzmann (composer/guitarist).

11/15/93	---	RA	Mr. Vain	Epic	20

CULTURE CLUB
British pop group formed in London in 1981: Boy George (vocals, b. George O'Dowd on 06/14/61 in Eltham, England), Roy Hay (guitar, keyboards, b. 08/12/61 in Southend-on-Sea, England), Mikey Craig (bass, b. 02/15/60 in London), Jon Moss (drums, b. 09/11/57 in London). Boy George recorded solo in 1987.

03/07/83	1(3)	18	Do You Really Want To Hurt Me?	Virgin	
06/20/83	6	12	Time (Clock Of The Heart)	Virgin	
09/19/83	8	14	I'll Tumble 4 Ya	Virgin	
12/12/83	12	13	Church Of The Poison Mind	Virgin	
01/30/84	1(7)	20	Karma Chameleon	Virgin	
04/16/84	8	13	Miss Me Blind	Virgin	
07/02/84	20	6	It's A Miracle	Virgin	
11/19/84	7	14	The War Song	Virgin	
01/21/85	28	5	Mistake No. 3	Virgin	
05/12/86	14	10	Move Away	Virgin	

CUMMINGS, Burton

DATE	PK	WK	TITLE	LABEL	RA

Canadian male singer/pianist/songwriter born on 12/31/47 in Winnipeg. Lead singer of Guess Who from 1965 to 1975. Won Juno Awards for Best New Male Vocalist in 1977, Male Vocalist of the Year in 1977 and 1980.

DATE	PK	WK	TITLE	LABEL	RA
12/18/76	2(3)	17	Stand Tall	Portrait	
04/30/77	11	14	I'm Scared	Portrait	
07/02/77	26	5	Never Had A Lady Before	Portrait	
08/06/77	30	7	Timeless Love	Portrait	
10/19/77	19	6	My Own Way To Rock	Portrait	
12/14/77	25	4	Your Backyard	Portrait	
09/06/78	6	16	Break It To Them Gently	Portrait	
07/16/80	8	6	Fine State Of Affairs	Portrait	
10/10/81	17	6	You Saved My Soul	Epic	
05/07/90	11	11	Take One Away	EMI	25

CURCI, Freddy
Canadian male pop singer. Former lead singer for Sheriff. Founded Alias with Sheriff bandmate Steve DeMarchi in 1990, became lead singer.

DATE	PK	WK	TITLE	LABEL	RA
06/06/94	36	1	Brown Eyed Girl	Capitol	40

CURE, The
British alternative rock group formed in 1976 in Crawley, England: Robert Smith (guitar, vocals, b. 04/21/59 in Blackpool, England), Laurence "Lol" Tolhurst (drums, b. 02/03/59). Line-up has changed over the years; other members in the 1980's included Simon Gallup (bass, b. 06/01/60 in Surrey, England), Boris Williams (drums, b. 04/24/57 in Versailles, France), Porl Thompson (guitar, b. 11/08/57 in London).

DATE	PK	WK	TITLE	LABEL	RA
11/27/89	26	3	Love Song	Elektra	
05/04/92	16	12	High	Elektra	29
07/27/92	12	14	Friday, I'm In Love	Elektra	2
11/02/92	27	5	A Letter To Elise	Elektra	
07/29/96	---	RA	Mint Car	Elektra	39

CUTTING CREW
British rock group: Nick Van Eede (vocals), Kevin Scott MacMichael (guitar), Colin Farley (bass), Martin Beedle (drums). Van Eede was lead singer of the Drivers in the early-1980's.

DATE	PK	WK	TITLE	LABEL	RA
06/08/87	1(2)	18	(I Just) Died In Your Arms	Virgin	
12/07/87	12	12	I've Been In Love Before	Virgin	

CYPRESS HILL
American rap formed in Los Angeles in 1988: B-Real (vocals, b. Louis Freese on 06/02/70 in Los Angeles), Sen Dog (vocals, b. Sennen Reyes on 11/20/65 in Havana, Cuba), DJ Muggs (DJ, b. Lawrence Muggerud on 01/28/68 in Queens, New York). Reyes' younger brother is rapper Mellow Man Ace.

DATE	PK	WK	TITLE	LABEL	RA
05/04/92	37	2	Hand On The Pump	Columbia	
10/11/93	3(1)	45	Insane In The Brain	Columbia	
02/14/94	14	18	Ain't Going Out Like That	Columbia	
11/13/95	9	22	Throw Your Set In The Air	Columbia	
09/20/98	21	12	Tequila Sunrise	Columbia	

CYRUS, Billy Ray

DATE	PK	WK	TITLE	LABEL	RA

American male country singer born on 08/25/61 in Flatwoods, Kentucky.

07/20/92	1(4)	23	Achy Breaky Heart	Mercury	23
10/19/92	17	5	Could've Been Me	Mercury	
09/27/93	11	17	In The Heart Of A Woman	Mercury	

D

D MOB - see DENNIS, Cathy

DA BRAT
American female rapper Shawntae Harris born circa 1974 in Chicago.

09/05/94	2(3)	39	Funkdafied	Chaos	
11/14/94	18	23	Fa All Y'All	Chaos	
07/24/95	30	6	Give It 2 You	Columbia	
07/20/97	10	15	Not Tonight *	Atlantic	
01/11/98	32	4	Sock It 2 Me **	Elektra	

* Lil' Kim featuring Da Brat, Left Eye, Missy "Misdemenaor" Elliott and Angie Martinez
** Missy "Misdemeanor" Elliott featuring Da Brat

DADDY FREDDY

| 07/01/91 | 26 | 9 | Daddy Freddy's In Town | Chrysalis | |

DAFT PUNK
French dance duo from Paris: Thomas Bangalter (b. 01/03/75) and Guy-Manuel de Homem-Christo (b. 02/08/74). Bangalter is also a member of Stardust.

| 05/18/97 | 31 | 5 | Da Funk | Virgin | 24 |
| 08/10/97 | 30 | 9 | Around The World | Virgin | 27 |

DAHLQUIST, Pat
Canadian female singer. Won the Juno Award for Best New Female Artist in 1976.

| 09/06/75 | 11 | 8 | Keep Our Love Alive | Columbia | |

DAILY, E.G.
American female dance singer/songwriter/actress Elizabeth Daily from Los Angeles. Appeared in the movie *Pee Wee's Big Adventure*. Provided the voice of Babe in the movie *Babe A Pig In The City* and the voice of Tommy Pickles in Nickelodeon's *Rugrats* television series.

| 08/25/86 | 32 | 8 | Say It, Say It | A&M | |

DALBELLO
Canadian female singer/songwriter born Lisa Dal Bello on 05/22/58 in Woodbridge, Ontario. Wrote lyrics for Nena's "99 Red Balloons", and composed songs for the soundtrack of the film *9 1/2 Weeks*. Won the Juno Award for Best New Female Vocalist in 1978.

DATE	PK	WK	TITLE	LABEL	RA
04/24/89	31	4	Tango	Capitol	

DALTERY, Roger
British male rock singer born Roger Harry Daltery on 03/01/44 in London. Founder and lead singer of The Who. Starred in several movies.

DATE	PK	WK	TITLE	LABEL	RA
12/02/85	38	2	After The Fire	WEA	

DAMIAN, Michael
American male rock singer/actor born Michael Weir on 04/26/62 in San Diego. Featured on television's *The Young & The Restless* as Danny Romalotti.

DATE	PK	WK	TITLE	LABEL	RA
07/03/89	2(1)	18	Rock On	Virgin	
09/04/89	35	1	Cover Of Love	Attic	
03/05/90	38	2	Was It Nothing At All	Attic	

DAMN YANKEES
American rock band formed in 1989 in New York City: Ted Nugent (guitar, vocals, b. 12/13/48 in Detroit), ex-Night Ranger member Jack Blades (bass, vocals, b. 04/24/54 in Palm, California), ex-Styx member Tommy Shaw (guitar, vocals, b. 09/11/53 in Montgomery, Alabama), Michael Cartellone (drums, b. 06/07/62 in Cleveland).

DATE	PK	WK	TITLE	LABEL	RA
03/25/91	27	3	High Enough	Warner	9
12/21/92	---	RA	Where You Goin' Now	Warner	19

D'ANGELO
American male R&B singer/producer born Michael D'Angelo Archer on 02/11/74 in Richmond, Virginia.

DATE	PK	WK	TITLE	LABEL	RA
11/06/95	35	2	Brown Sugar	EMI	

DANIELS, Charlie, Band
American band formed in 1971 led by Charlie Daniels (b. 1937 in Wilmington, North Carolina).

DATE	PK	WK	TITLE	LABEL	RA
10/03/79	10	4	The Devil Went Down To Georgia	Epic	

DANNY WILSON
British pop trio from Dundee, Scotland: Gary Clark (vocals, guitar), Kit Clark (keyboards, percussion), Ged Grimes (bass). Gary and Kit are brothers. Group named after the 1952 movie, *Meet Danny Wilson*.

DATE	PK	WK	TITLE	LABEL	RA
09/28/87	9	10	Mary's Prayer	Virgin	

D'ARBY, Terence Trent
American male pop/R&B singer born Terence Trent Darby on 03/15/62 in New York City. Joined the U.S. Army, assigned to Germany at Elvis Presley's old unit.

DATE	PK	WK	TITLE	LABEL	RA
05/09/88	2(2)	18	Wishing Well	Columbia	
09/05/88	11	14	Sign Your Name	Columbia	
11/01/93	---	RA	Delicate	Columbia	33

DARKNESS

DATE	PK	WK	TITLE	LABEL	RA
09/04/95	24	4	In My Dreams .... NuMuzik		

DAVID & DAVID
American duo from Los Angeles: David Baerwald and David Ricketts.

01/19/87	39	2	Welcome To The Boomtown .... A&M		

DAVIS, Alana
American female singer/songwriter born on 05/06/74 in New York City.

02/02/98	---	RA	32 Flavors .... Elektra		23

DAVIS, Mac
American male country-pop singer/songwriter born on 01/21/42 in Lubbock, Texas. Wrote "In The Ghetto" by Elvis Presley. Worked for Vee Jay Records and Liberty Records in 1960's. Own television show in 1974, *The Mac Davis Show*, made film debut, *North Dallas Forty*, in 1979.

06/04/80	5	10	It's Hard To Be Humble .... Casablanca		

DAVIS, Paul
American male pop singer/songwriter/producer born on 04/21/48 in Meridian, Mississippi. Survivor of shooting in Nashville on 07/30/86.

02/20/82	10	7	Cool Night .... Arista		
05/22/82	7	8	'65 Love Affair.. Arista		

DAWN
American pop vocal trio formed in 1970 in New York City: Tony Orlando (b. Michael Anthony Orlando Cassavitis on 04/03/44 in New York City), Telma Louise Hopkins (b. 10/28/48 in Louisville, Kentucky), Joyce Elaine Vincent-Wilson (b. 12/14/46 in Detroit). Orlando recorded solo, 1961-63. Hosted own TV show, *Tony Orlando & Dawn*, 1974-76. Hopkins acted in the television programs *Bosom Buddies*, *Gimme A Break*, and *Family Matters*.

08/02/75	28	2	Mornin' Beautiful * .... Elektra		
03/20/76	37	5	Cupid * .... Elektra		

* Tony Orlando & Dawn

DAYNE, Taylor
American female pop singer born Leslie Wunderman on 03/07/63 in Baldwin, New York.

03/07/88	3(2)	15	Tell It To My Heart .... Arista		
06/20/88	27	8	Prove Your Love .... Arista		
10/24/88	35	7	I'll Always Love You .... Arista		
02/13/89	22	8	Don't Rush Me .... Arista		
01/22/90	2(1)	14	With Every Beat Of My Heart .... Arista		
04/23/90	2(2)	15	Love Will Lead You Back .... Arista	5
07/23/90	3(1)	11	I'll Be Your Shelter .... Arista	2
10/22/90	14	12	Heart Of Stone... Arista	7
08/02/93	---	RA	Can't Get Enough Of Your Love .... Arista	4
11/15/93	---	RA	Send Me A Lover .... Arista	29

DATE	PK	WK	TITLE	LABEL	RA

D-CRU featuring Golden Child
Canadian dance/pop group based in Vancouver: Aimee Mackenzie (b. circa 1974), Nicole Hutton (b. circa 1974 in Vancouver), Damien Kyles (b. circa 1973 in Vancouver), Troy "Golden Child" Samson (b. circa 1974 in the Phillippines).

| 10/04/98 | 11 | 13 | Show Me | Dexter | 28 |
| 03/08/99 | --- | RA | Never Never | Dexter | 30 |

DC TALK
American Christian rock group formed in 1987 in Washington D.C.: Toby McKeehan, Michael Tait and Kevin Smith.

| 12/30/96 | --- | RA | Just Between You And Me | Virgin | 6 |

Hit Parade: #5 (12/23/96) / 10 wks.

DEAD OR ALIVE
British dance band formed in 1980 in Liverpool, England: Pete Burns (vocals, b. 08/05/59 in Liverpool), Tim Lever (keyboards, saxophone, b. 05/21/60), Steve McCoy (drums, b. 03/15/62), Mike Percy (bass, b. 03/11/61).

| 08/19/85 | 5 | 18 | You Spin Me Round (Like A Record) | Epic | |
| 02/16/87 | 34 | 6 | Brand New Lover | Epic | |

DEADEYE DICK
American rock group from New Orleans: Caleb Guillotte (guitar/vocals), Mark Miller (bass) and Billy Laundry (drums).

| 11/21/94 | --- | RA | New Age Girl | Hypnotic | 36 |

DeBARGE
American pop-R&B group consisting of members of the DeBarge family, formed Grand Rapids, Michigan in 1978: Bunny (vocals, b. 03/15/55 in Grand Rapids), El (vocals, keyboards, b. 06/04/61 in Grand Rapids), Marty (vocals, b. as Mark DeBarge on 06/19/59 in Grand Rapids), Randy (vocals, b. 08/06/58 in Grand Rapids), James (vocals, b. 08/22/63 in Grand Rapids). James and singer Janet Jackson were married for seven months in 1984.

| 05/27/85 | 2(1) | 15 | Rhythm Of The Night | Quality | |
| 08/19/85 | 9 | 10 | Who's Holding Donna Now | Quality | |

DeBARGE, Chico
American male R&B-funk singer born Jonathan DeBarge in 1966 in Grand Rapids, Michigan. Brother of DeBarge members.

| 03/16/87 | 37 | 4 | Talk To Me | Motown | |

DeBARGE, El
American male R&B-funk singer born Eldra DeBarge on 06/04/61 in Grand Rapids, Michigan. Lead singer of DeBarge, 1978-1988.

| 07/21/86 | 8 | 16 | Who's Johnny | MCA | |

DeBURGH, Chris
British male pop-rock singer born Christopher John Davidson on 10/15/48 in Argentina.

DATE	PK	WK	TITLE	LABEL	RA
12/25/82	18	7	Don't Pay The Ferryman	A&M	
07/23/84	29	12	High On Emotion	A&M	
12/08/86	1(8)	27	The Lady In Red	A&M	
02/06/89	33	7	Missing You	A&M	

DEE, Kiki - see Elton John

DEEE-LITE
American dance-pop group formed in 1986 in New York City: Lady Miss Kier (b. Kier Kirby in Youngstown, Ohio), Super DJ Dmitry (DJ, b. Dmitry Brill, circa 1964 in Kirovograd, Ukraine), Jungle DJ Towa Towa (b. Towa Tei, in Tokyo, Japan).

DATE	PK	WK	TITLE	LABEL	RA
12/03/90	---	RA	Groove Is In The Heart	Elektra	10
03/25/91	25	10	Power Of Love	Elektra	32
07/13/92	34	8	Runaway	Elektra	

DEEP BLUE SOMETHING
American rock band formed in 1992 in Denton, Texas: John Kirtland (drums, percussion), and brothers Toby Pipes(guitar, vocals) and Todd Pipes (vocals, bass), Kirk Tatom (guitar). Tatom was later replaced by Clay Bergus.

DATE	PK	WK	TITLE	LABEL	RA
12/04/95	---	RA	Breakfast At Tiffany's	WEA	4

DEES, Rick, & His Cast Of Idiots
American male disc jockey born Rigdon Osmond Dees III in Memphis in 1950. One of the world's top DJ's. Host of the syndicated radio show, *The Rick Dees Weekly Top 40*. Host of TV's *Solid Gold* (1984) and talk show *Into The Night* (1990-91).

DATE	PK	WK	TITLE	LABEL	RA
10/16/76	1(3)	14	Disco Duck Part 1	RSO	

DEF LEPPARD
British hard rock group formed in Sheffield, England in 1977: Joe Elliott (vocals, b. 08/01/59 in Sheffield), Pete Willis (guitar, b. 02/16/60), Rick Savage (bass, b. 12/02/60 in Sheffield), Rick Allen (drums, b. 11/01/63), Steve Clark (guitar, b. 04/23/60 in Hillsborough). Willis left in 1981, replaced by Phil Collen (guitar, b. 12/08/57 in Hackney, England). Allen lost left arm in car accident, 12/31/84, uses special equipment to play drums. Clark died on 01/08/91 in London of drug-alcohol-related causes, replaced by Vivian Campbell, formerly with Whitesnake.

DATE	PK	WK	TITLE	LABEL	RA
05/02/83	30	1	Photograph	Vertigo	
09/05/83	14	10	Rock Of Ages	Vertigo	
01/18/88	40	2	Animal	Vertigo	
04/04/88	15	12	Hysteria	Vertigo	
08/29/88	3(2)	20	Pour Some Sugar On Me	Vertigo	
10/24/88	2(1)	16	Love Bites	Vertigo	
02/20/89	9	15	Armageddon It	Vertigo	
05/01/89	22	9	Rocket	Vertigo	
06/15/92	2(2)	15	Let's Get Rocked	Vertigo	11
09/07/92	13	16	Make Love Like A Man	Vertigo	27
10/19/92	5	18	Have You Ever Needed Someone So Bad	Vertigo	2
02/22/93	20	11	Stand Up	Vertigo	13
10/18/93	---	RA	Two Steps Behind	Vertigo	2
02/21/94	4	22	Miss You In A Heartbeat	Vertigo	9

DATE	PK	WK	TITLE	LABEL	RA
12/04/95	19	16	When Love And Hate Collide	Mercury	10
07/01/96	9	13 h	Work It Out	Mercury	38
09/09/96	32	4 h	All I Want Is Everything	Mercury	

DEF SQUAD
American rap group formed in 1992: Erick Sermon, Reggie "Redman" Noble and Keith Murray.

DATE	PK	WK	TITLE	LABEL	RA
06/07/98	11	7	Full Cooperation	Def Jam	

DEL AMITRI
Scottish pop-rock group formed in 1983 in Glasgow: Justin Currie (vocals, bass, guitar, b. 12/11/64 in Glasgow), Iain Harvie (guitar, b. 05/19/62 in Glasgow), Andy Alston (keyboards, accordion), Brian McDermott (drums), David Cummings (guitar). McDermott left in 1994; Cummings left in 1996. Kris Dollimore (guitar), Mark Price (drums) joined in 1997.

DATE	PK	WK	TITLE	LABEL	RA
10/12/92	---	RA	Always The Last To Know	A&M	22
09/25/95	---	RA	Roll To Me	A&M	6

DELERIUM
Canadian dance duo from Vancouver: Bill Leeb and Rhys Fulber.

DATE	PK	WK	TITLE	LABEL	RA
07/21/97	---	RA	Euphoria (Firefly)	Nettwerk	30
05/10/99	---	RA	Silence	Nettwerk	28

DEMUS, Chaka, & Pliers
Jamaican male reggae duo consisting of DJ Chaka Demus and singer Everton "Pliers" Banner.

DATE	PK	WK	TITLE	LABEL	RA
06/06/94	---	RA	Twist & Shout	Island	17

DENNIS, Cathy
British female pop singer born in 1970 in Norwich, England. Vocalist for dance group, D MOB.

DATE	PK	WK	TITLE	LABEL	RA
04/02/90	---	RA	C'mon And Get My Love *	ffrr	23
03/18/91	13	9	Just Another Dream	Polydor	8
05/13/91	9	15	Touch Me (All Night Long)	Polydor	4
09/16/91	24	14	Too Many Walls	Polydor	7
02/24/92	17	9	Everybody Move	Polydor	38
10/19/92	9	10	You Lied To Me	London	20
02/15/93	24	9	Irresistible	Polydor	33

* D MOB introducing Cathy Dennis

DENVER, John
American country-pop singer/songwriter born John Henry Deutschendorf on 12/31/43 in Roswell, New Mexico. Wrote "Leaving On A Jet Plane". Member of the Chad Mitchell Trio in late-1960's. Done volunteer work for ecological causes and the ERA. Died on 10/12/97 when the plane he was flying crashed into Monterey Bay in California.

DATE	PK	WK	TITLE	LABEL	RA
06/14/75	3(1)	6	Thank God I'm A Country Boy	RCA	
10/25/75	2(2)	10	I'm Sorry	RCA	
11/29/75	9	10	Calypso	RCA	
01/31/76	13	6	Fly Away	RCA	

DATE	PK	WK	TITLE	LABEL	RA

DEPECHE MODE
British alternative rock band formed in 1980 in Basildon, England: Vince Clarke (keyboards, b. 07/03/60 in South Woodford, England), Andrew Fletcher (keyboards, b. 07/08/61 in Nottingham, England), Dave Gahan (vocals, b. 05/09/62 in Epping, England), Martin Gore (guitar, keyboards, b. 07/23/61 in Basildon), Alan Wilder (drums, keyboards, vocals, b. 06/01/59 in London). Clarke left in 1981 to form the bands, Yazoo and Erasure. Wilder left in 1995. Gahan arrested for heroin possession on 05/28/96.

DATE	PK	WK	TITLE	LABEL	RA
08/26/85	15	10	People Are People	Sire	
04/16/90	23	11	Personal Jesus	Sire	28
07/16/90	16	13	Enjoy The Silence	Sire	9
10/01/90	19	9	Policy Of Truth	Sire	9
04/05/93	4	14	I Feel You	Sire	22
07/19/93	13	15	Walking In My Shoes	Sire	32
02/16/97	3(1)	11	Barrel Of A Gun	Reprise	

Above is the domestic version. The "P1" version peaked at #19 on 02/16/97. The "P2" version peaked at #21 on 02/16/97. "P2" re-entered in 1998 and peaked at #28 on 09/20/98.

DATE	PK	WK	TITLE	LABEL	RA
05/04/97	14	16	It's No Good	Reprise	21
12/28/97	26	6	Home	Reprise	
09/27/98	5	20	Only When I Lose Myself	Reprise	

DES'REE
British female R&B-pop singer/songwriter born Des'ree Weeks on 11/30/68 in London.

DATE	PK	WK	TITLE	LABEL	RA
04/17/95	19	6	You Gotta Be	Epic	18
05/29/95	26	10	Feel So High	Epic	

DeSARIO, Teri
American female pop singer/songwriter from Miami.

DATE	PK	WK	TITLE	LABEL	RA
03/05/80	12	12	Yes, I'm Ready *	Casablanca	

* Teri DeSario with K.C.

DESTINY'S CHILD
American female R&B vocal group from Houston: Kelly, LaTavia, Le Toya, Beyonce.

DATE	PK	WK	TITLE	LABEL	RA
02/22/98	7	31	No, No, No	Columbia	38
07/25/99	10	5+	Bills, Bills, Bills	Columbia	

DEVO
American new-wave group formed in 1972 in Akron, Ohio: Jerry Casale (bass, vocals), Mark Mothersbaugh (vocals, keyboards, guitar), Bob "Bob I" Mothersbaugh (guitar, vocals), Bob "Bob II" Casale (keyboards, guitar, vocals), Alan Myers (drums). Myers left in 1984, David Kendrick (drums).

DATE	PK	WK	TITLE	LABEL	RA
11/29/80	14	12	Whip It	Warner	

DEVON
Canadian male rapper/singer/songwriter born Devon Martin in England. Raised in Malton, Ontario.

DATE	PK	WK	TITLE	LABEL	RA
11/30/92	35	3	Princess	Capitol	

DATE	PK	WK	TITLE	LABEL

DeVORZON & BOTKIN
American songwriting/producing/arranging duo of Barry DeVorzon (b. 07/31/34 in New York City) and Perry Botkin Jr. (b. 04/16/33 in New York City). Based in California.

| 01/01/77 | 3(1) | 16 | Nadia's Theme | A&M |

DEXY'S MIDNIGHT RUNNERS
British pop band formed in 1978 in Birmingham and led by Kevin Rowland (lead vocals, 08/17/53 in Wolverhampton, England). Comprised of eight members; line-up constantly changes. Rowland recorded solo in 1988.

| 02/21/83 | 9 | 15 | Come On Eileen | Mercury |

DeYOUNG, Dennis
American male pop singer born on 02/18/47 in Chicago. Former lead singer/keyboardist of Styx.

| 12/10/84 | 5 | 11 | Desert Moon | A&M |

DFS
Canadian dance group.

| 11/13/95 | 24 | 1 | Ou Eee Ou | PolyTel |

DIAMOND, Neil
American male pop-MOR singer/songwriter born Noah Kaminsky on 01/24/41 in Brooklyn, New York. Writer of The Monkees' "I'm A Believer". Signed with Bang Records in 1965, signed with Columbia Records for a record-breaking $5 million in 1973. Starred in the 1980 movie *The Jazz Singer*.

08/07/76	32	3	If You Know What I Mean	Columbia
01/25/78	9	12	Desiree	Columbia
12/13/78	1(2)	14	You Don't Bring Me Flowers *	Columbia
05/02/79	18	4	Forever In Blue Jeans	Columbia
03/19/80	14	4	September Morn	Columbia
12/20/80	7	12	Love On The Rocks	Capitol
04/11/81	7	8	Hello Again	Capitol
01/23/82	18	2	Yesterday's Songs	Columbia
11/20/82	11	5	Heartlight	Columbia

* Barbra Streisand/Neil Diamond

DIESEL
Dutch rock quartet featuring singer/guitarist Rob Vunderink.

| 10/10/81 | 10 | 11 | Sausalito Summernight | RCA |

DIGITAL UNDERGROUND
American rap group formed in 1988 in Oakland, California: Shock-G (vocals, b. Greg Jacobs on 08/25/63 in Queens, New York), Humpty Hump (vocals, b. Edward Ellington Humphrey on 05/25/66 in Tampa, Florida), Money B (vocals, b. Ronald Brooks on 09/22/69 in Oakland), DJ Fuze (DJ, b. David Scott in Syracuse, New York).

| 07/09/90 | 7 | 14 | Humpty Dance | Attic |

DATE	PK	WK	TITLE	LABEL	RA
10/25/93	23	8	Return Of The Crazy One	Attic	

DINO
American male pop singer born Dino Esposito on 07/20/63 in Encino, California. Former DJ/music director at KCEP in Las Vegas.

DATE	PK	WK	TITLE	LABEL	RA
10/23/89	25	7	I Like It	Island	
11/05/90	11	18	Romeo	Island	11
09/13/93	---	RA	Ooh Child	Island	20

DION, Celine
Canadian female pop singer born in 03/30/68 in Charlemange, Quebec. Popular Francophone recording artist in Quebec and France since age 13. Won the 1988 Eurovision Song Contest for Switzerland. First recorded in English in 1990. Married her manager Rene Angelil on 12/17/94 in Montreal. Won 19 Juno Awards including Best Female Vocalist in 1991, 1992, 1993, 1994, 1997, and 1999.

DATE	PK	WK	TITLE	LABEL	RA
05/14/90	24	4	(If There Was) Any Other Way	Columbia	27
09/17/90	38	1	Unison	Columbia	27
04/08/91	6	23	Where Does My Heart Beat Now	Columbia	23
05/20/91	17	12	The Last To Know	Columbia	13
09/02/91	---	RA	Have A Heart	Columbia	17
03/16/92	2(1)	34	Beauty And The Beast *	Columbia	21
06/22/92	3(1)	22	If You Asked Me To	Columbia	1
09/07/92	19	13	Nothing Broken But My Heart	Columbia	7
01/25/93	8	15	Love Can Move Mountains	Columbia	3
05/17/93	---	RA	Water From The Moon	Columbia	13
09/06/93	---	RA	Did You Give Enough Love	Columbia	19
10/04/93	---	RA	When I Fall In Love **	Columbia	31
03/14/94	1(12)	70	The Power Of Love	Columbia	1
05/16/94	7	42	Misled	Columbia	2
10/17/94	14	33	Think Twice	Columbia	15
05/06/96	1(1)	22 h	Because You Loved Me	Columbia	4
			SoundScan: #36 (11/03/96) / 1 wk.		
11/03/96	2(1)	33	It's All Coming Back To Me Now	Columbia	3
			Hit Parade: #3 (11/04/96) / 19 wks.		
02/17/97	---	RA	To Love You More	Columbia	15
04/14/97	---	RA	All By Myself	Columbia	9
11/30/97	12	6	Tell Him ***	Columbia	
05/03/98	14	13	My Heart Will Go On	Columbia	1
			Above is the remixes edition. Another version peaked at #33 on 02/22/98.		
01/17/99	37	1	I'm Your Angel ****	Jive	14

* Celine Dion & Peabo Bryson
** Celine Dion & Clive Griffin
*** Celine Dion & Barbra Streisand
**** R. Kelly & Celine Dion

DIONNE & FRIENDS - see JOHN, Elton; KNIGHT, Gladys; WARWICK, Dionne; WONDER, Stevie

DIRE STRAITS

DATE	PK	WK	TITLE	LABEL	RA

British rock group formed in London in 1977: Mark Knopfler (guitar, vocals, b. 08/12/49 in Glasgow, Scotland), David Knopfler (guitar, b. 12/27/52 in Glasgow), John Illsley (bass, b. 06/24/49 in Leicester, England), Pick Withers (drums, b. 04/04/48). David left in 1980, replaced by Hal Lindes (guitar); Alan Clark (keyboards), Terry Williams (drums), Tommy Mandel (keyboards) joined in 1982, Withers left in 1982; Mandel left in 1984; Guy Fletcher (keyboards) joined in 1985, Lindes and Clark left. Disbanded in 1985, re-forms in 1991. Mark Knopfler is the writer of Tina Turner's "Private Dancer" single.

04/04/79	10	8	Sultans Of Swing	Mercury	
12/18/82	10	12	Industrial Disease	Vertigo	
04/18/83	9	9	Twisting By The Pool	Vertigo	
07/29/85	10	14	Walk Of Life	Vertigo	
11/04/85	1(2)	13	Money For Nothing	Vertigo	
02/17/86	30	3	So Far Away	Vertigo	
11/04/91	16	10	Calling Elvis	Vertigo	10
02/17/92	32	4	Heavy Fuel	Vertigo	30

DISHWALLA
American rock quartet formed in 1993 in Santa Barbara, California: J.R. Richards (vocals, keyboards), Scot Alexander (bass), Rodney Browning (guitar), George Pendergast (drums). Named after entrepreneurial nomads in India.

| 07/08/96 | 11 | 19 h | Counting Blue Cars | A&M | 13 |

DIVINE
American R&B vocal trio: Nikki Bratcher (b. circa 1981; from Newark, New Jersey), Kia Thornton (b. circa 1981; from Inglewood, New Jersey), Tonia Tash (b. circa 1980; from Brooklyn, New York).

| 12/27/98 | 16 | 8 | Lately | Red Ant | 27 |

DIVINYLS
Australian rock-pop duo formed in 1980 in Sydney: Christina Amphlett (vocalist, b. 10/25 circa 1960, in Geelong, Australia), Mark McEntee (guitar, b. 07/16 circa 1961, in Perth, Australia). Originally a five-member band.

| 06/24/91 | 3(1) | 14 | I Touch Myself | Virgin | 9 |

DJ COMPANY
German techno-dance group: producers Stefan Benz, Louis Lasky, Paul Strand, January Ordu (vocals), Michael Fielder (dancer), Brian Thomas (dancer).

| 07/13/97 | 28 | 5 | Rhythm Of Love | Crave | |

D.J. JAZZY JEFF & THE FRESH PRINCE
American rap duo formed in 1986 in Philadelphia: Fresh Prince (vocals, b. Willard Smith on 09/25/69 in Philadelphia), Jazzy Jeff (DJ, b. Jeff Townes on 01/22/65 in Philadelphia). Smith appeared in the TV sitcom *The Fresh Prince of Bel-Air* and the movies *Six Degrees of Separation* (1993), *Bad Boys* (1995), *Independence Day* (1996), and *Wild Wild West* (1999). Smith pursued solo career in 1997.

09/26/88	15	15	Parents Just Don't Understand	Jive	
10/24/88	33	5	Nightmare On My Street	Jive	
02/05/90	13	13	I Think I Can Beat Mike Tyson	Jive	
09/02/91	3(2)	19	Summertime	Jive	13

| DATE | PK | WK | TITLE | LABEL | RA |

DJ KOOL
American male rapper John Bowman born circa 1960 in Washington D.C.

| 01/26/97 | 4 | 37 | Let Me Clear My Throat | American |

DJ LES & KOOL KAT

| 08/17/92 | 27 | 6 | Sugar Sugar | BGM |

DJ SHADOW
American male hip-hop singer born Josh Davis, circa 1972 in California.

| 06/01/97 | 40 | 1 | Midnight In A Perfect World | A&M |

DLUGOSCH, Borish

| 11/10/96 | 19 | 5 | Keep Pushin' | MAW |

Another version peaked at #20 on 11/23/97.

DMX
American male rapper Earl Simmons born in 1971 in Yonkers, New York. Lives in Teaneck, New Jersey.

| 04/19/98 | 22 | 9 | Get At Me Dog | Def Jam |

DNA featuring Suzanne Vega
British production team consisting of two disc jockeys from Bristol.

| 02/11/90 | 5 | 21 | Tom's Diner | A&M | 3 |

DOANE, Melanie
Canadian female pop/rock singer born in 1967 in Halifax. Won the 1999 Juno Award for Best New Solo Artist.

01/19/99	---	RA	Adam's Rib	Columbia	19
05/10/99	---	RA	Waiting For The Tide	Columbia	27
08/02/99	---	RA	Goliath	Columbia	21+

DR. ALBAN
Swedish male rapper born Alban Nwapa in Nigeria. Graduated as a dentist in Sweden. Owned the Alphabet Club record and clothes shop in Stockholm.

| 11/30/92 | --- | RA | It's My Life | Logic | 40 |

DOCTOR AND THE MEDICS
British rock band from London: The Doctor (lead vocals), The Anadin Brothers (Wendi and Collette), Richard Searle, Steve Maguire and Vom.

| 11/10/86 | 1(2) | 21 | Spirit In The Sky | I.R.S. |

DOCTOR DAVE

DATE	PK	WK	TITLE	LABEL	RA

| 07/27/87 | 33 | 6 | Vanna Pick Me A Letter | Electric | |

DR. HOOK
American rock group formed in Union City, New Jersey in 1968: Ray Sawyer (vocals, guitar, b. 02/01/37 in Chickasaw, Alabama), Dennis Locorriere (vocals, guitar, b. 06/13/49 in Union City), William Francis (keyboards, percussion, b. 01/16/42 in Mobile, Alabama), George Cummings (pedal steel guitar, b. 07/28/38 in Meridian, Mississippi), John "Jay" David (drums, b. 08/08/42 in Union City). Richard Elswit (guitar, b. 07/06/45 in New York State) and Jance Garfat (bass, b. 03/03/44 in California) joined in 1971. John Wolters (b. 04/28/45) replaced David in 1973. Cummings left in 1975, replaced by Bob "Wilard" Henke (guitar). Appeared in and performed soundtrack of several movies in 1970's.

04/10/76	5	11	Only Sixteen	Capitol	
10/02/76	2(1)	13	A Little Bit More	Capitol	
01/10/79	5	16	Sharing The Night Together	Capitol	
08/08/79	6	12	When You're In Love With A Beautiful Woman	Capitol	
12/12/79	22	12	Better Love Next Time	Capitol	
05/28/80	15	6	Sexy Eyes	Capitol	

DODGY
British rock trio formed in 1992: Nigel Clark (vocals, bass), Andy Miller (guitar), Matthew Priest (drums).

| 08/18/97 | --- | RA | Good Enough | A&M | 16 |

DOG'S EYE VIEW
American rock quartet from New York City: Peter Stuart (vocals, guitar), John Abbey (bass, cello, guitar), Oren Bloedow (guitar), Alan Bezozi (drums, percussion).

| 05/27/96 | 5 | 18 h | Everything Falls Apart | Columbia | 3 |

DOLBY, Thomas
British male vocalist/producer/multi-instrumentalist born Thomas Morgan Robertson on 10/14/58 in Cairo, Egypt. "Dolby" is a nickname first used by schoolmates. Produced albums by Joni Mitchell, George Clinton. Married to actress Kathleen Beller (Kirby Colby of *Dynasty*).

| 04/25/83 | 3(1) | 15 | She Blinded Me With Science | Capitol | |
| 04/16/84 | 15 | 10 | Hyperactive | Capitol | |

DOLCE, Joe
American male novelty singer born in 1947 in Painesville, Ohio.

| 04/04/81 | 19 | 2 | Shaddap You Face | MCA | |

DOMINO
American male rapper born Shawn Ivy in St. Louis, Missouri. Raised in Long Beach, California.

| 03/28/94 | 3(1) | 25 | Getto Jam | Columbia | |
| 09/07/97 | 33 | 3 | Baiia Baiia Conmigo | BMG | |

DONALDS, Andru
Jamaican male R&B singer from Kingston.

DATE	PK	WK	TITLE	LABEL	RA
02/13/95	---	RA	Mishale...EMI		1
07/17/95	---	RA	Tryin' To Tell Ya ....EMI		28

DOOBIE BROTHERS
American rock band formed in 1970 in San Jose, California: Tom Johnston (guitar, vocals, b. Visalia, California), John Hartman (drums, b. 03/18/50 in Falls Church, Virginia), Patrick Simmons (guitar, vocals, b. 01/23/50 in San Jose), Dave Shogren (bass, b. San Francisco). When Shogren left in 1971, Tiran Porter (bass) and Michael Hossack (drums, b. 09/18/50 in Patterson, New Jersey) were added. Keith Knudsen (b. 10/18/52 in Ames, Indiana) replaced Hossack in 1973. Jeff "Skunk" Baxter (guitar, b. 12/13/48 in Washington, D.C.) joined in 1974. Michael McDonald (keyboards, vocals, b. 12/02/52 in St. Louis) joined in 1975. Johnston left in 1977; Hartman, Baxter left in 1979, replaced by John McFee (guitar, b. 11/18/53 in Santa Cruz, California) and Chet McCracken (drums, b. 07/17/52 in Seattle). Cornelius Bumpus (saxophone, keyboards, b. 01/13/52). Disbanded in 1982, re-formed in 1988 with Johnston, Simmons, Hartman, Porter, Hossack, and Bobby LaKind (percussion). LaKind died 12/24/92 of cancer.

07/19/75	11	7	Take Me In Your Arms .... Warner
07/03/76	11	9	Takin' It To The Streets .... Warner
04/18/79	13	10	What A Fool Believes................................. Warner
06/27/79	17	10	Minute By Minute .... Warner
10/17/79	35	2	Dependin' On You.. Warner
11/01/80	2(2)	10	Real Love .... Warner
08/07/89	14	11	The Doctor... Capitol

DORE, Charlie
British female singer.

| 05/28/80 | 6 | 9 | Pilot Of The Airwaves ....WEA |

DOUBLE
Swiss pop duo: Kurt Maloo and Felix Haug.

| 05/26/86 | 2(1) | 18 | Captain Of Her Heart ....Polydor |

DOUCETTE
Canadian group featuring male vocalist/guitarist, Jerry Doucette, born in Montreal. To Vancouver in 1972. Won Juno Award for Most Promising Group of the Year in 1979.

| 06/14/78 | 33 | 2 | Mama Let Him Play .... A&M |
| 08/08/79 | 31 | 2 | Nobody... A&M |

DOUG & THE SLUGS
Canadian band formed in 1977, based in Vancouver: Doug Bennett (vocals, guitar), John Burton (guitar), Rick Baker (guitar), Steve Bosley (bass), Simon Kendall (keyboards), Wally Watson (drums).

07/09/80	19	1	Too Bad...Ritdong
03/28/83	23	5	Who Knows How To Make Love Stay..........Ritdong
05/23/83	30	3	Making It Work ....Ritdong
09/12/88	36	5	Tomcat Prowl ....Ritdong

DOYLE, Damhnait

DATE	PK	WK	TITLE	LABEL	RA

Canadian female rock singer born in December 1975 in Labrador City, Newfoundland. Native of St. John's, Newfoundland. Discovered while working at Duckworth/Latitude Records in St. John's.

| 04/22/96 | 24 | 12 h | A List Of Things.. | Latitude | 13 |
| 09/30/96 | --- | RA | Whatever You Need................................... | Latitude | 37 |

DREAM ACADEMY
British pop trio formed in London in 1983: Gilbert Gabriel (keyboards, b. 11/16/56 in Paddington, London), Nick Laird-Clowes (vocals, guitar, b. 02/05/57 in London), Kate St. John (vocals, oboe, saxophone, b. 10/02/57 in London).

| 02/10/86 | 10 | 12 | Life In A Northern Town............................... | Warner | |

DREAM WARRIORS
Canadian male rap duo: Capitol Q (b. Frank Lennon Alert on 08/10/c. 1969 in Port Of Spain, Trinidad), King Lou (b. Louis Robinson in Jamaica).

| 01/21/91 | 35 | 1 | Wash Your Face In My Sink.......................... | Island | |
| 04/01/91 | 12 | 15 | My Definition Of A Boombastic Jazz Style.... | Island | |

DRIVERS, The
British rock band fronted by singer/guitarist Nick Van Eede. Signed to the Dallcorte label in Toronto. Van Eede later moved to England. He formed and led Cutting Crew starting in the late-1980's.

| 05/09/83 | 24 | 4 | Tears On Your Anorak............................... | Dallcorte | |

DRU HILL
American R&B vocal group formed in 1993 in Baltimore: Mark "Sisqo" Andrews, James "Woody" Green, Tamir "Nokio" Ruffin, Larry "Jazz" Anthony. Named after Druid Hill Park in Baltimore.

10/27/96	19	5	Tell Me...	Island	
08/24/97	22	11	In My Bed...	Warner	
			The remixes version peaked at #36 on 11/23/97.		
01/25/98	35	2	We're Not Making Love No More................	LaFace	
02/08/98	38	3	5 Steps...	PolyGram	
11/15/98	16	9	How Deep Is Your Love	Island	27
02/28/99	11	10	These Are The Times.................................	Island	
07/04/99	9	4 +	You Are Everything...................................	Def Jam	

DUBOIS, Claude

| 12/27/78 | 23 | 2 | Le Blues Du Business Man .... | London | |

DUNDAS, David
British singer/actor born in Oxford, England.

| 02/26/77 | 9 | 20 | Jeans On.. | Chrysalis | |

DUPREE, Robbie
American male singer/songwriter born Robert Dupuis on 12/23/46 in Brooklyn, New York.

| 07/09/80 | 13 | 4 | Steal Away .... | Elektra | |

DATE	PK	WK	TITLE	LABEL	RA
10/04/80	9	7	Hot Rod Hearts	Elektra	

DURAN DURAN
British pop group formed in 1978 in Birmingham: Simon LeBon (vocals, b. 10/27/58 in Bushey, England), Andy Taylor (guitar, synthesizer, b. 02/16/61 in Dolver-Hampton, England), Nick Rhodes (keyboards, b. Nicholas James Bates on 06/08/62 in Birmingham), John Taylor (bass, b. Nigel John Taylor on 06/20/60 in Birmingham), Roger Taylor (drums, b. 04/26/60 in Birmingham). Became a trio in 1984 - LeBon, Rhodes, John Taylor. John Taylor and Andy Taylor left in 1985 to join Power Station. Rhodes, LeBon, Roger Taylor formed Arcadia in 1985. Steve Ferrone (guitar, b. 04/25/50 in Brighton, England) joined in 1986, left in 1988. Ex-Missing Persons member Warren Cuccurullo (guitar, b. 12/08/56 in Brooklyn, New York) joined in 1988. John Taylor left in 1997. Group named after a character in the movie *Barbarella*. None of the Taylors are related.

DATE	PK	WK	TITLE	LABEL	RA
03/21/83	2(5)	14	Hungry Like The Wolf	Capitol	
05/23/83	14	6	Rio	Capitol	
07/11/83	12	10	Is There Something I Should Know	Capitol	
01/16/84	7	15	Union Of The Snake	Capitol	
03/19/84	12	13	New Moon On Monday	Capitol	
06/25/84	4	17	The Reflex	Capitol	
12/03/84	4	17	The Wild Boys	Capitol	
03/11/85	24	7	Save A Prayer	Capitol	
07/22/85	3(1)	13	A View To A Kill	Capitol	
02/09/87	7	16	Notorious	Capitol	
12/19/88	10	13	I Don't Want Your Love *	Capitol	
02/27/89	34	1	All She Wants Is *	Capitol	
04/05/93	2(2)	31	Ordinary World	Capitol	1
06/14/93	2(1)	17	Come Undone	Capitol	2
10/04/93	---	RA	Too Much Information	Capitol	17
05/22/95	---	RA	White Lines	Capitol	13
05/05/97	---	RA	Out Of My Mind	Capitol	25
11/02/97	19	4	Electric Barbarella	Capitol	16

* Duranduran

DYLAN, Bob
American male folk-rock singer/songwriter/guitarist born Robert Allen Zimmerman on 05/24/41 in Duluth, Minnesota. The name "Dylan" taken from poet Dylan Thomas. Signed to Columbia Records in 1961. In motorcycle accident on 07/29/66. In several movies. Member of USA For Africa and Traveling Wilburys. His son Jakob is the lead singer of the Wallflowers.

DATE	PK	WK	TITLE	LABEL
10/03/79	28	2	Gotta Serve Somebody	Columbia

E

EAGLES
American rock group formed in 1971 in Los Angeles: Don Henley (drums, vocals, b. 07/22/47 in Gilmer, Texas), Glenn Frey (guitar, piano, vocals, b. 11/06/48 in Detroit), Bernie Leadon (guitar, banjo, mandolin, vocals, b. 07/19/47 in Minneapolis), Randy Meisner (bass, guitar, vocals, b. 03/08/46 in Scottsbluff, Nebraska). Don Felder (guitar, vocals, b. 09/21/47 in Gainesville, Florida) joined in 1974. Leadon replaced by Joe Walsh (guitar, vocals, b. 11/20/47 in Wichita, Kansas) in 1976. Meisner replaced by Timothy B. Schmit (bass, vocals, b. 10/30/47 in Sacramento, California). Disbanded in 1982. All members except Leadon had solo careers. Group re-formed in 1994.

DATE	PK	WK	TITLE	LABEL	RA
08/23/75	2(3)	10	One Of These Nights	Asylum	
11/08/75	3(3)	9	Lyin' Eyes	Asylum	
03/06/76	5	10	Take It To The Limit	Asylum	
03/12/77	1(1)	18	New Kid In Town	Asylum	
05/14/77	1(2)	19	Hotel California	Asylum	
07/16/77	6	14	Life In The Fast Lane	Asylum	
11/14/79	5	18	Heartache Tonight	Asylum	
01/23/80	20	4	The Long Run	Asylum	
05/14/80	13	3	I Can't Tell You Why	Asylum	
11/28/94	---	RA	Get Over It	Geffen	11
03/13/95	---	RA	Love Will Keep Us Alive	Geffen	13

EARL, Stacy
American female pop singer born on 12/28/62 in Boston.

02/03/92	---	RA	Love Me All Up	RCA	20
04/20/92	---	RA	Romeo And Juliet	RCA	16

EARLE, Steve
American male singer born on 01/17/55 in Fort Monroe, Virginia.

02/20/89	16	11	Copperhead Road	MCA	

EARTH, WIND & FIRE
American R&B group formed in 1969 in Chicago, based in Los Angeles. Various personnel, which included Maurice White (vocals, kalimba, drums, b. 12/19/41 in Memphis, Tennessee) and Philip Bailey (vocals, percussion, b. 05/08/51 in Denver). Group named after the three elements of White's astrological sign. Appeared in the movies *That's The Way Of The World* (1975) and *Sgt. Pepper's Lonely Hearts Club Band* (1978). Bailey, White, and fellow band members Wade Flemons and Ronnie Laws had solo careers.

06/14/75	8	2	Shining Star	Columbia	
01/17/76	25	2	Sing A Song	Columbia	
11/06/76	21	9	Getaway	Columbia	
11/01/78	32	4	Got To Get You Into My Life	Columbia	
02/07/79	8	10	September	Columbia	
06/27/79	16	16	Boogie Wonderland	Columbia	
10/17/79	9	6	After The Love Has Gone	Columbia	
03/14/83	24	6	Fall In Love With Me	Columbia	
10/11/93	---	RA	Sunday Morning	Reprise	32

EARTHTONES
Canadian pop/R&B vocal group from Calgary, formed in 1992: Dana Crawford, Tim Mason, Jesiahh, Chris Liscano and Scott Henderson. Disbanded by 1997.

01/30/95	---	RA	Move This Night	Passion	35

EAST COAST FAMILY
American R&B ensemble of recording artists assembled by Michael Bivins (New Edition, Bell Biv Devoe) featuring Bivins, Another Bad Creation, Boyz II Men, M.C. Brains.

12/21/92	22	10	1-4-All-4-1	MCA	

DATE	PK	WK	TITLE	LABEL	RA

EAST 17
British pop band formed in 1990 in London: Tony Mortimer (vocals, keyboards, b. 10/21/70 in London), Brian Harvey (lead vocals), John Hendy (keyboards, bass, vocals, b. 03/26/71 in London), Terry Coldwell (vocals). The name "East 17" is taken from the London postal code from which the band originates. Harvey was dismissed in January 1997; Mortimer left the same year.

| 09/11/95 | --- | RA | Let It Rain | London | 35 |

EASTON, Sheena
Scottish female pop singer/actress born on 04/27/59 in Bellshill, Glasgow, Scotland. Appeared in opening sequence of the James Bond movie *For Your Eyes Only* and the television program *Miami Vice*. Subject of the 1980 BBC-TV documentary *The Big Time*.

04/25/81	1(5)	12	Morning Train (Nine To Five)	EMI	
07/25/81	19	2	Modern Girl	EMI	
10/10/81	7	9	For Your Eyes Only	EMI	
03/06/82	13	6	You Could Have Been With Me	EMI	
03/14/83	2(1)	12	We've Got Tonight *	Liberty	
12/12/83	8	16	Telefone (Long Distance Love Affair)	EMI	
12/17/84	8	17	Strut	EMI	
03/04/85	20	7	Sugar Walls	EMI	
03/20/89	26	9	The Lover In Me	MCA	
06/24/91	21	11	What Comes Naturally	MCA	22

* Kenny Rogers & Sheena Easton

ECONOLINE CRUSH
Canadian rock group from Vancouver: Trevor Hurst (vocals), Robbie Morfitt (guitar), Ziggy (guitar), Ken Fleming (bass), Robert Wagner (drums).

| 01/12/98 | --- | RA | All That You Are | EMI | 15 |

EDWARDS, Jonathan
American male singer born on 07/28/46 in Minnesota.

| 09/07/77 | 33 | 2 | Carolina Caroline | Warner | |

EGAN, Walter
American male singer born on 07/12/48 in Jamaica, New York.

| 09/06/78 | 11 | 14 | Magnet And Steel | Columbia | |

EIGHT SECONDS
Canadian band formed in 1982 in Ottawa: Del Castillo (vocals), March Cesare (bass), Frank Levin (keyboards), Scott Milks (drums), Marc Parent (guitar).

| 02/23/87 | 12 | 17 | Kiss You (When It's Dangerous) | Polydor | |

EIKHARD, Shirley
Canadian female country/pop singer/songwriter born on 11/07/55 in Sackville, Nova Scotia. Wrote "Something To Talk About" by Bonnie Raitt.

DATE	PK	WK	TITLE	LABEL	RA

08/28/76	28	6	Say You Love Me...	Attic	

ELASTICA
British rock band formed in 1992 in London: Justine Frischman (lead vocals, guitar, b. 1968 in Twickenham, England), Donna Matthews (guitar, b. Newport, Wales), Annie Holland (bass, b. Brighton, England), Justin Welch (drums, b. 1972 in Nuneaton, England). Frischman is former the rhythm guitarist of Suede and a former student of architecture at London University.

05/29/95	---	RA	Connection	Geffen	14

ELECTRIC LIGHT ORCHESTRA
British orchestral rock band formed in 1971 in Birmingham by former members of The Move: Roy Wood (b. 11/08/47 in Birmingham), Bev Bevan (b. 11/24/46 in Birmingham), and Jeff Lynne (b. 12/30/47 in Birmingham). Wood left in the early-1970's to form Wizzard. Temporarily disbanded in 1983, reorganized in 1986 consisting of Lynne (vocals, guitar, keyboards), Bevan (drums), and Richard Tandy (keyboards, guitar, b. 03/26/48 in Birmingham). Lynne became a member of the Traveling Wilburys in 1988 and pursued a solo career in 1990.

01/31/76	6	10	Evil Woman......................................	United Artists
05/08/76	18	5	Strange Magic	United Artists
09/25/76	25	5	Showdown.......................................	United Artists
01/22/77	8	15	Livin' Thing	United Artists
04/02/77	25	7	Do Ya	United Artists
09/21/77	3(2)	12	Telephone Line	United Artists
01/11/78	10	16	Turn To Stone..................................	Jet
05/03/78	12	14	Sweet Talkin' Women	Jet
09/20/78	35	6	Mr. Blue Sky	Jet
08/22/79	8	16	Shine A Little Love	Jet
10/03/79	4	4	Don't Bring Me Down	Jet
07/02/80	11	5	I'm Alive...	MCA
10/04/80	5	8	All Over The World	MCA
09/19/81	2(2)	10	Hold On Tight	Jet
10/03/83	5	14	Rock N' Roll Is King	Jet

ELECTRONIC
British ad hoc techno duo formed in 1989 consisting of Johnny Marr (b. John Maher, on 10/31/63 in Manchester) and Bernard Sumner (b. 01/04/56 in Salford, England). Marr is the guitarist of The Smiths. Sumner is the former guitarist and vocalist of New Order. Neil Tennant of the Pet Shop Boys is an occasional singer of the group.

06/25/90	---	RA	Getting Away With It...................................	Warner	33

ELLIMAN, Yvonne
American female pop-disco vocalist born on 12/29/51 in Honolulu. Played Mary Magdalene in the rock opera and movie *Jesus Christ Superstar*.

01/15/77	13	10	Love Me..	RSO
05/28/77	18	8	Hello Stranger...............................	RSO
05/03/78	6	16	If I Can't Have You........................	RSO

ELLIOTT, Missy "Misdemeanor"
American female rapper/songwriter born in 1972 in Portsmouth, Virginia.

DATE	PK	WK	TITLE	LABEL	RA
07/20/97	10	15	Not Tonight *	Atlantic	
01/11/98	32	4	Sock It 2 Me **..	Elektra	
08/02/98	4	33	Make It Hot ***..	Elektra	
09/27/98	25	3	I Want You Back ****...................................	MCA	

* Lil' Kim featuring Da Brat, Left Eye, Missy "Misdemenaor" Elliott and Angie Martinez
** Missy "Misdemeanor" Elliott featuring Da Brat
*** Nicole featuring Missy "Misdemeanor" Elliott
**** Mel B. featuring Missy "Misdemeanor" Eliott

EMF
British rock-dance group formed in 1989 in Cinderford, England: James Atkin (vocals, b. 03/28/67 in Cinderford), Ian Dench (guitar, b. 08/07/64 in Cinderford), Derran "Derry" Brownson (keyboards, b. 11/10/70 in Cinderford), Zachary Foley (bass, b. 12/09/70 in Cinderford), Mark Decloedt (drums, b. 06/26/67 in Cinderford). EMF stands for "Epsom Mad Funkers".

| 06/24/91 | 2(5) | 23 | Unbelievable.. | Capitol | 2 |
| 10/14/91 | 22 | 11 | Lies .... | Capitol | 18 |

EMILIA
Swedish female pop singer born Emilia Rydberg on 01/05/78 in Sweden.

| 01/25/99 | --- | RA | Big Big World .... | Universal | 18 |

EMINEM
American male rapper born Marshall Mathers in Kansas City. Based in Detroit.

| 02/21/99 | 34 | 1 | Just Don't Give A F***............................ | Interscope | |
| 05/02/99 | 28 | 2 | My Name Is .... | Interscope | 26 |

EMJAY
Canadian female dance singer from Ottawa. Age 20 in 1995.

| 10/30/95 | 37 | 1 | Flying To The Moon................................. | NuMuzik | |

EMMETT, Rik
Canadian male rock singer/songwriter/guitarist born in 1953 in Toronto. Guitarist of Triumph, 1975-87.

| 12/24/90 | --- | RA | When A Heart Breaks .... | Duke Street | 29 |
| 03/25/91 | --- | RA | Saved By Love...................................... | Duke Street | 36 |

EMOTIONS
American R&B vocal trio formed in 1968 in Chicago consisting of sisters Wanda (b. 12/17/51 in Chicago), Sheila (b. 01/17/53), Jeanette (b. 1951 in Chicago) Hutchinson.

| 10/05/77 | 14 | 12 | Best Of My Love .... | Columbia | |

EN VOGUE
American female R&B vocal group formed on 07/18/88 in Oakland, California: Cindy Herron (b. 09/26/65 in San Francisco), Maxine Jones (b. 01/16/66 in Paterson, New Jersey), Terry Ellis (b. 09/05/66 in Houston), Dawn Robinson (b. 11/28/68 in New London, Connecticut). Herron is a former Miss Black California. Robinson left in 1997.

DATE	PK	WK	TITLE	LABEL	RA
08/06/90	9	12	Hold On	Atlantic	28
06/01/92	---	RA	My Lovin' (You're Never Gonna Get It)	EastWest	1
09/07/92	---	RA	Giving Him Something He Can Feel	EastWest	6
11/16/92	---	RA	Free Your Mind	EastWest	4
02/15/93	---	RA	Give It Up, Turn It Loose	EastWest	8
10/18/93	---	RA	Runaway Love	EastWest	25
02/02/97	5	21	Don't Let Go (Love)	EastWest	1
			Hit Parade: #26 (12/30/96) / 6 wks.		
08/04/97	---	RA	Whatever	EastWest	15

ENGLAND DAN & JOHN FORD COLEY
American pop duo consisting of Dan Seals (b. 02/08/48 in McCamey, Texas) and John Ford Coley (b. 10/13/48). Seals later became a country music star, his brother Jimmy is in Seals and Crofts.

DATE	PK	WK	TITLE	LABEL	RA
09/18/76	4	15	I'd Really Love To See You Tonight	Big Tree	
01/01/77	26	11	Nights Are Forever	Big Tree	
09/07/77	27	4	It's Sad To Belong	Big Tree	
12/14/77	33	2	Gone Too Far	Big Tree	
05/17/78	20	8	We'll Never Have To Say Goodbye Again	Big Tree	

ENGLAND UNITED
British collaboration of recording artists in honour of the 1998 World Cup British team: Ian McCulloch (Echo & The Bunnymen), Simone Fowler (Ocean Colour Scene), Tommy Scott (Space), Melanie Chisholm (Spice Girls).

DATE	PK	WK	TITLE	LABEL	RA
07/19/98	16	5	(How Does It Feel To Be) On Top of the World	London	

ENIGMA
British vocal/instrumental group led by producer Michael Cretu (b. 05/18/57 in Bucharest, Romania). Moved to Germany in 1975. Worked with Vangelis and The Art of Noise.

DATE	PK	WK	TITLE	LABEL	RA
03/18/91	1(3)	13	Sadeness Part 1	Virgin	7
06/24/91	18	15	Mea Culpa	Virgin	40
04/25/94	---	RA	Return To Innocence	Virgin	1

ENRIQUEZ, Jocelyn
American female dance singer born on 12/28/74 in San Francisco. Of Pilipino ancestry.

DATE	PK	WK	TITLE	LABEL	RA
01/19/97	12	12	Do You Miss Me?	Quality	38
06/08/97	26	7	Little Bit Of Ecstasy	Quality	

ENYA
Irish female vocalist born Eithne Ni Bhraonain on 05/17/61 in Gweedore, Ireland. Keyboardist in Irish family act, Clannad.

DATE	PK	WK	TITLE	LABEL	RA
04/03/89	10	14	Orinoco Flow (Sail Away)	WEA	
12/22/96	2(1)	10	The Christmas EP	Warner	
12/21/97	8	8	The Christmas EP (re-entry)	Warner	
12/20/98	9	8	The Christmas EP (re-entry)	Warner	

EPMD

DATE	PK	WK	TITLE	LABEL	RA

American rap duo formed in 1986 in Brentwood, New York: Erick "E Double E" Sermon (vocals, b. 11/25/68 in Bayshore, New York), Parrish "PMD" Smith (vocals, programmer, b. 05/13/68 in Smithtown, New York). Disbanded in 1993, both pursued solo careers. EPMD stands for "Erick and Parrish Making Dollars". Reunited in 1997.

| 10/12/92 | 30 | 10 | No Crossover | Columbia | |

ERASURE
British techno-pop duo formed in 1985 in London: Vince Clarke (synthesizer, b. 07/03/60 in South Woodford, England), Andy Bell (vocals, b. 04/25/64 in Peterborough, England). Clarke is a former member of Depeche Mode and Yazoo.

| 12/19/88 | 24 | 10 | Chains Of Love | Sire | |
| 08/22/94 | 19 | 18 | Always | Sire | 16 |

ERUPTION
British techno-funk group of Jamaican natives featuirng lead vocalists Precious Wilson and Lintel. Based in London.

| 07/26/78 | 15 | 12 | I Can't Stand The Rain | GRT | |

ESCAPE CLUB
British rock group from London formed in 1983: Trevor Steel (vocals), John Holliday (guitar), Johnnie Christo (bass), Milan Zekavica (drums).

12/19/88	4	18	Wild Wild West	Atlantic	
04/29/91	16	9	Call It Poison	Atlantic	40
08/19/91	---	RA	I'll Be There	Atlantic	20

ESTEFAN, Gloria, & Miami Sound Machine
American pop group formed in 1975 in Miami: Gloria Estefan (vocals, b. Gloria Fajardo on 09/01/57 in Havana, Cuba), Enrique "Kiki" Garcia (drums, b. 1958 in Cuba), Juan Marcos Avila (bass, b. 1956 in Cuba), Emilio Estefan Jr. (keyboards, percussion, b. 03/04/53 in Havana), Raul Murciano (saxophone, keyboards). Gloria immigrated to Miami in 1959, married Emilio on 09/01/78. On 03/20/90, a serious crash in Pennsylvania which involved their tour bus broke one of Gloria's vertebrae but recovered within a year.

03/17/86	1(2)	15	Conga *	Epic	
06/02/86	6	17	Bad Boy *	Epic	
09/22/86	13	12	Words Get In The Way *	Epic	
08/24/87	13	15	Rhythm Is Gonna Get You	Epic	
04/18/88	22	9	Can't Stay Away From You	Epic	
07/04/88	9	12	Anything For You	Epic	
09/12/88	15	10	1-2-3	Epic	
10/02/89	6	13	Don't Wanna Lose You **	Epic	
04/16/90	18	10	Here We Are	Epic	25
03/25/91	4	14	Coming Out Of The Dark **	Epic	6
01/20/92	---	RA	Live For Lovin' You **	Epic	29
11/23/92	25	13	Always Tomorrow **	Epic	
03/20/95	10	22	Turn The Beat Around **	Epic	22
04/03/95	---	RA	Everlasting Love	Epic	31
07/08/96	26	8 h	Reach **	Epic	

DATE	PK	WK	TITLE	LABEL	RA

* Miami Sound Machine
** Gloria Estefan

ESTUS, Deon
American male bassist born in Detroit. Formerly with George Michael, Wham!, and Marvin Gaye.

| 05/29/89 | 16 | 8 | Heaven Help Us .... Polydor | | |

ETERNAL
British female pop vocal quartet from London: Louise Nurding, Kelle Bryan, sisters Easther and Vernette Bennett.

| 06/13/94 | 3(1) | 34 | Stay .... EMI | 7 |

ETHERIDGE, Melissa
American female rock singer/songwriter born on 05/29/61 in Leavenworth, Kansas. Attended Berklee College of Music in Boston.

11/28/88	18	12	Bring Me Some Water .... Island	
11/20/89	30	10	No Souvenirs .... Island	
02/05/90	---	RA	Let Me Go .... Island	31
04/27/92	26	6	Ain't It Heavy .... Island	21
07/06/92	22	13	2001 .... Island	19
11/08/93	10	14	I'm The Only One .... Island	18
01/31/94	16	16	Come To My Window .... Island	22
03/27/95	---	RA	If I Wanted To .... Island	12
11/27/95	21	3	Your Little Secret .... Island	17
03/04/96	1(5)	16 h	I Want To Come Over .... Island	2
09/16/96	11	15 h	Nowhere To Go .... Island	14

EUROPE
Swedish rock quintet: Joey Tempest (vocals), Kee Marcello (guitar), John Leven (bass), Mic Michaeli (keyboards), Ian Haugland (drums).

04/20/87	1(1)	18	The Final Countdown .... Epic	
11/09/87	10	16	Carrie .... Epic	
10/17/88	32	2	Superstitious .... Epic	

EURYTHMICS
British pop/rock duo formed in 1980 in London: Annie Lennox (vocals, flute, b. 12/25/54 in Aberdeen, Scotland), Dave Stewart (guitar, keyboards, b. David A. Stewart on 09/09/52 in Sunderland, England). Both in the recording act, the Tourists. Stewart married Siobhan Fahey, former singer in Bananarama and Shakespear's Sister, on 08/01/87. Lennox and Stewart pursued solo careers.

10/03/83	1(3)	22	Sweet Dreams (Are Made Of This) .... RCA	
12/19/83	25	10	Love Is A Stranger .... RCA	
03/05/84	7	13	Here Comes The Rain Again .... RCA	
07/02/84	18	7	Who's That Girl? .... RCA	
12/24/84	32	7	Sexcrime (Nineteen Eighty-Four) .... Virgin	
07/01/85	3(2)	16	Would I Lie To You? .... RCA	
10/28/85	8	15	There Must Be An Angel (Playing With My Heart) RCA	
12/09/85	39	3	Sisters Are Doin' It For Themselves .... RCA	

DATE	PK	WK	TITLE	LABEL	RA
04/14/86	35	5	It's Alright (Baby's Coming Back)	RCA	
09/29/86	7	13	Missionary Man	RCA	
02/09/87	34	6	Thorn In My Side	RCA	
02/08/88	14	14	I Need A Man	RCA	
12/18/89	13	15	Don't Ask Me Why	RCA	

EVANS, Faith
American female R&B singer born in 1974 in Florida. Married to Notorious B.I.G., 1994-97.

DATE	PK	WK	TITLE	LABEL	RA
10/16/95	21	6	You Used To Love Me *	Arista	
06/22/97	1(13)	41	I'll Be Missing You **	Arista	4
01/24/99	8	23	Love Like This	Arista	24
03/14/99	12	13	Heartbreak Hotel ***	Arista	24

* Faith
** Puff Daddy & Faith Evans (featuring 112)
*** Whitney Houston featuring Faith Evans & Kelly Price

EVERCLEAR
American rock band from Portland, Oregon: Art Alexakis (vocals, guitar), Craig Montoya (bass, vocals), Greg Ekland (drums, vocals).

DATE	PK	WK	TITLE	LABEL	RA
04/22/96	22	11 h	Santa Monica (Watch The World Die)	Capitol	
02/16/98	---	RA	Everything To Everyone	Capitol	37

EVERLAST
American rapper/rock singer born Erik Schrody on 08/18/69 in Valley Stream, New York. Lead rapper of House of Pain.

DATE	PK	WK	TITLE	LABEL	RA
03/21/99	33	3	What It's Like	Tommy Boy	6+

EVERYTHING
American pop/rock band formed in 1989 at James Madison University in Virginia: Richard King Bradley (tenor saxophone, guitar, vocals, b. 04/24/70 in Richmond, Virginia), Nathan S. Brown (drums, percussion, lead vocals, b. 07/07/71 in Baltimore), Craig Edward Honeycutt (guitar, lead vocals, b. 04/08/70 in Washington D.C.), "Wolfe" Quinn (keyboards, organ, trombone, percussion, b. Washington D.C.), David Alan Slankard (bass, b. 01/07/70 in Fort Belvoir, Virginia), Stephen Marc Van Dam (guitar, alto saxophone, clarinet, vocals, b. 11/25/68 in Falls Church, Virginia).

DATE	PK	WK	TITLE	LABEL	RA
11/16/98	---	RA	Hooch	Sire	31

EVERYTHING BUT THE GIRL
British pop duo formed in 1981 in England: Tracey Thorn (vocals, b. 09/26/62 in Hertfordshire, England) and Ben Watt (guitar, keyboards, b. 12/06/62 in London, England).

DATE	PK	WK	TITLE	LABEL	RA
03/04/96	3(2)	19 h	Missing	Atlantic	1
			Retail Singles: #8 (02/12/96) / 16wks.		
07/29/96	10	13 h	Wrong	Atlantic	2

DATE	PK	WK	TITLE	LABEL	RA

EXILE
American pop group formed as the Fascinations in 1963 in Richmond, Kentucky, changed name to the Exiles in 1965 and to Exile in 1973. Nucleus of group features Jimmy Stokley (vocals), James Preston Pennington (guitar), Buzz Cornelison (keyboards). Recorded country music starting in 1983.

| 11/01/78 | 1(2) | 20 | Kiss You All Over.. | Warner | |

EXPOSE
American female dance-pop vocal trio formed in Miami in 1986: Jeanette Jurado (b. 11/14/66 in Los Angeles), Ann Curless (b. 10/07/65 in New York City), Gioia Carmen Bruno (b. 06/11/65 in Italy). Bruno left in 1992, replaced by Kelly Moneymaker (b. 06/04/65 in Fairbanks, Alaska).

04/27/87	17	11	Come Go With Me...	Arista	
08/17/87	22	9	Point Of No Return	Arista	
03/21/88	13	12	Seasons Change	Arista	
08/21/89	8	13	What You Don't Know..................................	Arista	
11/13/89	10	8	When I Looked At Him..................................	Arista	
03/19/90	15	10	Tell Me Why	Arista	36
06/25/90	33	4	Your Baby Never Looked Good In Blue	Arista	36
12/21/92	---	RA	I Wish The Phone Would Ring	Arista	24
07/05/93	---	RA	I'll Never Get Over You (Getting Over Me).....	Arista	19

EXTREME
American hard rock group formed in 1985 in Boston: Gary Cherone (vocals, b. 07/26/61 in Malden, Massachusetts), Nuno Bettencourt (guitar, b. 09/20/66 in Azores, Portugal), Pat Badger (bass, b. 07/22/67 in Boston), Paul Geary (drums, b. 07/24/61 in Medford, Massachusetts).

06/10/91	1(2)	39	More Than Words..	A&M	1
10/14/91	---	RA	Hole Hearted...	A&M	2
10/26/92	10	13	Rest In Peace	A&M	38
03/08/93	---	RA	Stop The World	A&M	40

F

FACHIN, Eria
Canadian female dance singer/songwriter born in 1950 in Hamilton, Ontario. Died of cancer on 05/09/96 in Oakville, Ontario.

| 06/20/88 | 32 | 7 | Savin' Myself .... | Power | |

FAGEN, Donald
American male vocalist born on 01/10/48 in Passaic, New Jersey. Backup vocalist/keyboardist in Jay & The Americans, formed Steely Dan in 1972.

| 12/11/82 | 14 | 6 | I.G.Y. (What A Wonderful World).............. | Warner | |

FAITH NO MORE
American rock band formed in San Francisco in 1982: Michael "Mike" Patton (vocals, b. 01/27/68 in Eureka, California), James "Jim" Martin (guitar, b. 07/21/61 in Oakland, California), Roddy Bottum (keyboards, b. 07/01/63 in Los Angeles), Billy Gould (bass, b. 04/23/63 in Los Angeles), Michael "Mike" Bordin (drums, b. 11/27/62 in San Francisco). Martin replaced by Dean Menta in 1994.

DATE	PK	WK	TITLE	LABEL	RA
10/29/90	19	5	Epic	Slash	23
05/03/93	21	6	Easy	Slash	36

FAITHLESS
British house music group: Rollo, Sister Bliss, Jamie Catto, Maxi Jazz.

| 03/30/97 | 6 | 20 | Insomnia | Arista | |

FALCO
Austrian male pop singer born Johann Holzel on 02/19/57 in Vienna. Died in a car crash on 02/07/98 near Puerto Plata, Dominican Republic.

01/17/83	9	11	Der Kommisar	A&M	
03/03/86	2(1)	17	Rock Me Amadeus	A&M	
04/28/86	8	11	Vienna Calling	A&M	

FALCON, Billy
American male rock singer/songwriter/guitarist born on 07/13/56 in Valley Stream, New York.

| 10/21/91 | --- | RA | Power Windows | Jambco | 38 |

FALTERMEYER, Harold
German male keyboardist/songwriter/arranger/producer born on 10/05/52 in Munich. Arranged and played keyboards on soundtracks to *Midnight Express* and *American Gigolo*.

| 07/22/85 | 6 | 13 | Axel F | MCA | |

FALTSKOG, Agnetha
Swedish female singer born on 04/05/50 in Jonkoping, Sweden. Member of ABBA.

| 11/07/83 | 26 | 4 | Can't Shake Loose | Polydor | |

FARM, The
British rock group formed in 1983 in Liverpool: Peter Hooton (vocals, b. 09/28/62 in Liverpool), Roy Boulter (drums, b. 07/02/64 in Liverpool), Steve Grimes (guitar, b. 06/04/62 in Liverpool), Ben Leach (keyboards, b. 05/02/69 in Liverpool), Keith Mullen (guitar), Carl Hunter (bass, b. 04/14/65 in Bootle, England).

| 11/25/91 | --- | RA | Groovy Train | Warner | 25 |

FARNHAM, John
Australian male singer born on 07/01/49 in Dagenham, England. Lead singer of Little River Band, 1983-87.

| 08/10/87 | 9 | 14 | You're The Voice | RCA | |
| 06/03/91 | --- | RA | That's Freedom | RCA | 32 |

FARRIS, Dionne
American female singer from Bordentown, New Jersey. Featured vocalist on Arrested Development's "Tennessee".

DATE	PK	WK	TITLE	LABEL	RA

05/29/95　　14　　13　　I Know .... Columbia　　1

FASTBALL
American rock trio formed in 1994 in Austin, Texas: Tony Michael Scalzo (bass, vocals, b. 05/06/64 in Honolulu, Hawaii), Miles Zuniga (guitar, vocals), and Joey Shyffield (drums).

06/15/98　　---　　RA　　The Way .... Hollywood　　1
12/07/98　　---　　RA　　Fire Escape .... Hollywood　26
08/02/99　　---　　RA　　Out Of My Head .... Hollywood　30+

FAT BOYS
American rap trio formed in 1983 in Brooklyn, New York: Mark "Prince Markie Dee" Morales, Darren "The Human Beat Box" Robinson, and Damon "Kool Rock-ski" Wimbley. Robinson died of a heart attack on 12/10/95.

10/19/87　　29　　3　　Wipe Out .... Polydor
09/12/88　　12　　14　　The Twist .... Polydor

FATBOY SLIM
British male dance singer born Norman Cook 07/13/63 in Bromley, England. Also recorded under other names such as the Mighty Dub Kats and Beats International.

09/13/98　　18　　1　　Rockafeller Skank .... ASWE
04/04/99　　34　　3　　Praise You .... Virgin　13

FENDER, Freddy
American male country-rock singer/guitarist born Baldemar Huerta on 06/04/37 in San Benito, Texas. Of Mexican ancestry.

10/04/75　　6　　9　　Wasted Days And Wasted Nights .... Dot

FERGUSON, Jay
American male vocalist born on 05/10/47 in Burbank, California. Former vocalist for Spirit, Jo Jo Gunne.

04/19/78　　17　　14　　Thunder Island .... Asylum

FERGUSSON, Maynard
Canadian jazz trumpeter born on 05/04/28 in Verdun, Quebec. To the United States in 1949.

08/24/77　　38　　2　　Gonna Fly Now .... Columbia

54.40
Canadian rock band formed in 1981 in Vancouver: Phil Comparelli (guitar, trumpet, vocals), Brad Merrit (bass), Darryl Neudorf (drums), Neil Osborne (vocals). Neudorf replaced by Matt Johnson in 1985. The name "54.40" originates from slogan used by U.S. President James Polk, who wanted to expand the U.S. border north past the 49th parallel.

06/22/92　　30　　4　　Nice To Luv You .... Columbia
05/02/94　　13　　16　　Blame Your Parents .... Columbia
06/03/96　　21　　11 h　Love You All .... Columbia
09/30/96　　20　　7 h　Lies To Me .... Columbia
08/24/98　　---　　RA　　Since When .... Columbia　18

| DATE | PK | WK | TITLE | LABEL | RA |

FINE YOUNG CANNIBALS
British pop trio formed in Birmingham, England in 1983: Roland Gift (vocals, b. 04/28/61 in Birmingham), and ex-English Beat members, Andy Cox (guitar, b. 01/25/56 in Birmingham) and David Steele (bass, keyboards, b. 09/08/60 in Isle of Wight, England). Band appeared in movie, *Tin Men*, Gift appeared in *Sammy and Rosie Get Laid* and *Scandal*.

04/14/86	13	10	Johnny Come Home .... I.R.S.
07/14/86	21	9	Suspicious Minds.. I.R.S.
05/01/89	1(2)	24	She Drives Me Crazy .... I.R.S.
07/31/89	3(2)	18	Good Thing... I.R.S.
10/16/89	19	9	Don't Look Back.. I.R.S.

FINN, Tim
New Zealand male vocalist born on 06/25/52 in Te Awamutu, New Zealand. Member of Split Enz and Crowded House, 1991-1993.

| 09/12/83 | 25 | 2 | Through The Years .... A&M |

FIREFALL
American country-rock band formed circa 1974 in Boulder, Colorado: Rick Roberts (guitar, vocals, b. 1950 in Florida), Jock Bartley (guitar, vocals, b. Kansas), Mark Andes (bass, b. 02/19/48 in Philadelphia), Larry Burnett (guitar, vocals, b. Washington, D.C.), Michael Clarke (drums, b. 06/03/44 in New York City, d. 12/19/93 in Treasure Island, Florida).

12/04/76	17	10	You Are The Woman .... Atlantic
11/16/77	26	10	Just Remember I Love You........................ Atlantic
01/10/79	17	6	Strange Way... Atlantic

FIREHOUSE
American rock group from North Carolina: C.J. Snare (vocals), Bill Leverty, Perry Richardson, Michael Foster.

07/08/91	11	15	Don't Treat Me Bad .... Epic	28
11/18/91	24	15	Love Of A Lifetime .... Epic	11
11/09/92	24	8	When I Look Into Your Eyes .... Epic	12
05/15/95	---	RA	I Live My Life For You .... Epic	30

FIRST BASE

| 04/29/96 | --- | RA | Love Is Paradise .... Ariola | 39 |
| 04/18/99 | 29 | 3 | The EP .... Ariola |

5IVE
British male pop vocal group formed in 1997 in London: Richard Neville (b. circa 1980 in Solihull, Birmingham, England), Scott Robinson (b. circa 1980 in Basildon, Essex, England), Richard Abidin Breen (b. 06/29/79 in Enfield, London, England), Jason Brown (b. 06/13/76 in Aldershot, Hampshire, England) and Sean Conlon (b. 1981 in Horsworth, Leeds, England).

07/19/98	10	15	When The Lights Go Out .... Arista	28
			Another version peaked at #11 on 07/05/98.
01/17/99	29	4	It's The Things You Do..................................Arista

DATE	PK	WK	TITLE	LABEL	RA

5000 VOLTS
British disco trio: Tina Charles, Martin Jay, Tony Eyers. Charles later pursued a solo career.

| 12/13/75 | 29 | 2 | I'm On Fire | Philips | |

FIXX, The
British techno-pop group based in London: Cy Curnin (vocals, piano), Jamie West-Oram (guitars), Rupert Greenall (keyboards), Adam Woods (drums), Dan K. Brown (bass).

10/22/84	25	8	Are We Ourselves?	Chrysalis	
10/03/83	8	18	One Thing Leads To Another	MCA	
08/18/86	39	2	Secret Separation	MCA	

FLACK, Roberta
American female R&B-pop singer born on 02/10/39 in Asheville, North Carolina. High school music teacher in 1960's in Farmville, North Carolina, and Washington D.C. Discovered by musician Les McCann.

05/31/78	2(2)	14	The Closer I Get *	Atlantic	
12/05/83	4	16	Tonight, I Celebrate My Love **	Capitol	
11/18/91	---	RA	Set The Night To Music ***	Atlantic	17

* Roberta Flack & Donny Hathaway
** Peabo Bryson & Roberta Flack
*** Robert Flack/Maxi Priest

FLEETWOOD MAC
British-American rock group formed in 1976 in London: Peter Green (guitar, vocals, b. Peter Greenbaum on 10/29/46 in London), Mick Fleetwood (drums, b. 06/24/47 in Redruth, England), John McVie (bass, b. 11/26/45 in London), Jeremy Spencer (guitar, vocals, b. 07/04/48 in West Hartlepool, England). Green and Spencer left in 1970. McVie's wife (1968-77), Christine McVie (vocals, keyboards, b. Christine Perfect on 07/12/43 in Birmingham, England) joined in 1970. Band relocated to California in 1974. Stevie Nicks (vocals, b. Stephanie Nicks on 05/26/48 in Phoenix) and Lindsey Buckingham (guitar, vocals, b. 10/03/47 in Palo Alto, California) joined in 1975, left in 1987. Nicks left in 1993. Bekka Bramlett, lead singer of Zoo, and Dave Mason joined in 1993. Christine McVie left in 1994. Christine McVie, Nicks, Buckingham had solo careers.

01/17/76	16	4	Over My Head	Reprise	
06/12/76	7	11	Rhiannon	Reprise	
04/16/77	7	15	Go Your Own Way	Warner	
07/02/77	1(2)	20	Dreams	Warner	
09/07/77	5	17	Don't Stop	Warner	
12/28/77	10	16	You Make Lovin' Fun	Warner	
11/14/79	10	12	Tusk	Warner	
02/20/80	6	8	Sara	Warner	
08/14/82	6	10	Hold Me	Warner	
11/06/82	11	5	Gypsy	Warner	
06/01/87	12	11	Big Love	Warner	
09/07/87	12	10	Seven Wonders	Warner	
11/23/87	21	12	Little Lies	Warner	
02/08/88	38	2	Everywhere	Warner	
06/18/90	30	6	Save Me	Warner	20

DATE	PK	WK	TITLE	LABEL	RA

FLOATERS
American R&B group from Detroit: Charles Clarke (vocals), Larry Cunningham, brothers Paul and Ralph Mitchell.

| 11/16/77 | 29 | 6 | Float On | GRT |

A FLOCK OF SEAGULLS
British pop band formed in 1980 in Liverpool, England: Mike Score (vocals, keyboards, b. 11/05/57 in Liverpool), Ali Score (drums, b. Alistair Score on 08/08/56 in Liverpool), Paul Reynolds (guitar, b. 08/04/62 in Liverpool), Frank Maudsley (bass, b. 11/10/59 in Liverpool).

| 09/11/82 | 19 | 4 | I Ran (So Far Away) | Jive/Quality |
| 06/20/83 | 16 | 7 | Wishing | Jive/Quality |

FLYING LIZARDS, The
Irish duo formed in 1978: David Cunningham (keyboards), Deborah Evans (vocals).

| 02/20/80 | 5 | 17 | Money | Virgin |

FLYING PICKETS
British a cappella vocal sextet: Rick Lloyd, Ken Gregson, Gareth Williams, David Brett, Brian Hibbard, Red Stripe. Hibbard has appeared on television's *Coronation Street* in Britain.

| 04/09/84 | 32 | 7 | Only You | Virgin |

FOGELBERG, Dan
American male folk-rock singer/songwriter born on 08/13/51 in Peoria, Illinois.

04/02/80	7	8	Longer	Full Moon
11/07/81	10	6	Hard To Say	Full Moon
03/13/82	12	8	Leader Of The Band	Full Moon

FOGERTY, John
American male rock singer/songwriter born on 05/28/45 in Berkeley, California. Former lead singer of Credence Clearwater Revival, 1959-1971.

| 03/11/85 | 10 | 15 | The Old Man Down The Road | Warner |
| 05/27/85 | 19 | 8 | Rock & Roll Girls | Warner |

FOGHAT
British blues-rock quartet formed in London in 1971 led by "Lonesome" Dave Peverett. Line-up in 1980 included Peverett (vocals, guitar), Craig MacGregor (bass), Eric Cartwright (guitar), Roger Earl (drums). Disbanded in 1984; reunited in 1993.

| 02/06/80 | 26 | 4 | Third-Time Lucky (First Time I Was A Fool) | Bearsville |

FOO FIGHTERS
American alternative rock group: Dave Grohl (vocals, drums), Pat Smear (guitar), Nate Mendel (bass), William Goldsmith (drums). Grohl is the former drummer of Nirvana. Group named inspired by the UFO-like apparitions reported by American pilots during World War II.

| 08/28/95 | --- | RA | This Is A Call | Capitol | 35 |

DATE	PK	WK	TITLE	LABEL	RA
05/13/96	16	14 h	Big Me .... Capitol		18

FOOL'S GARDEN
German pop group formed in 1991: Peter Freudenthaler (vocals, b. 02/19/63 in Pforzheim, Germany), Volker Hinkel (guitar, vocals, b. 06/21/68 in Calw, Germany), Roland Röhl (keyboards, b. 04/06/71 in Calw), Thomas Mangold (bass, b. 09/29/65 in Calw), Ralf Wochele (drums, percussion, backing vocals, b. 02/23/68 in Pforzheim).

| 09/14/97 | 11 | 12 | Lemon Tree .... Universal |

FORBERT, Steve
American male folk-rock singer/songwriter born in 1955 in Meridian, Mississippi.

| 02/20/80 | 10 | 8 | Romeo's Tune .... Epic |

FORCE M.D.'s
American R&B vocal group formed in 1979 as Dr. Rock and the M.C.'s in Staten Island, New York: Stevie D. (b. Steve Lundy on 12/15/65 in New York City), T.C.D. (b. Antoine Maurice Lundy on 02/03/65), Jesse Lee Daniels (b. 07/04/63), Trisco Pearson (b. circa 1963 in New York City), Mercury (b. Charles Richard Nelson in 1965 in New York City). Daniels left in 1987, rejoined in 1992; Pearson and Nelson were replaced in 1990.

| 06/09/86 | 21 | 11 | Tender Love.. Warner |

FORD, Lita
American female hard rock singer/guitarist born Rosanna Ford on 09/23/59 in London, England.

| 08/01/88 | 32 | 5 | Kiss Me Deadly... RCA |

FOREIGNER
American/British rock group formed in 1976 in New York City: Mick Jones (vocals, guitar, b. 12/27/44 in London), Ian McDonald (flute, keyboards, reeds, guitar, vocals, b. 06/25/46 in London), Al Greenwood (keyboards, synthesizer, b. New York City), Lou Gramm (vocals, b. Lou Grammatico on 05/02/50 in Rochester, New York), Ed Gagliardi (bass, b. 02/13/52 in New York City), Dennis Elliott (drums, b. 08/18/50 in London). Gagliardi replaced by Rick Wills in 1979; McDonald, Greenwood left in 1980. Gramm pursued a solo career starting in the late-1980's. Changes in the 1990's included Johnny Edwards replacing Gramm in 1991.

DATE	PK	WK	TITLE	LABEL	RA
07/23/77	12	13	Feels Like The First Time........................... Atlantic	
10/19/77	12	12	Cold As Ice .... Atlantic	
09/20/78	7	12	Hot Blooded... Atlantic	
11/29/78	9	14	Double Vision .... Atlantic	
10/17/79	15	4	Dirty White Boy.. Atlantic	
09/05/81	1(1)	13	Urgent .... Atlantic	
12/05/81	2(3)	14	Waiting For A Girl Like You .... Atlantic	
04/03/82	18	2	Juke Box Hero .... Atlantic	
03/25/85	1(2)	24	I Want To Know What Love Is .... Atlantic	
05/13/85	17	12	That Was Yesterday .... Atlantic	
03/07/88	19	13	Say You Will... Atlantic	
06/13/88	12	11	I Don't Want To Live Without You............. Atlantic	
05/15/95	---	RA	Until The End Of Time .... Atlantic	28

FORTE, John

DATE	PK	WK	TITLE	LABEL	RA

American male rapper/producer from New York City. Of Haitian ancestry.

| 06/21/98 | 35 | 2 | Ninety Nine | Columbia |

FOSTER, David
Canadian male keyboardist/composer/songwriter/singer born in Victoria, British Columbia. Produced and wrote recordings for Chicago and Barbra Streisand. Member of Skylark.

| 12/16/85 | 15 | 15 | Love Theme From "St. Elmo's Fire" | Atlantic |
| 07/21/86 | 32 | 6 | Best Of Me * | Atlantic |

   * David Foster/Olivia Newton-John

4 NON BLONDES
American rock band formed in 1989 in San Francisco: Linda Perry (vocals), Roger Rocha (guitar), Christa Hillhouse (bass), Dawn Richardson (drums).

| 07/19/93 | --- | RA | What's Up | Interscope | 24 |

411
Canadian dance group.

| 06/06/99 | 37 | 2 | Everybody's Free (To Wear Sunscreen) | Odeon |

4 P.M.
American male pop vocal quartet from Baltimore: Larry McFarland, Marty Ware, and brothers Rene and Roberto Pena.

| 03/06/95 | 1(7) | 34 | Sukiyaki | Next Plateau | 21 |

4 THE CAUSE
American R&B group from Chicago: siblings Ms. Lady (b. circa 1982) and J-Man (b. circa 1983), with their cousins Shorty (b. circa 1986) and Bennie (b. circa 1983). Formed circa 1993.

| 08/30/98 | 28 | 10 | Stand By Me | RCA |

FOUR SEASONS
American pop group formed as the Varietones in 1956 in Newark, New Jersey. Original line-up: Frankie Valli (vocals, b. Francis Casteluccio on 05/03/37 in Newark), Tommy DeVito (guitar, b. 06/19/36 in Belleville, New Jersey), Nick DeVito (guitar), Hank Majewski (bass). Briefly named the Four Lovers before changing the name to the Four Seasons (after a New Jersey cocktail lounge). Bob Gaudio (keyboards, b. 11/17/42 in Bronx, New York) joined in 1960 and a few personnel changes followed. By 1975, line-up included Valli, Don Ciccone (guitar, b. 02/28/46 in New York), Gerry Polci (drums, vocals, b. 1954 in Passaic, New Jersey), Gaudio, John Paiva.

11/15/75	4	9	Who Loves You	Warner	
04/10/76	1(2)	14	December 1963 (Oh, What A Night)	Warner	
11/07/94	---	RA	December 1963 (Oh, What A Night)	Curb	17

                 Above is a remix version of the 1976 original.

4 FOR THE CAUSE
American R&B group from Chicago: siblings Ms. Lady (b. circa 1983) and J-Man (b. circa 1984), and their cousins Shorty (b. circa 1986) and Bennie (b. circa 1984). Formed circa 1994.

DATE	PK	WK	TITLE	LABEL
08/30/98	28	10	Stand By Me	RCA

FOX, Samantha
British female pop singer born on 04/15/66 in London. Topless model for the *Daily Sun* newspaper in Britain.

03/02/87	1(7)	18	Touch Me (I Want Your Body)	Jive
05/18/87	27	7	Do Ya Do Ya (Wanna Please Me)	Jive
10/19/87	27	10	Nothing's Gonna Stop Me Now	Jive
03/07/88	35	5	I Surrender	Jive
07/11/88	8	13	Naughty Girls (Need Love Too)	Jive
02/27/89	10	14	I Wanna Have Some Fun	Jive
05/22/89	12	11	I Only Want To Be With You	Jive

FOXY
American dance band from Miami led by vocalist/guitarist Ish Ledesma, who later founded and produced Oxo and Company B. Four of five members from Cuba.

12/27/78	11	18	Get Off	TK

FRAMPTON, Peter
British male rock singer/songwriter/guitarist born on 04/22/50 in Beckenham, England. Former member of the Herd, Humble Pie, and formed Frampton's Camel; went solo in 1971. Survived serious car accident in the Bahamas in 1978.

04/24/76	5	12	Show Me The Way	A&M
09/11/76	8	9	Baby I Love Your Way	A&M
12/11/76	11	15	Do You Feel Like We Do	A&M
08/13/77	1(1)	16	I'm In You	A&M
10/19/77	15	12	Signed, Sealed, Delivered	A&M
01/11/78	28	4	Tried To Love	A&M
08/08/79	38	6	I Can't Stand It No More	A&M

FRANKIE AND THE KNOCKOUTS
American soft-rock quintet led by Franke Previte, native of New Brunswick, New Jersey.

05/23/81	14	3	Sweetheart	Millennium

FRANKIE GOES TO HOLLYWOOD
British pop-dance group formed in 1980 in Liverpool: Holly Johnson (vocals, b. William Johnson on 02/19/60 in Khartoum, Sudan), Paul Rutherford (vocals, b. 12/08/59 in Liverpool), Nasher Nash (guitar, b. Brian Nash on 05/20/63 in Liverpool), Mark O'Toole (bass, b. 01/06/64 in Liverpool), Peter Gill (drums, b. 03/08/64 in Liverpool).

07/02/84	23	13	Relax	Island
09/24/84	17	11	Two Tribes	Island
02/11/85	25	6	The Power Of Love	Island
05/20/85	39	2	Welcome To The Pleasure Dome	Island

FRANKLIN, Aretha

DATE	PK	WK	TITLE	LABEL	RA

American female R&B singer born on 03/25/42 in Memphis, Tennessee. Known as "The Queen Of Soul". Daughter of Reverend Cecil L. Franklin, pastor of Detroit's 4,500-member New Bethel Baptist Church and popular gospel singer. Raised in Detroit and Buffalo. In 1987, became first woman inducted into the Rock and Roll Hall of Fame. Made cameo appearance in the 1980 movie *The Blues Brothers*.

Date	PK	WK	Title	Label	RA
09/23/85	6	14	Freeway Of Love	Arista	
12/02/85	37	2	Who's Zoomin' Who	Arista	
11/17/86	24	9	Jumpin' Jack Flash	Arista	
05/18/87	9	13	I Knew You Were Waiting (For Me) *	Arista	
06/12/89	32	6	Through The Storm **	Arista	

* Aretha Franklin/George Michael
** Aretha Franklin/Elton John

FREAK NASTY
American male disc jockey Carlito Timmons born in Puerto Rico. Based in Atlanta.

04/13/97	14	6	Da' Dip	Tria	

FREDO, Michael
American male pop singer born in Elmira, New York.

07/25/99	21	1 +	This Time Around	Qwest	

FRENCH, Nicki
British female dance singer from Carlisle, England.

08/14/95	2(6)	25	Total Eclipse Of The Heart	Critique	4

FRENTE!
Australian pop-rock group formed in 1989 in Melbourne: Angie Hart (vocals), Tim O'Connor (bass), Simon Austin (guitar), Mark Picton (drums). O'Connor left in 1995; replaced by Bill McDonald (bass, guitar).

08/01/94	---	RA	Bizarre Love Triangle	Attic	23

FREW, Alan
Canadian male pop/rock singer born on 11/08/58 in Coatbridge, Scotland. Lead singer of Glass Tiger, early-1980's to 1993.

| 10/24/94 | --- | RA | Healing Hands | EMI | 5 |
| 02/20/95 | --- | RA | So Blind | EMI | 10 |

FREY, Glenn
American male pop-rock vocalist/songwriter/guitarist/pianist born on 11/06/48 in Detroit. Member of The Eagles. Made guest appearances on television's *Miami Vice* and *Wiseguy*.

11/13/82	13	5	The One You Love	Asylum	
04/08/85	15	22	The Heat Is On	MCA	
12/02/85	9	14	You Belong To The City	MCA	
11/14/88	8	15	True Love	MCA	

DATE	PK	WK	TITLE	LABEL	RA

FROZEN GHOST
Canadian rock band formed in 1985 consisting of Arnold Lanni (vocals, guitar, songwriter), Sammy D. Bartel (keyboards), John Bouvette (drums), and Wolf Hassel (bass). Lanni and Hassel were members of Sheriff.

10/31/88	39	1	Round And Round	WEA	
06/26/89	27	8	Dream Come True	WEA	
04/20/92	---	RA	Head Over Heels	WEA	23

FRUIT DE LA PASSION
Canadian dance group from Montreal.

06/15/97	2(1)	22	Tic Tic Tac	DEP	
08/24/97	27	4	Vai Vai Vai	DEP	

FUGEES
American hip-hop trio formed in 1994 in East Orange, New Jersey: Lauryn Hill (vocals, b. 05/25/75 in East Orange), Wyclef "Clef" Jean (rapper, guitar, producer, b. Whyclef Jean, on 10/17/72 in Haiti), Prakazrel "Pras" Michel (rapper, producer, b. 10/19/72 in Haiti). "Fugees" stands for refugees. All three later pursued solo careers. Hill played a role in *Sister Act II*.

07/29/96	9	14 h	Killing Me Softly	Columbia	2
09/30/96	---	RA	No Woman, No Cry	Columbia	29
03/16/97	39	1	Rumble In Jungle	NuMuzik	
11/09/97	7	21	Avenues *	Arista	

* Refugee Camp All Stars

FUN FACTORY
German pop/dance group from Hamburg: Marie-Anett (vocals; from France), Smooth T (rapper, dancer; from Italy), Rod D. (rapper; from the U.S.), Steve (dancer; from Germany). Formed in the early-1990's.

11/27/95	9	16	I Wanna B With U	Attic	19

FUNHOUSE

10/22/90	38	2	Kid N' Play	Attic	

FUNKDOOBIEST
American rap trio formed in 1991 in Los Angeles: Ralph "DJ Ralph M" Medrano, Jason "Sondoobie" Vasquez, Tyrone "Tomahawk Funk" Pachenco.

06/28/93	21	32	Bow Bow Bow	Epic	

FUNKY GREEN DOG
American techno-dance trio from New York City: singer Pamela Williams, with producers Oscar Gaetan and Ralph Falcon.

11/17/96	34	2	Fired Up!	MCA	

FU-SHNICKENS

DATE	PK	WK	TITLE	LABEL	RA

American rap trio from Brooklyn: Poc Fu, Chip Fu, Moc Fu. FU stands for "For Unity", Schnicken is an invented term meaning coalition.

| 08/23/93 | 15 | 25 | What's Up Doc | Jive | |

G

GABRIEL, Peter
British male rock singer/songwriter born on 02/13/50 in London, England. Lead singer of Genesis, 1966-1975.

09/20/80	8	6	Games Without Frontiers	Mercury	
12/18/82	16	7	Shock The Monkey	Geffen	
07/21/86	1(4)	21	Sledgehammer	Geffen	
10/27/86	40	1	In Your Eyes	Geffen	
03/16/87	18	11	Big Time	Geffen	
06/22/87	40	1	Don't Give Up *	Geffen	
11/23/92	---	RA	Diggin' In The Dirt	Geffen	19
02/15/93	---	RA	Steam	Geffen	1

* Peter Gabriel/Kate Bush

GABRIELLE
British female pop singer born Louise Gabrielle Bobb on 04/16/70. Based in South London, England.

| 12/06/93 | 3(2) | 35 | Dreams | Polydor | 8 |
| 06/13/94 | --- | RA | I Wish | Polydor | 38 |

GAGNON, Andre
Canadian male pianist/composer born on 08/01/42 in St. Pacome-de-Kamouraska, Quebec. Based in Montreal.

| 03/20/76 | 15 | 9 | Wow! | London | |

GAINES, Rosie
American R&B singer/keyboardist born in Pittsburg, California. Vocalist of Prince's New Power Generation.

| 08/28/95 | --- | RA | I Want U | Motown | 40 |

GALLANT, Patsy
Canadian female singer born in 1950 in Campbellton, New Brunswick. Host of the television program, *The Patsy Gallant Show*.

11/06/76	9	12	From New York To LA	Attic	
04/16/77	8	15	Are You Ready For Love	Attic	
10/05/77	7	10	Sugar Daddy	Attic	

GARBAGE
American alternative rock group formed in 1994 in Madison, Wisconsin: Shirley Manson (vocals, guitar),

| DATE | PK | WK | TITLE | LABEL | RA |

Steve Markes (guitar, bass, samples, loops), Duke Erikson (guitar, keyboards, bass), Butch Vig (drums, programming).

05/06/96	---	RA	Only Happy When It Rains........................ Geffen	39
09/23/96	28	4 h	Stupid Girl .... Geffen	17
02/11/97	---	RA	#1 Crush...EMI	30

GARFIELD
Canadian folk band: Garfield French (vocals), Dennis French (drums, percussion), Jacques Fillion (keyboards), Walter Lawrence (guitar, electric cello), Paul O'Donnell (guitar, harmonica, banjo), Chip Yarwood (flute, synthesizer).

| 12/04/76 | 36 | 2 | Give My Love To Anne............................. Mercury |

GARFUNKEL, Art
American male folk-pop singer/songwriter born on 11/05/41 in Forest Hills, New York. Member of duo, Simon & Garfunkel. In movies, *Catch-22, Carnal Knowledge*, and *Bad Timing/A Sensual Obsession*.

11/15/75	9	8	I Only Have Eyes For You....................... Columbia
03/08/78	8	12	(What A) Wonderful World *................... Columbia
08/08/79	34	2	Since I Don't Have You .... Columbia

* Art Garfunkel with James Taylor & Paul Simon

GARRETT, Leif
American male pop singer/actor born on 11/08/61 in Hollywood, California. Made film debut in 1969 film *Bob and Carol and Ted and Alice*. Own television series, *Three For The Road* in 1975.

03/08/78	26	8	Runaround Sue... Atlantic
05/03/78	22	4	Put Your Head On My Shoulder .... Atlantic
02/21/79	33	2	I Was Made For Dancin'.................. Scotti Brothers

GARFUNKEL, Art
American male folk-pop singer/songwriter born on 11/05/41 in New York City. Member of the duo Simon & Garfunkel. In movies, *Catch-22, Carnal Knowledge*, and *Bad Timing/A Sensual Obsession*.

11/15/75	9	8	I Only Have Eyes For You....................... Columbia
03/08/78	8	14	(What A) Wonderful World *................... Columbia
08/08/79	34	4	Since I Don't Have You .... Columbia

* Art Garfunkel with James Taylor & Paul Simon

GARRETT, Leif
American male pop singer/actor born on 11/08/61 in Hollywood, California. Made film debut in 1969 film *Bob and Carol and Ted and Alice*. Own television series, *Three For The Road* in 1975.

03/08/78	26	8	Runaround Sue... Atlantic
05/03/78	22	4	Put Your Head On My Shoulder .... Atlantic
02/21/79	33	2	I Was Made For Dancin'.................. Scotti Brothers

GATES, David
American male pop singer/songwriter/guitarist born on 12/11/40 in Tulsa, Oklahoma. Former lead singer

DATE	PK	WK	TITLE	LABEL	RA

of Bread.

| 05/03/78 | 3(2) | 14 | Goodbye Girl | Elektra | |
| 11/01/78 | 14 | 6 | Took The Last Train | Elektra | |

GAYE, Marvin
American male R&B singer born Marvin Pentz Gay Jr. on 04/02/39 in Washington, D.C. In recording act, Marquees in late-1950's. Recorded with Harvey Fuqua in the Moonglows. Signed to Motown in 1961. Married to Anna Gordy, sister of Motown founder/president Barry Gordy, Jr. (1961-75). Lived in Europe for three years due to taxation problems in U.S. in early-1980's. Fatally shot by father, an Apostolic preacher, after an argument on 04/01/84 in Los Angeles.

| 08/06/77 | 12 | 10 | Got To Give It Up (Part 1) | Motown | |
| 02/21/83 | 3(2) | 14 | Sexual Healing | Columbia | |

GAYLE, Crystal
American female country-pop singer born Brenda Gall Webb on 01/09/51 in Paintsville, Kentucky and raised in Wabash, Indiana. Sister of country singer, Loretta Lynn. In Bob Hope's *Road To China* TV show becoming first country artist to tour China, 1979.

| 11/30/77 | 6 | 20 | Don't It Make My Brown Eyes Blue | United Artists | |

GAYNOR, Gloria
American female disco-pop singer born on 09/07/49 in Newark, New Jersey.

| 04/04/79 | 4 | 16 | I Will Survive | Polydor | |

GEDDES, David
American male singer born on 07/01/50.

| 10/04/75 | 5 | 9 | Run Joey Run | Big Tree | |

GEILS, J., Band
American rock group formed in 1967 in Boston: Jerome Geils (guitar, b. 02/20/46 in New York City), Peter Wolf (vocals, b. Peter Blankfield on 03/07/46 in the Bronx, New York), Magic Dick (harmonica, b. Dick Salwitz on 05/13/45 in New London, Connecticut), Danny Klein (bass, b. 05/13/46 in New York City), Stephen Jo Bladd (drums, b. 07/13/42 in Boston), Seth Justman (keyboards, b. 01/27/51 in Washington, D.C.). Wolf left in 1983 for a solo career.

04/23/80	26	5	Come Back	EMI	
04/30/80	38	1	Love Stinks	EMI	
01/23/82	1(5)	16	Centerfold	EMI	
04/10/82	2(3)	13	Freeze-Frame	EMI	
02/07/83	24	3	I Do	EMI	

GENERAL PUBLIC
British pop group led by former English Beat vocalists Dave Wakeling (b. 02/19/56 in Birmingham, England), Ranking Roger (b. Roger Charlery on 02/21/61 in Birmingham). Disbanded in 1988, both pursued solo careers. Reunited in 1994.

| 02/18/85 | 16 | 10 | Tenderness | I.R.S. | |
| 06/06/94 | --- | RA | I'll Take You There | Epic | 3 |

DATE	PK	WK	TITLE	LABEL	RA

GENESIS
British rock group formed in 1966 in Godalming, England: Tony Banks (keyboards, b. 03/27/50 in East Hoathly, England), Michael Rutherford (guitar, bass, vocals, b. 10/02/50 in Guildford, England), Peter Gabriel (vocals, b. 02/13/50 in London), Anthony Phillips (guitar, b. 12/51 in Putney, England), Chris Stewart (drums, later replaced by John Mayhew in 1969). Phillips and Mayhew left in 1970, replaced by Steve Hackett (guitar, b. 02/12/50 in London) and Phil Collins (drums, b. 01/31/51 in London). Gabriel left in 1975, Collins replaced him as lead singer. Hackett left to pursue solo career in 1977 making Genesis a trio consisting of Collins, Rutherford, Banks. All three pursued solo careers. Rutherford formed Mike + The Mechanics, in 1985. Hackett formed GTR.

DATE	PK	WK	TITLE	LABEL	RA
08/09/78	19	10	Follow You Follow Me	Atlantic	
07/23/80	16	2	Misunderstanding	Atlantic	
11/21/81	4	9	No Reply At All	Atlantic	
02/20/82	8	5	Abacab	Atlantic	
08/14/82	14	3	Paperlate	Atlantic	
12/12/83	38	2	Mama	Atlantic	
02/13/84	10	15	That's All	Atlantic	
07/28/86	4	17	Invisible Touch	Atlantic	
11/17/86	20	8	Throwing It All Away	Atlantic	
03/02/87	13	8	Land Of Confusion	Atlantic	
04/13/87	39	5	Tonight, Tonight, Tonight	Atlantic	
07/20/87	15	10	In Too Deep	Atlantic	
12/23/91	---	RA	No Son Of Mine	Atlantic	3
04/06/92	7	13	I Can't Dance	Atlantic	3
06/22/92	---	RA	Hold On My Heart	Atlantic	5
09/21/92	---	RA	Jesus He Knows Me	Atlantic	5
01/25/93	---	RA	Never A Time	Atlantic	6

GEORGIA SATELLITES
American rock band formed in Atlanta in 1979: Dan Baird (guitar, vocals, b. 12/12/53 in California), Mauro Megellan (drums), Rick Price (bass, b. 08/15/51 in Atlanta), Rick Richards (guitar, b. 03/30/54 in Jasper, Georgia). Disbanded in 1991, re-formed in 1993.

DATE	PK	WK	TITLE	LABEL	RA
03/16/87	11	13	Keep Your Hands To Yourself	Elektra	
12/19/88	36	7	Hippy Hippy Shake	Elektra	

GERARDO
Ecuadorian male Latin rapper born Gerardo Mejia III on 04/16/65 in Guayaquil, Ecuador. Raps in Spanish and English. Moved to Glendale, California at age 12. Based in Los Angeles.

DATE	PK	WK	TITLE	LABEL	RA
05/13/91	31	4	Rico Sauve	Interscope	

GIANT
American rock quartet led by brothers Dann Huff (vocals) and David Huff (drums) from Nashville, Tennessee.

DATE	PK	WK	TITLE	LABEL	RA
06/25/90	31	3	I'll See You In My Dreams	A&M	23

GIANT STEPS
British pop duo: vocalist Campsie and multi-instrumentalist George McFarlane. Members of band, Grand Hotel and Quick.

DATE	PK	WK	TITLE	LABEL	RA
12/05/88	37	3	Another Lover	A&M	

DATE	PK	WK	TITLE	LABEL	RA

GIBB, Andy
British/Australian male pop singer born on 03/05/58 in Chorlton-Cum-Hardy, England. Briefly lived in Australia as a child. Youngest brother of the Bee Gees. Host of TV's *Solid Gold*, 1981-82, and appeared in Broadway's *Joseph and the Amazing Technicolor Dreamcoat*. Died on 03/10/88 in Oxford, England of a viral inflammation.

DATE	PK	WK	TITLE	LABEL
09/07/77	1(4)	21	I Just Want To Be Your Everything	RSO
02/22/78	2(4)	16	Love Is Thicker Than Water	RSO
06/28/78	2(2)	20	Shadow Dancing	RSO
09/20/78	9	8	An Everlasting Love	RSO
01/10/79	8	10	(Our Love) Don't Throw It All Away	RSO
02/06/80	35	2	Desire	RSO

GIBB, Barry
British male singer born on 09/01/47 in Douglas, Isle of Man, England. Member of the Bee Gees. Brother of fellow Bee Gees members Maurice and Robin Gibb.

DATE	PK	WK	TITLE	LABEL
04/04/81	15	3	What Kind Of Fool *	Columbia

* Barbra Streisand & Barry Gibb

GIBB, Robin
British male singer born on 12/22/49 in Douglas, Isle of Man, England. Member of the Bee Gees, twin brother of member Maurice Gibb.

DATE	PK	WK	TITLE	LABEL
09/17/84	20	12	Boys Do Fall In Love	Polydor

GIBBS, Terri
American female country singer/pianist born on 06/15/54 in Miami, Florida. Blind since birth. Returned to gospel music in 1986.

DATE	PK	WK	TITLE	LABEL
04/25/81	11	6	Somebody's Knockin'	MCA

GIBSON, Debbie
American pop singer/songwriter/pianist/actress born Deborah Gibson on 08/31/70 in Merrick, New York. Played Eponine in Broadway's *Les Miserables* and Sandy in the London stage production of *Grease*.

DATE	PK	WK	TITLE	LABEL	RA
10/19/87	6	16	Only In My Dreams	Atlantic	
02/01/88	10	14	Shake Your Love	Atlantic	
04/25/88	21	10	Out Of The Blue	Atlantic	
08/01/88	1(1)	17	Foolish Beat	Atlantic	
10/24/88	29	4	Staying Together	Atlantic	
03/20/89	5	16	Lost In Your Eyes	Atlantic	
06/12/89	15	9	Electric Youth	Atlantic	
12/24/90	17	9	Anything Is Possible	Atlantic	24

GILBERT, John

DATE	PK	WK	TITLE	LABEL
06/05/76	24	3	No Charge	Capitol

GILDER, Nick

| DATE | PK | WK | TITLE | LABEL | RA |

Canadian male rock vocalist born on 11/07/51 in London, England. Raised in Vancouver. Member of rock band Sweeney Todd.

| 10/18/78 | 2(6) | 24 | Hot Child In The City................................. Chrysalis |
| 01/24/79 | 21 | 8 | Here Comes The Night............................ Chrysalis |

GILL, Johnny
American male R&B singer born on 05/22/66 in Washington, D.C. Member of New Edition since 1988.

08/06/90	6	16	Rub You The Right Way .... Motown	17
10/15/90	---	RA	My My My .... Motown	33
07/26/93	7	18	The Floor .... Motown	37

GILL, Vince
American male country singer born Vince Grant Gill on 04/12/57 in Norman, Oklahoma.

| 02/27/95 | 18 | 19 | House Of Love.. A&M |

* Amy Grant & Vince Gill

GILLETTE
American female rapper born on 09/16/73 in Chicago. Member of 20 Fingers.

| 04/10/95 | --- | RA | Mr. Personality.. Zoo | 39 |
| 04/17/95 | 6 | 19 | Short Dick Man * .... Zoo |

* 20 Fingers featuring Gillette

GIN BLOSSOMS
American rock group from Tempe, Arizona: Robin Wilson (lead vocals), Phillip Rhodes (drums, vocals), Jesse Valenzuela (guitar, vocals), Bill Leen (bass), Scott Johnson (guitar).

10/25/93	---	RA	Hey Jealousy .... A&M	25
02/07/94	---	RA	Found Out About You .... A&M	4
08/15/94	---	RA	Until I Fall Away... A&M	34
12/12/94	---	RA	Allison Road .... A&M	17
09/25/95	---	RA	Til I Hear It From You .... A&M	1
04/08/96	1(4)	20 h	Follow You Down... A&M	1
07/15/96	23	5 h	Day Job.. A&M
10/07/96	25	6 h	As Long As It Matters..................................... A&M	36

GINA G
Australian female dance singer born in 1971 in Queensland, Australia.

| 01/26/97 | 22 | 11 | Ooh Aah...Just A Little Bit........................... Warner | 21 |

GINGER - see GRAPES OF WRATH

GINUWINE
American male R&B singer born Elgin Lumpkin, circa 1974 in Washington, D.C.

| 03/02/97 | 20 | 4 | Pony... Epic | 22 |

DATE	PK	WK	TITLE	LABEL	RA
			Two other versions peaked at #38 on 12/08/96 and #22 on 02/23/97.	..	
05/10/99	---	RA	What's So Different	550/Epic	25

GLASS TIGER
Canadian pop/rock band based in Newmarket, Ontario: Alan Frew (lead vocals, b. 11/08/58 in Coatbridge, Scotland), Al Connelly (guitar), Michael Hanson (drums), Wayne Parker (bass), Sam Reid (keyboards). Formed in 1982 as Tokyo; name changed to Glass Tiger in 1985. Hanson left band in 1988. Disbanded in 1993. Frew began recording solo in 1994.

DATE	PK	WK	TITLE	LABEL	RA
05/12/86	1(2)	21	Don't Forget Me (When I'm Gone)	Capitol	
07/21/86	17	17	Thin Red Line	Capitol	
11/24/86	11	19	Someday	Capitol	
02/23/87	21	9	You're What I Look For	Capitol	
05/04/87	31	4	I Will Be There	Capitol	
06/06/88	3(1)	15	I'm Still Searching	Capitol	
09/12/88	13	12	Diamond Sun	Capitol	
11/28/88	19	12	My Song	Capitol	
05/06/91	4	16	Animal Heart	Capitol	5
09/02/91	28	7	Rhythm Of Your Love	Capitol	11
11/11/91	39	1	My Town	Capitol	12
02/03/92	---	RA	Rescued (By The Arms Of Love)	Capitol	12
01/17/94	---	RA	Touch Of Your Hand	EMI	33

GO WEST
British pop duo of Peter Cox (vocals) and Richard Drummie (guitar, vocals).

DATE	PK	WK	TITLE	LABEL	RA
08/27/90	3(2)	11	King Of Wishful Thinking	EMI	1
01/25/93	28	14	Faithful	EMI	4
04/26/93	---	RA	What You Won't Do For Love	EMI	39

GODDESS
Dutch female singer from Amsterdam. Former backup vocalist for Joe Cocker and Falco.

DATE	PK	WK	TITLE	LABEL	RA
04/05/93	25	7	Sexual	Epic	

GODLEY & CREME
British pop duo: Kevin Godley (b. 10/07/45 in Manchester), Lol Creme (b. 09/19/47 in Manchester). Former members of 10cc and Hotlegs.

DATE	PK	WK	TITLE	LABEL	RA
09/30/85	8	12	Cry	Polydor	

GOGH VAN GO
American jazz group formed in the early-1990's in San Francisco: Connie Walkershaw (saxophone), Kelvin Burton (drums), Jamison Smeltz (vocals), Kate Regan (violin), Jesse Walkershaw (bass).

DATE	PK	WK	TITLE	LABEL	RA
10/18/93	---	RA	Say You Will	Star	39

GO-GOs, The
American female pop band formed in Hollywood, California in 1978: Belinda Carlisle (vocals, b. 08/17/58 in Hollywood), Charlotte Caffey (guitar, b. 10/21/53 in Santa Monica, California), Jane Wiedlin (guitar, b. 05/20/58 in Oconomowoc, Wisconsin), Margot Olaverra (bass), Elissa Bello (drums). Olaverra left in

DATE	PK	WK	TITLE	LABEL	RA

1980, replaced by Kathy Valentine (bass, b. 01/07/59 in Austin, Texas). Wiedlin left to record solo in 1984. Group disbanded in 1985. Carlisle pursued solo career. Reunited in 1990.

02/13/82	4	15	Our Lips Are Sealed	I.R.S.	
04/17/82	3(1)	12	We Got The Beat	I.R.S.	
09/04/82	10	8	Vacation	I.R.S.	
06/25/84	34	6	Head Over Heels	I.R.S.	

GOLD, Andrew
American male vocalist/pianist born on 08/02/51 in Burbank, California. Son of soundtrack composer Ernest Gold (*Exodus*) and singer Marni Nixon. Co-founded group, Bryndle in late-1960's. Member of pop group Wax.

07/16/77	7	16	Lonely Boy	Asylum	
05/17/78	6	8	Thank You For Being A Friend	Asylum	

GOLDEN EARRING
Dutch hard rock band formed in The Hague in 1961: George Kooymans (guitar, vocals, b. 03/11/48 in The Hague), Rinus Gerritsen (bass, keyboards, harmonica, b. 08/09/46 in The Hague), Barry Hay (vocals, flute, saxophone, b. 08/16/48 in Saizabad, Netherlands), Cesar Zuiderwijk (drums, b. 07/18/50 in The Hague).

04/25/83	12	10	Twilight Zone	21 Records	

GOLDIE
British dance producer born in 1965 in Wolverhampton, England. "Goldie" is short for his nickname "Goldilocks".

01/18/98	30	5	Digital	ffrr	

GOMM, Ian
British male singer born on 03/17/47 in Ealing, England.

10/17/79	28	2	Hold On	Epic	

GOO GOO DOLLS
American rock trio formed in 1985 in Buffalo, New York: Johnny Rzenzik (vocals, guitar, b. 12/05/65 in Buffalo), Robby Takac (bass), George Tutuska (drums). Tutuska was replaced by Mike Malinin in 1995.

03/11/96	34	6	Name	Elektra	1
04/08/96	31	8 h	Naked	Elektra	
07/29/96	39	3 h	Long Way Down	Elektra	
07/13/98	---	RA	Iris	Reprise	1
02/01/99	---	RA	Slide	Warner	3
07/26/99	---	RA	Black Balloon	Warner	30+

GOODMAN, Dickie
American male novelty singer born on 04/19/34 in Hewlett, New York. Comedy writer for Jackie Mason and head of music department at 20th Century Fox. Died on 11/06/89 of self-inflicted gunshot.

10/18/75	2(1)	7	Mr. Jaws	Cash	

DATE	PK	WK	TITLE	LABEL	RA

GOODMEN, The
Dutch production team of producers DJ Zki and Dobre from Amsterdam.

| 01/17/94 | 31 | 4 | Give It Up | ffrr | |

GOODY GOODY
American group featuring vocalist Denise Montana and a studio band from Philadelphia.

| 01/24/79 | 40 | 2 | No. 1 Dee Jay | Atlantic | |

GOWAN, Lawrence
Canadian male pop/rock singer/songwriter from Toronto. Born in Glasgow, Scotland. Played keyboards in Rhinegold, a Toronto progressive rock band.

05/13/85	12	15	A Criminal Mind *	Columbia	
07/22/85	9	12	(You're A) Strange Animal *	Columbia	
05/04/87	6	16	Moonlight Desires *	Columbia	
09/17/90	11	11	All The Lovers In The World *	Columbia	15
12/12/93	---	RA	(When There's) Time For Love	Columbia	10
02/28/94	---	RA	Dancing On My Own Ground	Columbia	17
06/13/94	---	RA	Souls Road	Columbia	20
11/06/95	---	RA	Guns And God	Select	32
09/23/96	---	RA	The Good Catches	Select	37

* Gowan

G.Q.
American R&B group from the Bronx, New York: Emmanuel Rahiem LeBlanc (vocals), Keith Crier, Herb Lane, Paul Service. Service left in 1980.

| 05/30/79 | 24 | 6 | Disco Nights | Capitol | |

GRAMM, John
Canadian male pop singer John Grammatikos from Toronto.

| 05/09/94 | 30 | 5 | The Blue & White | Quality | |

GRAMM, Lou
American male rock singer born Lou Grammatico on 05/02/50 in Rochester, New York. Lead singer of Foreigner, left in 1991.

| 04/13/87 | 18 | 14 | Midnight Blue | Atlantic | |
| 04/16/90 | --- | RA | True Blue Love | Atlantic | 26 |

GRAND FUNK
American hard rock band formed in Flint, Michigan in 1968: Mark Farner (guitar, vocals, b. 09/29/48 in Flint), Mel Schacher (bass, b. 04/03/51 in Owosso, Michigan), Don Brewer (drums, b. 09/03/48 in Flint). Craig Frost (keyboards, b. 04/20/48 in Flint) joined in 1972. Brewer and Farner were members of Terry Knight & The Pack; Schacher played bass with ? & The Mysterians. Group also known by original name, Grand Funk Railroad.

| 06/14/75 | 5 | 4 | Bad Time | Capitol | |

DATE	PK	WK	TITLE	LABEL	RA

GRANT, Amy
American female pop singer/songwriter born on 11/25/60 in Augusta, Georgia. Leading Contemporary Christian recording artist. Married to songwriter Gary Chapman, separated in December 1998.

01/19/87	4	21	The Next Time I Fall *	Full Moon	
06/06/91	2(1)	14	Baby Baby	A&M	2
08/26/91	15	11	Every Heartbeat	A&M	5
12/23/91	5	15	That's What Love Is For	A&M	7
04/06/92	10	11	Good For Me	A&M	4
06/22/92	---	RA	I Will Remember You	A&M	11
10/17/94	12	36	Lucky One	A&M	5
02/27/95	18	19	House Of Love **	A&M	
10/13/97	---	RA	Takes A Little Time	A&M	21

* Peter Cetera/Amy Grant
** Amy Grant & Vince Gill

GRANT, Eddy
British male pop singer born Edmond Montague Grant on 03/05/48 in Plaisance, Guyana. Lead singer of The Equals, 1967-72.

07/11/83	1(5)	18	Electric Avenue	Portrait	
10/17/83	11	14	I Don't Wanna Dance	Portrait	
08/27/84	9	11	Romancing The Stone	Portrait	

GRAPES OF WRATH
Canadian alternative rock band formed in 1983 based in Vancouver: Kevin Kane (vocals, guitar), Chris Hooper (vocals, drums), Tom Hooper (vocals, bass, guitar), Vincent Jones (keyboards). Named after the John Ford film of the same name. Kane left the group in 1992; the band's name changed to Ginger due to legal problems.

09/18/89	31	8	All The Things I Wasn't	Capitol	
11/04/91	14	7	I Am Here	Capitol	7
12/02/91	25	11	You May Be Right	Capitol	14
03/30/92	30	4	A Fishing Tale	Capitol	
12/05/94	---	RA	Solid Ground *	Nettwerk	36

* Ginger

GRATEFUL DEAD
American legendary psychedelic rock band formed in San Francisco in 1966 led by Jerry Garcia (vocals, guitar, b. 08/01/42 in San Francisco). Garcia died of a heart attack on 08/09/95 in Forest Knolls, California.

10/05/87	21	11	Touch Of Grey	Arista	

GRAVEDIGGAZ
American rap group from New York: Robert Diggs ("RZA", also a member of Wu-Tang Clan), Paul Huston ("Prince Paul" or "The Undertaker", also a member of Stetsasonic), Poetic ("Grym Reaper"), Arnold Hamilton ("Fruitkwan" or "The Gatekeeper").

09/05/94	11	25	Diary Of A Madman	Island	

DATE	PK	WK	TITLE	LABEL	RA

GREAT BIG SEA
Canadian Celtic-flavoured pop band from Petty Harbour, Newfoundland: Alan Doyle (vocals, guitar, bouzouki, mandolin, b. Petty Harbour), Bob Hallett (vocals, button accordion, tin whistle, fiddle, mandolin, mandola, b. St. John's, Newfoundland), Sean McCann (vocals, guitar, bodhran, snake drum, tin whistle, b. Carbonear, Newfoundland), Darrell Power (bass, vocals, b. Outer Cove, Newfoundland). Formed in 1991.

09/15/97	---	RA	When I'm Up (I Can't Get Down).....................WEA	17
01/05/98	---	RA	Ordinary Day ....WEA	31
07/26/99	---	RA	Consequence Free...................................... Warner	28+

GREAT WHITE
American rock group formed in Los Angeles in 1981: Tony Montana (bass), Andie Desbrow (drums), Michael Lardie (keyboards). Montana left in 1992.

09/18/89	13	11	Once Bitten, Twice Shy................................Capitol	
04/29/91	7	11	Call It Rock N' Roll...Capitol	

GRECO, Cyndi
American female singer born on 05/19/52, based in New York City.

07/17/76	24	5	Makin' Our Dreams Come True......... Private Stock	

GREEN, Al
American male R&B singer/songwriter born on 04/13/46 in Forest City, Arkansas. Originally with the gospel group the Greene Brothers. Returned to gospel music in 1980.

02/06/89	7	14	Put A Little Love In Your Heart *...................... A&M	

* Annie Lennox/Al Green

GREEN DAY
American rock trio formed in 1989 in Berkeley, California: Billie Joe Armstrong (vocals, guitar, b. 02/17/72 in San Pablo, California), Mike Dirnt (bass, b. Michael Pritchard on 05/04/72 in California), Tré Cool (drums, b. Frank Edwin Wright III on 12/09/72 in Germany).

11/14/94	---	RA	Basket Case ....Reprise	20
02/27/95	---	RA	When I Come Around ....Reprise	3
09/18/95	---	RA	J.A.R. ....Reprise	27
11/27/95	---	RA	Geek Stink Breath.......................................Reprise	36
02/23/98	---	RA	Good Riddance (Time Of Your Life)...........Reprise	12

GREGORASH, Joey
Canadian male vocalist born circa 1951 in Winnipeg. Hosted weekly television show *Young As You Are* in the late-1960's. Worked at radio station CHMM-FM in Winnipeg in the mid-1980's.

09/07/87	13	19	Together (The New Wedding Song) ....Attic	

GRIFFIN, Clive
British male pop-MOR singer born in London; raised in Surrey, England. Former back-up singer for Tears For Fears and Bobby Womack.

10/04/93	---	RA	When I Fall In Love * ....Columbia	31

DATE	PK	WK	TITLE	LABEL	RA

* Celine Dion & Clive Griffin

GROOVE CLUB
Canadian pop/dance group from Toronto: producers Earl Mclean and Paul Shango, with vocalist Tamara Watley.

07/08/96	---	RA	Upside Down	Isba	39

GROOVE THEORY
American R&B duo formed in 1991 in New York City: Amel Larrieux (vocals/songwriter, b. circa 1975), Bryce Wilson (multi-instrumentalist/producer). Larrieux was raised in New York City and Philadelphia.

02/19/96	8	16	Tell Me	Epic	29

GROSS, Henry
American male rock singer born on 04/01/51. Original lead guitarist for Sha Na Na.

| 05/29/76 | 1(1) | 15 | Shannon | Lifesong | |
| 08/28/76 | 38 | 3 | Springtime Mama | Lifesong | |

GRYNER, Emm
Canadian female rock singer born in 1975. Raised in Forest, Ontario; moved to Toronto at age 20. Of Pilipino and Irish ancestry.

10/05/98	---	RA	Summerlong	Mercury	27

GUNS N' ROSES
American hard rock band formed in 1985 in Los Angeles: Axl Rose (vocals, b. William Bailey on 02/06/62 in Lafayette, Indiana), Slash (guitar, b. Saul Hudson on 07/23/65 in Stoke-on-Trent, England), Duff McKagan (bass, b. Michael McKagan on 02/05/64 in Seattle), Steve Adler (drums, b. 01/22/65 in Cleveland), Izzy Stradlin (guitar, b. Jeffrey Isbell on 04/08/62 in Lafayette). Adler left in 1989, replaced by Matt Sorum (b. 11/19/60 in Long Beach, California). Stradlin left in 1992; Slash, McKagan, Sorum left in 1997.

10/10/88	4	20	Sweet Child O' Mine	Geffen	
01/16/89	30	9	Welcome To The Jungle	Geffen	
04/10/89	22	9	Paradise City	Geffen	
07/10/89	11	15	Patience	Geffen	
10/08/90	---	RA	Knockin' On Heaven's Door	DGC	40
08/12/91	2(7)	17	You Could Be Mine	Geffen	
11/11/91	6	13	Don't Cry	Geffen	6
02/24/92	---	RA	Live And Let Die	Geffen	34
09/14/92	---	RA	November Rain	Geffen	1
04/24/94	---	RA	Since I Don't Have You	Geffen	19
04/17/95	9	31	Sympathy For The Devil	Geffen	

GUYS NEXT DOOR
American pop quintet from Los Angeles: Patrick J. Dancy, Eddie Garcia, Bobby Leslie, Damon Sharpe, Chris Wolfe. Starred in own NBC-TV show.

10/22/90	37	5	I Was Made For You	Capitol	

DATE	PK	WK	TITLE	LABEL	RA

H

HADDAWAY
Trinidadian male dance singer/dancer born Nestor Alexander Haddaway, circa 1966 in Tobago. Raised in Washington, D.C., later moved to Cologne, Germany. Owner of a fashion company. Once a professional U.S. football player.

10/18/93	---	RA	What Is Love	RCA	8
03/07/94	---	RA	Life (Everybody Needs Somebody To Love)	RCA	6

HAIRCUT ONE HUNDRED
British rock group founded by vocalist Nick Heyward. Disbanded in 1983.

07/24/82	13	11	Love Plus One	Arista	

HALL, Daryl
American male pop singer born on 10/11/49 in Pottstown, Pennsylvania. Member of Daryl Hall & John Oates.

09/29/86	18	10	Dreamtime	RCA	

HALL, Daryl, & John Oates
American pop duo formed in Philadelphia in 1969: Daryl Hall (vocals, keyboards, guitar, b. Daryl Franklin Hohl on 10/11/49 in Pottstown, Pennsylvania), John Oates (vocals, guitar, b. 04/07/49 in New York City). Both were members of the group Gulliver. Hall was backup singer for various R&B groups in late-1960's.

06/05/76	19	8	Sara Smile	RCA	
11/06/76	8	11	She's Gone	Atlantic	
04/16/77	3(2)	15	Rich Girl	RCA	
04/18/81	2(3)	12	Kiss On My List	RCA	
07/18/81	7	9	You Make My Dreams	RCA	
11/07/81	1(1)	12	Private Eyes	RCA	
01/23/82	2(3)	15	I Can't Go For That	RCA	
05/08/82	6	7	Did It In A Minute	RCA	
12/25/82	1(3)	17	Maneater	RCA	
03/21/83	12	10	One On One	RCA	
12/26/83	20	13	Say It Isn't So	RCA	
04/30/84	13	9	Adult Education	RCA	
12/10/84	4	17	Out Of Touch	RCA	
02/25/85	6	13	Method Of Modern Love	RCA	
05/06/85	40	1	Some Things Are Better Left Unsaid	RCA	
06/20/88	14	11	Everything Your Heart Desires	Arista	
11/26/90	16	9	So Close	Arista	7
03/04/91	---	RA	Don't Hold Back Your Love	Arista	27

HALLIWELL, Geri
British female pop singer born Geraldine Halliwell on 08/06/72 in Watford, England. Member of the Spice Girls beginning in 1994 (nicknamed "Sexy Spice"/"Ginger"). Starred in the 1998 movie *Spice World*. Announced on 05/31/98 that she left the group.

DATE	PK	WK	TITLE	LABEL	RA
05/30/99	3(1)	11 +	Look At Me	EMI	24

HAMILTON, JOE FRANK & REYNOLDS
American trio: Don Hamilton, Joe Frank Carollo, Tommy Reynolds. All three were members of The T-Bones.

DATE	PK	WK	TITLE	LABEL
09/13/75	2(1)	11	Fallin' In Love	Playboy
02/14/76	25	5	Winners & Losers	Playboy

HAMMER
American male rapper born Stanley Kirk Burrell on 03/30/63 in Oakland, California. Known as M.C. Hammer, 1988-1991.

DATE	PK	WK	TITLE	LABEL	RA
07/02/90	1(3)	11	U Can't Touch This *	Capitol	3
10/01/90	2(1)	17	Have You Seen Her *	Capitol	6
11/12/90	---	RA	Pray	Capitol	7
12/23/91	---	RA	2 Legit 2 Quit	Capitol	28
05/16/94	27	13	It's All Good	Giant	

* M.C. Hammer

HAMMER, Jan
Czech male rock keyboardist born on 04/17/48 in Prague.

DATE	PK	WK	TITLE	LABEL
11/11/85	4	15	Miami Vice Theme	MCA

HANCOCK, Herbie
American male jazz-R&B keyboardist born on 04/12/40 in Chicago. Scored films *A Soldier's Story* (1984), *Round Midnight* (1986), *Jo Jo Dancer Your Life Is Calling* (1986), *Colors* (1987).

DATE	PK	WK	TITLE	LABEL
06/04/84	14	16	Rock It	Columbia

HANSIE

DATE	PK	WK	TITLE	LABEL
05/28/80	17	2	Automobile	Millennium

HANSON
American pop trio formed in 1992 in Tulsa, Oklahoma consisting of three brothers: Clarke Isaac (guitar, piano, vocals, b. 11/17/80), Jordan Taylor (keyboards, vocals, b. 03/14/83), Zachary Walker (drums, vocals, b. 10/22/85) Hanson. All three brothers were born in Tulsa.

DATE	PK	WK	TITLE	LABEL	RA
05/04/97	2(2)	12	MMMBop	Mercury	1
09/01/97	---	RA	Where's The Love	Mercury	1
02/08/98	3(1)	24	I Will Come To You	Mercury	8
03/15/98	3(1)	11	Weird	Mercury	35
05/24/98	10	11	Thinking Of You	Mercury	

HAPPY CLAPPERS

DATE	PK	WK	TITLE	LABEL
11/27/95	25	3	I Believe	NuMuzik

DATE	PK	WK	TITLE	LABEL	RA

HAPPY MONDAYS
British dance-rock group formed in 1984 in Manchester: brothers Shawn Ryder (vocals, b. 08/23/62 in Little Hulton, England), and Paul Ryder (bass, b. 04/24/64 in Manchester), Mark "Cow" Day (guitar, b. 12/29/61 in Manchester), Paul Davis (keyboards, b. 03/07/66 in Manchester), Gary "Gaz" Whelan (drums, b. 02/12/66 in Manchester), Mark "Bez" Berry (percussion, b. 04/18/64 in Manchester). Berry joined the group in 1985. The name inspired by New Order's "Blue Monday".

| 06/24/91 | --- | RA | Step On | Elektra | 34 |

HARDCASTLE, Paul
British male techno-dance keyboardist/producer born on 12/10/57 in London.

| 07/29/85 | 7 | 10 | 19 | Chrysalis | |

HARDY, Hagood
Canadian vibraphonist/composer born on 02/26/37 in Angola, Indiana. "The Homecoming" was used for a Salada Tea television commercial in the 1970's. Ran unsuccessfully in the 1995 Ontario election as the Liberal candidate against then-Premier Bob Rae. Died of cancer on 01/01/97 in Hamilton, Ontario.

| 11/01/75 | 5 | 15 | The Homecoming | Attic | |
| 04/30/77 | 32 | 6 | Maybe Tomorrow | Attic | |

HAREM SCAREM
Canadian rock band: Harry Hess (vocals, b. Harold John Hess, on 07/05/68), Mike Gionet (bass), Darren Smith (drums, b. 12/05/65), Pete Lesperance (guitar, b. 10/13/68). Barry Donaghy (b. 09/07/66) later replaced Gionet. "Harem Scarem" is the name of the first Buggs Bunny cartoon.

| 10/14/91 | --- | RA | Slowly Slipping Away | WEA | 39 |

HARLEQUIN
Canadian rock band formed in Winnipeg in 1975: George Belanger (vocals), John Hannah (guitar), Ralph James (bass), John White (keyboards), Denton Young (drums). Hannah replaced by Glen Willows; White replaced by Gary Golden; Young replaced David Budzak.

| 12/06/80 | 19 | 1 | Innocence | Epic | |

HARRISON, George
British male rock singer/guitarist. Born on 02/24/43 in Liverpool, England. Guitarist of the Beatles, 1962-70. Member of the 1988 supergroup Traveling Wilburys.

11/08/75	21	6	You	Apple	
01/08/77	35	2	This Song	Dark Horse	
04/02/77	38	4	Crackerbox Palace	Dark Horse	
05/16/79	16	8	Blow Away	Dark Horse	
07/11/81	2(1)	11	All Those Years Ago	Dark Horse	
12/28/87	2(6)	20	Got My Mind Set On You	Dark Horse	
04/11/88	27	9	When We Was Fab	Dark Horse	

HART, Corey
Canadian male pop singer/songwriter born Corey Mitchell Hart on 05/31/62 in Montreal. Raised in Spain, Mexico, and France. Has two children with singer Julie Masse.

| 04/02/84 | 24 | 12 | Sunglasses At Night | Aquarius | |

DATE	PK	WK	TITLE	LABEL	RA
10/08/84	40	3	She Got The Radio	Aquarius	
03/18/85	38	2	Lamp At Midnight	Aquarius	
07/08/85	1(9)	20	Never Surrender	Aquarius	
09/23/85	9	14	Boy In The Box	Aquarius	
01/27/86	4	14	Everything In My Heart	Aquarius	
03/17/86	33	3	Eurasian Eyes	Aquarius	
10/20/86	8	12	I Am By Your Side	Aquarius	
01/19/87	6	14	Can't Help Falling In Love	Aquarius	
08/17/87	19	9	2 Good 2 Be Enough	Aquarius	
08/15/88	7	14	In Your Soul	Aquarius	
11/21/88	29	3	Spot You In A Coalmine	Aquarius	
05/28/90	10	13	A Little Love	Aquarius	9
06/08/92	26	5	92 Days Of Rain	Sire	23
07/27/92	---	RA	Baby When I Call Your Name	Sire	20
11/11/96	---	RA	Black Cloud Rain	Columbia	11
04/21/97	---	RA	Tell Me	Columbia	9
09/15/97	---	RA	Third Of June	Columbia	14

HARTMAN, Dan
American male pop-dance singer/songwriter/multi-instrumentalist/producer born on 12/08/50 in Harrisburg, Pennsylvania. Bassist with the Edgar Winter Group, 1972-76. Died on 03/22/94 in Westport, Connecticut of a brain tumour.

DATE	PK	WK	TITLE	LABEL	RA
03/21/79	14	16	Instant Replay	Epic	
09/17/84	10	9	I Can Dream About You	MCA	

HARTT, Lisa, Band

DATE	PK	WK	TITLE	LABEL	RA
07/10/76	36	3	Old Time Movie	Rising	

HATHAWAY, Donny
American male R&B singer/songwriter/keyboardist/producer/arranger born on 10/01/45 in Chicago. Raised in St. Louis. Committed suicide by jumping from the 15th floor of the Essex House Hotel in New York City on 01/13/79. Gospel singer since age three. Studied fine arts in Howard University in Washington D.C.; classmate of Roberta Flack.

DATE	PK	WK	TITLE	LABEL	RA
05/31/78	2(2)	18	The Closer I Get	Atlantic	

HAWKES, Chesney
British male singer born Chesney Lee Hawkes on 09/22/71 in Windsor, England. Appeared in the 1991 film *Buddy's Song*.

DATE	PK	WK	TITLE	LABEL	RA
11/18/91	---	RA	The One And Only	Chrysalis	35

HAWKINS, Sophie B.
American female pop singer raised in Manhattan, New York. Her middle name is Ballantine.

DATE	PK	WK	TITLE	LABEL	RA
07/06/92	2(6)	24	Damn, I Wish I Was Your Lover	Columbia	2
09/07/92	30	3	California Here I Come	Columbia	33
11/28/94	4	35	Right Beside You	Columbia	3
03/04/96	18	8	As I Lay Me Down	Columbia	11
04/29/96	14	9 h	Only Love (The Ballad Of Sleeping Beauty)	Columbia	13

DATE	PK	WK	TITLE	LABEL	RA

HAYES, Issac
American male R&B singer/songwriter/keyboardist/producer born on 08/06/38 in Covington, Tennessee. Credited with laying the groundwork for disco in early-1970's. Session musician for artists on Stax label in 1960's. Appeared in films, *Truck Turner* (1974), *Escape From New York* (1981), *Robin Hood: Men In Tights* (1993), *It Could Happen To You* (1994). Composed movie scores of various films.

| 02/20/80 | 31 | 2 | Don't Let Go | Polydor | |

HAYWIRE
Canadian rock quintet from Charlottetown, P.E.I.: Paul MacAusland (vocals), Marvin Birt (guitar), Sean Kilbride (drums), David Rashed (keyboards), Ron Switzer (bass).

06/23/86	40	1	Bad Bad Boy	Attic	
11/09/87	21	11	Dance Desire	Attic	
05/23/88	38	2	Thinkin' About The Years	Attic	
08/17/92	---	RA	Buzz	Attic	16

HEAD, Murray
British male singer/songwriter. Appeared on the 1970 rock concept album *Jesus Christ Superstar*, in the movie *Sunday, Bloody Sunday*.

| 04/22/85 | 1(1) | 23 | One Night In Bangkok | Chess | |

HEADPINS
Canadian rock quartet formed by Chilliwack's Brian MacLeod and Ab Bryant in Vancouver in 1980: Darby Mills (vocals, from Vernon, British Columbia), Bryant, Matt Frenette, MacLeod. Broke up in 1986. Mills pursued solo career; MacLeod died in 1992.

| 09/25/82 | 11 | 4 | Don't It Make You Feel | Solid Gold | |

HEALEY, Jeff, Band
Canadian blues-rock band from Toronto: Jeff Healey (guitar, vocals, b. 03/25/66 in Toronto), Joe Rockman (bass, keyboards, b. 01/01/57 in Toronto), Tom Stephen (drums, b. 02/02/55 in Saint John, New Brunswick). Healey, blind since one years old, starred with Patrick Swayze in the film *Road Apples*.

07/31/89	10	16	Angel Eyes	Arista	
08/20/90	23	6	I Think I Love You Too Much	Arista	8
11/05/90	---	RA	While My Guitar Gently Weeps	Arista	28
04/01/91	36	2	How Long Can A Man Be Strong	Arista	16
12/28/92	---	RA	Cruel Little Number	Arista	27
05/10/93	---	RA	Lost In Your Eyes	Arista	11
07/24/95	---	RA	Angel	Arista	37

HEART
American/Canadian rock group formed in 1970 in Seattle: Ann Wilson (vocals, guitar, flute, b. 06/19/51 in San Diego), Nancy Wilson (vocals, guitar, mandolin, b. 03/16/54 in San Francisco), Roger Fisher (guitar, b. 02/14/50), Howard Lesse (keyboards, synthesizers, guitar, b. 06/13/51), Michael Derosier (drums, b. 08/24/51), Steve Fossen (bass, b. 11/15/49). Derosier, Fossen left in 1981; Mark Andes (bass, b. 02/19/48 in Philadelphia), Denny Carmassi (drums) joined in 1982, left in 1993. Relocated to Vancouver in 1975 when manager Mike Fisher was drafted in the U.S. military. Returned to Seattle in 1976. Roger joined Alias in 1990; Wilson sisters formed an acoustic group called the Lovemongers that same year.

DATE	PK	WK	TITLE	LABEL	RA
03/27/76	19	10	Crazy On You	Mushroom	
03/05/77	10	14	Dreamboat Annie	Mushroom	
09/07/77	13	15	Barracuda	Portrait	
12/27/78	28	8	Straight On	Portrait	
01/24/81	4	6	Tell It Like It Is	Capitol	
08/19/85	7	18	What About Love	Capitol	
12/23/85	26	11	Never	Capitol	
03/31/86	10	16	These Dreams	Capitol	
06/16/86	36	2	Nothin' At All	Capitol	
08/24/87	1(2)	17	Alone	Capitol	
11/02/87	16	9	Who Will You Run To	Capitol	
02/29/88	35	2	There's The Girl	Capitol	
06/11/90	1(2)	16	All I Wanna Do Is Make Love To You	Capitol	2
09/10/90	8	12	I Didn't Want To Need You	Capitol	15
12/10/90	1(1)	15	Stranded	Capitol	4
02/28/94	---	RA	Will You Be There (In The Morning)	Capitol	2
05/23/94	---	RA	The Woman In Me	Capitol	37

HEATWAVE
American/British group formed in 1973 in Kaiserslautern,Germany by brothers Johnnie (b. 07/03/49 in Dayton, Ohio) and Keith Wilder (b. Dayton). Johnnie became paraplegic after a car accident on 02/24/79.

DATE	PK	WK	TITLE	LABEL
12/14/77	12	16	Boogie Nights	Epic
07/26/78	33	2	The Groove Line	Epic

HEAVY D & THE BOYZ
American rap trio formed in 1984 in Mt. Vernon, New York: Dwight Meyers ("Heavy D". b. 05/24/67 in Jamaica), Edward Ferrell ("DJ Eddie F"), Glen Parrish ("G Wiz"). Appeared in the film *Who's The Man?* and the TV series *Roc*.

DATE	PK	WK	TITLE	LABEL	RA
10/07/91	---	RA	Now That We Found Love	Uptown	39
03/23/97	30	2	Big Daddy *	Uptown	

* Heavy D

HEIGHTS, The
American pop band consisting of cast members from the Fox Television program *The Heights*, led by vocalists/actors, Shawn Thompson and James Walters. Walters recorded solo in 1995.

DATE	PK	WK	TITLE	LABEL	RA
01/18/93	1(2)	19	How Do You Talk To An Angel	Capitol	3

HELIX
Canadian hard rock band from London, Ontario and Kitchener, Ontario formed in 1975: Brian Vollner (vocals), Paul Hackman (guitar), Daryl Gray (bass, keyboards), Brent and Brian Doerner (drums). Hackman died in a car accident in British Columbia in July 1992.

DATE	PK	WK	TITLE	LABEL	RA
12/03/84	22	10	Rock You	Capitol	
05/27/85	30	2	(Make Me Do) Anything You Want	Capitol	
02/25/91	33	4	Good To The Last Drop	Capitol	33

HEMINGWAY CORNER

DATE	PK	WK	TITLE	LABEL	RA

Canadian pop-MOR group formed in 1992: David Martin (vocals, guitar, percussion; from Atlanta), Johnny Douglas (bass, guitar, percussion; from Toronto). Douglas left after first album, replaced by Scott Dibble (guitar, bass, vocals) and Mark Sterling (guitar, harmonica, vocals) joined.

09/27/93	---	RA	Man On A Mission	Epic	21
09/25/95	---	RA	Big Sky	Epic	34
02/05/96	---	RA	Watch Over You	Epic	17
04/22/96	33	4 h	Make It Up As You Go	Epic	

HENLEY, Don
American male rock singer/songwriter/drummer born on 07/22/47 in Gilmer, Texas. Vocalist for the Eagles, went solo in 1982.

01/16/82	6	12	Leather And Lace *	Modern	
01/17/83	1(1)	12	Dirty Laundry	Asylum	
02/11/85	30	8	The Boys Of Summer	Geffen	
06/10/85	8	14	All She Wants To Do Is Dance	Geffen	
09/25/89	6	10	The End Of The Innocence	Geffen	
04/23/90	26	5	The Heart Of The Matter	Geffen	13
10/19/92	---	RA	Sometimes Love Just Ain't Enough **	MCA	3

* Stevie Nicks (with Don Henley)
** Patty Smyth with Don Henley

HERNANDEZ, Patrick
French male rock-disco singer from Guadeloupe. Born in 1949 in Paris.

| 08/22/79 | 1(2) | 34 | Born To Be Alive | Columbia | |

HI TEK 3 featuring Ya Kid K
Belgian dance trio: Kovali, El Sati, Yosev. Ya Kid K is female rapper, Manuella Kamosi of Technotronic.

| 06/04/90 | 4 | 13 | Spin That Wheel | SBK | |

HI-FIVE
American R&B vocal trio formed in 1989 in Waco, Texas: Tony Thompson (native of Oklahoma City), Roderick Clark, Russell Neal, Marcus Sanders, Toriano Easley (replaced in 1991 by Treston Irby). Clark and Neal left by 1993.

07/08/91	7	13	I Like The Way (The Kissing Game)	Jive	13
10/07/91	13	15	I Can't Wait Another Minute	Jive	21
10/12/92	---	RA	She's Playing Hard To Get	Jive	8
03/01/93	25	5	Quality Time	Jive	

HIGGINS, Bertie
American pop singer/songwriter born Elbert Higgins on 12/08/44 in Tarpon Springs, Florida.

| 04/10/82 | 13 | 7 | Key Largo | Kat Family | |

HILL, Dan
Canadian male pop-MOR singer/songwriter born on 06/03/54 in Toronto. Wrote songs for George Benson, Jeffrey Osborne, Tina Turner, and Celine Dion.

DATE	PK	WK	TITLE	LABEL	RA
08/09/75	24	2	You Make Me Want To Be	GRT	
11/02/77	3(4)	34	Sometimes When We Touch	GRT	
06/28/78	14	6	Let The Song Last Forever	GRT	
10/18/78	36	4	All I See Is Your Face	GRT	
07/27/87	24	11	Can't We Try	Columbia	
03/14/88	28	10	Never Thought	Columbia	

HILL, Lauryn
American female hip-hop singer born on 05/25/75 in East Orange, New Jersey. Vocalist of the Fugees. Played a role in *Sister Act II*.

DATE	PK	WK	TITLE	LABEL	RA
11/02/98	---	RA	Can't Take My Eyes Off Of You	Ruffhouse	15
11/23/98	---	RA	Doo Wop (That Thing)	Ruffhouse	16

HODGSON, Roger
British male rock singer/songwriter born on 03/21/50 in London. Lead singer of Supertramp.

DATE	PK	WK	TITLE	LABEL	RA
12/24/84	27	11	Had A Dream (Sleeping With The Enemy)	A&M	

HOFFS, Susanna
American female pop singer/guitarist born on 01/17/57 in Newport Beach, California. Former lead singer of The Bangles.

DATE	PK	WK	TITLE	LABEL	RA
04/01/91	26	4	My Side Of The Bed	Columbia	15

HOLMES, Rupert
American male pop singer/songwriter born on 02/24/47 in Cheshire, England. Wrote for The Platters, The Drifters, Gene Pitney. Arranged/produced for Barbra Streisand. Member of the group, Street People, in early-1970's.

DATE	PK	WK	TITLE	LABEL	RA
01/09/80	6	18	Escape (The Pina Colada Song)	Infinity	
04/16/80	4	6	Him	Infinity	

HOMETOWN BAND

DATE	PK	WK	TITLE	LABEL	RA
01/01/77	18	8	Flying	A&M	
03/19/77	24	8	I'm Ready	A&M	

HONEYDRIPPERS, The
American/British supergroup consisting of Led Zeppelin's Robert Plant and Jimmy Page, Nile Rodgers (formerly of Chic), Jeff Beck (formerly of The Yardbirds).

DATE	PK	WK	TITLE	LABEL	RA
01/14/85	2(1)	18	Sea Of Love	Es Paranza	
03/04/85	14	9	Rockin' At Midnight	Es Paranza	

HONEYMOON SUITE
Canadian rock band from Niagara Falls, Ontario: Johnny Dee (vocals), Dave Betts (drums), Ray Coburn (keyboards), Derry Grehan (guitar), Gary Lalonde (bass). Coburn left in 1987, replaced by Rob Preuss.

DATE	PK	WK	TITLE	LABEL	RA
10/01/84	23	8	New Girl Now	WEA	
03/31/86	16	11	Feel It Again	WEA	

DATE	PK	WK	TITLE	LABEL	RA
09/15/86	28	6	What Does It Take	WEA	
06/13/88	9	14	Love Changes Everything	WEA	
09/05/88	35	3	Lookin' Out For Number One	WEA	

HOOTERS
American rock group formed in 1978 in Philadelphia: Rob Hyman (vocals, keyboards), Eric Bazilian (vocals, guitar), John Lilley (guitar), Rob Miller (bass), David Uosikkinen (drums). Arrangers, musicians, background singers on *She's So Unusual* by Cyndi Lauper. Hyman co-wrote Cyndi Lauper's "Time After Time" with Lauper.

DATE	PK	WK	TITLE	LABEL	RA
11/18/85	35	3	And We Danced	Columbia	

HOOTIE & THE BLOWFISH
American pop/rock band formed at the University of South Carolina: Darius Carlos Rucker (vocals, b. 05/13/66 in Charleston, South Carolina), Mark Williams Bryan (guitar, b. 05/06/67 in Silver Spring, Maryland), Everett Dean Felber (bass, b. 06/09/67 in Bethesda, Maryland), James George "Soni" Sonefeld (drums, b. 10/20/64 in Lansing, Michigan).

DATE	PK	WK	TITLE	LABEL	RA
02/27/95	---	RA	Hold My Hand	Atlantic	12
06/26/95	---	RA	Let Her Cry	Atlantic	1
09/04/95	---	RA	Only Wanna Be With You	Atlantic	1
12/04/95	---	RA	I Go Blind	Atlantic	29
04/08/96	30	1	Time	Atlantic	4
05/13/96	1(8)	16 h	Old Man & Me (When I Get To Heaven)	Atlantic	2
08/26/96	3(2)	13 h	Tucker's Town	Atlantic	7
12/02/96	---	RA	Sad Caper	Atlantic	25
10/19/98	---	RA	I Will Wait	Atlantic	10

HOPE, Gavin
Canadian male R&B singer/songwriter born circa 1974 in Toronto; raised in Calgary. Member of The Nylons, 1994-97. Backing vocalist for Michael Bolton's 1991 Canadian tour. Appeared in the Toronto theatrical production of *Rent*.

DATE	PK	WK	TITLE	LABEL	RA
07/01/96	20	10 h	Can I Get Close?	Quality	22

HORNSBY, Bruce, & The Range
American group formed in 1984 in Los Angeles: Bruce Hornsby (vocals, keyboards, b. Bruce Randall Hornsby on 11/23/54 in Richmond, Virginia), David Mansfield (violin, mandolin, guitar), George Marinelli Jr. (guitar), Joe Puerta (bass), John Molo (drums). Mansfield replaced by Peter Harris in 1988. Harris left in 1990; The Range disbanded in 1993; Hornsby released solo album in 1993.

DATE	PK	WK	TITLE	LABEL	RA
02/09/87	4	18	The Way It Is	RCA	
03/16/87	35	3	Mandolin Rain	RCA	
07/18/88	11	13	The Valley Road	RCA	
09/03/90	31	3	Across The River	RCA	8

HOT
American interracial female trio: Gwen Owens, Cathy Carson, Juanita Curiel.

DATE	PK	WK	TITLE	LABEL	RA
07/02/77	4	14	Angel In Your Arms	Big Tree	

HOT CHOCOLATE

DATE	PK	WK	TITLE	LABEL	RA

British R&B group formed in London in 1970: Errol Brown (vocals, b. 11/12/48 in Kingston, Jamaica), Patrick Olive (guitar, percussion, bass, b. 03/22/47 in Grenada), Larry Ferguson (keyboards, b. 04/14/48 in Nassau, Bahamas), Harvey Hinsley (guitar, b. 01/19/48 in Northampton, England), Ian King (drums), Tony Wilson (bass, vocals, b. 10/08/47 in Trinidad). King left in 1973, replaced by Tony Connor (b. 04/06/47 in Romford, England). Wilson left in 1975. When Brown left to record solo in 1987, the group broke up.

| 02/14/76 | 1(1) | 12 | You Sexy Thing | Big Tree |
| 03/07/79 | 11 | 6 | Every 1's A Winner | Infinity |

HOTHOUSE FLOWERS

Irish alternative group formed in Dublin in 1986: Liam O'Maonlai (vocals, keyboards, harmonica, b. 11/07/64 in Dublin), Fiachna O'Braonain (guitar, b. 11/27/65 in Dublin), Peter O'Toole (bass, bouzouki, b. 04/01/65 in Dublin), Jerry Fehily (drums, b. 08/29/63 in Bishops Town, Ireland), Leo Barnes (saxophone, b. 10/05/65 in Dublin).

| 08/20/90 | 37 | 2 | Give It Up | London |
| 01/17/94 | 38 | 1 | Land * | Cargo |

* Crash Vegas/Hothouse Flowers/Daniel Lanois/Midnight Oil/Tragically Hip

HOUSE OF PAIN

American rap group formed in 1990 in Los Angeles: "Everlast" (vocals, b. Erik Schrody on 08/18/69 in Valley Stream, New York), Danny Boy (vocals, b. Daniel O'Connor on 12/12/68 in Los Angeles), DJ Lethal (DJ, b. Leor DiMant on 12/18/72 in Latvia).

09/28/92	13	11	Jump Around	Attic
01/18/93	13	12	Shamrocks & Shenanigans	Attic
05/03/93	24	10	Top O' The Morning To Ya	Attic
08/30/93	19	7	Who's The Man	Attic
10/20/96	33	3	Fed Up	Attic
01/31/99	20	4	Jump Around	Tommy Boy

featuring Jason Nevins remixes

HOUSTON, Thelma

American female R&B singer/actress from Leland, Mississippi. Born on 05/07/46. Starred in several movies.

| 04/16/77 | 4 | 21 | Don't Leave Me This Way | Motown |

HOUSTON, Whitney

American female R&B-pop singer/songwriter born on 08/09/63 in Newark, New Jersey. Daughter of gospel-R&B singer Cissy Houston, cousin of Dionne Warwick. Sang in family's church choir as a child. Model for *Glamour* and *Vogue* magazines. Starred in the movies *The Bodyguard*, *Waiting To Exhale*, and *The Preacher's Wife*. Married Bobby Brown on 07/18/92.

09/02/85	17	9	You Give Good Love	RCA
11/18/85	15	17	Saving All My Love For You	RCA
03/31/86	1(2)	17	How Will I Know?	Arista
06/02/86	3(3)	19	The Greatest Love Of All	Arista
06/29/87	1(6)	17	I Wanna Dance With Somebody (Who Loves Me)	Arista
10/12/87	4	15	Didn't We Almost Have It All	Arista

DATE	PK	WK	TITLE	LABEL	RA
01/25/88	12	14	So Emotional	Arista	
05/30/88	20	9	Where Do Broken Hearts Go	Arista	
10/10/88	40	1	Love Will Save The Day	Arista	
12/05/88	9	11	One Moment In Time	Arista	
12/24/90	4	13	I'm Your Baby Tonight	Arista	1
03/04/91	2(3)	15	All The Man That I Need	Arista	3
05/27/91	38	2	Miracle	Arista	27
09/09/91	---	RA	My Name Is Not Susan	Arista	35
03/01/93	---	RA	I'm Every Woman	Arista	2
03/08/93	22	7	I Will Always Love You	Arista	1

"I Will Always Love You" was released before "I'm Every Woman" and actually became an airplay hit first. "I Will Always Love You" peaked at #1 on 12/14/92.

DATE	PK	WK	TITLE	LABEL	RA
05/10/93	---	RA	I Have Nothing	Arista	1
08/23/93	---	RA	Run To You	Arista	19
12/27/93	---	RA	Something In Common *	MCA	19
02/07/94	---	RA	Queen Of The Night	Arista	36
03/11/96	2(1)	16	Exhale (Shoop, Shoop)	Arista	4
05/13/96	31	8 h	Count On Me **	Arista	
02/03/97	---	RA	I Believe In You And Me	Arista	33
03/30/97	9	8	Step By Step	Arista	13
03/14/99	12	19	Heartbreak Hotel ***	Arista	24
07/25/99	3(1)	7 +	It's Not Right But It's Okay	Arista	20+

Two other versions peaked at #32 on 06/06/99 and #8 on 07/25/99.

* Bobby Brown/Whitney Houston
** Whitney Houston/CeCe Winans
*** Whitney Houston featuring Faith Evans & Kelly Price

H-TOWN
American R&B vocal group from Houston: Shazam Conner, John "Dino" Conner, Darryl "GI" Jackson.

DATE	PK	WK	TITLE	LABEL
08/02/93	3(3)	14	Knockin' Da Boots	Attic
09/30/93	23	7	Lick U Up	Attic

HUMAN LEAGUE
British techno-pop group formed in Sheffield, England in 1977: Phil Oakey (vocals, synthesizers, b. 10/02/55 in Sheffield), Martyn Ware (synthesizer, b. 05/19/56 in Sheffield), Ian Craig Marsh (synthesizers, b. 11/11/56 in Sheffield), Phillip Adrian Wright (stage visuals, b. 06/30/56 in Sheffield). Ware, Marsh left in 1980; vocalists Suzanne Sulley (b. 03/22/63 in Sheffield) and Joanne Catherall (b. 09/18/62 in Sheffield), along with Ian Burden (bass, synthesizers) joined in 1982. Jo Callis (synthesizers) joined in 1981.

DATE	PK	WK	TITLE	LABEL	RA
05/08/82	1(1)	14	Don't You Want Me	Virgin	
02/28/83	16	9	Mirror Man	Virgin	
09/19/83	11	10	(Keep Feeling) Fascination	Virgin	
12/29/86	3(3)	18	Human	Virgin	
12/03/90	---	RA	Heart Like A Wheel	Virgin	37
05/15/95	---	RA	Tell Me When	EastWest	18

HUMPERDINCK, Engelbert

| DATE | PK | WK | TITLE | LABEL | RA |

British male MOR-pop singer born Thomas Arnold George Dorsey born on 05/02/36 in Madras, India. Raised in India where his father was a captain in the Royal Engineers; moved to Leicester, England. Stage name named after composer of *Hansel and Gretel*. Hosted own television variety show briefly in 1970. Recorded in German, Spanish, Italian.

| 01/22/77 | 4 | 17 | After The Lovin' | Epic |

HYNDE, Chrissie - see UB40

I

IAN, Janis
American female singer/songwriter born Janis Eddy Fink on 05/07/51 in New York City. Her last name, Ian is her brother's middle name.

| 09/20/75 | 3(2) | 11 | At Seventeen | Columbia |

ICEHOUSE
Australian rock quartet led by singer/guitarist Iva Davies. Name from Australian slang for an insane asylum.

| 02/08/88 | 32 | 6 | Crazy | Chrysalis |
| 05/30/88 | 7 | 12 | Electric Blue | Chrysalis |

ICICLE WORKS
British alternative band from Liverpool: Ian McNabb (vocals, guitar, b. 11/03/62), Chris Layhe (bass), and Chris Sharrock (drums).

| 06/25/84 | 21 | 7 | Whisper To A Scream (Birds Fly) | Arista |

IDLE EYES
Canadian rock band based in Vancouver: Tad Campbell (vocals), Miles Fox Hill (bass), Phil Robertson (drums), Glenn R. Smith (guitar), John Webster (keyboards).

| 06/10/85 | 18 | 10 | Tokyo Rose | WEA |

IDOL, Billy
American male rock singer born William Michael Albert Broad on 11/30/55 in Stanmore, Middlesex, England. Lead singer of punk groups, Chelsea (1976) and Generation X (1976-1981). Injured in motorcycle accident in 1990; appeared in the 1991 movie *The Doors*.

07/11/83	5	11	White Wedding	Chrysalis
12/26/83	24	7	Dancing With Myself	Chrysalis
03/19/84	11	14	Rebel Yell	Chrysalis
07/16/84	11	14	Eyes Without A Face	Chrysalis
11/19/84	10	12	Flesh For Fantasy	Chrysalis
01/14/85	22	5	Catch My Fall	Chrysalis
01/19/87	5	16	To Be A Lover	Chrysalis
06/22/87	23	12	Sweet Sixteen	Chrysalis
11/23/87	1(1)	21	Mony Mony	Chrysalis
02/01/88	30	6	Hot In The City	Chrysalis

DATE	PK	WK	TITLE	LABEL	RA
06/04/90	10	12	Cradle Of Love .... Chrysalis		5

IGLESIAS, Enrique
Spanish male Latin-pop singer born Enrique Iglesias Preysler on 05/08/75 in Madrid. Currently lives in Miami. Son of Julio Iglesias.

08/09/99	---	RA	Bailamos ....Interscope	22+

IGLESIAS, Julio
Spanish male MOR vocalist/songwriter born Julio Jose Iglesias de la Cueva on 09/23/43 in Madrid, Spain. Sold estimated 100 million records worldwide, recorded in English, Spanish, French, Italian, German, and Portuguese. Originally intended to become a professional soccer player in Spain until a near-fatal car accident. His son Enrique is a Latin-pop singer.

06/04/84	1(3)	19	To All The Girls I've Loved Before * .... Columbia
09/10/84	4	11	All Of You ** .... Columbia

* Julio Iglesias & Willie Nelson
** Julio Iglesias & Diana Ross

IMBRUGLIA, Natalie
Australian female pop singer born Natalie Jane Imbruglia on 02/04/75 in Sydney.

04/27/98	---	RA	Torn... RCA	1
09/07/98	---	RA	Wishing I Was There .... RCA	8

INDECENT OBSESSION
Australian pop band from Brisbane: David Dixon (vocals), Michael Szumowski, Andrew Coyne, Darryl Simms.

10/01/90	40	2	Tell Me Something .... MCA	

INDIO
Canadian singer/songwriter Gordon Peterson from Toronto.

09/11/89	38	3	Hard Sun .... A&M	

INFIDELS
Canadian duo, formerly the rock band, Alta Moda, based in Toronto and formed in 1991: Molly Johnson (vocals), Norman Orenstein (guitar).

11/25/91	25	6	100 Watt Bulb... I.R.S.	26
03/30/92	---	RA	Celebrate .... I.R.S.	7
06/22/92	---	RA	Without Love .... I.R.S.	30

INFORMATION SOCIETY
American techno-pop/dance band formed in Minneapolis in 1985: Kurt Valaquen (vocals), Paul Robb (songwriter), Amanda Kramer (keyboards), James Cassidy (bass). Kramer left in 1990.

12/05/88	11	12	What's On Your Mind (Pure Energy) ... Tommy Boy
03/13/89	38	1	Walking Away...................................... Tommy Boy

DATE	PK	WK	TITLE	LABEL	RA

INGRAM, James
American male R&B-pop singer/songwriter/multi-instrumentalist born 02/17/52 in Akron, Ohio. Moved to Los Angeles with band, Revelation Funk in mid-1970's. Produced, play keyboards, wrote songs for Ray Charles.

DATE	PK	WK	TITLE	LABEL	RA
02/21/83	2(1)	12	Baby, Come To Me *	Qwest	
12/03/84	18	8	What About Me? **	RCA	
04/20/87	6	15	Somewhere Out There ***	MCA	
12/10/90	28	4	I Don't Have The Heart	Warner	19

* Patty Austin/James Ingram
** Kenny Rogers/Kim Carnes/James Ingram
*** Linda Ronstadt/James Ingram

INNER CIRCLE
Jamaican reggae band formed in 1975 in Kingston, Jamaica: Calton Coffie (vocals), Touter Harvey, Lancelot Hall, brothers Ian and Roger Lewis, Lester Adderly. Adderly left in 1994.

DATE	PK	WK	TITLE	LABEL	RA
06/14/93	---	RA	Bad Boys	Big Beat	13
10/25/93	---	RA	Sweat (A La La La La Long)	Big Beat	14
09/19/94	---	RA	Games People Play	Big Beat	33

INOJ
American female R&B/pop singer born on 11/27/76 in Madison, Wisconsin; raised in Washington D.C.

DATE	PK	WK	TITLE	LABEL	RA
11/03/97	---	RA	Love You Down	Columbia	38
10/18/98	7	15	Time After Time	Columbia	13

INXS
Australian rock band formed in 1977 in Sydney: Garry Beers (bass, b. 06/22/57 in Sydney), Michael Hutchence (vocals, b. 01/22/60 in Sydney), Andrew Farriss (keyboards, guitar, b. 03/27/59 in Perth), Jon Farriss (drums, b. 08/10/61 in Perth), Tim Farriss (guitar, b. 08/16/57 in Perth), Kirk Pengilly (guitar, saxophone, vocals, b. 07/04/58 in Sydney). Hutchence committed suicide on 11/22/97 in Melbourne.

DATE	PK	WK	TITLE	LABEL	RA
06/25/84	22	8	Original Sin	Atco	
05/19/86	23	8	What You Need	Atlantic	
03/07/88	7	19	Need You Tonight	Atlantic	
05/16/88	8	14	Devil Inside	Atlantic	
08/08/88	5	15	New Sensation	Atlantic	
11/07/88	18	15	Never Tear Us Apart	Atlantic	
11/05/90	1(2)	15	Suicide Blonde	Atlantic	1
01/28/91	11	9	Disappear	Atlantic	2
04/15/91	---	RA	Bitter Tears	Atlantic	13
12/09/91	---	RA	Shining Star	Atlantic	34
10/12/92	---	RA	Not Enough Time	Atlantic	3
04/12/93	---	RA	Beautiful Girl	Atlantic	17
12/12/94	21	17	The Strangest Party	Polydor	
05/26/97	---	RA	Elegantly Wasted	Mercury	4

ISAAK, Chris
American male pop singer/songwriter/actor born on 06/26/56 in Stockton, California. Co-starred in the 1994 movie *Little Buddha*.

DATE	PK	WK	TITLE	LABEL	RA

02/11/91	10	9	Wicked Game..Reprise	2
06/14/93	---	RA	Can't Do A Thing (To Stop Me) ....Reprise	18
08/14/95	---	RA	Somebody's Cryin'.......................................Reprise	13

ISLEY BROTHERS
American R&B group formed in the early-1950's in Cincinnati, consisting of brothers, Rudolph (vocals, b. 04/01/39 in Cincinnati), Ronald (lead vocals, b. 05/21/41 in Cincinnati), O'Kelly (vocals, b. 12/25/37 in Cincinnati), Vernon (vocals). Vernon died in 1955 in a bicycle accident. Younger brothers, Ernie (bass, percussion, guitar, b. 03/07/52) and Marvin (bass, percussion, b. 08/18/53), Chris Jasper (keyboards, synthesizers), Everett Collins (drums) joined. Ernie, Marvin, and Jasper left in 1984 to form Isley, Jasper, Isley. O'Kelly died of a heart attack on 03/31/86 in Alpine, New Jersey, Rudolph left to join ministry shortly after. Group reunited in 1990; won copyright infringement suit against Michael Bolton concerning hit single, "Love Is A Wonderful Thing" in 1994.

| 09/06/75 | 22 | 4 | Fight The Power (Part 1).........................Columbia | |

ISLEY, Ronald
American male R&B singer born on 05/21/41. Lead vocalist of the Isley Brothers.

| 05/28/90 | 2(2) | 13 | This Old Heart Of Mine *............................. Warner | |

* Rod Stewart (with Ronald Isley)

IVAN
Canadian male pop singer Ivan Doroschuk. Lead singer of Men Without Hats.

| 07/14/97 | --- | RA | Open Your Eyes .... Tox | 12 |
| 12/22/97 | --- | RA | Superbadgirls ....Plug | 28 |

J

JA RULE
American male rapper born Jeffrey Atkins in 1978 in Queens, New York.

| 07/11/99 | 15 | 16 | Holla Holla...Def Jam | |

JACKS, Susan
Canadian female vocalist born Susan Pesklevits on 08/19/48 in Saskatoon, Saskatchewan. Recorded with husband Terry Jacks in the group Poppy Family. Divorced in 1973.

| 11/15/75 | 22 | 6 | Anna Marie ....Casino | |
| 05/21/80 | 14 | 1 | All The Tea In China .... Epic | |

JACKS, Terry
Canadian male vocalist born on 03/29/44 in Winnipeg. Based in Vancouver. Recorded with wife Susan Jacks in the group Poppy Family. Divorced in 1973. Won the 1975 Juno Award for Canadian Male Vocalist.

| 07/26/75 | 10 | 5 | Christina ....Quality | |

DATE	PK	WK	TITLE	LABEL	RA

JACKSON HAWKE
Canadian band formed as Hero in 1973 in Toronto: Chris Castle, Bob "Crow" Clarke, Gene Falbo, Garry Holt, Timi Ryan, Bob Yeoman.

DATE	PK	WK	TITLE	LABEL	RA
08/28/76	24	4	You Can't Dance	Columbia	
12/04/76	28	4	Into The Mystic	Columbia	

JACKSON, Freddie
American male R&B singer/songwriter born Freddie Anthony Jackson on 10/02/56 in New York City. Backup vocalist for R&B singers Evelyn "Champagne" King and Melba Moore.

DATE	PK	WK	TITLE	LABEL	RA
12/16/85	38	5	You Are My Lady	Capitol	

JACKSON, Janet
American female pop-R&B singer/songwriter born Janet Damita Jackson on 05/16/66 in Gary, Indiana. The youngest of the eight children of the Jackson family. Played lead roles in television sitcoms *Good Times* (played Penny Gordon Woods, 1977-79), *Diff'rent Stokes* (1981-82), *Fame*. Married to James DeBarge of the group DeBarge, 1984-85. Signed contract with Virgin Records in 1991 for more than $30 million. Made film debut in *Poetic Justice* in 1993. Signed a four-album deal with Virgin on 01/12/96 worth an estimated $80 million (U.S.).

DATE	PK	WK	TITLE	LABEL	RA
06/16/86	2(3)	17	What Have You Done For Me Lately	A&M	
09/08/86	3(1)	13	Nasty	A&M	
11/03/86	15	10	When I Think Of You	A&M	
02/23/87	20	5	Control	A&M	
04/06/87	14	10	Let's Wait Awhile	A&M	
10/30/89	1(2)	18	Miss You Much	A&M	
02/19/90	2(1)	14	Rhythm Nation	A&M	
03/19/90	3(1)	13	Escapade	A&M	1
06/04/90	7	11	Alright	A&M	5
08/13/90	27	3	Come Back To Me	A&M	4
10/15/90	9	13	Black Cat	A&M	3
02/11/91	---	RA	Love Will Never Do (Without You)	A&M	1
04/15/91	---	RA	State Of The World	A&M	11
09/07/92	4	17	The Best Things In Life Are Free *	A&M	4
05/31/93	1(6)	38	That's The Way Love Goes	Virgin	1
10/11/93	1(1)	25	If	Virgin	1
12/06/93	---	RA	Again	Virgin	2
03/14/94	---	RA	Because Of Love	Virgin	2
10/17/94	6	59	Any Time, Any Place	Virgin	12
12/26/94	---	RA	You Want This	Virgin	3
07/24/95	5	21	Scream **	Epic	10
11/06/95	1(2)	24	Runaway	A&M	2
03/11/96	---	RA	Twenty Foreplay	A&M	27
10/20/97	---	RA	Got Til It's Gone	Virgin	10
02/15/98	2(1)	25	Together Again ***	Virgin	1
05/31/98	18	11	I Get Lonely ***	Virgin	22

Above is the domestic version. Another version peaked at #28 (05/03/98).

DATE	PK	WK	TITLE	LABEL	RA
07/26/98	9	19	Go Deep ***	Virgin	2
09/21/98	---	RA	Luv Me, Luv Me ****	MCA	32
04/18/99	21	4	What's It Gonna Be?! *****	Elektra	27

| DATE | PK | WK | TITLE | LABEL | RA |

* Luther Vandross/Janet Jackson
** Michael Jackson & Janet Jackson
*** Janet
**** Shaggy featuring Janet
***** Busta Rhymes featuring Janet

JACKSON, Jermaine
American male R&B-pop singer born Jermaine La Jaune Jackson on 12/11/54 in Gary, Indiana. Fourth oldest of Jackson family; member of Jackson 5 until 1976. Married to Hazel Joy Gordy, daughter of Motown owner Barry Gordy Jr. in 1973; divorced in 1987. Reunited with The Jacksons in 1984.

| 10/29/84 | 6 | 13 | Dynamite | Arista |
| 01/21/85 | 39 | 1 | Do What You Do | Arista |

JACKSON, Joe
British male rock singer/songwriter/pianist born on 08/11/54 in Burton-upon-Trent, England.

09/19/79	7	10	Is She Really Going Out With Him?	A&M
12/12/79	24	6	I'm The Man	A&M
11/27/82	4	12	Steppin' Out	A&M
06/04/84	31	9	You Can't Get What You Want	A&M

JACKSON, Michael
American male pop-R&B singer/songwriter born Michael Joseph Jackson on 08/29/58 in Gary, Indiana. Known as "The King Of Pop". Seventh oldest of the Jackson children. Lead singer of Jackson 5 (later The Jacksons) beginning in 1964. Began production partnership during the filming of the 1978 movie, *The Wiz*, in which Jackson played the Scarecrow. Wrote and produced "Muscles" for Diana Ross. Jackson's 1982 album, sold 40 million copies worldwide becoming the best-selling album of all time. Seriously injured in 1984 when his hair caught fire while filming a Pepsi-Cola commercial. Co-wrote "We Are The World", the famine relief benefit single by USA For Africa, in 1985 with Lionel Richie. Starred in *Captain Eo*, a short sci-fi film shown exclusively in Disneyland in Anaheim, California, and Disney World in Orlando, Florida. Secured ATV music publishing catalogue, which included more than 250 songs written by John Lennon and Paul McCartney, for $47.5 million. Released autobiography, *Moonwalker*, in 1988. Signed a $65 million deal with Sony Corporation in 1991. Accused of sexually abusing a 13 year-old boy in 1993; settled out of court for undisclosed terms on 01/25/94. Married Lisa Marie Presley, daughter of Elvis Presley, on 05/26/94; Lisa Marie filed for divorce on 01/18/96.

11/14/79	2(2)	24	Don't Stop Til You Get Enough	Epic
01/23/80	4	17	Rock With You	Epic
05/07/80	3(2)	3	Off The Wall	Epic
07/23/80	10	5	She's Out Of My Life	Epic
12/18/82	8	7	The Girl Is Mine *	Epic
03/28/83	1(7)	20	Billie Jean	Epic
05/16/83	1(2)	19	Beat It	Epic
07/11/83	11	11	Wanna Be Startin' Something	Epic
09/26/83	17	8	Human Nature	Epic
12/05/83	24	7	P.Y.T. (Pretty Young Thing)	Epic
01/16/84	1(1)	19	Say Say Say **	Columbia
03/19/84	4	13	Thriller	Epic
09/21/87	2(2)	12	I Just Can't Stop Loving You	Epic
11/09/87	1(1)	15	Bad	Epic
01/25/88	3(3)	15	The Way You Make Me Feel	Epic
04/18/88	6	14	Man In The Mirror	Epic

DATE	PK	WK	TITLE	LABEL	RA
07/18/88	15	12	Dirty Diana	Epic	
12/16/91	1(8)	14	Black Or White	Epic	1
03/09/92	5	15	Remember The Time	Epic	1
06/08/92	13	16	In The Closet	Epic	6
08/24/92	21	9	Jam	Epic	8
04/12/93	17	11	Heal The World	Epic	22
06/14/93	20	16	Who Is It	Epic	4
09/27/93	3(1)	27	Will You Be There	Epic	6
07/24/95	5	21	Scream ***	Epic	10
12/04/95	2(7)	30	You Are Not Alone	Epic	6
04/27/97	4	7	Blood On The Dance Floor	Epic	12

* Michael Jackson/Paul McCartney
** Paul McCartney/Michael Jackson
*** Michael Jackson & Janet Jackson

JACKSONS

American R&B-pop group formed in 1964 in Gary, Indiana: Sigmund Esco (Jackie) Jackson (vocals, b. 05/04/51 in Gary), Toriano Adaryll (Tito) Jackson (guitar, vocals, b. 10/15/53 in Gary), Marlon David Jackson (vocals, b. 03/12/57 in Gary), Jermaine La Jaune Jackson (vocals, bass, b. 12/11/54 in Gary), Michael Joe Jackson (lead vocals, b. 08/29/58 in Gary). Known as The Jacksons, 1968-75. Jermaine replaced by Steven Randall (Randy) Jackson (vocals, keyboards, b. 10/29/61 in Gary) joined in 1975. Jermaine rejoined in 1984 for the group's 1984 *Victory* album and tour. In the mid-1970's, sisters Maureen "Rebbie", La Toya, and Janet were part of the Jackson Family, which included the Jackson 5. Marlon went solo in 1987; Randy recorded as Randy and the Gypsies starting in 1989; Rebbie, Michael, and Janet recorded solo. Michael and Janet became recording superstars.

DATE	PK	WK	TITLE	LABEL
04/02/77	5	16	Enjoy Yourself	Epic
05/16/79	4	12	Shake Your Body Down	Epic
08/13/84	6	11	State Of Shock	Epic
10/22/84	7	10	Torture	Epic

JACYNTHE

Canadian female dance singer born circa 1980 in Quebec. Pronounced "Jah-saint".

DATE	PK	WK	TITLE	LABEL	RA
02/22/99	---	RA	Give It Up *	KLM	29

* Jacynthe featuring KC

JADE

American R&B-pop vocal trio formed in 1991 in Los Angeles: Joi Marshall, Tonya Kelly, Di Reed. Kelly, Marshall are from Chicago; Reed was born in Houston.

DATE	PK	WK	TITLE	LABEL	RA
11/30/92	23	10	I Wanna Love You	Giant	30
04/19/93	19	10	Don't Walk Away	Giant	13
10/18/93	34	4	All Thru The Night *	Giant	
02/20/95	---	RA	Every Day Of The Week	Giant	37

* POV & Jade

JAGGER, Mick

British male rock singer/songwriter born Michael Phillip Jagger on 07/26/43 in Dartford, England. Lead singer of the Rolling Stones. Appeared in movies, *Ned Kelly* (1970) and *Freejack* (1992). Married to

DATE	PK	WK	TITLE	LABEL	RA

Nicaraguan fashion model Bianca Perez Morena de Macias, 1971-1980. Married actress/model Jerry Hall on 11/24/90, the marriage was annulled on 07/09/99.

03/25/85	12	13	Just Another Night	Columbia	
06/17/85	40	2	Lucky In Love	Columbia	
11/04/85	5	18	Dancing In The Street *	Capitol	
10/19/87	38	2	Let's Work	Columbia	
03/08/93	13	9	Sweet Thing	Atlantic	39

* David Bowie/Mick Jagger

JALE
Canadian rock band formed in 1992 in Halifax: Jennifer Pierce (guitar, vocals), Alyson MacLeod (drums, vocals), Laura Stein (bass, vocals), Eve Hartling (guitar, vocals). Mike Belitsky later replaced MacLeod. The band's name is an acronym of the members' first names.

09/02/96	---	RA	All Ready	Sub Pop	33

JAM & SPOON
German male dance instrumental/production duo from Frankfurt consisting of Jam El Mar and Mark Spoon.

11/06/95	32	2	Angel	Quality

JAMES
British alternative rock group formed in 1983: Tim Booth (vocals, b. 02/04/60), Jim Glennie (guitar, b. 10/10/63), Dave Baynton-Power (drums, b. 01/29/61), Larry Gott (b. 07/24/57), Mark Hunter (keyboards, b. 11/05/68), Saul Davies (guitar, violin, b. 06/28/65), Andy Diagram (trumpet). Based in Manchester.

06/29/97	24	4	Tomorrow	Fontana

JAMES, Colin
Canadian male rock singer/songwriter born Colin Munn in 1964 in Regina Saskatchewan. Won Juno Awards for Best Male Vocalist in 1991 and 1996 and Most Promising Male Vocalist in 1989.

11/14/88	15	11	Voodoo Thing	Virgin	
01/23/89	34	8	Five Long Years	Virgin	
09/10/90	12	11	Just Came Back	Virgin	10
02/18/91	---	RA	Give It Up	Virgin	38
12/27/93	---	RA	Cadillac Baby	Virgin	39
04/15/96	23	8 h	Real Stuff	WEA	

JAMES, John
Canadian male pop-dance singer from Toronto. Born circa 1963.

02/04/91	21	4	Yo Baby Yo *	Attic	
03/08/93	---	RA	Supernatural	Attic	39

* Tarzan Dan and the John James Jungle Posse

JAMES, Rick
American male R&B-funk singer/songwriter/keyboardist/guitarist/producer born James Johnson on 02/01/48 in Buffalo, New York. Formed and fronted Mynah Birds, which included Neil Young, in the

DATE	PK	WK	TITLE	LABEL	RA

1960's in Toronto. Produced Teena Marie, Temptations, Mary Jane Girls, Eddie Murphy. Charged and arrested in 1991 along with a girlfriend for physically assaulting women.

| 10/18/78 | 22 | 14 | You & I | Motown | |

JAMIROQUOI

British dance group formed in 1989 in London: Jason Kay (vocals), Stuart Zender (bass), Derrick McKenzie (drums), Simon Katz (guitar), Toby Smith (keyboards), Wallis Buchanan (digeridoo).

| 09/13/93 | 35 | 4 | When You Gonna Learn | Columbia | |
| 06/13/99 | 10 | 8 + | Canned Heat | Columbia | 35 |

JANET - see JACKSON, Janet

JANZ, Paul

Canadian male pop singer born in Three Hills, Alberta. Recorded with brothers as the German-based band, Deliverance. Won the 1985 Juno Award for Most Promising Male Vocalist.

07/22/85	33	4	Go To Pieces	A&M	
01/18/88	26	8	Believe In Me	A&M	
04/02/90	7	12	Every Little Tear	A&M	16
08/06/90	12	15	Rocket To My Heart	A&M	18
11/12/90	28	7	Stand	A&M	35
11/30/92	---	RA	Wind Me Up	Attic	35

JARS OF CLAY

American Christian rock group from Nashville: Dan Paul Haseltine (lead vocals, b. 01/12/73, from Winter Springs, Florida), Matt Odmark (guitar, background vocals, b. 01/25/74, from Rochester, New York), Steve Mason (guitar, bass, background vocals, b. 07/08/75, from Decatur, Illinois), Charlie Lowell (synthesizer, organ, piano, background vocals, b. 10/21/73, from Rochester, New York).

| 07/08/96 | 8 | 11 h | Flood | RCA | 13 |

JAY JAY

| 01/26/97 | 30 | 2 | Do You Really Love Me | NuMuzik | |

JAY-Z

American male rapper born Jason Carter in Brooklyn, New York.

02/08/98	40	1	Sunshine	DJ Line	
02/28/99	7	17	Hard Knock Life	Def Jam	
			Another version peaked at #35 on 12/20/98.		
03/08/99	---	RA	Can I Get A... *	Def Jam	31

* Jay-Z featuring Amil & JA

JD

American male producer Jermaine Dupree born circa 1972. Produced numerous acts such as Usher, Mariah Carey, Aretha Franklin, TLC, Aaliyah, and Mase; CEO of So So Def Productions.

| 04/19/98 | 28 | 8 | Party Continues | Columbia | |

DATE	PK	WK	TITLE	LABEL	RA

JEACOCKE, Sheree
Canadian female pop singer. Former session musician and backup vocalist for Gordon Lightfoot, Glass Tiger, and Kim Mitchell.

02/05/90	9	12	Woman's Work *	RCA	
04/16/90	36	1	Before We Fall *	RCA	
08/30/93	---	RA	Miss My Love	RCA	29
12/12/94	---	RA	Serious	RCA	22

* Sheree

JEAN, Wyclef
American male rapper born Whyclef Jean on 10/17/72 in Haiti. Moved to Brooklyn, New York at age 9. Member of The Fugees.

06/15/97	6	14	We Trying To Stay Alive	Columbia
03/29/98	4	36	Gone Til November	Columbia
08/30/98	18	5	Cheated (To All The Girls)	Columbia

JEFFERSON STARSHIP
American rock group formed in San Francisco in 1965. Name changed to Jefferson Starship in 1974: Grace Slick (vocals, keyboards, b. Grace Barnett Wing on 10/30/39 in Chicago), John Barbata (drums), Papa John Creach (fiddle, b. 05/28/17 in Beaver Falls, Pennsylvania, d. 02/22/94 in Los Angeles), Paul Kantner (guitar, vocals, b. 03/12/41 in San Francisco), Peter Kangaroo (bass, b. Peter Kaukonen, Craig Chaquico (guitar, b. 09/26/54 in Sacremento, California), Pete Sears (bass, b. England). Marty Balin (vocals, b. Martyn Jerel Buchwald on 01/30/43 in Cincinnati) joined in 1975. Several personnel changes followed including the 1979 addition of Mickey Thomas (vocals, b. Cairo, Georgia). Renamed Starship in 1985 consisting of Slick, Barbata, Kangaroo, Chaquico, Thomas, Sears, Don Baldwin (drums). Slick left in 1988. Jefferson Airplane with 1966-74 lineup including Slick reformed in 1989. Starship disbanded in 1990. Inducted into the Rock And Roll Hall of Fame in 1996.

11/15/75	5	9	Miracles	Grunt
10/02/76	7	13	With Your Love	Grunt
05/31/78	16	8	Count On Me	Grunt
08/09/78	22	6	Runaway	Grunt
12/12/79	19	10	Jane	Grunt
01/20/86	4	18	We Built This City *	Grunt
04/21/86	8	18	Sara *	Grunt
04/27/87	1(3)	17	Nothing's Gonna Stop Us Now *	Grunt
09/21/87	22	11	It's Not Over ('Til It's Over) *	Grunt
10/09/89	31	4	It's Not Enough *	RCA

* Starship

JESUS JONES
British alternative rock group formed in 1988 in London: Mike Edwards (vocals, guitar, b. 06/22/64 in London), Jerry De Borg (guitar, b. 10/30/63 in London), Barry D (keyboards, b. Iain Baker on 09/29/65 in Surrey, England), Al Jaworski (bass, b. 01/31/66 in Plymouth, England), Gen (drums, b. Simon Matthews on 04/23/64 in Wiltshire, England).

06/10/91	8	18	Right Here, Right Now	SBK	11
11/25/91	29	11	Real Real Real	SBK	7
03/08/93	28	8	The Devil You Know	Perverse	24

DATE	PK	WK	TITLE	LABEL	RA

JETS, The
American pop group formed in 1984 in Minneapolis consisting of eight brothers and sisters of the Wolfgramm family: Leroy (guitar, vocals, b. 07/19/65 in Tonga), Eddie (keyboards, vocals, saxophone, drums), Eugene (vocals, percussion, b. 09/24/67 in Samoa), Rudy (drums, vocals, b. 03/01/69 in Salt Lake City, Utah), Haini (vocals, b. 01/25/68 in San Francisco), Kathi (vocals, keyboards, b. 09/06/70 in San Diego), Elizabeth (vocals, b. 08/19/72 in Salt Lake City), Moana (keyboards, percussion, vocals, b. 10/13/73 in Salt Lake City). Family originated from Tonga in the South Pacific. Eugene quitted group to form the Boys Club in 1988.

DATE	PK	WK	TITLE	LABEL	RA
07/28/86	17	8	Crush On You	MCA	
03/30/87	17	14	You Got It All	MCA	
09/21/87	15	12	Cross My Broken Heart	MCA	
05/09/88	16	13	Rocket 2 U	MCA	
07/25/88	22	10	Make It Real	MCA	

JETT, Joan, & The Blackhearts
American rock band: Joan Jett (lead vocals, b. Joan Larkin, 11/22/60 in Philadelphia), Ricky Byrd (guitar), Gary Ryan (bass), Lee Crystal (drums).

DATE	PK	WK	TITLE	LABEL	RA
03/20/82	1(7)	17	I Love Rock N' Roll	Boardwalk	
06/19/82	5	9	Crimson & Clover	Broadwalk	
11/07/88	21	7	I Hate Myself For Loving You	CBS Associated	
03/19/90	21	7	Dirty Deeds	CBS Associated	

JEWEL
American female pop singer/songwriter/poet born Jewel Kilcher on 05/23/74 in Payson, Utah. Raised in Homer, Alaska, based in San Diego. Wrote poetry book *A Night Without Armor: Poems* in 1998.

DATE	PK	WK	TITLE	LABEL	RA
08/26/96	6	17 h	Who Will Save Your Soul	Atlantic	5
03/17/97	---	RA	You Were Meant For Me	Atlantic	5
10/27/97	---	RA	Foolish Games	Atlantic	5
01/04/99	---	RA	Hands	Atlantic	3
05/17/99	---	RA	Down So Long	Atlantic	19

JIGSAW
British pop-rock quartet from England: Des Dyer (lead vocals), Clive Scott, Tony Campbell, Barrie Bernard.

DATE	PK	WK	TITLE	LABEL	RA
12/27/75	3(2)	10	Sky High	Chelsea	

JITTERS, The
Canadian rock band from Toronto: Danny Levy (guitar, vocals), Glenn Martin (drums), Blair Packham (vocals, guitar).

DATE	PK	WK	TITLE	LABEL	RA
11/30/87	35	8	Last Of The Red Hot Fools	Capitol	
10/08/90	29	4	Til The Fever Breaks	Capitol	36

JIVE BUNNY & THE MASTERMIXERS
British dance group: DJ Les Hemstock and mixers John Pickles, Andy Pickles (John's son) and Ian Morgan.

DATE	PK	WK	TITLE	LABEL	RA
12/25/89	1(4)	13	Swing The Mood	Atco	

DATE	PK	WK	TITLE	LABEL	RA

JK
Polish female dance singer born Maria Simlat on 01/02/71 in Cracovia, Poland.

| 05/22/95 | 24 | 23 | You & I | Quality | |

JODECI
American R&B vocal group formed in 1988 in Charlotte, North Carolina: K-Ci (b. Cedric Hailey on 09/02/69 in Charlotte), Jo-Jo (b. Joel Hailey on 06/10/71 in Charlotte), Devante Swing (b. Donald DeGrate on 09/29/69 in Newport News, Virginia), Mr. Dalvin (b. Dalvin DeGrate on 07/23/71 in Newport News, Virginia). K-Ci, Devante Swing were arraigned on charges of aggravated sexual contact and weapons possession in Teaneck, New Jersey, in 1993. K-Ci & Jo-Jo recorded by themselves in the late-1990's.

| 02/10/92 | 38 | 1 | Forever My Lady | MCA | |

JOE PUBLIC
American R&B band from Buffalo, New York: Kevin "Kev" Scott (vocals), Joe "J.R." Carter, Joseph "Jake" Sayles, Dwight "Dew" Wyatt.

| 06/15/92 | 4 | 18 | Live And Learn | Columbia | 12 |
| 08/24/92 | 23 | 12 | I Miss You | Columbia | |

JOEE
Canadian male pop-dance singer/songwriter born Joey Desimone in 1973 in Toronto. Based in Maple, Ontario.

08/28/95	22	3	Died In Your Arms *	Quality	
01/04/98	6	19	Angel	Popular	
05/10/98	15	8	If I Could	Popular	
01/25/99	---	RA	Do You Right	Popular	19

* Intonation featuring Joee

JOEL, Billy
American male pop singer/songwriter/pianist born William Martin Joel on 05/09/49 in Hicksville, New York. A boxer for three years before singing career. Member of various bands before recording solo in 1973. Involved in serious motorcycle accident in 1982 in Long Island, New York. Married supermodel Christie Brinkley on 03/23/85, divorced in 1994. Toured Soviet Union in 1987. Filed lawsuits against various business associates in the 1990's.

02/22/78	6	20	Just The Way You Are	Columbia	
06/14/78	38	2	Movin' Out	Columbia	
07/26/78	17	12	Only The Good Die Young	Columbia	
11/15/78	16	8	She's Always A Woman	Columbia	
01/10/79	6	12	My Life	Columbia	
06/13/79	8	12	Honesty	Columbia	
05/28/80	10	12	You May Be Right	Columbia	
07/09/80	1(1)	7	It's Still Rock And Roll To Me	Columbia	
10/04/80	13	6	Don't Ask Me Why	Columbia	
11/14/81	12	5	Say Goodbye To Hollywood	Columbia	
11/20/82	4	7	Pressure	Columbia	
02/14/83	24	4	Allentown	Columbia	
10/17/83	4	13	Tell Her About It	Columbia	

DATE	PK	WK	TITLE	LABEL	RA
12/19/83	3(1)	16	Uptown Girl	Columbia	
02/27/84	20	8	An Innocent Man	Columbia	
06/04/84	35	4	The Longest Time	Columbia	
09/30/85	15	10	You're Only Human (Second Wind)	Columbia	
08/18/86	40	2	Modern Woman	Columbia	
11/03/86	12	17	A Matter Of Trust	Columbia	
02/02/87	35	4	This Is The Time	Columbia	
12/11/89	2(2)	20	We Didn't Start The Fire	Columbia	
03/26/90	5	13	I Go To Extremes	Columbia	3
10/05/92	14	7	All Shook Up	Epic	
10/18/93	7	38	The River Of Dreams	Columbia	3
01/24/94	22	15	All About Soul	Columbia	10
08/24/97	36	1	To Make You Feel My Love	Columbia	

JOHN, Elton

British male pop singer/songwriter/pianist born Reginald Kenneth Dwight on 03/25/47 in Pinner, England. In 1966, formed Bluesology, backup band for visiting American soul acts like Patti LaBelle and the Bluebelles. Long John Baldry hired Bluesology as backup band in 1966. Changed name to Elton John, named after group members saxophonist Elton Dean and John Baldry. Later made Elton Hercules John legal name (Hercules is a childhood nickname). Began working with lyricist Bernie Taupin (b. 05/22/50 in Sleaford, England). Godfather of Sean Ono Lennon, son of John Lennon and Yoko Ono. Sotheby's of London auctioned off 2,000 of John's items in 1988 netting over $20 million. Founded the Elton John AIDS Foundation to raise funds for AIDS research. Inducted into the Rock and Roll Hall of Fame in 1994.

DATE	PK	WK	TITLE	LABEL
06/07/75	1(1)	6	Pinball Wizard	Polydor
06/07/75	9	2	Philadelphia Freedom	MCA
08/23/75	3(3)	10	Someone Saved My Life Tonight	MCA
11/29/75	1(4)	14	Island Girl	MCA
02/28/76	9	9	Grow Some Funk/Feel Like A Bullet	MCA
06/12/76	26	4	Love Song	MCA
08/14/76	1(6)	17	Don't Go Breaking My Heart *	Rocket
01/01/77	7	11	Sorry Seems To Be The Hardest Word	Rocket
03/19/77	16	10	Bite Your Lip	Rocket
05/31/78	35	4	Ego	MCA
09/05/79	10	16	Mama Can't Buy You Love	MCA
07/16/80	7	8	Little Jeannie	MCA
07/04/81	10	4	Nobody Wins	Geffen
05/22/82	5	9	Empty Garden (Hey Hey Johnny)	Geffen
10/02/82	8	6	Blue Eyes	Geffen
07/11/83	7	12	I'm Still Standing	Geffen
10/10/83	29	1	Kiss The Bride	Geffen
02/20/84	6	15	I Guess That's Why They Call It Blues	Geffen
08/20/84	4	16	Sad Songs (Say So Much)	Geffen
10/22/84	28	5	Who Wears These Shoes	Geffen
02/24/86	1(3)	23	That's What Friends Are For **	Arista
04/14/86	1(4)	25	Nikita	Geffen
01/26/87	37	2	Heartache Around The World	Geffen
07/27/87	14	8	Flames Of Paradise ***	Epic
02/22/88	20	15	Candle In The Wind	MCA
08/29/88	1(3)	17	I Don't Wanna Go On With You Like That	MCA
12/12/88	18	13	A Word In Spanish	MCA
06/12/89	32	6	Through The Storm ****	Arista

DATE	PK	WK	TITLE	LABEL	RA
10/16/89	29	9	Healing Hands	MCA	
03/19/90	24	9	Sacrifice	MCA	18
07/16/90	---	RA	Club At The End Of The Street	MCA	26
01/21/91	14	10	You Gotta Love Someone	MCA	10
03/16/92	1(1)	25	Don't Let The Sun Go Down On Me *****	Columbia	2
08/31/92	---	RA	The One	MCA	2
12/21/92	20	12	The Last Song	MCA	18
05/03/93	---	RA	Simple Life	MCA	8
08/01/94	1(9)	45	Can You Feel The Love Tonight	Hollywood	5
02/13/95	7	31	Circle Of Life	Hollywood	21
06/19/95	2(1)	28	Believe	Rocket	3
08/21/95	---	RA	Made In England	Rocket	17
04/29/96	35	9 h	Please	Rocket	
10/28/96	16	11 h	You Can Make History (Young Again)	MCA	31
09/14/97	22	3	Something About The Way You Look Tonight	Rocket	38
09/21/97	1(45)	97 +	Candle In The Wind 1997/		17
			Something About The Way You Look Tonight	Rocket	
			Two other versions peaked at #20 on 09/28/97 and at #23 on 01/04/98.		
02/28/99	4	19	Written In The Stars ******	Rocket	

* Elton John & Kiki Dee
** Dionne & Friends
*** Jennifer Rush/Elton John
**** Aretha Franklin/Elton John
***** George Michael & Elton John
****** Elton John & Leann Rimes

JOHN, Robert
American male singer born Robert John Pedrick, Jr. in 1946 in Brooklyn, New York. First recorded in 1958 as Bobby Pedrick, Jr.

| 10/17/79 | 2(4) | 18 | Sad Eyes | Capitol | |

JOHNNY HATES JAZZ
British/American pop trio: Clark Datchler (vocals), Calvin Hayes, Mike Nocito. Datchler (left in 1988, replaced by producer Phil Thornalley), Hayes are British, Nocito is American.

| 06/13/88 | 3(3) | 14 | Shattered Dreams | Virgin | |

JOHNSON, Debbie
Canadian female dance singer from Toronto born in Trinidad. To Canada at age ten. Toured with family as a member of the group Johnson Family (later Sweet Ecstasy).

| 01/27/92 | 29 | 9 | I'll Respect You | Aquarius | 26 |

JOHNSON, Don
American male singer/actor born on 12/15/49 in Flat Creek in Missouri. Played Sonny Crockett on the television series, *Miami Vice*. Divorced, remarried, separated from actress Melanie Griffith.

| 11/17/86 | 7 | 18 | Heartbeat | Epic | |

| DATE | PK | WK | TITLE | LABEL | RA |

JOHNSON, Michael
American male MOR-pop singer born on 08/08/44 in Alamosa, Colorado and raised in Denver. In the Chad Mitchell Trio with John Denver in 1968.

| 08/09/78 | 17 | 10 | Bluer Than Blue | EMI |

JOLI, France
Canadian female pop vocalist from Dorion, Quebec born in 1963.

| 12/12/79 | 16 | 4 | Come To Me | TGO |

JON & VANGELIS
British/Greek duo: English vocalist Jon Anderson (lead singer of Yes), Greek keyboardist Evangelos Papathanassiou (recorded later as Vangelis).

| 11/21/81 | 5 | 13 | Friends Of Mr. Cairo | Polydor |

JON B.
American male R&B vocalist from Pasadena, California, born circa 1976 in Rhode Island.

| 07/24/95 | 25 | 12 | Someone To Love * | Epic |

* Jon B./Babyface

JONES, Howard
British male techno-pop vocalist/songwriter/keyboardist born John Howard Jones on 02/23/55 in Southampton, England.

04/30/84	16	8	New Song	WEA	
07/22/85	18	11	Things Can Only Get Better	WEA	
07/21/86	12	15	No One Is To Blame	WEA	
12/22/86	26	10	You Know I Love You...Don't You?	WEA	
06/19/89	17	12	Everlasting Love	WEA	
06/08/92	---	RA	Lift Me Up	WEA	10

JONES, Oran "Juice"
American male R&B singer born in 1959 in Houston, raised in New York City.

| 01/19/87 | 8 | 15 | The Rain | Def Jam |

JONES, Ricki Lee
American female jazz-pop singer/songwriter born on 11/08/54 in Chicago. Won a Grammy Award for Best New Artist in 1979.

| 06/27/79 | 10 | 14 | Chuck E's In Love | Warner |

JONES, Tom
British male pop vocalist born Thomas Jones Woodward on 06/07/40 in Pontypridd, Wales. Performed in the 1960's as Tommy Scott; formed trio Senators in 1963. Changed name after the film *Tom Jones* in 1964. Own TV show *This Is Tom Jones*, 1969-71.

| 04/16/77 | 14 | 11 | Say You'll Stay Until Tomorrow | Epic |

DATE	PK	WK	TITLE	LABEL	RA
02/27/89	27	11	Kiss *	Polydor	
12/24/94	---	RA	If I Only Knew	Warner	29

* Art Of Noise/Tom Jones

JORDAN, Jeremy
American male pop singer born Don Henson on 09/19/73 in Hammond, Indiana, raised in Calumet City, Illinois.

DATE	PK	WK	TITLE	LABEL	RA
04/19/93	7	16	The Right Kind Of Love	Giant	14
06/28/93	---	RA	Wannagirl	Giant	8

JORDAN, Keven
Canadian male singer. Won the 1992 Juno Award for Most Promising Male Vocalist of the Year.

DATE	PK	WK	TITLE	LABEL	RA
04/01/91	40	1	No Sign Of Rain	Columbia	
10/14/91	---	RA	Just Another Day	Columbia	36

JORDAN, Montell
American male R&B singer born on 12/03/68 in Los Angeles.

DATE	PK	WK	TITLE	LABEL	RA
07/10/95	1(2)	28	This Is How We Do It	PMP	7
09/25/95	23	8	Something 4 Da Honeyz	PMP	

JORDAN, Sass
Canadian female rock singer born in 1962 in Birmingham, England. Based in Montreal. Former backup singer for The Box. Won the 1989 Juno Award for Most Promising Female Vocalist.

DATE	PK	WK	TITLE	LABEL	RA
03/27/89	22	8	Tell Somebody	Aquarius	
09/18/89	39	1	Stranger Than Paradise	Aquarius	
01/22/90	16	9	So Hard	Aquarius	
03/23/92	14	12	Make You A Believer	Aquarius	14
07/13/92	---	RA	I Want To Believe	Aquarius	39
10/12/92	---	RA	You Don't Have To Remind Me	Aquarius	21
12/21/92	---	RA	Goin' Back Again	Aquarius	37
09/05/94	---	RA	Sun's Gonna Rise	Aquarius	22
01/26/98	---	RA	Do What I Can	Aquarius	23
05/11/98	---	RA	Desire	Aquarius	36

JOURNEY
American rock band formed in 1973 in San Francisco. Line-up in the late-1970's: Neal Schon (vocals, guitar, b. 02/27/54 in San Mateo, California), Ross Valory (bass, b. 02/02/49 in San Francisco), Gregg Rolie (vocals, keyboards, b. 06/17/47), Steve Smith (drums, b. 08/21/54 in Los Angeles), Steve Perry (vocals, b. 01/22/49 in Hanford, California). Rolie left in 1981, later joined Jefferson Starship and Whitesnake, replaced by Jonathan Cain (of the Babys). Smith, Valory left in 1986. Perry, Cain, Schon had solo careers.

DATE	PK	WK	TITLE	LABEL	RA
11/28/79	14	10	Lovin', Touchin', Squeezin'	Columbia	
10/10/81	3(1)	11	Who's Crying Now	Columbia	
12/19/81	5	10	Don't Stop Believin'	Columbia	
03/13/82	2(4)	12	Open Arms	Columbia	
05/02/83	11	11	Separate Ways	Columbia	

DATE	PK	WK	TITLE	LABEL	RA
06/27/83	26	2	Faithfully	Columbia	
03/25/85	24	6	Only The Young	Geffen	
12/09/96	---	RA	When You Love A Woman	Columbia	4
04/14/97	---	RA	If He Should Break Your Heart	Columbia	35

JT MONEY
American male rapper Jeff Thompkins from Miami.

05/23/99	25	2	Who Dat	PRR

JULUKA
British/South African vocal/instrumental group.

01/23/84	29	2	Scatterlings Of Africa	Warner

JUMP 'N THE SADDLE
American band based in Chicago, led by vocalist Peter Quinn.

01/16/84	30	3	The Curly Shuffle	Atlantic

JUNIOR M.A.F.I.A.
American rap/R&B group formed in 1995 in Brooklyn, New York: Chris Wallace (Notorious B.I.G.), Little Caesar, Chico, Nino Brown, Trife, Larency, MC Klepto, MC Little Kim (Big Momma). M.A.F.I.A. stands for Masters At Finding Intelligent Attitudes. Notorious B.I.G. and Lil' Kim had successful solo careers.

11/27/95	24	3	Player's Anthem	Atlantic

JUNKHOUSE
Canadian rock band from Hamilton, Ontario: Tom Wilson (vocals), Dan Achen (guitar), Russ Wilson (bass), Ray Farrugia (drums).

11/08/93	30	1	Out Of My Head	Epic
03/21/94	22	7	The Sky Is Falling	Epic

JUVET, Patrick
French male vocalist.

11/16/77	25	4	Ou Sont Les Femmes	Polydor

K

KAJAGOOGOO
British pop quintet led by Limahl (Chris Hamill), who left in 1983 to pursue solo career. Replaced by Nick Beggs.

06/27/83	11	10	Too Shy	Capitol

KAMOZE, Ini
Jamaican male dance-reggae singer/songwriter/author/playwright born on 10/09/57 in St. Mary, Jamaica.

DATE	PK	WK	TITLE	LABEL	RA
02/27/95	33	4	Here Comes The Hotstepper	Columbia	7

KANSAS
American rock group formed in Topeka, Kansas in 1970: Kerry Livgren (guitar, keyboards, synthesizers, b. 09/18/49 in Kansas), Steve Walsh (keyboards, synthesizer, vocals, b. 06/15/51 in St. Joseph, Missouri), Robby Steinhardt (violin, vocals, b. 05/25/50 in Mississippi), Richard Williams (guitar, b. 02/01/51 in Kansas), Phil Ehart (drums, b. 02/04/50 in Kansas), Dave Hope (bass, b. 10/07/49 in Kansas). Walsh replaced in 1981 by John Elefante (vocals, keyboards, b. 1958 in Levittown, New York). Group re-formed in 1986 with Walsh, Ehart, Williams, Steve Morse (guitar), Billy Greer (bass).

04/16/77	13	12	Carry On Wayward Son	Kirshner	
03/22/78	6	14	Dust In The Wind	Kirshner	

KAOMA
French group of singers, musicians, and dancers, led by keyboardist/arranger Jean-Claude Bonaventure. Based in Paris.

04/30/90	6	23	Lambada	Epic	

KATRINA & THE WAVES
American/British pop group formed in 1981 in England: Katrina Leskanich (vocals, guitar, b. 1960 in Topeka, Kansas), British-born Kimberley Rew (guitar), American-born Vince de la Cruz (bass), British-born Alex Cooper (drums).

07/22/85	2(1)	15	Walking On Sunshine	Attic	
10/07/85	29	6	Do You Want Crying	Attic	
06/02/86	29	10	Is That It?	Attic	
09/25/89	21	9	That's The Way	Attic	

KAYLE
Canadian female pop/dance singer from Coquitlam, British Columbia. Raised in Nova Scotia.

06/06/99	40	2	A Little Sumthin' Sumthin'	Robbins	27+

KC & THE SUNSHINE BAND
American pop-dance group formed in 1973 in Hialeah, Florida: Harry Wayne Casey (vocals, keyboards, b. 01/31/51 in Hialeah), Richard Finch (bass, b. 01/25/54 in Indianapolis, Indiana), Jerome Smith (guitar, b. 06/18/53 in Miami), Robert Johnson (drums, b. 03/21/53 in Miami), Fermin Coytisolo (congas, b. 12/31/51 in Havana, Cuba), Ronnie Smith (trumpet, b. 1952 in Hialeah), Denvil Liptrot (saxophone), James Weaver (trumpet), Charles Williams (trombone, b. 11/18/54 in Rockingham, North Carolina). First recorded in 1973 as KC and the Sunshine Junkanoo Band. Casey and Finch wrote the 1974 hit "Rock Your Baby" for George McCrae. Casey involved in a serious car crash in 1982; went solo in 1984.

09/27/75	1(1)	14	Get Down Tonight	RCA	
12/27/75	1(3)	14	That's The Way I Like It	RCA	
10/09/76	3(1)	15	Shake Your Booty	RCA	
06/25/77	2(2)	17	I'm Your Boogie Man	RCA	
10/05/77	5	16	Keep It Comin' Love	RCA	
07/26/78	32	2	It's The Same Old Song	RCA	
01/09/80	3(2)	22	Please Don't Go	TK	
03/05/80	12	12	Yes, I'm Ready *	Casablanca	
02/22/99	---	RA	Give It Up **	KLM	29

DATE	PK	WK	TITLE	LABEL	RA

* Teri DeSario with K.C.
** Jacynthe featuring KC

K-CI & JOJO
American R&B vocal duo from Tiny Grove, North Carolina consisting of brothers Joel ("JoJo") (b. 06/10/71 in Charlotte, North Carolina) and Cedric ("K-Ci") (b. 09/02/69 in Charlotte) Hailey. Members of the vocal quartet Jodeci.

04/12/98	9	6	All My Life	MCA	8
			Two other versions peaked at #23 on 05/17/98 and at #39 on 07/26/98.		
07/19/99	---	RA	Tell Me It's Real	MCA	25+

KEAN, Sherry
Canadian female singer. Former member of the group Sharks.

| 04/09/84 | 28 | 8 | I Want You Back | Capitol | |

KEANE BROTHERS
Canadian duo consisting of John (born circa 1965) and Tom (born circa 1964), sons of label owner Bob Keane.

| 02/12/77 | 25 | 6 | Sherry | 20th Century | |

KEEDY
American female dance singer from Milwaukee, born on 07/26/65 in Abilene, Texas.

| 06/10/91 | 39 | 1 | Save Some Love | RCA | 29 |

KEITH, Lisa
American female pop singer/songwriter from Minneapolis. Vocalist on Herb Alpert's "Diamonds".

| 11/15/93 | 21 | 14 | Better Than You | A&M | 13 |

KELLY, R.
American male R&B singer/producer born Robert Kelly on 01/08/69 in Chicago. Married Aaliyah on 08/31/94.

02/02/97	27	4	I Believe I Can Fly	Jive	
			Another version peaked at #33 on 03/23/97.		
07/27/97	19	8	Gotham City	Jive	32
01/17/99	37	1	I'm Your Angel *	Jive	14
03/08/99	---	RA	Home Alone	Jive	40
06/27/99	10	7 +	Did You Ever Think	Jive	

* R. Kelly & Celine Dion

KEMP, Tara
American female dance-pop singer/songwriter from San Francisco.

| 05/06/91 | 34 | 3 | Hold You Tight | Giant | 17 |

DATE	PK	WK	TITLE	LABEL	RA
07/22/91	---	RA	Piece Of My Heart..	Giant	30

KENDALLS, The
American country father-daughter duo from St. Louis, Missouri, formed in 1969: Royce Kendall (vocals, guitar, b. Royce Kykendall on 09/25/34 in St. Louis), Jeannie Kendall (vocals, guitar, b. 11/30/54 in St. Louis).

| 12/14/77 | 23 | 4 | Heaven's Just A Sin Away............................... | RCA | |

KENNY G
American male jazz saxophonist born Kenneth Gorelick on 06/05/56 in Seattle. Played in Barry White's Love Unlimited Orchestra at age 17. Graduated from the University of Washington with an accounting degree. Signed with Arista Records in early-1980's.

| 08/10/87 | 20 | 10 | Songbird.. | Arista | |
| 07/19/93 | --- | RA | By The Time This Night Is Over *................... | Arista | 23 |

* Kenny G with Peabo Bryson

KERSHAW, Nik
British male pop singer/songwriter/multi-instrumentalist born on 03/01/58 in Bristol, England.

| 07/02/84 | 7 | 17 | Wouldn't It Be Good.. | MCA | |

KHALEEL
American male hip-hop act Bob Khaleel from Los Angeles. Raised in the Bronx.

| 02/08/99 | --- | RA | No Mercy .... | Hollywood | 29 |

KHAN, Chaka/Rufus
American female R&B singer born Yvette Marie Stevens on 03/23/53 in Great Lakes, Illinois. Lead singer of the group, Rufus. Went solo in 1978. Her daughter, Milini is a member of the group, Pretty In Pink.

04/10/76	26	7	Sweet Thing *..	ABC	
12/24/84	4	16	I Feel For You **...	Warner	
11/03/96	35	2	Missing You ***...	Elektra	

* Rufus featuring Chaka Khan
** Chaka Khan
*** Brandy, Tamia, Gladys Knight & Chaka Khan

KID N' PLAY
American rap duo formed in 1988 in Queens, New York: Kid (Christopher Reid, b. 04/05/64 in Bronx, New York) and Play (Christopher Martin on 07/10/62 in Queens). Starred in the movies *House Party*, *House Party 2*, *Class Act*. Stars of own Saturday morning cartoon show.

| 02/03/92 | 17 | 17 | Ain't Gonna Hurt Nobody .... | Attic | |

KIHN, Greg, Band
American pop band formed in 1975 in Berkeley, California: Greg Kihn (vocals, guitar, b. 1952, Baltimore), Robbie Dunbar (guitar), Larry Lynch (drums, vocals), Steve Wright (bass, vocals). Dunbar re-

DATE	PK	WK	TITLE	LABEL	RA

placed by Dave Carpender in 1976, who in turn was replaced by Greg Douglass in 1982. Gary Phillips (keyboards) joined in 1980. Kihn is a writer of screenplay, novels and a newsletter editor.

| 08/15/81 | 15 | 4 | The Breakup Song .... Beserkley | | |
| 04/25/83 | 6 | 13 | Jeopardy.. Beserkley | | |

KILLER BUNNIES

| 01/12/98 | --- | RA | I Can't Talk The Heartbreak .... Universal | 37 |

KILLJOYS, The
Canadian rock trio from Hamilton, Ontario, formed in 1992: Mike Trebilcock (guitar, vocals), Gene Champagne (drums), Shelley Woods (bass). Won the 1997 Juno Award for Best New Group.

| 10/07/96 | 35 | 3 h | Soaked .... WEA | |

KIM, Andy
Canadian male singer/songwriter born Andrew Youakim on 12/05/46 in Montreal. Recorded as Baron Longfellow in 1980 and Longfellow in the 1990's.

| 10/16/76 | 22 | 8 | Harlem .... Ice | |
| 12/30/91 | --- | RA | Powerdrive * .... Ice | 39 |

* Longfellow

KING, Ben E.
American male R&B singer born Benjamin Earl Nelson on 09/23/38 in Henderson, North Carolina. Joined the Five Clowns in 1956, which in 1959 became the new Drifters. Wrote and sang lead on the group's "There Goes By Baby" in 1959; became lead singer soon after. Recorded solo in 1960. "Stand By Me" re-released in 1986 after it was featured in the Rob Reiner-directed film of the same name.

| 01/19/87 | 10 | 17 | Stand By Me .... Atlantic | |

KING, Carole
American female pop singer/songwriter born Carole Klein on 02/09/40 in Brooklyn, New York. Wrote music to "Will You Love Me Tomorrow?", "Up On The Roof". Married to lyricist Gerry Goffin, 1958-68. Neil Sedaka's 1958 hit, "Oh! Carol" was inspired by King. Wrote "The Loco-Motion" with Goffin for their 17 year-old babysitter, Little Eva (Boyd) in 1962. King's Tapestry album won four Grammy Awards. Daughter Louise Goffin began solo career in 1979.

| 04/24/76 | 30 | 4 | Only Love Is Real .... Ode | |

KING, Diana
Jamaican female dancehall-hip hop singer born circa 1974 in Spanish Town, St. Catherine Parish, Jamaica. Lives in Kingston.

| 08/21/95 | 7 | 36 | Shy Guy .... Columbia | 8 |
| 10/19/97 | 34 | 1 | I Say A Little Prayer .... Columbia | 24 |

KING, Evelyn "Champagne"
American female pop-R&B singer born on 06/29/60 in the Bronx, New York.

| 10/18/78 | 18 | 16 | Shame.. RCA | |

| DATE | PK | WK | TITLE | LABEL | RA |

KINKS, The
British rock group formed in London in 1963: Ray Davies (guitar, vocals, b. 06/21/44 in London), Dave Davies (guitar, vocals, b. 02/03/47 in London), Mick Avory (drums, b. 02/15/44 in London), Pete Quaife (bass, b. 12/27/43 in Tavistock, England). Numerous line-up changes since 1963. Ray and Dave formed the nucleus of the group. Ray appeared in the 1986 movie, *Absolute Beginners*.

09/19/79	39	2	(Wish I Could Fly Like) Superman	Arista	
07/11/83	6	14	Come Dancing	Arista	
10/31/83	20	8	Don't Forget To Dance	Arista	

KISH
Canadian male rapper Andrew Kishino from Toronto. Of Japanese ancestry. Age 20 in 1991.

06/10/91	---	RA	I Rhyme The World In 80 Days	A&M	37
08/26/91	30	9	She's A Flirt	A&M	

KISS
American hard rock group formed in 1972 in New York City: Gene Simmons (vocals, bass, b. Gene Klein on 08/25/49 in Haifa, Israel), Paul Stanley (guitar, vocals, b. Stanley Eisen on 01/20/52 in Queens, New York), Peter Criss (drums, vocals, b. Peter Crisscoula on 12/20/47 in Brooklyn, New York), Ace Frehley (guitar, b. Paul Frehley on 04/27/51 in Bronx, New York). Known for wearing distinctive make-up until 1983 when the group removed make-up for the first time. Criss replaced by Eric Carr (b. 07/12/50 in Brooklyn, died of cancer on 11/24/91 in New York City); Frehley replaced in 1982 by Vinnie Vincent, who was replaced by Mark St. John in 1984. St. John replaced by Bruce Kulick in 1986; Carr replaced by Eric Singer in 1991.

01/17/76	11	10	Rock And Roll All Nite	Casablanca	
05/22/76	15	8	Shout It Out Loud	Casablanca	
11/27/76	1(1)	16	Beth	Casablanca	
03/19/77	13	11	Hard Luck Woman	Casablanca	
06/18/77	22	7	Calling Dr. Love	Casablanca	
08/13/77	26	4	Christine Sixteen	Casablanca	
09/05/79	1(2)	16	I Was Made For Loving You	Casablanca	
04/30/90	22	10	Forever	Mercury	11

KLF, The
British dance/pop group formed in 1987 in England: Bill Drummond (synthesizers, samplers, b. William Butterworth on 04/29/53 in South Africa), Jimmy Cauty (guitar, b. 1954 in England). Drummond played in Big In Japan and managed Echo and the Bunnymen and Teardrop Explodes. KLF stands for "Kopyright Liberation Front", a reference to sampling without proper copyright clearance.

09/16/91	---	RA	3 AM Eternal	RCA	13
03/23/92	1(6)	17	Justified And Ancient *	RCA	1

* The KLF Featuring Tammy Wynette

KLYMAXX
American pop/R&B band founded by producer Bernadette Cooper in Los Angeles in 1979: Cooper (drums), Lorena Porter Shelby (vocals), Joyce "Fenderella" Irby (vocals). 1990 line-up: Shelby, Cheryl Cooley (guitar), Robbin Grider (keyboards).

02/03/86	15	15	I Miss You	MCA	

| DATE | PK | WK | TITLE | LABEL | RA |

KMFDM
German industrial rock band. Core members are Sascha Konietzko, En Esch, and Gunter Schulz. Disbanded in late-1998. "KMFDM" is an acronym for "Kein Mehrheit für die Mitleid" (translates roughly to "no pity for the majority").

Date	PK	WK	Title	Label
03/01/98	18	5	MDFMK	TVT/Wax Trax

KNACK, The
American rock group formed in 1978 in Los Angeles: Doug Fieger (guitar, vocals, b. 08/20/52 in Detroit), Berton Averre (guitar, b. 12/13 in Van Nuys, California), Bruce Gary (drums, b. 04/07/52 in Burbank, California), Prescott Niles (bass, b. 05/02 in New York City).

Date	PK	WK	Title	Label
09/19/79	1(2)	22	My Sharona	Capitol
10/17/79	3(2)	14	Good Girls Don't	Capitol
03/19/80	15	2	Baby Talks Dirty	Capitol

KNIGHT, Gladys, and the Pips
American R&B group formed in 1952 in Atlanta led by Gladys Knight (vocals, b. 05/28/44 in Atlanta). Line-up in 1975 included Knight, Edward Patten (vocals, b. 08/02/39 in Atlanta), Mermald "Budda" Knight (vocals, b. 09/04/42 in Atlanta), William Guest (06/02/41 in Atlanta). Gladys appeared in the 1976 movie *Pipe Dreams* and co-starred in the TV series *Charlie and Co.*

Date	PK	WK	Title	Label
07/26/75	17	7	The Way We Were/Try To Remember	Buddah
02/24/86	1(3)	23	That's What Friends Are For *	Arista
11/03/96	35	2	Missing You **	Elektra

* Dionne & Friends
** Brandy, Tamia, Gladys Knight & Chaka Khan

KNIGHT, Jordan
American male pop singer born on 05/15/70 in Worcester, Massachusetts. Former member of New Kids On The Block.

Date	PK	WK	Title	Label	RA
04/25/99	11	17	Give It To You	Interscope	38

KNOPFLER, Mark
British male rock singer/guitarist/songwriter born on 08/12/49 in Glasgow, Scotland. Guitarist/vocalist of Dire Straits.

Date	PK	WK	Title	Label
04/29/96	32	5 h	Darling Pretty	Vertigo

KNUCKLEHEADS, The
Canadian novelty group of studio musicians led by vocalist Roy Kenner. Produced by former Guess Who producer Jack Richardson.

Date	PK	WK	Title	Label
01/16/84	32	7	The Curly Shuffle	Attic

KON KAN
Canadian dance duo from Toronto: Barry Harris (guitar, piano) and Kevin Wynne (vocals). Wynne left in 1989. Name is a play on the radio business term, Can Con (Canadian Content).

Date	PK	WK	Title	Label
04/03/89	19	9	I Beg Your Pardon	Atlantic
09/04/89	38	2	Harry Houdini	Atlantic

DATE	PK	WK	TITLE	LABEL	RA
04/19/93	---	RA	Sinful Wishes .... Hypnotic		26

KOOL & THE GANG
American R&B-pop group formed in 1964 in Jersey City, New Jersey: Robert "Kool" Bell (vocals, bass, b. 10/08/50 in Youngstown, Ohio), Ronald Bell (tenor saxophone, b. 11/01/51 in Youngstown), Dennis "Dee Tee" Thomas (saxophone, flute, b. 02/09/51 in Jersey City), Claydes Smith (guitar, b. 09/06/48 in Jersey City), Robert "Spike" Mickens (trumpet, b. Jersey City), Rickey Westfield (keyboards, b. Jersey City), George "Funky" Brown (drums, b. 01/05/48 in Jersey City). Clifford Adams (trombone) joined in 1976; Westfield left in 1977. James "J.T." Taylor (lead vocals, b. 08/16/53 in South Carolina) joined in 1979; Curtis Williams (keyboards) and Michael Ray (trumpet) joined in 1980. J.T. Taylor left in 1989 to record solo.

DATE	PK	WK	TITLE	LABEL
02/06/80	4	14	Ladies Night .... De-Lite
04/30/80	27	5	Too Hot .... De-Lite
03/07/81	6	12	Celebration .... De-Lite
04/02/84	13	12	Joanna .... De-Lite
04/15/85	40	2	Misled .... De-Lite
07/22/85	13	16	Fresh .... De-Lite
10/14/85	2(3)	21	Cherish .... De-Lite
02/09/87	25	8	Victory .... Mercury

KORGIS
British pop duo consisting of James Warren and Andy Davis.

DATE	PK	WK	TITLE	LABEL
01/17/81	16	2	Everybody's Got To Learn Sometime .... Elektra

KORN
American hard rock group formed in 1992 in Bakersfield, California: Jonathan Houseman Davis (vocals, bagpipes), James "Munky" Shaffer (guitar), Brian "Head" Welch (guitar), Reginald "Fieldy Snuts" Arvizu (bass), David Silveria (drums).

DATE	PK	WK	TITLE	LABEL
06/01/97	36	1	A.D.I.A.S. .... Epic
03/14/99	30	4	A.D.I.A.S. (re-entry) .... Epic
05/09/99	26	7	Freek On A Leash .... Sony Import

KRAVITZ, Lenny
American male rock singer/songwriter/multi-instrumentalist born Leonard Albert Kravitz on 05/26/64 in New York City. Married to actress Lisa Bonet (of TV's *Cosby Show*), 1987-1993. Son of actress Roxie Roker (1929-1995), who played Helen Willis in TV's *The Jeffersons*.

DATE	PK	WK	TITLE	LABEL	RA
08/26/91	4	17	It Ain't Over Til It's Over .... Virgin		2
02/10/92	36	2	Stand By My Woman .... Virgin		
05/31/93	---	RA	Are You Gonna Go My Way .... Virgin		4
09/27/93	---	RA	Believe .... Virgin		3
12/20/93	---	RA	Heaven Helps .... Virgin		11
11/27/95	20	10	Rock And Roll Is Dead .... Virgin		24
04/15/96	34	8 h	Can't Get You Off Of My Mind .... Virgin		31
05/03/99	---	RA	Fly Away .... Virgin		7
07/19/99	---	RA	American Woman .... Virgin/Maverick		40

KREVIAZUK, Chantal
Canadian female pop/rock singer born on 05/18/73 in Winnipeg. Injured in a car accident in Italy in 1994.

DATE	PK	WK	TITLE	LABEL	RA
12/30/96	---	RA	God Made Me	Epic	22
01/26/98	---	RA	Surrounded	Columbia	14
02/14/99	22	7	Leaving On A Jet Plane	Columbia	34

Another version peaked at #31 on 12/13/98.

KRIS KROSS
American rap duo formed in 1991 in Atlanta: Chris Kelly (vocals, b. 08/11/78 in Englewood, New Jersey), Chris Smith (vocals, b. 01/10/79 in Atlanta). Known for wearing clothes backward. Appeared in the film *Who's The Man?* and a few TV programs.

DATE	PK	WK	TITLE	LABEL	RA
05/25/92	1(6)	14	Jump	Columbia	13
08/24/92	4	18	Warm It Up	Columbia	25
10/26/92	21	6	I Missed The Bus	Columbia	
09/27/93	4	27	Alright	Columbia	
03/04/96	23	9	Tonite's The Night	Columbia	

KRISTINE

DATE	PK	WK	TITLE	LABEL	RA
01/29/77	31	3	Photo Album	Power Exchange	

KRISTINE W.
American female dance singer born in Pasco, Washington.

DATE	PK	WK	TITLE	LABEL	RA
07/22/96	---	RA	One More Try	RCA	38

KWS
British dance trio from Nottingham, England: Chris King, Winnie Williams, "Mystic Meg" St. Joseph.

DATE	PK	WK	TITLE	LABEL	RA
10/19/92	1(3)	23	Please Don't Go	ffrr	10

KYPER
American male rapper born Randall Kyper in Baton Rouge, Louisiana.

DATE	PK	WK	TITLE	LABEL	RA
10/22/90	27	8	Tic Tac Toe	Atlantic	

L

LA BOUCHE
German pop/dance duo: D. Lane McCray Jr., Melanie Thompson.

DATE	PK	WK	TITLE	LABEL	RA
10/31/94	---	RA	Sweet Dreams	RCA	33
02/26/96	---	RA	Be My Lover	RCA	23
07/08/96	---	RA	Sweet Dreams (re-entry)	RCA	16
12/09/96	---	RA	Fallin' In Love	RCA	10
			Hit Parade: #38 (12/09/96) / 1 wk.		
06/14/98	35	2	You Won't Forget Me	RCA	

LABELLE, Patti

DATE	PK	WK	TITLE	LABEL	RA

American female R&B singer born Patricia Louise Holt on 10/04/44 in Philadelphia. Vocalist of LaBelle, 1961-1976. Appeared in the movie *A Soldier's Story*, as well as many stage productions.

| 07/28/86 | 2(3) | 19 | On My Own * | MCA | |

* Patti LaBelle/Michael McDonald

LAID BACK
Danish pop duo consisting of Tim Stahl (keyboards) and John Guldberg (guitar).

| 04/30/84 | 34 | 12 | Sunshine Reggae | Sire | |
| 07/02/84 | 28 | 3 | White Horse | Sire | |

LAKE, Greg
British male rock singer/bassist/guitarist born on 11/10/48 in Bournemouth, England. Member of the rock groups Emerson, Lake and Palmer, and King Crimson.

| 11/02/77 | 30 | 4 | C'est La Vie | Atlantic | |

LAMOND, George
American male R&B singer born George Garcia on 02/25/67 in Washington, D.C. Raised in the Bronx, New York.

| 03/11/91 | 34 | 5 | No Matter What | Columbia | |

LANDS, Wendy
Canadian female pop/rock singer/songwriter born Wendy Dawn Lands in Montreal.

| 10/07/96 | --- | RA | Little Sins | EMI | 22 |
| 05/26/97 | --- | RA | Angels And Ordinary Men | EMI | 15 |

LANG, Jonny
American male blues rock singer/guitarist born Jon Langseth on 01/29/81 in Fargo, North Dakota. Currently based in Minneapolis.

| 06/23/97 | --- | RA | Lie To Me | A&M | 34 |

LANG, k.d.
Canadian female singer born Katherine Dawn Lang on 11/02/61 in Consort, Alberta. In 1992, she declared her lesbianism raising controversy. Won Juno Awards for Most Promising Female Vocalist in 1985 and Female Vocalist of the Year in 1989.

02/15/88	8	15	Crying *	Virgin	
06/29/92	---	RA	Constant Craving	Sire	18
01/31/94	---	RA	Just Keep Me Movin'	Sire	24
02/05/96	---	RA	If I Were You	Sire	19

* Roy Orbison/k.d. lang

LANOIS, Daniel - see VARIOUS ARTISTS

LARSON, Nicolette

| DATE | PK | WK | TITLE | LABEL | RA |

American female singer born on 07/17/52 in Helena, Montana, raised in Kansas City. Session vocalist for Neil Young, Linda Ronstadt, and Van Halen. Died of cerebral edema on 12/16/97.

| 02/07/79 | 15 | 6 | Lotta Love.. Warner |

LAST, James, Band
German cabaret band led by producer/arranger/conductor James Last, born on 04/17/29 in Bremen, Germany.

| 06/04/80 | 10 | 6 | The Seduction (Love Theme) .... Polydor |

LATOUR
American male house music producer William LaTour from Chicago.

| 07/08/91 | 3(2) | 12 | People Are Still Having Sex........................ Polydor |

LAUPER, Cyndi
American female pop singer/songwriter born Cynthia Anne Stephanie Lauper on 06/22/53 in New York City. Lead singer/songwriter of Blue Angel, a New York rock group, in early-1980's. Appeared in the movies *Vibe* (1988) and *Life with Mikey* (1993). Married actor David Thornton on 11/24/91.

04/02/84	1(6)	24	Girls Just Wanna Have Fun .... Portrait
06/25/84	1(3)	16	Time After Time... Portrait
10/01/84	4	16	She Bop... Portrait
12/17/84	9	12	All Through The Night................................ Portrait
02/04/85	40	2	Money Changes Everything....................... Portrait
07/08/85	5	16	Goonies 'R' Good Enough.......................... Portrait
11/24/86	1(1)	18	True Colors.. Portrait
02/16/87	7	12	Change Of Heart... Portrait
05/04/87	31	7	What's Going On .... Portrait
07/31/89	12	11	I Drove All Night...Epic

LAWRENCE, Joey
American male actor/pop singer born on 04/20/76 in Montgomery, Pennsylvania. Appeared on the television program *Gimme A Break*, 1983-87 and starred in the TV series *Blossom*, 1991-94.

| 05/17/93 | --- | RA | Nothin' My Love Can't Fix .... Impact | 14 |

LE CLICK
Swedish female dance/pop singer Kayo Shekoni. Of Nigerian and Swedish ancestry.

| 06/15/97 | 26 | 11 | Call Me .... Logic |

LED ZEPPELIN
British heavy-metal group formed in 1968 as the New Yardbirds: Jimmy Page (guitar, b. James Patrick Page on 01/09/44 in Heston, England), John Paul Jones (bass, b. John Baldwin on 01/03/46 in Sidcup, England), Robert Plant (vocals, b. 08/20/48 in Bromwich, England), John "Bonzo" Bonham (drums, b. John Henry Bonham on 05/31/48 in Redditch, England). Page was a member of the band's predecessor, The Yardbirds. Re-named Led Zeppelin allegedly by Keith Moon in 1969. Founded Swan Song label in 1974. Plant and family seriously injured in a car accident in Rhodes, Greece on 08/04/75. Group appeared in the 1976 concert movie *The Song Remains The Same*. Bonham died of asphyxiation on 09/25/80 in Windsor, England. Group disbanded in 1980. Plant and Page formed the Honeydrippers in 1984. Page also a member of The Firm, 1984-86. Plant recorded solo.

DATE	PK	WK	TITLE	LABEL RA

| 02/20/80 | 16 | 4 | Fool In The Rain | Swan Song |

LEE, Johnny
American male country singer/songwriter/guitarist born John Lee Ham on 07/03/46 in Texas City, Texas. In 1979, made screen debut in the TV movie *The Girls In The Office*. Married to actor Charlene Tilton, 1982-84.

| 09/27/80 | 17 | 5 | Lookin' For Love | Full Moon |

LEILA K
Swedish female rapper born circa 1972 in Stockholm. Her background is Arabic Muslim.

| 04/30/90 | 17 | 9 | Got To Get | Arista |

LEKAKIS, Paul
American male dance singer/model/dancer born on 10/22/65 in Yonkers, New York.

| 06/22/87 | 2(2) | 15 | Boom Boom (Let's Go Back To My Room) | RCA |

LEN
Canadian pop/hip-hop group from Toronto: siblings Marc "Burger Pimp" Costanzo and Sharon Costanzo, with Halifax, Nova Scotia natives DRock and DJ Mooves. Formed in 1995.

| 08/02/99 | --- | RA | Steal My Sunshine | Work | 1+ |

LENNON, John
British male vocalist/songwriter born John Winston Lennon on 10/09/40 in Liverpool, England. Founding member of The Beatles, 1964-70. Married Cynthia Powell on 08/23/62; their son Julian (a recording artist in 1980's) was born on 04/08/63; divorced Powell on 11/08/68. Married Yoko Ono, daughter in a wealthy Japanese banking family, on 03/20/69. Both Lennon and Ono performed with Eric Clapton, Alan White, and Klaus Voorman as Plastic Ono Band in 1969. Moved to New York City in 1971. Battled with U.S. Immigration, which sought his deportation on the basis of a previous drug arrest and his association with the American political left, 1972-1976. Became permanent resident of U.S. in 1976. Fatally shot on 12/08/80 in New York City. Inducted in Rock and Roll Hall of Fame in 1994.

12/13/80	1(7)	15	(Just Like) Starting Over	Geffen
02/28/81	1(5)	11	Woman	Geffen
05/30/81	5	10	Watching The Wheels	Geffen
02/27/84	11	11	Nobody Told Me	Polydor

LENNON, Julian
British male pop singer/songwriter born John Charles Julian Lennon on 04/08/63 in Liverpool, England. Son of John and Cynthia Lennon. Inspiration of The Beatles' 1968 hit "Hey Jude".

| 12/17/84 | 15 | 12 | Valotte | Atlantic |
| 04/15/85 | 8 | 14 | Too Late For Goodbyes | Atlantic |

LENNOX, Annie
British female singer/songwriter born on 12/25/54 in Aberdeen, Scotland. Lead singer of the Eurythmics.

| 02/06/89 | 7 | 13 | Put A Little Love In Your Heart * | A&M |

DATE	PK	WK	TITLE	LABEL	RA
06/29/92	---	RA	Why...	Arista	8
10/26/92	---	RA	Walking On Broken Glass.............................	Arista	1
03/01/93	---	RA	Little Bird	Arista	4
05/15/95	---	RA	No More "I Love You's"	Arista	1
09/04/95	---	RA	A Whiter Shade Of Pale................................	Arista	31

* Annie Lennox/Al Green

LEVEL 42
British pop band formed in 1980 in London: Mark King (bass, vocals, b. 10/20/58 in Cowes, England), Phil Gould (drums, b. 02/28/57 in Hong Kong), Boon Gould (guitar, b. Roland Gould on 03/04/55 in Shanklin, England), Mike Lindup (keyboards, vocals, b. 03/17/59 in London). The Goulds are brothers, left in 1987; replaced by Alan Murphy (guitar), Gary Husband (drums, vocals). Murphy died of AIDS on 10/19/89.

06/09/86	5	17	Something About You	Polydor
06/29/87	8	15	Lessons In Love..	Polydor
10/12/87	35	5	Running In The Family................................	Polydor

LEVERT
American R&B vocal group formed in 1982 in Cleveland consisting of brothers Gerald (b. 07/13/66) and Sean Levert (b. 09/28/68), and Marc Gordon (b. 09/08/64).

| 11/30/87 | 14 | 14 | Casanova .... | Atlantic |

LEVERT, Gerald
American male R&B singer born on 07/13/66. Member of Levert.

| 10/10/94 | 30 | 9 | I'd Give Anything.. | EastWest |

LEWIS, Donna
Welsh female pop singer from Cardiff.

09/23/96	2(4)	18 h	I Love You Always Forever.........................	Atlantic	1
			SoundScan: #39 (11/17/96) / 1 wk.		
02/03/97	---	RA	Without Love	Atlantic	5

LEWIS, Huey, & The News
American pop/rock band formed in 1979 in Marin County, California: Huey Lewis (vocals, harmonica, b. Hugh Cregg III on 07/05/50 in New York City), Chris Hayes (guitar, b. 11/24/57 in California), Mario Cipollina (bass, b. 11/10/54 in California), Bill Gibson (drums, b. 11/13/51 in California), Sean Hopper (keyboards, b. 03/31/53 in California), Johnny Colla (saxophone, guitar, b. 07/02/52 in California). Lewis and Hopper played in country-rock group Clover before forming The News.

04/24/82	7	8	Do You Believe In Love............................	Chrysalis
12/26/83	14	14	Heart & Soul	Chrysalis
03/26/84	6	14	I Want A New Drug...................................	Chrysalis
07/02/84	9	14	The Heart Of Rock & Roll.........................	Chrysalis
09/17/84	9	10	If This Is It	Chrysalis
09/23/85	3(3)	17	Power Of Love	Chrysalis
10/06/86	3(2)	16	Stuck With You..	Chrysalis
01/26/87	9	15	Hip To Be Square	Chrysalis
03/09/87	27	7	Jacob's Ladder	Chrysalis

DATE	PK	WK	TITLE	LABEL	RA
10/03/88	6	16	Perfect World..	Chrysalis	
07/08/91	12	16	Couple Days Off	EMI	
09/16/91	---	RA	Hit Me Like A Hammer................................	Capitol	27

LFO
American pop vocal trio formed in 1996 in Orlando, Florida: Richard Burton Cronin (b. 08/30/74 in Boston), Devin Lima (b. March 18), Bradley David Fischetti (b. 09/11/75 in New York City). "LFO" stands for "Lyte Funky Ones".

07/25/99	17	2 +	Summer Girls	Arista	38 +

LIA
Canadian female dance singer from Quebec.

10/09/95	29	4	Private Fantasy...	NuMuzik	

LIGHTER SHADE OF BROWN
American Hispanic rap duo from Riversdale, California: Robert "ODM" (One Dope Mexican) Guitterez, Bobby "DTTX" (Don't Try To Xerox) Ramirez.

06/06/94	3(1)	31	Hey D.J.	Mercury	

LIGHTFOOT, Gordon
Canadian male folk-pop singer/songwriter born on 11/17/38 in Orillia, Ontario. Wrote songs for Peter, Paul & Mary, Johnny Cash. Wrote and produced commercial jingles in Toronto, 1958-60. Appeared on CBC-TV's *Country Hoedown*. Received Order of Canada in 1970. Winner of eleven Juno Awards including Male Vocalist of the Year in 1972, 1973, and 1975.

11/06/76	5	19	The Wreck Of The Edmund Fitzgerald	Reprise	
04/30/77	19	10	Race Among The Ruins	Reprise	
04/05/78	18	10	The Circle Is Small	Warner	

LIL' KIM
American female rapper Kimberly Jones from New York City. Member of Junior M.A.F.I.A.

07/20/97	10	15	Not Tonight *	Atlantic	

* Lil' Kim featuring Da Brat, Left Eye, Missy "Misdemenaor" Elliott and Angie Martinez

LIL LOUIS
American male producer/dance club disc jockey Louis Burns, born and raised in Chicago.

01/29/90	32	2	French Kiss	Epic	

LIMAHL
British male singer Chris Hamill. Ex-lead singer of Kajagoogoo.

07/22/85	17	9	Never Ending Story......................................	Capitol	

LINEAR
American dance trio based in Miami: Charlie "Steele" Pennachio (vocals) and Joey Restivo (percussion) (both from New York), and Wyatt Pauley (guitar) (from Ecuador).

DATE	PK	WK	TITLE	LABEL	RA
06/11/90	21	7	Sending All My Love	Warner	15
09/24/90	30	4	Don't You Come Crying	Atlantic	
07/13/92	30	8	TLC	Atlantic	35

LIPPS INC
American dance-funk outfit formed in Minneapolis in 1977: Steven Greenberg (multi-instrumentalist, producer, vocals, b. 10/24/50 in St. Paul, Minnesota), Cynthia Johnson (lead vocals, b. 04/06/56 in St. Paul), David Rivkin (guitar), Tom Riopelle (guitar), Terry Grant (bass), Ivan Rafowitz (keyboards). Johnson was Miss Black Minnesota in 1976.

| 06/04/80 | 1(7) | 13 | Funkytown | Casablanca | |

LISA LISA & CULT JAM With Full Force
American pop-R&B trio formed in 1984 in New York City: Lisa Lisa (vocals, b. Lisa Velez on 01/15/67 in New York City), Spanador (guitar, b. Alex Mosely in 1962 in New York City), Mike Hughes (drums, b. 1963 in New York City).

08/10/87	4	16	Head To Toe	Columbia	
11/16/87	7	13	Lost In Emotion	Columbia	
04/11/94	16	14	Skip To My Lu *	Pendulum	

* Lisa Lisa

LITTLE RIVER BAND
Australian country-pop band formed in Melbourne in 1975: Beeb Birtles (guitar, b. Holland), Graham Goble (guitar, b. 1944, Australia), Glenn Shorrock (lead vocals, b. England), Roger McLachlan (bass, b. New Zealand), Derek Pellicci (drums, b. England), Rick Formosa (guitar, b. Italy). Formosa, McLachlan left in 1977, replaced by David Briggs (guitar, vocals), George McArdale (bass, left in 1979). Wayne Nelson (vocals, bass) joined in 1980. Steve Housden (guitar) replaced Briggs in 1982. John Farnham (vocals, b. England) replaced Shorrock in 1982. Pellicci left in 1985, replaced by Steven Prestwich (drums). David Hirschfelder (keyboards) joined in 1985. In 1988, Farnham, Hirschfelder, Prestwich left; Shorrock, Pellicci returned.

12/14/77	34	4	Help Is On Its Way	Capitol	
04/19/78	30	2	Happy Anniversary	Capitol	
10/18/78	5	12	Reminiscing	Capitol	
04/04/79	18	6	Lady	Capitol	
10/03/79	7	6	Lonesome Loser	Capitol	
01/09/80	12	8	Cool Change	Capitol	
10/24/81	7	9	The Night Owls	Capitol	
02/20/82	13	4	Take It Easy On Me	Capitol	
01/31/83	17	4	The Other Guy	Capitol	
07/18/83	30	3	We Two	Capitol	

LIVE
American rock band formed in 1991 in York, Pennsylvania: Ed Kowalczyk (vocals, b. 07/17/71 in Lancaster, Pennsylvania), Chad Taylor (guitar, b. 11/24/70 in York), Patrick Dahlheimer (bass, b. 05/30/71 in York), Chad Gracey (drums, b. 07/23/71 in York).

| 06/12/95 | --- | RA | Lightning Crashes | Radioactive | 5 |
| 09/29/97 | --- | RA | Turn My Head | Radioactive | 38 |

| DATE | PK | WK | TITLE | LABEL | RA |

LIVING COLOR
American rock band formed in 1983 in Brooklyn, New York: Corey Glover (vocals, b. 11/06/64 in Brooklyn), William Calhoun (drums, b. 07/22/64 in Brooklyn, New York), Vernon Reid (guitar, b. 08/22/58 in London, England), Muzz Skillings (bass, b. Manuel Skillings on 01/06/60 in Queens, New York). Skillings left, Doug Wimbish (bass, b. 09/22/56 in Hartford, Connecticut) joined in 1992.

| 06/12/89 | 30 | 6 | Cult Of Personality | Epic |

LIVING IN A BOX
British pop band based in Sheffield, England consisting of Richard Darbyshire (vocals/guitar, b. 03/08/60 in Stockport, Cheshire, England), Marcus Vere (keyboards, b. 01/29/62) and Anthony Critchlow (drums).

| 09/28/87 | 16 | 12 | Living In A Box | Chrysalis |

L.L. COOL J
American male rapper born James Todd Smith on 08/16/68 in Queens, New York. "L.L. Cool J" stands for Ladies Love Cool James. Appeared in the movies *The Hard Way* (1991) and *Toys* (1992).

05/06/91	14	13	Around The Way Girl	Def Jam	
09/02/91	9	17	Mama Said Knock You Out	Def Jam	
10/14/91	34	10	Six Minutes Of Pleasure	Def Jam	
05/03/93	25	12	How I'm Coming	Def Jam	
07/26/93	20	6	Pink Cookies	Def Jam	
09/27/93	38	2	Stand By Your Man	Def Jam	
03/04/96	14	7	Hey Lover	Def Jam	
10/20/96	3(1)	7	Lougin'	Def Jam	
02/23/97	33	2	Ain't Nobody	Def Jam	
11/09/97	37	2	Phenomenon	Def Jam	23

LOEB, Lisa and Nine Stories
American pop band based in New York: Dallas native Lisa Loeb (vocals, b. circa 1969), Tim Bright (guitar), Joe Quigley (bass), Jonathan Feinberg (drums, left in 1994). Discovered by actor Ethan Hawke. Loeb later pursued solo career.

10/10/94	26	15	Stay (I Missed You)	RCA	3
10/30/95	---	RA	Do You Sleep *	Geffen	5
03/11/96	---	RA	Taffy *	Geffen	39
09/02/96	---	RA	Waiting For Wednesday *	Geffen	12
01/19/98	---	RA	I Do *	Geffen	6

* Lisa Loeb

LOGGINS, Kenny
American male pop/rock singer/songwriter born 01/07/48 in Everett, Washington. Member of Gator Creek and Second Helping in the late-1960's. Member of the duo Loggins and Messina (1972-76). Went solo in 1977.

11/01/78	5	14	Whenever I Call You "Friend"	Columbia
02/06/80	12	6	This Is It	Columbia
10/18/80	8	9	I'm Alright	Columbia
10/30/82	7	7	Don't Fight It	Columbia
04/02/84	5	21	Footloose	Columbia

DATE	PK	WK	TITLE	LABEL	RA
08/06/84	36	2	I'm Free .... Columbia		
05/20/85	34	3	Vox Humana .... Columbia		
09/01/86	8	14	Danger Zone .... Columbia		
10/10/88	31	4	Nobody's Fool .... Columbia		

LONDON, Paul

10/20/96	14	9	Ti Amo .... Capitol		

LONDON QUIREBOYS
British hard rock band led by vocalist Spike and featuring bassist Nigel Mogg.

07/30/90	10	13	7 O'Clock .... Capitol		29
12/03/90	27	9	Hey You .... Capitol		

LONDONBEAT
British/American soul-pop band consisting of vocalists Jimmy Helms, George Chandler, Jimmy Chambers, and multi-instrumentalist/producer Willy M. Helms and Chandler are American, Chambers is from Trinidad.

04/08/91	1(4)	13	I've Been Thinking About You .... Anxious		1
07/29/91	19	12	A Better Love .... Anxious		3
05/17/93	---	RA	You Bring On The Sun .... RCA		34
05/01/95	---	RA	Come Back .... RCA		7

LOPEZ, Jennifer
American female pop singer/actress born on 07/24/70 in the Bronx, New York. Starred in several movies including *Selena* and *Anaconda*. Provided voice for the animated movie *Antz*.

06/13/99	2(3)	11 +	If You Had My Love 550/Work		1+

LORD TARIZ & PETER GUNZ
American rap duo from New York City: Sean Hamilton ("Lord Tariq") and Peter Panky ("Peter Gunz").

04/05/98	6	21	Deja Vu (Uptown Baby) .... Columbia		

LORENZ, Trey
American male pop-soul singer born on 01/19/69 in Florence, South Carolina. Attended New York's Fairleigh Dickinson University, earned advertising degree. Back-up singer for Mariah Carey.

11/30/92	14	15	Someone To Hold .... Epic		11
02/22/93	19	6	Photograph Of Mary .... Epic		

LORING, Gloria
American female pop singer/actress born on 12/10/46. Played Liz Curtis on the TV soap opera *Days Of Our Lives*. Married to actor Alan Thicke for 14 years.

09/22/86	5	16	Friends And Lovers * .... Epic		

* Gloria Loring & Carl Anderson

DATE	PK	WK	TITLE	LABEL	RA

LOS DEL MAR
Canadian dance group from Quebec featuring singer/dancer Wil Veloz (b. circa 1969 in Cuba, raised in New York City). Veloz left by 1996.

07/24/95	1(9)	31	Macarena	Quality	34

LOS DEL RIO
Spanish flamenco guitar duo formed in 1962: Antonio Romero Monge and Rafael Ruiz Perdigones (both born in 1948 in Dos Hermanas, Spain). "Macarena" was remixed by the Miami production team of the Bayside Boys (consisting of Carlos De Yarza and Mike Triay).

11/03/96	8	10	Macarena (Bayside Boys Mix)	RCA	

LOS LOBOS
American Hispanic group formed in East Los Angeles in 1973: Cesar Rosas (guitar, vocals, b. 09/26/54 in Los Angeles), David Hidalgo (guitar, accordion, vocals, b. 10/06/54 in Los Angeles), Luis "Louie" Perez (drums, b. 01/29/53 in Los Angeles), Conrad R. Lozano (bass, b. 03/21/51 in Los Angeles). Steve Berlin (saxophone, b. 09/14/55 in Philadelphia) joined in 1984.

09/21/87	1(7)	20	La Bamba	Warner	
12/14/87	27	8	Come On, Let's Go	Warner	

LOS UMBRELLOS
Danish dance trio from Copenhagen: Al Agami (vocals; from the African country of Lado), Mai-Britt Grondahl Vingsoe (vocals), Grith Hojfeldt (vocals).

10/19/97	30	4	No Tengo Dinero	Virgin	

LOST & PROFOUND
Canadian pop/rock group from Calgary: Lisa Boudreau (vocals), Terry Tompkins (guitar, vocals), Curtis Driedger, Allen Baekeland, David Quinton-Steinberg (drums), Anton Evans (bass), Vic D'Arsie (keyboards).

04/18/94	---	RA	Miracles Happen	Polydor	31
08/01/94	---	RA	Invitation	Polydor	29

LOUGHEED, Lisa
Canadian female dance-pop singer born circa 1969. Provided voice for soundtrack of the animated series *The Raccoons*.

05/11/92	31	9	World Love	WEA	31
08/17/92	---	RA	Love Vibe	WEA	28
11/16/92	---	RA	Love You By Heart	WEA	36
09/20/93	---	RA	Won't Give Up My Music	WEA	30

LOUIE LOUIE
American male pop singer/songwriter/dancer Louie Cordero from Southern California. Played Madonna's boyfriend in "Borderline" video.

07/30/90	15	9	Sitting In The Lap Of Luxury	WTG	15

LOVE & ROCKETS

DATE	PK	WK	TITLE	LABEL	RA

British alternative rock trio formed in 1985: Daniel Ash (guitar, vocals, b. 07/31/57 in Northampton, England), and brothers Kevin Haskins (drums, b. 07/19/60 in Northampton) and David J (bass, b. David J. Haskins 04/24/57 in Northampton). All three were members of Bauhaus, 1979-84. The group name comes from the underground comic book series.

DATE	PK	WK	TITLE	LABEL	RA
12/23/85	17	13	Ball Of Confusion	Vertigo	
09/11/89	3(1)	13	So Alive	Vertigo	

LOVE & SAS
Canadian female R&B-dance duo from Toronto: Vancouver native Lovena Fox and Toronto native Saskia Garel. Garel is originally from Jamaica; in the Toronto theatrical production of *Rent*.

DATE	PK	WK	TITLE	LABEL	RA
03/30/92	29	8	Call My Name	RCA	40
07/13/92	---	RA	Don't Stop Now	RCA	13
10/12/92	---	RA	Once In A Lifetime	RCA	38

LOVE INC.
Canadian dance trio: Simone Demny, Chris Sheppard, Brad Daymond. Sheppard is a member of BKS and is a disc jockey with a nationally-syndicated dance radio program.

DATE	PK	WK	TITLE	LABEL	RA
04/19/98	6	16	Broken Bones	Vik.	12
09/20/98	19	21	You're A Superstar	Vik.	14
12/21/98	---	RA	Homeless	Vik.	33
06/07/99	---	RA	Who Do You Love	Vik.	37

LOVERBOY
Canadian rock group based in Vancouver, formed in 1978 in Calgary: Mike Reno (vocals), Paul Dean (guitar), Matt Frenette (drums), Doug Johnson (keyboards), Scott Smith (bass). Won the Juno Award for Group of the Year, 1982, 1983, 1984.

DATE	PK	WK	TITLE	LABEL	RA
10/18/80	17	6	The Kid Is Hot Tonite	Columbia	
03/07/81	5	14	Turn Me Loose	Columbia	
01/16/82	10	11	Working For The Weekend	Columbia	
05/29/82	10	12	When It's Over	Columbia	
08/08/83	14	10	Hot Girls In Love	Columbia	
10/24/83	28	3	Queen Of The Broken Hearts	Columbia	
11/11/85	9	12	Lovin' Every Minute Of It	Columbia	
11/17/86	30	8	Heaven In Your Eyes	Columbia	
11/02/87	24	10	Notorious	Columbia	

LOWE, Nick
British male pop singer born on 03/25/49 in Woodbridge, England. Member of Rockpile. Married to Carlene Carter, 1979-90.

DATE	PK	WK	TITLE	LABEL	RA
09/19/79	9	18	Cruel To Be Kind	Columbia	

LOX, The
American rap trio from Yonkers, New York: Shawn "Sheek" Jacobs, Jayson Phillips, David Styles. "LOX" stands for "Living Off Experience".

DATE	PK	WK	TITLE	LABEL	RA
05/03/98	21	11	Money, Power & Respect	Arista	

| DATE | PK | WK | TITLE | LABEL | RA |

L.T.D.
American R&B-funk band formed in 1968 in Greensboro, North Carolina. Led by vocalist Jeffrey Osborne (b. 03/09/48 in Providence, Rhode Island). Core members included Osborne, Billy Osborne (vocals, keyboards), Henry Davis (keyboards), Jimmie Davis (keyboards), John McGhee (guitar). Band included large horn section. Osborne left in 1980; later went solo. Disbanded in 1982. L.T.D. stands for Love, Togetherness and Devotion.

| 02/08/78 | 10 | 8 | (Every Time I Turn) Back In Love Again | A&M | |

LUBA
Canadian female singer/songwriter born Luba Kowalchyk in 1958 in Montreal. Won the Juno Award for Female Vocalist of the Year in 1985, 1986, 1987.

04/04/83	16	9	Everytime I See Your Picture	Capitol	
03/04/85	26	6	Storm Before The Calm	Capitol	
07/21/86	15	14	How Many (Rivers To Cross)	Capitol	
02/08/88	4	19	When A Man Loves A Woman	Capitol	
12/11/89	11	14	Giving Away A Miracle	Capitol	
03/12/90	22	7	Little Salvation	Capitol	15

LUCAS
Danish male rapper/producer born Lucas Secon, circa 1970 in Copenhagen.

| 12/12/94 | --- | RA | Lucas With The Lid Off | Warner | 12 |

LUHRMANN, Baz
Australian male film director BazMark Luhrmann born in 1964.

| 06/20/99 | 32 | 1 | Everybody's Free (To Wear Sunscreen) | Capitol | 16 |

LUKE featuring 2 Live Crew
American rap group formed in Miami in 1985: Luke Skyywalker (vocals, b. Luther Campbell on 12/22/60 in Miami), Fresh Kid Ice (vocals, b. Christopher Wong-Won in Trinidad), Brother Marquis (vocals, b. Mark Ross in New York City), Mr. Mixx (DJ, b. David Hobbs in California).

| 09/17/90 | 18 | 5 | Banned In The USA | Luke Skyywalker | |

LYELL, Ray, & The Storm
Canadian rock band led by Ray Lyell from Hamilton, Ontario.

| 05/28/90 | --- | RA | Carry Me | Spy | 34 |

LYNN, Cheryl
American female R&B singer born on 03/11/57 in Los Angeles. Discovered after appearing on the television program *The Gong Show*.

| 03/07/79 | 19 | 4 | Got To Be Real | Columbia | |

LYNNE, Jeff
British male rock singer born on 12/30/47 in Birmingham, England. Leader of the Electric Light Orchestra and The Move. Otis Wilbury of the Traveling Wilburys.

DATE	PK	WK	TITLE	LABEL	RA
08/13/90	31	6	Every Little Thing .... Reprise		29

LYNYRD SKYNYRD
American rock band formed in 1966 in Jacksonville, Florida. Original line-up consisted of Ronnie Van Zant (vocals, b. 01/15/49), Gary Rossington (guitar), Allen Collins (guitar), Billy Powell (keyboards), Leon Wilkeson (bass), Bob Burns (drums). Members met in high school; named band after Leonard Skinner, their gym teacher. Van Zant and Gaines killed in an airplane crash on 10/20/77 in Gillsburg, Mississippi. Group disbanded soon after. Rossington and Collins in Rossington Collins Band, 1980-82. Collins paralyzed after a car crash in 1986, died of pneumonia on 01/23/90 in Jacksonville. Group re-formed in 1991 with three new members.

| 03/22/78 | 31 | 4 | What's Your Name .... MCA | |

M

M
British techno-pop band formed in Paris, France, and led by folk singer Robin Scott. Featured various session musicians including Level 42's Mark King. Name taken from the signs for Paris Metro.

| 10/03/79 | 1(12) | 28 | Pop Muzik .... Sire | |

M PEOPLE
British pop/dance trio from Manchester: Mike Pickering (keyboards, programming; b. March 1958 in Manchester), Heather Small (vocals, b. 01/20/65 in London), Paul Heard (keyboards, programming; b. 10/05/60 in Hammersmith, London).

| 07/04/94 | --- | RA | Movin' On Up .... RCA | 8 |
| 11/14/94 | --- | RA | One Night In Heaven .... RCA | 27 |

MacGREGOR, Mary
American female pop singer born on 05/06/48 in St. Paul, Minnesota.

| 02/12/77 | 4 | 16 | Torn Between Two Lovers .... Ariola | |

MacISAAC, Ashley
Canadian fiddle player born on 02/24/75 in Creignish, Nova Scotia. Won the 1996 Juno Award for Best New Solo Artist.

| 05/29/95 | 5 | 28 | Square Dance Song (I Wanna Go Higher) * ... A&M | |
| 03/18/96 | 28 | 8 h | Sleepy Maggie .... A&M | 13 |

* BKS featuring Ashley MacIsaac

MacLEAN, Kenny
Canadian male rock singer born in Scotland. Keyboardist/bassist of Platinum Blonde.

| 04/23/90 | --- | RA | Don't Look Back .... Justin | 31 |

MAD COBRA
Jamaican male reggae rapper Ewart Everton Brown born on 03/31/68 in Kingston, raised in St. Mary's, Jamaica.

DATE	PK	WK	TITLE	LABEL	RA
02/15/93	1(3)	15	Flex	Columbia	

MADNESS
British pop group formed in 1978 in London: Graham "Suggs" McPherson (vocals, b. 01/13/61 in Hastings, England), Lee Thompson (saxophone, b. 10/05/57 in St. Pancras, England), Chris Foreman (guitar, b. 08/08/58 in London), Mike Barson (keyboards, b. 05/21/58 in London), Daniel Woodgate (drums, b. 10/19/60 in London), Mike Bedford (bass, b. 08/24/61 in London), Chas Smash (emcee, trumpet, b. Cathal Smythe on 01/14/59). Disbanded in 1986, re-forms in 1988.

DATE	PK	WK	TITLE	LABEL	RA
08/22/83	4	14	Our House	Geffen	

MADONNA
American female pop singer/songwriter/actress born Madonna Louise Veronica Ciccone on 08/16/58 in Bay City, Michigan. Attended the University of Michigan for dance studies. Moved to New York City in 1978 and became member of Alvin Ailey dance troupe. Member of the band Breakfast Club in the early-1980's. Married to actor Sean Penn from 1985 to 1989. Appeared in the movies *Vision Quest, Desperately Seeking Susan, Shanghai Surprise, Dick Tracy, Evita*. Appeared in Broadway play *Speed-The-Plow*. Oversaw the film *Truth or Dare*, a documentary of her Blond Ambition Tour. In 1992, signed a multi-million-dollar deal with Time Warner releasing all albums, films, and books under her Maverick production company. Released controversial nude photo book *Sex* in 1992. Her daughter Lourdes Maria Ciccone was born on 10/14/96; the father is her boyfriend, trainer Carlos Leon.

DATE	PK	WK	TITLE	LABEL	RA
02/06/84	34	4	Holiday	Sire	
09/10/84	22	8	Borderline	Sire	
11/12/84	16	9	Lucky Star	Sire	
01/21/85	1(3)	20	Like A Virgin	Sire	
04/29/85	5	15	Material Girl	Sire	
06/10/85	4	17	Crazy For You	Geffen	
07/22/85	19	12	Angel	Sire	
10/14/85	5	12	Dress You Up	Sire	
06/16/86	1(5)	20	Live To Tell	Sire	
08/18/86	1(6)	19	Papa Don't Preach	Sire	
11/24/86	2(5)	15	True Blue	Sire	
02/23/87	4	12	Open Your Heart	Sire	
06/15/87	1(1)	18	La Isla Bonita	Sire	
09/07/87	1(2)	16	Who's That Girl	Sire	
11/16/87	2(1)	15	Causing A Commotion	Sire	
05/15/89	1(3)	16	Like A Prayer	Sire	
08/07/89	4	13	Express Yourself	Sire	
11/06/89	11	14	Cherish	Sire	
04/23/90	22	6	Keep It Together	Sire	8
05/21/90	1(3)	11	Vogue	Sire	1
08/27/90	2(1)	11	Hanky Panky	Sire	3
12/24/90	2(4)	12	Justify My Love	Sire	1
04/22/91	4	12	Rescue Me	Sire	3
08/17/92	1(6)	19	This Used To Be My Playground	Sire	1
11/16/92	2(1)	17	Erotica	Maverick	2
02/01/93	1(2)	22	Deeper And Deeper	Maverick	2
04/05/93	5	13	Bad Girl	Maverick	8
09/20/93	1(1)	15	Rain	Maverick	3
08/15/94	13	37	I'll Remember	Maverick	1
11/07/94	1(9)	46	Secret	Maverick	1

DATE	PK	WK	TITLE	LABEL	RA
04/24/95	1(1)	36	Take A Bow	Maverick	2
05/29/95	17	21	Bedtime Stories	Maverick	24
10/02/95	9	31	Human Nature	Maverick	33
02/12/96	17	9	You'll See	Maverick	3
06/17/96	31	4 h	Love Don't Live Here Anymore	Maverick	22
11/10/96	2(1)	24	You Must Love Me	Maverick	24
02/16/97	1(6)	32	Don't Cry For Me Argentina	Maverick	3
03/08/98	2(6)	32	Frozen	Maverick	1
06/14/98	7	14	Ray Of Light	Maverick	3
			Domestic version above. Import edition peaked at #29 on 09/27/98.		
08/30/98	18	4	Drowned/Substitute For Love	Maverick	
11/01/98	6	14	The Power of Good-bye	Maverick	6
			Another version peaked at #37 on 12/13/98.		
05/09/99	6	13 +	Nothing Really Matters	Maverick	13
			"CD2" peaked at #19 on 03/07/99; "CD1" peaked at #26 on 03/07/99. Another version peaked at #27 on 03/21/99.		
07/05/99	---	RA	Beautiful Stranger	Maverick	3+

MAESTRO FRESH-WES

Canadian male rapper born Wes Williams in 1968 in Toronto. Raised in North York. First rap artist to perform at the Juno Awards. Began recording as Maestro in 1998.

DATE	PK	WK	TITLE	LABEL	RA
04/09/90	1(1)	18	Let Your Backbone Slide	Attic	11
06/25/90	5	13	Drop The Needle	Attic	24
09/03/90	29	3	Private Symphony	Attic	
07/22/91	5	15	Conductin' Thangs	Attic	33
11/22/98	13	10	Stick To Your Vision *	Attic	
04/11/99	26	4	416/905 (T.O. Party Anthem) **	Attic	39

* Maestro
** Maestro featuring Latoya & Miranda

MAISONETTES, The

DATE	PK	WK	TITLE	LABEL	RA
08/15/83	28	6	Heartache Avenue	Quality	

MAJIK

DATE	PK	WK	TITLE	LABEL	RA
10/11/98	15	2	Sky's The Limit	EMI	

MANCHESTER, Melissa

American female pop-MOR singer/songwriter born on 02/15/51 in Bronx, New York. Enrolled in a seminar taught by Paul Simon in New York University in the early-1970's. Former backup vocalist for Bette Midler. In the movie *For The Boys* and the TV show *Blossom*.

DATE	PK	WK	TITLE	LABEL	RA
08/23/75	4	11	Midnight Blue	Arista	
04/04/79	16	2	Don't Cry Out Loud	Arista	
10/16/82	6	12	You Should Hear How She Talks About You	Arista	

MANGIONE, Chuck

DATE	PK	WK	TITLE	LABEL RA

American male flugelhornist/composer born 11/29/40 in Rochester, New York.

| 06/14/78 | 7 | 12 | Feels So Good | A&M |

MANHATTAN TRANSFER
American vocal group formed in New York City in 1972: Tim Hauser (b. 1940 in Troy, New York), Alan Paul (b. 1949 in Newark, New Jersey), Janis Siegel (b. 1953 in Brooklyn, New York), Laurel Masse (b. 1954). Masse replaced by Cheryl Bentyne (b. 01/17/54 in Mount Vernon, Washington) in 1979.

12/27/75	12	4	Operator	Atlantic
04/30/80	24	1	Twilight Zone	Atlantic
08/01/81	5	9	Boy From New York City	Atlantic

MANHATTANS
American R&B vocal group formed in 1961 in Jersey City, New Jersey. Line-up in mid-1970's: Winfred "Blue" Lovett (b. 11/16/43 in New Jersey), Edward "Sonny" Bivins (b. 01/15/42 in New Jersey), Kenneth Kelley (b. 01/09/43 in New Jersey), Richard Taylor (b. 1940, d. 12/07/87), Gerald Alston (b. 11/08/42). Taylor left in 1977 to pursue religious interests, became Islam. Regina Belle recorded with the group in 1987, went solo in 1988. Alston went solo in 1988.

| 07/31/76 | 2(4) | 17 | Kiss And Say Goodbye | Columbia |
| 09/13/80 | 9 | 2 | Shining Star | Columbia |

MANILOW, Barry
American male pop-MOR singer/songwriter born Barry Alan Pinkus on 06/17/46 in Brooklyn, New York. Hired as musical director of the CBS-TV show *Callback*; conducted and arranged for Ed Sullivan productions. Was pianist/arranger/musical director for Bette Midler. Wrote commercial jingles for various companies. Produced Dionne Warwick's "I'll Never Love This Way Again".

09/06/75	24	4	Could It Be Magic	Arista
01/24/76	1(1)	14	I Write The Songs	Arista
05/22/76	19	9	Trying To Get The Feeling	Arista
11/13/76	36	3	This One's For You	Arista
03/19/77	7	16	Weekend In New England	Arista
08/13/77	4	15	Looks Like We Made It	Arista
12/14/77	32	2	Daybreak	Arista
04/19/78	9	12	Can't Smile Without You	Arista
08/23/78	3(4)	16	Copacabana (At The Copa)	Arista
11/15/78	15	10	Ready To Take A Chance	Arista
12/12/79	21	6	Ships	Arista
05/09/83	13	8	Some Kind Of Friend	Arista
01/30/84	15	7	Read 'Em And Weep	Arista

MANN, Herbie
American jazz flutist born Herbert Jay Soloman on 04/16/30 in Brooklyn, New York.

| 06/28/75 | 18 | 3 | Hijack | Atlantic |

MANN, Manfred
South African/British rock group formed in 1964 in England. Re-formed in 1971 in England as Manfred Mann's Earth Band: Manfred Mann (keyboards, b. Michael Lubowitz, on 10/21/40 in Johannesburg), Mick Rogers (vocals, guitar, b. Michael Oldroyd on 09/20/46), Colin Pattenden (bass), Chris Slade (drums, b. 10/30/46). Chris Thompson (guitar, vocals, b. 03/09/48 in New Zealand), Dave Flett (guitar),

DATE	PK	WK	TITLE	LABEL	RA

Pat King (bass), Steve Waller (guitar), John Lingwood (drums) joined in 1975. Waller, Flett departed soon after joining.

| 02/12/77 | 1(4) | 16 | Blinded By The Light | Warner | |
| 04/16/84 | 16 | 8 | Runner | Arista | |

MANNING, Dayna
Canadian female pop/rock singer born in 1980 in Stratford, Ontario.

| 11/10/97 | --- | RA | My Addiction | EMI | 25 |

MANSON, Marilyn
American male shock rocker born Brian Warner on 01/05/69 in Canton, Ohio. Once produced by Trent Reznor of Nine Inch Nails.

| 04/27/97 | 10 | 24 | Get Your Gunn | Interscope | |
| 05/04/97 | 5 | 32 | Lunchbox | Interscope | |

MARCY PLAYGROUND
American alternative rock band from New York City: John Wozniak (vocals, songwriter), Dylan Keefe (bass), Dan Reiser (drums). Named after a children's playground at Marcy Open School in Minneapolis, the school Wozniak attended as a youth.

| 05/04/98 | --- | RA | Sex & Candy | Capitol | 3 |

MARDONES, Benny
American male pop vocalist from Savage, Maryland.

| 09/13/80 | 5 | 4 | Into The Night | Polydor | |

MARIE, Teena
American white female R&B singer/songwriter/keyboardist/guitarist/producer/actor born Mary Christine Brockert 03/05/57 in Santa Monica, California. Raised in Venice, California.

| 04/22/85 | 15 | 11 | Lovergirl | Epic | |

MARKY MARK & THE FUNKY BUNCH
American pop band formed in Boston in 1991: Marky Mark (vocals, b. Mark Wahlberg on 06/05/71 in Dorchester, Massachusetts), Scott Russ (dancer, b. 04/06/69 in Boston), Hector Barrons (dancer, b. 05/14/67 in Boston), Terry Yancy (DJ, b. 09/11/69 in Boston). Wahlberg is the younger brother of Donnie Wahlberg of the New Kids On The Block. Wahlberg starred in the films *The Basketball Diaries* (1995) and *Boogie Nights* (1997).

10/14/91	3(1)	13	Good Vibrations	Interscope	10
01/20/92	---	RA	Wildside	Interscope	30
11/16/92	17	6	You Gotta Believe *	Interscope	

* Marky Mark

MARLEY, Bob, and the Wailers

DATE	PK	WK	TITLE	LABEL	RA

Jamaican reggae band formed in 1963 in Jamaica featuring Bob Marley (vocals, guitar, b. Robert Nesta Marley, on 02/06/45 in St. Ann's Parish, Jamaica), the most celebrated reggae singer in history. Marley died of cancer on 05/11/81 in Miami.

| 11/30/92 | 22 | 9 | Iron Lion Zion | Island | |

MARMALADE
Scottish pop quintet led by vocalist Dean Ford (Thomas McAleese).

| 06/05/76 | 38 | 1 | Falling Apart At The Seams | Ariola | |

M.A.R.R.S.
British electro-funk band: Martyn Young, Steve Young, Alex Kane, Rudi Kane, and mixers Chris "CJ" Mackintosh and DJ Dave Dorrell. The Youngs are brothers; the Kanes are brothers as well.

| 02/29/88 | 1(4) | 21 | Pump Up The Volume | Vertigo | |

MARSHALL TUCKER BAND
American Southern rock band formed in 1971 in Spartanburg, South Carolina: Toy Caldwell (steel guitar, vocals, b. 1948), George McCorkle (rhythm guitar), Doug Gray (lead vocals, b. 05/02/48 in Spartanburg), Paul Riddle (drums), Jerry Eubanks (multi-instrumentalist, vocals, b. 03/09/50 in Spartanburg), Tommy Caldwell (bass, vocals, b. 1950). Tommy died of an automobile accident on 04/28/80 in Spartanburg; replaced by Franklin Wilkie; Toy died of respiratory failure on 02/23/94 in Moore, South Carolina.

| 07/02/77 | 17 | 9 | Heard It In A Love Song | Capricorn | |

MARSHALL, Amanda
Canadian female rock singer born on 08/29/72 in Toronto. Discovered by singer Jeff Healey.

01/15/96	---	RA	Let It Rain	Epic	14
04/01/96	3(2)	14 h	Birmingham	Epic	10
07/29/96	5	17 h	Fall From Grace	Epic	11
10/28/96	13	16 h	Beautiful Goodbye	Epic	16
05/12/97	---	RA	Dark Horse	Epic	12
07/14/97	---	RA	Sitting On The Top Of The World	Epic	8
11/03/97	---	RA	Trust Me (This Is Love)	Epic	37
01/25/99	---	RA	Believe In You	Epic	16
07/05/99	---	RA	Love Lift Me	Epic	13+

MARTHA & THE MUFFINS
Canadian pop group from Toronto formed in 1977: Martha Johnson (vocals, keyboards), Martha Ladly (vocals, keyboards, trombone), Carl Finkle (bass), brothers Mark Gane (guitar) and Tim Gane (drums), Andy Haas (saxophone).

| 07/09/80 | 6 | 8 | Echo Beach | Virgin | |
| 06/23/86 | 39 | 2 | Song In My Head * | Current/Wake | 14 |

* M+M

MARTIKA
American female pop singer/writer/actor/dancer born Marta Marrera on 05/18/69, based in Los Angeles. Starred in the TV program *Kids, Incorporated*. In the 1982 movie musical *Annie*.

DATE	PK	WK	TITLE	LABEL	RA
09/04/89	4	15	Toy Soldiers .... Columbia		
11/13/89	21	6	I Feel The Earth Move........................... Columbia		
10/14/91	5	15	Love...Thy Will Be Done .... Columbia		3
02/27/92	24	8	Martika's Kitchen .... Columbia		15

MARTIN, Billie Ray
German female dance singer raised in Hamburg, Germany. Former lead singer of the group, Electribe 101.

07/24/95	9	24	Your Loving Arms .... Warner		

MARTIN, Marilyn
American female pop singer raised in Louisville, Kentucky. Background vocalist for Kenny Loggins, Stevie Nicks, and Tom Petty.

12/16/85	1(2)	23	Separate Lives * .... Atlantic		

   * Phil Collins/Marilyn Martin

MARTIN, Moon
American male pop singer/songwriter/guitarist John Martin from Oklahoma. Wrote Robert Palmer's "Bad Case Of Loving You".

10/17/79	27	4	Rolene .... Capitol		

MARTIN, Ricky
Puerto Rican male Latin pop singer/actor born Enriquez Martin IV on 12/24/71 in San Juan, Puerto Rico. Played Miguel on the television soap opera *General Hospital*. Member of the group Menudo, 1984-89.

| 05/02/99 | 1(3) | 14 + | Livin' La Vida Loca................................... Columbia | | 1+ |
| 05/16/99 | 25 | 13 | Cup of Life... Sony Import | | |

MARTINEZ, Nancy
Canadian female dance-pop singer/actress from Montreal.

03/02/87	35	5	For Tonight... Atlantic		

MARTINEZ, Rosco
Cuban male rock singer born in Oriente Holguin, Cuba. Moved to Plantation, Florida at age six.

05/16/94	---	RA	Neon Moonlight.. RCA		37

MARTINO, Al
American male vocalist born Alfred Cini on 10/07/27 in Philadelphia. Popular recording artist of 1960's. Portrayed singer Johnny Fontane in the 1972 movie, *The Godfather*.

12/13/75	13	6	Volare .... Capitol		

MARX, Richard
American male pop-MOR singer/songwriter born Richard Noel Marx on 09/16/63 in Chicago. Began singing commercials jingles at age five. Backup singer for Lionel Richie in the early-1980's. Married

DATE	PK	WK	TITLE	LABEL	RA

Animotion lead singer/actress Cynthia Rhodes on 01/08/89.

DATE	PK	WK	TITLE	LABEL	RA
09/07/87	9	11	Don't Mean Nothing	EMI-Manhattan	
11/30/87	36	4	Should've Known Better	EMI-Manhattan	
04/18/88	9	13	Endless Summer Nights	EMI-Manhattan	
08/15/88	25	11	Hold On To The Nights	EMI-Manhattan	
07/24/89	7	14	Satisfied	EMI	
10/02/89	1(2)	16	Right Here Waiting	EMI	
12/18/89	8	15	Angelia	EMI	
03/19/90	12	8	Too Late To Say Goodbye	EMI	9
07/02/90	34	2	Children Of The Night	EMI	7
12/09/91	19	16	Keep Coming Back	Capitol	2
05/11/92	5	19	Hazard	Capitol	4
07/27/92	---	RA	Take This Heart	Capitol	10
12/07/92	---	RA	Chains Around My Heart	Capitol	27
03/14/94	---	RA	Now And Forever	Capitol	7
09/19/94	---	RA	The Way She Loves Me	Capitol	20

MARY JANE GIRLS
American female funk-dance-R&B group: Joanne McDuffie, Candice Ghant, Kim Wuletich, Yvette Marina. Formed and produced by Rick James.

DATE	PK	WK	TITLE	LABEL
07/29/85	6	8	In My House	Quality

MAS, Carolyne
American female rock singer/guitarist from the Bronx, New York.

DATE	PK	WK	TITLE	LABEL
10/17/79	37	4	Stillsane	Mercury

MASE
American male rapper born Mason Betha on 08/27/78 in Jacksonville, Florida.

DATE	PK	WK	TITLE	LABEL	RA
09/14/97	2(11)	46	Mo Money, Mo Problems *	Arista	14
11/23/97	3(1)	21	Feel So Good	Arista	14
12/21/97	2(6)	31	Been Around The World **	Arista	
			Another version peaked at #9 on 12/07/97.		
03/22/98	12	11	What You Want	Arista	
09/13/98	17	4	Lookin' At Me	Arista	
09/27/98	21	4	Top Of The World ***	Atlantic	27
11/08/98	17	13	Love Me ****	Arista	

* Notorious B.I.G. featuring Puff Daddy & Mase
** Puff Daddy & the Family (featuring Notorious B.I.G. and Mase)
*** Brandy featuring Mase
**** 112 featuring Mase

MASON, Dave
British male pop singer/composer/guitarist born on 05/10/46 in Worcester, England. Member of Traffic. Joined Fleetwood Mac in 1993.

DATE	PK	WK	TITLE	LABEL
11/30/77	14	10	We Just Disagree	Columbia

DATE	PK	WK	TITLE	LABEL	RA

MASSE, Julie
Canadian female pop/Francophone singer born on 06/03/70 in Ville Lemoyne, Quebec. Mother of Corey Hart's two children.

01/16/95	---	RA	One More Moment	Surge	12

MATCHBOX 20
American rock group formed as Tabitha's Secret in the early-1990's in Orlando, Florida: Rob Thomas (vocals), Kyle Cook (lead guitar), Adam Gaynor (guitar), Brian Yale (bass), Paul Doucette (drums).

11/10/97	---	RA	Push	Lava	7
04/27/98	---	RA	3 am	Lava	3
07/20/98	---	RA	Real World	Lava	7
03/29/99	---	RA	Back 2 Good	Atlantic	17

MATHIS, Johnny
American male R&B-MOR-pop singer born John Royce Mathis on 09/30/35 in San Francisco. Enrolled in professional opera lessons at age 13; studied to become physical education teacher. In 1956, invited to the Olympic track trials in Berkeley. First recordings were jazz-influenced; Columbia A&R head convinced him to perform pop ballads. Sang "Without Us", theme from TV's *Family Ties*.

06/14/78	9	12	Too Much, Too Little, Too Late *	Columbia	
07/11/79	39	2	The Last Time I Felt Like This **	Columbia	

* Johnny Mathis/Deniece Williams
** Johnny Mathis/Jane Olivor

MATTHEWS, Dave, Band
South African/American rock band: Dave Matthews (vocals, guitar), Leroi Moore (saxophone), Boyd Tinsley (violin), Stefan Lessard (bass), Carter Beauford (drums).

06/26/95	---	RA	What Would You Say	RCA	21
11/06/95	---	RA	Ants Marching	RCA	28
06/24/96	24	5 h	Too Much	RCA	
10/21/96	27	8	So Much To Say	RCA	33

MATTHEWS, Ian
British male vocalist born Ian Matthew MacDonald in Lincolnshire, England in 06/16/46. Founder of Matthews' Southern Comfort.

02/21/79	18	6	Shake It	Mushroom	

MAX-A-MILLION
American dance trio based in Chicago consisting of Jamaican-raised Duran Esteyez (b. Trinidad), A'Lisa B (b. Leland, Mississippi), Tommye (b. Chicago). Produced by 20 Fingers.

09/25/95	7	13	Fat Boy	RCA	31
03/18/96	---	RA	Sexual Healing	RCA	17

MAXWELL
American male R&B singer born on 05/23/73 in Brooklyn. Of West Indian-Puerto Rican heritage.

DATE	PK	WK	TITLE	LABEL RA
06/27/99	26	5	Fortunate	Columbia

McCAIN, Edwin
American male rock singer/songwriter/guitarist born in Charleston, South Carolina. Back-up band also named Edwin McCain: Larry Chaney (guitar), Scott Bannevich (bass), Dave Harrison (drums) and Craig Shields (saxophone).

08/02/99	---	RA	I Could Not Ask For More	Atlantic 27+

McCALL, C.W.
American male country/pop singer born William Fries on 11/15/28 in Audubon, Iowa. Worked for Bozell and Jacobs advertising agency in Omaha, Nebraska when he created character "C.W. McCall" for an ad campaign for the Mertz Baking Company.

01/31/76	1(2)	12	Convoy	MGM

McCANN, Denise
Canadian female disco singer born in 1950 in Iowa. In the early-1980's, became lead singer of the Headpins and married Randy Bachman of Bachman Turner Overdrive.

02/05/77	31	4	Tattoo Man	Polydor
08/13/77	36	1	I Don't Wanna Forget You	Polydor

McCANN, Peter
American male singer/songwriter from Connecticut. Wrote Jennifer Warnes' "The Right Time Of The Night".

09/07/77	4	14	Do You Wanna Make Love	20th Century

McCARTNEY, Paul, & Wings
British male pop/rock singer/songwriter/bassist born James Paul McCartney 06/18/42 in Liverpool. Founder, vocalist of The Beatles. Married American photographer Linda Eastman on 03/12/69. Only ex-Beatle to have successful permanent band, Wings (1971-81). Original line-up: Paul, Linda McCartney (keyboards, vocals, b. Linda Louise Eastman on 09/24/42 in Scarsdale, New York), Denny Laine (guitar, vocals, keyboards, b. Brian Hines on 10/29/44), Denny Seiwell (drums). Guitarist Henry McCullough joined in 1972, he and Seiwell left in 1973. Jimmy McCulloch (guitar, b. 1953 in Glasgow, d. 09/27/79 in London), Geoff Britton (drums), Joe English (drums, b. 02/07/49 in Rochester, New York) joined in 1974. English and McCulloch left in 1976. Drummer Steve Holly and vocalist Laurence Juber joined in 1978. McCartney appeared in the 1984 movie *Give My Regards To Broad Street*. Copyright owner of entire Buddy Holly catalogue. Linda died of breast cancer on 04/17/98 in Arizona.

07/26/75	1(2)	10	Listen To What The Man Said	Capitol
12/27/75	15	2	Venus And Mars Rock Show	Capitol
06/05/76	1(3)	14	Silly Love Songs	Capitol
08/28/76	2(3)	14	Let 'Em In	Capitol
04/30/77	22	6	Maybe I'm Amazed	Capitol
07/09/77	23	9	Seaside Woman *	Epic
03/08/78	2(2)	32	Girl's School/Mull Of Kintyre	Capitol
06/14/78	4	16	With A Little Luck	Capitol
06/13/79	10	16	Goodnight Tonight	Columbia
08/22/79	24	8	Getting Closer	Columbia
10/03/79	13	4	Arrow Through Me	Columbia
06/11/80	5	9	Coming Up	Columbia

DATE	PK	WK	TITLE	LABEL	RA
05/29/82	1(5)	14	Ebony & Ivory **	Columbia	
09/11/82	8	9	Take It Away ***	Columbia	
12/18/82	8	7	The Girl Is Mine ****	Epic	
01/16/84	1(1)	19	Say Say Say *****	Columbia	
03/12/84	11	10	So Bad ***	Columbia	
12/24/84	11	12	No More Lonely Nights ***	Columbia	
02/03/86	24	6	Spies Like Us ***	Capitol	
08/07/89	23	10	My Brave Face ***	Capitol	
03/08/93	32	4	Hope Of Deliverance ***	Capitol	27
07/21/97	---	RA	The World Tonight	Capitol	21

* Suzy And The Red Stripes
** Paul McCartney (with Stevie Wonder)
*** Paul McCartney
**** Michael Jackson/Paul McCartney
***** Paul McCartney/Michael Jackson

McCLINTON, Delbert
American male singer born on 11/04/40 in Lubbock, Texas. Leader of The Ron-Dels.

DATE	PK	WK	TITLE	LABEL
02/28/81	14	5	Giving It Up For Your Love	Capitol

McCOO, Marilyn, & Bill Davis Jr.
American husband-wife R&B-pop duo consisting of Marilyn McCoo (b. 09/30/43 in Jersey City, New Jersey) and Bill Davis Jr. (b. 06/26/40 in St. Louis). Original members of Fifth Dimension; left group to form duo in 1975. McCoo hosted TV's *Solid Gold*, 1981-84.

DATE	PK	WK	TITLE	LABEL
01/08/77	11	16	You Don't Have To Be A Star	ABC

McCOY, Van
American male pianist/producer/songwriter/singer born on 01/06/44 in Washington, D.C. Produced and wrote for Aretha Franklin, Gladys Knight and the Pips, Peaches and Herb, Melba Moore. Died of a heart attack on 07/06/79 in Englewood, New Jersey.

DATE	PK	WK	TITLE	LABEL
08/09/75	1(1)	12	The Hustle *	Avco

* Van McCoy & The Soul City Symphony

McCRAE, Gwen
American female R&B singer born on 12/21/43 in Pensacola, Florida. First recorded with husband George who later became her manager.

DATE	PK	WK	TITLE	LABEL
08/16/75	10	8	Rockin' Chair	RCA

McDONALD, Michael
American male singer/keyboardist born on 12/02/52 in St. Louis. Former member of Steely Dan; former vocalist and keyboardist of The Doobie Brothers.

DATE	PK	WK	TITLE	LABEL
10/16/82	7	7	I Keep Forgettin'	Warner
07/28/86	2(3)	19	On My Own *	MCA
10/06/86	25	9	Sweet Freedom	MCA

| DATE | PK | WK | TITLE | LABEL | RA |

* Patti LaBelle/Michael McDonald

McDOWELL, Ronnie
American male country singer/songwriter/guitarist born Ronald Dean McDowell on 03/26/50 in Fountain Head, Tennessee.

| 10/05/77 | 2(6) | 16 | The King Is Gone | GRT | |

McFADDEN & WHITEHEAD
American R&B vocal/songwriting duo: Gene McFadden (b. 1948 in Philadelphia) and John Whitehead (b. 1948 in Philadelphia).

| 08/22/79 | 26 | 4 | Ain't No Stoppin' Us Now | Philadelphia International | |

McFERRIN, Bobby
American male jazz vocalist born on 03/11/50 in New York City. Human one-man band; able to vocally reproduce musical sounds and tones normally made by musical instruments. Sang TV's *The Cosby Show* theme and several TV commercials.

| 10/24/88 | 1(4) | 19 | Don't Worry, Be Happy | EMI-Manhattan | |

McGUINN, Roger
American male vocalist/guitarist born James Joseph McGuinn III on 07/13/42 in Chicago. Former member of The Byrds and McGuinn, Clark & Hillman.

| 04/29/91 | 35 | 1 | King Of The Hill | Arista | |

McINTYRE, Joey
American male pop singer born on 12/31/72 in Needham, Massachusetts. Former member of New Kids On The Block.

| 03/14/99 | 14 | 14 | Stay The Same | Columbia | |

MCJ & COOL G
Canadian dance-rap-R&B duo based in Montreal, originally from Halifax, Nova Scotia: James "MCJ" McQuaid, Richard "Cool G" Gray.

11/26/90	33	6	So Listen	Capitol	27
02/04/91	6	15	Smooth As Silk	Capitol	25
04/05/93	37	4	No Sexx With My Sister	Capitol	

McKENNITT, Loreena
Canadian female Celtic/folk singer/harpist born on 02/17/57 in Morden, Manitoba. Founded the Quinlan Road label in 1985. Currently based in Stratford, Ontario.

| 03/22/98 | 16 | 23 | The Mummer's Dance | Quinlan Road | 13 |

McKENZIE, Bob & Doug
Canadian comic act consisting of comedians/actors Rick Moranis (b. 04/18/54 in Toronto) and Dave Thomas (b. 06/20/49 in St. Catharines, Ontario). Doug (played by Thomas) and Bob (played by Moranis) were characters on the TV show *SCTV*, portraying "typical" Canadians. Moranis later starred in movies such as *Ghostbusters*, *Spaceballs*, and *Honey, I Shrunk The Kids*. Thomas is the brother of singer Ian Thomas.

DATE	PK	WK	TITLE	LABEL	RA
12/26/81	5	7	Take Off .... Anthem		

McKNIGHT, Brian
American male R&B singer/songwriter born on 06/05/69 in Buffalo, New York.

05/17/93	6	14	Love Is * .... Polydor		
10/04/93	19	22	One Last Cry .... Mercury		31
04/26/98	12	11	Anytime .... Motown		13
01/31/99	21	5	Hold Me .... Motown		

* Vanessa Williams & Brian McKnight

McLACHLAN, Sarah
Canadian female rock singer/guitarist/pianist born on 01/28/68 in Halifax, Nova Scotia. Currently lives in Vancouver. Founder of the all-female Lilith Fair tour. Won the 1998 Juno Award for Female Vocalist of the Year.

11/25/91	---	RA	Into The Fire .... Nettwerk		40
12/13/93	---	RA	Posession... Nettwerk		36
11/14/94	---	RA	Good Enough .... Nettwerk		19
09/04/95	---	RA	I Will Remember You............................... Nettwerk		23
09/21/97	32	2	Building A Mystery .... Nettwerk		1
02/16/98	---	RA	Sweet Surrender .... Nettwerk		4
07/12/98	7	12	Adia... Nettwerk		3
02/08/99	---	RA	Angel... Nettwerk		13
07/26/99	---	RA	I Will Remember You............................... Nettwerk		14+
			Live version; recorded in Porland, Oregon.		

McLAREN, Malcolm
British male vocalist born on 01/22/46 in London. Formed the punk groups, the Sex Pistols and Bow Wow Wow. Fostered early careers of Boy George and Adam Ant.

01/14/85	31	1	Madam Butterfly .... Virgin		

McLEAN, Don
American male singer/songwriter/poet born on 10/02/45 in New Rochelle, New York. McLean was the subject of Roberta Flack's 1973 hit, "Killing Me Softly With His Song".

03/28/81	6	7	Crying... Millennium		

McLEAN, Penny
German female singer born in Klagenforn, Germany. Member of Silver Convention.

02/28/76	31	4	Lady Bump .... Columbia		

M.C. LYTE
American female rapper born Lana Moorer on 10/11/71 in Queens, New York. Raised in Brooklyn.

02/23/97	11	15	Cold Rock A Party .... Elektra		

M.C. MIKER "G" AND DEE JAY SVEN

DATE	PK	WK	TITLE	LABEL	RA

Dutch male vocal/instrumental rap duo.

| 05/04/87 | 17 | 16 | Holiday Rap | Power/Electric | |

McNARLAND, Holly
Canadian female singer born circa 1973. Based in Vancouver. Won the 1998 Juno Award for Best New Solo Artist.

| 08/18/97 | --- | RA | Numb | MCA | 35 |

MEAT LOAF
American male rock singer/actor born Marvin Lee Aday on 09/27/51 in Dallas. Appeared in several plays including a West Coast production of *Hair*, and in films like *Americathon* (1979), *Roadie* (1980), and *Spice World* (1997).

06/28/78	4	16	Two Out Of Three Ain't Bad	Epic	
11/29/78	6	20	Paradise By The Dashboard Light	Epic	
02/07/79	29	6	You Took The Words	Epic	
11/01/93	---	RA	I'd Do Anything For Love (But I Won't Do That)	MCA	4
03/28/94	---	RA	Rock & Roll Dreams Come Through	MCA	8
06/13/94	---	RA	I'd Lie For You (And That's The Truth)	MCA	12

MECO
American male disco producer/multi-instrumentalist born Meco Monardo on 11/29/39 in Johnsonburg, Pennsylvania. A total of 75 musicians played in "Star Wars Theme/Cantina Band".

| 10/05/77 | 1(6) | 26 | Star Wars Theme/Cantina Band | Millennium | |
| 03/22/78 | 13 | 10 | Theme From "Close Encounters Of A Third Kind" | Millennium | |

MEDEIROS, Glenn
American male pop singer born on 06/24/70 and raised in Lawai, Hawaii.

| 07/20/87 | 2(1) | 19 | Nothing's Gonna Change My Love For You | A&M | |
| 08/27/90 | --- | RA | She Ain't Worth It * | MCA | 3 |

* Glenn Medeiros featuring Bobby Brown

MEDINA, Carol
Canadian female dance singer/songwriter/actor born on 10/25/66 in Melbourne, Australia.

03/28/94	24	22	And The Song Goes	Quality	
10/03/94	---	RA	I Had A Dream	Quality	35
05/22/95	25	14	Tell Me You Love Me	Quality	39
07/03/95	24	10	You Don't Know (Where My Lips Have Been)	Quality	35
04/08/96	---	RA	You Never Done It Like That	Quality	29

MEDLEY, Bill
American male singer born on 09/19/40 in Santa Ana, California. Member of Righteous Brothers.

| 01/25/88 | 2(1) | 16 | (I've Had) The Time Of My Life * | RCA | |

DATE	PK	WK	TITLE	LABEL	RA

* Bill Medley/Jennifer Warnes

MEDLEY, Sue
Canadian female singer born in 1962 in Courtenay, British Columbia. Won the 1991 Juno Award for Most Promising Female Vocalist.

07/09/90	38	4	Dangerous Times	Mercury	19
08/27/90	33	4	That's Life	Mercury	31
07/13/92	31	7	When The Stars Fall	Mercury	34

MEISNER, Randy
American male singer/bassist born on 03/08/46 in Scottsbluff, Nebraska. Member of Poco (1968-69), Rick Nelson's Stone Canyon Band (1969-71), Eagles (1971-77).

| 03/21/81 | 16 | 2 | Hearts On Fire | Epic | |

MEL B - see ELIOTT, Missy "Misdemeanor"

MELANIE C - see ADAMS, Bryan

MELENDEZ, Lisette
American female dance singer from East Harlem, New York.

| 11/18/91 | 35 | 4 | A Day In My Life | CBS Associated | |

MELLENCAMP, John Cougar
American male rock singer/songwriter born on 10/07/51 in Seymour, Indiana. Christened Johnny Cougar by David Bowie's manager, Tony DeFries. Married model Elaine Irwin on 09/05/92. Directed and starred in the 1992 film *Falling From Grace*.

04/25/81	6	7	Ain't Even Done With The Night *	Riva	
07/17/82	1(1)	15	Hurt So Good *	Riva	
09/18/82	1(5)	14	Jack & Diane *	Riva	
12/05/83	12	15	Crumblin' Down	Riva	
02/13/84	11	9	Pink Houses	Riva	
06/25/84	20	7	The Authority Song	Riva	
10/28/85	4	10	Lonely Ol' Night	Riva	
01/27/86	21	9	Small Town	Riva	
05/05/86	6	14	R.O.C.K. In The U.S.A.	Riva	
11/16/87	1(1)	15	Paper In Fire	Mercury	
02/01/88	4	16	Cherry Bomb	Mercury	
04/18/88	12	11	Check It Out	Mercury	
07/25/88	14	10	Rooty Toot Toot	Mercury	
12/05/88	14	12	Rave On	Elektra	
06/26/89	8	14	Pop Singer	Mercury	
10/09/89	36	1	Jackie Brown	Mercury	
11/25/91	7	20	Get A Leg Up **	Mercury	9
04/06/92	26	6	Again Tonight **	Mercury	20
10/04/93	---	RA	What If I Came Knocking	Mercury	16
12/13/93	14	18	Human Wheels **	Mercury	6
08/15/94	3(5)	53	Wild Night **	Mercury	4
01/16/95	18	19	Dance Naked **	Mercury	8

DATE	PK	WK	TITLE	LABEL	RA
09/09/96	1(8)	18	Key West Intermezzo (I Saw You First)	Mercury	3
02/10/97	---	RA	Just Another Day	Mercury	11
01/12/98	---	RA	Without Expression	Mercury	26
11/09/98	---	RA	Your Life Is Now	Columbia	16

* John Cougar
** John Mellencamp

MELLOW MAN ACE
American Hispanic rapper born Ulpiano Sergio Reyez on 04/12/67 in Cuba. Raised in Southgate, California. Brother of "Sen Dog" of Cypress Hill.

| 09/24/90 | 24 | 8 | Mentirosa | Capitol | |

MELVIN, Harold, And The Blue Notes
American R&B vocal group formed in Philadelphia in 1955. By 1975, line-up included Harold Melvin (b. 06/25/39 in Philadelphia), Bernard Wilson, Jesse Gillis Jr., Franklin Peaker, Roosevelt Brodie, Lawrence Brown, Teddy Pendergrass, Jerry Cummings. Pendergrass left in 1976, replaced by David Eho. Dwight Johnson and Bill Spratley joined in 1977. Melvin died of a stoke on 03/24/97.

| 06/21/75 | 15 | 2 | Bad Luck (Part 1) | Columbia | |

MEN AT WORK
Australian rock group formed in 1979 in Melbourne, Australia: Colin Hay (vocals, guitar, b. 06/29/53 in Scotland), Ron Strykert (guitar, vocals, b. 08/18/57 in Australia), Jerry Speiser (drums, vocals, b. Australia), Greg Ham (saxophone, flute, vocals, keyboards, b. 09/27/53 in Australia), John Rees (bass, vocals, b. Australia).

07/24/82	4	15	Who Can It Be Now?	Columbia	
10/23/82	1(3)	14	Down Under	Columbia	
01/24/83	19	5	Be Good Johnny	Columbia	
06/13/83	6	15	Overkill	Columbia	
08/08/83	26	7	It's A Mistake	Columbia	
10/24/83	26	5	Dr. Heckyll & Mr. Jive	Columbia	

MEN WITHOUT HATS
Canadian pop band formed in 1980 in Montreal consisting of Ivan Doroschuk (vocals/songwriter) and his two brothers, Stefan (guitar/violin), and Colin (keyboards), and Allan McCarthy (drums). Doroschuk later pursued a solo career under the name "Ivan".

04/11/83	24	7	The Safety Dance	Backstreet	
02/22/88	1(1)	20	Pop Goes The World	Mercury	
04/11/88	34	4	Moonbeam	Mercury	
12/25/89	21	10	Hey Men	Mercury	
02/26/90	30	5	In The 21st Century	Mercury	33

MENDES, Sergio
Brazilian conductor/pianist born on 02/11/41 in Niteroi, Brazil. Leader of Brasil '66, a Latin-styled musical group in the late-1960's.

| 08/08/83 | 7 | 12 | Never Gonna Let You Go | A&M | |

| DATE | PK | WK | TITLE | LABEL | RA |

MENS ROOM
Canadian pop group consisting of three female vocalists. Formed by then-Solid Gold President Neill Dixon.

| 06/13/83 | 20 | 7 | Sign Of The Times | Solid Gold | |

MENTAL AS ANYTHING
Australian rock group led by keyboardist Andrew "Greedy" Smith. Consists of five members.

| 07/03/82 | 20 | 2 | Too Many Times | Solid Gold | |

MERCHANT, Natalie
American female pop-rock singer/songwriter born on 10/26/63 in Jamestown, New York. Lead singer of the 10,000 Maniacs, 1981-1993.

11/06/95	---	RA	Carnival	Elektra	10
03/18/96	18	14 h	Wonder	Elektra	3
08/19/96	7	17 h	Jealousy	Elektra	9
07/06/98	---	RA	Kind & Generous	Elektra	19

METALLICA
American heavy metal band formed in 1981 in Los Angeles: James Alan Hetfield (vocals, guitar, b. 08/03/63 in Los Angeles), Ron McGovney (bass), Dave Mustaine (guitar, b. 09/13/61 in La Mesa, California), Lars Ulrich (drums, b. 12/16/63 in Gentoss, Copenhagen, Denmark). Mustaine, McGovney left in 1983, replaced by Kirk Hammett (guitar, b. 11/18/62 in San Francisco) and Clifford Lee Burton (bass, b. 02/10/62). Burton died on 09/27/86 in a bus accident in Sweden; replaced by Jason Newsted (bass, b. 03/04/63 in Battle Creek, Michigan).

10/21/91	1(2)	17	Enter Sandman	Elektra	
02/17/92	11	15	The Unforgiven	Elektra	
05/04/92	4	11	Nothing Else Matters	Elektra	30
07/20/92	20	7	Whenever I May Roam	Elektra	
11/23/92	34	5	Sad But True	Elektra	
11/03/96	7	23	Hero Of The Day	Elektra	
11/03/96	21	15	Until It Sleeps	Elektra	
			Hit Parade: #23 (07/22/96) / 10 wks.		
02/23/97	14	9	King Nothing	Elektra	
11/16/97	4	18	The Memory Remains	Elektra	

METHENY, Pat, Group - see BOWIE, David

METHOD MAN
American male rapper Clifford Smith born in Staten Island, New York. Member of Wu-Tang Clan.

09/25/95	1(5)	37	I'll Be There For You/You're All I Need (To Get By) *	Def Jam	
			Re-entered and peaked at #40 on 08/17/97.		
11/20/95	7	12	How High	Def Jam	
03/07/99	25	3	Judgement Day (Remixes)	Def Jam	

* Method Man featuring Mary J. Blige

DATE	PK	WK	TITLE	LABEL	RA

METRO, Tanto
Jamaican male reggae singer Mark Wolfe.

| 07/25/99 | 9 | 5+ | Everyone Falls In Love * .... VP | | |

* Tanto Metro & Devonte

MIAMI SOUND MACHINE - see ESTEFAN, Gloria/Miami Sound Machine

MICHAEL, George
British male pop singer/songwriter born Georgios Kyriacos Panayiotou on 06/25/63 in London. Former member of the duo, Wham!, 1983-86. Began taking legal action to terminate his contract with Sony Music in 1992 due to dispute over marketing of Michael's image; court rejected Michael's claim in June 1994; repealed two months later. Charged with lewd conduct in Los Angeles in 1998.

06/23/86	3(4)	14	A Different Corner .... Columbia	
05/18/87	9	13	I Knew You Were Waiting (For Me) * .... Arista	
08/31/87	2(3)	19	I Want Your Sex .... Columbia	
11/30/87	1(12)	19	Faith .... Columbia	
03/28/88	3(2)	16	Father Figure .... Columbia	
07/11/88	2(1)	13	One More Try .... Columbia	
09/26/88	6	13	Monkey .... Columbia	
01/23/89	7	14	Kissing A Fool .... Columbia	
11/19/90	1(1)	19	Praying For Time .... Columbia	1
01/21/91	2(2)	19	Freedom .... Columbia	2
03/04/91	15	6	Waiting For The Day .... Columbia	9
03/16/92	1(1)	25	Don't Let The Sun Go Down On Me ** ..... Columbia	2
07/27/92	3(3)	11	Too Funky .... Columbia	1
06/14/93	---	RA	Somebody To Love *** .... Hollywood	4
08/02/93	---	RA	Killer/Papa Was A Rollin' Stone .... Hollywood	12
04/01/96	7	6	Jesus To A Child .... Dreamworks	7
			Hit Parade: #9 (03/08/96) / 11 wks.	
06/10/96	5	15 h	Fastlove .... Dreamworks	1

* Aretha Franklin/George Michael
** George Michael & Elton John
*** George Michael And Queen

MICHEL, Pras
Haitian male rapper/producer born Prakazrel Michel on 10/19/72 in Haiti. Member of the Fugees.

07/12/98	4	29	Ghetto Supastar (That Is What You Are)* .. Interscope	13
			Another version peaked at #35 on 06/28/98.	

* Pras Michel featuring ODB & introducing Mya

MICHEL'LE
American female R&B singer Michel'le Toussant from Los Angeles, born circa 1972. Former backing singer of the World Class Wreckin Cru.

| 04/23/90 | 35 | 1 | No More Lies .... Ruthless | |

| DATE | PK | WK | TITLE | LABEL | RA |

MIDDLETON, Tom
Canadian male singer.

| 08/07/76 | 9 | 15 | I Need A Harbour .... Columbia | |

MIDLER, Bette
American female pop-MOR singer/actress born on 12/01/45 in Paterson, New Jersey. Raised in Oahu, Hawaii. Appeared in Broadway's *Fiddler On The Roof* and a Seattle production of *Tommy*. Won the Grammy Award for Best New Artist in 1973. Barry Manilow was her piano accompanist in the 1970's. Her memoirs of her first world tour, *A View from a Broad*, was a best-selling book. Appeared in the movies *The Rose* (1979), *Down and Out in Beverly Hills* (1986), *Ruthless People* (1987), *Beaches* (1989), and *For The Boys* (1991).

07/23/80	2(1)	9	The Rose .... Atlantic	
07/10/89	2(3)	19	Wind Beneath My Wings .... Atlantic	
12/24/90	---	RA	From A Distance .... Atlantic	12

MIDNIGHT OIL
Australian rock band formed in 1976 in Sydney: Peter Garrett (vocals), Rob Hirst (drums, vocals), Jim Moginie (guitar, keyboards), Martin Rotsey (guitar), Peter Gifford (bass). Garrett ran for a seat in the Australian senate in 1984 as a Nuclear Disarmament Party candidate. Garrett is a university graduate in law, but never practised as a lawyer.

06/27/88	1(2)	20	Beds Are Burning .... Columbia	
05/07/90	2(2)	15	Blue Sky Mine .... Columbia	7
05/24/93	34	4	Truganini .... Columbia	12
01/17/94	38	1	Land * .... Cargo	

* Crash Vegas/Hothouse Flowers/Daniel Lanois/Midnight Oil/Tragically Hip

MIGHTY DUB KATS
British male dance singer born Norman Cook 07/13/63 in Bromley, England. Also recorded under other names such as Fatboy Slim and Beats International.

| 02/05/96 | 22 | 14 | Magic Carpet Ride .... Mercury | |
| 03/16/97 | 36 | 2 | It's Just Another .... Quality | |

MIGHTY MIGHTY BOSSTONES
American rock band from Boston: Dicky Barrett (vocals), Joe Gittleman (bass), Joe Sirois (drums), Nate Albert (guitar), Kevin Lenear (horns), Tim Burton (horns), Dennis Brockenborough (horns), Ben Carr (dancer).

| 11/03/97 | --- | RA | The Impression That I Get .... Mercury | 23 |

MIGHTY POPE
Canadian male disco singer, Jamaican-born Earl Heedram.

| 03/05/77 | 30 | 2 | Whatever Goes Around .... RCA | |

MIKE & THE MECHANICS
British pop group formed in 1985: Mike Rutherford (guitar, bass, vocals, b. 10/02/50 in Guildford, England), Paul Carrack (vocals, keyboards, b. 04/22/51 in Sheffield, England), Paul Young (vocals, b.

DATE	PK	WK	TITLE	LABEL	RA

06/17/47 in Manchester), Adrian Lee (keyboards, b. 09/09/47 in London), Peter Van Hook (drums, b. 06/04/50 in London). Carrack was a member of Ace and Squeeze.

03/31/86	15	10	Silent Running	Atlantic	
07/21/86	16	11	All I Need Is A Miracle	Atlantic	
04/10/89	4	17	The Living Years	Atlantic	

MILES, Robert
Italian dance club disc jockey/instrumentalist born Roberto Concina on 11/03/69 in Fluerier, Switzerland. His parents are Italian. Moved to Italy at age 10.

10/20/96	9	16	Children	Arista	7
			Hit Parade: #38 (07/29/96) / 4 wks.		
10/20/96	24	5	Fable	Arista	
11/24/96	2(3)	37	One & One	Arista	15

MILLER, Steve, Band
American blues-rock band formed in 1966 in San Francisco featuring vocalist/guitarist/songwriter Steve Miller (b. 10/05/43 in Milwaukee). At age 12, founded blues band, The Marksmen. At University of Wisconsin, founded blues-rock band, the Ardells, later known as the Fabulous Night Trains. All three bands included singer Boz Scaggs. Miller studied literature at the University of Copenhagen.

07/24/76	4	13	Take The Money And Run *	Capitol	
11/13/76	2(1)	16	Rock N' Me *	Capitol	
03/05/77	13	13	Fly Like An Eagle *	Capitol	
07/09/77	3(1)	16	Jet Airliner	Capitol	
10/19/77	40	2	Jungle Love	Capitol	
12/28/77	14	14	Swingtown	Capitol	
07/24/82	1(2)	17	Abracadabra	Capitol	
08/23/93	---	RA	Wide River	Polydor	23

* Steve Miller

MILLI VANILLI
German/French pop group formed in 1988 in Munich, Germany by producer Frank Farian, best known for forming Boney M. Rob Pilatus (b. 06/08/65 in New York City), Fabrice Morvan (b. 05/14/66 in France) originally known as vocalists. The band's 1990 Juno Award for International Album of the Year and 1990 Best New Artist Grammy were withdrawn when it was revealed the duo were not the singers on the Milli Vanilli album *Girl You Know It's True*. Actual singers were U.S. Army veteran Charles Shaw, John Davis, and Brad Howe. Farian released an album by the trio without Pilatus and Farian (who, in turn, recorded an album using their own vocals). Pilatus died of a drug overdose on 04/02/98 in Frankfurt, Germany.

05/15/89	1(1)	18	Girl You Know It's True	Arista	
08/14/89	1(1)	16	Baby Don't Forget My Number	Arista	
11/06/89	1(1)	19	Girl I'm Gonna Miss You	Arista	
12/11/89	1(4)	19	Blame It On The Rain	Arista	
03/26/90	2(2)	13	All Or Nothing	Arista	5

MILLS, Darby
Canadian female rock singer from Vernon, British Columbia. Former lead singer of the Headpins.

DATE	PK	WK	TITLE	LABEL	RA
08/26/91	---	RA	Cry To Me	WEA	34
02/24/92	---	RA	Give It All Up	WEA	40

MILLS, Frank
Canadian male pianist/composer/arranger born on 06/27/42 in Montreal. Former member of The Bells, 1968-70.

04/18/79	16	18	Music Box Dancer	Polydor	
11/28/79	13	14	Peter Piper	Polydor	

MILSAP, Ronnie
American male country singer/songwriter/multi-instrumentalist born on 01/16/46 in Robbinsville, North Carolina. Blind since birth.

11/16/77	16	6	It's Almost Like A Song	RCA	
07/04/83	27	2	Stranger In My House	RCA	

MINISTRY
American alternative rock band formed in Chicago in 1981 led by Al "Hypo Luxa" Jourgensen (vocals, guitar, b. Allen Jourgensen on 10/09/58 in Havana, Cuba). Personnel fluctuated over the years.

03/18/96	21	12	Fall	Interscope	

MINOGUE, Kylie
Australian female pop singer/actress born on 05/28/68 in Melbourne, Australia. Played Charlene Ramsey in the Australian television show *Neighbours*, 1986-89.

11/14/88	25	1	I Should Be So Lucky	Geffen	
12/26/88	1(4)	23	The Locomotion	Geffen	

MINOR, Morris, & The Majors
British male dance vocal group.

07/18/88	28	9	Stutter Rap	Virgin	

MINT CONDITION
American R&B-funk group formed in 1986 in Minneapolis: Stokley Williams (vocals), Homer O'Dell, Larry Waddell, Jeffrey Allen, Keri Lewis, Ricky Kinchen.

04/27/92	32	6	Breaking My Heart	Island	31

MIRACLES
American R&B group formed in 1957 in Detroit, Michigan. Line-up in 1975: William Griffin (lead vocals, b. 08/15/50 in Detroit), Ronnie White (baritone, b. 04/05/39 in Detroit), Bobby Rogers (tenor, b. 02/19/40 in Detroit), Warren "Pete" Moore (bass, b. 11/19/39 in Detroit). Popular in the late-1950's, 1960's, and early-1970's. Smokey Robinson was lead vocalist, 1957-72.

01/31/76	24	5	Love Machine	Motown	

MR. BIG
American pop-rock band formed in 1988 in Los Angeles: Eric Martin (vocals, b. 10/10/60 in Long Island, New York), Paul Gilbert (guitar, b. 11/06/66 in Pittsburgh), Billy Sheehan (bass, b. 03/19/53 in Buffalo),

DATE	PK	WK	TITLE	LABEL	RA

Pat Torpey (drums, b. 12/13/59).

03/30/92	---	RA	To Be With You	Atlantic	1
06/15/92	---	RA	Just Take My Heart	Atlantic	18
11/29/93	---	RA	Wild World	Atlantic	9

MR. MISTER
American pop-rock band formed in 1982 in Los Angeles: Richard Page (vocals), Steve George (keyboards), Pat Mastelotto (drums), Steve Farris (guitar). Farris left in 1989; replaced by Buzz Feiten. Page is a popular songwriter; wrote Madonna's "I'll Remember".

01/20/86	2(1)	14	Broken Wings	RCA	
04/07/86	2(1)	16	Kyrie	RCA	
06/16/86	30	7	Is It Love?	RCA	
10/19/87	31	2	Something Real (Inside Me/Inside You)	RCA	

MR. PRESIDENT
German dance trio from Bremen, Germany: Daniela "Lady Danii" Haak (b. circa 1975), Judith "T" Hildebrandt (b. circa 1978), Delroy "Lazy Dee" Rennalds (b. circa 1968).

01/05/97	24	13	Coco Jamboo	Warner	39

MITCHELL, Kim
Canadian male rock singer/songwriter/guitarist born on 07/10/52 in Sarnia, Ontario. Former lead singer of the band Max Webster. Won Juno Awards for Most Promising Male Vocalist of the Year in 1983 and Male Vocalist of the Year in 1990. "Go For Soda" was the 1985 theme for Mothers Against Drunk Driving in the United States.

09/24/84	34	6	Go For Soda	Alert	
01/14/85	28	1	All We Are	Alert	
08/25/86	20	12	Patio Latterns	Alert	
03/23/87	25	8	Easy To Tame	Alert	
09/18/89	15	12	Rock N' Roll Duty	Alert	
12/11/89	23	12	Rocklandwonderland	Alert	
02/05/90	33	4	Expedition Sailor	Alert	27
10/22/90	28	8	I Am A Wild Party	Alert	38
07/27/92	36	7	America	Alert	19

MITSOU
Canadian female Francophone/pop singer born Mitsou-Miel-Rioux Gélinas on 09/01/70 in Loretteville, Quebec.

10/05/92	---	RA	Deep Kiss	Isba	19
02/08/93	---	RA	Heading West	Hollywood	32
03/07/94	---	RA	Everybody Say Love	Isba	29
06/20/94	---	RA	Loving Me Is Not A Sin	Isba	14

MIX MASTER MIKE

02/07/99	26	2	Suprize Packidge	Asphodel	

MODERN TALKING

DATE	PK	WK	TITLE	LABEL	RA

German dance/pop duo formed in 1984 in Berlin: Dieter Bohlen (b. 02/07/54 in Berne, Switzerland), Thomas Anders (b. 03/01/63 in Münstermaifeld/Eifel, Germany). Disbanded in 1987. Reunited in 1998.

| 03/23/87 | 34 | 6 | Brother Louie | Ariola | |

MOFFATTS, The
Canadian pop group from Victoria, British Columbia consisting of brothers Scott (b. Scott Andrew Moffatt on 03/30/83 in Winnipeg), Clint (b. Clinton Thomas John Moffatt), Dave (b. David Michael William Moffatt), Bob (b. Robert Franklin Peter Moffatt) Moffatt. Clint, Dave, and Bob are triplets born on 03/08/84 in Vancouver. Performed as a country act, 1994-98.

05/17/98	5	14	I'll Be There For You	EMI	12
10/19/98	---	RA	Miss You Like Crazy	EMI	19
03/15/99	---	RA	Girl Of My Dreams	EMI	20
05/16/99	36	3	Until You Loved Me	Capitol	20

MOIST
Canadian rock group: David Usher (vocals, b. 04/24/66 in Oxford, England), Jeff Pearce (bass, b. Jeffrey Howard Pearce on 04/25/67), Kevin Young (keyboards, b. Kevin Thompson Young on 09/18/66), Mark Makoway (guitar, b. Mark Andrew Makowy on September 12; changed the spelling of his last name, to clear up mispronunciations). Paul Wilcox (drums, b. Paul Matthew Wilcox on 02/13/70). Won the 1995 Juno Award for Best New Group.

07/11/94	---	RA	Push	EMI	30
11/21/94	---	RA	Silver	EMI	12
02/13/95	---	RA	Believe Me	EMI	14
11/11/96	12	15 h	Leave It Alone	EMI	23
04/21/97	---	RA	Resurrection	EMI	28
11/09/97	16	16	Gasoline	Capitol	

MONEY, Eddie
American male rock singer born Edward Mahoney on 03/02/49 in Brooklyn, New York. Studied to become police officer at the New York Police Academy when he started his career in music.

06/14/78	12	12	Baby Hold On	Columbia	
01/19/87	26	14	Take Me Home Tonight	Columbia	
12/19/88	20	12	Walk On Water	Columbia	
02/19/90	20	7	Peace In Our Time	Columbia	7
03/09/92	---	RA	I'll Get By	Columbia	26

MONICA
American female R&B vocalist born Monica Arnold on 10/24/80 in Atlanta.

09/25/95	5	28	Don't Take It Personal	Arista	
06/08/97	33	3	For You I Will	Atlantic	20
05/24/98	1(15)	47	The Boy Is Mine *	Atlantic	1
10/11/98	6	23	The First Night	Arista	6
02/14/99	10	6	Angel Of Mine	Arista	5

* Brandy & Monica

MONIFAH
American female R&B/dance singer born in New York City. In off-Broadway production of *Midsummer's*

DATE	PK	WK	TITLE	LABEL	RA

Night Dream at age 10.

11/08/98	14	12	Touch It .... Uptown	11

Another version peaked at #25 on 02/14/99.

MONKEES, The
American pop group formed in 1965 in Los Angeles, disbanded in 1969. Re-formed in 1986: David Jones (vocals, b. 12/30/45 in Manchester, England), Peter Tork (bass, vocals, b. Peter Thorkelson on 02/13/44 in Washington, D.C.), Mickey Dolenz (drums, vocals, b. George Michael Dolenz on 03/08/45 in Tarzana, California, drums, vocals). Group was popular mostly in 1960's when the group was a quartet with guitarist/vocalist Michael Nesmith (vocals, guitar, b. Robert Michael Nesmith on 12/30/42 in Houston).

09/29/86	33	1	That Was Then, This Is Now .... Arista

MONO
British dance duo formed in 1996: Martin Virgo (producer), Siobhan DeMare (vocals).

02/08/98	33	2	Life In Mono .... Mercury

MONSTER MAGNET
American rock band from Red Bank, New Jersey: Dave Wyndorf (vocals/guitar), Ed Mundell (lead guitar), Joe Calandra (bass), Jon Kleiman (drums, percussion).

08/16/98	38	3	Space Lord .... A&M

MOODY BLUES
British rock group formed in Birmingham, England in 1964: Denny Laine (guitar, vocals, b. Brian Hines on 10/29/44 in Tyseley, England), Ray Thomas (flute, vocals, b. 12/29/42 in Stourport-on-Severn, England), Mike Pinder (keyboards, vocals, b. 12/27/41 in Birmingham), Clint Warwick (bass, b. Clinton Eccles on 06/25/40 in Birmingham), Graeme Edge (drums, b. 03/30/42 in Rochester, England). Laine and Warwick left in 1966, replaced by Justin Hayward (vocals, guitar, b. David Justin Hayward on 10/14/46 in Swindon, England), John Lodge (bass, vocals, b. 07/20/45 in Birmingham). Laine joined Wings in 1971. Patrick Moraz (keyboards, b. 06/24/48 in Morges, Switzerland) replaced Pinder in 1978. Moraz left in 1992.

08/08/81	1(4)	13	Gemini Dream .... Threshold
10/17/81	3(1)	9	The Voice .... Threshold
10/03/83	22	7	Sitting At The Wheel .... Threshold
07/28/86	33	7	Your Wildest Dreams .... Polydor
09/12/88	30	6	I Know You're Out There Somewhere .... Polydor

MOORE, Dorothy
American female R&B-gospel singer born in 1946 in Jackson, Mississippi. Lead singer of The Poppies.

07/03/76	2(4)	14	Misty Blue .... Malaco

MOORE, Mae
Canadian female singer/songwriter from Brandon, Manitoba. Wrote Loverboy's "Heaven In Your Eyes".

02/22/93	36	3	Because Of Love .... Epic	28
07/24/95	---	RA	Genuine .... Epic	23
10/23/95	---	RA	Watermark .... Epic	32

DATE	PK	WK	TITLE	LABEL	RA
03/04/96	29	7 h	Love Won't Find Us Here	Columbia	

MORALES, David
American male dance remixer born circa 1961 in Brooklyn, New York.

DATE	PK	WK	TITLE	LABEL	RA
10/25/93	37	5	Gimme Luv	Mercury	

MORISSETTE, Alanis
Canadian female singer/songwriter born Alanis Nadine Morissette on 06/01/74 in Ottawa. Started career recording dance music simply as Alanis, switched to alternative rock in 1995. Starred on the Nickolodeon cable-TV children series *You Can't Do That On Television*, at age 12. Winner of nine Juno Awards including Most Promising Female Vocalist in 1992 and Best Female Vocalist in 1996.

DATE	PK	WK	TITLE	LABEL	RA
07/08/91	4	14	Too Hot *	MCA	6
10/07/91	---	RA	Feel Your Love *	MCA	9
12/23/91	---	RA	Walkaway *	MCA	18
03/23/92	---	RA	Plastic *	MCA	34
11/30/92	9	17	An Emotion Away *	MCA	10
03/15/93	---	RA	Real World	MCA	23
06/21/93	---	RA	No Apologies	MCA	28
09/25/95	---	RA	You Oughta Know	Maverick	3
12/18/95	---	RA	Hand In My Pocket	Maverick	2
04/22/96	2(1)	16 h	Ironic	Maverick	2
			Retail Singles: #15 (03/18/96) / 4 wks.		
07/29/96	1(3)	17 h	You Learn	Maverick	1
			SoundScan: #20 (11/17/96) / 12 wks.		
11/25/96	1(1)	17 h	Head Over Feet	Maverick	2
06/08/98	---	RA	Uninvited	Reprise	6
11/01/98	1(1)	27	Thank U	Maverick	1
02/22/99	---	RA	Unsent	Maverick	8
04/04/99	30	3	Joining You	Maverick	30
08/02/99	---	RA	So Pure	Maverick	18+

* Alanis

MORRISON, Mark
American male R&B singer born in Leicester, England. Sentenced to three months in prison for weapons possession in 1997.

DATE	PK	WK	TITLE	LABEL	RA
03/23/97	6	26	Return Of The Mack	Atlantic	6

MORRISSEY
British male alternative rock singer/songwriter born Stephen Patrick Morrissey on 05/22/59 in Davyhulme, Lancashire, England. Former lead singer of The Smiths. A music journalist for the British music magazine *Record Mirror* in the late-1970's.

DATE	PK	WK	TITLE	LABEL	RA
05/16/94	---	RA	The More You Ignore Me, The Closer I Get	Sire	35

MOTELS, The
American pop band formed in 1972 in Berkeley, California led by Martha Davis (vocals/songwriter, b. 01/15/51 in Berkeley). Various personnel changes over the years; six member band in the early-1980's. Disbanded in 1987.

DATE	PK	WK	TITLE	LABEL	RA
07/31/82	6	12	Only The Lonely..	Capitol	
11/14/83	17	10	Suddenly Last Summer...............................	Capitol	
10/07/85	35	5	Shame..	Capitol	

MÖTLEY CRÜE

American hard rock band formed in 1981 in Los Angeles: "Tommy Lee" Bass (drums, b. 10/03/62 in Athens, Greece), Mick Mars (guitar, vocals, b. Bob Deal, on 04/03/55 in Terre Haute, Indiana), Vince Neil (b. Vincent Neil Wharton on 02/08/61 in Hollywood, California), Nikki Sixx (bass, b. Frank Carlton Serafino Ferranno on 12/11/58 in San Jose, California). Lee married to actress Heather Locklear (1986-1993), married *Baywatch* actress Pamela Anderson on 02/19/95. Sixx married singer Vanity in 1987. Neil left in 1992, replaced by John Corabi (vocals, b. 04/26/59 in Philadelphia).

DATE	PK	WK	TITLE	LABEL	RA
09/23/85	22	10	Smokin' In The Boys Room........................	Elektra	
07/27/87	23	7	Girls, Girls, Girls..	Elektra	
11/27/89	7	13	Dr. Feelgood..	Elektra	
06/25/90	22	10	Without You...	Elektra	25
08/20/90	24	4	Don't Go Away Mad (Just Go Away)..........	Elektra	36
10/21/91	6	17	Primal Scream...	Elektra	

MOXY

Canadian hard rock band from Toronto: Buddy Caine, Earl Johnson, Terry Juric, Buzz Sherman (d. 06/16/83 of motorcycle accident), Bill Wade.

DATE	PK	WK	TITLE	LABEL	RA
12/11/76	28	7	Take It Or Leave It.....................................	Polydor	

MOXY FRÜVOUS

Canadian alternative rock band formed in 1990 in Toronto: Mike Ford (vocals, guitar, piano, percussion), Murray Foster (vocals, guitar, bass), David Matheson (vocals, guitar, banjo, keyboards, harmonica, saxophone, accordion), Jian "Jean" Ghomeshi (vocals, percussion, drums, flute).

DATE	PK	WK	TITLE	LABEL	RA
06/23/97	---	RA	Get In My Car..	WEA	33

MOYET, Alison

British female singer/songwriter born Genevieve Alison-Jane "Alf" Moyet on 06/18/61 in Basildon, Essex, England. Vocalist in the group Yaz.

DATE	PK	WK	TITLE	LABEL	RA
05/13/85	19	12	Invisible..	Columbia	

MOZZ, The

DATE	PK	WK	TITLE	LABEL	RA
11/01/93	33	6	Mad Money..	Virgin	

M.T.S.

American dance group from Miami: Melissa Hamm, Tonia Lee, Tony Delaney.

DATE	PK	WK	TITLE	LABEL	RA
10/27/96	23	5	I'll Be Alright..	Popular	

MULLEN, Larry - see CLAYTON, Adam, & Larry Mullen

MULLINS, Shawn

American male rock singer born on 03/08/68 in Atlanta.

DATE	PK	WK	TITLE	LABEL	RA
12/21/98	---	RA	Lullaby	Columbia	6

MURPHEY, Michael
American male country singer/songwriter/guitarist/actor born on 03/13/45 in Dallas. Recorded in the late-1960's in the group the Lewis and Clark Expedition. Began using his full name, Michael Martin Murphey to distinguish himself from actor Michael Murphy in 1982.

06/28/75	3(3)	12	Wildfire	Epic	

MURPHY, Eddie
American male comedian/actor/R&B-pop singer born on 04/03/61 in Brooklyn, New York. Made television debut as a cast member of *Saturday Night Live*, 1980-83. Starred in movies, *Beverly Hills Cop*, *Beverly Hills Cop II*, *Beverly Hills Cop III*, *48 Hours*, and *The Nutty Professor*.

02/17/86	9	12	Party All The Time	Columbia	

MURPHY, Peter
British male alternative rock singer born on 07/11/57 in Northhampton, England. Former lead singer of the gothic rock group Bauhaus.

05/14/90	---	RA	Cuts You Up	Beggars Banquet	31

MURPHY, Walter, And The Big Apple Band
American orchestra led by pianist Walter Murphy (b. 1952 in New York City). Murphy is conservatory-trained musician and is a former arranger for Doc Severinsen and *The Tonight Show* Orchestra.

09/18/76	3(1)	20	A Fifth Of Beethoven	Private Stock	

MURRAY, Anne
Canadian female country-pop singer born Morna Anne Murray on 06/20/45 in Springhill, Nova Scotia. One of Canada's most successful recording artists of all time. Sold over 25 million records, won 25 Juno and four Grammy Awards. Appeared on CBC-TV's *Singalong Jubilee* and *Let's Go*. Physical education teacher in Prince Edward Island in the late-1960's. Appeared on Glen Campbell's American TV show in the 1970's. Hosted the Juno Awards in the 1990's. Received the Juno Hall of Fame Award in 1993.

04/05/78	27	10	Walk Right Back	Capitol
07/12/78	7	30	You Needed Me	Capitol
03/21/79	10	6	I Just Fall In Love Again	Capitol
06/27/79	20	12	Shadows In The Moonlight	Capitol
02/20/80	40	2	Broken Hearted Me	Capitol
11/08/80	19	2	Could I Have This Dance	Capitol
03/17/86	17	11	Now And Forever (You And Me)	Capitol
10/07/96	27	10 h	What Would It Take	EMI

MUSICAL YOUTH
British pop-reggae band formed circa 1979 in Birmingham, England: Dennis Seaton (vocals, b. 1967), Kelvin Grant (guitar, vocals, b. 1971), Michael Grant (keyboards, vocals, b. 1969), Patrick White (bass, vocals, b. 1968), Junior Waite (drums, vocals, b. 1967). The Whites and The Waites and two sets of brothers. Patrick died in February 1993 after he collapsed due to a mystery virus.

02/28/83	1(1)	10	Pass The Dutchie	MCA
01/16/84	29	1	She's Trouble	MCA

DATE	PK	WK	TITLE	LABEL	RA

MUSIQUE
American disco trio: Christine Wiltshire, Gina Tharps, Mary Seymour.

| 11/29/78 | 7 | 18 | In The Bush .... Prelude | | |

MY BRILLIANT BEAST
Canadian band from Toronto: Julia Galios (vocals, keyboards), Jonathan Gallivan (guitar, bass, piano, backing vocals, drums, percussion), B!ron (keyboards, drums, percussion).

| 10/30/95 | --- | RA | Fall Away....................................... Random Sound | 30 |

MYA
American female R&B singer born Maya Angelou in 1980 in Washington, D.C.

04/19/98	39	1	It's All About Me....................................... Interscope	
07/12/98	4	29	Ghetto Supastar (That Is What You Are)*.. Interscope	13
			Another version peaked at #35 on 06/28/98.	
02/28/99	35	1	Take Me There **................................... Interscope	15

* Pras Michel featuring ODB & introducing Mya
** Blackstreet & Mya

MYERS, Billie
British female pop singer born on 06/14/70 in Coventry, England.

| 04/27/98 | --- | RA | Kiss The Rain .... Unviersal | 5 |
| 07/06/98 | --- | RA | Tell Me .... Unviersal | 35 |

MYLES, Alannah
Canadian female rock singer/songwriter/guitarist born on 12/25/55 in Toronto. Grew up in Toronto and Buckhorn, Ontario. Won the 1990 Juno Award for Most Promising Female Vocalist.

08/14/89	11	16	Love Is... Atlantic	
10/30/89	9	13	Black Velvet.. Atlantic	
02/12/90	38	2	Still Got This Thing .... Atlantic	
05/07/90	6	12	Lover Of Mine .... Atlantic	3
11/23/92	7	17	Song Instead Of A Kiss............................ Atlantic	2
02/22/93	---	RA	Our World Our Times .... Atlantic	25
08/23/93	---	RA	Sonny Say You Will .... Atlantic	27

N

NAKED EYES
British pop-rock duo formed in 1982 in London: Pete Byrne (vocals), Rob Fisher (keyboards/ synthesizer). Disbanded in 1984, Fisher later in duo Climie Fisher.

| 05/09/83 | 12 | 10 | Always Something There (To Remind Me) .. Capitol | |
| 10/10/83 | 9 | 9 | Promises, Promises................................... Capitol | |

NATE DOGG

DATE	PK	WK	TITLE	LABEL	RA

American male rapper. Cousin of Snoop Doggy Dogg.

| 01/19/97 | 39 | 2 | Never Leave Me Alone | Death Row | |

NATÉ, Ultra
American female R&B/dance singer born in 1968 in Baltimore. Ultra Naté is her real name.

| 11/09/97 | 10 | 18 | Free | Strictly Rhythm | 32 |

NATURAL SELECTION
American funk-pop duo from Minneapolis: Elliott Erikson (vocals), Frederick Thomas (keyboards).

| 11/25/91 | 6 | 13 | Do Anything | East West | 6 |
| 02/10/92 | --- | RA | Hearts Don't Think (They Feel)! | East West | 25 |

NAUGHTON, David
American male singer/dancer/actor born on 02/13/51 in West Hartford, Connecticut. Starred in the movie *An American Werewolf In London* (1981) and the television shows *Makin' It* and *My Sister Sam*.

| 08/08/79 | 15 | 12 | Makin' It | RSO | |

NAUGHTY BY NATURE
American rap trio formed in 1986 in East Orange, New Jersey: Treach (vocals, b. Anthony Criss on 12/02/70 in East Orange), Vinnie (vocals, b. Vincent Brown on 09/17/70 in East Orange), Kay Gee (DJ, b. Kier Gist on 09/15/69 in East Orange).

12/30/91	12	8	O.P.P.	Tommy Boy	34
04/20/92	10	14	Everything's Gonna Be Alright	Tommy Boy	
07/13/92	21	13	Guard Your Grill	Tommy Boy	
03/08/93	1(5)	20	Hip Hop Hooray	Tommy Boy	
07/26/93	11	21	It's On	Tommy Boy	
03/21/94	25	17	Written On Ya Kitten	Tommy Boy	
06/19/95	15	15	Craziest	Tommy Boy	

NAZARETH
Scottish hard rock band formed in 1968 in Dunfermline, Scotland: Dan McCafferty (vocals), Manny Charlton (guitar), Darrel Sweet (drums), Pete Agnew (bass). Billy Rankin (guitar) and John Locke (keyboards) joined in 1981.

| 03/20/76 | 2(1) | 12 | Love Hurts | A&M | |

N'DOUR, Youssou
Senegalese male World Music singer born on 10/01/59 in Dakar, Senegal.

| 10/10/94 | --- | RA | 7 Seconds * | Columbia | 9 |

 * Youssou N'Dour/Neneh Cherry

NELSON
American rock duo formed in 1988 in Los Angeles consisting of identical twin sons of rock star Rick Nelson: Matthew Gray Nelson (vocals, bass, b. 09/20/67 in Los Angeles), Gunnar Eric Nelson (vocals, guitar, b. 09/20/67 in Los Angeles).

DATE	PK	WK	TITLE	LABEL	RA
10/29/90	13	11	(Can't Live Without Your) Love And Affection	DGC	12
12/17/90	34	7	After The Rain	DGC	8

NELSON, Willie
American male country singer/songwriter born on 04/30/33 in Fort Worth, Texas. Wrote Patsy Cline's "Crazy". Played bass for Ray Price. In movies such as *The Electric Horseman* (1979). Elected to the Country Music Hall Of Fame in 1993.

DATE	PK	WK	TITLE	LABEL
06/26/82	17	5	Always On My Mind	Columbia
06/04/84	1(3)	19	To All The Girls I've Loved Before *	Columbia

* Julio Iglesias & Willie Nelson

NENA
German pop band from Hagen, formed in 1982 in Berlin: Gabriele "Nena" Kerner (vocals, b. 03/26/60), Rolf Brendel (drums), Jurgen Dehmel (bass), Joern-Uwe Fahrenkrog-Peterson (keyboards), Carlos Karges (guitar).

DATE	PK	WK	TITLE	LABEL
03/19/84	1(2)	22	99 Luftballons	Epic

NEON PHILHARMONIC
American chamber-sized orchestra consisting of Nashville Symphony Orchestra musicians led by conductor Tupper Saussy and vocalist Don Gant. Gant died on 03/06/87 at age 44.

DATE	PK	WK	TITLE	LABEL
03/20/76	27	5	So Glad You're A Woman	London

NETZWERK
American dance group led by Simone Jackson, born in Portchester, New York.

DATE	PK	WK	TITLE	LABEL
09/25/95	21	5	Memories	NuMuzik

NEVIL, Robbie
American male pop singer/songwriter/guitarist born on 10/02/60 in Los Angeles. Wrote songs for Pointer Sisters, Sheena Easton, Vanity, and Eddie Kendricks.

DATE	PK	WK	TITLE	LABEL	RA
02/09/87	2(6)	17	C'est La Vie	Manhattan	
05/04/87	26	11	Dominoes	Manhattan	
09/14/87	30	10	Wot's It To Ya	Manhattan	
09/16/91	25	5	Just Like You	EMI	21

NEVILLE, Aaron
American male R&B singer born on 01/24/41 in New Orleans.

DATE	PK	WK	TITLE	LABEL	RA
08/26/91	21	9	Everybody Plays The Fool	A&M	27
06/28/93	---	RA	Don't Take Away My Heaven	A&M	33
01/17/94	18	9	The Grand Tour	A&M	
10/17/94	19	10	Betcha By Golly Wow	A&M	

NEVILLE BROTHERS, The

DATE	PK	WK	TITLE	LABEL	RA

American R&B group formed in 1977 in New Orleans consisting of brothers Arthur (keyboards, vocals, b. 12/17/37), Charles (vocals, percussion, saxophone, b. 1939), Aaron (vocals, percussion, b. 01/24/41), Cyril (percussion, vocals, b. 10/10/48) Neville.

| 08/13/90 | 1(2) | 16 | Bird On A Wire | A&M | |

NEW CITY JAM BAND
Canadian band popular in the mid-1970's.

| 03/20/76 | 16 | 6 | Lazy Love | Smile | |

NEW EDITION
American R&B-pop vocal group formed circa 1981 in Boston: Bobby Brown (b. Bobby Bradsford Brown on 02/07/66 in Boston), Michael Bivins (b. 08/10/68 in Boston), Ricky Bell (b. 09/18/67 in Boston), Ronnie DeVoe (b. 11/17/67 in Boston), Ralph Tresvant (b. 05/16/68 in Boston). Johnny Gill (b. 1965 in Washington, D.C.) replaced Brown in 1988. Brown, Gill, Tresvant eventually pursued solo careers. The remaining members formed the trio Bell Biv Devoe in 1988.

07/18/83	14	9	Candy Girl	London	
03/11/85	34	4	Mr. Telephone Man	MCA	
10/20/96	13	5	Hit Me Off	MCA	
01/27/97	---	RA	I'm Still In Love With You	MCA	30

NEW KIDS ON THE BLOCK
American pop vocal group formed in 1985 in Boston: Donnie Wahlberg (b. 08/17/69 in Boston), Jonathan Knight (b. 11/29/68 in Worcester, Massachusetts), Jordan Knight (b. 05/15/70 in Worcester), Danny Wood (b. 05/14/69 in Boston), Joe McIntyre (b. 12/31/72 in Needham, Massachusetts). Created by producer Maurice Starr, who founded and produced New Edition. Group recorded as NKOTB in 1992. Disbanded in 1994. Knight and McIntyre pursued solo careers in 1999.

04/03/89	16	10	You Got It (The Right Stuff)	Columbia	
08/07/89	21	7	I'll Be Loving You (Forever)	Columbia	
10/09/89	7	16	Hangin' Tough	Columbia	
11/13/89	7	15	Cover Girl	Columbia	
12/18/89	36	5	Didn't I (Blow Your Mind)	Columbia	
02/05/90	6	14	This One's For The Children	Columbia	
02/12/90	20	6	You Got It (The Right Stuff)	Columbia	
06/25/90	1(4)	19	Step By Step	Columbia	1
09/24/90	5	24	Tonight	Columbia	5
12/03/90	10	15	Let's Try It Again	Columbia	
02/25/91	---	RA	Games	Columbia	27
04/27/92	6	9	If You Go Away *	Columbia	
02/14/94	3(1)	13	Dirty Dawg *	Columbia	
08/15/94	18	13	Never Let You Go *	Columbia	

* NKOTB

NEW ORDER
British techo-dance/modern rock band formed in 1980 in Manchester: Peter Hook (bass, b. 02/13/56 in Salford, England), Bernard Sumner (guitar, b. Bernard Albrecht on 01/04/56 in Salford), Stephen Morris (drums, b. 10/28/57 in Macclesfield, England), Gillian Gilbert (keyboards, b. 01/27/61 in Manchester). Group known as Joy Division, 1976-80, led by Ian Curtis (b. 07/15/56 in Macclesfield, d. 05/18/80 in Macclesfield). Sumner joined the group Electronics in 1989. Hook formed the group Monaco in 1996.

DATE	PK	WK	TITLE	LABEL	RA
06/21/93	6	22	Regret	London	4
11/29/93	38	3	World	London	40
09/04/95	30	3	Blue Monday '95	London	

NEW RADICALS
American rock group led by singer/songwriter/producer Gregg Alexander (native of Grosse Point, Michigan).

02/01/99	---	RA	You Get What You Give	MCA	4

NEWMAN, Randy
American male singer/composer/pianist born on 11/28/44 in New Orleans. Composer of several film soundtracks including *Ragtime*, *Three Amigos*, and *Parenthood*.

02/08/78	1(2)	14	Short People	Warner	

NEWSBOYS
Australian Christian rock group: John James (vocals), Peter Furler (drums), Jody Davis (guitar), Phil Joel (bass), Jeff Frankenstein (keyboards), Duncan Phillips (drums). James left in 1996; Furler replaced him as vocalist.

07/15/96	---	RA	Take Me To Your Leader	Virgin	20

NEWTON, Juice
American female country-pop singer/songwriter/guitarist born Judy Kay Newton on 02/18/52 in Virginia Beach, Virginia. Formed Juice Newton & The Silver Spur in 1973. Fronted the band until it disbanded in 1978.

05/09/81	2(3)	11	Angel Of The Morning	Capitol	
09/05/81	5	9	Queen Of Hearts	Capitol	
07/10/82	8	8	Love's Been A Little Bit Hard On Me	Capitol	

NEWTON-JOHN, Olivia
British/Australian female pop singer/actress born on 09/26/48 in Cambridge, England. Raised in Melbourne, Australia. Granddaughter of Nobel Prize-winning German physicist Max Born. Won the 1974 Female Vocalist of the Year Award from the Country Music Association. Appeared in several movies including *Grease* (1978), *Xanadu* (1980), *Two Of A Kind* (1983). Married actor Matt Lattanzi in 1984. Opened a chain of clothing stores called Koala Blue in 1984. Successfully underwent treatment for breast cancer in 1992.

08/23/75	9	8	Please Mr. Please	MCA	
04/30/77	24	12	Sam	MCA	
05/31/78	1(6)	24	You're The One That I Want *	RSO	
09/20/78	3(4)	18	Hopelessly Devoted To You	RSO	
09/20/78	4	16	Summer Nights *	RSO	
03/07/79	10	8	A Little More Love	MCA	
07/23/80	6	4	Magic	MCA	
10/18/80	6	10	Xanadu	MCA	
12/26/81	2(4)	14	Physical	MCA	
04/17/82	4	11	Make A Move On Me	MCA	
11/13/82	2(1)	10	Heart Attack	MCA	
01/16/84	5	19	Twist Of Fate	MCA	

DATE	PK	WK	TITLE	LABEL	RA
12/09/85	25	9	Soul Kiss	MCA	
07/21/86	32	8	Best Of Me **	Atlantic	
12/30/96	---	RA	Grease Megamix *	Polydor	30

* John Travolta & Olivia Newton-John
** David Foster/Olivia Newton-John

NEXT
American R&B trio formed in 1992 in Minneapolis: T-Low (b. circa 1975), R.L. (b. circa 1978), Tweety (b. circa 1977).

DATE	PK	WK	TITLE	LABEL	RA
05/03/98	3(1)	24	Too Close	Arista	3
			Another version peaked at #34 on 07/19/98.		
01/10/99	25	1	I Still Love You	Arista	

NICKS, Stevie
American female pop/rock singer/songwriter born Stephanie Nicks on 05/26/48 in Phoenix. Recorded with Lindsey Buckingham in 1973. Vocalist in Fleetwood Mac, 1975-93.

DATE	PK	WK	TITLE	LABEL	RA
10/03/81	2(1)	11	Stop Draggin' My Heart Around *	Modern	
01/16/82	6	12	Leather And Lace **	Modern	
04/24/82	11	4	Edge Of Seventeen	Modern	
08/15/83	17	3	Stand Back	Modern	
02/03/86	14	13	Talk To Me	Modern	
08/07/89	27	5	Room's On Fire	Modern	
07/11/94	---	RA	Maybe Love Will Change Your Mind	Modern	33

* Stevie Nicks (with Tom Petty & The Heartbreakers)
** Stevie Nicks (with Don Henley)

NICOLE
American female rapper/R&B singer born Nicole Wray, circa 1980 in Salinas, California. Later moved to Portsmouth, Virginia. Discovered by Missy "Misdemeanor" Elliott.

DATE	PK	WK	TITLE	LABEL	RA
08/02/98	4	33	Make It Hot *	Elektra	

* Nicole featuring Missy "Misdemeanor" Elliott

NIGHT
British sextet led by Stevie Lange and Chris Thompson, vocalist/guitarist of Manfred Mann's Earth Band.

DATE	PK	WK	TITLE	LABEL	RA
10/03/79	19	6	Hot Summer Nights	Planet	

NIGHT RANGER
American rock group formed in 1981 in San Francisco: Kelly Keagy (vocals, drums), Jack Blades (vocals, bass), Jeff Watson (guitar), Brad Gillis (guitar), Alan "Fitz" Gerald (keyboards). Group disbanded in 1989. Blades and Gillis were members of Rubicon. Blades joined the Damn Yankees.

DATE	PK	WK	TITLE	LABEL	RA
07/30/84	3(1)	12	Sister Christian	Epic	
07/15/85	38	5	Sentimental Street	MCA	

NIGHTINGALE, Maxine

DATE	PK	WK	TITLE	LABEL	RA

British female pop singer born on 11/02/52 in Wembly, England. Appeared in productions of *Hair* and *Jesus Christ Superstar* in the early-1970's.

| 04/24/76 | 1(1) | 13 | Right Back Where We Started From | United Artists | |
| 10/03/79 | 3(2) | 12 | Lead Me On | RCA | |

NIGRINI, Ron
Canadian male folk singer born in 1948.

| 08/14/76 | 22 | 8 | I'm Easy | Attic | |

NINE INCH NAILS
American industrial rock group formed in 1987 in Cleveland: Michael Trent Reznor (vocals, keyboards, guitar, bass, drums, b. 05/17/65 in Mercer, Pennsylvania), Danny Lohner (keyboards, guitar, bass), Charlie Clouser (keyboards), Chris Vrenna (drums). Reznor once produced Marilyn Manson.

01/26/97	25	16	March of the Pigs	Nothing	
05/18/97	2(4)	46	Perfect Drug	Nothing	
07/25/99	1(1)	1 +	The Day The World Went Away	Nothing	

95 SOUTH
American rap group from Miami: Church's, Black, Lemonhead, Bootyman, K-Knock. Named after an American interstate highway.

| 10/25/93 | 1(1) | 18 | Whoot, There It Is | Hypnotic | |

98 DEGREES
American male R&B vocal group from Cincinnatti: Jeffrey Brandon Timmons ("Jeff") (tenor, b. 04/30/73 in Canton, Ohio), Nicholas Scott Lachey ("Nick") (tenor, b. 11/09/73 in Harlan, Kentucky), Andrew John Lachey ("Drew") (baritone, b. 08/08/76 in Cincinnati), Justin Paul Jeffre "Justin" (bass, b. 02/25/73 in Mount Clemens, Michigan). Nick and Drew are brothers.

09/14/97	7	22	Invisible Man	Motown	5
02/01/98	23	9	Was It Something I Didn't Say	Motown	
10/18/98	5	36	Because Of You	Motown	13
04/26/99	---	RA	The Hardest Thing	Motown	12

NIRVANA
American alternative rock band formed in 1987 in Aberdeen, Washington: Kurt Cobain (vocals, guitar, b. Kurt Donald Cobain on 02/20/67 in Hoquiam, Washington), Krist "Chris" Novoselic (bass, b. Krist Anthony Novoselic on 05/16/65 in Compton, California), Dave Grohl (drums, b. 01/14/69 in Warren, Ohio), Early members also included Jason Everman (guitar), Chad Channing (b. 01/31/67 in Santa Rosa, California). Guitarist Pat Smear played on the band's last tour. Cobain shot himself to death in 04/05/94. Grohl and Smear left in 1994 to form the Foo Fighters. Cobain's widow (married on 02/24/92) is rock singer/actress Courtney Love.

02/17/92	---	RA	Smells Like Teen Spirit	DGC	17
05/04/92	---	RA	Come As You Are	DGC	33
12/19/94	---	RA	About A Girl	DGC	9
03/06/95	---	RA	The Man Who Sold The World	DGC	22

NITTY GRITTY DIRT BAND

| DATE | PK | WK | TITLE | LABEL | RA |

American country-rock band formed in 1966 in Long Beach, California led by Jeff Hanna (vocals, guitar, b. 07/11/47 in Detroit) and John McEuen (vocals, mandolin, guitar, b. 12/19/45 in Long Beach). Jackson Browne was an original member of the band.

| 04/16/80 | 10 | 9 | An American Dream | United Artists | |

NO DOUBT
American ska-pop group formed in 1987 in Los Angeles: Gwen Stefani (vocals, b. 10/03/69 in Fullerton, California), Eric Stefani (keyboards), Tony Kanal (bass, b. 08/27/70 in Kingsbury, England), Adrian Young (drums, b. 08/26/69 in Long Beach, California), Tom Dumont (guitar, b. 01/11/68 in Los Angeles). The Stefanis are siblings. Eric left in 1995.

06/03/96	---	RA	Just A Girl	Interscope	34
10/21/96	---	RA	Spiderwebs	Interscope	22
02/23/97	30	1	Don't Speak	Interscope	1
06/16/97	---	RA	Sunday Morning	Interscope	36

NO MERCY
American male dance trio: Ariel and Gabriel Hernandez from Miami, Marty Cintron from New York City. Ariel and Gabriel are brothers.

| 10/20/96 | 1(7) | 34 | Where Do You Go? | Arista | 4 |

Hit Parade: #18 (10/28/96) / 11 wks.

| 03/24/97 | --- | RA | Please Don't Go | Arista | 21 |

NOLAN, Kenny
American male singer/songwriter based in Los Angeles. Wrote "My Eyes Adore You", "Lady Marmalade". Led the group The Eleventh Hour.

| 04/02/77 | 13 | 15 | I Like Dreamin' | 20th Century | |

NOMAD
British dance pop trio: Sharon Dee Clarke (vocals, b. circa 1965), rapper MC Mikee Freedom (b. circa 1969 in Bristol, England), Damon Rochefort (b. circa 1965 in Cardiff, Wales).

| 10/28/91 | 6 | 15 | (I Wanna Give You) Devotion | Capitol | |

NORMAN, Chris - see QUATRO, Suzi

NORTHERN LIGHTS
Canadian ensemble of 56 celebrities formed in 1985 to raise money for famine victims in Ethiopia: Bryan Adams, Paul Anka, Carroll Baker, Veronique Beliveau, Doug Bennett, Salome Bey, Liona Boyd, John Candy, Robert Charlebois, Tom Cochrane, Bruce Cockburn, Burton Cummings, Lisa Dal Bello, Claude Dubois, Rik Emmett, Wayne Gretzky, Corey Hart, Ronnie Hawkins, Dan Hill, Honeymoon Suite, Tommy Hunter, Paul Hyde, Martha Johnson, Geddy Lee, Eugene Levy, Gordon Lightfoot, Murray McLauchlan, Frank Mills, Joni Mitchell, Kim Mitchell, Anne Murray, Bruce Murray, Aldo Nova, Catherine O'Hara, Oscar Petersen, Carole Pope, Lorraine Segato, Paul Shaffer, Graham Shaw, Jane Siberry, Liberty Silver, Wayne St. John, Ian Thomas, Jim Vallance, Neil Young, Zappacosta.

| 04/29/85 | 1(4) | 14 | Tears Are Not Enough | Columbia | |

NORTHERN PIKES

DATE	PK	WK	TITLE	LABEL	RA

Canadian quartet from Saskatoon, Saskatchewan formed in 1984: Meryl Bryck (vocals, guitar), Bryan Potvin (vocals, guitar), Jay Semko (vocals, bass), Don Schmid (drums). Disbanded in 1993. Semko recorded solo in 1995.

08/31/87	27	8	Teenland	Virgin	
07/30/90	3(3)	14	She Ain't Pretty	Virgin	15
10/15/90	21	10	Girl With A Problem	Virgin	24
01/21/91	---	RA	Kiss Me You Fool	Virgin	35
12/28/92	33	9	Twister	Virgin	33

NOTORIOUS B.I.G.
American male rapper Christopher Wallace born in 05/21/72 in Brooklyn, New York. Fronted Junior M.A.F.I.A. Married to singer Faith Evans, 1994-97. Arrested for drug and firearms charges on 07/23/96 in Teaneck, New Jersey. Shot to death on 03/09/97 in Los Angeles.

09/25/95	3(1)	32	One More Chance	Arista	
04/20/97	14	11	Runnin' *	Mergela	
05/18/97	3(1)	10	Hypnotize	Arista	
09/14/97	2(11)	46	Mo Money, Mo Problems **	Arista	14
09/14/97	20	10	Hypnotize	Arista	
12/21/97	2(6)	31	Been Around The World ***	Arista	
			Another version peaked at #9 on 12/07/97.		
01/04/98	11	15	Sky's The Limit	Arista	

* 2Pac, Notorious B.I.G., Radio, Dramacydal & Stretch
** Notorious B.I.G. featuring Puff Daddy & Mase
*** Puff Daddy & the Family (featuring Notorious B.I.G. and Mase)

NOVA, Aldo
Canadian male rock singer/songwriter/producer. Played guitar in Jon Bon Jovi's "Blaze Of Glory".

| 04/24/82 | 9 | 12 | Fantasy | Portrait | |

NOVA, Heather
Bermudan female pop/rock singer/songwriter born Heather Frith in 1968 in Bermuda.

| 09/14/98 | --- | RA | London Rain | Work | 16 |

'N SYNC
American pop vocal quintet formed in Orlando in 1995: James Lansten "Lance" Bass (b. 05/04/79 in Clinton, Mississippi), Joseph "Joey" Anthony Fatone, Jr. (b. 01/28/77 in Brooklyn, New York), Christopher "Chris" Alan Kilpatrick (b. 10/17/71 in Clarion, Pennsylvania), Joshua "JC" Scott Chasez (b. 08/08/76 in Washington D.C.), Justin Randall Timberlake (b. 01/31/81 in Memphis). "'N SYNC' is the last letter in the names of the members: JustiN, ChriS, JoeY, LansteN, JC.

03/15/98	2(2)	26	I Want You Back	RCA	3
08/03/98	---	RA	Tearin' Up My Heart	RCA	4
02/28/99	3(2)	15	(God Must Have Spent) A Little More Time On You	RCA	12
05/03/99	---	RA	I Drive Myself Crazy	RCA	17

N-TRANCE

DATE	PK	WK	TITLE	LABEL	RA

British dance group from Manchester, England consisting of Kevin O'Toole and Dale Longworth. Rapper Ricarddo Da Force featured on "Stayin' Alive". Da Force rapped for dance group KLF in late-1980's.

| 02/05/96 | 1(9) | 22 | Stayin' Alive | Quality | 29 |
| 02/23/98 | --- | RA | Do Ya Think I'm Sexy | Universal | 39 |

NU FLAVOR
American R&B vocal group from Long Beach, California: Frank Pangelinan (tenor), Jacob Ceniceros (bass/tenor), Anthony DaCosta (tenor), Rico Luna (alto).

| 02/01/98 | 28 | 5 | Heaven | Warner | |

NU SHOOZ
American R&B-pop group from Portland, Oregon featuring lead vocalist Valerie Day and her husband, guitarist/songwriter John Smith.

| 08/18/86 | 2(1) | 16 | I Can't Wait | Atlantic | |
| 11/10/86 | 22 | 7 | Point Of No Return | Atlantic | |

NUMAN, Gary
British synthesized techno-rock artist born Gary Anthony James Webb on 03/08/58 in Hammersmith, England.

| 04/23/80 | 3(10) | 17 | Cars | Beggers Banquet | |

NYLONS, The
Canadian à cappella quartet formed in 1978 in Toronto. Line-up in 1987: Marc Connors (b. 04/15/49 in Ottawa), Paul Cooper (b. 02/20/50 in Chattanooga, Tennessee), Claude Morrison (b. 10/11/52 in Toronto), Arnold Robinson. Other members throughout the years included Gavin Hope (b. circa 1974 in Toronto), Ralph Cole, Denis Simpson, and Micah Barnes. Connors died of viral pneumonia on 03/25/91 in Toronto, replaced by Billy Newton-Davis (b. 04/26/51 in Cleveland). Hope and Newton-Davis have recorded solo.

| 07/27/87 | 21 | 9 | Kiss Him Goodbye | Attic | |

O

OAK RIDGE BOYS
American country vocal group formed in 1945 as the Oak Ridge Quartet, re-formed in 1956. Became the Oak Ridge Boys in 1961. From 1972 to 1987, line-up included Joe Bonsall (tenor vocals, piano, b. 05/18/48 in Philadelphia), Duane Allen (lead tenor, guitar, piano, b. 04/29/43 in Taylortown, Texas), Richard Sterban (bass vocals, trumpet, b. 04/24/43 in Camden, New Jersey), William Lee Golden (baritone, guitar, b. 01/12/39 in Brewton, Alabama). Steve Sanders replaced Golden in 1987. Sanders shot himself to death on 06/10/98 in Cape Coral, Florida.

| 08/08/81 | 10 | 5 | Elvira | MCA | |

OASIS
British alternative rock band from Manchester: Liam Gallagher (vocals, b. 09/21/72 in Manchester), Noel Gallagher (guitar, vocals, b. 05/29/67 in Manchester), Paul Arthurs (guitar, b. 06/23/65 in Manchester), Paul McGuigan (bass, b. 05/09/71 in Manchester).

DATE	PK	WK	TITLE	LABEL	RA
03/18/96	3(2)	15 h	Wonderwall	Epic	1
			Retail Singles: #28 (03/04/96) / 7 wks.		
06/03/96	10	13 h	Champagne Supernova	Epic	18
09/02/96	19	8 h	Don't Look Back In Anger..............................	Epic	19
07/20/97	3(3)	15	D'You Know What I Mean	Epic	39
11/10/97	---	RA	Don't Go Away..	Epic	23

OCASEK, Ric
American male rock singer born Richard Otcasek on 03/23/49 in Baltimore. Lead vocalist/songwriter/guitarist of The Cars. Appeared in the film *Made In Heaven* (1987). Married model/actress Paulina Porizkova in 1989.

DATE	PK	WK	TITLE	LABEL
12/22/86	23	11	Emotion In Motion.......................................	Geffen

OCEAN, Billy
British male R&B-pop singer born Leslie Sebastian Charles on 01/21/50 in Fyzabad, Trinidad.

DATE	PK	WK	TITLE	LABEL
05/29/76	8	9	Love Really Hurts Without You	Ariola
12/10/84	3(1)	15	Caribbean Queen (No More Love On The Run)	Jive
03/18/85	4	15	Loverboy..	Jive
07/22/85	10	19	Suddenly	Jive
03/10/86	2(1)	17	When The Going Gets Tough, The Tough Get Going	Jive
06/23/86	9	14	There'll Be Sad Songs (To Make You Cry)........	Jive
10/06/86	27	4	Love Zone..	Jive
04/25/88	1(5)	20	Get Outta My Dreams, Get Into My Car	Jive
08/22/88	14	11	Color Of Love	Jive
01/22/90	39	3	Licence To Chill	Jive

O'CONNOR, Sinead
Irish female singer/songwriter/actress born on 12/12/66 in Glenageary, Ireland. Appeared in the 1989 Irish film *Hush-a-Bye Baby*.

DATE	PK	WK	TITLE	LABEL	RA
04/09/90	16	6	Nothing Compares 2 U	Chrysalis	1
08/06/90	---	RA	The Emperor's New Clothes...................	Chrysalis	16
10/19/92	14	4	Success Has Made A Failure Of Our Home	Chrysalis	

OCTAVIAN
Canadian group formed in Ottawa in 1969 as Octavius: Daryl Alguire (vocals), Warren Barbour (guitar), Kirk Darrow (drums), Bill Gavreau (lead guitar), Ray Lessard (bass), Rob McDonald (keyboards), and John Pulkinen (vocals). Disbanded in 1979.

DATE	PK	WK	TITLE	LABEL
08/02/75	22	2	Round And Round	MCA
07/23/77	13	8	Can't Stop Myself From Loving You	MCA

O'DAY, Alan
American male singer/songwriter/pianist born on 10/03/40 in Hollywood, California. Wrote Helen Reddy's "Angie Baby" and The Righteous Brothers' "Rock And Roll Heaven".

DATE	PK	WK	TITLE	LABEL
07/16/77	1(3)	17	Undercover Angel	Atlantic

ODB - see MICHEL, Pras

DATE	PK	WK	TITLE	LABEL	RA

ODDS, The
Canadian rock group formed in 1987 in Vancouver: Craig Northey (vocals, guitar, keyboards), Doug Elliott (bass, vocals), Pat Steward (drums, percussion), Steven Drake (vocals, guitars, keyboards), Paul Brennan (drums). Brennan left in 1995.

11/25/91	---	RA	Love Is The Subject	Zoo	32
03/20/95	---	RA	Truth Untold	WEA	37
06/12/95	---	RA	Eat My Brain	WEA	32
09/18/95	---	RA	Satisfied	WEA	20
12/23/96	---	RA	Someone Who's Cool	WEA	30
05/02/97	---	RA	You Make Me Mad	WEA	36

OFFSPRING, The
American rock group formed in 1986 in Orange County, California: Brian "Dexter" Holland (vocals, guitar, b. 12/29/65), Ron Welty (drums, b. 02/01/71 in Long Beach, California), Greg Kriesel (bass, b. 01/20/65 in Glendale, California), Kevin "Noodles" Wasserman (guitar, b. 02/04/63 in Los Angeles).

| 02/21/99 | 18 | 3 | Pretty Fly (For A White Guy) | Columbia | 12 |
| 05/24/99 | --- | RA | Why Don't You Get A Job | Columbia | 35 |

OH WELL

| 07/16/90 | 26 | 9 | Radar Love | Capitol | |

OHIO PLAYERS
American R&B group formed in 1959 in Dayton, Ohio: Billy Beck (keyboards), Clarence Satchell (saxophone, flute), Jimmy "Diamond" Williams (drums, percussion), Leroy "Sugar" Bonner (guitar, vocals), Marvin Pierce (trumpet), Marshall Jones (bass), Ralph "Pee Wee" Middlebrooks (trumpet).

| 01/17/76 | 8 | 10 | Love Rollercoaster | Mercury | |

O'JAYS
American R&B vocal group formed in 1958 in Canton, Ohio: Bobby Massey, Walter Williams, Eddie Levert, Bill Isles, William Powell. Isles left in 1965, Massey left in 1972. Powell left in 1976 and died in 1977, replaced by Sammy Strain.

| 02/14/76 | 13 | 8 | I Love Music | Columbia | |
| 07/26/78 | 10 | 10 | Use Ta Be My Girl | Philadelphia International | |

OLIVE
British pop trio formed in 1995 in Buxton, England: Ruth-Ann Boyle (vocals, b. 1971 in Sunderland, England), Tim Kellett (keyboards), Robin Taylor-Firth (programming). Kellett was the keyboardist for Simply Red.

| 11/23/97 | 17 | 18 | You're Not Alone | RCA | |

OLIVOR, Jane - see MATHIS, Johnny

OLLIE & JERRY
American dance-R&B duo: Ollie Brown, Jerry Knight (formerly of Raydio).

| 09/03/84 | 13 | 9 | Breakin'...There's No Stopping Us | Polydor | |

DATE	PK	WK	TITLE	LABEL	RA

OMC
New Zealand pop group formed in 1995 in Auckland. Led by Pauly Fuemana, who led OMC's predecessor, the Otara Millionaires Club.

| 10/20/96 | 17 | 5 | How Bizarre | Polydor | 1 |
| 04/14/97 | --- | RA | Right On | Polydor | 37 |

ONE
Canadian reggae-pop band from Toronto led by Chris Taylor. Taylor left by 1996; replaced by former King Apparatus vocalist Chris Murray.

| 10/03/94 | 10 | 13 | Wide Load | Virgin | |
| 12/19/94 | --- | RA | 54-46 | Virgin | 39 |

ONE TO ONE
Canadian pop duo from Ottawa: Leslie Howe and Louise Reny.

03/10/86	12	13	There Was A Time	WEA Bonaire	
06/16/86	28	6	Angel In My Pocket	WEA Bonaire	
12/26/88	25	11	Hold Me Now	WEA Bonaire	
03/16/92	25	9	Peace Of Mind *	A&M	13
06/22/92	---	RA	Memory Lane	A&M	27

* One 2 One

112
American R&B vocal group from Atlanta: Daron, Q, Slim, Mike.

11/03/96	17	19	Only You	Arista	
06/22/97	1(13)	41	I'll Be Missing You *	Arista	4
11/08/98	17	13	Love Me **	Arista	
05/31/99	---	RA	Anywhere	Arista	38

* Puff Daddy & Faith Evans (featuring 112)
** 112 featuring Mase

OPUS
Austrian pop-rock group led by singer Herwig Rudisser.

| 12/23/85 | 1(7) | 20 | Live Is Life | Polydor | |

ORBISON, Roy
American pop-rock singer born on 04/23/36 in Vernon, Texas. Mainly popular in the 1960's. Attended North Texas State University with Pat Boone. Lead singer of The Teen Kings in the late-1950's. Toured with The Beatles in England in 1963. Career on hold after his wife Claudette died in a motorcycle accident on 06/07/66. Two sons died in a fire in 1968. Inducted into the Rock and Roll Hall of Fame in 1987. Member of the supergroup Traveling Wilburys in 1988. Died of a heart attack on 12/06/88 in Hendersonville, Tennessee.

02/15/88	8	15	Crying *	Virgin	
03/20/89	1(1)	17	You Got It	Virgin	
06/15/92	22	12	I Drove All Night	MCA	

DATE	PK	WK	TITLE	LABEL

* Roy Orbison/k.d. lang

ORBITAL
British techno-dance duo formed in 1987 in Sevenoaks, Kent, England consisting of brothers Phillip (b. 01/09/64 in Dartford, England) and Paul (b. 05/19/68 in Dartford) Hartnoll. Named after a road in England.

03/30/97	18	12	Saint	ffrr

ORCHESTRAL MANOEUVRES IN THE DARK
British electropop group formed in 1978 in London: Andy McCluskey (vocals, keyboards, b. 06/24/59 in Wirral, England), Paul Humphreys (vocals, keyboards, b. 02/27/60 in London), Martin Cooper (saxophone, keyboards), Malcolm Holmes (drums), Neil Weir (horns), Graham Weir (horns). Disbanded in 1988, re-formed in 1991 with McCluskey but without Humphreys.

02/24/86	36	2	Secret	Virgin
06/09/86	16	14	If You Leave	Virgin
12/01/86	14	16	(Forever) Live And Die	Virgin
05/23/88	29	7	Dreaming	Virgin

ORGY
American metal band formed in 1997 in Los Angeles: Jay Gordon (vocals), Amir Derakh (synthesizer), Ryan Shuck (guitar), Paige Haley (bass), Bobby Hewitt (drums).

02/28/99	5	22 +	Blue Monday	Reprise

ORLEANS
American pop group formed in 1972 in New York City: Lance Hoppen (bass), Wells Kelly (organ, vocals, drums), Larry Hoppen (vocals, keyboards, guitar), Jerry Marotta (drums, percussion), John Hall (guitar, vocals). Hall and Marotta left in 1977, replaced by Bob Leinback (keyboards, vocals) and R.A. Martin (keyboards, vocals).

11/01/75	3(1)	7	Dance With Me	Asylum
10/30/76	4	15	Still The One	Asylum
06/27/79	15	10	Love Takes Time	MCA

ORR, Benjamin
American male pop singer born Benjamin Orzechowski on 08/09/55 in Cleveland. Bassist/vocalist of The Cars.

03/02/87	40	1	Stay The Night	Elektra

OSBORNE, Jeffrey
American male R&B singer/songwriter born on 03/09/48 in Providence, Rhode Island. Member of L.T.D., 1970-1980.

02/13/84	29	3	Stay With Me Tonight	A&M
09/07/87	36	4	Love Power *	Arista

* Dionne Warwick/Jeffrey Osborne

DATE	PK	WK	TITLE	LABEL	RA

OSBORNE, Joan
American female pop-rock singer born on 07/08/62 in Anchorage, Kentucky.

| 02/05/96 | 4 | 18 h | One Of Us | Mercury | 1 |

OSBOURNE, Ozzy
American male heavy metal singer born John Michael Osbourne on 12/03/48 in Birmingham, England. Former lead singer of Black Sabbath. Appeared in the 1986 movie *Trick Or Treat*.

12/09/91	26	18	No More Tears	Epic	
04/27/92	20	20	Mama I'm Coming Home	Epic	
08/02/93	32	5	Changes	Epic	

OSMOND, Donny
American male pop singer/songwriter/actor born Donald Clark Osmond on 12/09/57 in Ogden, Utah. Vocalist and drummer of The Osmonds, a group consisting of his siblings. Appeared in the theatrical production *Joseph and the Amazing Technicolor Dreamcoat*.

07/03/89	5	15	Soldier Of Love	Capitol	
09/18/89	23	10	Sacred Emotion	Capitol	
12/24/90	30	6	Love Is A Fire	Capitol	18

OSMOND, Donny & Marie
American brother and sister duo: Donny (b. Donald Clark Osmond on 12/09/57 in Ogden, Utah), Marie (b. Olive Marie Osmond on 10/13/59 in Ogden, Utah) Osmond. Hosted own variety television series, 1976-78. Starred in the movie *Goin' Coconuts*.

| 04/24/76 | 14 | 6 | Deep Purple | MGM | |

OTHER ONES, The
Australian/German rock group: Jayney Klimek (lead vocals), Alf Klimek, Johnny Klimek, Andreas Schwarz-Ruszcynski, Stephan Gottwald, Uwe Hoffmann. The Klimeks are from Australia, the other members are from Germany.

| 06/29/87 | 31 | 3 | We Are What We Are | Virgin | |

OUR LADY PEACE
Canadian rock band formed in 1993 in Toronto: Raine Maida (vocals, guitar), Mike Turner (guitar), Jeremy Taggart (drums), Chris Eacrett (bass). Eacrett left in 1995, replaced by Duncan Coutts (bass, keyboards, cello). Won the 1998 Juno Award for Group of the Year.

| 07/14/97 | --- | RA | Clumsy | Columbia | 23 |

OUTFIELD, The
British rock trio: Tony Lewis (lead vocals, bass), John Spinks (guitar, keyboards, vocals), Alan Jackman (drums). Jackman left by 1990.

| 06/09/86 | 39 | 2 | Your Love | Columbia | |
| 01/28/91 | --- | RA | For You | MCA | 16 |

OUTHERE BROTHERS
American dance duo from Chicago consisting of singer/lyricist Malik and producer Hula.

DATE	PK	WK	TITLE	LABEL	RA
09/04/95	28	4	Boom! Boom! Boom! .... NuMuzik		

OXO
American pop-rock quartet led by Ish "Angel" Ledesma, a former member of Foxy.

| 05/02/83 | 15 | 7 | Whirly Girl .... Geffen | | |

OZARK MOUNTAIN DAREDEVILS
American country-rock group from Springfield, Missouri: Larry Lee (keyboards, guitar), Steve Cash (harp), John Dillon (guitar), Michael Granda (bass) form the core of the group.

| 06/07/75 | 7 | 2 | Jackie Blue .... A&M | | |

P

PABLO CRUISE
American pop-rock group: Dave Jenkins (guitar, bass, vocals), Cory Lerios (keyboards, vocals), Bud Cockrell (bass, vocals), Steve Price (drums). In 1977, Cockrell replaced by Bruce Day, who in turn was replaced by John Pierce in 1980. Guitarist/vocalist Angelo Rossi joined in 1980.

08/13/77	16	16	Whatcha Gonna Do? .... A&M		
09/06/78	13	12	Love Will Find A Way .... A&M		
01/09/80	18	8	I Want You Tonight.. A&M		
09/26/81	14	5	Cool Love .... A&M		

PAGE, Martin
British male pop singer/songwriter born on 09/23/59 in Southampton, Hampshire, England. Co-wrote "We Built This City" by Starship, "These Dreams" by Heart, and "King Of Wishful Thinking" by Go West.

| 04/24/95 | --- | RA | In The House Of Stone And Light .... Mercury | | 7 |

PAGE, Jimmy - see PUFF DADDY

PAGE, Tommy
American male pop singer born on 05/24/69 in West Caldwell, New Jersey.

| 05/14/90 | 5 | 9 | I'll Be Your Everything..Sire | | 8 |
| 07/02/90 | 23 | 7 | When I Dream Of You ....Sire | | |

PAGLIARO, Michel
Canadian male singer born on 11/09/48 in Montreal.

| 11/08/75 | 16 | 7 | What The Hell I Got .... Columbia | | |
| 04/30/77 | 33 | 4 | Dock Of The Bay .... Columbia | | |

PAIGE, Jennifer
American female singer born on 09/03/73 in Marietta, Georgia.

DATE	PK	WK	TITLE	LABEL	RA
09/27/98	2(3)	16	Crush .... Hollywood		1

PALMER, Robert
British male rock singer born Alan Palmer on 01/19/49 in Batley, England. Raised on the island of Malta. Lead singer of the supergroup The Power Station in 1985.

DATE	PK	WK	TITLE	LABEL	RA
10/03/79	5	6	Bad Case Of Loving You............................. Island		
01/24/81	17	4	Looking For Clues....................................... Island		
05/05/86	7	18	Addicted To Love.. Island		
08/18/86	16	12	I Didn't Mean To Turn You On...................... Island		
09/19/88	1(3)	19	Simply Irresistible .... EMI-Manhattan		
12/24/90	18	9	You're Amazing ....EMI		17
05/06/91	19	9	Mercy Mercy Me (The Ecology)/I Want You......EMI		5
12/05/94	---	RA	Know By Now ....EMI		26

PAPERBOY
American male rapper M. Johnson born circa 1973 in Los Angeles.

DATE	PK	WK	TITLE	LABEL	RA
04/26/93	4	20	Ditty... Next Plateau		

PARACHUTE CLUB
Canadian pop group based in Toronto formed in 1982: Keith Brownstone (guitar), Billy Bryans (drums, percussion), Lauri Conger (keyboards, synthesizer, vocals), Margo Davidson (saxophone, percussion, vocals), Dave Gray (guitar), Julie Masi (percussion, vocals), Lorraine Segato (vocals, guitar, percussion), Steve Webster (bass). Won Juno Awards for Most Promising Group of the Year in 1984 and Group of the Year in 1985.

DATE	PK	WK	TITLE	LABEL	RA
10/31/83	18	8	Rise Up .... Current		
02/18/85	11	13	At The Feet Of The Moon............................... RCA		
01/26/87	31	8	Love Is Fire... RCA		

PARKER, Ray, Jr./Raydio
American male R&B-pop singer/songwriter born on 05/01/54 in Detroit. Started music career as a session guitarist/writer, worked with Stevie Wonder, Barry White, and Herbie Hancock. Formed Raydio in 1978: Arnell Carmichael (keyboards, vocals), Darren Carmichael (guitar), Larry Tolbert (drums), Charles Fearing (guitar), Jerry Knight (later member of Ollie & Jerry). Parker went solo in 1982.

DATE	PK	WK	TITLE	LABEL	RA
05/31/78	13	12	Jack And Jill *..Arista		
08/22/79	15	8	You Can't Change That * ....Arista		
06/20/81	8	9	A Woman Needs Love ** ....Arista		
06/19/82	11	9	The Other Woman ***....................................Arista		
02/21/83	19	3	Bad Boy ***..Arista		
03/12/84	30	9	I Still Can't Get Over Loving You ***..............Arista		
08/27/84	1(5)	18	Ghostbusters *** ....Arista		
02/25/85	38	2	Jamie *** ....Arista		
12/09/85	36	3	Girls Are More Fun *** ....Arista		

* Raydio
** Ray Parker Jr. & Raydio
*** Ray Parker Jr.

PARLIAMENT

DATE	PK	WK	TITLE	LABEL RA

American R&B-funk aggregation of musicians formed as The Parliaments in the mid-1950's by lead vocalist George Clinton.

| 09/04/76 | 24 | 11 | Tear The Roof Off The Sucker | Casablanca |

PARR, John
British male pop-rock singer/songwriter born in Nottingham, England.

| 10/14/85 | 3(2) | 16 | St. Elmo's Fire (Man In Motion) | Atlantic |

PARSONS, Alan, Project
British pop duo formed in 1975 in London: producer/engineer Alan Parsons (keyboards, guitar, b. 1949 in England) and lyricist/manager Eric Woolfson (vocals). Parsons engineered The Beatles' Abbey Road and Pink Floyd's "Dark Side Of The Moon". Project records with various vocalists.

08/22/81	11	8	Time	Arista
09/04/82	5	14	Eye In The Sky	Arista
06/04/84	20	9	Don't Answer Me	Arista

PARTLAND BROTHERS
Canadian pop duo from Colgan, Ontario, consisting of brothers Chris (vocals, guitar) and G.P. Partland (vocals, percussion).

| 12/08/86 | 27 | 11 | Soul City | Capitol |

PARTNERS IN KRYME
American rap duo from New York: DJ James "Keymaster Snow" Alpern, rapper Richard "MC Golden Voice" Usher. Met while studying speech communications at Syracuse University. Kryme stands for Keeping Rhythm Your Motivating Energy.

| 07/09/90 | 6 | 10 | Turtle Power | SBK 21 |

PARTON, Dolly
American female country singer/songwriter born Dolly Rebecca Parton on 01/19/46 in Locust Ridge, Sevier County, Tennessee. Became a regular on a Knoxville radio station at age 10. Appeared in the Grand Ole Opry at age 12. In Porter Wagoner's syndicated country music show, 1967-74. Wrote "I Will Always Love You" recorded by Parton and later Whitney Houston (Houston's version is one of the best-selling singles worldwide of all time). Starred in the movies *9 To 5*, *The Best Little Whorehouse In Texas*, and *Steel Magnolias*. In 1985, opened Dollywood, an amusement park in Pigeon Forge, Tennessee.

02/08/78	2(2)	14	Here You Come Again	RCA
03/07/81	2(1)	9	9 To 5	RCA
11/14/83	1(9)	22	Islands In The Stream *	RCA

* Kenny Rogers & Dolly Parton

PASSENGERS - see U2

PAYOLAS
Canadian group based in Vancouver, formed in 1982: Paul Hyde (vocals, b. 05/21/55), Bob Rock (vocals), Chris Taylor (drums), Larry Wilkins (bass). Disbanded in 1985. Hyde and Rock continued recording as Rock & Hyde. Won the 1993 Juno Award for Most Promising Group of the Year.

DATE	PK	WK	TITLE	LABEL	RA
08/14/82	3(3)	12	Eyes Of A Stranger	A&M	
09/26/83	13	9	Never Said I Loved You *	A&M	
06/10/85	32	9	You're The Only Love **	A&M	

* Payola$ with Carol Pope
** Paul Hyde & The Payolas

PEACH UNION
British pop trio formed in 1991 in London: Lisa Lamb (vocals), Pascal Gabriel (keyboards, programming), Paul Statham (keyboards, programming).

DATE	PK	WK	TITLE	LABEL	RA
10/20/97	---	RA	On My Own	Mute	2

PEACHES & HERB
American R&B duo formed in 1965 in Washington, D.C.: Herb Fame (b. Herbert Feemster in 1942 in Washington) and Francine Barker (last name: Hurd, b. 1947 in Washington). Barker replaced briefly by Marlene Mack, 1968-69. Disbanded in 1970. Re-formed in 1977 with Fame and vocalist Linda Green.

DATE	PK	WK	TITLE	LABEL	RA
05/02/79	9	10	Shake Your Groove Thing	Polydor	
06/13/79	1(2)	16	Reunited	Polydor	
06/11/80	8	9	I Pledge My Love	Polydor	

PEARL JAM
American rock band formed in 1990 in Seattle: Eddie Vedder (vocals, b. Edward Mueller on 12/23/66 in Evanston, Illinois), Jeff Ament (bass, b. 03/10/63 in Big Sandy, Montana), Stone Gossard (guitar, 07/20/66 in Seattle), Dave Krusen (drums), Mike McCready (guitar, b. 04/05/65 in Seattle). Krusen replaced by Dave Abbruzzese (b. 05/17/64) in 1991. Abbruzzese left in 1994, replaced by Jack Irons. Responsible for popularizing the Seattle "grunge" sound.

DATE	PK	WK	TITLE	LABEL	RA
01/24/94	---	RA	Daughter	Epic	23
03/20/95	---	RA	Better Man	Epic	8
04/01/96	12	12	Merkinball	Epic	
09/30/96	15	9 h	Who You Are	Epic	
01/12/97	31	1	I Got ID	Epic	
01/11/98	2(2)	9	Given To Fly	Epic	
05/17/98	7	15	Wishlist	Epic	
06/13/99	1(6)	7 +	Last Kiss	Epic	21+

PEBBLES
American female R&B singer/songwriter/producer born Perri Alette McKissack on 08/29/65 in Oakland, California. Nicknamed "Pebbles" by godfather after cartoon character Pebbles Flintstones. Married to singer/songwriter/producer L.A. Reid of The Deele. Formed R&B group TLC.

DATE	PK	WK	TITLE	LABEL	RA
06/06/88	20	12	Girlfriend	MCA	
08/08/88	32	8	Mercedes Boy	MCA	
11/19/90	19	6	Giving You The Benefit	MCA	13

PEE WEE HERMAN
American male children's actor/comedian Paul Reubenfeld in 08/27/52 in Peekskill, New York. In the movies *Pee-wee's Big Adventure* (1985), *Pee-wee's Big Top* (1988), and TV's *Pee-wee's Playhouse*. Charged with indecent exposure on 07/26/91 in Sarasota, Florida.

DATE	PK	WK	TITLE	LABEL	RA
08/24/87	39	2	Surfin' Bird .... Columbia		

PEEPLES, Nia
American female R&B singer/actress born on 12/10/61. Played Nicole Chapman in the TV series *Fame*. Hosted American version of the TV show *Top Of The Pops* and music video dance TV program *Party Machine*. Married to R&B singer Howard Hewett, 1989-93.

12/16/91	10	10	Street Of Dreams .... Virgin		17

PENISTON, Ce Ce
American female R&B singer born on 09/06/69 in Dayton, Ohio. Won Miss Black Arizona pageant in 1989.

02/10/92	1(2)	18	Finally .... A&M		5
04/20/92	8	18	We Got A Love Thang .... A&M		9
07/06/92	14	12	Keep On Walkin' .... A&M		29
10/19/92	32	2	Inside That I Cried .... A&M		
03/07/94	10	30	I'm In The Mood .... A&M		40

PENN, Michael
American male rock singer/songwriter born on 08/01/58 in New York City. Based in Los Angeles. Older brother of actor Sean Penn, son of actor/director Leo Penn and actress Eileen Ryan.

04/16/90	8	10	No Myth .... RCA		13

PERFECT GENTLEMEN
American R&B teen trio produced by New Edition and New Kids On The Block producer Maurice Starr: Corey Blakely, Maurice Starr, Jr. (Starr's son), Tyrone Sutton.

06/25/90	6	12	Ooh La La .... Columbia		26

PERRY, Steve
American male rock singer/songwriter born on 01/22/49 in Hanford, California. Lead singer of Journey since 1977.

07/02/84	2(3)	21	Oh Sherrie .... Columbia		
08/13/84	40	2	She's Mine .... Columbia		
09/12/94	---	RA	You Better Wait .... Columbia		6

PET SHOP BOYS
British techno-pop/dance duo formed in 1981 in London: Neil Tennant (vocals, b. Neil Francis Tennant on 07/10/54 in Gosforth, England) and Chris Lowe (keyboards, b. Christopher Sean Lowe on 10/04/59 in Blackpool, England). Met in 1981 when Lowe was an architecture student and Tennant was a journalist (later wrote for British music magazine *Smash Hits*). Released documentary film *It Couldn't Happen Here* in 1988. Tennant recorded with the group Electronic in 1989.

06/02/86	1(2)	17	West End Girls .... EMI		
09/08/86	26	3	Opportunities (Let's Make Lots Of Money) .... EMI		
12/07/87	4	17	It's A Sin .... EMI		
03/21/88	2(1)	13	What Have I Done To Deserve This * .... EMI		
05/30/88	1(4)	18	Always On My Mind .... EMI-Manhattan		
01/16/89	9	14	Domino Dancing .... EMI-Manhattan		

DATE	PK	WK	TITLE	LABEL	RA
11/19/90	18	12	So Hard	Capitol	27
07/01/91	18	9	Where The Streets Have No Name	Capitol	
08/30/93	6	27	Can You Forgive Her	Capitol	11
12/20/93	---	RA	Go West	EMI	7
03/28/94	---	RA	I Wouldn't Normally Do This Kind Of Thing	EMI	24

* Pet Shop Boys/Dusty Springfield

PETTY, Tom, And The Heartbreakers
American rock group formed in 1975 in Los Angeles: Tom Petty (vocals, guitar, b. 10/20/52 in Gainesville, Florida), Mike Campbell (guitar, b. 02/01/54 in Gainesville), Benmont Tench (keyboards, b. 09/07/54 in Gainesville), Ron Blair (bass, b. 09/16/52 in Macon, Georgia), Stan Lynch (drums, b. 05/21/55 in Gainesville). Blair left in 1982, replaced by Howie Epstein (bass, b. 07/21/55). Lynch replaced by Steve Ferrone in 1994.

DATE	PK	WK	TITLE	LABEL	RA
02/20/80	14	8	Don't Do Me Like That	Backstreet	
04/16/80	8	9	Refugee	Backstreet	
06/27/81	7	8	The Waiting	Backstreet	
10/03/81	2(1)	11	Stop Draggin' My Heart Around *	Modern	
12/25/82	17	3	You Got Lucky	Backstreet	
06/10/85	25	5	Don't Come Around Here No More	MCA	
07/24/89	13	12	I Won't Back Down **	MCA	
10/02/89	40	3	Running Down A Dream **	MCA	
08/26/91	---	RA	Learning To Fly	MCA	10
02/28/94	---	RA	Mary Jane's Last Dance	MCA	28
02/06/95	---	RA	You Don't Know How It Feels **	Warner	9
03/11/96	---	RA	Waiting For Tonight **	MCA	20
09/30/96	3(1)	12 h	Walls **	Warner	15

* Stevie Nicks (with Tom Petty & The Heartbreakers)
** Tom Petty

PHATTS AND SMALL

DATE	PK	WK	TITLE	LABEL	RA
06/13/99	11	9 +	Turn-a-round	DanceNet	

Another version, credited to Phats And Small present Mutant Disco, peaked at #28 on 05/23/99.

PHILLIPS, Esther
American female R&B singer/multi-instrumentalist born Esther Mae Jones on 12/23/35 in Galveston, Texas. R&B superstar of the 1940's to the 1960's. Died of kidney and liver failure on 08/07/84 in Torrance, California.

DATE	PK	WK	TITLE	LABEL	RA
11/15/75	16	7	What A Diff'rence A Day Makes	Kudu	

PHILOSOPHER KINGS
Canadian R&B-flavoured pop group from Toronto: Gerald Eaton (vocals), Jon Levine (piano), Brian West (guitar), Jason Levine (bass), James McCollum (guitar). Won the 1996 Juno Award for Best New Group. Jason Levine and McCollum formed the animated pop duo Prozzäk in 1998.

DATE	PK	WK	TITLE	LABEL	RA
06/12/95	---	RA	Charms	Epic	4
04/13/98	---	RA	Hurts To Love You	Columbia	10
06/29/98	---	RA	Cry	Columbia	13

DATE	PK	WK	TITLE	LABEL	RA
04/05/99	---	RA	You Stepped On My Life ....Columbia		24

PIG

| 12/13/98 | 29 | 1 | Pig X-Mas Song.. Indy |

PILOT
Scottish trio: David Paton (lead singer, guitar), Bill Lyall (keyboards, d. of AIDS in 1989), Stuart Tosh (drums).

| 07/26/75 | 5 | 10 | Magic ....EMI |

PINK FLOYD
British progressive rock group formed in 1965 in London: David Gilmour (guitar, vocals, b. 03/06/44 in Cambridge, England), Syd Barrett (guitar, vocals, b. Roger Keith Barrett on 01/06/46 in Cambridge), Richard Wright (keyboards, vocals, b. 07/28/45 in London), Roger Waters (bass, vocals, b. 09/06/44 in Surrey, England), Nick Mason (drums, b. 01/27/45 in Birmingham, England). Barrett left in 1969, Waters left in 1984. All five members have recorded solo. Inducted into the Rock and Roll Hall of Fame in 1996.

03/19/80	1(5)	23	Another Brick In The Wall ....Columbia	
06/06/94	---	RA	Keep Talking...Columbia	11
08/22/94	8	22	Take It Back ....Columbia	18

P.J.
Canadian male dance club D.J./remixer Paul Jacobs from Toronto. Attended Osgoode Law School in Toronto when "Happy Days" was charting.

| 11/24/96 | 7 | 14 | Happy Days...Koch |

PLANET SOUL
American/Cuban dance duo formed in Miami in 1995 consisting of Miami-raised producer/songwriter George Acosta (b. circa 1971 in Cuba) and vocalist Nadine Renee.

| 03/18/96 | 7 | 20 | Set U Free ....Quality |

PLANT, Robert
British male rock singer born on 08/20/48 in Bromwich, England. Lead singer of Led Zeppelin and The Honeydrippers.

11/21/83	16	8	Big Log...Es Paranza	
07/25/88	13	12	Tall Cool One ....Es Paranza	
05/28/90	20	9	Hurting Kind..Es Paranza	33
09/27/93	---	RA	29 Palms ....Es Paranza	25

PLATINUM BLONDE
Canadian rock quartet from Toronto: Mark Holmes (vocals), Sergio Galli (guitar), Kenny MacLean (keyboards/bass), Chris Steffer (percussion). Formed in the early-1980's as a Police tribute band. Recorded as The Blondes in 1990. MacLean later recorded solo.

| 03/12/84 | 34 | 5 | Doesn't Really Matter...............................Columbia |
| 01/14/85 | 17 | 2 | Not In Love...Columbia |

DATE	PK	WK	TITLE	LABEL	RA
09/16/85	2(4)	17	Crying Over You	Columbia	
12/16/85	18	11	Situation Critical	Columbia	
02/03/86	26	7	Somebody Somewhere	Columbia	
11/23/87	11	14	Contact	Columbia	

PLAYA
American R&B trio from Kentucky: Black (b. circa 1975), Smokey (b. circa 1977), Static (b. circa 1975).

01/18/98	34	1	Don't Stop The Music	Def Jam	

PLAYAHITTY
French dance-pop singer Mario (b. circa 1971 in French Guiana). Named Miss Guiana in 1991.

07/17/95	---	RA	The Summer Is Magic	Future-Tell	31
10/23/95	36	2	1-2-3 (Train With Me)	Quality	

PLAYER
American pop-rock group formed in Los Angeles: Peter Beckett (vocals, guitar), John Crowley (vocals, guitar), Ronn Moss (bass), John Friesen (drums), Wayne Cooke (keyboards). Moss plays Ridge Forrester in the TV soap *The Bold & Beautiful*. Crowell started recording Country music in 1988. Beckett joined Little River Band by 1992.

01/25/78	4	18	Baby Come Back	Polydor	

PLUTO
Canadian rock group formed in 1993 in Vancouver: Ian Jones (guitar, vocals), John Ounpuu (bass, vocals), Rolf Hetherington (guitar), Jason Leigh (drums).

07/15/96	39	1 h	Paste	Virgin	
09/14/98	---	RA	Goodbye Girl	Virgin	22

PM DAWN
American rap-pop duo formed in 1989 in Jersey City, New Jersey: brothers Prince Be (vocals, b. Attrell Cordes on 05/19/70 in Jersey City), DJ Minutemix (DJ, b. Jarrett Cordes on 07/17/71 in Jersey City). PM Dawn means "from the darkest hour comes light".

12/23/91	2(4)	16	Set Adrift On Memory Bliss	Island	2
03/23/92	21	10	Paper Doll	Island	19
11/23/92	15	17	I'd Die Without You	Island	6
03/29/93	21	9	Plastic	Island	
05/31/93	2(2)	18	Looking Through Patient Eyes	Island	1
09/06/93	---	RA	The Ways Of The Wind	Island	16
02/07/94	4	22	You Got Me Floatin'	Island	
11/13/95	38	2	Downtown Venus	Island	8

POCO
American country-rock band formed in 1968 in Los Angeles. Line-up in the 1970's: Paul Cotton (guitar, vocals, b. 02/26/43 in Los Angeles), Steve Chapman (drums), Rusty Young (guitar, b. 02/23/46 in Long Beach, California), Charlie Harrison (bass), Kim Bullard (keyboards). Re-formed in 1989 with ex-members Young, Jim Messina (guitar, vocals, b. 12/05/47 in Maywood, California), George Grantham (drums, vocals, b. 11/20/47 in Cordell, Oklahoma), Richie Furay (guitar, vocals, b. 05/09/44 in Yellow Springs, Ohio), Randy Meisner (bass, vocals, b. 03/08/46 in Scottsbluff, Nebraska). Meisner and ex-

DATE	PK	WK	TITLE	LABEL	RA

member Timothy B. Schmidt (bass, vocals, b. 10/03/47 in Sacramento, California) later joined The Eagles. Messina was a member of Loggins & Messina and Buffalo Springfield.

04/18/79	19	2	Crazy Love	ABC	
12/04/89	30	11	Call It Love	RCA	

POINTER SISTERS
American pop/R&B vocal group formed in 1971 in Oakland, California consisting of sisters Ruth (b. 03/19/46 in Oakland), Anita (b. 01/23/48 in East Oakland), Bonnie (b. 07/11/51 in East Oakland, California), and June (b. 11/30/53 in East Oakland) Pointer. Backup vocals for Elvin Bishop, Boz Scaggs, Sylvester. Appeared in the 1976 movie *Car Wash*. Bonnie left to pursue solo career in 1978.

03/21/79	6	14	Fire	Planet	
11/08/80	4	9	He's So Shy	Planet	
08/15/81	2(3)	12	Slow Hand	Planet	
04/03/82	11	5	Should I Do It	Planet	
05/21/84	28	7	Automatic	Planet	
08/13/84	4	14	Jump (For My Love)	Planet	
12/03/84	19	7	I'm So Excited	Planet	
02/18/85	4	17	Neutron Dance	Planet	
09/16/85	23	7	Dare Me	RCA	

POINTER, Bonnie
American female R&B singer born on 07/11/50 in East Oakland, California. Member of the Pointer Sisters, 1971-78.

10/31/79	12	4	Heaven Must Have Sent You	Motown	

POISON
American hard rock group formed in 1983 in Harrisburg, Pennsylvania: Bret Michaels (vocals, guitar, b. Bret Michael Sychak on 03/15/63 in Harrisburg), Bobby Dall (bass, vocals, b. Robert Kuy Kendall on 11/02/65 in Miami), Rikki Rockett (drums, b. Richard Ream on 08/08/61 in Mechanicsburg, Pennsylvania), C.C. DeVille (guitar, vocals, b. Bruce Anthony Johannesson on 05/14/62 in Brooklyn, New York). Richie Kotzen (b. 02/03/70 in Reading, Pennsylvania) replaced DeVille in 1991. DeVille returned in 1996.

06/22/87	14	10	Talk Dirty To Me	Capitol	
02/20/89	2(1)	18	Every Rose Has Its Thorn	Enigma	
05/01/89	14	12	Your Mama Don't Dance	Enigma	
08/27/90	1(3)	16	Unskinny Bop	Enigma	3
11/26/90	1(2)	17	Something To Believe In	Enigma	2
04/08/91	---	RA	Ride The Wind	Enigma	39
03/15/93	15	9	Stand	Capitol	18

POLICE, The
British rock trio formed in 1977 in England: Sting (bass, vocals, saxophone, keyboards, b. Gordon Sumner on 10/02/51 in Wallsend, England), Stewart Copeland (drums, b. 07/16/52 in Alexandria, Egypt), Andy Summers (guitar, b. Andrew Somers on 12/31/42 in Poulton-Le-Fylde, England). Disbanded in 1984. Sting began solo career in 1985. Copeland composed film scores for Oliver Stone's *Wall Street* and *Talk Radio*, recorded with the rock band Animal Logic.

01/09/80	8	16	Message In A Bottle	A&M	
11/29/80	6	11	Don't Stand So Close To Me	A&M	

DATE	PK	WK	TITLE	LABEL	RA
01/24/81	5	11	De Do Do Do, De Da Da Da	A&M	
11/14/81	1(1)	14	Every Little Thing She Does Is Magic	A&M	
02/13/82	11	7	Spirits In The Material World	A&M	
08/15/83	1(5)	23	Every Breath You Take	A&M	
10/10/83	4	13	King Of Pain	A&M	
12/19/83	35	5	Synchronicity II	A&M	
02/13/84	27	7	Wrapped Around Your Finger	A&M	
12/22/86	32	7	Don't Stand So Close To Me '86	A&M	
01/18/98	26	6	Roxanne '97 - Puff Daddy Remix *	A&M	

Another version peaked at #29 on 01/18/98.

* Sting & The Police

PORN KINGS

01/05/97	11	26	Up To No Good	Warner	

PORTISHEAD

British dance group formed in 1993 in Bristol, England: Beth Gibbons (vocals, b. 01/04/65 in Devon, England), Geoff Barrow (programming, drums, keyboards, b. 12/09/71 in Walton-In-Gordano, England), Adrian Utley (musical director, guitar, bass, keyboards, b. 1958).

04/17/95	---	RA	Sour Times	London	22
05/02/99	17	33 +	Glorytimes	London	

PORTRAIT

American R&B vocal quartet formed in the early-1990's in Los Angeles: Eric Kirland, Michael Angelo Saulsberry (both from Los Angeles), Irving Washington III (from Providence, Rhode Island), Phillip Johnson (from Tulsa, Oklahoma).

04/12/93	29	12	Here We Go Again	Capitol	25

POSITIVE K

American male rapper Darryl Gibson born circa 1967 in The Bronx, New York. Adopted the name Positive Knowledge Allah after converting to Islam in 1982.

02/15/93	11	15	I Got A Man	Island	

POST, Mike

American producer/composer born on 09/29/44 in Los Angeles. Composer of several television and movie scores. Orchestra leader for TV's *Andy Williams Show* (1969-71), *The Mac Davis Show* (1974-76).

08/23/75	5	8	The Rockford Files	MGM	

POV

American R&B/hip-hop group from New Jersey: Marc Sherman ("The Rapper Extraordinaire") (b. circa 1974), Hakim "HB" Bell (b. circa 1975), Lincoln "Link" DeVulgt (b. Virgin Islands), Ewarner "E" Mills (b. circa 1974). "POV" is an abbreviation for Point of View. Bell's father is Robert "Kool" Bell (Kool & The Gang).

10/18/93	34	4	All Thru The Night *	Giant	

DATE	PK	WK	TITLE	LABEL	RA

* POV & Jade

POWDER BLUES
Canadian rock group from Vancouver: Tom Lavin (guitar), Jack Lavin (bass, keyboards), Mark Hasselbach (trumpet), Duris Maxwell (drums), Wayne Kozak (saxophone), Gordie Bertram (saxophone), David Woodward (saxophone). Formed in 1978. Won the 1981 Juno Award for Most Promising Group of the Year.

| 09/19/81 | 6 | 8 | Thirsty Ears | Liberty | |

POWER STATION
British/American rock supergroup formed in 1985: Robert Palmer (vocals, b. Alan Palmer on 01/19/49 in Batley, England), Tony Thompson (drums), John Taylor (bass, b. 06/20/60 in Birmingham, England), Andy Taylor (guitar, b. 02/16/61 in Dolver-Hampton, England). Both Taylors are from Duran Duran. Thompson was a member of Chic.

| 05/06/85 | 9 | 13 | Some Like It Hot | Capitol | |
| 09/16/85 | 21 | 11 | Get It On (Bang A Gong) | Capitol | |

PRATT & McCLAIN
American pop group featuring Truett Pratt and Jerry McClain, with backup vocals from the group Brother Love.

| 06/12/76 | 5 | 12 | Happy Days | Reprise | |

PREMIER

| 08/22/94 | --- | RA | Open Up Your Heart | A&M | 32 |

PRESIDENTS OF THE UNITED STATES OF AMERICA, The
American alternative rock trio formed in 1991 in Seattle: Chris Ballew (vocals), Dave Dederer (guitar), Jason Finn (drums). Disbanded in 1997.

| 11/27/95 | --- | RA | Lump | Columbia | 28 |
| 04/08/96 | 28 | 7 h | Peaches | Columbia | 28 |

PRESLEY, Elvis
American male rock & roll singer/songwriter born on 01/08/35 in East Tupelo, Mississippi. Widely known as "The King Of Rock N' Roll", the top recording artist of the rock era (1955-present). Primarily popular in the 1950's and the 1960's. Made American television debut on 01/28/56 on *Stage Show*. In 1957, performed at three concerts in Canada (his only concert tour outside the United States). Served two years in the U.S. Army, 1958-60. Married Priscilla Beaulieu on 05/01/67, had only child, Lisa Marie, on 02/01/68, who later married pop superstar Michael Jackson. Priscilla and Presley divorced on 10/11/73; Priscilla later pursued acting career in the 1980's. Starred in 31 feature films beginning in 1956. Died of a heart failure caused by prescription drug abuse on 08/16/77 at his Graceland estate in Memphis, Tennessee. In 1986, was one of the first ten performers inducted into the Rock And Roll Hall Of Fame.

06/05/76	35	3	Hurt	RCA	
04/02/77	29	4	Moody Blue	RCA	
11/02/77	10	8	Way Down	RCA	
12/14/77	2(6)	18	My Way	RCA	
04/05/78	20	12	Unchained Melody	RCA	

DATE	PK	WK	TITLE	LABEL	RA

PRESTON, Billy
American male R&B singer/keyboardist born on 09/09/46 in Houston. Regular on TV's Shindig. Wrote Joe Cocker's "You Are So Beautiful". Sideman for Little Richard, Ray Charles, the Beatles, and the Rolling Stones.

| 05/07/80 | 6 | 8 | With You I'm Born Again * | Quality | |

* Billy Preston/Syreeta

PRETENDERS, The
British/American rock band formed in 1978 in London: Chrissie Hynde (vocals, guitar, b. 09/07/51 in Akron, Ohio), Pete Farndon (bass, b. 06/12/52 in Hereford, England), James Honeyman-Scott (guitar, b. 11/04/56 in Hereford), Martin Chambers (drums, b. 09/04/51 in Hereford). Honeyman-Scott died of a drug overdose on 06/16/82, replaced by Robbie McIntosh. Farndon died of a drug overdose on 04/14/83 in London, replaced by Malcolm Foster. Changes include the addition of guitarist Adam Seymour, bassist Andy Hobson in 1993.

05/14/80	15	4	Brass In Pocket	Sire	
04/11/83	5	12	Back On The Chain Gang	Sire	
03/05/84	19	12	Middle Of The Road	Sire	
12/29/86	15	12	Don't Get Me Wrong	Sire	
07/04/94	---	RA	Night In My Veins	Sire	11
11/07/94	---	RA	I'll Stand By You	Sire	14

PRETTY POISON
American dance band from Philadelphia formed by Camden, New Jersey natives Jade Starling (vocals) and Whey Cooler.

| 02/22/88 | 11 | 17 | Catch Me (I'm Falling) | Virgin | |

PRIEST, Maxi
British male reggae singer born Max Alfred Elliott on 06/10/60 in London.

02/20/89	3(3)	13	Wild World	Virgin	
11/05/90	8	20	Close To You	Virgin	5
09/16/96	9	11 h	That Girl *	Virgin	2
			SoundScan: #14 (10/20/96) / 8 wks.		
12/02/96	---	RA	Watching The World Go By	Virgin	28

* Maxi Priest featuring Shaggy

PRIMAL SCREAM
Scottish rock band formed in 1986: Bobby Gillespie (vocals, b. 06/22/64 in Scotland), Denise Johnson (vocals), Robert Young (guitar), Andrew Innes (guitar), Martin Duffy (keyboards), David Hood (bass), Roger Hawkins (drums).

| 06/13/94 | --- | RA | Rocks | Sire | 22 |

PRIMITIVE RADIO GODS
American male alternative rock singer Chris O'Connor.

| 10/07/96 | 4 | 15 h | Standing Outside A Broken Phone Booth With Money In My Hand | Work | 2 |

DATE	PK	WK	TITLE	LABEL	RA

PRINCE

American male pop-R&B singer/songwriter/multi-instrumentalist/actor/producer born Prince Rogers Nelson on 06/07/58 in Minneapolis. Self-taught guitar, piano, and drums by age 14. Had his own band in high school called Grand Central. Discovered the groups Vanity 6 and The Time. Starred in the movies *Purple Rain* (1984), *Under The Cherry Moon* (1986), *Sign 'O' The Times* (1987), *Graffiti Bridge* (1989). Opened own label and studio, both named Paisley Park in 1985. Wrote Sinead O'Connor's "Nothing Compares 2 U" and Sheena Easton's "Sugar Walls". Credited The Revolution, a six-member band, with playing on his records, 1984-87. Unveiled his new band, New Power Generation (NPG), an eight-member band in January 1991. *Billboards* rock ballet, choreographed by Joffrey Ballet of New York to Prince's music. Announced he would no longer record with the NPG and changed his name to an unpronounceable symbol combining both male and female symbols on 06/07/93. Paisley Records out of business in February 1994 after Warner Brothers dropped its distribution deal with the label. Married NPG member Mayte Garcia on 02/14/96. Their first son died shortly after birth in October 1996.

DATE	PK	WK	TITLE	LABEL	RA
06/06/83	5	14	Little Red Corvette	Warner	
08/22/83	6	9	1999	Warner	
11/28/83	27	3	Delirious	Warner	
08/13/84	1(2)	17	When Doves Cry	Warner	
10/22/84	4	11	Let's Go Crazy *	Warner	
12/03/84	3(1)	13	Purple Rain *	Warner	
02/18/85	14	7	I Would Die 4 U *	Warner	
07/01/85	8	11	Raspberry Beret *	Paisley Park	
05/05/86	4	18	Kiss *	Paisley Park	
05/04/87	5	11	Sign 'O' The Times	Paisley Park	
12/07/87	22	7	U Got The Look	Paisley Park	
03/07/88	33	6	I Could Never Take The Place Of Your Man	Warner	
06/06/89	30	8	Alphabet Street	Warner	
08/21/89	1(2)	15	Batdance	Warner	
10/16/89	31	3	Partyman	Warner	
09/10/90	5	11	Thieves In The Temple	Paisley Park	4
09/30/91	25	10	Gett Off **	Paisley Park	
12/02/91	3(4)	16	Cream **	Paisley Park	2
03/02/92	12	15	Diamonds And Pearls **	Paisley Park	5
05/25/92	---	RA	Money Don't Matter 2 Night **	Paisley Park	10
08/31/92	11	14	Sexy MF **	Paisley Park	
11/16/92	5	15	My Name Is Prince **	Paisley Park	
02/15/93	3(1)	15	7 **	Paisley Park	5
05/10/93	---	RA	Morning Papers **	Paisley Park	8
11/08/93	7	22	Pink Cashmere	Paisley Park	24
05/30/94	---	RA	The Most Beautiful Girl In The World	NPG	6
10/03/94	20	17	Let It Go	Warner	10
10/09/95	25	4	I Hate You	Warner	
02/05/96	---	RA	Gold	Warner	39
01/20/97	---	RA	Betcha By Golly Wow	NPG	9
03/10/97	---	RA	The Holy River	NPG	31

* Prince & The Revolution
** Prince & The New Power Generation

PRINGLE, Peter

Canadian male singer born in 1955. Raised in Toronto, sang with the Canadian Opera Company.

DATE	PK	WK	TITLE	LABEL
02/08/78	17	10	You Really Got Me Needing You Now	Warner

DATE	PK	WK	TITLE	LABEL	RA

PRISM
Canadian rock band formed in 1976 in Vancouver: Ron Tabak (vocals), John Hall (keyboards), Allan Harlow (bass), Lindsay Mitchell (guitar), Rocket Norton (drums). Won the 1981 Juno Award for Group of the Year. Disbanded in 1982. Tabak died in a car accident in 1984.

12/28/77	23	12	Spaceship Superstar	GRT	
08/23/78	28	6	Take Me Away	GRT	
09/05/79	26	6	Armageddon	GRT	
05/21/80	11	9	Night To Remember	Capitol	

PROCLAIMERS
Scottish pop/rock duo formed in 1983 in Edinburgh consisting of brothers Craig and Charlie Reid.

08/23/93	---	RA	I'm Gonna Be (500 Miles)	Chrysalis	6

PRODIGY
British techno-dance group formed in 1991 in Braintree, England: Keith Flint (vocals, dancer), Liam Howlett (programming), Maxim Reality (MC), Leeroy Thornhill (dancer).

03/02/97	3(6)	39	Firestarter	XL	
			Another version peaked at #12 on 01/12/97.		
06/29/97	3(1)	49	Breathe	XL	
11/23/97	12	12	Smack My Bitch Up	XL	
10/05/97	37	2	Voodoo People	XL	
10/12/97	32	3	Poison	XL	

PROPELLERHEADS
British electronica/dance duo formed in 1996 in Bath, England: Alex Gifford (keyboards, bass, DJ), Will White (drums, DJ). Gifford once played piano for Van Morrison.

05/03/98	2(1)	12	Bang On	Dreamworks	

PROTOTYPE

09/05/83	22	7	Video Kids	Mercury	

PROZZÄK
Canadian animated pop duo formed in 1998. Consists of characters Simon (vocals) and Milo (guitar, keyboards). Simon and Milo are really Philosopher Kings members Jason Levine and James McCollum respectively. Based in Toronto.

12/28/98	---	RA	Omobolasire	Epic	37
04/19/99	---	RA	Sucks To Be You	Epic	20
07/05/99	---	RA	Strange Disease	Epic	38

PSEUDO ECHO
Australian rock group from Melbourne led by vocalist Brian Canham.

08/24/87	2(1)	17	Funky Town	RCA	

PUBLIC ENEMY

DATE	PK	WK	TITLE	LABEL	RA

American rap group formed in 1982 in Garden City, New Jersey: Chuck D (vocals, b. Carlton Ridenhour on 08/01/60 in New York), Flavor Flav (vocals, b. William Drayton on 03/16/59 in New York), Terminator X (DJ, b. Norman Lee Rogers on 08/25/66 in New York), Professor Griff (minister of information, b. Richard Griffin). Disbanded briefly in 1989 after Griff made controversial remarks against Jews. Griff left in 1989, band continued to record. Flavor Flav was charged with attempted murder after shooting at a neighbour in Bronx, New York.

| 01/20/92 | 12 | 19 | Can't Truss It | Def Jam | |

PUFF DADDY

American male rapper/producer/record company executive born Sean Combs on 11/09/69 in New York City. Became CEO of the record label Bad Boy Entertainment at age 24.

04/27/97	1(8)	38	Can't Nobody Hold Me Down	Arista	
06/22/97	1(13)	41	I'll Be Missing You *	Arista	4
12/21/97	2(6)	33	Been Around The World **	Arista	
			Another version peaked at #9 on 12/07/97.		
06/21/98	7	13	Come With Me ***	Columbia	

* Puff Daddy & Faith Evans (Featuring 112)
** Puff Daddy & the Family (featuring Notorious B.I.G. and Mase)
*** Puff Daddy featuring Jimmy Page

PURSUIT OF HAPPINESS

Canadian rock group formed in 1986 in Edmonton: Moe Berg (vocals, guitar), Tam Amabile (vocals), Tasha Amabile (vocals), Susan Murumets (vocals, replaced later by Kris Abbott), Dave Gilby (drums), Rachel Oldfield (vocals), Johnny Sinclair (bass, vocals, later replaced by Brad Barker), Leslie Stanwyck (vocals). Sinclair (bass), Tim Timleck (drums). Stanwyck and Sinclair later became founding members of Universal Honey in 1992.

04/20/87	38	2	I'm An Adult Now	WEA	
05/01/89	30	4	She's So Young	Chrysalis	
07/16/90	---	RA	Two Girls In Love	Chrysalis	40
10/18/93	30	1	Pressing Lips	Mercury	

Q

Q

American pop quartet from Beaver Falls, Pennsylvania led by Robert Peckman and Don Garvin, both formerly of the group Jaggerz.

| 06/18/77 | 14 | 9 | Dancing Man | Epic | |

QUAD CITY DJ'S

American hip-hop duo formed in 1996 in Jacksonville, Florida: Lana LaFleur (vocals), Johnny "Jayski" McGowan (singer/producer).

| 10/28/96 | --- | RA | C'mon 'N' Ride It (The Train) | Atlantic | 22 |

QUARTERFLASH

DATE	PK	WK	TITLE	LABEL	RA

American rock group formed in 1980 in Portland, Oregon: Rindy Ross (vocals, saxophone), her husband, Marv Ross (vocals, guitar), Jack Charles (vocals, guitar), Rick DiGiallonardo (keyboards), Brian David Willis (drums), Rick Gooch (bass).

01/16/82	9	13	Harden My Heart	Geffen	
04/10/82	17	2	Find Another Fool	Geffen	
08/29/83	23	2	Take Me To Heart	Geffen	

QUATRO, Suzi
American female rock singer born Suzi Quatrocchio on 06/03/50 in Detroit. Played Leather Tuscadero, a semi-regular character on TV's *Happy Days* in 1977. Her older sister Patti played bass in the all-female group Fanny. Hosted British TV show *Gas* in 1983; later starred in the London production of *Annie Get Your Gun*.

05/30/79	8	8	Stumblin' In *	RSO	

* Suzi Quatro & Chris Norman

QUEEN
British rock group formed in 1971 in England: Freddie Mercury (vocals, piano, b. Frederick Bulsara on 09/05/46 in Zanzibar, Tanzania), Brian May (guitar, b. 07/19/47 in Hampton Hill, England), John Deacon (bass, b. 08/19/51 in Leicester, England), Roger Meddows-Taylor (drums, b. 07/26/49 in Norfolk, England). Mercury died of AIDS on 11/24/91 in London.

04/24/76	3(1)	15	Bohemian Rhapsody	Elektra	
07/31/76	16	11	You're My Best Friend	Elektra	
02/05/77	8	14	Somebody To Love	Elektra	
04/05/78	2(2)	26	We Are The Champions	Elektra	
03/19/80	2(2)	16	Crazy Little Thing Called Love	Elektra	
10/18/80	1(4)	14	Another One Bites The Dust	Elektra	
01/16/82	7	12	Under Pressure *	Elektra	
07/03/82	3(2)	11	Body Language	Elektra	
04/23/84	11	11	Radio Ga Ga	Capitol	
07/02/84	27	5	I Want To Break Free	Capitol	
07/17/89	32	5	I Want It All	Capitol	
03/18/91	16	7	Headlong	Hollywood	
05/11/92	---	RA	Bohemian Rhapsody	Hollywood	13
06/14/93	---	RA	Somebody To Love **	Hollywood	4
01/22/96	---	RA	Too Much Love Will Kill You	Hollywood	27

* Queen & David Bowie
** George Michael and Queen

QUEENSRYCHE
American rock band formed in 1981 in Bellevue, Washington: Chris DeGarmo (b. 06/14/63 in Wenatchee, Washington), Eddie Jackson (bass, b. 01/29/61 in Robstown, Texas), Scott Rockenfield (drums, b. 06/15/63 in Seattle), Geoff Tate (vocals, b. 01/14/59 in Stuttgart, Germany), Michael Wilton (guitar, b. 02/23/62 in San Francisco).

05/27/91	6	14	Silent Lucidity	EMI	8

QUIET RIOT

DATE	PK	WK	TITLE	LABEL

American rock group from Los Angeles formed in 1975 in Burbank, California: Kevin DuBrow (vocals, b. 10/29/55 in Los Angeles), Carlos Cavazo (guitar, b. 07/08/57 in Atlanta), Frankie Banali (drums, b. 11/14/53 in Queens, New York), Rudy Sarzo (bass, b. 11/09/52 in Havana, Cuba). Sarzo replaced by Chuck Wright in 1985. DuBrow and Wright left group in 1987, replaced by Paul Shortino (vocals) and Sean McNabb (bass). DuBrow returned in 1990. Disbanded in 1989; re-formed in 1991.

| 01/23/84 | 4 | 16 | Cum On Feel The Noize | Epic |
| 09/24/84 | 37 | 2 | Mama Weer All Crazee Now | Epic |

R

RABBITT, Eddie
American male country singer/songwriter born Edward Thomas on 11/27/44 in Brooklyn, New York. Moved to Nashville in 1968. Big break came in 1970 when Elvis Presley recorded his song "Kentucky Rain". Died of lung cancer on 05/07/98 in Nashville.

10/18/80	14	3	Drivin' My Life Away	Elektra
02/14/81	6	9	I Love A Rainy Night	Elektra
10/10/81	16	3	Step By Step	Elektra
01/30/82	19	2	Someone Could Lose A Heart Tonight	Elektra

RADIOHEAD
British rock group formed in 1991 in Oxford, England: Thom E. Yorke (vocals, guitar, b. 10/07/68 in Wellingborough, England), Jonny Greenwood (guitar, keyboards, b. 11/05/71 in Oxford), Ed O'Brien (guitar, b. Edward John O'Brien on 04/15/68 in Oxford), Colin Greenwood (bass, b. 06/26/69 in Oxford), Phil Selway (drums, b. 05/23/64 in Hemingford Grey, England).

10/04/93	---	RA	Creep	Capitol	34
04/22/96	25	5 h	High & Dry	Capitol	33
09/21/97	39	1	Carma Please Version 1	Koch	
02/08/98	37	1	No Surprises	PID	

RAES, The
Canadian disco duo consisting of the husband-wife team of Robbie and Cherrill Rae from St. Thomas, Ontario.

| 09/07/77 | 14 | 10 | Que Sera Sera | A&M |
| 02/21/79 | 27 | 6 | A Little Lovin' | A&M |

RAFFERTY, Gerry
Scottish male pop singer/songwriter born on 04/16/47 in Paisley, Scotland. Former lead singer of Stealers Wheel.

06/28/78	5	18	Baker Street	United Artists
11/15/78	8	10	Right Down The Line	United Artists
02/21/79	28	2	Home And Dry	United Artists
07/11/79	24	8	Days Gone Down	United Artists
09/19/79	31	4	Get It Right Next Time	United Artists

RAGE
British pop/dance group.

DATE	PK	WK	TITLE	LABEL	RA
04/12/93	25	12	Run To You .... Quality		

RAITT, Bonnie
American female blues-rock singer/songwriter/guitarist born on 11/08/49 in Burbank, California. Her father is Broadway actor/singer John Raitt. Won four Grammies for her 1989 album *Nick Of Time*. Married actor Michael O'Keefe on 04/28/91.

09/09/91	10	10	Something To Talk About........................... Capitol	9
11/04/91	30	4	I Can't Make You Love Me .... Capitol	37
05/16/94	---	RA	Love Sneakin' Up On You .... Capitol	12
12/25/95	---	RA	Rock Steady *... Capitol	11

* Bonnie Raitt & Bryan Adams

RANKIN FAMILY
Canadian Celtic group consisting of five siblings from Inverness County, Cape Breton, Nova Scotia: Carol Jean "Cookie" (vocals, percussion), Heather (vocals, piano, percussion), Jimmy (vocals, acoustic guitar, percussion), John Morris (vocals, piano, fiddle, guitar), Raylene (vocals, percussion) Rankin. All were born in Mabou, Nova Scotia. Won the 1994 Juno Awards for Group of the Year and Canadian Entertainer of the Year.

04/05/93	---	RA	Fare Thee Well Love..EMI	25

RANKS, Shabba
Jamaican dancehall-reggae singer born Rexton Ralston Fernando Gordon on 01/17/66 in Saint Ann's Parish, Jamaica.

09/14/92	14	17	Mr. Loverman .... Epic
01/18/93	2(2)	19	Slow & Sexy .... Epic
02/21/94	9	13	Family Affair .... Epic

RATT
American heavy metal band formed in 1981 in Los Angeles: Bobby Blotzer (drums, b. 10/22/58), Robbin Crosby (guitar), Juan Croucier (bass, b. 08/22/59), Warren De Martini (guitar, b. 04/10/63), Stephen Pearcy (vocals, b. 07/03/56). Disbanded in 1992.

10/01/84	9	9	Round And Round .... Atlantic

RAWLS, Lou
American male R&B singer born on 12/01/35 in Chicago. In the Pilgrim Travelers gospel group in the mid-1950's. Laid in coma for five days after a serious car accident in 1958. In the movies *At Last* and *Believe In Me*. His voice was used in three *Garfield The Cat* television specials.

09/25/76	1(1)	16	You'll Never Find Another Love Like Mine Columbia

RAY, GOODMAN & BROWN
American R&B vocal trio formed as The Moments in the mid-1960's in Hackensack, New Jersey: Harry Ray (b. 12/15/46 in Hackensack), Al Goodman (b. 03/31/47 in Jackson, Mississippi), William Brown (b. 06/30/46 in Perth Amboy, New Jersey). Ray died of a stroke on 10/01/92.

05/07/80	9	6	Special Lady .... Polydor

| DATE | PK | WK | TITLE | LABEL | RA |

RAY, Jimmy
British male pop singer born in Walthamstow, East London, England. Lives in London.

| 03/15/98 | 20 | 9 | Are You Jimmy Ray? | Epic | 3 |

RAYDIO - see PARKER, Ray, Jr./Raydio

REA, Chris
British male pop singer/songwriter born on 03/04/51 in Middlesborough, England.

| 10/18/78 | 4 | 8 | Fool (If You Think It's Over) | United Artists | |

READY FOR THE WORLD
American funk-R&B group formed in 1982 in Flint, Michigan: Melvin Riley, Jr. (lead vocals), Gordon Strozier, Gregory Potts, Willie Triplett, John Eaton, Gerald Valentine.

| 12/02/85 | 3(2) | 16 | Oh Sheila | MCA | |
| 03/23/87 | 27 | 3 | Love You Down | MCA | |

REAL LIFE
Australian quartet led by vocalist David Sterry.

| 04/02/84 | 22 | 11 | Send Me An Angel | MCA | |

REAL McCOY
German dance trio from Berlin formed in 1990: Olaf "O-Jay" Jeglitza, Patricia "Patsy" Petersen, Vanessa Mason. Known as M.C. Sar And The Real McCoy, 1990-95.

04/17/95	18	19	Another Night	Arista	8
05/22/95	13	21	Runaway	Arista	6
08/21/95	---	RA	Come And Get Your Love	Arista	5
02/02/97	28	7	Automatic Lover	NuMuzik	
04/13/97	8	17	One More Time	Arista	19

REALITY
American dance duo from Chicago including Bad Boy Bill, who has own radio show on B96 in Chicago.

| 05/30/94 | 18 | 29 | Yolanda | Quality | |

REALWORLD

| 03/07/94 | --- | RA | We All Need | fre | 35 |
| 08/01/94 | --- | RA | Throwing It All Away | fre | 30 |

REBEL PEBBLES
American pop band from Los Angeles: Rachel Murray (vocals), Karen Blankfeld, Robin Fox, Cheryl Bullock.

| 07/01/91 | 29 | 7 | Dream Lover | I.R.S. | 32 |

RED HOT CHILI PEPPERS

DATE	PK	WK	TITLE	LABEL	RA

American alternative rock group formed in 1983 in Hollywood, California: Michael "Flea" Balzary (bass, b. 10/16/62 in Melbourne, Australia), Jack Irons (drums, b. 07/18/62 in Los Angeles), Anthony Kiedis (vocals, b. 11/01/62 in Grand Rapids, Michigan), Hillel Slovak (guitar, b. 04/13/62 in Haifa, Israel). Slovak died of a drug overdose on 06/25/88 in Los Angeles, replaced by a succession of guitarists: Blackbyrd McKnight, John Frusciante (b. 03/05/70 in New York City), Arik Marshall (b. 02/13/67 in Los Angeles), Jesse Tobias, Dave Navarro (b. 06/07/67 in Santa Monica, California). Irons left in 1988, replaced by D.H. Peligro, who in turn was replaced by Chad Smith (b. 10/25/62 in St. Paul, Minnesota) in 1989. Frusciante recorded solo in 1994.

06/29/92	---	RA	Under The Bridge	Warner	2
11/15/93	1(1)	33	Soul To Squeeze	Warner	18
11/13/95	---	RA	My Friends	Warner	27

RED RIDER - see COCHRANE, Tom, & Red Rider

REDDY, Helen
Australian female pop singer/songwriter born 10/25/41 in Melbourne. Began performing at age four with her show-business parents. Had her own Australian TV show, *Helen Reddy Sings*. To New York in 1966. Hosted NBC-TV's *The Midnight Special* in the 1970's. Appeared in the movies *Airport 1975* (1974), *Pete's Dragon* (1977), and *Sgt. Pepper's Lonely Hearts Club Band* (1978). Served as California's commissioner of parks and recreation in the mid-1970's.

10/25/75	15	7	Ain't No Way To Treat A Lady	Capitol
03/13/76	37	3	Somewhere In The Night	Capitol
08/24/77	17	9	You're My World	Capitol

REDNEX
Swedish techno-dance quartet from Stockholm formed in 1994 by producer/songwriter Pat Reiniz: vocalists Ken Tacky and Mary Joe, fiddle-players Billy Ray and Bobby Sue.

| 05/29/95 | 18 | 9 | Cotton Eye Joe | Jive | 17 |

REEL 2 REAL featuring The Mad Stuntman
American rap-dance duo from New York City: producer Erick Morillo (b. circa 1972 in New York City) and rapper Mark "The Mad Stuntman" Quashie (b. circa 1969 in Trinidad).

| 07/04/94 | 13 | 29 | I Like To Move It | Quality |
| 10/24/94 | 6 | 40 | Go On Move '94 | Quality |

RE-FLEX
British rock quartet founded by keyboardist Paul Fishman.

| 03/19/84 | 22 | 14 | The Politics Of Dancing | Capitol |

REFRESHMENTS, The
American rock group formed in 1993 in Tempe, Arizona: Roger Meade Clyne (lead vocals, guitar), P.H. Naffah (drums), Arthur Eugene "Buddy" Edwards III (bass), Brian David Blush (lead guitar).

| 07/22/96 | 26 | 9 h | Banditos | Mercury |

REGATTA
Canadian rock trio from Toronto: Chris Smith (vocals, guitar), Matthew Gerrard (bass), Greg Critchley (drums).

DATE	PK	WK	TITLE	LABEL	RA
03/19/90	26	8	Wherever You Run	RCA	

REGINA
American female pop singer Regina Richards from New York.

10/13/86	25	9	Baby Love	Atlantic	

R.E.M.
American alternative rock band formed in 1980 in Athens, Georgia: Michael Stipe (vocals, b. John Michael Stipe on 01/04/60 in Decatur, Georgia), Peter Buck (guitar, b. Peter Lawrence Buck on 12/06/56 in Berkeley, California), Mike Mills (bass, vocals, b. Michael Edward Mills on 12/17/56 in Orange, California), Bill Berry (drums, b. William Thomas Berry on 07/31/58 in Duluth, Minnesota). The most popular college-rock band of the 1980's.

DATE	PK	WK	TITLE	LABEL	RA
12/07/87	14	13	The One I Love	I.R.S.	
05/01/89	16	11	Stand	Warner	
05/06/91	16	6	Losing My Religion	Warner	1
10/28/91	17	12	Shiny Happy People	Warner	2
12/21/92	10	12	Drive	Warner	6
03/15/93	9	11	Man On The Moon	Warner	5
11/22/93	---	RA	Everybody Hurts	Warner	11
10/17/94	10	24	What's The Frequency, Kenneth?	Warner	3
02/20/95	---	RA	Bang And Blame	Warner	3
06/19/95	---	RA	Strange Currencies	Warner	12
10/07/96	10	8 h	E-Bow The Letter	Warner	38
			SoundScan: #29 (10/20/96) / 4 wks.		
11/24/96	22	3	Bittersweet Me	Warner	31

REMBRANDTS, The
American pop duo formed in 1991 in Los Angeles: Danny Wilde and Phil Solem. Solem left in 1996.

05/06/91	---	RA	Just The Way It Is Baby	Atco	11
07/10/95	---	RA	I'll Be There For You	EastWest	1
02/05/96	27	16	This House Is Not A Home	EastWest	27

RENO, Mike
Canadian male rock singer. Lead singer of Loverboy.

08/06/84	3(1)	12	Almost Paradise *	Columbia	

* Mike Reno & Ann Wilson

REO SPEEDWAGON
American rock-pop band formed in 1968 in Champaign, Illinois: Kevin Cronin (vocals, b. 10/06/51 in Evanston, Illinois), Gary Richrath (guitar, b. 10/18/49 in Peoria, Illinois), Bruce Hall (bass, b. 05/03/53 in Champaign), Neal Doughty (keyboards, b. 07/29/46 in Evanston), Alan Gratzer (drums, b. 11/09/48 in Syracuse, New York). Gratzer left in 1988, replaced by Graham Lear. Band named after a high-speed fire engine.

03/07/81	3(3)	14	Keep On Lovin' You	Epic	
05/23/81	3(3)	13	Take It On The Run	Epic	
08/08/81	15	4	Don't Let Him Go	Epic	

DATE	PK	WK	TITLE	LABEL	RA
08/07/82	5	7	Keep The Fire Burnin'	Epic	
04/15/85	5	15	Can't Fight This Feeling	Epic	
06/10/85	40	1	One Lonely Night	Epic	

REPUBLICA
British rock group formed in 1994 in London: Saffron (lead vocals), Tim Dorney (keyboards), Jonny Male (guitar), Pete Riley (drums), Dave Barborossa (drums), Andy Todd (keyboards). Barborossa and Todd left in 1997.

11/18/96	---	RA	Ready To Go	RCA	26

RESTLESS HEART
American country group from Nashville, formed in 1984: Larry Stewart (lead vocals), John Dittrich (drums, vocals, b. 04/07/51), Dave Innis (piano, b. 04/09/59), Greg Jennings (guitar, b. 10/02/54), and Paul Gregg (bass, vocals, b. 12/03/54). Stewart and Innis left in 1993. Disbanded in 1996.

01/25/93	---	RA	When She Cries	RCA	14
05/24/93	---	RA	Tell Me What You Dream	RCA	30

RHEOSTATICS
Canadian rock group formed in 1980 in Etobicoke, Ontario: Martin Tielli (vocals, lead guitar), Dave Bidini (vocals, rhythm guitar), Tim Vesely (vocals, bass, acoustic guitar, accordion and piano), Don Kerr (drums).

12/12/94	---	RA	Claire	Sire	28

RHYTHM HERITAGE
American studio group from Los Angeles, assembled by producers Steve Barri and Michael Omartian (keyboards). Vocals by Oren and Luther Waters.

02/14/76	21	8	Theme From "SWAT"	ABC	

RICH, Tony, Project
American male R&B singer/songwriter/multi-instrumentalist Tony Rich, born Anthony Jeffries on 11/19/71 in Detroit. Based in Atlanta.

04/22/96	5	21 h	Nobody Knows	LaFace	3
09/09/96	26	9 h	Like A Woman	LaFace	12

RICHARD, Cliff
British male pop/rock and roll singer/actor/guitarist born Harry Rodger Webb on 10/14/40 in Lucknow, India. To England in 1948. In 1958, formed backup band, the Drifters (name later changed to the Shadows) and changed his name to Cliff Richard. Began recording a series of gospel albums in 1966. The Shadows disbanded in 1969. Starred in various films such as *Expresso Bongo* (1960), *The Young Ones* (1961), *Summer Holiday* (1963), and *Wonderful Life* (1964).

09/25/76	3(1)	17	Devil Woman	Rocket	
01/09/80	9	14	We Don't Talk Anymore	EMI	
11/29/80	2(1)	12	Dreaming	EMI	
03/28/81	5	9	A Little In Love	EMI	

RICHIE, Lionel

DATE	PK	WK	TITLE	LABEL	RA

American male pop-R&B singer/songwriter born on 06/20/49 in Tuskegee, Alabama. Former lead singer of the Commodores. Appeared in the 1978 movie *Thank God It's Friday*. Co-wrote USA for Africa's "We Are The World" with Michael Jackson in 1985.

DATE	PK	WK	TITLE	LABEL	RA
09/12/81	1(4)	13	Endless Love *	Motown	
12/25/82	2(3)	14	Truly	Motown	
04/04/83	5	12	You Are	Motown	
11/14/83	2(9)	23	All Night Long (All Night)	Motown	
02/20/84	15	14	Running With The Night	Motown	
05/28/84	3(4)	21	Hello	Motown	
09/03/84	8	13	Stuck On You	Motown	
12/17/84	25	8	Penny Lover	Motown	
02/10/86	1(2)	19	Say You, Say Me	Motown	
08/25/86	2(3)	18	Dancing On The Ceiling	Motown	
12/29/86	23	8	Love Will Conquer All	Motown	
03/09/87	9	13	Ballerina Girl/Deep River Woman	Motown	
06/01/87	34	3	Se La	Motown	
07/13/92	10	16	Do It To Me	Motown	14
05/20/96	24	11 h	Don't Wanna Lose You	Mercury	

* Diana Ross & Lionel Richie

RIFF
American male vocal group from Paterson, New Jersey: Kenny Kelly, Steve Capers, Jr., Anthony Fuller, Dwayne Jones, Michael Best. Appeared in the 1989 movie *Lean On Me*.

DATE	PK	WK	TITLE	LABEL	RA
06/15/92	10	18	White Men Can't Jump	SBK	

RIGHT SAID FRED
British duo formed in 1987: brothers Richard (vocals) and Fred Fairbrass (guitar) and Rob Manzoli (guitar). "Right Said Fred" is the title of a 1962 British top ten single by Bernard Cribbins.

DATE	PK	WK	TITLE	LABEL	RA
02/24/92	1(3)	11	I'm Too Sexy	Virgin	3
05/18/92	---	RA	Don't Talk Just Kiss	Virgin	6
07/27/92	---	RA	Deeply Dippy	Virgin	30

RIGHTEOUS BROTHERS
American R&B/pop vocal duo formed in 1962 in Los Angeles: Bill Medley (b. 09/19/40 in Santa Ana, California), Bobby Hatfield (b. 08/10/40 in Beaver Dam, Wisconsin). "Righteous" is from a popular American slang term. Recorded as the Parmours in 1962. A regular on TV's *Shindig!* Broke up in 1968; Hatfield performed with Jimmy Walker, Medley went solo. Reunited in 1974. Medley retired for five years after the murder of his wife in 1976.

DATE	PK	WK	TITLE	LABEL	RA
02/11/91	15	10	Unchained Melody	Capitol	6

RIMES, Leann
American female country/pop singer born on 08/28/82 in Jackson, Mississippi. Raised in Garland, Texas.

DATE	PK	WK	TITLE	LABEL	RA
08/24/97	2(1)	39	How Do I Live	Curb	39
02/28/99	4	19	Written In The Stars *	Rocket	

* Elton John & Leann Rimes

DATE	PK	WK	TITLE	LABEL	RA

RITCHIE FAMILY
American disco group featuring various session singers and musicians named after arranger/producer Ritchie Rome.

| 10/18/75 | 14 | 7 | Brazil | Able | |

RIVERS, Johnny
American male rock and roll singer/songwriter/producer born John Ramistella on 11/07/42 in New York City. Name changed to Rivers by New York DJ Alan Freed in 1958. Primarily popular in the 1960's and the early-1970's. Founded own Soul City label in 1966.

| 09/27/75 | 18 | 7 | Help Me Rhonda | Epic | |
| 10/05/77 | 4 | 12 | (Slow Dancin') Swayin' To The Music | Polydor | |

ROB BASE & D.J. E-Z ROCK
American rap duo formed in 1982 in New York City: Rob Base (vocals, b. Robert Ginyard on 05/18/67 in New York City), D.J. E-Z Rock (DJ, b. Rodney Bryce on 06/29/67 in New York City).

| 09/25/89 | 8 | 15 | Joy & Pain | Mercury | |

ROBERTS, Austin
American male singer/songwriter born on 09/19/45 in Newport News, Virginia. Collaborator on the cartoon series *Scooby Doo* and *Josie & The Pussycats*.

| 10/11/75 | 8 | 7 | Rocky | Private Stock | |

ROBERTS, David

| 09/25/82 | 14 | 4 | Boys Of Autumn | Elektra | |

ROBERTS, Juliet
British female pop/R&B singer/songwriter raised in London.

| 05/23/94 | 13 | 27 | I Want You | Reprise | 28 |

ROBERTSON, Robbie
Canadian male rock singer born on 07/05/43 in Montreal. His father is Jewish and his mother is Mohawk Aboriginal. Former member of The Band. Acted in the 1980 movie *Carny*. Won the 1989 Juno Award for Male Vocalist of the Year.

| 11/25/91 | --- | RA | What About Now | Geffen | 10 |
| 02/17/92 | --- | RA | Go Back To Your Woods | Geffen | 29 |

ROBIN S
American female R&B-pop singer Robin Stone from Jamaica, New York.

| 06/28/93 | 3(5) | 18 | Show Me Love | Atlantic | 16 |
| 10/18/93 | 10 | 10 | Love For Love | Atlantic | |

ROBINSON, Smokey
American male R&B singer/songwriter born William Robinson on 02/19/40 in Detroit. Lead vocalist of The Miracles, 1957-72. First became a Vice-President of Motown in 1961, held position on and off, until

| DATE | PK | WK | TITLE | LABEL | RA |

finally resigning in 1988. Many artists have covered his songs including the Beatles and the Rolling Stones. Married to Claudette Rogers, formerly of The Miracles, 1963-85.

02/06/80	39	2	Cruisin'	Tamla
05/30/81	2(2)	10	Being With You	Tamla
07/13/87	34	3	Just To See Her	MCA

ROBINSON, Vicki Sue
American female disco singer born in 1955 in Philadelphia. Appeared in the original Broadway productions of *Hair* and *Jesus Christ Superstar*.

| 09/25/76 | 26 | 10 | Turn The Beat Around | RCA |

ROBYN
Swedish female pop singer born Robin Miriam Carlsson on 06/12/79 in Stockholm.

08/31/97	5	22	Do You Know (What It Takes)	RCA	1
01/19/98	---	RA	Show Me Love	RCA	2
05/11/98	---	RA	Do You Really Want Me? (Show Respect)	RCA	7

ROCK & HYDE
Canadian rock duo: Bob Rock and Paul Hyde (b. 05/21/55). Both were members of the Payolas, 1982-85.

| 04/27/87 | 13 | 9 | Dirty Water | Capitol |
| 08/10/87 | 35 | 6 | I Will | Capitol |

ROCKELL
American female techno-dance singer born in 1977 in New York City.

| 02/23/97 | 12 | 10 | I Fell In Love | RCA | 38 |
| 07/27/97 | 6 | 29 | In A Dream | RCA |

ROCKWELL
American male R&B singer born Kennedy Gordy on 03/15/64 in Detroit. Son of Berry Gordy, Jr., chairman of Motown.

| 04/09/84 | 2(3) | 15 | Somebody's Watching Me | Motown |

ROGER
American male R&B singer born Roger Troutman in Hamilton, Ohio. Leader of the family funk group Zapp.

| 03/28/88 | 22 | 10 | I Want To Be Your Man | Reprise |

ROGERS, Kenny
American male country singer/songwriter born Kenneth Donald Rogers on 08/21/38 in Houston. Sang with the Scholars in high school in 1958. Joined the Bobby Doyle Trio at the University of Houston. Member of the groups New Christy Minstrels and the First Edition. Starred in the movies *The Gambler* (1980) and *Six Pack* (1982). Published two photography books. Opened a fast food chicken restaurant chain in the late-1980's; closed in the late-1990's. Spearheaded the 1986 Hands Across America charity event. Started a gambling website in the late-1990's.

DATE	PK	WK	TITLE	LABEL	RA
07/09/77	4	15	Lucille	United Artists	
11/02/77	19	4	Daytime Friends	United Artists	
03/07/79	14	8	The Gambler	United Artists	
07/11/79	8	14	She Believes In Me	United Artists	
11/28/79	20	12	You Decorated My Life	United Artists	
01/23/80	2(6)	13	Coward Of The County	United Artists	
05/28/80	7	11	Don't Fall In Love With A Dreamer *	United Artists	
12/06/80	2(2)	13	Lady	Liberty	
08/08/81	7	9	I Don't Need You	Liberty	
03/14/83	2(1)	12	We've Got Tonight **	Liberty	
11/14/83	1(9)	22	Islands In The Stream ***	RCA	
12/03/84	18	8	What About Me? ****	RCA	

* Kenny Rogers/Kim Carnes
** Kenny Rogers & Sheena Easton
*** Kenny Rogers & Dolly Parton
**** Kenny Rogers/Kim Carnes/James Ingram

ROLLING STONES

British rock group formed in 1962 in London: Mick Jagger (vocals, b. Michael Phillip Jagger on 07/26/43 in Dartford, England), Keith Richards (guitar, vocals, b. 12/18/43 in Dartford), Brian Jones (guitar, b. Lewis Brian Hopkins-Jones on 02/28/42 in Cheltenham, England), Bill Wyman (bass, b. William Perks on 10/24/36 in London), Charlie Watt (drums, b. 06/02/41 in Islington, England). Self-proclaimed "World's Greatest Rock & Roll Band". Mick Taylor (b. 01/17/48 in Welwyn Garden City, England) replaced Jones, who left the group and died shortly after on 07/03/69 in a drowning accident. Taylor left in 1975 and later pursued a solo career; replaced by Ron Wood (guitar, vocals, b. 06/01/47 in Hillingdon, England). Wyman left in 1992, replaced in 1994 by Darryl Jones. Inducted into the Rock and Roll Hall of Fame in 1989.

DATE	PK	WK	TITLE	LABEL	RA
06/26/76	11	13	Fool To Cry	Rolling Stones	
06/28/78	6	20	Miss You	Rolling Stones	
11/01/78	10	10	Beast Of Burden	Rolling Stones	
09/13/80	1(1)	6	Emotional Rescue	Rolling Stones	
11/22/80	11	8	She's So Cold	Rolling Stones	
10/10/81	1(4)	12	Start Me Up	Rolling Stones	
01/30/82	3(1)	7	Waiting On A Friend	Rolling Stones	
01/16/84	14	12	Undercover Of The Night	Rolling Stones	
05/19/86	2(1)	16	Harlem Shuffle	Rolling Stones	
07/14/86	26	2	One Hit (To The Body)	Rolling Stones	
11/13/89	13	14	Mixed Emotions	Rolling Stones	
01/22/90	13	9	Rock And A Hard Place	Rolling Stones	
04/02/90	29	3	Almost Hear You Sigh	Rolling Stones	28
04/29/91	13	9	High Wire	Rolling Stones	26
09/05/94	---	RA	Love Is Strong	Virgin	2
02/20/95	---	RA	You Got Me Rocking	Virgin	21
03/13/95	9	19	Out Of Tears	Virgin	6
12/04/95	25	13	Like A Rolling Stone	Virgin	
10/06/97	---	RA	Anybody Seen My Baby	Virgin	9
02/22/98	38	1	Saint Of Me	Virgin	

ROMANTICS, The

| DATE | PK | WK | TITLE | LABEL | RA |

American rock group formed in 1977 in Detroit: Wally Palmer (guitar, vocals, b. 04/27/53 in Hamtramck, Michigan), Cos Canter (guitar, b. 07/25/54 in Havana, Cuba), Richard Cole (bass, vocals), David Patratos (drums; replaced by ex-Blondie Clem Burke).

| 02/06/84 | 2(3) | 19 | Talking In Your Sleep .... Nemperor |

RONSTADT, Linda
American female pop singer/songwriter born 07/15/46 in Tucson, Arizona. Formed and recorded with the Stone Poneys in the late-1960's. Went solo in 1968; her backup musicians once consisted of the four original members of the Eagles. Played Mabel in the opera *The Pirates of Penzance* in Central Park, New York City, in 1980; starred in the movie version in 1983.

06/28/75	7	6	When Will I Be Loved .... Capitol	
12/13/75	18	6	Heatwave.. Asylum	
11/27/76	13	12	That'll Be The Day .... Asylum	
01/11/78	5	18	Blue Bayou .... Asylum	
01/25/78	13	14	It's So Easy .... Asylum	
04/05/78	24	4	Poor Poor Pitiful Me .... Asylum	
01/24/79	15	8	Ooh Baby Baby .... Asylum	
04/02/80	18	9	How Do I Make You .... Asylum	
05/21/80	19	2	Hurts So Bad .... Asylum	
04/20/87	6	15	Somewhere Out There * .... MCA	
04/16/90	---	RA	All My Life ** .... Elektra	18
07/23/90	40	1	When Something Is Wrong With My Baby .. Elektra	

* Linda Ronstadt/James Ingram
** Linda Ronstadt & Aaron Neville

ROOTS
American rap group formed in 1987 in Philadelphia: Tariz "Black Thought" Trotter (vocals), Malik B. (vocals), Leonard Hubbard (bass), B.R.O.theR. ?uestion/?uestlove (drums), Rahzel the Godfather of Noyze (vocals, percussion), Kamla (keyboards).

| 04/19/99 | --- | RA | You Got Me * .... MCA | 40 |

* Roots featuring Erykah Badu

ROSE ROYCE
American R&B backing band formed in 1973 in Los Angeles. Backed Edwin Starr and The Temptations. Lead vocalist Gwen Dickey joined in 1976.

| 02/12/77 | 2(2) | 14 | Car Wash .... MCA |
| 06/18/77 | 16 | 7 | I Wanna Get Next To You .... MCA |

ROSS, Diana
American female R&B-pop singer born Diane Ernestine Ross on 03/26/44 in Detroit. Lead singer of The Supremes, 1961-70. Nominated for an Oscar for Best Actress in 1972 for starring in *Lady Sings The Blues*. Also appeared in the movies *The Wiz* and *Mahogany*. Changed from Motown to RCA in 1981. Married Norwegian businessman Arne Naess in 02/01/86. Returned to Motown in 1989 to become a corporate officer and co-owner.

| 01/31/76 | 4 | 10 | Theme From Mahogany (Do You Know Where You're Going To) .... Motown |

DATE	PK	WK	TITLE	LABEL	RA
07/03/76	1(1)	14	Love Hangover	Motown	
10/18/80	2(2)	10	Upside Down	Motown	
09/12/81	1(4)	13	Endless Love *	Motown	
01/16/82	18	1	Why Do Fools Fall In Love	RCA	
09/10/84	4	11	All Of You **	Columbia	
10/29/84	20	9	Swept Away	RCA	
05/20/85	29	3	Missing You	RCA	
05/12/86	25	15	Chain Reaction	RCA	

* Diana Ross & Lionel Richie
** Julio Iglesias & Diana Ross

ROTH, David Lee
American male hard rock singer/songwriter born on 10/10/55 in Bloomington, Indiana. Former lead singer of Van Halen. Recorded solo beginning in 1985.

DATE	PK	WK	TITLE	LABEL	RA
02/25/85	7	15	California Girls	Warner	
05/27/85	9	17	Just A Gigolo/I Ain't Got Nobody	Warner	
04/11/88	6	15	Just Like Paradise	Warner	

ROUGH TRADE
Canadian rock sextet formed in 1974 based in Toronto: Carole Pope (vocals), John Cessine (percussion), Marv Kanarek (percussion), Happy Roderman (bass), Sharon Smith (piano), Kevan Staples (guitar).

DATE	PK	WK	TITLE	LABEL	RA
05/16/81	17	4	High School Confidential	True North	
12/05/81	16	8	All Touch	True North	
01/24/83	25	2	Crimes Of Passion	True North	

ROULA
American female dance singer produced by the production team 20 Fingers.

DATE	PK	WK	TITLE	LABEL	RA
07/24/95	2(3)	23	Lick It	SOS	

ROVERS, The
Canadian band formed as Irish Rovers in 1964 in Calgary consisting of Jimmy Ferguson (vocals), Wilcil McDowell (accordion), brothers Will Millar (vocals, guitar, banjo), George Millar (guitar), and their cousin, Joe Millar (accordion, bass).

DATE	PK	WK	TITLE	LABEL	RA
02/07/81	8	16	Wasn't That A Party	Epic	

ROXETTE
Swedish pop duo formed in 1986 in Sweden: Marie Fredriksson (vocals, b. 05/29/58 in Östra Ljungby, Sweden) and Per Gessle (guitar, vocals, b. 02/12/59 in Halmstad, Sweden).

DATE	PK	WK	TITLE	LABEL	RA
06/12/89	1(1)	20	The Look	EMI	
08/28/89	4	18	Dressed For Success	EMI	
11/20/89	1(2)	17	Listen To Your Heart	EMI	
03/05/90	2(2)	12	Dangerous	EMI	2
06/18/90	2(1)	11	It Must Have Been Love	EMI	1
05/06/91	1(5)	16	Joyride	EMI	1
08/12/91	3(3)	15	Fading Like A Flower	EMI	2

DATE	PK	WK	TITLE	LABEL	RA
11/11/91	9	23	Spending My Time	EMI	9
04/06/92	---	RA	Church Of Your Heart	EMI	12
09/21/92	11	17	How Do You Do	EMI	9
06/28/93	13	15	Almost Unreal	Capitol	18
06/27/94	3(7)	30	Sleeping In My Car	Capitol	2
09/05/94	---	RA	Crash! Boom! Bang!	Capitol	16

ROXY MUSIC
British art rock band formed in 1971 in London. Core included Bryan Ferry (vocals, keyboards, b. 09/26/45 in Washington, England), Phil Manzanera (b. Phillip Targett-Adams on 01/31/51 in London), Andy Mackay (saxophone, oboe, b. 07/23/46 in London). Disbanded in 1983. Ferry later pursued solo career.

| 04/17/76 | 18 | 6 | Love Is The Drug | Atco | |

ROZALLA
Zimbabwean female dance singer born Rozalla Miller on 03/18/64 in Ndola, Zambia.

| 10/12/92 | 5 | 14 | Everybody's Free (To Feel Good) | Columbia | |
| 01/31/94 | 19 | 13 | I Love Music | Epic | |

RTZ
American rock group formed in 1989 in Boston: Brad Delp (vocals, b. 06/12/51 in Boston), Barry Goudreau (guitar, b. 11/29/51 in Boston), Brian Maes (keyboards), Tim Archibald (bass), David Stefanelli (drums). Delp and Goudreau were members of Boston. RTZ is an abbreviation for Return To Zero.

| 03/16/92 | --- | RA | Until Your Love Comes Back Around | Giant | 34 |

RUBICON
American group led by horn player Jerry Martini, formerly of Sly & The Family Stone, 1966-76. Group included Jack Blades and Brad Gillis of Night Ranger.

| 05/03/78 | 32 | 2 | I'm Gonna Take Care Of Everything | 20th Century | |

RUFFIN, David
American male R&B singer born Davis Eli Ruffin on 01/18/41 in Meridian, Mississippi. Vocalist of The Temptations, 1963-1968. Died of a drug overdose on 06/01/91 in Philadelphia.

| 12/27/75 | 19 | 2 | Walk Away From Love | Motown | |

RUFFNECK
American dance group.

| 04/01/96 | 11 | 9 | Everybody Be Somebody | Quality | |

RUFUS - see KHAN, Chaka/Rufus

RUHNKE, Craig
Canadian male singer/songwriter born in Toronto. Formed record label, Pinnacle Records.

| 07/31/76 | 40 | 1 | Summer Love | United Artists | |

DATE	PK	WK	TITLE	LABEL	RA

RUMBLE
Canadian male rapper based in Toronto.

08/02/93	22	11	Safe..	Island	

RUN-D.M.C.
American rap trio formed in 1981 in Hollis, Queens, New York: Joseph "Run" Simmons (vocals, b. 11/14/64), Darryl "D.M.C." McDaniels (vocals, b. 05/31/64), Jam Master Jay (turntables, programming, b. Jason Mizell on 01/21/65).

10/20/86	4	15	Walk This Way	London	
06/14/93	7	16	Down With The King	Attic	
09/06/93	24	8	Ooh, Whatcha Gonna Do...............................	Attic	
07/05/98	3(8)	34	It's Like That *...	Smile	

Another version peaked at #39 on 02/07/99.

* Run-D.M.C. vs. Jason Nevins

RUPAUL
American male dance singer RuPaul Andre Charles from New York, originally from Atlanta. Transvestite, stands 190 cm without heels.

05/07/93	12	20	Supermodel (You Better Work)	Isba	
07/19/93	31	5	Back To My Roots	Isba	
11/15/93	30	6	A Space Shady..	Isba	

RUSH
Canadian hard rock trio formed in 1969 in Toronto: Geddy Lee (vocals/bass/guitar/keyboards, b. Gary Lee Weinrib on 07/29/53 in Toronto), Alex Lifeson (guitar, b. Alex Zivojinovich, 08/27/53 in Surnie, British Columbia), Neil Peart (drums, b. 09/12/52 in Hamilton, Ontario). Won Juno Awards for Most Promising Group of the Year in 1975 and Group of the Year in 1978 and 1979. Received the Juno Hall of Fame Award in 1994.

02/08/78	14	6	Closer To The Heart...................................	Polydor	
02/20/80	33	2	The Spirit Of Radio	Anthem	
05/02/81	16	5	Limelight..	Anthem	
11/13/82	1(1)	10	New World Man	Anthem	
05/07/90	---	RA	The Pass	Anthem	29
01/20/92	---	RA	Roll The Bones	Anthem	39
10/07/96	33	7 h	Test For Echo	Anthem	

RUSH, Jennifer
American female pop singer from Queens, New York.

06/09/86	9	21	The Power Of Love	Epic	
07/27/87	14	8	Flames Of Paradise *......................................	Epic	

* Jennifer Rush/Elton John

RUSSELL, Leon
American male rock singer/songwriter/multi-instrumentalist born on 04/02/41 in Lawton, Oklahoma. Formed Shelter Records in 1970 and Paradise label in 1976. Wrote "Superstar" and "This Masquerade".

DATE	PK	WK	TITLE	LABEL	RA
11/15/75	21	5	Lady Blue .... Shelter		

RYTHM SYNDICATE
American R&B group from Connecticut: Evan Rogers (vocals), Carl Sturken (guitar), John Nevin, Rob Mingrino, Kevin Cloud. Rogers and Sturken produced Donny Osmond's "Soldier Of Love" and "Sacred Emotion". Changed name to Rhythm Syndicate in 1992.

DATE	PK	WK	TITLE	LABEL	RA
08/12/91	---	RA	P.A.S.S.I.O.N. .... Impact		10
11/04/91	---	RA	Hey Donna.. Impact		18
11/09/92	34	4	I Wanna Make Love To You .... Impact		

S

SADE
British female vocalist born Helen Folasade Adu on 01/16/59 in Ibadan, Nigeria. Former member of the group Pride. Name pronounced shar-day.

DATE	PK	WK	TITLE	LABEL	RA
03/25/85	28	8	Hang On To Your Love .... Portrait		
06/17/85	8	11	Smooth Operator .... Portrait		
02/17/86	19	8	The Sweetest Taboo .... Portrait		
08/29/88	31	7	Paradise .... Epic		
02/22/93	15	16	No Ordinary Love....................................... Epic		13
05/17/93	33	4	Kiss Of Life .... Epic		
10/04/93	38	3	Cherish The Day .... Epic		

SAGA
Canadian rock group: Michael Sadler (vocals), Ian Crichton (guitar), Jim Crichton (bass), Steve Negus (drums), Peter Rachon (keyboards, replaced by Jim Gilmour). Won the 1982 Juno Award for Most Promising Group of the Year.

DATE	PK	WK	TITLE	LABEL	RA
01/30/82	18	3	Wind Him Up .... Maze		

SAIGON KICK
American rock group formed in 1988 in Miami: Matt Kramer (vocals), Jason Bieler (guitar), Tom DeFile (bass), Phi Varone (drums). DeFile was replaced by Chris McLernon in 1993.

DATE	PK	WK	TITLE	LABEL	RA
11/30/92	---	RA	Love Is On The Way .... Atlantic		26

SALT-N-PEPA
American rap trio formed in 1985 in Queens, New York: Cheryl "Salt" James (b. 03/28/69 in Brooklyn, New York), Sandy "Pepa" Denton (b. 09/09/69 in Kingston, Jamaica), Deidre "Dee Dee" "Spinderella" Roper (DJ, b. 08/03/71 in New York City).

DATE	PK	WK	TITLE	LABEL	RA
05/23/88	2(1)	27	Push It.. London		
07/02/90	33	6	Expression.. ffrr		
12/30/91	10	10	Let's Talk About Sex .... Next Plateau		22
06/15/92	28	11	You Showed Me... Next Plateau		
11/30/92	26	13	Start Me Up .... Next Plateau		
11/29/93	2(3)	20	Shoop... Next Plateau		30
02/21/94	3(5)	33	Whatta Man .... Next Plateau		13

| DATE | PK | WK | TITLE | LABEL | RA |

SAMBORA, Richie
American male rock singer/guitarist born on 07/11/59 in Woodbridge, New Jersey. Guitarist of Bon Jovi.

| 10/14/91 | 32 | 5 | Ballad Of Youth | Mercury | |

SANDBOX
Canadian rock band from New Glasgow, Nova Scotia: Paul Murray (lead vocals, b. 04/09/71 in New Glasgow), Jason "Jay" Archibald (guitar, vocals, b. 08/21/71 in Pictou, Nova Scotia), Scott MacFarlane (bass, vocals b. 05/11/73 in Halifax, Nova Scotia), Troy Shanks (drums, piano, b. 06/12/71 in Halifax), Mike Smith (guitar, vocals, b. 08/27/72 in New Glasgow).

| 08/14/95 | --- | RA | Curious | Latitude | 31 |

SANFORD/TOWNSEND BAND, The
American rock band from Los Angeles led by Ed Sanford and John Townsend.

| 09/21/77 | 17 | 10 | Smoke From A Distant Fire | Warner | |

SANG, Samantha
Australian female pop singer born Cheryl Gray on 08/05/53 in Melbourne.

| 03/08/78 | 3(6) | 22 | Emotion | Private Stock | |

SANTA ESMERALDA
American/French disco studio project produced by Nicolas Skorsky and Jean-Manuel de Scarano.

| 03/22/78 | 7 | 26 | Don't Let Me Be Understood | JC Enterprises | |

SANTANA
American Latin-rock group formed in 1967 in San Francisco: Carlos Santana (guitar, vocals, percussion, b. 07/20/47 in Autlán de Navarro, Mexico), Gregg Rolie (keyboards, vocals, b. 06/17/47 in Seattle), David Brown (bass, b. 02/15/47 in New York), Michael Shrieve (drums, b. 07/06/49 in San Francisco), Mike Carabello (percussion, b. 11/18/47 in San Francisco), Jose Chepito Areas (percussion, b. 07/25/46 in Leon, Nicaragua), Neal Schon (guitar, b. 02/27/54), Thomas "Coke" Escovedo (percussion, b. 04/30/41, d. 07/13/85 in California), Tom Rutley (bass).

| 07/04/81 | 13 | 6 | Winning | Columbia | |
| 10/09/82 | 12 | 6 | Hold On | Columbia | |

SANTERS
Canadian rock trio: brothers Rick (vocals, guitar) and Mark Santers (drums, vocals), with Rick Lazaroff (bass).

| 04/09/84 | 37 | 6 | All Right Now | Ready | |

SANTIAGO, Lina
American female singer born on 09/05/78 in Los Angeles.

| 05/06/96 | --- | RA | Feels So Good | Universal | 33 |

SASH!
German dance disc jockey from Cologne. A former record shop assistant and computer electrician.

DATE	PK	WK	TITLE	LABEL	RA
08/16/98	34	3	Stay	London	
08/16/98	38	2	It's My Life	Wind	

SAVAGE GARDEN
Australian male pop duo formed in 1993 in Brisbane: Darren Hayes (vocals, b. 05/08/72 in Brisbane), Daniel Jones (instruments, b. 07/22/73 in Essex, England).

DATE	PK	WK	TITLE	LABEL	RA
03/30/97	1(4)	16	I Want You	Columbia	1
08/11/97	---	RA	To The Moon And Back	Columbia	9
03/15/98	17	6	Truly, Madly, Deeply	Columbia	2
			Another version peaked at #21 (03/08/98).		
06/22/98	---	RA	Break Me Shake Me	Columbia	34
03/14/99	1(3)	20 +	The Animal Song	Columbia	5

SAYER, Leo
British male pop singer/songwriter born Gerard Hugh Sayer on 05/21/48 in Shoreham-by-Sea, England. Headed a group named Patches before solo career.

DATE	PK	WK	TITLE	LABEL
01/22/77	1(2)	17	You Make Me Feel Like Dancing	Warner
05/28/77	1(3)	20	When I Need You	Warner
09/21/77	8	14	How Much Love	Warner
11/30/77	23	6	Thunder In My Heart	Warner
12/13/80	3(5)	11	More Than I Can Say	Warner
03/28/81	14	3	Living In A Fantasy	Warner

SCAGGS, Boz
American male pop/rock singer/songwriter born William Royce Scaggs on 06/08/44 in Ohio. Met Steve Miller while a student at St. Mark's Preparatory School in Dallas. Fronted Miller's band, the Marksmen, then the Ardells (later Fabulous Knight Trains). Joined R&B group the Wigs in 1963. Opened Slim's nightclub in San Francisco in the mid-1980's.

DATE	PK	WK	TITLE	LABEL
11/06/76	11	13	Lowdown	Columbia
05/28/77	4	14	Lido Shuffle	Columbia
11/01/80	14	7	Look What You've Done To Me	Columbia
02/14/81	18	3	Miss Sun	Columbia

SCANDAL featuring Patty Smyth
American rock group formed in 1982 in New York City: Patty Smyth (vocals, b. 06/26/57 in New York City), Zack Smith (guitar), Ivan Elias (bass), Benji King (keyboards), Frankie LaRocka (drums). Smyth later recorded solo.

DATE	PK	WK	TITLE	LABEL
10/15/84	3(3)	15	The Warrior	Columbia

SCARBURY, Joey
American male pop singer born on 06/07/55 in Ontario, California. Session vocalist for producer/composer Mike Post.

DATE	PK	WK	TITLE	LABEL
08/15/81	3(3)	11	Theme From "Greatest American Hero"	Elektra

SCATMAN JOHN
American male techno-dance singer/songwriter John Larkin. Born on 03/13/42 in El Monte, California, raised in El Sereno, California. Also a jazz musician.

DATE	PK	WK	TITLE	LABEL	RA
09/25/95	22	12	Scatman (Ski-Ba-Bop-Ba-Dop-Bop)	RCA	18

SCHILLING, Peter
German male pop singer/songwriter born on 01/28/56 in Stuttgart, Germany.

01/23/84	1(1)	19	Major Tom (Coming Home)	WEA	

SCHWARTZ, Eddie
Canadian male pop/rock singer/songwriter born in 1949. Wrote Pat Benatar's "Hit Me With Your Best Shot", Doobie Brothers' "The Doctor", Paul Carrack's "Don't Shed A Tear", and Gowan's "All The Lovers In The World". Won the 1982 Juno Award for Most Promising Male Vocalist.

02/20/82	9	5	All Our Tomorrows..	A&M	
05/28/84	40	4	Strike...	WEA	

SCORPIONS
German rock band formed in 1971 in Hanover, Germany: Lothar Heimberg (bass), Klaus Meine (lead vocals, b. 05/25/48 in Hanover), Jurgen Rosenthal (drums), Michel Schenker (guitar, b. 01/10/55 in Savstedt, Germany), Rudolf Schenker (guitar, b. 08/31/48 in Hildesheim, Germany).

07/23/84	35	2	Rock You Like A Hurricane	Mercury	
08/19/91	4	12	Wind Of Change................................	Mercury	8
12/16/91	9	17	Send Me An Angel	Mercury	36
04/18/94	---	RA	Under The Same Sun	Mercury	24

SCRITTI POLITTI
British pop trio formed in 1978 in Leeds, England: Green Gartside (vocals, b. Green Strohmeyer-Gartside on 06/22/56 in Cardiff, Wales), David Gamson (guitar), and Fred Maher (drums).

01/20/86	40	2	Perfect Way..	Warner	

SEAL
British male pop singer/songwriter born Sealhenry Samuel on 02/19/63 in London. Of Nigerian and Brazilian ancestry. Has a degree in architecture.

08/05/91	---	RA	Crazy..	ZTT	4
10/21/91	---	RA	Future Love Paradise	ZTT	28
08/08/94	---	RA	Prayer For The Dying	ZTT	1
12/12/94	---	RA	Newborn Friend	ZTT	4
11/27/95	10	26	Kiss From A Rose	ZTT	5
03/18/96	10	13 h	Don't Cry	ZTT	6
12/23/96	---	RA	Fly Like An Eagle	ZTT	2
01/18/99	---	RA	Human Being..	Warner	37

SEALS & CROFTS
American MOR-pop duo formed in 1969 in California: Jim Seals (guitar, saxophone, fiddle, vocals, b. 10/17/41 in Sidney, Texas), Dash Crofts (drums, vocals, mandolin, keyboards, guitar, b. 08/14/40 in Cisco, Texas). Both were former members of the groups Dean Beard and The Champs. Seals' younger brother is country singer Dan Seals (England Dan & John Ford Coley).

07/31/76	3(2)	13	Get Closer	Warner	

DATE	PK	WK	TITLE	LABEL	RA

SEALS, Dan
American male country singer/songwriter/multi-instrumentalist born on 02/08/48 in McCamey, Texas. Seals' older brother is Jim Seals (Seals & Crofts).

| 04/21/86 | 22 | 14 | Bop | Capitol | |

SEBASTIAN, John
American male pop singer/songwriter born on 03/17/44 in New York City. Founding member and lead vocalist of the Lovin' Spoonful.

| 05/22/76 | 3(1) | 13 | Welcome Back | Reprise | |

SECADA, Jon
American male pop singer/songwriter born Juan Secada on 10/04/63 in Havana, Cuba. Raised in Hialeah, Florida. Earned a master's degree in jazz at the University of Miami. Backup singer for Gloria Estefan tour; co-wrote "Coming Out Of The Dark" with Estefan. Released Spanish versions of a few of his English albums. Starred as Danny Zuko in a 1995 Broadway production of *Grease*.

08/17/92	4	18	Just Another Day	SBK	2
10/26/92	12	19	Do You Believe In Us	SBK	1
04/12/93	---	RA	Angel	SBK	4
08/23/93	---	RA	I'm Free	SBK	5
06/27/94	1(5)	40	If You Go	SBK	1
10/17/94	---	RA	Whipped	SBK	22
01/23/95	---	RA	Mental Picture	SBK	35
05/19/97	---	RA	Too Late, Too Soon/Amandolo	SBK	11

SEDAKA, Neil
American male pop singer/songwriter born on 03/13/39 in Brooklyn, New York. Wrote Captain & Tennille's "Love Will Keep Us Together", Connie Francis' "Stupid Cupid". Began songwriting partnership with Howard Greenfield at age 13, split in 1973. Began recording on Elton John's Rocket label in 1974.

10/25/75	1(5)	14	Bad Blood	Polydor	
02/21/76	8	12	Breaking Up Is Hard To Do	Polydor	
06/05/76	13	9	Love In The Shadows	Polydor	

SEDUCTION
American dance-pop vocal trio from New York: Idalis Leon (b. 06/15/66), April Harris (b. 03/25/67), Michelle Visage (b. 09/20/68). Leon left in 1990; replaced by Sinoa Loren (b. 12/06/66).

| 03/05/90 | 3(1) | 10 | Two To Make It Right | Vendetta | 6 |
| 05/21/90 | 31 | 3 | Heartbeat | Vendetta | 33 |

SEGER, Bob
American male rock singer/songwriter born on 05/06/45 in Dearborn, Michigan. Member of several local Michigan bands in the 1960's. Left music from 1969-70 to attend college. Formed the backing band Silver Bullet Band in 1976: Drew Abbott (guitar), Robyn Robbins (keyboards), Alto Reed (saxophone), Chris Campbell (bass), Charlie Allen Martin (drums).

03/12/77	21	10	Night Moves	Capitol	
07/26/78	11	12	Still The Same *	Capitol	
10/04/78	12	16	Hollywood Nights *	Capitol	

DATE	PK	WK	TITLE	LABEL	RA
01/24/79	16	8	We've Got Tonite *	Capitol	
04/16/80	5	5	Fire Lake	Capitol	
09/27/80	11	6	You'll Accomp'ny Me	Capitol	
10/31/81	5	10	Tryin' To Live My Life Without You	Capitol	
02/21/83	13	7	Shame On The Moon *	Capitol	
05/09/83	16	3	Even Now *	Capitol	
12/26/83	36	5	Old Time Rock N' Roll *	Capitol	
01/14/85	20	1	Understanding *	Capitol	
04/14/86	27	7	American Storm *	Capitol	
07/28/86	39	3	Like A Rock *	Capitol	
08/03/87	3(3)	16	Shakedown	MCA	
10/07/91	22	13	The Real Love *	Capitol	21
01/20/92	---	RA	The Fire Inside	Capitol	36

* Bob Seger & The Silver Bullet Band

SEIKO
Japanese female pop singer born Noriko Kanda circa 1963. Discovered at a Sony Music talent contest at age 16. Scored 24 consecutive number one singles in Japan, 1980-88.

08/20/90	2(1)	19	The Right Combination *	Columbia	

* Seiko And Donnie Wahlberg

SELENA
American female Latin/pop singer born Selena Quintanilla on 04/16/71 in Lake Jackson, Texas. Married to her guitarist Chris Pérez. Shot to death on 03/31/95 in Corpus Christi, Texas.

09/18/95	---	RA	I Could Fall In Love	EMI	17
01/29/96	---	RA	Dreaming Of You	EMI	32

SEMBELLO, Michael
American male pop singer/songwriter born on 04/17/54 in Philadelphia. Session guitarist/producer/composer/vocalist. Guitarist on Stevie Wonder's albums, 1974-79.

09/19/83	1(3)	18	Maniac	Casablanca	

SEMISONIC
American rock band formed in 1994 in Minneapolis: Dan Wilson (vocals, guitar), John Munson (bass, vocals), Jake Slichter (drums, keyboards).

09/28/98	---	RA	Closing Time	MCA	5

SETZER, Brian, Orchestra
American big band musical group led by Brian Setzer (b. 04/10/59 in Long Island, New York). Setzer is a former vocalist/guitarist of the Stray Cats. Consists of sixteen members.

11/02/98	---	RA	Jump Jive And Wail	Interscope	28

702

| DATE | PK | WK | TITLE | LABEL | RA |

American female R&B vocal trio formed in 1995, based in Las Vegas: sisters Irish (b. June 2) and Lemisha "Mimi" Grinstead (b. 06/30/c. 1978), Kameelah "Butterfly" Williams (b. 03/08/c. 1978). "702" is the area code for Las Vegas. Discovered by Michael Bivins of New Edition and Bell Biv Devoe.

| 05/23/99 | 5 | 10 + | Where My Girl's At | Motown | 15+ |

SHAGGY

Jamaican male reggae singer/songwriter born Orville Richard Burrell on 10/22/68 in Kingston, Jamaica.

09/06/93	1(2)	20	Oh Carolina	Virgin	17
09/25/95	6	24	Boombastic	Virgin	
09/16/96	9	11 h	That Girl *	Virgin	2
			SoundScan: #14 (10/20/96) / 8 wks.		
09/21/98	---	RA	Luv Me, Luv Me **	MCA	32

* Maxi Priest & Shaggy
** Shaggy feat. Janet

SHAI

American R&B vocal group formed in 1990 in Washington, D.C.: Garfield A. Bright (b. 10/21/69 in Nashville, Tennessee), Marc Gay (b. 01/21/69 in Miami), Carl Martin (b. 08/29/70 in Lafayette, Louisiana), Darnell Van Rensalier (b. 05/17/70 in Patterson, New Jersey). "Shai" is Egyptian for "personification of destiny".

| 01/25/93 | 10 | 14 | If I Ever Fall In Love | Gasoline Alley | 11 |
| 08/30/93 | --- | RA | Baby I'm Yours | Gasoline Alley | 36 |

SHAKESPEAR'S SISTER

British/American pop band: Siobhan Fahey (b. Siobhan Marie Deidre-Fahey on 09/10/58 in Dublin, Ireland), and Marcella Detroit (b. Marcella Levy on 06/21/58 in Detroit). Fahey, a former member of Bananarama, married Dave Stewart of the Eurythmics in 1987. Disbanded in 1993.

| 09/28/92 | 2(2) | 16 | Stay | London | 9 |
| 03/01/93 | 11 | 13 | I Don't Care | London | 13 |

SHALAMAR

American dance-R&B vocal group formed in 1977 in Los Angeles: Jeffrey Daniels (b. 08/24/57 in Los Angeles), Jody Watley (b. 01/30/59 in Chicago), Howard Hewett (b. 10/01/57 in Akron, Ohio). Daniels and Watley left in 1984, replaced by Delisa Davis and Micki Free. Hewett replaced by Sidney Justin in 1985. Watley and Daniels were dancers on TV's Soul Train. Watley and Hewett later pursued solo careers.

| 08/24/77 | 28 | 10 | Uptown Festival | Sout |

SHAMEN, The

Scottish techno-pop dance band from Aberdeen: Colin Angus (bass, b. 08/24/61 in Aberdeen), Peter Stephenson (b. 03/01/62 in Ayrshire, Scotland), Keith McKenzie (b. 08/30/61 in Aberdeen) and William Sinnott (bass, b. 12/23/60 in Glasgow). Sinnott drowned and died off the coast of Gomera, Canary Islands on 05/22/91.

03/16/92	12	9	Move Any Mountain	Epic
10/19/92	22	11	LSI (Love, Sex, Intelligence)	Epic
06/21/93	35	3	Boss Drum	Epic

DATE	PK	WK	TITLE	LABEL	RA

SHAMPOO
British punk-rock duo formed in 1994 in Plumstead, England: Jacqui Blake and Carrie Askew.

02/20/95	---	RA	Trouble	EMI	29

SHANICE
American female R&B singer born Shanice Wilson on 05/14/73 in Pittsburgh. As a child, appeared in Kentucky Fried Chicken commercials with jazz singer Ella Fitzgerald.

03/23/92	2(3)	15	I Love Your Smile	Motown	5
04/27/92	23	1	I'm Crying	Motown	
02/15/93	23	15	Saving Forever For You	Motown	6
09/05/94	16	7	Somewhere	Motown	

SHANNON
American R&B-dance singer from Washington, D.C.

04/16/84	13	13	Let The Music Play	Unidisc	

SHARKEY, Feargal
Irish male singer born on 08/13/58 in Derry, Northern Ireland. Former lead singer of the Irish pop-punk group The Undertones.

04/14/86	7	16	A Good Heart	Virgin	

SHE MOVES
American female pop vocal trio from New York City: Carla, Danielle, Diana.

12/08/97	---	RA	Breaking All The Rules	Geffen	22

SHEIK, Duncan
American male singer/songwriter born on 11/18/69 in Hilton Head, South Carolina.

03/24/97	---	RA	Barely Breathing	Atlantic	13

SHEILA E
American female R&B singer/drummer/percussionist born Sheila Escovedo on 12/12/57 in Oakland, California. Protegee of singer Prince. Uncle Thomas "Coke" Escovedo played percussion in Santana. Recorded and toured with Lionel Richie, Diana Ross, Marvin Gaye, and Herbie Hancock in the 1970's and 1980's.

11/12/84	3(3)	14	The Glamorous Life	Warner	
01/28/85	31	4	The Belle Of St. Mark	Warner	
03/31/86	20	9	A Love Bizarre	Warner	

SHEPARD, Vonda
American female pop singer/songwriter/pianist born on 07/07/63 in New York City. Raised in Southern California. Backing vocalist and keyboardist for Rickie Lee Jones, Al Jarreau, and Jackson Browne. Played the resident singer on the TV series *Ally McBeal*.

06/08/98	---	RA	Searchin' My Soul	550/Epic	7

DATE	PK	WK	TITLE	LABEL	RA

SHEREE - see JEACOCKE, Sheree

SHERIFF
Canadian rock band formed in Toronto in 1979: Freddy Curci (vocals), Steve De Marchi (guitar), Rob Elliott (drums), Wolf Hassel (bass), Arnold Lanni (keyboards). Lanni and Hassel formed Frozen Ghost in 1985. Curci and De Marchi formed Alias.

| 02/28/83 | 5 | 11 | When I'm With You | Capitol | |
| 04/03/89 | 14 | 9 | When I'm With You (re-issue) | Capitol | |

SHOOTER

| 09/20/75 | 29 | 1 | Train | GRT | |

SILK
American male R&B vocal group formed in the early-1990's in Atlanta: Timothy Cameron, Jimmy Gates, Jr., Johnathen Rasboro, Gary Jenkins, Gary Glenn.

| 05/24/93 | --- | RA | Freak Me | Elektra | 19 |

SILVER
American country-rock quintet led by John Batdorf. Organist Brent Mydland (d. 07/26/90 of a drug overdose at age 37) was later a member of Grateful Dead.

| 10/23/76 | 17 | 8 | Wham Bam | Arista | |

SILVER CONVENTION
German studio disco group assembled by producer Michael Kunze and writer/arranger Silvester Levay, and consisting of female vocalists Penny McLean, Ramona Wolf, Linda Thompson.

| 12/27/75 | 2(2) | 10 | Fly Robin Fly | Columbia | |
| 06/26/76 | 1(1) | 13 | Get Up And Boogie | Columbia | |

SILVERCHAIR
Australian rock group formed in 1992 in Newcastle, Australia: Daniel Johns (vocals, guitar), Ben Gillies (drums), Chris Joannou (bass, vocals).

| 04/11/99 | 27 | 6 | Anthem For The Year 2000 | Sony Import | |

SIMON & GARFUNKEL
American folk-pop duo formed in 1962 in New York City: Paul Simon (guitar, vocals, b. 10/13/41 in Newark, New Jersey), Arthur Garfunkel (vocals, b. 11/05/41 in Forest Hills, New York). Met in grade six in Forest Hills. Simon studied English Literature, Garfunkel studied architecture in the early-1960's. Disbanded in 1970.

| 12/27/75 | 7 | 8 | My Little Town | Columbia | |

SIMON, Carly
American female pop singer/songwriter born on 06/25/45 in New York City. Her father is the co-founder of the Simon & Schuster publishing company. Recorded with sister Lucy as The Simon Sisters in the mid-1960's. Married singer James Taylor on 11/03/72, divorced in 1983. In 1993, *Romulus Hunt*, her opera for children, debuted in New York City. Author of several children books.

DATE	PK	WK	TITLE	LABEL	RA
10/05/77	3(2)	20	Nobody Does It Better................................	Elektra	
07/12/78	10	10	You Belong To Me	Elektra	
11/15/80	10	8	Jesse..	Warner	

SIMON, Paul
American male singer/songwriter born on 10/13/41 in Newark, New Jersey. In the duos Tom & Jerry and Simon & Garfunkel with singer Art Garfunkel. Appeared in the 1977 Woody Allen movie Annie Hall. Married to actress Carrie Fisher, 1983-85. Recording in South Africa in 1985-6 prompted the United Nations and the African National Congress to blacklist Simon until he vowed in 1987 not to record in South Africa again. Married singer Edie Brickell in 1992.

DATE	PK	WK	TITLE	LABEL	RA
02/21/76	1(3)	14	50 Ways To Leave Your Lover	Columbia	
02/08/78	7	20	Slip Sliding Away	Columbia	
03/08/78	8	14	(What A) Wonderful World *	Columbia	
10/04/80	4	9	Late In The Evening	Warner	
11/03/86	19	11	You Can Call Me Al..................................	Warner	
12/17/90	25	9	The Obvious Child	Warner	

* Art Garfunkel with James Taylor & Paul Simon

SIMPLE MINDS
Scottish rock band formed in 1978 in Glasgow: Jim Kerr (vocals, b. 07/09/59 in Glasgow), Charles Burchill (guitar, keyboards, b. 11/27/59 in Glasgow), Mick McNeil (keyboards, b. 07/20/58 in Glasgow), Mel Gaynor (drums, b. 05/29/59 in Glasgow), John Giblin (bass), Robin Clark (vocals), Sue Hadjopoulos (percussion). Kerr married Chrissie Hynde (of the Pretenders) on 05/05/84, later divorced; married British actress Patsy Kensit on 01/03/92.

DATE	PK	WK	TITLE	LABEL	RA
06/03/85	2(3)	16	Don't You (Forget About Me)........................	Virgin	
12/23/85	3(4)	16	Alive & Kickin'	Virgin	
03/10/86	26	7	Sanctify Yourself...	Virgin	
07/01/91	33	7	See The Lights...	Virgin	21
03/27/95	---	RA	She's A River	Virgin	3

SIMPLY RED
British blue-eyed soul group formed in 1982 in Manchester: Mick Hucknall (vocals, b. Michael James Hucknall on 06/08/60 in Denton, England), Sylvan Richardson (guitar), Fritz McIntyre (keyboards, b. 09/02/56 in Birmingham), Tony Bowers (bass, b. 10/31/52), Chris Joyce (drums, b. 11/10/57 in Manchester), Tim Kellett (horns, keyboards, b. 07/23/64 in Knaresborough, England). Kellett formed Olive in 1995.

DATE	PK	WK	TITLE	LABEL	RA
07/07/86	5	17	Holding Back The Years.............................	Elektra	
05/18/87	25	11	The Right Thing	Elektra	
08/21/89	3(3)	16	If You Don't Know Me By Now....................	Elektra	
11/25/91	---	RA	Something Go Me Started........................	EastWest	6
02/24/92	---	RA	Stars..	EastWest	15
11/20/95	26	1	Fairground	EastWest	28

SIMPSONS, The
American animated television family on Fox network's *The Simpsons*. Bart (the voice of Nancy Cartwright), Homer (Dan Castellaneta), Marge (Julie Kavner), Lisa (Yeardley Smith), Maggie (Matt Groening). Groening is the show's creator.

DATE	PK	WK	TITLE	LABEL	RA
02/04/91	---	RA	Do The Bartman .... Geffen		4

SIN WITH SEBASTIAN
German male dance singer Sebastian Roth from Hamburg.

| 03/04/96 | 16 | 8 | Shut Up (And Sleep With Me) .... RCA | | |

SIR MIX-A-LOT
American male rapper born Anthony Ray on 08/12/63 in Seattle. Starred in the television show *The Watcher*.

| 09/14/92 | 5 | 12 | Baby Got Back................................. Def American | | |

SISTER HAZEL
American rock group formed in 1994 in Gainesville, Florida: Ken Block (lead vocals, acoustic guitar), Andrew Copeland (vocals, acoustic guitar), Jeff Beres (bass, vocals), Ryan Newell (guitar), Mark Trojanowski (drums). Named after an African American woman who ran Sister Hazel's Rescue Mission in Gainesville during the 1970's and 1980's.

| 08/04/97 | --- | RA | All For You .... Universal | | 12 |

SISTER SLEDGE
American R&B-pop vocal quartet formed in the late-1950's: sisters Joni (b. 1957), Kathie (b. 1959), Kim (b. 1958), and Debra (b. 1955) Sledge. All four sisters were born in Philadelphia.

05/16/79	10	12	He's The Greatest Dancer .... Atlantic		
07/11/79	4	14	We Are Family... Atlantic		
02/06/80	24	2	Got To Love Somebody .... Atlantic		

666
German techno-dance group.

| 02/07/99 | 9 | 44 + | Paradox.. DJ Line | | |

SIXPENCE NONE THE RICHER
American pop/rock group formed in the early-1990's in New Braunfels, Texas: Leigh Nash (vocals, b. as Leigh Bingham), Dale Baker (drums), Matt Slocum (guitar), Justin Cary (bass), Sean Kelly (guitar). Nash and Slocum are from New Braunfels, Texas; Baker is from Branson, Missouri. Band's name comes from a passage from C.S. Lewis' book *Mere Christianity*.

| 03/28/99 | 4 | 23 + | Kiss Me .... Squint | | 1+ |

Another version peaked at #34 on 03/21/99.

SKEE-LO
American male rapper born Antoine Roundtree, circa 1975 in Los Angeles.

| 12/04/95 | 20 | 15 | I Wish... Attic | | |

SKID ROW
American hard rock group formed in 1986 in New Jersey: Peterborough, Ontario native Sebastian Bach (vocals, b. Sebastian Bierk on 04/03/68 in Bahamas), Dave "Snake" Sabo (guitar), Scotti Hill (guitar), Rachel Bolan (bass, b. 02/09/64), Rob Affuso (drums, b. 03/01/63).

DATE	PK	WK	TITLE	LABEL	RA
10/30/89	5	13	18 & Life	Atlantic	
02/12/90	---	RA	I Remember You	Atlantic	12

SKY, Amy
Canadian female MOR singer/songwriter/actress born in 1960 in Toronto. Married to singer/songwriter husband Marc Jordan. Starred in the Toronto production of the musical *Blood Brothers*. Graduated from the University of Toronto in music theory.

05/26/97	---	RA	Til You Love Somebody	Iron	24

SKY
Canadian pop duo from Montreal consisting of Antoine Sicotte and James Renald.

11/15/98	4	24	Some Kinda Wonderful	EMI	18
04/25/99	4	14 +	Love Song	EMI	1
06/28/99	---	RA	Push	EMI	13+

SLADE
British rock group formed in 1968 in Wolverhampton, England: Noddy Holder (vocals, guitar, b. Neville Holder on 06/15/50 in Walsall, England), Dave Hill (guitar, b. 04/04/52 in Fleet Castle, England), Jimmy Lea (bass, piano, b. 06/14/52 in Wolverhampton), Don Powell (drums, b. 09/10/50 in Bilston, England).

06/25/84	13	16	Run Runaway	CBS	
09/17/84	21	5	My Oh My	CBS	

SLOAN
Canadian alternative rock band formed in 1991: Jay Ferguson (guitar, vocals, b. 10/14/68 in Halifax), Chris Murphy (bass, vocals, b. 11/07/68 in Charlottetown, P.E.I.), Patrick Pentland (guitar, vocals, b. 09/20/69 in Northern Ireland), Andrew Scott (drums, vocals, b. 11/15/67 in Ottawa). Based in Halifax.

10/10/94	---	RA	Coax Me	DGC	37
10/28/96	---	RA	Everything You've Done Wrong	Murderecords	17

SLY FOX
American dance duo: Gary "Mudbone" Cooper (P-Funk) and Michael Carmacho.

05/26/86	1(1)	21	Let's Go All The Way	Capitol	

SMART E's
British techno-pop band from Romford, Essex, England: Tom Orton, Chris "Luna C" Howell, Nick Arnold.

02/08/93	12	12	Sesame's Treat	Warner	

SMASH MOUTH
American rock band formed in 1994 in San Jose, California: Steve Harwell (vocals), Greg Camp (guitars), Paul De Lisle (bass), Kevin Coleman (drums).

12/08/97	---	RA	Walkin' On The Sun	Interscope	2
08/10/98	---	RA	Can't Get Enough Of You Baby	Elektra	7
07/05/98	18	9	The Fonz	Interscope	

DATE	PK	WK	TITLE	LABEL	RA
08/09/99	---	RA	All Star .... Interscope		2+

SMASHING PUMPKINS
American grunge rock group formed in 1989 in Chicago: Billy Corgan (vocals, guitar, b. 03/17/67 in Chicago), James Iha (guitar, b. 03/26/68 in Elk Grove, Illinois), D'Arcy Wretzky (bass, b. 05/01/68 in South Haven, Michigan), Jimmy Chamberlain (drums, b. 06/10/64 in Joliet, Illinois). Touring keyboardist Jonathan Melvoin died of a heroin overdose on 07/12/96 in New York City; Chamberlain was dismissed from the band after being charged with possession of a controlled substance.

05/30/94	---	RA	Disarm... Virgin	12
12/04/95	6	19	Bullet With Butterfly Wings .... Virgin	
03/04/96	5	18 h	1979 .... Virgin	2
			Retail Singles: #8 (04/01/96) / 6 wks.	
08/19/96	6	12 h	Tonight Tonight... Virgin	31
01/12/97	24	2	Cherub Rock... Page	
01/12/97	30	1	Today .... Page	
01/12/97	34	1	Lull .... Page	
03/03/97	---	RA	Thirty-Three.. Virgin	22
07/05/98	9	14	Ava Adore... Virgin	
			Another version peaked at #30 on 06/28/98.	
10/18/98	13	11	Perfect... Virgin	33

SMITH, Charlene
Canadian female dance singer from Toronto.

02/26/96	---	RA	Let It Slide .... China	37

SMITH, Michael W.
American male Christian rock singer/songwriter/keyboardist born Michael Whitaker Smith in Kenova, West Virginia.

07/22/91	---	RA	Place In This World .... Reunion	19
11/23/92	---	RA	I Will Be Here For You .... Reunion	31

SMITH, Patti
American female punk rock singer born on 12/31/46 in Chicago. Poet/playwright, wrote several poetry books. Once married to ex-MC5 guitarist Fred "Sonic" Smith (died late-1994).

07/12/78	31	2	Because The Night.. Arista	

SMITH, Rex
American male singer/actor born on 09/19/56 in Jacksonville, Florida. Starred in several Broadway musicals and movies such as *The Pirates Of Penzance* and *Streethawk*. Appeared in the Toronto production of *Sunset Boulevard*.

07/11/79	1(2)	14	You Take My Breath Away .... Columbia	

SMITH, Will
American male rapper/actor born Willard Smith on 09/25/69 in Philadelphia. Member of D.J. Jazzy Jeff & The Fresh Prince. Appeared in the TV sitcom *The Fresh Prince of Bel-Air* and the movies *Bad Boys* (1995), *Independence Day* (1996), *Men In Black* (1997), and *Wild Wild West* (1999).

08/25/97	---	RA	Men In Black... Columbia	1

DATE	PK	WK	TITLE	LABEL	RA
03/22/98	22	5	Gettin' Jiggy Wit It	Columbia	10
08/10/98	---	RA	Just The Two Of Us	Columbia	14
01/04/99	---	RA	Miami	Columbia	5
07/11/99	2(3)	3+	Wild Wild West	Columbia	3+

SMITHEREENS
American rock group formed in 1980 in Carteret, New Jersey: Pat DiNizio (guitar, vocals), Jim Babjak (guitar, vocals), Dennis Diken (drums, vocals), Mike Mesaros (bass, vocals).

04/13/92	---	RA	Too Much Passion	Capitol	24

SMOKIE
British pop-rock quartet: Chris Norman (vocals), Alan Silson (guitar), Terry Utley (bass), Pete Spencer (drums).

04/30/77	9	15	Living Next Door To Alice	RSO	

SMYTH, Patty
American female rock singer born on 06/26/57 in New York City. Former vocalist of Scandal.

10/19/92	---	RA	Sometimes Love Just Ain't Enough *	MCA	3
03/01/93	---	RA	No Mistakes	MCA	10

* Patty Smyth with Don Henley

SNAP!
American/German dance duo formed by Frankfurt-based producers/composers Michael Muenzing and Luca Anzilotti: vocalist Penny Ford (former member of SOS Band and Klymaxx), rapper Turbo B (b. Maurice Durron Butler on 04/30/67 in Pittsburgh). Ford left by 1992 to pursue solo career; replaced by Thea Austin. Turbo B and Austin left in 1992, both replaced by Niki Harris, backing singer for Madonna. Austin became the lead singer of Soulsearcher in 1999.

07/30/90	2(1)	13	The Power	Arista	6
11/05/90	5	10	Ooops Up	Arista	29
10/26/92	---	RA	Rhythm Is A Dancer	Arista	3
04/19/93	18	13	Exterminate	Arista	

SNEAKER PIMPS
British trip-hop trio formed in 1995 in Manchester: Kelli Dayton (vocals, b. 1975), Chris Corner (guitar), Liam Howe (keyboards). Dayton is Anglo-Indonesian.

10/05/97	37	3	Spin Spin Sugar	Virgin	

SNIFF N' THE TEARS
British rock group led by Paul Roberts (vocals) and Loz Netto (guitar).

09/19/79	6	8	Driver's Seat	Atlantic	

SNOW
Canadian male reggae singer born Darrin O'Brien on 10/30/69 in North York, Ontario.

DATE	PK	WK	TITLE	LABEL	RA
03/22/93	1(2)	11	Informer...	EastWest	6
07/05/93	---	RA	Girl I've Been Hurt...................................	EastWest	8
05/22/95	30	8	Anything For You	EastWest	
11/20/95	20	3	Sexy Girl	EastWest	

S.O.A.P.
Danish female pop duo formed in 1997: Line (b. 06/26/82) and Heidi (b. 10/18/79) Sørensen. Both were born in Malaysia.

06/08/98	---	RA	This Is How We Party	Crave	24

SOCCIO, Gino
Canadian techno-disco singer/multi-instrumentalist/producer born in 1955 in Montreal.

05/30/79	22	4	Dancer...	Celebration	

SOFT CELL
British techno-pop duo formed in 1980 in Leeds, England: Marc Almond (vocals, b. Peter Marc Almond on 07/09/59 in Southport, England), David Ball (synthesizer, b. 05/03/59 in Blackpool, England). Disbanded in 1984. Almond pursued solo career in 1988.

02/27/82	1(3)	15	Tainted Love..	Vertigo	

SOHO
British dance trio from London: Jacqueline and Pauline Cuff (vocals), Timothy Brinkhurst (guitar). The Cuffs are twins.

11/26/90	---	RA	Hippy Chick	Atco	33

SOMETHIN' FOR THE PEOPLE
American R&B vocal trio formed in 1990 in Oakland, California: Jeff "Fuzzy" Young, Curtis "Sauce" Wilson, Rochad "Cat Daddy" Holiday. Based in Los Angeles. Young and Wilson are both natives of Oakland; Holiday is a native of Los Angeles.

11/30/97	7	21	My Love Is The Shhh....	Warner	20

SOUL ASYLUM
American rock group formed in 1983 in Minneapolis: Dave Pirner (vocals, guitar, b. 04/16/64 in Green Bay, Wisconsin), Daniel Murphy (guitar, b. 07/12/62 in Duluth, Minnesota), Karl Mueller (bass, b. 07/27/62 in Minneapolis), Grant Young (drums, b. 01/05/64 in Iowa City, Iowa). Pirner appeared in the 1994 movie *Reality Bites*. Young replaced by Sterling Campbell (formerly of Duran Duran) in 1995. Campbell left in 1997.

09/06/93	---	RA	Runaway Train	Columbia	1
08/21/95	---	RA	Misery...	Columbia	2
03/04/96	14	10 h	Promises Broken	Columbia	19

SOUL ATTORNEYS
Canadian rock trio from Quebec City: Jacques Gaines (vocals), Eric Filto (keyboards, backing vocals, programming), Mathieu "Rocket" Dandurand (guitar).

07/29/96	21	9 h	These Are The Days	Epic	15
01/20/97	---	RA	So They Say	Epic	16

DATE	PK	WK	TITLE	LABEL	RA
05/19/97	---	RA	See The People	Epic	30

S.O.U.L. SYSTEM
American dance group produced by Robert Clivilles and David Cole of C&C Music Factory. Features vocalist Michelle Visage (b. 09/20/68) of Seduction.

DATE	PK	WK	TITLE	LABEL	RA
02/08/93	---	RA	It's Gonna Be A Lovely Day	Arista	24

SOUL II SOUL
British dance-soul group formed in 1982 in London: Jazzie B. (DJ, vocals, b. Beresford Romeo on 01/26/63 in London), Nellee Hooper (programming), Caron Wheeler (vocals, b. 01/19/63 in London), Simon Law (keyboards), Daddae (b. Phillip Harvey on 02/28/64 in London). Before joining Soul II Soul, Wheeler was a background vocalist for Phil Collins, Erasure, and Elvis Costello.

DATE	PK	WK	TITLE	LABEL
10/02/89	5	24	Keep On Movin'	Virgin
02/05/90	1(3)	25	Back To Life *	Virgin
03/12/90	15	7	Jazzie's Groove	Virgin
05/07/90	40	3	Get A Life	Virgin

* Soul II Soul featuring Caron Wheeler

SOUL, David
American male singer/actor born David Solberg on 08/28/43 in Chicago. Played Ken Hutchinson on TV's *Starsky & Hutch*, 1975-79. Appeared on *The Merv Griffin Show* as "The Covered Man" (wore a ski mask).

DATE	PK	WK	TITLE	LABEL
04/30/77	1(2)	14	Don't Give Up On Us	Private Stock

SOULSEARCHER
American dance trio: Marc Pomeroy (keyboards), Brian Tappert (producer), Thea Austin (vocals). Austin was briefly the lead singer of Snap! in 1992.

DATE	PK	WK	TITLE	LABEL
07/18/99	34	1	Can't Get Enough	Sugarfoot

SOUNDGARDEN
American grunge rock band formed in 1984 in Seattle: Matt Cameron (drums, b. 11/28/62 in San Diego), Chris Cornell (vocals, b. 07/20/64 in Seattle), Kim Thayil (guitar, b. 09/04/60 in Seattle), Ben Shepherd (bass, b. Hunter Shepherd on 09/20/68 in Okinaw, Japan). Former bassist Jason Everman played guitar in Nirvana before joining in 1989. Disbanded in 1997. Group named after a sculpture in a Seattle park.

DATE	PK	WK	TITLE	LABEL	RA
09/19/94	---	RA	Black Hole Sun	A&M	3
07/01/96	36	2 h	Pretty Noose	A&M	
09/09/96	31	4 h	Burden In My Hand	A&M	

SOUP DRAGONS
Scottish pop-rock band formed in 1985 in Belshill, Scotland: Sean Dickson (vocals, b. 03/21/67 in Glasgow), Jim McCulloch (guitar, b. 05/19/66 in Glasgow), Sushil Dade (bass, b. 07/15/66 in Glasgow), Paul Quinn (drums). McCulloch, Dade, and Quinn left in 1994.

DATE	PK	WK	TITLE	LABEL	RA
10/26/92	38	1	Divine Thing	Mercury	32

SOUTHER, J.D.

DATE	PK	WK	TITLE	LABEL	RA

American male pop singer John David Souther born in Detroit, raised in Amarillo, Texas.

| 12/12/79 | 9 | 16 | You're Only Lonely | Columbia | |
| 05/09/81 | 9 | 8 | Her Town Too * | Columbia | |

* James Taylor with J.D. Souther

SPACE MONKEYS
British alternative dance group formed in 1994: Tony Pipes (DJ, beats, keyboards, samples), Chas Morrison (drums, vocals, percussion), Richard McNevin-Duff (vocals, guitar, loops), Dom Morrisson (bass, sub bass). Based in Manchester.

| 02/09/98 | --- | RA | Sugar Cane | Interscope | 34 |

SPACEHOG
British/American rock band formed in 1994 in New York City: brothers Anthony (bass) and Royston Langdon (vocals), Jonny Cragg (drums), Richard Steel (guitar). The Langdons are from Leeds, England.

| 04/22/96 | 17 | 13 h | In The Meantime | Elektra | 29 |

SPANDAU BALLET
British pop-dance band formed in 1979 in London: Tony Hadley (vocals, keyboards, b. 06/02/60 in London), Gary Kemp (guitar, keyboards, b. 10/16/59 in London), Martin Kemp (bass, b. 10/10/61 in London), Steve Norman (guitar, saxophone, percussion, b. 03/25/60 in London), John Keeble (drums, b. 07/06/59 in London). The Kemp brothers starred in the 1990 film *The Krays*. Disbanded in 1990. Gary appeared in the 1992 film *The Bodyguard* and on TV's *Larry Sanders Show*.

10/31/83	1(2)	19	True	Chrysalis	
12/26/83	21	11	Gold	Chrysalis	
10/01/84	20	7	Only When You Leave	Chrysalis	

SPEARS, Britney
American female pop singer born Britney Jeau Spears on 12/02/81 in Kentwood, Louisiana. Member of the television show *The Mickey Mouse Club* at age 11.

| 11/29/98 | 1(2) | 21 | ...Baby One More Time | Jive | 1 |
| 06/14/99 | --- | RA | Sometimes | Jive | 7+ |

SPENCER, Tracie
American female R&B singer born on 07/12/76 in Waterloo, Iowa. Winner of TV's *Star Search* singing competition in 1986.

| 05/06/91 | 7 | 15 | This House | Capitol | 18 |
| 07/01/91 | 37 | 4 | This Time Make It Funky | Capitol | |

SPICE GIRLS
British female pop vocal group formed in 1994 in London: Posh Spice (b. Victoria Addams on 04/17/74 in Hertfordshire, England), Baby Spice (b. Emma Lee Bunton on 01/21/76 in Finchley, England), Sporty Spice/Mel C (b. Melanie Jayne Chisholm on 01/12/74 in Widnes, England), Scary Spice/Mel B (b. Melanie Brown on 05/29/75 in Leeds, England), Sexy Spice/Ginger (b. Geraldine Halliwell on 08/06/72 in Watford, England). Starred in the 1998 movie *Spice World*. Halliwell announced on 05/31/98 that she

DATE	PK	WK	TITLE	LABEL	RA

left the group; later pursued solo career. Addams married professional soccer player David Beckham on 07/04/99.

02/16/97	37	4	Wannabe	Virgin	3
05/05/97	---	RA	Say You'll Be There	Virgin	3
08/25/97	---	RA	2 Become 1	Virgin	5
12/28/97	2(1)	30	Spice Up Your Life	Virgin	6
02/08/98	9	13	Too Much	Virgin	16
06/14/98	35	2	Stop	Virgin	3
08/09/98	24	10	Viva Forever	Virgin	3

"Pt. 1" version is above. "Pt. 2" peaked at #32 on 08/02/98. Another version peaked at #38 on 08/16/98.

12/13/98	1(13)	33 +	Goodbye	Virgin	16

SPIN DOCTORS

American rock group formed in 1988 in New York City: Chris Barron (vocals, b. Christopher Barron Gross on 02/05/68 in Hawaii), Aaron Comess (drums, b. 04/24/68 in Arizona), Mark Burton White (bass, b. 07/07/62 in New York City), Eric Schenkman (guitar, b. 12/12/63 in Massachusetts). Schenkman replaced in 1994 by Anthony Krizan. Krizan replaced in 1997 by Erin Tabib.

12/14/92	---	RA	Little Miss Can't Be Wrong	Epic	30
04/05/93	---	RA	Two Princes	Epic	1
09/13/93	---	RA	How Could You Want Him	Epic	40
09/05/94	---	RA	You Let Your Heart Go Too Fast	Epic	11

SPINNERS

American R&B vocal group formed in 1957 in Detroit. Line-up in 1975: Bobbie Smith (b. 04/10/36 in Detroit), Pervis Jackson (b. May 16), Henry Fambrough (b. 05/10/38 in Detroit), Billy Henderson (b. 08/09/39 in Detroit), Phillipé Wynne (b. Philip Walker on 04/03/38 in Cincinnatti). Wynne left in 1977, replaced by John Edwards. Wynne died of a heart attack on 07/13/84 in Oakland, California.

11/15/75	6	13	Games People Play	Atlantic
01/22/77	5	16	The Rubberband Man	Atlantic
04/23/80	4	10	Working My Way Back To You	Atlantic

SPIRIT OF THE WEST

Canadian folk group formed in 1993 in Vancouver: Geoffrey Kelly (b. Scotland), John Mann (b. Calgary), Hugh McMillan (b. Calgary), Vince Ditrich (b. Deathfridge, Alberta). McMillan joined the group in 1986; Ditrich joined in 1990.

08/28/95	---	RA	Tell Me What I Think	WEA	32

SPLIT ENZ

New Zealand pop band formed in 1972 in Auckland: brothers Tim (vocals, piano, b. 06/25/52 in Te Awamutu, New Zealand) and Neil Finn (guitar, vocals, b. 05/27/58 in Te Awamutu), Malcolm Green (drums, b. 01/25/53), Eddie Rayner (keyboards), Noel Crombie (percussion), Nigel Griggs (bass, b. 08/18/49). Tim later pursued a solo career, married actress Greta Scacchi in 1985. The Finns were in the group Crowded House.

12/20/80	5	13	I Got You	A&M
08/01/81	17	3	One Step Ahead	A&M
06/12/82	6	10	Six Months In A Leaky Boat	A&M

DATE	PK	WK	TITLE	LABEL RA

SPOONS
Canadian pop group formed in 1979 in Burlington, Ontario: Gordon Deppe (vocals, guitar), Colin Cripps (guitar), Sandy Horne (bass), Rob Preuss (keyboards, replaced by Scott MacDonald), Derrick Ross (drums, replaced by Ian Hendry).

12/26/83	31	6	Old Emotions	Ready
11/05/84	38	2	Tell No Lies	Ready

SPORTY THIEVZ
American hip-hop trio: King Kirk (a.k.a. Thieven Stealberg), Big Dubez (a.k.a. Safecracker), Marlon Brando (a.k.a. Robin Hood). Brando is not the actor of the same name.

06/13/99	3(1)	7+	No Pigeons	Columbia

Another version peaked at #5 on 05/30/99. Credited to Sporty Thieves featuring Mr. Woods.

SPRINGFIELD, Dusty
British female pop singer/guitarist born Mary O'Brien on 04/16/39 in London. Mainly popular in the 1960's. Died of breast cancer on 03/02/99 in London.

03/21/88	2(1)	13	What Have I Done To Deserve This *	Capitol

* Pet Shop Boys/Dusty Springfield

SPRINGFIELD, Rick
Australian male rock singer/actor born on 08/23/49 in Sydney. First recorded with the Australian teen idol band Zoot. Played Dr. Noah Drake on the television soap opera *General Hospital* in the early-1980's. Appeared in the 1984 movie *Hard To Hold*.

07/18/81	4	12	Jessie's Girl	RCA
11/07/81	19	3	I've Done Everything For You	RCA
02/27/82	15	3	Love Is Alright Tonite	RCA
05/15/82	1(2)	12	Don't Talk To Strangers	RCA
06/27/83	16	4	Affair Of The Heart	RCA
09/12/83	29	2	Human Touch	RCA
05/28/84	12	10	Love Somebody	RCA
02/04/85	39	2	Bruce	Mercury
06/03/85	28	2	Celebrate Youth	RCA
05/02/88	34	3	Rock Of Life	RCA

SPRINGSTEEN, Bruce
American male rock singer/songwriter/guitarist born on 09/23/49 in Freehold, New Jersey. Performed in local clubs in New Jersey and New York in 1960's. Wrote "Blinded By The Light" by Manfred Mann's Earth Band and "Fire" by the Pointer Sisters. His E-Street Band formed in 1973, consisting of Clarence Clemons (saxophone), David Sancious, Danny Federici (keyboards), Gary Tallent (bass), Vini Lopez (drums). Sancious and Lopez replaced by Roy Bittan and Max Weinberg. Steve Van Zandt joined in 1975 as guitarist. A court injunction prevented Springsteen from recording from 1976 to 1977. Married to model/actress Julianne Phillips from 1985 to 1989. Stopped performing with E-Street Band in 1989. Married Patti Scialfa in 1991.

07/26/78	37	2	Prove It All Night	Columbia
12/20/80	2(4)	13	Hungry Heart	Columbia
03/14/81	19	2	Fade Away	Columbia

DATE	PK	WK	TITLE	LABEL	RA
07/09/84	7	23	Dancing In The Dark	Columbia	
10/15/84	16	9	Cover Me	Columbia	
02/18/85	15	9	Born In The U.S.A.	Columbia	
05/06/85	18	12	I'm On Fire	Columbia	
07/08/85	37	6	Glory Days	Columbia	
11/18/85	14	8	I'm Goin' Down	Columbia	
01/20/86	22	7	My Hometown	Columbia	
12/29/86	19	9	War *	Columbia	
03/16/87	31	2	Fire *	Columbia	
10/26/87	12	14	Brilliant Disguise	Columbia	
01/18/88	24	10	Tunnel Of Love	Columbia	
05/09/88	39	1	One Step Up	Columbia	
04/20/92	4	12	Human Touch/ Better Days	Columbia	2
07/13/92	33	8	57 Channels	Columbia	
05/02/94	1(3)	52	Streets Of Philadelphia	Columbia	5
03/27/95	---	RA	Murder Incorporated	Columbia	26
08/14/95	27	10	Secret Garden	Columbia	
05/12/97	---	RA	Secret Garden (re-release)	Columbia	17

* Bruce Springsteen & The E Street Band

SPUNKADELIC
Canadian R&B duo consisting of Ray Guiste and Ali Whittaker from Toronto.

DATE	PK	WK	TITLE	LABEL	RA
03/11/91	23	8	Boomerang	SBK	31

SQUEEZE
British pop-rock band formed in 1974 in London. Paul Carrack was lead singer, 1981-82. Disbanded in 1982. Re-formed in 1985, line-up included Chris Difford (guitar, vocals, b. 11/04/54 in London), Glenn Tilbrook (guitar, vocals, b. 08/31/57 in London), Julian "Jools" Holland (keyboards, vocals, b. 01/24/55), Gilson Lavis (drums, b. 06/27/51 in Bedford, England), Keith Wilkinson (bass, vocals, b. 09/24/54 in Southfield, England). Difford, Tilbrook, Holland, and Lavis were in the original line-up.

DATE	PK	WK	TITLE	LABEL	RA
12/14/87	26	11	Hourglass	A&M	

SQUIER, Billy
American male rock singer born on 05/12/50 in Wellesley Hills, Massachusetts.

DATE	PK	WK	TITLE	LABEL	RA
08/22/81	9	7	The Stroke	Capitol	
09/25/82	19	1	Emotions In Motion	Capitol	
09/10/84	21	8	Rock Me Tonight	Capitol	

STACEY Q
American female dance singer Stacey Swain of Los Angeles.

DATE	PK	WK	TITLE	LABEL	RA
12/01/86	2(3)	21	Two Of Hearts	Atlantic	

STALLONE, Frank
American male pop singer/actor born on 07/30/50 in Philadelphia. Brother of actor Sylvester Stallone.

DATE	PK	WK	TITLE	LABEL	RA
09/26/83	25	2	Far From Over	RSO	

DATE	PK	WK	TITLE	LABEL	RA

STAMPEDERS
Canadian rock band formed in 1963 in Calgary, based in Toronto: Rick Dodson, Ronnie King, Kim Berly. Won the 1972 Juno Award for Vocal Instrumental Group of the Year.

07/26/75	7	7	Hit The Road Jack	MWC	
06/12/76	21	9	Playing In The Band	MWC	

STANSFIELD, Lisa
British female pop-R&B singer born on 04/11/66 in Rochdale, England. Founder of the group Blue Zone.

04/16/90	1(5)	17	All Around The World	Arista	2
07/02/90	37	4	You Can't Deny It	Arista	10
10/15/90	---	RA	This Is The Right Time	Arista	22
01/20/92	---	RA	Change	Arista	8

STAPLE SINGERS
American R&B vocal group formed in 1953 as a gospel outfit: Roebuck "Pops" Staples (b. 12/02/15 in Winona, Mississippi), his son Pervis Staples (b. 1935 in Mississippi) and daughters Mavis (b. 1940 in Chicago), Cleo (b. 1934 in Mississippi), and Yvonne Staples (b. 1939 in Chicago). Pervis left in 1971.

01/10/76	7	12	Let's Do It Again	Curtom	

STARBUCK
American pop-rock group led by vocalist Bruce Blackman.

07/17/76	4	11	Moonlight Feels Right	Private Stock	

STARDUST
French dance group led by Thomas Bangalter (b. 01/03/75). Bangalter is also a member of Daft Punk.

11/22/98	2(1)	37 +	Music Sounds Better With You	Virgin	24
			Two other versions peaked at #21 on 10/11/98 and #2 on 10/18/98.		

STARLAND VOCAL BAND
American pop quartet from Washington, D.C.: husband and wife Bill and Taffy Danoff, John Carroll and future wife Margot Chapman. Bill co-wrote "Take Me Home, Country Roads" with singer John Denver.

07/10/76	1(5)	15	Afternoon Delight	RCA	

STARR, Ringo
British male rock singer/drummer born Richard Starkey, Jr. on 07/07/40 in Liverpool. Played drums in Rory Storm and the Hurricanes in the early-1960's. Drummer of The Beatles, 1962-70. First recorded solo in 1970. Appeared in the films *Candy, The Magic Christian, 200 Motels, Born To Boogie, Blindman, That'll Be The Day, Cave Man, Give My Regards To Broad Street* and in a 1985 TV production of *Alice in Wonderland*. Married actress Barbara Bach in 1981.

11/20/76	34	5	A Dose Of Rock N' Roll	Atlantic	

STARS ON 45
Dutch aggregation of studio vocalists and musicians assembled by producer Jaap Eggermont.

DATE	PK	WK	TITLE	LABEL	RA
07/04/81	1(3)	12	Medley...	Radio	

STARS ON 54
American/Dutch one-time collaboration for the 1998 movie *54*: Ultra Naté (b. 1968 in Baltimore), Amber, Jocelyn Enriquez (b. 12/28/74 in San Francisco).

10/25/98	7	22	If You Could Read My Mind	Tommy Boy	3
			Another version peaked at #32 on 03/28/99.		

STARSHIP - see JEFFERSON STARSHIP

STATON, Candi
American female R&B singer born Canzata Maria Staton on 05/13/40 in Hanceville, Alabama. Once married to singer Clarence Carter. Recorded gospel music in the 1980's and 1990's. Started hosting her own variety TV show *Say Yes* in 1996.

| 09/11/76 | 30 | 5 | Young Hearts Run Free .... | Warner | |

STEELE, Chrissy
Canadian female heavy metal singer.

| 09/16/91 | 18 | 10 | Love You Till It Hurts .... | Capitol | |

STEELY DAN
American jazz-styled pop group formed in 1972 in Los Angeles led by Walter Becker (bass, guitar, vocals, b. 02/20/50 in Queens, New York) and Donald Fagen (keyboards, vocals, b. 01/10/48 in Passaic, New Jersey). Featured various session musicians including singer Michael McDonald (later of the Doobie Brothers). Becker and Faggen originally in Bad Rock Group along with comedian/actor Chevy Chase, who played drums.

04/05/78	14	10	Peg...	ABC	
11/01/78	31	2	Josie...	ABC	
02/14/81	3(2)	10	Hey, Nineteen	MCA	
04/25/81	20	3	Time Out Of Mind	MCA	

STEREO MC's
British alternative rock trio formed in the late-1980's in London: Rob Birch (vocals, b. Robert Charles Birch on 06/11/61 in Ruddington, England), Nick "The Head" Hallam (synthesizers, computers, b. 06/11/62 in Nottingham), Owen "If" Rossiter (percussion, b. Ian Frederick Rossiter on 03/20/59 in Newport, Wales). Touring/video vocalists include Cath Coffey (b. Catherine Muthomi Coffey, circa 1965 in Kenya), Verona Davis (b. 02/18/52 in London), Andrea Groves (b. 11/07/57 in London).

| 06/21/93 | 23 | 2 | Connected .... | Island | 10 |
| 07/19/93 | 22 | 5 | Step It Up .... | Island | 9 |

STEVENS, Martin
Canadian male disco singer from Quebec.

| 09/06/78 | 22 | 14 | Love Is In The Air...................................... | Columbia | |

STEVENS, Suzanne

DATE	PK	WK	TITLE	LABEL	RA

Canadian female singer from Montreal.

| 07/03/76 | 40 | 1 | Knowing You Knowing When | Capitol | |

STEVIE B
American male R&B singer Steven Bernard Hill born and raised in Miami. Self-taught musician.

09/25/89	19	7	In My Eyes	A&M	
02/04/91	2(4)	17	Because I Love You (The Postman Song)	A&M	6
04/22/91	---	RA	I'll Be By Your Side	A&M	33
09/06/98	25	6	If You Leave Me Now	Indy	

STEWART, Al
British male folk-rock singer/composer born on 09/05/45 in Glasgow, Scotland.

| 04/02/77 | 2(2) | 22 | Year Of The Cat | Janus |
| 11/29/78 | 11 | 10 | Time Passages | Arista |

STEWART, Amii
American female disco singer/dancer/actress born in 1956 in Washington, D.C. In the Broadway musical *Bubbling Brown Sugar*. Her niece is singer Sinitta.

| 05/02/79 | 2(6) | 22 | Knock On Wood | Arista |

STEWART, Jermaine
American male pop singer raised in Chicago. Backing vocals for Shalamar and Boy George.

| 12/24/84 | 34 | 8 | The Word Is Out | Virgin |
| 09/01/86 | 11 | 13 | We Don't Have To Take Our Clothes Off | Virgin |

STEWART, John
American male vocalist born on 09/05/39 in San Diego. Member of The Kingston Trio, 1961-67. Wrote "Daydream Believer".

| 09/05/79 | 8 | 12 | Gold | RSO |
| 10/03/79 | 36 | 2 | Midnight Wind | RSO |

STEWART, Rod
British male rock singer/songwriter born Roderick David Stewart on 01/10/45 in London. Played with Jimmy Powell and the Five Dimensions, Hoochie Coochie Men, and Shotgun Express (members included future Fleetwood Mac members Peter Green and Mick Fleetwood). Member of the Jeff Beck Group, 1967-69. First recorded solo in 1969. Member of Faces/Small Faces, 1969-75. Married to actress Alana Hamilton, 1979-84. Lived with model Kelly Emberg for six years, married model Rachel Hunter on 12/15/90. Donates royalties of his song, "Da Ya Think I'm Sexy" to UNICEF.

12/18/76	1(7)	20	Tonight's The Night (Gonna Be Alright)	Warner
04/16/77	26	8	First Cut Is The Deepest	Warner
08/13/77	23	8	Killing Of Georgie	Warner
01/25/78	2(2)	20	You're In My Heart (The Final Acclaim)	Warner
04/05/78	10	14	Hot Legs	Warner
06/28/78	19	8	I Was Only Joking	Warner
02/21/79	1(8)	22	Da Ya Think I'm Sexy	Warner

DATE	PK	WK	TITLE	LABEL	RA
06/13/79	6	12	Ain't Love A Bitch	Warner	
02/07/81	2(3)	14	Passion	Warner	
12/12/81	1(6)	14	Young Turks	Warner	
03/20/82	3(2)	9	Tonight I'm Yours (Don't Hurt Me)	Warner	
08/22/83	7	13	Baby Jane	Warner	
08/13/84	13	13	Infatuation	Warner	
11/05/84	12	12	Some Guys Have All The Luck	Warner	
09/01/86	3(1)	17	Love Touch	Warner	
08/08/88	2(2)	16	Lost In You	Warner	
11/14/88	7	17	Forever Young	Warner	
05/01/89	17	9	My Heart Can't Tell Me No	Warner	
08/21/89	22	5	Crazy About Her	Warner	
02/12/90	27	5	Downtown Train	Warner	
05/28/90	2(2)	13	This Old Heart Of Mine *	Warner	3
05/06/91	6	15	Rhythm Of My Heart	Warner	1
10/14/91	23	11	The Motown Song	Warner	4
12/09/91	---	RA	Broken Arrow	Warner	10
06/21/93	3(1)	17	Have I Told You Lately	Warner	1
10/18/93	9	27	Reason To Believe	Warner	4
12/27/93	6	32	All For Love **	A&M	
02/21/94	---	RA	Having A Party	Warner	22
08/14/95	---	RA	Leave Virginia Alone	Warner	12
11/06/95	---	RA	This	Warner	34
03/04/96	25	9 h	So Far Away	Lava	

* Rod Stewart (with Ronald Isley)
** Bryan Adams/Rod Stewart/Sting

STIGERS, Curtis
American male MOR singer/saxophonist born in Boise, Idaho.

DATE	PK	WK	TITLE	LABEL	RA
12/02/91	---	RA	I Wonder Why	Arista	20

STING
British male rock singer/songwriter/bassist born Gordon Matthew Sumner on 10/02/51 in Wallsend, England. Lead singer/bassist of The Police. Appeared in the films *Dune*, *Stormy Monday*, and *Plenty* and in the Broadway revival of *The Threepenny Opera*. Toured with other artists to benefit Amnesty International. Established the Rainforest Foundation for environmental causes concerning the endangered Brazilian rainforest.

DATE	PK	WK	TITLE	LABEL	RA
08/19/85	8	17	If You Love Somebody, Set Them Free	A&M	
10/21/85	26	7	Fortress Around Your Heart	A&M	
12/14/87	6	14	We'll Be Together	A&M	
03/28/88	29	5	Be Still My Beating Heart	A&M	
03/18/91	4	13	All This Time	A&M	1
07/27/92	11	12	It's Probably Me *	A&M	33
04/05/93	7	16	If I Ever Lose My Faith In You	A&M	2
08/02/93	---	RA	Fields Of Gold	A&M	3
11/08/93	---	RA	Nothin' 'Bout Me	A&M	4
12/27/93	6	32	All For Love **	A&M	1
12/12/94	---	RA	When We Dance	A&M	20
04/10/95	---	RA	This Cowboy Song	A&M	37

DATE	PK	WK	TITLE	LABEL	RA
04/01/96	9	10 h	Let Your Soul Be Your Pilot	A&M	23
07/01/96	10	13 h	You Still Touch Me	A&M	24
11/11/96	---	RA	I'm So Happy I Can't Stop Crying	A&M	40
01/18/98	26	6	Roxanne '97 - Puff Daddy Remix ***	A&M	

Another version peaked at #29 on 01/18/98.

* Sting & Eric Clapton
** Bryan Adams/Rod Stewart/Sting
*** Sting & The Police

STINGLY, Byron

05/11/97	35	2	Get Up	Quality	

STOCKWOOD, Kim

Canadian female pop singer/songwriter born on 11/11/65 in St. John's, Newfoundland. Currently lives in Toronto.

10/23/95	---	RA	She's Not In Love	EMI	19
02/19/96	---	RA	Enough Love	EMI	17
09/16/96	8	14 h	Jerk	EMI	8
03/03/97	---	RA	You Won't Remember This	EMI	15
05/03/99	---	RA	12 Years Old	EMI	8

STONE TEMPLE PILOTS

American rock group formed in 1987 in San Diego as Mighty Joe Young: Weiland (vocals, b. Scott Weiland on 10/27/67 in Santa Cruz, California), Eric Kretz (drums, b. 06/07/66 in Santa Cruz), brothers Dean (guitar, b. 08/23/61 in New Jersey) and Robert DeLeo (bass, b. 02/02/66 in New Jersey).

09/06/93	---	RA	Plush	Atlantic	35
08/22/94	---	RA	Vasoline	Atlantic	37
11/07/94	---	RA	Interstate Love Song	Atlantic	20
05/13/96	29	6 h	Big Bang Baby	Atlantic	
07/29/96	34	4 h	Trippin' On A Hole	Atlantic	

STONEBOLT

Canadian rock band formed in Vancouver in the mid-1970's: David Wills (vocals), Danny Atchison (bass), Brian Lousley (drums), Roy Roper (guitar), and Jon Webster (keyboards). Disbanded in 1983.

11/01/78	15	12	I Will Still Love You	Parachute

STRAIGHT LINES

02/13/82	5	11	Letting Go	Epic

STRANGE ADVANCE

Canadian rock trio: Drew Arnott, Paul Iverson, Darryl Kromm.

04/11/83	28	1	Kiss In The Dark	Capitol
03/25/85	30	6	We Run	Capitol
04/25/88	30	9	Love Becomes Electric	Capitol

DATE	PK	WK	TITLE	LABEL	RA

STRATAVARIOUS

| 06/05/76 | 33 | 5 | I Got Your Love | Polydor | |

STRAY CATS
American rock group formed in 1979 in Massapequa, New York: Brian Setzer (guitar, vocals, b. 04/10/59 in Long Island, New York), Slim Jim Phantom (drums, b. Jim McDonell on 03/20/61), Lee Rocker (bass, vocals, b. Lee Drucker in 1961). Disbanded in 1984, re-formed in 1986. Formed the trio Phantom, Rocker, and Slick in 1985. Setzer played Eddie Cochran in the movie *La Bamba* in 1987. Setzer founded the 16-piece swing Brian Setzer Orchestra in 1994.

12/11/82	4	15	Rock This Town	EMI	
03/07/83	7	12	Stray Cat Strut	EMI	
10/24/83	3(1)	14	(She's) Sexy & 17	EMI	
01/16/84	28	7	I Won't Stand In Your Way	EMI	

STREETHEART
Canadian rock band from Winnipeg: Paul Dean (guitar), Matt Frenette (drums), Daryl Gutheil (keyboards), John Hannah (guitar), Ken Shields (vocals), Kim Sinnaeve (bass). Won the 1980 Juno Award for Most Promising Group of the Year.

| 01/23/80 | 10 | 12 | Under My Thumb | Atlantic | |
| 04/10/82 | 16 | 5 | What Kind Of Love Is This | Capitol | |

STREISAND, Barbra
American female pop-MOR singer/actress born Barbara Joan Streisand on 04/24/42 in New York City. Top-selling female artist in recording history. Debuted on Broadway in 1962's *I Can Get It For You Wholesale*. Starred as Fanny Brice in *Funny Girl* on Broadway. A death threat before a 1967 concert in New York City caused retirement from concert appearances for more than 20 years. Starred in the movies *Funny Girl, Hello, Dolly!, The Way We Were, A Star Is Born, The Prince of Tides*. Married to actor Elliott Gould, 1963-71. Became the first woman to co-write, direct, produce, and star in a film of her own, *Yentl*, in 1983. Founded the Barbra Streisand Foundation to support liberal political causes in 1987.

03/19/77	1(6)	21	Love Theme From "A Star Is Born" (Evergreen)	Columbia	
08/13/77	9	10	My Heart Belongs To Me	Columbia	
12/13/78	1(2)	14	You Don't Bring Me Flowers *	Columbia	
09/19/79	8	12	The Main Event/Fight	Columbia	
11/28/79	3(6)	12	No More Tears (Enough Is Enough) **	Columbia	
11/15/80	1(4)	13	Woman In Love	Columbia	
01/24/81	7	9	Guilty	Columbia	
04/04/81	15	3	What Kind Of Fool ***	Columbia	
12/15/96	5	9	I Finally Found Someone ****	Columbia	27
11/30/97	12	6	Tell Him *****	550/Epic	36
07/04/99	12	4 +	I've Dreamed Of You	Columbia	

* Barbra Streisand/Neil Diamond
** Donna Summer/Barbra Streisand
*** Barbra Streisand & Barry Gibb
**** Bryan Adams & Barbra Streisand
***** Celine Dion & Barbra Streisand

DATE	PK	WK	TITLE	LABEL	RA

STRIKE

| 03/02/97 | 28 | 2 | My Love Is For Real | Quality | |

STYX

American rock band formed in 1963 in Chicago: James Young (guitar, vocals, b. 11/14/48 in Chicago), Tommy Shaw (guitar, vocals, b. 09/11/53 in Montgomery, Alabama), Dennis DeYoung (keyboards, vocals, b. 02/18/47 in Chicago), and twin brothers Chuck (bass, vocals), John Panozzo (drums,) (both b. 09/20/47 in Chicago). Disbanded in 1984, re-formed in 1990 and 1996. DeYoung and Shaw pursued solo careers in 1984. Shaw returned in 1996. John died on 07/17/96.

05/01/76	31	3	Lorelei	A&M	
01/25/78	14	12	Come Sail Away	A&M	
12/13/78	30	6	Blue Collar Man	A&M	
07/11/79	31	4	Renegade	A&M	
12/12/79	1(4)	24	Babe	A&M	
03/14/81	2(5)	13	The Best Of Times	A&M	
06/06/81	8	10	Too Much Time On My Hands	A&M	
04/25/83	2(2)	17	Mr. Roboto	A&M	
06/20/83	9	8	Don't Let It End	A&M	
02/25/91	9	13	Show Me The Way	A&M	8
06/24/91	---	RA	Love At First Sight	A&M	29

SUEDE

British male vocal/instrumental group.

| 07/05/93 | 22 | 12 | Metal Mickey | Columbia | |

SUGAR RAY

American pop/rock group formed in the mid-1990's in Orange County, California: Mark McGrath (vocals), Rodney Sheppard (guitar), Murphy Karges (bass), Craig "DJ Homicide" Bullock (DJ), Stan Frazier (drums).

10/13/97	---	RA	Fly	Lava	1
04/04/99	29	3	Every Morning	Lava	1
08/09/99	---	RA	Someday	Lava	20+

SUGARHILL GANG

American rap group formed in 1977 in New York City: Master Gee (b. Guy O'Brien in 1963 in New York City), Wonder Mike (b. Michael Wright in 1958 in Englewood, New Jersey), Big Bank Hank (b. Henry Jackson in 1958 in Bronx, New York).

| 01/23/80 | 1(8) | 18 | Rapper's Delight | Quality | |

SUMMER, Donna

American female pop-R&B singer born Adrian Donna Gaines on 12/31/48 in Boston. Appeared in Munich, Germany production of Hair at age 18. In European production of *Porgy and Bess*. Appeared in the 1978 disco film *Thank God It's Friday*. Married Bruce Sudano, lead singer of Brooklyn Dreams, in 1980. Last name is an Anglicized surname of her ex-husband, Austrian actor Helmut Somer.

| 02/21/76 | 2(2) | 14 | Love To Love You Baby | Oasis | |
| 11/16/77 | 4 | 20 | I Feel Love | Casablanca | |

DATE	PK	WK	TITLE	LABEL	RA
09/20/78	10	34	Last Dance	Casablanca	
11/29/78	1(2)	18	MacArthur Park	Casablanca	
04/04/79	11	8	Heaven Knows	Casablanca	
06/27/79	1(2)	22	Hot Stuff	Casablanca	
08/08/79	2(2)	16	Bad Girls	Casablanca	
11/28/79	12	12	Dim All The Lights	Casablanca	
11/28/79	3(6)	12	No More Tears (Enough Is Enough) *	Columbia	
03/19/80	9	13	On The Radio	Casablanca	
11/22/80	2(1)	13	The Wanderer	Geffen	
09/12/83	5	18	She Works Hard For The Money	Mercury	
10/08/84	37	4	There Goes My Baby	Geffen	
07/31/89	4	12	This Time I Know It's For Real	Atlantic	

* Donna Summer/Barbra Streisand

SUMMER, Henry Lee
American male rock singer from Brazil, Indiana.

DATE	PK	WK	TITLE	LABEL	RA
05/23/88	17	9	I Wish I Had A Girl	CBS Associated	
09/04/89	31	5	Hey Baby	CBS Associated	

SUNSCREEM
British techno-pop group: Lucia Holm (vocals; native of Maidstone, England), Paul Carnell (keyboards), Rob Fricker (bass), Sean Wright (drums), Darren Woodford (guitar).

DATE	PK	WK	TITLE	LABEL	RA
05/17/93	13	17	Love U More	Columbia	24
08/02/93	29	5	Pressure Us	Columbia	

SUPERTRAMP
British rock group formed in 1969: Roger Hodgson (vocals, bass, guitar, b. 03/21/50 in London), Richard Davies (keyboards, vocals, b. 07/22/44 in England), John Helliwell (saxophone, b. 02/15/45 in Todmorden, England), Dougie Thomson (bass, b. 03/24/51 in Glasgow, Scotland), Bob Siebenberg (drums). Re-formed in 1996.

DATE	PK	WK	TITLE	LABEL	RA
09/21/77	16	14	Give A Little Bit	A&M	
03/08/78	39	4	Dreamer	A&M	
06/27/79	2(2)	22	The Logical Song	A&M	
09/05/79	6	12	Goodbye Stranger	A&M	
11/28/79	10	14	Take The Long Way Home	A&M	
11/15/80	11	4	Dreamer	A&M	
12/11/82	1(2)	13	It's Raining Again	A&M	
02/28/83	30	1	Crazy	A&M	
06/10/85	35	3	Cannonball	A&M	

SURFACE
American R&B group formed in 1983 in West Orange, New Jersey: David Townsend (vocals, keyboards, guitar, b. 05/17/54 in Englewood, California), David "Pic" Conley (bass, saxophone, percussion, keyboards, flute, vocals, b. 12/27/53 in Newark, New Jersey), Karen Copeland. Copeland died on 12/05/88 in New Jersey, replaced by Bernard Jackson (vocals, b. 07/11/59 in Stamford, Connecticut).

DATE	PK	WK	TITLE	LABEL	RA
02/25/91	18	12	The First Time	Columbia	12

DATE	PK	WK	TITLE	LABEL	RA

SURVIVOR
American hard rock band from Chicago: David Bicker (vocals), Jim Peterik (keyboards, b. 11/11/50), Frank Sullivan (guitar). Bassist Stephan Ellis and drummer Marc Droubay joined in 1981.

08/07/82	1(6)	16	Eye Of The Tiger	Scotti Brothers	
12/24/84	16	10	I Can't Hold Back	Scotti Brothers	
05/06/85	35	4	High On You	Scotti Brothers	
09/02/85	30	7	The Search Is Over	Scotti Brothers	
02/03/86	16	16	Burning Heart	Scotti Brothers	

SVEN GALI
Canadian band formed in 1987 in Hamilton, Ontario: Dave Wanless (vocals), Dee Corniles (guitar), Andy Frank (guitar), Shawn "TT" Maher (bass), Gregg Gerson (drums).

| 07/05/93 | --- | RA | Love Don't Live Here Anymore | BMG | 27 |

SWAY
Canadian pop-dance band from Ottawa consisting of various session musicians.

| 03/28/88 | 7 | 16 | Hands Up | Virgin | |

SWAYZE, Patrick
American male actor/singer/dancer born on 08/18/52 in Houston. Starred in several movies including *Red Dawn*, *Dirty Dancing*, *Road House*, and *Ghost*.

| 03/28/88 | 5 | 13 | She's Like The Wind | RCA | |

SWEAT, Keith
American male R&B singer/songwriter born on 07/22/61 in New York City.

| 10/27/96 | 15 | 16 | Twisted | Elektra | 31 |
| 02/02/97 | 16 | 19 | Nobody | Elektra | 33 |

SWEENEY TODD
Canadian rock group: Nick Gilder (vocals, b. 11/07/51 in London, England) and James McCulloch (guitar). Gilder replaced by Bryan Adams (b. 11/05/59 in Kingston, Ontario) in 1976.

| 06/26/76 | 7 | 16 | Roxy Roller | London | |

SWEET
British hard rock band formed in 1968 in London: Brian Connolly (vocals, b. 10/05/49 in Hamilton, Scotland), Mick Tucker (vocals, drums, b. 07/17/48 in Middlesex), Andy Scott (guitar, keyboards, vocals, b. 07/30/49 in Wexham, Wales), Steve Priest (bass, vocals, harmonica, b. 02/23/50 in Middlesex). Connolly left in 1978, replaced by Gary Moberley. Disbanded in 1981. Connolly died of renal failure on 02/10/97.

10/04/75	1(2)	11	Ballroom Blitz	Capitol	
01/17/76	2(1)	16	Fox On The Run	Capitol	
04/03/76	12	8	Action	Capitol	
07/12/78	11	8	Love Is Like Oxygen	Capitol	

SWEET SENSATION

DATE	PK	WK	TITLE	LABEL	RA

American female trio from New York City: Betty LeBron, and sisters Margie and Mari Fernandez. Mari replaced by Sheila Bega in 1989.

| 06/04/90 | 24 | 9 | Love Child | Atco | |
| 10/22/90 | 20 | 8 | If Wishes Came True | Atco | 13 |

SWEETBOX
American female dance singer/rapper Tina Harris, born in Maryland.

| 11/22/98 | 39 | 1 | Everything's Gonna Be Alright | BMG | 19 |

SWING OUT SISTER
British dance-pop band formed circa 1986 in Manchester: Corinne Drewery (vocals, b. 09/21/59), Andy Connell (keyboards), Martin Jackson (drums). Jackson left in 1988.

| 09/28/87 | 14 | 14 | Breakout | Mercury | |
| 10/26/92 | --- | RA | Am I The Same Girl | Mercury | 19 |

SWIRL 360
American pop/rock duo from Jacksonville, Florida consisting of twin brothers Denny (guitar, vocals) and Kenny Scott (guitar, vocals).

| 08/02/98 | 25 | 6 | Hey Now Now | Mercury | 12 |

SWV
American female R&B vocal trio formed in 1989 in New York City: Cheryl "Coko" Gamble, Tamara "Taj" Johnson, Leanne "Lelee" Lyons.

05/31/93	---	RA	I'm So Into You	RCA	22
07/26/93	---	RA	Weak	RCA	13
10/11/93	---	RA	Right Here/Human Nature	RCA	13
10/27/96	29	4	You're The One	RCA	33
10/12/97	16	6	Someone	RCA	

SYBIL
American female R&B singer Sybil Lynch from Paterson, New Jersey.

| 02/05/90 | 14 | 11 | Don't Make Me Over | Attic | |

SYLK-E-FYNE featuring Chili
American female rapper from Los Angeles, with male rapper Chili.

| 05/03/98 | 10 | 8 | Romeo & Juliet | RCA | |

SYLVERS
American R&B group formed in 1972 in Memphis. Consists of ten brothers and sisters: Olympia-Ann, Leon, Charmaine, James, Edmund, Ricky, Angelia, Pat, Jonathon, and Foster Sylvers. Leon formed the group Dynasty in 1979. Disbanded in 1985.

05/01/76	1(4)	14	Boogie Fever	Capitol	
02/05/77	1(1)	15	Hot Line	Capitol	
08/13/77	15	5	High School Dance	Capitol	

| DATE | PK | WK | TITLE | LABEL | RA |

SYLVESTER
American male disco-R&B singer born Sylvester James in September 1944 in Los Angeles. Appeared in the movie *The Rose*. Died on 12/16/88 at age 41 of AIDS-related complications.

| 01/10/79 | 26 | 12 | Dance (Disco Heat) .... Fantasy |

SYLVIA
American female country singer/songwriter born Sylvia Kirby on 12/09/56 in Kokomo, Indiana.

| 12/18/82 | 14 | 11 | Nobody .... RCA |

SYREETA - see PRESTON, Billy

T

TACO
German male singer born Taco Ockerse to Dutch parents in 1955 in Jakarta, Indonesia.

| 06/13/83 | 4 | 17 | Putting On The Ritz .... RCA |

TAKE THAT
British pop vocal group from Manchester: Gary Barlow (b. 01/20/71 in Fordsham, England), Howard Donald (b. Howard Paul Donald on 04/28/68 in Manchester), Mark Owen (b. Mark Anthony Owen on 01/27/72 in Oldham, England), Jason Orange (b. Jason Thomas Orange on 07/10/70 in Manchester), Robbie Williams (b. Robert Peter Maximillian Williams on 02/13/74 in Stoke-On-Trent, England). Williams left in July 1995. Disbanded in 1996. Barlow and Williams later pursued solo careers.

| 04/05/93 | 20 | 8 | It Only Takes A Minute .... RCA | |
| 12/18/95 | 7 | 18 | Back For Good .... RCA | 4 |

TALK TALK
British rock group formed in 1981 in London: Mark Hollis (vocals, keyboards, b. 1955 in London), Simon Brenner (keyboards), Paul Webb (bass, b. 01/16/62), Lee Harris (drums).

| 05/28/84 | 37 | 5 | It's My Life .... Capitol |
| 05/19/86 | 34 | 5 | Life's What You Make It .... Capitol |

TALKING HEADS
American rock group formed in 1975 in New York City: David Byrne (vocals, guitar, b. 05/14/52 in Dumbarton, Scotland), Tina Weyworth (bass, synthesizer, b. Martina Weyworth on 11/22/50 in Coronado, California), Chris Frantz (drums, b. 05/08/51 in Fort Campbell, Kentucky), Jerry Harrison (keyboards, guitar, b. Jerimiah Harrison on 02/21/49 in Milwaukee).

| 11/14/83 | 10 | 13 | Burning Down The House .... Sire |

TAMIA
Canadian female R&B singer/songwriter/actress born Tamia Washington on 05/09/76 in Windsor, Ontario.

| 11/03/96 | 35 | 2 | Missing You * .... Elektra |
| 04/05/98 | 12 | 16 | Imagination .... Qwest |

DATE	PK	WK	TITLE	LABEL

| 09/20/98 | 40 | 1 | So Into You.. | Qwest |

* Brandy, Tamia, Gladys Knight & Chaka Khan

TARZAN DAN
Canadian male disc jockey/video jockey Dan Freeman born in Toronto. DJ at radio stations AM106 Calgary, CHOG Toronto, Power 88.5 Newmarket, Ontario, Kiss 92 Toronto. At CFTR Toronto when "Yo Baby Yo" was released. Host of YTV's countdown show, *Hit List with Tarzan Dan*, 1991-97.

| 02/04/91 | 21 | 4 | Yo Baby Yo *.. | Attic |

* Tarzan Dan And The John James Jungle Posse

TASTE OF HONEY, A
American soul-disco group, formed in 1972 in Los Angeles: Janice Marie Johnson (vocals, guitar), Hazel Payne (vocals, bass), Perry Kimble (keyboards), Donald Johnson (drums). Re-formed in 1980 with Johnson and Payne.

| 10/18/78 | 1(4) | 30 | Boogie Oogie Oogie..................................... | Capitol |
| 06/27/81 | 4 | 9 | Sukiyaki.. | Capitol |

TAVARES
American R&B group formed circa 1959 in New Bedford, Massachusetts: brothers Ralph (b. 12/10/48), Arthur "Pooch" (b. 11/12/46), Feliciano "Butch" (b. 05/18/53), Perry Lee "Tiny" (b. 10/24/54), Antone "Chubby" Tavares (b. 06/02/47).

| 11/15/75 | 23 | 7 | It Only Takes A Minute................................ | Capitol |
| 10/02/76 | 14 | 11 | Heaven Must Be Missing An Angel............ | Capitol |

TAYLOR, Andy
British male pop-rock singer born on 02/16/61 in Dolver-Hampton, England. Guitarist of Duran Duran and The Power Station.

| 08/25/86 | 33 | 8 | Take It Easy .... | Atlantic |

TAYLOR, James
American male pop-adult contemporary singer/songwriter/guitarist. Born on 03/12/48 in Boston. Began career as a member of the Fabulous Corsairs in 1964. Married singer Carly Simon on 11/03/72, divorced in 1983. In the 1973 movie *Two Lane Blacktop*.

09/13/75	4	10	How Sweet It Is..	Warner
09/21/77	2(2)	15	Handy Man	Columbia
01/25/78	11	10	Your Smiling Face	Columbia
03/08/78	8	14	(What A) Wonderful World *	Columbia
05/09/81	9	8	Her Town Too **	Columbia

* Art Garfunkel with James Taylor & Paul Simon
** James Taylor with J.D. Souther

TAYLOR, Johnnie
American male R&B singer born on 05/05/38 in Crawsfordsville, Arkansas. Made recording debut with the Five Echoes in 1955. Lead singer of the Soul Stirrers, 1957-63.

DATE	PK	WK	TITLE	LABEL	RA
05/15/76	2(1)	13	Disco Lady..Columbia		

TBTBT
Canadian rap-R&B group: Ishaka "Shaka-D" Dodd (age 11 in 1993), Jeremy "L.J." Robinson (age 14), Frankie "Styles" Scarcelli (age 12), Al Cox (age 13).

12/06/93	18	17	One Track Mind ....Isba		
08/15/94	12	35	Get Down To It ....Isba		

TEARS FOR FEARS
British rock duo formed in 1982 in Bath, England: Roland Orzabal (vocals, guitar, b. Roland Orzabal de la Quintana on 08/22/61 in Portsmouth, England), Curt Smith (bass, vocals, b. 06/24/61 in Bath). Keyboardist Ian Stanley played on the band's records. Smith left in 1992. Name inspired by psychotherapist Arthur Janov's "primal scream" theory.

08/08/83	20	8	Change..Vertigo		
11/14/83	19	7	Pale Shelter (You Don't Give Me Love)........Vertigo		
04/08/85	1(4)	17	Shout..Vertigo		
06/10/85	1(2)	14	Everybody Wants To Rule The World ....Vertigo		
09/16/85	11	12	Head Over Heels ....Vertigo		
10/30/89	10	9	Sowing The Seeds Of Love ....Fontana		
02/26/90	---	RA	Woman In Chains....................................Fontana	11	
05/21/90	---	RA	Advice For The Young ....Fontana	37	
04/27/92	25	5	Laid So Low (Tears Roll Down).................Fontana	28	
08/23/93	6	23	Break It Down Again ....Fontana	4	
12/13/93	30	11	Goodnight Song.......................................Fontana		

TEAZE
Canadian band formed in 1975 in Windsor, Ontario: Mark Bradac, Brian Danter, Mike Kozak, Chuck Price.

05/03/78	29	8	Sweet Misery .... London		

TECHNOTRONIC
Belgian dance-house music group formed by American producer Jo Bogaert in 1989 in Aalst, Belgium: Bogaert (synthesizer, b. Thomas de Quincy on 05/05/56), Ya Kid K (vocals, b. Manuela Barbara Kamosi on 01/26/72 in Kinshasa, Zaire), MC Eric (vocals, b. 08/19/68 in Cardiff, Wales). Zairian-born fashion model Felly posed as the lead singer in videos and was featured on the group's album cover.

12/25/89	5	10	Pump Up The Jam * ....SBK		
04/16/90	4	15	Get Up! (Before The Night Is Over) **.............SBK	6	
07/16/90	15	7	This Beat Is Technotronic ....SBK		
11/19/90	36	4	Rockin' Over The Beat ....SBK		
08/31/92	2(2)	12	Move This ** ....SBK	10	

* Technotronic Featuring Felly
** Technotronic Featuring Ya Kid K

TEENAGE HEAD
Canadian rock band from Hamilton, Ontario: Frank Kerr (vocals), Gord Lewis (vocals), Steve Mahon (drums), Nick Stipanitz (bass).

04/30/80	37	1	Something On My Mind ....Attic		

DATE	PK	WK	TITLE	LABEL	RA

TEMPERANCE
Canadian dance trio formed in 1994 in Toronto: Lorraine Reid (lead vocals, b. 1977 in Toronto), Mystah Munroe (b. Curtneil Anthony Munroe in Clarendon, Jamaica), Nick Fiorucci (native of Toronto).

| 07/27/98 | --- | RA | Hands Of Time * | Hi-Bias | 34 |
| 03/22/99 | --- | RA | Dancing In The Key Of Love | Hi-Bias | 31 |

* Temperence featuring Lorraine

TENANTS, The
Canadian band from Scarborough: Gary Brown (vocals), Andy McLean (vocals), Derek Gassyt (drums), Fraser MacDougall (keyboards), Lewis Mele (bass).

| 05/02/83 | 29 | 2 | Sheriff | Epic | |

10CC
British pop group formed in 1972 in Manchester: Eric Stewart (guitar, vocals, b. 01/20/45), Lol Creme (guitar, vocals, bass, b. Lawrence Creme on 09/19/47), Graham Gouldman (guitar, vocals, bass, keyboards, b. 05/10/46), Kevin Godley (drums, vocals, keyboards, b. 10/07/45). All were born in Manchester. Gouldman and Stewart were in the Mindbenders. Godley and Creme left in 1976 (later recorded as the duo Godley & Creme), replaced by drummer Paul Burgess. Burgess left in 1977, Rick Fenn (vocals, guitar), Tony O'Malley (keyboards), and Stuart Tosh (drums, vocals, percussion) joined that same year. Disbanded in 1982; re-formed in 1991.

08/02/75	3(1)	9	I'm Not In Love	Mercury	
04/16/77	2(2)	17	The Things We Do For Love	Philips	
12/27/78	30	2	Dreadlock Holiday	Polydor	

10,000 MANIACS
American pop/rock group formed in 1981 in Jamestown, New York: Natalie Merchant (vocals, b. 10/26/63 in Jamestown), Robert Buck (guitar, b. 08/03/58 in Jamestown), Steven Gustafson (bass, b. 04/10/57 in Madrid, Spain), Dennis Drew (keyboards, b. 08/08/57 in Buffalo, New York), Jerry Augustyniak (drums, b. 09/02/58 in Lackawanna, New York). Merchant left in 1993; later pursued a solo career. Mary Ramsey replaced Merchant.

| 01/24/94 | --- | RA | Because The Night | Elektra | 6 |
| 08/25/97 | --- | RA | More Than This | Geffen | 14 |

TERMINATOR X
American male rapper born Norman Lee Rogers on 08/25/66 in New York City. Member of the rap group Public Enemy.

| 06/20/94 | 26 | 18 | Hell Comes Down | Columbia | |

TESLA
American rock/metal band formed in 1984 in Sacramento, California: Jeff Keith (vocals), Tommy Skeoch (guitar), Frank Hannon (guitar), Brian Wheat (bass), Troy Luccketta (drums). Skeoch left in 1995. Disbanded in 1996.

| 03/18/91 | --- | RA | Signs | Geffen | 28 |

TEX, Joe

DATE	PK	WK	TITLE	LABEL	RA

American male R&B singer born Joseph Arrington Jr. on 08/08/33 in Rogers, Texas. Became a Muslim minister in 1972 and adopted the surname Hazziez. Died of a heart attack on 08/12/82 in Navasota, Texas.

| 08/24/77 | 23 | 8 | Ain't Gonna Bump No More (With No Big Fat Woman) | Epic | |

TEXAS
Scottish pop/rock group formed in 1987 in Glasgow: Sharleen Spiteri (vocals, guitar), Ally McErlaine (guitar), John McElhone (bass), Stuart Kerr (drums, vocals).

| 07/28/97 | --- | RA | Say What You Want | Mercury | 33 |

THIN LIZZY
Irish rock group formed in 1970 in Dublin: Philip Lynott (bass, vocals, b. 08/20/51 in Dublin), Brian Downey (drums, b. 01/27/51 in Dublin), and guitarists Brian Robertson (b. 09/12/56 in Glasgow, Scotland) and Scott Gorham (b. 03/17/51 in Santa Monica, California). Disbanded in 1983. Lynott died of heart failure on 01/04/86 in Dublin.

| 07/31/76 | 14 | 12 | The Boys Are Back In Town | Vertigo | |

THIRD EYE BLIND
American rock band formed in 1994 in San Francisco: Stephan Jenkins (vocals), Kevin Cadogan (guitars), Arion Salazar (bass), Brad Hargreaves (drums). Jenkins is a graduate of the University of California - Berkeley.

07/21/97	---	RA	Semi-Charmed Life	Elektra	4
03/09/98	---	RA	How's It Gonna Be	Elektra	25
12/28/98	---	RA	Jumper	Elektra	20

38 SPECIAL
American Southern-rock group formed in 1975 in Jacksonville, Florida: Donnie Van Zant (vocals), Don Barnes (guitar, vocals), Jeff Carlisli (guitar), Ken Lyons (bass), Jack Grondin (drums), Steve Brookins (drums). Larry Junstrom (bass, guitar) replaced Lyons in 1979. Barnes and Brookins left in 1987, replaced by Danny Chauncey (guitar) and Max Carl (drums). Carl left in 1991, Scott Hoffman (drums) and Bobby Capps (keyboards) joined and Barnes returned that same year.

07/31/82	7	9	Caught Up In You	A&M	
11/26/84	16	11	Teacher Teacher	Capitol	
05/29/89	39	3	Second Chance *	A&M	

* Thirty Eight Special

THOMAS, B.J.
American male singer born on 08/07/42 in Hugo, Oklahoma.

| 06/07/75 | 17 | 2 | (Hey Won't You Play) Another Somebody Done Somebody Wrong Song | Quality | |
| 10/05/77 | 15 | 10 | Don't Worrry Baby | MCA | |

THOMAS, Evelyn
American female dance singer born in 1953 in Chicago.

DATE	PK	WK	TITLE	LABEL	RA
08/27/84	32	2	High Energy	Polydor	

THOMAS, Ian
Canadian male pop singer/songwriter born in Hamilton, Ontario. Producer at CBC Radio in early-1970's. Wrote songs for America, Chicago, and Santana. Brother of comedian and actor Dave Thomas. Won the 1974 Juno Award for Most Promising Male Vocalist.

DATE	PK	WK	TITLE	LABEL
05/29/76	34	3	Liars	GRT
05/28/77	24	9	Right Before Your Eyes	GRT
06/14/78	25	10	Coming Home *	GRT
08/22/79	32	4	Pilot	GRT

* Ian Thomas Band

THOMPSON TWINS
British pop trio formed in 1977 in Chesterfield, England: Tom Bailey (lead vocals, keyboards, b. 06/18/57 in Halifax, England), Alannah Currie (percussion, saxophone, vocals, b. 09/20/59 in Auckland, New Zealand), Joe Leeway (percussion, vocals, b. 11/15/57 in London). Leeway left in 1986.

DATE	PK	WK	TITLE	LABEL
05/30/83	25	4	Lies	Arista
05/07/84	3(3)	17	Hold Me Now	Arista
07/30/84	12	11	Doctor! Doctor!	Arista
11/05/84	29	4	You Take Me Up	Arista
11/18/85	12	10	Lay Your Hands On Me	Arista
03/17/86	13	9	King For A Day	Arista

THP ORCHESTRA
Canadian disco group formed in 1977 led by Wayne St. John, a former backup singer for Anne Murray and Ocean and a former member of the cast of *Hair*. Group named after Three Hat Productions, a music production company. Won the 1977 Juno Award for Best New Group.

DATE	PK	WK	TITLE	LABEL
03/13/76	4	10	Theme From "SWAT"	RCA
01/22/77	6	14	Fighting On The Side Of Love	RCA

3DEEP
American/Canadian pop trio: C.J. Huyer (lead vocals, b. circa 1972 in Pickering, Ontario), Eddie Cibrian, Joshua Morrow. Both Cibrian and Morrow are American television actors. Cibrian plays Cole Deschannel on *Sunset Beach*; Morrow plays Nicholas Newman on TV's *The Young And The Restless*.

DATE	PK	WK	TITLE	LABEL	RA
06/28/98	14	24	Into You	Beatfactory	38
02/08/99	---	RA	Never Gonna Give Up	Beatfactory	31

TIA

DATE	PK	WK	TITLE	LABEL
07/13/97	10	10	Slip N' Slide	ICH

TICTOC

DATE	PK	WK	TITLE	LABEL
10/17/83	27	6	Twenty Questions	Dallcorte

TIFFANY

| DATE | PK | WK | TITLE | LABEL | RA |

American female pop singer born Tiffany Renee Darwish on 10/02/71 in Norwalk, California. Provided the voice of Judy Jetson in the 1990 film *The Jetsons: The Movie*.

12/14/87	4	18	I Think We're Alone Now	MCA
02/29/88	2(3)	17	Could've Been	MCA
05/02/88	4	13	I Saw Him Standing There	MCA
02/20/89	14	17	All This Time	MCA

TIKARAM, Tanita
British female singer.

| 04/24/89 | 37 | 5 | Twist In My Sobriety | WEA |

'TIL TUESDAY
American pop-rock group formed in 1983 in Boston: Aimee Mann (vocals, bass, b. 08/09/60 in Richmond, Virginia), Robert Holmes (guitar, b. 03/31/59 in Hampton, England), Joey Pesce (keyboards, b. 04/14/62 in Bronx, New York), Michael Hausman (drums, b. 06/12/60 in Philadelphia). Pesce left in 1986, replaced by Michael Montes. Guitarists Clayton Scobel and Jon Brion joined that same year.

| 08/26/85 | 16 | 11 | Voices Carry | Epic |

TIMBALAND & MAGOO
American hip-hop duo from Norfolk, Virginia: Timbaland, Magoo. Timbaland is a music producer of several hit recordings such as Ginuwine's "Pony". Magoo has written several songs on albums for Ginuwine and Missy "Misdemeanor" Elliott.

| 10/05/97 | 28 | 8 | Up Jumps Da Boogie | Atlantic |
| 05/17/98 | 29 | 5 | Clock Strikes | Atlantic |

TIMBUK 3
American husband-and-wife rock duo formed in 1984 in Madison, Wisconsin: Pat (vocals, guitar, harmonica, bass, b. 08/06/52 in Green Bay, Wisconsin) and Barbara Kooyman MacDonald (vocals, guitar, harmonica, violin, b. 10/04/57 in Wausau, Wisconsin). Disbanded in 1995.

| 02/09/87 | 18 | 9 | The Future's So Bright I Gotta Wear Shades | I.R.S. |

TIME, The
American R&B-funk group formed in 1981 in Minneapolis: Morris Day (vocals, b. circa 1958 in Springfield, Illinois), Jesse Johnson (guitar, vocals, b. 05/29/60 in Rock Island, Illinois), Jellybean Johnson (drums), Paul "St. Paul" Peterson (keyboards, vocals), Mark Cardenas (keyboards), Jerry Hubbard (bass), Jerome Benton (vocals, percussion). Producers Jimmy Jam (b. James Harris III on 06/06/59 in Minneapolis) and Terry Lewis (b. 11/24/56 in Omaha, Nebraska) were members, 1981-83. Group toured with Prince in the early-1980's, appeared in his movie *Purple Rain* in 1984. Disbanded in 1984, re-formed in 1990 and again in 1995.

| 03/18/85 | 9 | 11 | Jungle Love | Warner | |
| 09/17/90 | 15 | 12 | Jerk Out | Paisley Park | 23 |

TIMELORDS
British techno-dance duo: Bill Drummond and Jimmy Cauty. Became The KLF in 1989.

| 07/22/91 | 39 | 1 | Doctorin' The Tardis | Somersault |

DATE	PK	WK	TITLE	LABEL	RA

TIMEX SOCIAL CLUB
American rap group from Berkeley, California: Michael Marhsall (lead vocals), Marcus Thompson (backing vocals, keyboards), Alex Hill (backing vocals, keyboards).

| 10/20/86 | 2(5) | 19 | Rumors | A&M | |

TIMMY T
American male pop singer born Timmy Torres on 09/23/67 in Fresno, California.

| 04/15/91 | --- | RA | One More Try | Quality | 5 |

TITI, Lysette

| 02/08/98 | 29 | 2 | Young, Sad & Blue | Frew | |

TKA
American rap trio from New York City: Anthony "Tony" Ortiz, Louis "Kayel" Sharpe, and Ralph "Aby" Cruz. Kayel recorded solo as K7.

| 09/14/92 | 32 | 5 | Maria | Isba | |

TLC
American hip-hop/R&B trio formed in 1991 in Atlanta: Tionne "T-Boz" Watkins (vocals, b. 04/26/70 in Des Moines, Iowa), Lisa Nicole "Left Eye" Lopes (vocals, b. 05/27/71 in Philadelphia), and Rozonda "Chilli" Thomas (b. 02/27/71). Founded and managed by Pebbles. Lopes was charged with felony arson after setting fire to her boyfriend Andre Rison's (a receiver for the Atlanta Falcons football team) house on 06/09/94.

08/31/92	---	RA	Baby, Baby, Baby	LaFace	7
11/30/92	---	RA	What About Your Friends	LaFace	14
04/17/95	17	25	Creep	LaFace	18
06/05/95	---	RA	Red Light Special	LaFace	13
09/25/95	8	25	Waterfalls	LaFace	1
01/15/96	---	RA	Diggin' On You	LaFace	3
04/18/99	32	4	No Scrubs	LaFace	1+
05/23/99	22	10	Silly Ho	LaFace	
08/09/99	---	RA	Unpretty	LaFace	11+

TOAD THE WET SPROCKET
American rock quartet formed in 1988 in San Lafaceta Barbara, California: Glen Phillips (vocals, guitar), Tony Nichols (guitar), Dean Dinning (bass, keyboards), Randy Guss (drums). Name taken from a Monty Python skit.

09/14/92	---	RA	All I Want	Columbia	17
02/15/93	---	RA	Walk On The Water	Columbia	18
06/06/94	37	1	Fall Down	Columbia	14
11/14/94	---	RA	Something's Always Wrong	Columbia	24
12/04/95	---	RA	Good Intentions	Reprise	6

TOBIAS, Ken
Canadian male singer/songwriter born and raised in Saint John, New Brunswick. Wrote songs for Anne Murray and The Bells.

DATE	PK	WK	TITLE	LABEL	RA
12/27/75	20	6	Every Bit Of Love..Attic		
05/08/76	28	6	Give A Little Love..Attic		

TOBY BEAU
American pop quintet from Texas: Balde Silva (vocals), Danny McKenna, Rob Young, Steve Zipper, Ron Rose.

09/06/78	15	8	My Angel Baby... RCA		

TOMMY TUTONE
American rock band from San Francisco led by vocalist Tommy Heath and lead guitarist Jim Keller.

05/29/82	2(3)	10	867-5309/Jenny .... Columbia		

TONE LOC
American male rapper born Anthony Terrell Smith on 03/03/66 in Los Angeles. Provided voice in the animated movie *Bebe's Kids* and appeared in the movies *Posse* and *Poetic Justice*.

03/13/89	2(1)	18	Wild Thing .... Island		
06/12/89	3(1)	17	Funky Cold Medina .... Island		

TONIC
American rock group formed in 1993 in Los Angeles: Emerson Hart (vocals, guitar), Jeff Russo (guitar), Dan Lavery (bass), Kevin Shepard (drums).

10/20/97	---	RA	If You Could Only See .... A&M	7	

TONY! TONI! TONE!
American R&B-rap trio formed in 1986 in Oakland, California: brothers Dwayne and Raphael Wiggins, and cousin Timothy Christian. Appeared in the movie *House Party 2*.

02/04/91	18	4	Feels Good...Polydor		
04/22/91	40	1	It Never Rains (In Southern California)........Polydor		
09/27/93	1(2)	22	If I Had No Loot .... Mercury	12	
12/13/93	5	26	Anniversary .... Mercury	22	
02/03/97	---	RA	Let's Get Down .... Mercury	28	

TORONTO
Canadian rock band from Toronto: Holly Woods (vocals), Brian Allen (guitar), Sharon Alton (guitar), Nick Costlello (bass), Jim Fox (drums).

08/21/82	6	11	Your Daddy Don't Know ....Solid Gold		
11/20/82	17	4	Start Tellin' The Truth ....Solid Gold		
08/08/83	27	4	Girls Night Out..Solid Gold		

TOTO
American pop-rock group formed in 1978 in Los Angeles: Bobby Kimball (lead vocals, b. Robert Toteaux on 03/29/47 in Vinton, Louisiana), David Paich (keyboards, vocals, b. 06/25/54 in Los Angeles), Steve Lukather (guitar, vocals, b. 10/21/57 in Los Angeles), David Hungate (bass, b. Los Angeles), and brothers Steve (keyboards, b. 09/02/57 in Hartford, Connecticut) and Jeff Porcaro (drums, b. 04/01/54 in Hartford). Hungate replaced by Mike Porcaro in 1983. Kimball left in 1984, replaced by Dennis "Fergie"

DATE	PK	WK	TITLE	LABEL	RA

Frederiksen, who in turn was replaced by Joseph Williams in 1986. Jeff Porcaro died of a heart attack on 08/05/92 in Holden Hills, California.

Date	PK	WK	Title	Label
01/24/79	6	14	Hold The Line	Columbia
04/16/80	11	13	99	Columbia
07/03/82	1(2)	14	Rosanna	Columbia
02/14/83	2(1)	17	Africa	Columbia
05/09/83	10	9	I Won't Hold You Back	Columbia
01/21/85	23	6	Stranger In Town	Columbia
10/20/86	34	6	I'll Be Over You	Columbia
05/23/88	35	3	Pamela	Columbia

TOUCH & GO
British/American dance group consisting of studio musicians. Formed by British producer David Lowe, with record label owners Charlie Gillett and Gorton Nelki. British singer Vanessa Lancaster appears in the video of "Would You...?"; however, the female voice on the record is actually an unknown American actress.

Date	PK	WK	Title	Label
01/24/99	10	17	Would You...?	V2

TOULOUSE
Canadian trio of female backup singers from Montreal: Heather Gauthier, Judi Richards, Lorri Zimmerman.

Date	PK	WK	Title	Label
07/09/77	28	5	It Always Happens This Way	Magique

TOWNSELL, Lidell
American DJ/mixer from Chicago.

Date	PK	WK	Title	Label
07/13/92	4	27	Nu Nu	Isba

TOWNSHEND, Pete
British male rock singer/songwriter born Peter Dennis Blandford Townshend on 05/19/45 in London. Lead guitarist/vocalist/songwriter of The Who. Wrote and produced *Tommy*, the first successful rock opera.

Date	PK	WK	Title	Label
09/13/80	6	2	Let My Love Open The Door	Atco
02/10/86	7	15	Face The Face	Atco

T'PAU
British pop group formed in 1986 consisting of Carol Decker (vocals, b. 09/10/57 in London), Ronnie Rogers (guitar), Michael Chetwood (keyboards), Paul Jackons (bass), and Tim Burgess (drums).

Date	PK	WK	Title	Label
08/24/87	5	19	Heart And Soul	Virgin
04/18/88	24	12	China In Your Hand	Virgin

TQ
American male rapper born Terrance Quaites in Mobile, Alabama. Moved to Compton, California. Lead singer of the R&B group Coming of Age.

Date	PK	WK	Title	Label
10/25/98	10	14	Westside	Epic

DATE	PK	WK	TITLE	LABEL	RA

TRAGICALLY HIP

Canadian rock band formed in 1983 in Kingston, Ontario: Gordon Downie (vocals), Bobby Baker (guitar), Johnny Fay (drums), Paul Langlois (guitar), Gord Sinclair (bass). Name originated from ex-Monkee Michael Nesmith's "Elephant Parts" video. Winner of 11 Juno Awards including Most Promising Group of the Year in 1990, Group of the Year in 1995 and 1997, and Canadian Entertainer of the Year in 1991, 1993, and 1995.

DATE	PK	WK	TITLE	LABEL	RA
04/09/90	---	RA	Boots Or Hearts	MCA	28
05/13/91	---	RA	Little Bones	MCA	18
11/30/92	---	RA	Locked In The Trunk Of A Car	MCA	25
04/26/93	---	RA	Courage	MCA	11
01/17/94	38	1	Land *	Cargo	
11/28/94	---	RA	Grace Too	MCA	25
02/20/95	---	RA	Greasy Jungle	MCA	28
07/08/96	1(1)	19 h	Ahead By A Century	MCA	6
08/19/96	14	11 h	Gift Shop	MCA	34
04/07/97	---	RA	Flamenco	Universal	32
09/07/98	---	RA	Poets	Universal	29

* Crash Vegas/Hothouse Flowers/Daniel Lanois/Midnight Oil/Tragically Hip

TRAMMPS

American disco-R&B group formed in the mid-1960's in Philadelphia: Earl Young (drums, bass vocals), Jimmy Ellis (lead tenor vocals), Robert Upchurch (baritone vocals), Stanley Wade (bass, tenor vocals), Harold Wade (guitar, tenor vocals).

DATE	PK	WK	TITLE	LABEL	RA
07/12/78	13	10	Disco Inferno	Atlantic	

TRAVELING WILBURYS

American-British supergroup formed in 1988 in Los Angeles composed of superstars posing as a group of brothers: Nelson (guitar, vocals; George Harrison, b. 02/25/43 in Liverpool, England), Lucky (guitar, vocals; Bob Dylan, b. Robert Allen Zimmerman on 05/24/41 in Duluth, Minnesota), Otis (guitar, vocals, bass; Jeff Lynne, b. 12/30/47 in Birmingham, England), Charlie T.(guitar, vocals; Tom Petty, b. 10/20/52 in Gainesville, Florida), and Lefty (guitar, vocals; Roy Orbison, b. 04/23/36 in Vernon, Texas). Jim Keltner played drums on the group's records. Orbison died of a heart attack on 12/06/88 in Hendersonville, Texas. Members were re-named in 1990: Spike (Harrison), Boo (Dylan), Clayton (Lynne), Muddy (Petty).

DATE	PK	WK	TITLE	LABEL	RA
01/30/89	6	16	Handle With Care	Wilbury	
05/01/89	29	4	End Of The Line	Wilbury	
12/24/90	13	11	She's My Baby	Wilbury	

TRAVOLTA, John

American male actor/singer born on 02/18/54 in Englewood, New Jersey. Starred as Vinnie Barbarino in the television sitcom *Welcome Back Kotter*. Starred in numerous films including *Saturday Night Fever, Grease, Urban Cowboy, Look Who's Talking, Pulp Fiction,* and *Phenomenon.* Married actress Kelly Preston on 09/05/91.

DATE	PK	WK	TITLE	LABEL	RA
08/07/76	4	14	Let Her In	RCA	
05/31/78	1(6)	24	You're The One That I Want *	RSO	
09/20/78	4	16	Summer Nights *	RSO	
12/30/96	---	RA	Grease Megamix *	Polydor	30

DATE	PK	WK	TITLE	LABEL	RA

* John Travolta & Olivia Newton-John

TRESVANT, Ralph
American male R&B-pop singer born on 05/16/68 in Boston, and raised in Roxbury, Massachusetts. Member of New Edition.

03/11/91	3(2)	14	Sensitivity	MCA	10

TRIO
German new wave group formed in 1979: Stephan Remmler (vocals, keyboards), Kralle Krawinkel (guitar), Peter Behrehns (percussion).

01/17/83	5	9	Da Da Da	Mercury	

TRIPLETS, The
American pop trio: triplet sisters Diana, Sylvia, and Vicky Villegas; all born on 04/18/65.

05/27/91	22	11	You Don't Have To Go Home Tonight	Mercury	20

TRIPPING DAISY
American pop-rock band from Dallas: Tim DeLaughter (vocals), Wes Berggren (guitar), Mark Pirro (bass), Bryan Wakeland (drums).

10/02/95	---	RA	I Got A Girl	Island	19

TRIUMPH
Canadian hard rock band formed in 1975 in Toronto consisting of Rik Emmett (guitar), Mike Levine (bass), Gil Moore (vocals, drums). Disbanded in 1987; Emmett went solo. Reunited in 1992 without Emmett.

09/19/79	29	2	Hold On	Attic	
11/28/81	12	7	Magic Power	Attic	
03/16/87	26	4	Just One Night	MCA	

TROCCOLI, Kathy
American female Contemporary Christian/pop singer from New York City.

05/25/92	23	10	Everything Changes	Geffen	7

TROIANO, Domenic
Canadian male guitarist born on 01/17/46 in Mondugno, Italy. Former guitarist of The James Gang, and the Guess Who.

07/25/79	28	6	We All Need Love	Capitol	

TROOPER
Canadian rock group formed in 1972 in Vancouver. Original line-up: Ramon McGuire (vocals), Brian Smith (guitar). Tommy Stewart (drums) joined in 1972, Harry Kalinsky (bass) joined in 1974. Kalinsky was replaced by Doni Underhill in 1976. Frank Ludwig (piano) joined in 1976. Ludwig was replaced by Rob Deans in 1979. Won the 1980 Juno Award for Group of the Year.

01/31/76	23	6	General Hand Grenade	Legend	

DATE	PK	WK	TITLE	LABEL	RA
09/11/76	15	10	Two For The Show..................................Legend		
06/18/77	30	6	Santa Maria..MCA		
08/24/77	12	14	We're Here For A Good Time.......................MCA		
04/19/78	10	14	Oh Pretty Lady..MCA		
10/18/78	10	12	Round Round We Go......................................MCA		
11/15/78	23	10	Raise A Little Hell ....MCA		
09/05/79	33	2	Boys In The Sports Car..................................MCA		
01/09/80	27	14	3 Dressed Up As A 9......................................MCA		
04/23/80	36	9	Janine..MCA		

TRUBBLE
British dance outfit featuring English female rapper/singer/dancer/choreographer Cherzia, with the Dancing Baby. The Dancing Baby is a computer-generated digital image first created on the Internet in 1995 and subsequently appeared on the TV show *Ally McBeal*.

01/31/99	15	4	Dancing Baby (Ooga-Chaka) .... Island		

TRUE, Andrea, Connection
American disco group led by vocalist Andrea True (b. Nashville). Wrote commercials for television and radio after moving to New York City in 1968.

07/10/76	3(3)	15	More More More ....Buddah		

TRU-G'Z
Canadian pop/dance group.

03/02/98	---	RA	Picture Me Leaving You .... Paladin/Spinner	32	

TU
Canadian pop duo consisting of twins Amanda and Cassandra DiBlassi (b. circa 1968).

11/30/87	13	16	Stay With Me .... RCA		

TUBES, The
American theatre-rock group formed in the late-1960's in Phoenix: Fee Waybill (lead vocals, b. John Waldo on 09/17/50 in Omaha, Nebraska), Bill Spooner (guitar, b. 04/16/49 in Phoenix), Roger Steen (guitar, b. 11/13/49 in Pipestone, Minnesota), Vince Welnick (keyboards, b. 02/21/51 in Phoenix), Michael Cotten (keyboards, b. 01/25/50 in Kansas City), Prairie Prince (drums, b. 05/07/50 in Charlotte, North Carolina), Rick Anderson (bass, b. 08/01/47 in St. Paul, Minnesota), Re Styles (vocals, b. 03/03/50).

07/18/83	16	10	She's A Beauty ....Capitol		

TUCKER, Louise
Dutch female classical-pop vocalist.

05/23/83	2(3)	19	Midnight Blue.. PolyGram		

TUESDAYS
Norwegian female pop group formed in 1993: Hege "The Hedge" Solli (guitar, b. 01/09/74 in Larvik, Norway), Laila Samuels (lead vocals, b. 06/03/76 in Oslo, Norway), Linda Gustafsson (percussion, b. 02/10/74 in Karlskog, Sweden); Kristin Werner (keyboards, b. 06/26/74 in Larvik, Norway), Veslemoy "May" Hole (bass, b. 09/04/74 in Larvik, Norway).

DATE	PK	WK	TITLE	LABEL	RA

| 04/20/98 | --- | RA | It's Up To You | Arista | 13 |

TURNER, Tina
American female pop-R&B singer/actress born Annie Mae Bullock on 11/26/39 in Brownsville, Tennessee. Performed with husband Ike Turner during the duration of their marriage, 1958-78. Changed name to Tina Turner in the late-1950's. First recorded in 1960. Later formed the "Ike and Tina Turner Revue" with nine musicians and the Inkettes, three female background vocalists. Disbanded in 1974. Tina made a comeback in the mid-1980's. Appeared in the films *Tommy* (1975) and *Mad Max Beyond Thunderdome* (1985). Inducted into the Rock and Roll Hall of Fame along with Ike in 1991. The 1993 film *What's Love Got To Do With It* is based on her autobiography.

03/19/84	40	3	Let's Stay Together	Capitol	
10/01/84	1(1)	18	What's Love Got To Do With It	Capitol	
11/19/84	8	11	Better Be Good To Me	Capitol	
03/11/85	17	10	Private Dancer	Capitol	
09/16/85	1(4)	16	We Don't Need Another Hero	Capitol	
12/16/85	12	11	It's Only Love *	A&M	
12/23/85	5	12	One Of The Living	Capitol	
10/27/86	9	11	Typical Male	Capitol	
12/08/86	36	2	Two People	Capitol	
04/13/87	28	6	What You Get Is What You See	Capitol	
10/30/89	2(1)	16	The Best	Capitol	
02/05/90	25	6	Steamy Windows	Capitol	32
07/26/93	---	RA	I Don't Want To Fight	Capitol	1
11/08/93	---	RA	Why Must We Wait Until Tonight?	Capitol	28
02/12/96	16	9	Goldeneye	Virgin	
10/07/96	23	9 h	Missing You	Virgin	35

* Bryan Adams/Tina Turner

TUXEDO JUNCTION
American female disco studio group formed by producers W. Michael Lewis and Laurin Rinder. Consisted of Jamie Edlin, Marilyn Jackson, Sue Allen, Marti McCall.

| 08/09/78 | 27 | 4 | Chattanooga Choo Choo | Butterfly | |

TWAIN, Shania
Canadian female country singer born Eilleen Regina Edwards on 08/28/65 in Windsor, Ontario. Married to record producer Robert John "Mutt" Lange.

12/08/96	1(9)	60	God Bless The Child	Mercury	
10/05/97	4	25	Love Gets Me Every Time	Mercury	
02/08/98	12	20	Don't Be Stupid (You Know I Love You)	Mercury	26
05/10/98	2(4)	15	You're Still The One	Mercury	6
			Another version peaked at #10 on 08/23/98.		
12/13/98	4	8	From This Moment On	Mercury	26
			Another version peaked at #29 on 02/14/99.		
05/30/99	8	13 +	That Don't Impress Me Much	Mercury	2+
			Another version peaked at #27 on 06/13/99.		
08/09/99	---	RA	You've Got A Way	Mercury	29+

T.W.D.Y.

DATE	PK	WK	TITLE	LABEL	RA
06/20/99	30	2	Player's Holiday	Thump	

20 FINGERS
American production team from Chicago: Manfred "Manny" Mohr (keyboards/songwriter), Charlie Baby (producer/songwriter/keyboards), Onofrio Lollino, J.J. Flores. Lead rapper is Sandra Gillette (b. 09/16/73 in Chicago).

| 04/17/95 | 6 | 19 | Short Dick Man | Zoo |

TWILLEY, Dwight
American male rock singer/songwriter/pianist born on 06/06/51 in Tulsa, Oklahoma. Formed the Dwight Twilley Band with fellow Tulsa native Phil Seymour, who died of lymphoma on 08/17/93 (age 41) in Tarzana, California.

| 05/14/84 | 30 | 7 | Girls | Capitol |

TWISTED SISTER
American heavy metal group formed in 1973 in Ho-Ho-Kus, New Jersey: Dee Snider (vocals, b. 03/15/55 in Massapequa, New York), Jay Jay French (guitar, b. John Segall on 07/20/54 in New York City), Mark "The Animal" Mendoza (bass, b. 07/13/56 in Long Island, New York), Eddie Ojeda (guitar, b. 08/05/54 in Bronx, New York), A.J. Pero (drums, b. 10/14/59 in New York City). Pero left in 1987, replaced by Joe Franco.

| 11/12/84 | 6 | 17 | We're Not Gonna Take It | Atlantic |

2 IN A ROOM
American dance duo from Washington Heights, New York: rapper Rafael "Dose" Vargas and remixer Roger "Rog Nice" Pauletta.

| 12/24/90 | 1(6) | 11 | Wiggle It | Virgin |

2 LIVE CREW - see LUKE FEATURING 2 LIVE CREW

2 RUDE
Canadian male rapper/producer Richard Rude from Toronto.

| 06/21/99 | --- | RA | Thinkin' About You * | I.L.L. Vibe | 26 |

* 2 Rude featuring LaToya & Miranda

2 UNLIMITED
Dutch techno-dance duo from Amsterdam: rapper Ray Slijngaard (b. 1971) and singer Anita Dels (b. 1972). Dels left in 1996.

07/20/92	15	10	Twilight Zone	Quality
12/14/92	26	7	The Magic Friend	Quality
05/24/93	1(1)	24	No Limit	Quality
08/23/93	7	19	Tribal Dance	Quality
08/22/94	5	29	The Real Thing	Quality
07/03/95	22	11	Here I Go	Quality
03/18/96	17	6	Do What's Good For Me	Quality

DATE	PK	WK	TITLE	LABEL	RA

2nu
American group from Seattle: Jock Blaney (vocals), Mike Nealy, Tom Martin, Phil DeVault. Blaney was production director of Seattle radio station KPLZ in 1990.

| 04/01/91 | 31 | 6 | This Is Ponderous | Atlantic | |

2PAC
American male rapper/actor born Tupac Amaru Shakur on 06/16/71 in Bronx, New York. Former member of Digital Underground. Acted in the movies *Nothing But Trouble* and *Poetic Justice*. Shot in a drive-by shooting on 09/07/96 in Las Vegas. Died six days later on 09/13/96.

04/22/96	---	RA	California Love	Island	35
10/27/96	11	13	How Do U Want It	Death Row	
01/12/97	28	5	I Ain't Mad At Cha	Wind	
04/20/97	14	11	Runnin' *	Mergela	
04/05/98	26	11	Do For Love	Jive	
02/28/99	14	12	Changes	Interscope	35

* 2Pac, Notorious B.I.G., Radio, Dramacydal & Stretch

TYLER, Bonnie
British female rock singer born Gaynor Hopkins on 06/08/53 in Skewen, South Wales. Distinctive husky voice was caused by a 1976 operation to remove nodules on throat.

06/14/78	1(4)	22	It's A Heartache	RCA	
06/27/83	2(8)	31	Total Eclipse Of The Heart	Columbia	
05/14/84	17	9	Holding Out For A Hero	Columbia	

U

UB40
British reggae group formed in 1978 in Birmingham: Ali Campbell (lead vocals, guitar, b. 02/15/59), Astro (vocals, b. Terence Wilson on 06/24/57), James Brown (drums, b. 11/20/57), Robin Campbell (guitar, vocals, b. 12/25/54), Earl Falconer (bass, b. 01/23/59), Norman Hassan (percussion, b. 01/26/58), Brian Travers (saxophone, b. 02/07/59), Mickey Virtue (keyboards, b. 01/19/57). All were born in Birmingham, England. Name taken from the British Unemployment Benefits, Form 40.

02/13/84	3(3)	15	Red Red Wine	Virgin	
11/11/85	13	13	I Got You Babe *	Virgin	
12/24/90	---	RA	The Way You Do The Things You Do	Virgin	34
07/22/91	---	RA	Here I Am	Virgin	36
07/12/93	1(8)	17	Can't Help Falling In Love	Virgin	1
11/15/93	---	RA	Higher Ground	Virgin	40

* UB40 with Chrissie Hynde

UGLY KID JOE
American rock band formed in 1990 in Isla Vista, California: Whitfield Crane (vocals, b. 01/19/68 in Palo Alto, California), Klaus Eichstadt (guitar, b. 12/19/67 in Redwood City, California), Mark Davis (drums, b.

DATE	PK	WK	TITLE	LABEL	RA

04/22/64 in Phoenix), Cordell Crockett (bass, b. 01/21/65 in Livermore, California), Dave Fortman (guitar, b. 07/11/67 in Orlando, Florida). Disbanded in 1996.

| 05/25/92 | --- | RA | Everything About You .... Mercury | 21 |
| 04/26/93 | 1(4) | 20 | Cats In The Cradle..................................... Mercury | 8 |

ULLMAN, Tracey
British female comedian/pop singer/actress born on 12/30/59 in Buckinghamshire, England. Starred in own variety Fox network television show *The Tracey Ullman Show*, 1987-90. Appeared in the movies *I Love You To Death* and *Give My Regards To Broad Street*.

| 05/14/84 | 7 | 13 | They Don't Know.. MCA | |

ULTRAVOX
British electro-pop group formed in 1973 in London: Midge Ure (vocals, guitar, b. James Ure on 10/10/53 in Gambusland, Scotland), Chris Cross (bass, b. Christopher Allen on 07/14/52 in London), Billy Currie (keyboards, synthesizer, violin, b. 04/01/52 in Huddersfield, England), Warren Cann (drums, b. 05/20/52 in Victoria, British Columbia). Ure went solo in 1985. Disbanded in 1987.

| 09/10/84 | 25 | 6 | Dancing With Tears In My Eyes .... Chrysalis | |

UNCLE SAM
American male R&B singer born Sam Turner in Detroit.

| 02/22/98 | 31 | 3 | I Don't Ever Want To See You Again............... Epic | |

UNDERWORLD
British electronica/dance trio formed in 1986 in London: Karl Hyde (vocals, guitar, electronics), Rick Smith (keyboards, programming), Darren Emerson (DJ).

| 09/07/97 | 23 | 4 | Born Slippy... TVT | |

Above is the remixes version. Another version peaked at #36 on 03/23/97.

UNIQUE II

| 06/22/97 | 30 | 3 | Break My Stride .... Columbia | 27 |

UNIVERSAL HONEY
Canadian rock group formed in 1992: Leslie Stanwyck (guitar, vocals), Simon Craig (guitar), Johnny Sinclair (bass), Tim Timleck (drums). Stanwyck and Sinclair are former members of the Pursuit of Happiness.

| 08/15/94 | --- | RA | Just Before Mary Goes .... Martane | 37 |

UNV
American soul vocal quartet from Detroit: brothers John and Shawn Powe, John Clay, Demetrius Peete. UNV stands for United Nubian Voices.

| 10/04/93 | 26 | 6 | Something's Going On.......................................Sire | |

URBAN COOKIE COLLECTIVE

DATE	PK	WK	TITLE	LABEL	RA

British dance group based in Manchester: Rohan Heath (songwriter/keyboards), Diane Charlemagne (vocals), Simon Bentall (percussion), Peter Samms (dancer).

| 05/30/94 | 19 | 29 | Feels Like Heaven | Quality | |

URBAN DANCE SQUAD
Dutch dance group from Amsterdam: Rude Boy (rapper, singer, b. Patrick Remington), Magic Stick (drums), DJ DNA (programming), Silly Sil (bass), Tres Manos (guitar, b. Rene van Barneveld).

| 03/18/91 | --- | RA | Deeper Shade Of Soul | Arista | 36 |

URE, Midge
British male singer born on 10/10/53 in Gambusland, Scotland. Lead singer/guitarist of Ultravox, 1980-87. Co-writer of Band Aid's "Do They Know It's Christmas?". Musical director of the Prince's Trust benefit concerts.

| 03/17/86 | 12 | 12 | If I Was | Chrysalis | |

URGE OVERKILL
American rock band formed in 1986 in Evanston, Illinois: National "Nash" Kato (guitar, vocals), Eddie "King" Roeser (guitar, bass, vocals), Blackie Onassis (drums). Roeser left in 1996.

| 12/19/94 | --- | RA | Girl You'll Be A Woman Soon | MCA | 26 |

USA FOR AFRICA
American ensemble of 45 celebrities formed in 1985 to raise money for famine victims in the United States and Ethiopia: Dan Aykroyd, Harry Belafonte, Lindsey Buckingham, Kim Carnes, Ray Charles, Bob Dylan, Sheila E., Bob Geldof, Daryl Hall and John Oates, James Ingram, Jackie Jackson, LaToya Jackson, Marlon Jackson, Michael Jackson, Randy Jackson, Tito Jackson, Al Jarreau, Waylon Jennings, Billy Joel, Cyndi Lauper, Huey Lewis and the News, Kenny Loggins, Bette Midler, Willie Nelson, Jeffrey Osborne, Steve Perry, the Pointer Sisters, Lionel Richie, Smokey Robinson, Kenny Rogers, Diana Ross, Paul Simon, Bruce Springsteen, Tina Turner, Dionne Warwick, and Stevie Wonder. Raised a total of $44 million for famine relief.

| 05/06/85 | 3(3) | 11 | We Are The World | Columbia | |

USHER
American male R&B singer/songwriter/actor born Raymond Usher IV on 10/14/79 in Chattanooga, Tennessee.

10/05/97	7	8	You Make Me Wanna	LaFace	8
03/01/98	6	10	Nice & Slow	LaFace	35
09/13/98	19	14	My Way	LaFace	

USHER, David
Canadian male rock singer born on 04/24/66 in Oxford, England. Raised in Kingston, Ontario. Earned Bachelor's degree in Political Science at Vancouver's Simon Fraser University. Co-founder/lead singer of Moist since 1992. Recorded solo in 1998.

| 05/25/98 | --- | RA | Forest Fire | EMI | 16 |

US3
British jazz/rap duo formed in 1992 in London: Mel Simpson, Geoff Wilkinson.

DATE	PK	WK	TITLE	LABEL	RA
04/04/94	---	RA	Cantaloop (Flip Fantasia)......................................EMI		12

U2

Irish rock band formed in 1976 in Dublin: Bono (vocals, guitar, b. Paul Hewson on 05/10/60 in Dublin), The Edge (guitar, keyboards, vocals, b. David Evans on 08/08/61 in Barking, England), Adam Clayton (bass, b. 03/13/60 in Oxford, England), Larry Mullen (drums, b. 10/31/61 in Dublin). Met at Mount Temple High School in Dublin. Signed to Island Records in 1980. Joined Sting, Peter Gabriel, Lou Reed, and others for the Amnesty International Conspiracy of Hope Tour. In the 1988 concert tour documentary film *Rattle and Hum*. Initiated Passengers project with Brian Eno, Howie B, and others in 1995.

DATE	PK	WK	TITLE	LABEL	RA
11/12/84	33	9	Pride (In The Name Of Love) .... Island		
05/11/87	2(3)	16	With Or Without You .... Island		
08/03/87	11	15	I Still Haven't Found What I'm Looking For... Island		
10/19/87	14	9	Where The Streets Have No Name .... Island		
02/01/88	28	4	In God's Country .... Island		
11/21/88	2(1)	19	Desire .... Island		
03/06/89	15	13	Angel Of Harlem .... Island		
11/25/91	3(1)	12	The Fly .... Island		
02/24/92	4	19	Mysterious Ways .... Island		1
06/15/92	3(1)	17	One .... Island		1
08/31/92	---	RA	Even Better Than The Real Thing................. Island		4
01/18/93	---	RA	Who's Gonna Ride Your Wild Horses........... Island		10
08/23/93	---	RA	Numb .... Island		11
11/15/93	---	RA	Lemon .... Island		9
01/24/94	5	19	Stay (Faraway, So Close) .... Island		13
07/24/95	11	30	Hold Me, Thrill Me, Kiss Me, Kill Me .... Atlantic		1
02/09/97	1(1)	23	Discotheque.. Island		6
			Two other versions peaked at #18 and #20 on 02/16/97.		
02/09/97	19	3	One (re-release).. Island		
02/09/97	26	2	Who's Gonna Ride Your Wild Horses (re-release) .... Island		
02/09/97	39	1	The Fly (re-release)....................................... Island		
03/09/97	32	1	Wide Awake In America................................ Island		
03/23/97	38	1	Miss Sarajevo *... Island		36
			Peaked on the airplay chart on 01/22/96.		
04/20/97	2(1)	17	Staring At The Sun .... Island		5
07/06/97	4	24	Last Night On Earth .... Island		
10/12/97	4	26	Please/Popheart Live E.P............................. Island		
11/16/97	10	10	Please .... Island		
10/25/98	1(1)	23	Sweetest Thing .... Island		4
			Above is "Pt. 1" version. "Pt. 2" peaked at #2 on 11/08/98.		

* Passengers

V

VALDY

Canadian male folk singer/songwriter, Valdemar Horsdal, born in 1946 in Ottawa.

DATE	PK	WK	TITLE	LABEL	RA
10/09/76	25	7	Peter And Lou	A&M	

VALLI, Frankie
American male pop singer born Francis Castellucio on 05/03/37 in Newark, New Jersey. Recorded solo for the first time in 1953 as Frank Valley. Founded own group, the Varietones (later The Four Lovers and then The 4 Seasons) in 1955.

DATE	PK	WK	TITLE	LABEL	RA
07/26/75	11	7	Swearin' To God	Private Stock	
08/09/78	1(6)	18	Grease	RSO	

VAN HALEN
American hard rock group formed in 1974 in Pasadena, California: David Lee Roth (vocals, b. 10/10/55 in Bloomington, Indiana), Eddie Van Halen (guitar, vocals, b. 01/26/55 in Nijmegen, Netherlands), Alex Van Halen (drums, b. 05/08/53 in Nijmegen), Michael Anthony (bass, b. 06/20/55 in Chicago). Roth left in 1985 to record solo, replaced by Sammy Hagar (vocals, b. 10/13/47 in Monterey, California). The two Van Halens are brothers; arrived in Pasadena in 1967. Eddie married actress Valerie Bertinelli (TV's *One Day At A Time*) in 1981; composed and played the guitar solo in Michael Jackson's "Beat It". Hagar left in June 1996, replaced by Gary Cherone, formerly of Extreme.

DATE	PK	WK	TITLE	LABEL	RA
04/10/82	14	5	Pretty Woman	Warner	
03/05/84	2(3)	26	Jump	Warner	
05/28/84	23	6	I'll Wait	Warner	
08/27/84	17	9	Panama	Warner	
05/12/86	9	16	Why Can't This Be Love	Warner	
07/04/88	34	6	Black And Blue	Warner	
10/10/88	34	3	When It's Love	Warner	
12/02/91	10	13	Top Of The World	Warner	31
05/15/95	---	RA	Can't Stop Loving You	Warner	8
10/09/95	---	RA	Not Enough	Warner	27
07/01/96	34	5 h	Human Beings	Warner	

VAN HELDEN, Armand
American male dance remixer born in the Netherlands. Based in New York City.

DATE	PK	WK	TITLE	LABEL	RA
11/03/96	19	4	Funk Phenomenon	RBR	
04/11/99	11	7	You Don't Know Me	NuMuzik	

Another version peaked at #13 on 03/28/99.

VANDROSS, Luther
American male R&B singer/songwriter/producer born Luther Ronzoni Vandross on 04/20/51 in New York City. Former commercial jingle singer, then backing vocalist/arranger for Ringo Starr, Carly Simon, Donna Summer, Barbra Streisand and others. Appeared in the 1993 movie *Meteor Man*.

DATE	PK	WK	TITLE	LABEL	RA
07/22/91	8	14	Power Of Love/Love Power	Epic	12
10/18/93	33	5	Heaven Knows	Epic	
09/07/92	4	17	The Best Things In Life Are Free *	A&M	4
04/17/95	14	40	Endless Love **	Epic	8

* Luther Vandross/Janet Jackson
** Luther Vandross/Mariah Carey

VANGELIS

DATE	PK	WK	TITLE	LABEL	RA

Greek male pop/MOR keyboardist/composer born Evangalos Odyssey Papathanassiou on 03/29/43 in Valos, Greece. Formed band Aphrodite's Child with singer Demis Roussos in the late-1960's. Recorded with Yes lead vocalist Jon Anderson as Jon and Vangelis in the early-1980's.

| 05/08/82 | 10 | 10 | Chariots Of Fire - Titles | Polydor | |

VANILLA ICE
American male rapper from Dallas. Born Robert Van Winkle on 10/31/68 in Miami Lakes, Florida. Starred in the movie *Cool As Ice*.

11/19/90	5	13	Ice Ice Baby	SBK	8
12/24/90	6	9	Play That Funky Music	SBK	10
04/01/91	5	10	I Love You	SBK	

VANNELLI, Gino
Canadian male pop singer/songwriter born on 06/16/52 in Montreal. Studied music theory at McGill University. His brother, Ross, is a producer. Won Juno Awards for Most Promising New Male Artist in 1975 and Male Artist of the Year in 1976 and 1979.

11/20/76	32	4	Love Of My Life	A&M	
11/29/78	16	14	I Just Wanna Stop	A&M	
06/13/81	5	11	Living Inside Myself	Arista	
07/01/85	6	18	Black Cars	Polydor	
09/30/85	14	13	Hurts To Be In Love	Polydor	
05/04/87	10	14	Wild Horses	Polydor	
12/10/90	35	2	The Time Of Day	Polydor	25

VANWARMER, Randy
American male MOR-pop singer/songwriter/guitarist. Born Randall Van Wormer on 03/30/55 in Indiana Hills, Colorado. Recorded country music in 1988.

| 07/11/79 | 2(2) | 14 | Just When I Needed You Most | Bearsville | |

VARIOUS ARTISTS

| 05/18/97 | 27 | 3 | Club Culture Volume 1 | Mercury | |
| 02/01/98 | 20 | 14 | Dogwhistle Kwikmix | BMG | |

VAUGHAN BROTHERS
American blues-rock duo consisting of guitarists Stevie Vaughan (b. 10/03/54 in Dallas) and his older brother, Jimmy (b. 03/20/51 in Dallas). Jimmy was lead guitarist of The Fabulous Thunderbirds; Stevie was lead guitarist of his own band Double Trouble. Stevie was killed in a helicopter crash on 08/27/90 in East Troy, Wisconsin.

| 12/24/90 | 32 | 7 | Tick Tock | Epic | |

VEGA, Suzanne
American female folk-styled alternative music singer/songwriter/guitarist born on 08/12/59 in New York City.

10/05/87	5	17	Luka	A&M	
02/11/90	5	21	Tom's Diner *	A&M	3
11/16/92	27	4	Blood Makes Noise	A&M	

| DATE | PK | WK | TITLE | LABEL | RA |

* DNA featuring Suzanne Vega

VELVA BLU

| 10/05/97 | 12 | 9 | Barbie Girl .... Groove |

VENGABOYS

Spanish dance group formed in the mid-1990's: Denice (b. 10/20/73), Kim (b. 04/01/76), Roy (b. 07/31/75), Robin (b. 01/01/78).

| 02/21/99 | 8 | 25 | We Like To Party .... Groovilicious/Isba | 28 |
| 08/09/99 | --- | RA | Boom, Boom, Boom, Boom!! ..... Groovilicious/Isba | 39+ |

VERA, Billy, and the Beaters

American R&B-styled band formed in 1979 in Los Angeles led by vocalist/songwriter Billy Vera (b. William McCord on 05/28/44 in Riverside, California, raised in Westchester County, New York). In the movies *Buckaroo Banzai* and *The Doors*.

| 03/23/87 | 2(3) | 16 | At This Moment ....Rhino |

VERUCA SALT

American alternative rock band formed in 1993 in Chicago: Louise Post (guitar, vocals), Stephen L. Lack (bass), Nina Gordon (guitar, vocals), Jim Shapiro (drums, vocals). Post and Gordon left in 1998. Shapiro left in 1996, replaced by Stacy Jones.

| 04/20/97 | 39 | 1 | Blow It Out Your Ass It's Veruca Salt .... Geffen |

VERVE, The

British alternative rock group formed in 1991 in England: Richard Ashcroft (vocals, guitar), Nick McCabe (guitar), Peter Salisbury (drums), Simon Jones (bass), Simon Tong (guitar, keyboards).

09/14/97	31	1	Drugs Don't Work V2 ....DOM
			Above is "V2" version. "V1" version peaked at #35 (09/14/97).
01/12/98	---	RA	Bittersweet Symphony .... Virgin	12

VERVE PIPE

American rock group formed in 1991 in East Lansing, Michigan: Brian Vander Ark (vocals, guitar), Brian Stout (guitar, vocals), A.J. Dunning (guitar), Doug Corella (percussion, keyboards), Donny Brown (drums, vocals). Stout left in 1993.

| 07/21/97 | --- | RA | The Freshman .... RCA | 9 |

VICTORIA, C.B.

Canadian female singer.

| 10/30/76 | 28 | 6 | I Don't Believe In Miracles............................... GRT |

VILLAGE PEOPLE

American disco vocal group formed by French producer Jacques Morali in 1977 in New York City: Victor Willis (lead vocals), David Hodo (b. 07/07/47), Felipe Rose (b. 01/12/54), Randy Jones, Glenn Hughes (b. 07/18/50 in the Bronx, New York), Alex Briley (b. 04/12/51). Willis left in 1979; replaced by Ray

DATE	PK	WK	TITLE	LABEL	RA

Simpson. Numerous line-up changes over the years. Members dressed in various costumes such as a police officer, cowboy, a construction worker, and a biker.

11/01/78	4	38	Macho Man	Casablanca	
01/10/79	2(8)	30	YMCA	Casablanca	
04/18/79	1(2)	16	In The Navy	Casablanca	
07/11/79	36	4	Go West	Casablanca	

V.I.P.
Canadian male pop vocal group formed circa 1991 in Barrie, Ontario: Marty Beecroft (b. circa 1976; tenor), Glenn Coulson (b. circa 1975; baritone), Joe Heslip (b. circa 1975; bass), Peter Luciano (b. circa 1974; tenor). Originally called U4ia, later changed name to Natural Reaction, changed to V.I.P. in early-1998.

| 09/21/98 | --- | RA | Just My Luck | VM | 21 |

VITAMIN C
American female pop singer Colleen Fitzpatrick. Former lead singer of Eve's Plum.

| 08/09/99 | --- | RA | Smile | Elektra | 36+ |

VOICE OF THE BEEHIVE
British pop group formed in London by California-born sisters Melissa (vocals) and Tracey (vocals, guitar) Belland. Line-up includes Britons Mike Jones (guitar), Martin Brett (bass) and former Madness member Dan Woodgate (drums). The Bellands are the daughters of Bruce Belland, member of the Four Preps.

| 07/01/96 | 31 | 4 h | Scary Kisses | EastWest | 11 |
| 10/28/96 | --- | RA | So Hard | EastWest | 28 |

VOICES OF THEORY
American R&B group from Philadelphia: Melchi, James, Hector, David, Mike G. Formed in the early-1990's.

| 08/09/98 | 22 | 11 | Say It | H.O.L.A. | |

VOISINE, Roch
Canadian male MOR-pop singer born in 1963 in St. Basile, New Brunswick. Won the 1994 Juno Award for Male Vocalist of the Year.

02/19/90	14	15	Helene	Star	
09/27/93	25	10	Oochigeas	Star	
12/27/93	---	RA	I'll Always Be There	Star	8
03/28/94	22	13	Lost Without You	Star	7
09/12/94	---	RA	Shout Out Loud	Star	10
01/30/95	---	RA	She Picked On Me	Star	16
01/20/97	---	RA	Kissing Rain	R.V.	20
05/26/97	---	RA	Deliver Me	R.V.	20
09/01/97	---	RA	Shed A Light	R.V.	39

DATE	PK	WK	TITLE	LABEL	RA

W

WAGNER, Jack
American male actor/pop singer born on 10/03/59 in Washington, Missouri. Played Frisco Jones on the television soap opera *General Hospital*, later appeared in TV's *Santa Barbara*.

| 02/04/85 | 5 | 14 | All I Need | Qwest | |

WAITE, John
British male rock singer born on 07/04/55 in Lancashire, England. Lead singer of The Babys and Bad English.

| 10/08/84 | 1(3) | 17 | Missing You | Capitol | |

WAKELIN, Johnny & The Kirshasa Band
British group led by singer/songwriter Johnny Wakelin.

| 09/06/75 | 25 | 1 | Black Superman | Pye | |

WAKELING, Dave
British male pop singer/guitarist born on 02/19/56 in Birmingham, England. Guitarist and vocalist for The English Beat, 1978-83, and General Public (since 1984).

| 05/30/88 | 35 | 7 | She's Having A Baby | MCA | |

WALKER, Chris
American male R&B singer born in Houston.

| 05/18/92 | --- | RA | Take Time | Pendulum | 32 |

WALLFLOWERS, The
American rock band formed in 1990 in Los Angeles: Jakob Dylan (vocals, guitar, b. 12/09/69), Rami Jaffee (piano, organ), Michael Ward (guitar), Greg Richling (bass), Mario Calire (drums). Dylan is the son of Bob Dylan.

09/02/96	28	5 h	6th Avenue Heartache	Interscope	25
04/07/97	---	RA	One Headlight	Interscope	4
09/08/97	---	RA	The Difference	Interscope	12
06/22/98	---	RA	Heroes	Interscope	12

WALL OF VOODOO
American electronic-rock group from Los Angeles led by singer Stanard Ridgway.

| 06/06/83 | 19 | 6 | Mexican Radio | A&M | |

WALSH, Joe
American male rock singer/songwriter/guitarist born on 11/20/47 in Wichita, Kansas. Member of The James Gang, 1969-71, and the Eagles, 1975-82. Formed his own band, Barnstorm, 1972-75.

| 09/06/78 | 5 | 12 | Life's Been Good | Asylum | |

DATE	PK	WK	TITLE	LABEL	RA
07/23/80	13	1	All Night Long .... Elektra		

WALTERS, Jamie
American male singer/actor born in June 1969 in Boston. Appeared in the 1991 movie *Shout* and the television series *The Heights*. Former lead singer of The Heights.

05/01/95	---	RA	Hold On .... Atlantic		4

WALTONS, The
Canadian pop trio formed in the mid-1980's: Jason "Walton" Plumb (vocals, acoustic guitar, b. circa 1969), Keith Nakonechny (vocals, bass), Dave Cooney (drums). Based in Toronto. Won the 1994 Juno Award for Best New Group.

04/05/93	---	RA	Colder Than You..WEA		36
08/02/93	---	RA	In The Meantime..WEA		39
05/15/95	---	RA	End Of The World...WEA		20

WANG CHUNG
British pop-rock group formed in 1982 in London: Jack Hues (vocals, guitar, keyboards), Nick Feldman (bass, keyboards), Darren Costin (drums). Costin left in 1985. Original name is Huang Chung.

07/02/84	6	17	Dance Hall Days .... Geffen	
01/20/86	33	2	To Live And Die In L.A. .... Geffen	
02/02/87	1(1)	18	Everybody Have Fun Tonight .... Geffen	
04/06/87	8	12	Let's Go .... Geffen	
09/21/87	38	2	Hypnotize Me.. Geffen	

WAR
American funk-R&B band formed in 1969 in Long Beach, California: Lonnie Jordan (keyboards, vocals, b. Leroy Jordan on 11/21/48 in San Diego), Howard Scott (guitar, vocals, b. 03/15/46 in San Pedro, California), Charles Miller (saxophone, clarinet, b. 06/02/39 in Olathe, Kansas), Harold Brown (drums, percussion, b. 03/17/46 in Long Beach), Lee Oskar (harmonica, b. Oskar Levetin Hansen on 03/24/46 in Copenhagen, Denmark), Thomas "Papa Dee" Allen (keyboards, vocals, b. 07/18/31 in Wilmington, Delaware).

09/06/75	9	8	Why Can't We Be Friends................. United Artists	
11/29/75	12	8	Low Rider .... United Artists	
09/25/76	28	7	Summer .... United Artists	

WARD, Anita
American female R&B-disco singer born on 12/20/57 in Memphis, Tennessee.

07/25/79	1(4)	18	Ring My Bell .... TK	

WARD, Christopher
Canadian male vocalist/songwriter born in 1950 in Toronto. Host of CBC-TV's *Catch Up!* in late-1970's. Video jockey at MuchMusic television network in 1980's. Wrote songs for Alannah Myles.

06/25/77	25	6	Once In A Long Time............................... Warner	
06/28/78	30	4	Maybe Your Heart................................... Warner	

WARNES, Jennifer

DATE	PK	WK	TITLE	LABEL	RA

American female pop-MOR singer/songwriter born Jennifer Jeane Warnes on 03/03/47 in Seattle, raised in Orange County, California. Lead actress in the Los Angeles production of *Hair*.

05/28/77	9	9	Right Time Of The Night	Arista	
11/27/82	1(2)	15	Up Where We Belong *	Island	
03/23/87	24	3	Ain't No Cure For Love	Attic	
01/25/88	2(1)	16	(I've Had) The Time Of My Life **	RCA	

* Joe Cocker and Jennifer Warnes
** Bill Medley/Jennifer Warnes

WARRANT
American hard rock band formed in 1984 in Los Angeles: Jani Lane (vocals, b. Johnny Lane on 02/01/64), Erik Turner (guitar, b. 03/31/64), Joey Allen (guitar, b. 06/23/64), Jerry Dixon (bass, b. 09/15/64), Steven Sweet (drums, b. 10/29/65).

11/06/89	4	16	Heaven	Columbia	
04/09/90	15	9	Sometimes She Cries	Columbia	24
11/26/90	2(2)	21	Cherry Pie	Columbia	
02/18/91	15	9	I Saw Red	Columbia	21
05/04/92	21	12	We Will Rock You	Columbia	
10/12/92	31	3	Machine Gun	Columbia	

WARREN G
American male rapper born Warren Griffin III, circa 1971 in Long Beach, California. Half-brother of Dr. Dre.

| 01/12/97 | 32 | 1 | What's Love Got To Do With It | Interscope |

WARWICK, Dionne
American female R&B singer born Marie Dionne Warwick on 12/12/40 in East Orange, New Jersey. Cousin of singer Whitney Houston. Attended Hartt College of Music in Hartford, Connecticut. Recorded as Dionne Warwicke, 1971-74. Popularized compositions of Burt Bacharach and Hal David. Co-hosted the music television show *Solid Gold*, 1980-81, 1985-86. Engaged in various business pursuits in the 1990's including an interior design firm, a fragrance, a television production company, and the Psychic Friends Network.

10/31/79	7	8	I'll Never Love This Way Again	Arista
12/25/82	16	8	Heartbreaker	Arista
02/24/86	1(3)	23	That's What Friends Are For *	Arista
09/07/87	36	4	Love Power **	Arista

* Dionne & Friends
** Dionne Warwick/Jeffrey Osborne

WAS (NOT WAS)
American R&B group formed in 1980 in Detroit: Don Was (bass, b. Donald Fagenson on 09/13/52 in Detroit), David Was (saxophone, flute, b. David Weiss on 10/26/52 in Detroit), Sweet Pea Atkinson (vocals, b. 09/20/45 in Oberlin, Ohio), Sir Harry Bowens (vocals, b. 10/08/49 in Detroit), Donald Ray Mitchell (vocals, b. 04/12/57 in Detroit). Name taken from a word game. Don Was is a prolific producer (Bonnie Raitt's *Nick Of Time*). Disbanded in 1993; re-formed in 1998.

| 05/15/89 | 6 | 14 | Walk The Dinosaur | Fontana |

| DATE | PK | WK | TITLE | LABEL | RA |

WASHINGTON, Sarah

| 09/27/93 | 34 | 7 | I Will Always Love You ....Quality |

WATCHMEN
Canadian rock band formed in 1988 in Winnipeg: Danny Greaves (vocals), Joey Serlin (guitar), Peter Loewen (bass), Sammy Kohn (drums).

| 02/20/95 | --- | RA | All Uncovered .... MCA | 30 |

WATERFRONT
British pop-rock duo from Cardiff, Wales: Chris Duffy (vocals), Phil Cillia (guitar). Name taken from the movie *On The Waterfront*.

| 07/24/89 | 22 | 8 | Cry ....Polydor |

WATERS, Crystal
American female R&B-dance singer born in 1964 in Philadelphia. From South New Jersey. Majored in computer science at Howard University. Her father is jazz musician Jr. Waters.

08/12/91	9	15	Gypsy Woman (She's Homeless).............. Mercury	26
08/15/94	4	37	100% Pure Love .... Mercury	9
04/21/97	---	RA	Say...If You Feel Alright .... Mercury	17

WATERS, Roger
British male rock bassist/vocalist born on 09/06/44 in Surrey, England. Bassist/vocalist of Pink Floyd.

| 11/09/92 | 39 | 2 | What God Wants (Part 1) ....Columbia |

WATLEY, Jody
American female R&B-pop singer born on 01/30/59 in Chicago. Vocalist of Shalamar, 1977-84 and dancer on the television show *Soul Train*. Her godfather is Jackie Wilson.

06/22/87	4	17	Looking For A New Love .... MCA	
01/18/88	33	4	Don't You Want Me.. MCA	
06/19/89	6	13	Real Love .... MCA	
10/09/89	24	9	Friends .... MCA	
02/12/90	---	RA	Everything .... MCA	21
05/11/92	---	RA	I'm The One You Need................................... MCA	12

WEDNESDAY
Canadian pop group from Oshawa, Ontario: Randy Begg, John Dufek, Mike O'Neil, Paul Andrew-Smith.

| 02/14/76 | 19 | 7 | Loving You Baby..Skyline |
| 01/08/77 | 36 | 6 | Ruby Baby ....Skyline |

WEEZER
American alternative rock band formed in 1992 in Los Angeles: Rivers Cuomo (vocals, guitar), Brian Bell (guitar, vocals), Matt Sharp (bass, vocals), Pat Wilson (drums).

| 02/13/95 | --- | RA | Buddy Holly .... DGC | 8 |

| DATE | PK | WK | TITLE | LABEL | RA |

WELCH, Bob
American male rock singer born on 07/31/46 in Los Angeles. Guitarist/vocalist of Fleetwood Mac, 1971-74. His father, Robert L. Welch, was a movie/TV producer.

| 01/25/78 | 15 | 12 | Sentimental Lady | Capitol | |
| 05/17/78 | 10 | 14 | Ebony Eyes | Capitol | |

WEST END GIRLS
Canadian pop vocal trio formed in Vancouver in 1991: Camille Henderson, Aimee MacKenzie, and Silvana Petrozzi. Henderson, daughter of Chilliwack's Bill Henderson left in 1993. Replaced by Celia-Louise Martin. Janele Woodley replaced Petrozzi in 1992. MacKenzie later joined the group D-Cru.

06/24/91	1(1)	16	Not Like Kissin' You	Johnny Jet	13
09/23/91	25	8	I Want You Back	Johnny Jet	16
02/10/92	33	10	Say You'll Be Mine	Johnny Jet	23
04/13/92	---	RA	Show Me The Way	Johnny Jet	34
07/26/93	18	16	R U Sexin' Me	Johnny Jet	
11/22/93	---	RA	State Of The Heart	Johnny Jet	34
03/14/94	---	RA	Pure	Johnny Jet	29

WET WET WET
Scottish pop quartet formed in 1982 in Glasgow: Marti Pellow (vocals, b. Mark McLoughlin on 03/23/66 in Cydebank, Scotland), Graeme Clarke (bass, b. 04/15/66 in Glasgow), Tom Cunningham (drums, b. 06/22/65 in Glasgow), Neil Mitchell (keyboards, b. 06/08/67 in Helensborough, Scotland). Based in Clydebank.

| 12/05/94 | 3(1) | 33 | Love Is All Around | London | 7 |

WET WILLIE
American rock band from Mobile, Alabama led by brothers Jack (bass) and Jimmy Hall (vocals).

| 09/05/79 | 39 | 2 | Weekend | Epic | |

WHAM!
British pop duo formed in 1982 in London: George Michael (vocals, b. Georgios Kyriacos Panayiotou on 06/25/63 in London), Andrew Ridgeley (guitar, b. 01/26/63 in Windlesham, England). Disbanded in 1986; Michael started solo career that same year, Ridgeley started recording solo in 1990.

11/19/84	2(9)	23	Wake Me Up Before You Go Go	Columbia	
02/04/85	2(7)	22	Careless Whisper *	Columbia	
06/24/85	5	13	Everything She Wants	Columbia	
09/16/85	12	11	Freedom	Columbia	
02/03/86	6	13	I'm Your Man	Columbia	
09/01/86	6	11	Edge Of Heaven	Columbia	

* Wham! featuring George Michael

WHIGFIELD
Danish female dance singer born Sannia Charlotte Carlson in 1970 in Skarlskar, Denmark.

| 04/03/95 | 11 | 39 | Saturday Night | Quality | 6 |
| 04/03/95 | --- | RA | Another Day | Quality | 21 |

DATE	PK	WK	TITLE	LABEL	RA
07/10/95	3(2)	21	Think Of You	Quality	
11/27/95	8	27	Big Time	Quality	

WHISPERS, The
American R&B vocal group formed in 1962 in Los Angeles: twins Walter and Wallace Scott (b. 09/03/43 in Fort Worth, Texas), Nicholas Caldwell (b. 04/05/44 in Loma Linda, California), Marcus Hutson (b. 01/08/43 in Los Angeles), Leaveil Degree (b. 07/31/48 in New Orleans; replaced Gordy Harmon in 1974).

| 05/14/80 | 10 | 2 | And The Beat Goes On | RCA | |

WHITE LION
American hard rock group formed in 1983 in Brooklyn, New York: Vito Bratta (guitar), Greg D'Angelo (drums), James Lomenzo (bass), Mike Tramp (vocals, b. Denmark). Lomenzo and D'Angelo left in 1991; replaced by Tommy Caradonna (bass), Jimmy DeGrasso (drums).

| 06/13/88 | 39 | 2 | Wait | Atlantic | |
| 03/27/89 | 8 | 11 | When The Children Cry | Atlantic | |

WHITE TOWN
British male techno-dance singer/multi-instrumentalist Jyoti Mishra (b. 07/30/66 in Rourkela, India). Moved to Derby, England in 1969.

| 04/13/97 | 13 | 3 | Your Woman | Chrysalis | 1 |

WHITE, Barry
American male R&B singer/songwriter/keyboardist/producer born on 09/12/44 in Galveston, Texas. Formed Love Unlimited in 1969; later became leader of Love Unlimited Orchestra.

| 12/28/77 | 26 | 6 | It's Ecstasy When You Lay Down | GRT | |
| 02/27/95 | 15 | 19 | Practice What You Preach | A&M | 40 |

WHITE, Karyn
American female R&B singer born Karyn Lay Vonne White on 10/14/65 in Los Angeles. Session work as backup vocalist for Julio Iglesias, the Commodores, Bobby Brown, and Sheena Easton. Married producer/songwriter Terry Lewis in 1990.

05/22/89	15	8	Superwoman	Warner	
09/25/89	22	8	Secret Rendezvous	Warner	
12/02/91	8	7	Romantic	Warner	5
02/17/92	---	RA	The Way I Feel About You	Warner	7

WHITESNAKE
British hard rock group formed in 1978 in Yorkshire, England. Line-up in 1987: David Coverdale (vocals, b. 09/22/49 in Saltburn, England), John Sykes (guitar, b. 07/29/59 in England), Neil Murray (bass), Aynsley Dunbar (drums, b. 1946 in Liverpool), Don Airey (keyboards). Coverdale is the former vocalist of Deep Purple, 1973-76.

11/02/87	9	18	Here I Go Again	Geffen	
01/18/88	12	15	Is This Love	Geffen	
12/25/89	28	6	Fool For Your Lovin'	Geffen	
03/19/90	39	1	The Deeper The Love	Geffen	40

DATE	PK	WK	TITLE	LABEL	RA

WHITTAKER, Roger
British male MOR singer born on 03/22/36 in Nairobi, Kenya.

| 06/21/75 | 11 | 6 | The Last Farewell | RCA | |

WHO, The
British rock group formed in 1964 in London: Peter Dennis Blandford "Pete" Townshend (guitar, vocals, b. 05/19/45 in London), Roger Harry Daltrey (vocals, b. 03/01/44 in London), John Alec Entwistle (bass, French horn, vocals, b. 10/09/44 in London), Keith John Moon (drums, b. 08/23/47 in London). Townshend created the 1969 rock opera *Tommy*, which was performed by the band several times and became a movie in 1975. Second rock opera *Quadrophenia* was released in 1973 and became a movie in 1979. All members had solo careers. Moon died of a drug overdose on 09/07/78 in London. A concert documentary film of the group, The *Kids Are Alright* was released in 1979. Eleven concertgoers were trampled to death at the group's concert in Cincinnati on 12/03/79. Disbanded in 1982. Inducted into the Rock and Roll Hall of Fame in 1990.

03/06/76	6	10	Squeeze Box	MCA	
10/18/78	11	10	Who Are You	MCA	
05/09/81	6	9	You Better You Bet	Warner	
10/30/82	10	6	Athena	Warner	

WIEDLIN, Jane
American female pop singer/actor born on 05/20/58 in Oconomowoc, Wisconsin. Guitarist of the Go-Go's. Made cameo appearances in the movies *Clue* and *Star Trek 4: The Voyage Home*.

| 08/22/88 | 13 | 11 | Rush Hour | EMI-Manhattan | |

WILD CHERRY
American R&B-funk group formed in the early-1970's in Steubenville, Ohio: Robert Parissi (lead vocals, guitar), Bryan Bassett (guitar), Mark Avsec (keyboards), Allen Wentz (bass), Ron Beitle (drums).

| 10/02/76 | 1(2) | 17 | Play That Funky Music | Epic | |

WILD ORCHID
American female vocal trio from Los Angeles: Stacy Ferguson, Stefanie Ridel, Renee Sandstrom.

| 10/28/96 | --- | RA | At Night I Pray | RCA | 29 |
| 05/05/97 | --- | RA | Talk To Me | RCA | 38 |

WILD STRAWBERRIES
Canadian husband-and-wife pop duo formed in 1989 in Toronto: Roberta Carter Harrison (vocals), Ken Harrison (keyboards).

06/20/94	---	RA	Crying Shame	Strawberry	30
04/15/96	17	11 h	Heroine	Nettwerk	24
07/29/96	31	5 h	I Don't Want To Think About It	Nettwerk	23

WILDE, Coleman
Canadian male singer.

| 08/28/89 | 15 | 11 | It Doesn't Matter | Attic | |

DATE	PK	WK	TITLE	LABEL	RA

WILDE, Kim
British female singer born Kim Smith on 11/18/60 in Chiswick, London, England. Daughter of 1950's pop idol Marty Wilde.

| 07/13/87 | 1(2) | 17 | You Keep Me Hangin' On | MCA | |

WILDER, Matthew
American male singer/songwriter/keyboardist born and raised in New York City. Session work for Rickie Lee Jones and Bette Midler.

| 02/20/84 | 4 | 18 | Break My Stride | Epic | |

WILL TO POWER
American pop trio from Miami: Bob Rosenberg (son of singer Gloria Mann), Dr. J, Suzi Carr. Rosenberg and Dr. J were disc jockeys in the Miami area. By 1990, Dr. J and Carr left and Elin Michaels joined.

| 01/23/89 | 1(2) | 15 | Baby, I Love Your Way/Freebird Medley | Epic | |
| 02/25/91 | 3(2) | 12 | I'm Not In Love | Epic | 6 |

WILLI ONE BLOOD
American male reggae/dancehall singer from New York City.

| 02/13/95 | --- | RA | Whiney Whiney | RCA | 39 |

WILLIAMS, Deniece
American female pop-R&B singer/songwriter born Deniece Chandler on 06/03/51 in Gary, Indiana. Began recording in the early-1960's. Member of Wonderlove, Stevie Wonder's backup group, 1972-75. Began recording gospel in 1986.

| 06/14/78 | 9 | 12 | Too Much, Too Little, Too Late * | Columbia | |
| 07/16/84 | 1(1) | 15 | Let's Hear It For The Boy | Columbia | |

* Johnny Mathis/Deniece Williams

WILLIAMS, John
American male orchestra conductor/composer born on 02/08/32 in New York City. Composed soundtrack to various movies like *Star Wars*, *Superman*, and *Close Encounters of the Third Kind*. Conductor of the Boston Pops Orchestra, 1980-93. His son, Joseph, was a vocalist of Toto, 1986-90.

| 03/08/78 | 18 | 12 | Theme From "Close Encounters Of A Third Kind" | Arista | |

WILLIAMS, Robbie
British male dance/pop singer born Robert Peter Maximillian Williams on 02/13/74 in Stoke-On-Trent, England. Former member of Take That (left in 1995).

| 05/17/99 | --- | RA | Milennium | Capitol | 6 |

WILLIAMS, Vanessa
American female pop-R&B singer born on 03/18/63 in Tarrytown, New York. In 1983, became the first black woman to be crowned Miss America. Resigned in July 1984 when nude photographs of her were published in *Penthouse* Magazine. Married Ramon Hervey (manager of Babyface, later Williams' man-

DATE	PK	WK	TITLE	LABEL	RA

ager) on 01/02/87. A host on VH-1 video music television channel. Appeared in the movies *Harley Davidson & The Marlboro Man* and *Eraser*. Made Broadway debut in *Kiss Of The Spider Woman* in 1995.

DATE	PK	WK	TITLE	LABEL	RA
05/15/89	28	4	Dreamin'	Polydor	
11/25/91	37	1	Running Back To You	Mercury	36
05/04/92	1(2)	15	Save The Best For Last	Mercury	3
07/13/92	14	14	Just For Tonight	Mercury	18
11/09/92	35	6	Work To Do	Polydor	
05/17/93	6	14	Love Is *	Polydor	4
02/13/95	14	19	The Sweetest Days	Mercury	16
11/20/95	10	29	Colors Of The Wind	Hollywood	19

* Vanessa Williams & Brian McKnight

WILLIAMS, Vivienne
Canadian female R&B singer.

DATE	PK	WK	TITLE	LABEL	RA
01/18/93	---	RA	My Temptation	Benchmark	24
06/21/93	---	RA	Look Me In The Eyes	Isba	34

WILLIS, Bruce
American male actor/singer born on 03/19/55 in Penns Grove, New Jersey. Starred as David Addison on the television show *Moonlighting*. Starred in *Die Hard* movies, and provided voice in the *Look Who's Talking* movies. Married actress Demi Moore on 11/21/87; separated by June 1998.

DATE	PK	WK	TITLE	LABEL	RA
03/09/87	4	14	Respect Yourself	Motown	

WILSON PHILLIPS
American pop vocal trio formed in 1989 in Los Angeles: Chynna Phillips (b. 02/12/68 in Los Angeles), Carnie Wilson (b. 04/29/68 in Los Angeles), Wendy Phillips (b. 10/16/69 in Los Angeles). Phillips is the daughter of John and Michelle Phillips of the Mamas and the Papas; the Wilsons are the daughters of Brian Wilson of the Beach Boys. Phillips left in 1993, recorded solo in 1995. Carnie began hosting her own television talk show in 1995, cancelled in 1996. Chynna married actor William Baldwin on 09/09/95.

DATE	PK	WK	TITLE	LABEL	RA
07/16/90	4	11	Hold On	SBK	5
09/10/90	1(5)	18	Release Me	SBK	2
12/10/90	3(1)	19	Impulsive	SBK	4
04/15/91	---	RA	You're In Love	SBK	2
08/05/91	---	RA	The Dream Is Still Alive	SBK	6
06/29/92	9	14	You Won't See Me Cry	SBK	5
09/14/92	23	10	Give It Up	SBK	20

WILSON, Ann
American female rock singer/guitarist born on 06/19/50 in San Diego. Lead singer of Heart.

DATE	PK	WK	TITLE	LABEL	RA
08/06/84	3(1)	12	Almost Paradise *	Columbia	
04/10/89	27	9	Surrender To Me **	Capitol	

* Mike Reno & Ann Wilson
** Ann Wilson/Robin Zander

DATE	PK	WK	TITLE	LABEL	RA

WILSON, Meri
American female singer born in Japan and raised in Marietta, Georgia.

| 11/02/77 | 27 | 4 | Telephone Man | GRT | |

WINANS, CeCe - see HOUSTON, Whitney

WINGFIELD, Pete
British keyboardist born on 05/07/48.

| 01/10/76 | 10 | 4 | Eighteen With A Bullet | Island | |

WINK
American male dance act, remixer, DJ Josh Wink (b. circa 1970 in Philadelphia). Co-founder of the Ovum Recordings label.

| 10/30/95 | 32 | 1 | Higher State Of Conciousness | Quality | |

WINWOOD, Steve
British male rock singer/keyboardist/guitarist born on 05/12/48 in Birmingham, England. Lead singer of the Spencer Davis Group (1963-67), Blind Faith (1969), and Traffic (1967-74, 1994).

05/09/81	3(1)	12	While You See A Chance	Island	
09/25/82	20	1	Still In The Game	Island	
09/29/86	11	13	Higher Love	Island	
01/25/88	32	8	Valerie	Island	
08/08/88	1(3)	17	Roll With It	Virgin	
11/21/88	14	11	Don't You Know What The Night Can Do?	Virgin	
12/10/90	27	10	One And Only Man	Virgin	11

WOLF, Peter
American male rock singer born Peter Blankfield on 03/07/46 in The Bronx, New York. Lead singer of the J. Geils Band, 1967-83. Married actress Faye Dunaway on 08/07/74, divorced in 1979.

| 09/10/84 | 18 | 9 | Lights Out | Capitol | |

WOMACK & WOMACK
American husband-and-wife R&B vocal/songwriting/production duo: Cecil Womack (guitars, vocals, b. 1947 in Cleveland), Linda Cooke (keyboards, vocals, b. 1952). Womack's brother is R&B singer Bobby Womack; Cooke's father is Sam Cooke.

| 07/31/89 | 29 | 6 | Tear Drops | Island | |

WONDER, Stevie
American male R&B singer/songwriter/multi-instrumentalist/producer born Steveland Judkins Morris on 05/13/50 in Saginaw, Michigan. Blind since birth. Backup vocalist when first signed to Motown in 1960. First recorded in 1962 as "Little Stevie Wonder". Married to singer Syreeta Wright, 1970-72. At age 21, first Motown artist to win complete artistic control of his recordings. Toured with the Rolling Stones in 1972. Left in coma for four days on 08/16/73 after a serious car accident. In the movie *Bikini Beach*. Inducted into the Rock and Roll Hall of Fame in 1989.

| 01/29/77 | 4 | 19 | I Wish | Tamla | |

DATE	PK	WK	TITLE	LABEL	RA
06/18/77	1(2)	20	Sir Duke	Tamla	
12/12/79	18	8	Send One Your Love	Tamla	
03/14/81	15	3	I Ain't Gonna Stand For It	Tamla	
03/20/82	6	9	That Girl	Tamla	
05/29/82	1(5)	14	Ebony & Ivory *	Columbia	
10/29/84	1(11)	26	I Just Called To Say I Love You	Motown	
02/11/85	38	2	Love Light In Flight	Motown	
10/14/85	1(7)	22	Part Time Lover	Tamla	
02/03/86	39	3	Go Home	Tamla	
02/24/86	1(3)	23	That's What Friends Are For **	Arista	
12/21/87	40	1	Skeletons	Motown	

* Paul McCartney (with Stevie Wonder)
** Dionne & Friends

WONDERS
American fictitious band from the 1996 movie *That Thing You Do!*. The single "That Thing You Do" is performed by studio musicians (Mike Viola, lead vocals).

12/02/96	---	RA	That Thing You Do	Epic	7

WORLD ON EDGE
Canadian pop quartet from Montreal: Rob Meyer (vocals), Steph Thompson (bass), Peter Hopkins (guitar), Jon Daniels (keyboards).

01/28/91	16	5	Still Beating	Virgin	19
03/18/91	39	2	Only The Lonely	Virgin	27
08/19/91	18	12	Wash The Rain	Virgin	17
10/28/91	---	RA	Standing Push & Fall	Virgin	23
01/20/92	---	RA	Little Lack Of Love	Virgin	32

WRECKX-N-EFFECT
American rap group born circa 1987 in New York City: Markell Riley (DJ), Aquil Davidson (rapper). Former member Brandon Mitchell shot to death in 1990.

02/08/93	---	RA	Rump Shaker	MCA	30

WRESTLERS, The

02/17/86	38	2	Land Of 1,000 Dances	CBS	

WRIGHT, Gary
American male pop-rock singer/songwriter/keyboardist born on 04/26/43 in Creskill, New Jersey. Child actor, featured in various TV and radio commercials. Appeared in TV's *Captain Video* at age seven. In Broadway's *Fanny*. Member of Spooky Tooth.

04/03/76	1(1)	13	Dream Weaver	Warner	
07/17/76	6	11	Love Is Alive	Warner	
09/19/81	15	3	Really Wanna Know You	Warner	

DATE	PK	WK	TITLE	LABEL	RA

XSCAPE
American R&B group formed in Atlanta: sisters LaTocha and Tamika Scott, Kandi Burruss, Tameka Cottle.

02/07/94	3(2)	40	Just Kickin' It	Columbia	
05/23/94	7	24	Understanding	Columbia	

XTC
British alternative rock band formed in 1977 in Swindon, England: Andy Partridge (vocals, synthesizer, b. 12/11/53 in Swindon), Colin Moulding (bass, b. 08/17/55 in Swindon), Terry Chambers (drums, b. 07/18/55 in Swindon), Dave Gregory (keyboards).

04/02/80	15	9	Making Plans For Nigel	PolyGram	

YA KID K
Zairian female dance-house singer born Manuela Barbara Kamosi on 01/26/72 in Kinshasa. Vocalist in Technotronic and Hi Tek 3.

04/16/90	4	15	Get Up! (Before The Night Is Over) *	SBK	
06/04/90	4	13	Spin That Wheel **	SBK	
08/31/92	2(2)	12	Move This *	SBK	10
12/28/92	34	7	Let This Housebeat Drop	SBK	

* Technotronic featuring Ya Kid K
** Hi Tek 3 featuring Ya Kid K

YAKI-DA
Swedish female pop duo: Linda Schonberg, Marie Knutsen.

07/10/95	---	RA	I Saw You Dancing	London	16

YAKOO BOYZ
Canadian techno-dance duo from Guelph, Ontario: Brad Ferringo and Trevor Magee.

05/15/95	4	26	Pipe Dreamz	Quality	

YANKOVIC, "Weird Al"
American male novelty singer/accordionist born Alfred Matthew Yankovic on 10/24/59 in Lynwood, California. Recorded parodies of popular songs. Starred in the 1989 movie *UHF*.

04/16/84	6	13	Eat It	Rock N' Roll	
07/29/85	35	4	Like A Surgeon	Rock N' Roll	
06/08/92	5	10	Smells Like Nirvana	Scotti Brothers	
08/24/92	26	6	You Don't Love Me	Scotti Brothers	
02/14/94	5	22	Jurassic Park	Attic	

DATE	PK	WK	TITLE	LABEL	RA

YES
British rock group formed in 1968 in London: Jon Anderson (vocals, percussion, b. 10/25/44 in Accrington, England), Peter Banks (guitar, vocals), Tony Kaye (keyboards, b. 01/11/45 in Leicester, England), Chris Squire (bass, vocals, b. 03/04/48 in London), William Scott "Bill" Bruford (drums, b. 05/17/49 in Sevenoaks, England). Several personnel changes followed including the addition of Steve Howe (b. 04/08/47 in London) and Geoffrey Downes, who later formed the nucleus of the group Asia. Anderson recorded with Vangelis in 1980. Group re-formed in 1983: Anderson, Kaye, Squire, Alan White (drums, b. 06/14/49 in Pelton, England; originally joined in 1972), Trevor Rabin (guitar, b. 01/13/54 in Johannesburg, South Africa). Re-named Anderson, Bruford, Wakeman, Howe after members of the group (Rick Wakeman was a member in the 1970's). Anderson left in 1990. Group re-formed in 1991, and again in 1993.

01/30/84	7	21	Owner Of A Lonely Heart	Atco	
12/14/87	30	8	Love Will Find A Way	Atco	

YOUNG M.C.
American male rapper born Marvin Young on 05/10/67 in London, England. Raised in Queens, New York. Co-writer of Tone Loc's "Wild Thing" and "Funky Cold Medina". Graduated from the University of Southern California with an economics degree.

12/04/89	1(1)	15	Bust A Move	Island	
02/12/90	5	16	Principal's Office	Island	20
05/14/90	21	7	I Come Off	Island	
09/02/91	17	9	That's The Way Love Goes	Capitol	

YOUNG, John Paul
Australian male pop singer/songwriter/pianist born in Glasgow, Scotland in 1953.

11/01/78	22	6	Love Is In The Air	Scotti Brothers	

YOUNG, Karen
American female disco artist born circa 1951, died on 01/26/91 in Philadelphia of a bleeding stomach ulcer.

01/10/79	29	10	Hot Shot	Telon	

YOUNG, Neil
Canadian male folk/rock singer/songwriter/guitarist born on 11/12/45 in Toronto. Raised in Winnipeg. In the Detroit band Mynah Birds, whose lead singer is Rick James. Member of Buffalo Springfield, 1966-69. Went solo in 1969 with backing band Crazy Horse. Member of Crosby, Stills, Nash & Young, 1970-71 (briefly reunited in 1988). Appeared in the 1987 movie *Made In Heaven*. Inducted into the Rock and Roll Hall of Fame in 1995.

03/01/93	---	RA	Harvest Moon	Reprise	24
08/19/96	40	1 h	Big Time	Reprise	

YOUNG, Paul
British male pop singer/songwriter/guitarist born on 01/17/56 in Luton, England.

11/14/83	27	7	Wherever I Lay My Hat (That's My Home)	Columbia	
05/14/84	35	5	Come Back And Stay	Columbia	
08/26/85	1(1)	20	Everytime You Go Away	Columbia	
11/18/85	16	8	I'm Gonna Tear Your Playhouse Down	Columbia	

DATE	PK	WK	TITLE	LABEL	RA
10/22/90	12	12	Oh Girl .... Columbia		6
01/27/92	21	11	Senza Una Donna * .... London		36
03/30/92	---	RA	What Becomes Of The Broken Hearted.......... MCA		11

* Zucchero featuring Paul Young

Z

ZAGER, Michael, Band
American disco studio group led by keyboardist/writer/arranger Michael Zager (b. 1943 in Jersey City, New Jersey). Member of the group Ten Wheel Drive.

| 05/31/78 | 19 | 24 | Let's All Chant .... Quality | | |

ZANDER, Robin
American male rock singer born on 01/23/53 in Loves Park, Illinois. Lead singer of Cheap Trick.

| 04/10/89 | 27 | 9 | Surrender To Me * .... Capitol | | |

* Ann Wilson/Robin Zander

ZAPPACOSTA
Canadian male singer/songwriter, Alfie Zappacosta. Won the 1984 Juno Award for Most Promising Male Vocalist.

| 03/23/87 | 40 | 4 | Nothing Could Stand In Your Way .... Capitol | | |
| 12/17/90 | 36 | 6 | Letterback... Capitol | | 24 |

ZEVON, Warren
American male rock singer/songwriter/pianist. Born on 01/24/47 in Chicago to Russian parents. In the duo Lyme & Cybelle with female vocalist Tule Livingston. Keyboardist/bandleader for the Everly Brothers.

| 05/31/78 | 7 | 8 | Werewolves In London................................ Asylum | | |

ZHANE
American R&B-dance duo formed in 1990 in Philadelphia: Renee Neufville, Jean Norris.

12/13/93	---	RA	Hey Mr. D.J. .... Epic		39
05/09/94	2(1)	38	Groove Thang..Motown		33
06/20/94	31	2	Sending My Love ....Motown		
02/20/95	---	RA	Shame... Jive		31

ZILBA, Mary
Canadian female dance singer.

| 11/24/97 | --- | RA | Do Me Right... Spinner | | 26 |

ZUCCHERO
Italian male vocalist/guitarist Adelmo Fornaciari.

DATE	PK	WK	TITLE	LABEL	RA
01/27/92	21	11	Senza Una Donna *	London	36

* Zucchero featuring Paul Young

ZZ TOP
American rock trio formed in 1969 in Houston: Billy Gibbons (vocals, guitar, b. 12/16/49 in Houston), Dusty Hill (vocals, bass, b. 05/19/49 in Dallas), Frank Beard (drums, b. 06/11/49 in Frankston, Texas). Appeared in the 1990 movie *Back To The Future III*.

DATE	PK	WK	TITLE	LABEL	RA
09/20/75	12	7	Tush	London	
07/30/84	11	11	Legs	Warner	
12/16/85	14	13	Sleeping Bag	Warner	
03/10/86	37	2	Stages	Warner	
06/25/90	10	16	Doubleback	Warner	22
05/18/92	11	11	Viva Las Vegas	Warner	
10/28/96	28	7 h	What's Up With That	RCA	

THE HITS
An alphabetical listing, by song title, of every record that hit the national singles chart from 1975 to the present.

A

- 82 **Abacab** Genesis
- 94 **About A Girl** Nirvana
- 82 **Abracadabra** Steve Miller Band
- 92 **Achy Breaky Heart** Billy Ray Cyrus
- 90 **Across The River** Bruce Hornsby & The Range
- 76 **Action** Sweet
- 86 **Action Speaks Louder Than Words** Action
- 99 **Adam's Rib** Melanie Doane
- 86 **Addicted To Love** Robert Palmer
- 98 **Adia** Sarah McLachlan
- 97 **A.D.I.A.S.** Korn
- 84 **Adult Education** Daryl Hall & John Oates
- 90 **Advice For The Young** Tears For Fears
- 83 **Affair Of The Heart** Rick Springfield
- 83 **Africa** Toto
- 89 **After All** Cher/Peter Cetera
- 85 **After The Fire** Roger Daltery
- 79 **After The Love Has Gone** Earth, Wind & Fire
- 77 **After The Lovin'** Engelbert Humperdinck
- 90 **After The Rain** Nelson
- 76 **Afternoon Delight** Starland Vocal Band
- 94 **Afternoons & Coffeespoons** Crash Test Dummies
- 93 **Again** Janet Jackson
- 92 **Again Tonight** John Mellencamp
- 84 **Against All Odds (Take A Look At Me Now)** Phil Collins
- 95 **Age Ain't Nothin' But A Number** Aaliyah
- 96 **Ahead By A Century** Tragically Hip
- 81 **Ain't Even Done With The Night** John Cougar Mellencamp
- 94 **Ain't Going Out Like That** Cypress Hill
- 77 **Ain't Gonna Bump No More (With No Big Fat Woman)** Joe Tex
- 92 **Ain't Gonna Hurt Nobody** Kid N' Play
- 94 **Ain't Got Nothin' If You Ain't Got Love** Michael Bolton
- 92 **Ain't It Heavy** Melissa Etheridge
- 79 **Ain't Love A Bitch** Rod Stewart
- 87 **Ain't No Cure For Love** Jennifer Warnes
- 79 **Ain't No Stoppin' Us Now** McFadden & Whitehead
- 75 **Ain't No Way To Treat A Lady** Helen Reddy
- 97 **Ain't Nobody** L.L. Cool J
- 79 **Ain't That A Shame** Cheap Trick
- 85 **Alive & Kickin'** Simple Minds
- 78 **Alive Again** Chicago
- 92 **All 4 Love** Color Me Badd
- 94 **All About Soul** Billy Joel
- 90 **All Around The World** Lisa Stansfield
- 76 **All By Myself** Eric Carmen
- 97 **All By Myself** Celine Dion
- 97 **All Cried Out** Allure
- 88 **All Fired Up** Pat Benatar
- 93 **All For Love** Bryan Adams/Rod Stewart/Sting
- 97 **All For You** Sister Hazel
- 94 **All I Do** Jane Child
- 98 **All I Have To Give** Backstreet Boys
- 85 **All I Need** Jack Wagner
- 86 **All I Need Is A Miracle** Mike & The Mechanics
- 78 **All I See Is Your Face** Dan Hill
- 95 **All I Wanna Do** Sheryl Crow
- 90 **All I Wanna Do Is Make Love To You** Heart
- 92 **All I Want** Toad The Wet Sprocket
- 96 **All I Want Is Everything** Def Leppard
- 90 **All My Life** Linda Ronstadt & Aaron Neville
- 98 **All My Life** K-Ci & Jo Jo
- 80 **All Night Long** Joe Walsh
- 83 **All Night Long (All Night)** Lionel Richie
- 83 **All Of My Heart** ABC
- 84 **All Of You** Julio Iglesias & Diana Ross
- 90 **All Or Nothing** Milli Vanilli
- 82 **All Our Tomorrows** Eddie Schwartz
- 80 **All Out Of Love** Air Supply
- 80 **All Over The World** Electric Light Orchestra
- 96 **All Ready** Jale
- 83 **All Right** Christopher Cross
- 84 **All Right Now** Santers
- 89 **All She Wants Is** Duranduran
- 85 **All She Wants To Do Is Dance** Don Henley
- 92 **All Shook Up** Cheap Trick
- 92 **All Shook Up** Billy Joel
- 99 **All Star** Smash Mouth
- 93 **All That She Wants** Ace Of Base
- 98 **All That You Are** Econoline Crush
- 90 **All The Lovers In The World** Gowan
- 91 **All The Man That I Need** Whitney Houston
- 80 **All The Tea In China** Susan Jacks
- 89 **All The Things I Wasn't** Grapes Of Wrath
- 96 **All The Way Live** Coolio
- 89 **All This Time** Tiffany
- 91 **All This Time** Sting
- 81 **All Those Years Ago** George Harrison
- 84 **All Through The Night** Cyndi Lauper
- 93 **All Thru The Night** POV & Jade
- 81 **All Touch** Rough Trade
- 95 **All Uncovered** The Watchmen
- 85 **All We Are** Kim Mitchell
- 83 **Allentown** Billy Joel
- 94 **Allison Road** Gin Blossoms
- 99 **Almost Doesn't Count** Brandy

Year	Song	Artist
90	Almost Hear You Sigh	Rolling Stones
84	Almost Paradise	Mike Reno & Ann Wilson
93	Almost Unreal	Roxette
87	Alone	Heart
97	Alone	Bee Gees
85	Along Comes A Woman	Chicago
89	Alphabet Street	Prince
90	Alright	Janet Jackson
93	Alright	Kris Kross
95	Alternative Girlfriend	Barenaked Ladies
87	Always	Atlantic Starr
94	Always	Erasure
95	Always	Bon Jovi
96	Always Be My Baby	Mariah Carey
82	Always On My Mind	Willie Nelson
88	Always On My Mind	Pet Shop Boys
83	Always Something There (To Remind Me)	Naked Eyes
92	Always The Last To Know	Del Amitri
92	Always Tomorrow	Gloria Estefan
92	Am I The Same Girl	Swing Out Sister
86	Amanda	Boston
94	Amazing	Aerosmith
92	America	Kim Mitchell
80	An American Dream	Nitty Gritty Dirt Band
89	American Dream	Crosby Stills Nash & Young
86	American Storm	Bob Seger
99	American Woman	Lenny Kravitz
98	Amnesia	Chumbawamba
80	And The Beat Goes On	The Whispers
94	And The Song Goes...	Carol Medina
85	And We Danced	Hooters
85	Angel	Madonna
88	Angel	Aerosmith
93	Angel	Jon Secada
95	Angel	Jeff Healey Band
95	Angel	Jam & Spoon
98	Angel	Joee
99	Angel	Sarah McLachlan
80	Angel Eyes	ABBA
89	Angel Eyes	Jeff Healey Band
86	Angel In My Pocket	One To One
77	Angel In Your Arms	Hot
89	Angel Of Harlem	U2
99	Angel Of Mine	Monica
81	Angel Of The Morning	Juice Newton
89	Angelia	Richard Marx
96	Angeline Is Coming Home	The Badlees
97	Angels And Ordinary Men	Wendy Lands
88	Animal	Def Leppard
91	Animal Heart	Glass Tiger
99	The Animal Song	Savage Garden
75	Anna Marie	Susan Jacks
93	Anniversary	Tony! Toni! Tone!
94	Anniversary Song	Cowboy Junkies
80	Another Brick In The Wall	Pink Floyd
95	Another Day	Whigfield
89	Another Day In Paradise	Phil Collins
88	Another Lover	Giant Steps
95	Another Night	Real McCoy
80	Another One Bites The Dust	Queen
76	Another Rainy Day In New York City	Chicago
93	Another Sad Love Song	Toni Braxton
99	Anthem For The Year 2000	Silverchair
95	Ants Marching	Dave Matthews Band
94	Any Time, Any Place	Janet Jackson
97	Anybody Seen My Baby	Rolling Stones
99	Anything But Down	Sheryl Crow
88	Anything For You	Gloria Estefan & Miami Sound Machine
95	Anything For You	Snow
90	Anything Is Possible	Debbie Gibson
98	Anytime	Brian McKnight
94	Anytime You Need A Friend	Mariah Carey
76	Anyway You Want It	Charity Brown
99	Anywhere	112
97	Anywhere For You	Backstreet Boys
86	April Fool	Chalk Circle
84	Are We Ourselves?	The Fixx
93	Are You Gonna Go My Way	Lenny Kravitz
98	Are You Jimmy Ray?	Jimmy Ray
77	Are You Ready For Love	Patsy Gallant
98	Are You That Somebody?	Aaliyah
79	Armageddon	Prism
89	Armageddon It	Def Leppard
78	Arms Of Mary	Chilliwack
91	Around The Way Girl	L.L. Cool J
97	Around The World	Daft Punk
93	Arranged Marriage	Apache Indian
79	Arrow Through Me	Paul McCartney & Wings
81	Arthur's Theme (The Best That You Can Do)	Christopher Cross
96	As I Lay Me Down	Sophie B. Hawkins
96	As Long As It Matters	Gin Blossoms
97	As Long As You Love Me	Backstreet Boys
80	Ashes To Ashes	David Bowie
96	Astroplane	BKS
96	At Night I Pray	Wild Orchid
75	At Seventeen	Janis Ian
85	At The Feet Of The Moon	Parachute Club
87	At This Moment	Billy Vera And The Beaters
82	Athena	The Who
84	The Authority Song	John Cougar Mellencamp
84	Automatic	Pointer Sisters
97	Automatic Lover	Real McCoy

80	**Automobile** Hansie	95	**Ballad Of Peter Pumpkinhead** Crash Test Dummies
98	**Ava Adore** Smashing Pumpkins	91	**Ballad Of Youth** Richie Sambora
97	**Avenues** Refugee Camp All Stars	87	**Ballerina Girl/Deep River Woman** Lionel Richie
85	**Axel F** Harold Faltermeyer	75	**Ballroom Blitz** Sweet

B

79	**Babe** Styx	96	**Banditos** The Refreshments
95	**Baby** Brandy	95	**Bang And Blame** R.E.M.
91	**Baby Baby** Amy Grant	98	**Bang On** Propellerheads
95	**Baby Baby** Corona	90	**Banned In The USA** Luke featuring 2 Live Crew
78	**Baby Come Back** Player	97	**Barbie Girl** Aqua
83	**Baby Come To Me** Patty Austin/ James Ingram	97	**Barbie Girl** Velva Blu
92	**Baby Doll** Big House	97	**Barely Breathing** Duncan Sheik
89	**Baby Don't Forget My Number** Milli Vanilli	77	**Barracuda** Heart
92	**Baby Got Back** Sir Mix-A-Lot	97	**Barrel Of A Gun** Depeche Mode
78	**Baby Hold On** Eddie Money	94	**Basket Case** Green Day
76	**Baby I Love Your Way** Peter Frampton	89	**Batdance** Prince
94	**Baby I Love Your Way** Big Mountain	83	**Be Good Johnny** Men At Work
89	**Baby I Love Your Way/Freebird Medley** Will To Power	96	**Be My Lover** La Bouche
93	**Baby I'm Yours** Shai	85	**Be Near Me** ABC
90	**Baby It's Tonight** Jude Cole	88	**Be Still My Beating Heart** Sting
83	**Baby Jane** Rod Stewart	98	**Beach Ball** Nalin & Kane
86	**Baby Love** Regina	81	**The Beach Boys Medley** Beach Boys
98	**...Baby One More Time** Britney Spears	78	**Beast Of Burden** Rolling Stones
80	**Baby Talks Dirty** The Knack	83	**Beat It** Michael Jackson
77	**Baby What A Big Surprise** Chicago	82	**The Beatles' Movie Medley** The Beatles
92	**Baby When I Call Your Name** Corey Hart	93	**Beautiful Girl** INXS
92	**Baby, Baby, Baby** TLC	96	**Beautiful Goodbye** Amanda Marshall
99	**Back 2 Good** Matchbox 20	95	**Beautiful Life** Ace Of Base
94	**Back And Forth** Aaliyah	99	**Beautiful Stranger** Madonna
95	**Back For Good** Take That	92	**Beauty And The Beast** Celine Dion & Peabo Bryson
83	**Back On The Chain Gang** The Pretenders	91	**Because I Love You** Stevie B
90	**Back To Life** Soul II Soul featuring Caron Wheeler	93	**Because Of Love** Mae Moore
93	**Back To My Roots** RuPaul	94	**Because Of Love** Janet Jackson
98	**Back To You** Bryan Adams	98	**Because Of You** 98°
87	**Bad** Michael Jackson	78	**Because The Night** Patti Smith
86	**Bad Bad Boy** Haywire	94	**Because The Night** 10,000 Maniacs
75	**Bad Blood** Neil Sedaka	98	**Because We Want To** Billie
83	**Bad Boy** Ray Parker Jr.	96	**Because You Loved Me** Celine Dion
86	**Bad Boy** Miami Sound Machine	93	**Bed Of Roses** Bon Jovi
93	**Bad Boys** Inner Circle	88	**Beds Are Burning** Midnight Oil
79	**Bad Case Of Loving You** Robert Palmer	95	**Bedtime Stories** Madonna
79	**Bad Girl** Donna Summer	97	**Been Around The World** Puff Daddy & The Family (featuring Notorious B.I.G. And Mase)
93	**Bad Girl** Madonna	97	**Beetlebum** Blur
75	**Bad Luck (Part 1)** Harold Melvin And The Blue Notes	90	**Before We Fall** Sheree
88	**Bad Medicine** Bon Jovi	81	**Being With You** Smokey Robinson
75	**Bad Time** Grand Funk	93	**Believe** Lenny Kravitz
97	**Baiia Baiia Conmigo** Domino	95	**Believe** Elton John
99	**Bailamos** Enrique Iglesias	99	**Believe** Cher
78	**Baker Street** Gerry Rafferty	88	**Believe In Me** Paul Janz
85	**Ball Of Confusion** Love & Rockets	99	**Believe In You** Amanda Marshall
		95	**Believe Me** Moist
		85	**The Belle Of St. Mark** Sheila E
		89	**The Best** Tina Turner
		86	**Best Of Me** David Foster/Olivia Newton-John

77	Best Of My Love Emotions	92	Blowing Kisses In The Wind Paula Abdul
81	The Best Of Times Styx		
92	The Best Things In Life Are Free Luther Vandross/Janet Jackson	94	The Blue & White John Gramm
		78	Blue Bayou Linda Ronstadt
94	Betcha By Golly Wow Aaron Neville	78	Blue Collar Man Styx
97	Betcha By Golly Wow Prince	82	Blue Eyes Elton John
76	Beth Kiss	84	Blue Jean David Bowie
81	Bette Davis Eyes Kim Carnes	99	Blue Monday Orgy
84	Better Be Good To Me Tina Turner	95	Blue Monday '95 New Order
88	Better Be Home Soon Crowded House	90	Blue Sky Mine Midnight Oil
		78	Bluer Than Blue Michael Johnson
91	A Better Love Londonbeat	82	Body Language Queen
79	Better Love Next Time Dr. Hook	99	Body Movin' Beastie Boys
95	Better Man Pearl Jam	76	Bohemian Rhapsody Queen
96	Better Off As We Are Blue Rodeo	92	Bohemian Rhapsody Queen
93	Better Than You Lisa Keith	96	Bohemian Rhapsody The Braids
96	Big Bang Baby Stone Temple Pilots	77	Boogie Child Bee Gees
99	Big Big World Emilia	76	Boogie Fever Sylvers
97	Big Daddy Heavy D	77	Boogie Nights Heatwave
93	Big Gun AC/DC	78	Boogie Oogie Oogie A Taste Of Honey
89	Big League Tom Cochrane & Red Rider		
		79	Boogie Wonderland Earth, Wind & Fire
83	Big Log Robert Plant		
87	Big Love Fleetwood Mac	79	(Boogie Woogie) Dancin' Shoes Claudja Barry
96	Big Me Foo Fighters		
95	Big Sky Hemingway Corner	87	Boom Boom (Let's Go Back To My Room) Paul Lekakis
87	Big Time Peter Gabriel		
95	Big Time Whigfield	95	Boom! Boom! Boom! Outhere Brothers
96	Big Time Neil Young		
83	Billie Jean Michael Jackson	99	Boom, Boom, Boom, Boom!! Vengaboys
99	Bills Bills Bills Destiny's Child		
90	Bird On A Wire The Neville Brothers	95	Boombastic Shaggy
96	Birmingham Amanda Marshall	91	Boomerang Spunkadelic
91	Biscuit's In The House Biscuit	92	Boot Scootin' Boogie Brooks & Dunn
97	Bitch Meredith Brooks	90	Boots Or Hearts Tragically Hip
77	Bite Your Lip Elton John	86	Bop Dan Seals
91	Bitter Tears INXS	84	Borderline Madonna
96	Bittersweet Me R.E.M.	85	Born In The U.S.A. Bruce Springsteen
98	Bittersweet Symphony The Verve	97	Born Slippy Underworld
94	Bizarre Love Triangle Frente	79	Born To Be Alive Patrick Hernandez
88	Black And Blue Van Halen	89	Born To Be My Baby Bon Jovi
99	Black Balloon Goo Goo Dolls	93	Boss Drum The Shamen
85	Black Cars Gino Vannelli	93	Both Sides Of The Story Phil Collins
90	Black Cat Janet Jackson	94	The Bottle The Christians
96	Black Cloud Rain Corey Hart	80	Boulevard Jackson Browne
94	Black Hole Sun Soundgarden	93	Bow Bow Bow Funkdoobiest
91	Black Or White Michael Jackson	81	Boy From New York City Manhattan Transfer
75	Black Superman Johnny Wakelin & The Kirshasa Band		
		85	Boy In The Box Corey Hart
89	Black Velvet Alannah Myles	86	Boy Inside The Man Tom Cochrane
89	Blame It On The Rain Milli Vanilli	98	The Boy Is Mine Brandy & Monica
94	Blame Your Parents 54.40	76	The Boys Are Back In Town Thin Lizzy
90	Blaze Of Glory Jon Bon Jovi		
95	Blind Man Aerosmith	84	Boys Do Fall In Love Robin Gibb
77	Blinded By The Light Manfred Mann	79	Boys In The Sports Car Trooper
92	Blood Makes Noise Suzanne Vega	82	Boys Of Autumn David Roberts
97	Blood On The Dancefloor Michael Jackson	85	The Boys Of Summer Don Henley
		87	Brand New Lover Dead Or Alive
79	Blow Away George Harrison	80	Brass In Pocket Pretenders
97	Blow It Out Your Ass It's Veruca Salt Veruca Salt	75	Brazil Ritchie Family
		93	Break It Down Again Tears For Fears

78	**Break It To Them Gently** Burton Cummings	89	**Call It Love** Poco
98	**Break Me Shake Me** Savage Garden	91	**Call It Poison** Escape Club
84	**Break My Stride** Matthew Wilder	91	**Call It Rock N' Roll** Great White
97	**Break My Stride** Unique II	80	**Call Me** Blondie
88	**Breakaway** Big Pig	91	**Call Me** Acosta Russell
84	**Breakdance** Irene Cara	97	**Call Me** Le Click
95	**Breakfast At Tiffany's** Deep Blue Something	92	**Call My Name** Love & Sas
92	**Breakin' My Heart** Mint Condition	77	**Calling Dr. Love** Kiss
84	**Breakin'...There's No Stopping Us** Ollie & Jerry	91	**Calling Elvis** Dire Straits
		77	**Calling Occupants** Carpenters
		75	**Calypso** John Denver
97	**Breaking All The Rules** She Moves	99	**Can I Get A...** Jay-Z feat. Amil & Ja
92	**Breaking My Heart** Mint Condition	96	**Can I Get Close?** Gavin Hope
76	**Breaking Up Is Hard To Do** Neil Sedaka	95	**Can I Touch You...There?** Michael Bolton
87	**Breakout** Swing Out Sister	94	**Can We Talk?** Tevin Campbell
81	**The Breakup Song** Greg Kihn	94	**Can You Feel The Love Tonight** Elton John
97	**Breathe** Prodigy	93	**Can You Forgive Her** Pet Shop Boys
94	**Breathe Again** Toni Braxton	76	**Can't Catch Me** Bim
93	**Brian Wilson** Barenaked Ladies	95	**Can't Cry Anymore** Sheryl Crow
98	**Brick** Ben Folds Five	93	**Can't Do A Thing** Chris Isaak
77	**Brick House** Commodores	85	**Can't Fight This Feeling** REO Speedwagon
87	**Brilliant Disguise** Bruce Springsteen		
98	**Brimful of Asha** Cornershop	99	**Can't Get Enough** Soulsearcher
88	**Bring Me Some Water** Melissa Etheridge	98	**Can't Get Enough Of You Baby** Smash Mouth
91	**Broken Arrow** Rod Stewart	93	**Can't Get Enough Of Your Love** Taylor Dayne
98	**Broken Bones** Love Inc.		
80	**Broken Hearted Me** Anne Murray	96	**Can't Get You Off Of My Mind** Lenny Kravitz
86	**Broken Wings** Mr. Mister		
95	**Brokenhearted** Brandy	87	**Can't Help Falling In Love** Corey Hart
87	**Brother Louie** Modern Talking	93	**Can't Help Falling In Love** UB40
94	**Brown Eyed Girl** Freddy Curci	92	**Can't Let Go** Mariah Carey
95	**Brown Sugar** D'Angelo	98	**Can't Let Her Go** Boyz II Men
85	**Bruce** Rick Springfield	90	**(Can't Live Without Your) Love And Affection** Nelson
95	**Buddy Holly** Weezer		
93	**Buddy X** Neneh Cherry	97	**Can't Nobody Hold Me Down** Puff Daddy
89	**Buffalo Stance** Neneh Cherry		
97	**Building A Mystery** Sarah McLachlan	83	**Can't Shake Loose** Agnetha Faltskog
95	**Bullet With Butterfly Wings** Smashing Pumpkins	78	**Can't Smile Without You** Barry Manilow
96	**Burden In My Hand** Soundgarden	88	**Can't Stay Away From You** Gloria Estefan & Miami Sound Machine
83	**Burning Down The House** Talking Heads		
		90	**Can't Stop** After 7
86	**Burning Heart** Survivor	77	**Can't Stop Dancing** Captain & Tennille
89	**Bust A Move** Young M.C.	90	**Can't Stop Fallin' Into Love** Cheap Trick
97	**Butterfly** Mariah Carey		
97	**Butterfly Kisses** Bob Carlisle	95	**Can't Stop Loving You** Van Halen
92	**Buzz** Haywire	77	**Can't Stop Myself From Loving You** Octavian
93	**By The Time This Night Is Over** Kenny G		
		91	**Can't Stop This Thing We Started** Bryan Adams

C

		98	**Can't Take My Eyes Off Of You** Lauryn Hill
93	**Cadillac Baby** Colin James		
77	**California Girl** Chilliwack	92	**Can't Truss It** Public Enemy
85	**California Girls** David Lee Roth	87	**Can't We Try** Dan Hill
92	**California Here I Come** Sophie B. Hawkins	88	**Candle In The Wind** Elton John
		97	**Candle In The Wind 1997** Elton John
96	**California Love** 2Pac	83	**Candy Girl** New Edition
99	**Call And Answer** Barenaked Ladies	99	**Canned Heat** Jamiroquai

85	Cannonball Supertramp		88	China In Your Hand T'Pau
94	Cantaloop (Flip Fantasia) US3		80	Chiquitita ABBA
86	Captain Of Her Heart Double		90	Chocolate Box Bros
77	Car Wash Rose Royce		91	Chocolate Cake Crowded House
85	Careless Whisper Wham! featuring George Michael		93	Chok There Apache Indian
			94	Choose Color Me Badd
84	Caribbean Queen (No More Love On The Run) Billy Ocean		75	Christina Terry Jacks
			77	Christine Sixteen Kiss
97	Carma Please Version 1 Radiohead		96	Christmas Blues Holly Cole Trio
95	Carnival Natalie Merchant		97	Christmas Blues Holly Cole Trio
77	Carolina Caroline Jonathan Edwards		96	The Christmas EP Enya
91	Caroline Concrete Blonde		97	The Christmas EP Enya
87	Carrie Europe		98	The Christmas EP Enya
90	Carry Me Ray Lyell & The Storm		91	The Christmas Song Natalie Cole
90	Carry On The Box		85	Christmas Time Bryan Adams
77	Carry On Wayward Son Kansas		79	Chuck E's In Love Ricki Lee Jones
80	Cars Gary Numan		83	Church Of The Poison Mind Culture Club
87	Casanova Levert			
88	Catch Me (I'm Falling) Pretty Poison		92	Church Of Your Heart Roxette
85	Catch My Fall Billy Idol		88	Circle In The Sand Belinda Carlisle
93	Cats In The Cradle Ugly Kid Joe		78	The Circle Is Small Gordon Lightfoot
82	Caught Up In You 38 Special		95	Circle Of Life Elton John
87	Causing A Commotion Madonna		85	C-I-T-Y John Cafferty & The Beaver Brown Band
92	Celebrate Infidels			
85	Celebrate Youth Rick Springfield		94	Claire Rheostatics
81	Celebration Kool & The Gang		98	Clock Strikes Timbaland & Magoo
82	Centerfold J. Geils Band		80	Clones Alice Cooper
77	C'est La Vie Greg Lake		90	Close To You Maxi Priest
87	C'est La Vie Robbie Nevil		78	The Closer I Get Roberta Flack & Donny Hathaway
99	C'est La Vie B*Witched			
86	Chain Reaction Diana Ross		96	Closer To Free Bodeans
96	Chains Tina Arena		78	Closer To The Heart Rush
92	Chains Around My Heart Richard Marx		87	Closer Together The Box
			98	Closing Time Semisonic
88	Chains Of Love Erasure		99	Cloud #9 Bryan Adams
96	Champagne Supernova Oasis		90	Club At The End Of The Street Elton John
83	Change Tears For Fears			
92	Change Lisa Stansfield		97	Club Culture Volume 1 Various Artists
87	Change Of Heart Cyndi Lauper		97	Clumsy Our Lady Peace
96	Change The World Eric Clapton		96	C'mon 'N' Ride It (The Train) Quad City DJ's
97	A Change Would Do You Good Sheryl Crow			
			90	C'mon And Get My Love D-Mob featuring Cathy Dennis
93	Changes Ozzy Osbourne			
99	Changes 2Pac		94	Coax Me Sloan
82	Chariots Of Fire - Titles Vangelis		80	Cocaine Eric Clapton
95	Charms Philosopher Kings		97	Coco Jamboo Mr. President
78	Chattanooga Choo Choo Tuxedo Junction		77	Cold As Ice Foreigner
			89	Cold Hearted Paula Abdul
98	Cheated (To All The Girls) Wyclef Jean		97	Cold Rock A Party M.C. Lyte
			93	Colder Than You The Waltons
88	Check It Out John Cougar Mellencamp		88	Color Of Love Billy Ocean
85	Cherish Kool & The Gang		97	Color Of Love Amber
89	Cherish Madonna		95	Colors Of The Wind Vanessa Williams
93	Cherish The Day Sade		79	Come And Get Your Love Long John Baldry
88	Cherry Bomb John Cougar Mellencamp			
			95	Come And Get Your Love Real McCoy
90	Cherry Pie Warrant		92	Come As You Are Nirvana
97	Cherub Rock Smashing Pumpkins		80	Come Back J. Geils Band
96	Children Robert Miles		95	Come Back Londonbeat
90	Children Of The Night Richard Marx		84	Come Back And Stay Paul Young
83	China Girl David Bowie		90	Come Back To Me Janet Jackson

83	**Come Dancing** The Kinks		95	**Craziest** Naughty By Nature
87	**Come Go With Me** Expose		83	**Crazy** Supertramp
83	**Come On Eileen** Dexy's Midnight Runners		88	**Crazy** Icehouse
87	**Come On Let's Go** Los Lobos		91	**Crazy** Seal
78	**Come Sail Away** Styx		94	**Crazy** Aerosmith
79	**Come To Me** France Joli		89	**Crazy About Her** Rod Stewart
94	**Come To My Window** Melissa Etheridge		95	**Crazy Cool** Paula Abdul
78	**Come Together** Aerosmith		85	**Crazy For You** Madonna
93	**Come Undone** Duran Duran		85	**Crazy In The Night (Barking At Airplanes)** Kim Carnes
98	**Come With Me** Puff Daddy featuring Jimmy Page		80	**Crazy Little Thing Called Love** Queen
78	**Coming Home** Ian Thomas Band		79	**Crazy Love** Poco
91	**Coming Out Of The Dark** Gloria Estefan		76	**Crazy On You** Heart
80	**Coming Up** Paul McCartney		91	**Cream** Prince & The New Power Generation
96	**A Common Disaster** Cowboy Junkies		93	**Creep** Radiohead
94	**Completely** Michael Bolton		95	**Creep** TLC
91	**Conductin' Thangs** Maestro Fresh-Wes		90	**Crime Against Love** Barney Bentall & The Legendary Hearts
86	**Conga** Miami Sound Machine		83	**Crimes Of Passion** Rough Trade
93	**Connected** Stereo MCs		97	**Criminal** Fiona Apple
95	**Connection** Elastica		85	**A Criminal Mind** Gowan
99	**Consequence Free** Great Big Sea		82	**Crimson & Clover** Joan Jett & The Heartbreakers
92	**Constant Craving** k.d. lang		87	**Cross My Broken Heart** The Jets
87	**Contact** Platinum Blonde		90	**Cruel Crazy Beautiful World** Johnny Clegg & Savuka
87	**Control** Janet Jackson		92	**Cruel Little Number** Jeff Healey Band
76	**Convoy** C.W. McCall		84	**Cruel Summer** Bananarama
80	**Cool Change** Little River Band		98	**Cruel Summer** Ace Of Base
81	**Cool Love** Pablo Cruise		79	**Cruel To Be Kind** Nick Lowe
82	**Cool Night** Paul Davis		80	**Cruisin'** Smokey Robinson
78	**Copacabana (At The Copa)** Barry Manilow		90	**Cruising For Bruising** Basia
89	**Copperhead Road** Steve Earl		83	**Crumblin' Down** John Cougar Mellencamp
94	**Cornflake Girl** Tori Amos		98	**Crush** Jennifer Paige
97	**Cosmic Girl** Jamiroquai		86	**Crush On You** The Jets
95	**Cotton Eye Joe** Rednex		85	**Cry** Godley & Creme
96	**Could Be Good** Bass Line Syndicate		89	**Cry** Waterfront
94	**Could I Be Your Girl** Jann Arden		98	**Cry** Philosopher Kings
80	**Could I Have This Dance** Anne Murray		91	**Cry For Help** Rick Astley
75	**Could It Be Magic** Barry Manilow		91	**Cry To Me** Darby Mills
88	**Could've Been** Tiffany		93	**Cryin'** Aerosmith
92	**Could've Been Me** Billy Ray Cyrus		81	**Crying** Don McLean
77	**Couldn't Get It Right** Climax Blues Band		88	**Crying** Roy Orbison/k.d. lang
78	**Count On Me** Jefferson Starship		93	**The Crying Game** Boy George
96	**Count On Me** Whitney Houston		85	**Crying Over You** Platinum Blonde
96	**Counting Blue Cars** Dishwalla		94	**Crying Shame** Wild Strawberries
91	**Couple Days Off** Huey Lewis & The News		97	**C U When You Get There** Coolio
93	**Courage** Tragically Hip		89	**Cult Of Personality** Living Color
89	**Cover Girl** New Kids On The Block		84	**Cum On Feel The Noize** Quiet Riot
84	**Cover Me** Bruce Springsteen		98	**Cup of Life** Ricky Martin
89	**Cover Of Love** Michael Damian		76	**Cupid** Tony Orlando & Dawn
80	**Coward Of The County** Kenny Rogers		95	**Curious** Sandbox
77	**Crackerbox Palace** George Harrison		84	**The Curly Shuffle** Jump 'N The Saddle
90	**Cradle Of Love** Billy Idol		84	**The Curly Shuffle** The Knuckleheads
94	**Crash! Boom! Bang!** Roxette		83	**Cuts Like A Knife** Bryan Adams
96	**Crawl** Tom Cochrane		90	**Cuts You Up** Peter Murphy

83	**Da Da Da** Trio		81	**De Do Do Do, De Da Da Da** The Police
77	**Da Doo Ron Ron** Shaun Cassidy		90	**Deadbeat Club** The B-52s
97	**Da Funk** Daft Punk		97	**Dear M.F.** Big Sugar
79	**Da Ya Think I'm Sexy** Rod Stewart		95	**December** Collective Soul
97	**Da' Dip** Freak Nasty		76	**December 1963 (Oh, What A Night)** Four Seasons
91	**Daddy Freddy's In Town** Daddy Freddy		94	**December 1963 (Oh, What A Night)** Four Seasons
92	**Damn, I Wish I Was Your Lover** Sophie B. Hawkins		92	**Deep In My Soul** Acosta Russell
79	**Dance (Disco Heat)** Sylvester		92	**Deep Kiss** Mitsou
78	**Dance Dance Dance** Chic		76	**Deep Purple** Donny & Marie Osmond
87	**Dance Desire** Haywire		91	**Deep Shade Of Soul** Urban Dance Squad
84	**Dance Hall Days** Wang Chung		93	**Deeper And Deeper** Madonna
96	**Dance Into The Light** Phil Collins		95	**A Deeper Shade Of Love** Camille
77	**Dance Little Lady Dance** Tina Charles		90	**The Deeper The Love** Whitesnake
95	**Dance Naked** John Mellencamp		92	**Deeply Dippy** Right Said Fred
75	**Dance With Me** Orleans		98	**Deja Vu (Uptown Baby)** Lord Tariq & Peter Gunz
78	**Dance With Me** Peter Brown		93	**Delicate** Terence Trent D'Arby
97	**Dancehall Queen** Beenie Man		83	**Delirious** Prince
79	**Dancer** Gino Soccio		97	**Deliver Me** Roch Voisine
98	**Dancing Baby** Baby Talk		79	**Dependin' On You** Doobie Brothers
99	**Dancing Baby (Ooga-Chaka)** Trubble		83	**Der Kommisar** After The Fire
84	**Dancing In The Dark** Bruce Springsteen		83	**Der Kommisar** Falco
99	**Dancing In The Key Of Love** Temperance		84	**Desert Moon** Dennis DeYoung
94	**Dancing In The Moonlight** Baha Men		80	**Desire** Andy Gibb
85	**Dancing In The Street** David Bowie/ Mick Jagger		88	**Desire** U2
77	**Dancing Man** Q		98	**Desire** Sass Jordan
94	**Dancing On My Own Ground** Lawrence Gowan		78	**Desiree** Neil Diamond
86	**Dancing On The Ceiling** Lionel Richie		94	**Deuces Are Wild** Aerosmith
77	**Dancing Queen** ABBA		88	**Devil Inside** INXS
88	**Dancing Under A Latin Moon** Candi		79	**The Devil Went Down** Charlie Daniels Band
83	**Dancing With Myself** Billy Idol		76	**Devil Woman** Cliff Richard
84	**Dancing With Tears In My Eyes** Ultravox		93	**The Devil You Know** Jesus Jones
96	**Danger** Blahzay Blahzay		95	**Diamond Dreams** Base Is Bass
86	**Danger Zone** Kenny Loggins		89	**Diamond Mine** Blue Rodeo
90	**Dangerous** Roxette		88	**Diamond Sun** Glass Tiger
90	**Dangerous Times** Sue Medley		87	**Diamonds** Herb Alpert
85	**Dare Me** Pointer Sisters		92	**Diamonds & Pearls** Prince
90	**Dare To Fall In Love** Brent Bourgeois		94	**Diary Of A Madman** Gravediggaz
97	**Dark Horse** Amanda Marshall		82	**Did It In A Minute** Daryl Hall & John Oates
94	**Darling Be Home Soon** Barra MacNeils		99	**Did You Ever Think** R. Kelly
96	**Darling Pretty** Mark Knopfler		93	**Did You Give Enough Love** Celine Dion
94	**Daughter** Pearl Jam		89	**Didn't I (Blow Your Mind)** New Kids On The Block
88	**Day After Day** Blue Rodeo		87	**Didn't We Almost Have It All** Whitney Houston
91	**A Day In My Life** Lisette Melendez		95	**Died In Your Arms** Intonation featuring Joee
96	**Day Job** Gin Blossoms		97	**The Difference** Wallflowers
87	**Day-In Day-Out** David Bowie		86	**A Different Corner** George Michael
99	**The Day The World Went Away** Nine Inch Nails		96	**Diggin' A Hole** Big Sugar
77	**Daybreak** Barry Manilow		92	**Diggin' In The Dirt** Peter Gabriel
98	**Daydreamin'** Tatyana Ali		96	**Diggin' On You** TLC
79	**Days Gone Down** Gerry Rafferty		86	**Digging Your Scene** Blow Monkeys
77	**Daytime Friends** Kenny Rogers		98	**Digital** Goldie
77	**Dazz** Brick			

79	**Dim All The Lights** Donna Summer	94	**Do You Wanna Get Funky** C&C Music Factory
94	**Dirty Dawg** NKOTB		
90	**Dirty Deeds** Joan Jett	77	**Do You Wanna Make Love** Peter McCann
88	**Dirty Diana** Michael Jackson		
83	**Dirty Laundry** Don Henley	85	**Do You Want Crying** Katrina & The Waves
87	**Dirty Water** Rock & Hyde		
79	**Dirty White Boy** Foreigner	89	**The Doctor** Doobie Brothers
91	**Disappear** INXS	89	**Dr. Feelgood** Mötley Crüe
94	**Disarm** Smashing Pumpkins	83	**Dr. Heckyll & Mr. Jive** Men At Work
76	**Disco Duck Part 1** Rick Dees & His Cast Of Idiots	84	**Doctor! Doctor!** Thompson Twins
		91	**Doctorin' The Tardis** Timelords
78	**Disco Inferno** Trammps	79	**Does Your Mother Know** ABBA
76	**Disco Lady** Johnnie Taylor	84	**Doesn't Really Matter** Platinum Blonde
79	**Disco Nights** G.Q.		
97	**Discotheque** U2	98	**Dogwhistle Kwikmix** Various Artists
94	**Distant Sun** Crowded House	90	**Doing The Do** Betty Boo
93	**Ditty** Paperboy	76	**Dolannes Melodie** Jean-Claude Borelly
92	**Divine Thing** Soup Dragons		
91	**Do Anything** Natural Selection	89	**Domino Dancing** Pet Shop Boys
98	**Do For Love** 2Pac	87	**Dominoes** Robbie Nevil
92	**Do I Have To Say The Words?** Bryan Adams	84	**Don't Answer Me** Alan Parsons Project
79	**Do It Or Die** Atlanta Rhythm Section	80	**Don't Ask Me Why** Billy Joel
92	**Do It To Me** Lionel Richie	89	**Don't Ask Me Why** Eurythmics
90	**Do Me!** Bell Biv Devoe	88	**Don't Be Cruel** Cheap Trick
97	**Do Me Right** Mary Zilba	98	**Don't Be Stupid (You Know I Love You)** Shania Twain
80	**Do That To Me One More Time** Captain & Tennille		
		79	**Don't Bring Me Down** Electric Light Orchestra
91	**Do The Bartman** The Simpsons		
85	**Do They Know It's Christmas?** Band Aid	85	**Don't Come Around Here No More** Tom Petty & The Heartbreakers
90	**Do They Know It's Christmas?** Band Aid II	83	**Don't Cry** Asia
		91	**Don't Cry** Guns N' Roses
97	**Do To You** Bryan Adams	96	**Don't Cry** Seal
98	**Do What I Can** Sass Jordan	97	**Don't Cry For Me Argentina** Madonna
85	**Do What You Do** Jermaine Jackson	79	**Don't Cry Out Loud** Melissa Manchester
96	**Do What's Good For Me** 2 Unlimited		
77	**Do Ya** Electric Light Orchestra	80	**Don't Do Me Like That** Tom Petty
95	**Do Ya** Barney Bentall	87	**Don't Dream It's Over** Crowded House
87	**Do Ya Do Ya (Wanna Please Me)** Samantha Fox		
		80	**Don't Fall In Love With A Dreamer** Kenny Rogers/Kim Carnes
96	**Do Ya Own Thing** Camille		
98	**Do Ya Think I'm Sexy** N-Trance	76	**Don't Fear The Reaper** Blue Oyster Cult
82	**Do You Believe In Love** Huey Lewis & The News		
		82	**Don't Fight It** Kenny Loggins
92	**Do You Believe In Us** Jon Secada	86	**Don't Forget Me (When I'm Gone)** Glass Tiger
91	**Do You Feel Like I Feel** Belinda Carlisle		
		83	**Don't Forget To Dance** The Kinks
76	**Do You Feel Like We Do** Peter Frampton	86	**Don't Get Me Wrong** The Pretenders
		87	**Don't Give Up** Peter Gabriel/Kate Bush
97	**Do You Know (What It Takes)** Robyn		
88	**Do You Love Me** Contours	77	**Don't Give Up On Us** David Soul
97	**Do You Miss Me** Jocelyn Enriquez	97	**Don't Go Away** Oasis
97	**Do You Really Love Me** Jay Jay	90	**Don't Go Away Mad (Just Go Away)** Mötley Crüe
98	**Do You Really Want Me? (Show Respect)** Robyn		
		76	**Don't Go Breaking My Heart** Elton John/Kiki Dee
83	**Do You Really Want To Hurt Me?** Culture Club		
		91	**Don't Hold Back Your Love** Daryl Hall & John Oates
90	**Do You Remember?** Phil Collins		
99	**Do You Right** Joee	77	**Don't It Make My Brown Eyes Blue** Crystal Gayle
95	**Do You Sleep?** Lisa Loeb		

82	Don't It Make You Feel Headpins	98	Doo Wop (That Thing) Lauryn Hill
88	Don't Know What You Got Cinderella	76	A Dose Of Rock N' Roll Ringo Starr
97	Don't Leave Me Blackstreet	78	Double Vision Foreigner
77	Don't Leave Me This Way Thelma Houston	90	Doubleback ZZ Top
80	Don't Let Go Issac Hayes	99	Down So Long Jewel
97	Don't Let Go (Love) En Vogue	82	Down Under Men At Work
81	Don't Let Him Go REO Speedwagon	93	Down With The King Run-D.M.C.
83	Don't Let It End Styx	90	Downtown Train Rod Stewart
78	Don't Let Me Be Understood Santa Esmeralda	95	Downtown Venus PM Dawn
92	Don't Let The Sun Go Down On Me George Michael & Elton John	78	Dreadlock Holiday 10cc
		89	Dream Come True Frozen Ghost
		91	The Dream Is Still Alive Wilson Phillips
78	Don't Look Back Boston	91	A Dream Like Mine Bruce Cockburn
89	Don't Look Back Fine Young Cannibals	91	Dream Lover Rebel Pebbles
		76	Dream On Aerosmith
90	Don't Look Back Kenny MacLean	94	Dream On Dreamer Brand New Heavies
96	Don't Look Back In Anger Oasis		
85	Don't Lose My Number Phil Collins	80	Dream Police Cheap Trick
90	Don't Make Me Over Sybil	76	Dream Weaver Gary Wright
87	Don't Mean Nothing Richard Marx	77	Dreamboat Annie Heart
82	Don't Pay The Ferryman Chris DeBurgh	78	Dreamer Supertramp
		80	Dreamer Supertramp
89	Don't Rush Me Taylor Dayne	96	Dreamer's Dream Tom Cochrane
88	Don't Shed A Tear Paul Carrack	89	Dreamin' Vanessa Williams
97	Don't Speak Clueless	79	Dreaming Blondie
97	Don't Speak No Doubt	80	Dreaming Cliff Richard
80	Don't Stand So Close To Me The Police	88	Dreaming OMD
		96	Dreaming Of You Selena
86	Don't Stand So Close To Me '86 The Police	93	Dreamlover Mariah Carey
		77	Dreams Fleetwood Mac
77	Don't Stop Fleetwood Mac	93	Dreams Gabrielle
81	Don't Stop Believin' Journey	94	Dreams The Cranberries
92	Don't Stop Now Love & Sas	86	Dreamtime Daryl Hall & John Oates
76	Don't Stop The Music Bay City Rollers	85	Dress You Up Madonna
98	Don't Stop The Music Playa	89	Dressed For Success Roxette
79	Don't Stop Til You Get Enough Michael Jackson	97	Drinking In L.A. Bran Van 3000
		84	Drive The Cars
93	Don't Take Away My Heaven Aaron Neville	92	Drive R.E.M.
		79	Driver's Seat Sniff N' The Tears
95	Don't Take It Personal Monica	80	Drivin' My Life Away Eddie Rabbitt
92	Don't Talk Just Kiss Right Said Fred	90	Drop The Needle Maestro Fresh-Wes
82	Don't Talk To Strangers Rick Springfield	98	Drowned World/Substitute For Love Madonna
89	Don't Tell Me Lies Breathe	97	Drugs Don't Work The Verve
91	Don't Treat Me Bad Firehouse	88	Dude (Looks Like A Lady) Aerosmith
94	Don't Turn Around Ace Of Base	78	Dust In The Wind Kansas
93	Don't Walk Away Jade	84	Dynamite Jermaine Jackson
90	Don't Wanna Fall In Love Jane Child	75	Dynomite-Part 1 Tony Camillo's Bazuka
89	Don't Wanna Lose You Gloria Estefan		
96	Don't Wanna Lose You Lionel Richie	97	D'You Know What I Mean Oasis
77	Don't Worrry Baby B.J. Thomas		
88	Don't Worry, Be Happy Bobby McFerrin		

E

85	Don't You (Forget About Me) Simple Minds	96	The Earth, The Sun, The Rain Color Me Badd
90	Don't You Come Crying Linear	94	Ease My Mind Arrested Development
88	Don't You Know What The Night Can Do? Stevie Winwood	77	Easy Commodores
		93	Easy Faith No More
82	Don't You Want Me Human League	85	Easy Lover Phillip Bailey/Phil Collins
88	Don't You Want Me Jody Watley	87	Easy To Tame Kim Mitchell
		84	Eat It "Weird Al" Yankovic
		95	Eat My Brain Odds

82	**Ebony & Ivory** Paul McCartney (With Stevie Wonder)	82	**Even The Nights Are Better** Air Supply
78	**Ebony Eyes** Bob Welch	78	**An Everlasting Love** Andy Gibb
96	**E-Bow The Letter** R.E.M.	89	**Everlasting Love** Howard Jones
80	**Echo Beach** Martha & The Muffins	95	**Everlasting Love** Gloria Estefan
85	**Edge Of A Dream** Joe Cocker	79	**Every 1's A Winner** Hot Chocolate
86	**Edge Of Heaven** Wham!	75	**Every Bit Of Love** Ken Tobias
82	**Edge Of Seventeen** Stevie Nicks	83	**Every Breath You Take** The Police
77	**Edge Of Universe** Bee Gees	95	**Every Day Of The Week** Jade
78	**Ego** Elton John	91	**Every Heartbeat** Amy Grant
82	**867-5309/Jenny** Tommy Tutone	89	**Every Little Step** Bobby Brown
89	**18 & Life** Skid Row	90	**Every Little Tear** Paul Janz
96	**18 Til I Die** Bryan Adams	90	**Every Little Thing** Jeff Lynne
76	**Eighteen With A Bullet** Pete Wingfield	81	**Every Little Thing She Does Is Magic** The Police
85	**Election Day** Arcadia	99	**Every Morning** Sugar Ray
83	**Electric Avenue** Eddy Grant	89	**Every Rose Has Its Thorn** Poison
97	**Electric Barbarella** Duran Duran	95	**Every Shade Of Blue** Bananarama
88	**Electric Blue** Icehouse	78	**(Every Time I Turn) Back In Love Again** L.T.D.
89	**Electric Youth** Debbie Gibson	81	**Every Woman In The World** Air Supply
97	**Electro Bank** Chemical Brothers		
97	**Elegantly Wasted** INXS	97	**Everybody (Backstreet's Back)** Backstreet Boys
81	**Elvira** Oak Ridge Boys		
78	**Emotion** Samantha Sang	96	**Everybody Be Somebody** Ruffneck
92	**An Emotion Away** Alanis	90	**Everybody Everybody** Black Box
86	**Emotion In Motion** Ric Ocasek	87	**Everybody Have Fun Tonight** Wang Chung
80	**Emotional Rescue** Rolling Stones		
91	**Emotions** Mariah Carey	93	**Everybody Hurts** R.E.M.
82	**Emotions In Motion** Billy Squier	92	**Everybody Move** Cathy Dennis
90	**The Emperor's New Clothes** Sinead O'Connor	91	**Everybody Plays The Fool** Aaron Neville
82	**Empty Garden (Hey Hey Johnny)** Elton John	94	**Everybody Say Love** Mitsou
		85	**Everybody Wants To Rule The World** Tears For Fears
89	**The End Of The Innocence** Don Henley	92	**Everybody's Free (To Feel Good)** Rozalla
89	**End Of The Line** Traveling Wilburys		
92	**End Of The Road** Boyz II Men	99	**Everybody's Free (To Wear Sunscreen)** Baz Luhrmann
95	**End Of The World** The Waltons		
81	**Endless Love** Diana Ross & Lionel Richie	99	**Everybody's Free (To Wear Suncreen)** 411
95	**Endless Love** Luther Vandross/Mariah Carey	81	**Everybody's Got To Learn Sometime** Korgis
88	**Endless Summer Nights** Richard Marx	94	**Everyday** Phil Collins
		83	**Everyday I Write The Book** Elvis Costello/The Attractions
92	**Enid** Barenaked Ladies		
90	**Enjoy The Silence** Depeche Mode	97	**Everyday Is A Winding Road** Sheryl Crow
77	**Enjoy Yourself** Jacksons		
82	**Enough Is Enough** April Wine	92	**Everyday People** Arrested Development
96	**Enough Love** Kim Stockwood		
91	**Enter Sandman** Metallica	99	**Everyone Falls In Love** Tanto Metro
99	**The EP** First Base	91	**Everyone's A Winner** Bootsauce
90	**Epic** Faith No More	90	**Everything** Jody Watley
92	**Erotica** Madonna	92	**Everything About You** Ugly Kid Joe
90	**Escapade** Janet Jackson	92	**Everything Changes** Kathy Troccoli
80	**Escape (The Pina Colada Song)** Rupert Holmes	96	**Everything Falls Apart** Dog's Eye View
89	**Eternal Flame** Bangles	91	**(Everything I Do) I Do It For You** Bryan Adams
97	**Euphoria (Firefly)** Delerium		
86	**Eurasian Eyes** Corey Hart	87	**Everything I Own** Boy George
92	**Even Better Than The Real Thing** U2	86	**Everything In My Heart** Corey Hart
83	**Even Now** Bob Seger		

85	Everything She Wants Wham!		95	Fat Boy Max-A-Million
98	Everything To Everyone Everclear		88	Father Figure George Michael
96	Everything You've Done Wrong Sloan		96	Fed Up House Of Pain
88	Everything Your Heart Desires Daryl Hall & John Oates		99	Feel Alright Troy Brown
			86	Feel It Again Honeymoon Suite
			75	Feel Like Makin' Love Bad Company
92	Everything's Gonna Be Alright Naughty By Nature		97	Feel So Good Mase
			95	Feel So High Des'ree
98	Everything's Gonna Be Alright Sweetbox		91	Feel Your Love Alanis
			75	Feelings Morris Albert
97	Everytime I Close My Eyes Babyface		91	Feels Good Tony! Toni! Tone!
83	Everytime I See Your Picture Luba		94	Feels Like Heaven Urban Cookie Collective
85	Everytime You Go Away Paul Young			
88	Everywhere Fleetwood Mac		77	Feels Like The First Time Foreigner
98	Everywhere Bran Van 3000		78	Feels So Good Chuck Mangione
76	Evil Woman Electric Light Orchestra		96	Feels So Good Lina Santiago
96	Exhale (Shoop Shoop) Whitney Houston		76	Fernando ABBA
			93	Fields Of Gold Sting
90	Expedition Sailor Kim Mitchell		77	Fiesta Raffaella Carra
97	Experience Prodigy		76	A Fifth Of Beethoven Walter Murphy And The Big Apple Band
89	Express Yourself Madonna			
90	Expression Salt-N-Pepa		94	54-46 One
93	Exterminate Snap		92	57 Channels Bruce Springsteen
82	Eye In The Sky Alan Parsons Project		76	50 Ways To Leave Your Lover Paul Simon
82	Eye Of The Tiger Survivor			
82	Eyes Of A Stranger The Payola$		75	Fight The Power (Part 1) Isley Brothers
84	Eyes Without A Face Billy Idol			
			77	Fighting On The Side Of Love THP Orchestra
	F			
			87	The Final Countdown Europe
94	Fa All Y'All Da Brat		92	Finally CeCe Peniston
96	Fable Robert Miles		82	Find Another Fool Quarterflash
86	Face The Face Pete Townshend		84	Fine Fine Day Tony Carey
81	Fade Away Bruce Springsteen		80	Fine State Of Affairs Burton Cummings
91	Fading Like A Flower Roxette			
95	Fairground Simply Red		79	Fire Pointer Sisters
87	Faith George Michael		87	Fire Bruce Springsteen & The E Street Band
92	Faithful Go West			
83	Faithfully Journey		81	Fire And Ice Pat Benatar
96	Fall Ministry		98	Fire Escape Fastball
95	Fall Away My Brilliant Beast		92	The Fire Inside Bob Seger
94	Fall Down Toad The Wet Sprocket		80	Fire Lake Bob Seger
96	Fall From Grace Amanda Marshall		89	Fire Woman The Cult
83	Fall In Love With Me Earth, Wind & Fire		96	Fired Up! Funky Green Dog
			97	Firestarter Prodigy
75	Fallin' In Love Hamilton, Joe Frank & Reynolds		77	First Cut Is The Deepest Rod Stewart
			98	The First Night Monica
96	Fallin' In Love La Bouche		91	The First Noel Crash Test Dummies
76	Falling Apart Marmalade		91	The First Time Surface
97	Falling In Love (Is Hard On The Knees) Aerosmith		92	A Fishing Tale Grapes Of Wrath
			94	5 Days In May Blue Rodeo
75	Fame David Bowie		89	Five Long Years Colin James
94	Family Affair Shabba Ranks		98	5 Steps Dru Hill
76	Fanny (Be Tender With My Love) Bee Gees		97	Fix Blackstreet
			88	The Flame Cheap Trick
94	Fantastic Voyage Coolio		97	Flamenco Tragically Hip
82	Fantasy Aldo Nova		87	Flames Of Paradise Jennifer Rush/ Elton John
95	Fantasy Mariah Carey			
83	Far From Over Frank Stallone		83	Flashdance...What A Feelin' Irene Cara
93	Fare Thee Well Love Rankin Family			
88	Fast Car Tracy Chapman		84	Flesh For Fantasy Billy Idol
96	Fastlove George Michael			

93	**Flex** Mad Cobra		97	**The Freshman** Verve Pipe
86	**Flippin' To The "A" Side** Cats Can Fly		92	**Friday, I'm In Love** The Cure
77	**Float On** Floaters		89	**Friends** Jody Watley
96	**Flood** Jars Of Clay		86	**Friends And Lovers** Gloria Loring/Carl Anderson
93	**The Floor** Johnny Gill		91	**Friends Forever** Candi & The Backbeat
91	**The Fly** U2		81	**Friends Of Mr. Cairo** Jon & Vangelis
97	**The Fly** U2		90	**From A Distance** Bette Midler
97	**Fly** Sugar Ray		76	**From New York To LA** Patsy Gallant
77	**Fly At Night** Chilliwack		98	**From This Moment On** Shania Twain
76	**Fly Away** John Denver		98	**Frozen** Madonna
99	**Fly Away** Lenny Kravitz		98	**Full Cooperation** Def Squad
77	**Fly Like An Eagle** Steve Miller		96	**Funk Phenomenon** Armand Van Helden
96	**Fly Like An Eagle** Seal		94	**Funkdafied** Da Brat
75	**Fly Robin Fly** Silver Convention		89	**Funky Cold Medina** Tone Loc
77	**Flying** Hometown Band		87	**Funky Town** Pseudo Echo
95	**Flying To The Moon** Emjay		80	**Funkytown** Lipps Inc.
96	**Follow You Down** Gin Blossoms		91	**Future Love Paradise** Seal
78	**Follow You Follow Me** Genesis		87	**The Future's So Bright, I Gotta Wear Shades** Timbuk 3
98	**The Fonz** Smash Mouth			
78	**Fool (If You Think It's Over)** Chris Rea			

G

89	**Fool For Your Lovin'** Whitesnake		79	**The Gambler** Kenny Rogers
80	**Fool In The Rain** Led Zeppelin		91	**Games** New Kids On The Block
76	**Fool To Cry** Rolling Stones		75	**Games People Play** Spinners
76	**Fooled Around And Fell In Love** Elvin Bishop		94	**Games People Play** Inner Circle
88	**Foolish Beat** Debbie Gibson		80	**Games Without Frontiers** Peter Gabriel
97	**Foolish Games** Jewel		93	**Gangsta Bitch** Apache
84	**Footloose** Kenny Loggins		93	**Gansta** Bell Biv Devoe
87	**For Tonight** Nancy Martinez		95	**Gansta's Paradise** Coolio featuring LV
91	**For You** The Outfield		97	**Gasoline** Moist
97	**For You I Will** Monica		95	**Geek Stink Breath** Green Day
81	**For Your Eyes Only** Sheena Easton		95	**Gel** Collective Soul
98	**Forest Fire** David Usher		81	**Gemini Dream** Moody Blues
90	**Forever** Kiss		76	**General Hand Grenade** Trooper
96	**Forever** Mariah Carey		99	**Genie In A Bottle** Christina Aguilera
79	**Forever In Blue Jeans** Neil Diamond		95	**Genuine** Mae Moore
92	**Forever Love** Color Me Badd		90	**Georgia On My Mind** Michael Bolton
92	**Forever My Lady** Jodeci		91	**Get A Leg Up** John Mellencamp
88	**Forever Young** Rod Stewart		90	**Get A Life** Soul II Soul
89	**Forever Your Girl** Paula Abdul		98	**Get At Me Dog** DMX
86	**(Forever) Live And Die** OMD		93	**Get Away** Bobby Brown
85	**Fortress Around Your Heart** Sting		76	**Get Closer** Seals & Crofts
99	**Fortunate** Maxwell		79	**Get Down** Gene Chandler
94	**Found Out About You** Gin Blossoms		96	**Get Down (You're The One For Me)** Backstreet Boys
97	**4 Seasons Of Loneliness** Boyz II Men		94	**Get Down To It** TBTBT
99	**416/905 (T.O. Party Anthem)** Maestro feat. Latoya & Miranda		75	**Get Down Tonight** KC & The Sunshine Band
76	**Fox On The Run** Sweet		91	**Get Here** Oleta Adams
93	**Freak Me** Silk		97	**Get In My Car** Moxy Fruvous
97	**Free** Ultra Nate		85	**Get It On (Bang A Gong)** Power Station
96	**Free As A Bird** The Beatles		79	**Get It Right Next Time** Gerry Rafferty
96	**Free To Decide** The Cranberries		78	**Get Off** Foxy
92	**Free Your Mind** En Vogue		88	**Get Outta My Dreams, Get Into My Car** Billy Ocean
85	**Freedom** Wham!		94	**Get Over It** Eagles
91	**Freedom** George Michael			
99	**Freek On A Leash** Korn			
85	**Freeway Of Love** Aretha Franklin			
82	**Freeze-Frame** J. Geils Band			
90	**French Kiss** Lil Louis			
85	**Fresh** Kool & The Gang			

96	Get Together Big Mountain	76	Give Me Your Money Bachman-Turner Overdrive
97	Get Up Byron Stingly		
76	Get Up And Boogie Silver Convention	76	Give My Love To Anne Garfield
90	Get Up! (Before The Night Is Over) Technotronic featuring Ya Kid K	92	Give U My Heart Babyface
		98	Given To Fly Pearl Jam
97	Get Your Gunn Marilyn Manson	89	Giving Away A Miracle Luba
76	Getaway Earth, Wind & Fire	92	Giving Him Something He Can Feel En Vogue
85	Getcha Back Beach Boys		
91	Gett Off Prince & The New Power Generation	81	Giving It Up For Your Love Delbert McClinton
98	Gettin' Jiggy Wit It Will Smith	89	Giving Up On Love Rick Astley
90	Getting Away With It Electronic	90	Giving You The Benefit Pebbles
79	Getting Closer Paul McCartney & Wings	84	The Glamorous Life Sheila E.
		83	Gloria Laura Branigan
94	Getto Jam Domino	85	Glory Days Bruce Springsteen
98	Ghetto Supastar (That Is What You Are) Pras Michel featuring ODB & introducing Mya	86	Glory Of Love Peter Cetera
		99	Glorytimes Portishead
		92	Go Back To Your Woods Robbie Robertson
89	Ghost Town Cheap Trick		
84	Ghostbusters Ray Parker Jr.	98	Go Deep Janet
96	Gift Shop Tragically Hip	84	Go For Soda Kim Mitchell
93	Gimme Luv David Morales	86	Go Home Stevie Wonder
80	Gimme Some Lovin' Blues Brothers	94	Go On Move '94 Reel 2 Real
96	Gin Palace Barney Bentall	85	Go To Pieces Paul Janz
89	Girl I'm Gonna Miss You Milli Vanilli	79	Go West Village People
93	Girl I've Been Hurt Snow	93	Go West Pet Shop Boys
82	The Girl Is Mine Michael Jackson/Paul McCartney	77	Go Your Own Way Fleetwood Mac
		96	God Bless The Child Shania Twain
95	A Girl Like You Edwyn Collins	96	God Made Me Chantal Kreviazuk
79	Girl Of My Dreams Bram Tchaikovsky	99	(God Must Have Spent) A Little More Time On You 'N Sync
99	Girl Of My Dreams The Moffatts		
90	Girl With A Problem Northern Pikes	94	God Shuffled His Feet Crash Test Dummies
89	Girl You Know It's True Milli Vanilli		
94	Girl You'll Be A Woman Soon Urge Overkill	92	Goin' Back Again Sass Jordan
		79	Gold John Stewart
78	Girl's School/Mull Of Kintyre Paul McCartney & Wings	83	Gold Spandau Ballet
		96	Gold Prince
88	Girlfriend Pebbles	76	Golden Years David Bowie
99	Girlfriend/Boyfriend Blackstreet featuring Janet	96	Goldeneye Tina Turner
		99	Goliath Melanie Doane
84	Girls Dwight Twilley	98	Gone Til November Wyclef Jean
94	Girls & Boys Blur	77	Gone Too Far England Dan & John Ford Coley
85	Girls Are More Fun Ray Parker Jr.		
84	Girls Just Wanna Have Fun Cyndi Lauper	77	Gonna Fly Now Maynard Fergusson
		91	Gonna Make You Sweat (Everybody Dance Now) C&C Music Factory Featuring Freedom Williams
83	Girls Night Out Toronto		
87	Girls, Girls, Girls Mötley Crüe		
77	Give A Little Bit Supertramp	95	Good Better Than Ezra
76	Give A Little Love Ken Tobias	96	The Good Catches Up Lawrence Gowan
95	Give It 2 You Da Brat		
92	Give It All Up Darby Mills	92	Good Enough Bobby Brown
99	Give It To You Jordan Knight	94	Good Enough Sarah McLachlan
90	Give It Up Hothouse Flowers	97	Good Enough Dodgy
91	Give It Up Colin James	92	Good For Me Amy Grant
92	Give It Up Wilson Phillips	96	Good Friday Black Crowes
94	Give It Up The Goodmen	79	Good Girls Don't The Knack
99	Give It Up Jacynthe featuring KC	86	A Good Heart Feargal Sharkey
93	Give It Up Turn It Loose En Vogue	95	Good Intentions Toad The Wet Sprocket
96	Give Me One Reason Tracy Chapman		
80	Give Me The Night George Benson	95	Good Mother Jann Arden
		92	Good Stuff The B-52's

89	Good Thing Fine Young Cannibals		95	Hand In My Pocket Alanis Morissette
79	Good Times Chic		92	Hand On The Pump Cypress Hill
89	Good Times Tom Cochrane		89	Handle With Care Traveling Wilburys
94	Good Times Edie Brickell		99	Hands Jewel
93	Good Times With Bad Boys Boy Krazy		98	Hands Of Time Temperence featuring Lorraine
91	Good To The Last Drop Helix		90	Hands On Lee Aaron
91	Good Together Candi & The Backbeat		88	Hands To Heaven Breathe
91	Good Vibrations Marky Mark & The Funky Bunch		88	Hands Up Sway
			77	Handy Man James Taylor
98	Goodbye Spice Girls		91	Hang In Long Enough Phil Collins
78	Goodbye Girl David Gates		85	Hang On To Your Love Sade
98	Goodbye Girl Pluto		89	Hangin' Tough New Kids On The Block
79	Goodbye Stranger Supertramp		90	Hanky Panky Madonna
93	Goodnight Song Tears For Fears		77	Happier Paul Anka
79	Goodnight Tonight Paul McCartney & Wings		78	Happy Anniversary Little River Band
			76	Happy Days Pratt & McClain
83	Goody Two Shoes Adam Ant		96	Happy Days P.J.
85	Goonies 'R' Good Enough Cyndi Lauper		84	Hard Habit To Break Chicago
			99	Hard Knock Life Jay-Z
87	Got My Mind Set On You George Harrison		77	Hard Luck Woman Kiss
			94	Hard Luck Woman Garth Brooks
97	Got Til It's Gone Janet		89	Hard Sun Indio
79	Got To Be Real Cheryl Lynn		91	Hard To Handle Black Crowes
90	Got To Get Leila K		81	Hard To Say Dan Fogelberg
76	Got To Get You Into My Life The Beatles		82	Hard To Say I'm Sorry Chicago
			97	Hard To Say I'm Sorry Az Yet featuring Peter Cetera
78	Got To Get You Into My Life Earth, Wind & Fire		82	Harden My Heart Quarterflash
77	Got To Give It Up (Part 1) Marvin Gaye		99	The Hardest Thing 98°
			76	Harlem Andy Kim
80	Got To Love Somebody Sister Sledge		86	Harlem Shuffle Rolling Stones
97	Gotham City R. Kelly		89	Harry Houdini Kon Kan
79	Gotta Go Home Boney M		93	Harvest Moon Neil Young
79	Gotta Serve Somebody Bob Dylan		94	Hasn't Hit Me Yet Blue Rodeo
94	Grace Too Tragically Hip		90	Haunted Heart Alias
92	Grade Nine Barenaked Ladies		91	Have A Heart Celine Dion
94	The Grand Tour Aaron Neville		98	Have Fun, Go Mad! Blair
78	Grease Frankie Valli		93	Have I Told You Lately Rod Stewart
96	Grease Megamix John Travolta & Olivia Newton-John		92	Have You Ever Needed Someone So Bad Def Leppard
95	Greasy Jungle Tragically Hip		95	Have You Ever Really Loved A Woman? Bryan Adams
86	The Greatest Love Of All Whitney Houston		99	Have You Ever? Brandy
90	Groove Is In The Heart Deee-Lite		90	Have You Seen Her M.C. Hammer
78	The Groove Line Heatwave		92	Hazard Richard Marx
94	Groove Thang Zhane		88	Hazy Shade Of Winter Bangles
88	Groovy Kind Of Love Phil Collins		96	He Liked To Feel It Crash Test Dummies
91	Groovy Train The Farm		80	He's So Shy Pointer Sisters
76	Grow Some Funk/Feel Like A Bullet Elton John		79	He's The Greatest Dancer Sister Sledge
92	Guard Your Grill Naughty By Nature		96	Head Over Feet Alanis Morissette
81	Guilty Barbra Streisand & Barry Gibb		84	Head Over Heels Go-Go's
95	Guns And God Lawrence Gowan		85	Head Over Heels Tears For Fears
82	Gypsy Fleetwood Mac		92	Head Over Heels Frozen Ghost
91	Gypsy Woman (She's Homeless) Crystal Waters		97	Head Over Heels Allure
			87	Head To Toe Lisa Lisa & Cult Jam With Full Force

H

84	Had A Dream (Sleeping With The Enemy) Roger Hodgson		93	Heading West Mitsou
			91	Headlong Queen

93	**Heal The World** Michael Jackson	81	**Her Town Too** James Taylor with J.D. Souther
89	**Healing Hands** Elton John		
94	**Healing Hands** Alan Frew	95	**Here Comes The Hotstepper** Ini Kamoze
77	**Heard It In A Love Song** Marshall Tucker Band		
		79	**Here Comes The Night** Nick Gilder
83	**Heart & Soul** Huey Lewis & The News	84	**Here Comes The Rain Again** Eurythmics
87	**Heart And Soul** T'Pau		
82	**Heart Attack** Olivia Newton-John	91	**Here I Am (Come And Take Me)** UB40
90	**Heart Like A Wheel** Human League		
79	**Heart Of Glass** Blondie	81	**Here I Am (Just When I Thought I Was Over You)** Air Supply
84	**The Heart Of Rock & Roll** Huey Lewis & The News		
		95	**Here I Go** 2 Unlimited
90	**Heart Of Stone** Cher	87	**Here I Go Again** Whitesnake
90	**Heart Of Stone** Taylor Dayne	90	**Here We Are** Gloria Estefan & Miami Sound Machine
90	**Heart Of The Matter** Don Henley		
92	**Hearts Don't Think (They Feel)!** Natural Selection	91	**Here We Go** C&C Music Factory Presents Freedom Williams and Zelma Davis
87	**Heartache Around The World** Elton John		
		93	**Here We Go Again** Portrait
83	**Heartache Avenue** The Maisonettes	78	**Here You Come Again** Dolly Parton
79	**Heartache Tonight** Eagles	93	**Hero** David Crosby
86	**Heartbeat** Don Johnson	94	**Hero** Mariah Carey
90	**Heartbeat** Seduction	96	**Hero Of The Day** Metallica
99	**Heartbreak Hotel** Whitney Houston (feat. Faith Evans & Kelly Price)	98	**Heroes** Wallflowers
		96	**Heroine** Wild Strawberries
80	**Heartbreaker** Pat Benatar	89	**Hey Baby** Henry Lee Summer
82	**Heartbreaker** Dionne Warwick	99	**Hey Boy Hey Girl** Chemical Brothers
82	**Heartlight** Neil Diamond	78	**Hey Deanie** Shaun Cassidy
81	**Hearts** Marty Balin	94	**Hey D.J.** Lighter Shade Of Brown
95	**Hearts Filthy Lesson** David Bowie	91	**Hey Donna** Rythm Syndicate
81	**Hearts On Fire** Randy Meisner	93	**Hey Jealousy** Gin Blossoms
87	**Hearts On Fire** Bryan Adams	99	**Hey Leonardo (She Likes Me For Me)** Blessid Union Of Souls
85	**The Heat Is On** Glenn Frey		
82	**Heat Of The Moment** Asia	96	**Hey Lover** L.L. Cool J
87	**Heat Of The Night** Bryan Adams	89	**Hey Men** Men Without Hats
75	**Heatwave** Linda Ronstadt	93	**Hey Mr. D.J.** Zhane
85	**Heaven** Bryan Adams	81	**Hey, Nineteen** Steely Dan
89	**Heaven** Warrant	98	**Hey Now Now** Swirl 360
98	**Heaven** Nu Flavor	91	**Hey Stoopid** Alice Cooper
89	**Heaven Help Us** Deon Estus	75	**(Hey Won't You Play) Another Somebody Done Somebody Wrong Song** B.J. Thomas
93	**Heaven Helps** Lenny Kravitz		
86	**Heaven In Your Eyes** Loverboy		
87	**Heaven Is A Place On Earth** Belinda Carlisle	75	**Hey You** Bachman Turner Overdrive
		90	**Hey You** London Quireboys
79	**Heaven Knows** Donna Summer	92	**High** The Cure
93	**Heaven Knows** Luther Vandross	96	**High & Dry** Radiohead
76	**Heaven Must Be Missing An Angel** Tavares	84	**High Energy** Evelyn Thomas
		91	**High Enough** Damn Yankees
79	**Heaven Must Have Sent You** Bonnie Pointer	84	**High On Emotion** Chris Deburgh
		85	**High On You** Survivor
77	**Heaven's Just A Sin Away** The Kendalls	81	**High School Confidential** Rough Trade
92	**Heavy Fuel** Dire Straits	77	**High School Dance** Sylvers
90	**Helene** Roch Voisine	91	**High Wire** Rolling Stones
94	**Hell Comes Down** Terminator X	93	**Higher Ground** UB40
84	**Hello** Lionel Richie	86	**Higher Love** Stevie Winwood
81	**Hello Again** Neil Diamond	97	**Higher Love** Capitol Sound
77	**Hello Stranger** Yvonne Elliman	95	**Higher State Of Conciousness** Wink
92	**Helluva** Brotherhood Creed	91	**Highwire** Rolling Stones
77	**Help Is On Its Way** Little River Band	75	**Hijack** Herbie Mann
75	**Help Me Rhonda** Johnny Rivers	80	**Him** Rupert Holmes

93	Hip Hop Hooray Naughty By Nature		78	Hot Legs Rod Stewart
87	Hip To Be Square Huey Lewis & The News		77	Hot Line Sylvers
90	Hippy Chick Soho		80	Hot Rod Hearts Robbie Dupree
88	Hippy Hippy Shake Georgia Satellites		79	Hot Shot Karen Young
91	Hit Me Like A Hammer Huey Lewis & The News		79	Hot Stuff Donna Summer
			79	Hot Summer Nights Night
96	Hit Me Off New Edition		77	Hotel California Eagles
80	Hit Me With Your Best Shot Pat Benatar		87	Hourglass Squeeze
			90	House Of Fire Alice Cooper
75	Hit The Road Jack Stampeders		95	House Of Love Amy Grant & Vince Gill
82	Hold Me Fleetwood Mac		92	How About That Bad Company
99	Hold Me Brian McKnight		90	How Am I Supposed To Live Without You Michael Bolton
84	Hold Me Now Thompson Twins			
88	Hold Me Now One To One		96	How Bizarre OMC
95	Hold Me, Thrill Me, Kiss Me, Kill Me U2		89	How Can I Fall Breathe
			90	How Can We Be Lovers Michael Bolton
95	Hold My Hand Hootie & The Blowfish		93	How Could You Want Him Spin Doctors
79	Hold On Ian Gomm			
79	Hold On Triumph		77	How Deep Is Your Love Bee Gees
82	Hold On Santana		98	How Deep Is Your Love Dru Hill
90	Hold On En Vogue		97	How Do I Live LeAnn Rimes
90	Hold On Wilson Phillips		80	How Do I Make You Linda Ronstadt
95	Hold On Jamie Walters		96	How Do U Want It 2Pac
77	Hold On Baby Charity Brown		92	How Do You Do Roxette
92	Hold On My Heart Genesis		93	How Do You Talk To An Angel The Heights
81	Hold On Tight Electric Light Orchestra			
88	Hold On To The Nights Richard Marx		98	(How Does It Feel To Be) On Top Of The World England United
79	Hold The Line Toto			
91	Hold You Tight Tara Kemp		95	How High Method Man
75	Holdin' On To Yesterday Ambrosia		93	How I'm Coming L.L. Cool J
86	Holding Back The Years Simply Red		75	How Long Ace
84	Holding Out For A Hero Bonnie Tyler		91	How Long Can A Man Be Strong Jeff Healey Band
91	Hole Hearted Extreme			
97	Hole In My Soul Aerosmith		86	How Many (Rivers To Cross) Luba
84	Holiday Madonna		79	How Much I Feel Ambrosia
87	Holiday Rap M.C. Miker "G" And Dee Jay Sven		77	How Much Love Leo Sayer
			75	How Sweet It Is James Taylor
99	Holla Holla Ja Rule		91	How To Dance Bingoboys featuring Princessa
78	Hollywood Nights Bob Seger			
97	The Holy River Prince		86	How Will I Know Whitney Houston
97	Home Depeche Mode		79	How You Gonna See Me Now Alice Cooper
99	Home Alone R. Kelly			
79	Home And Dry Gerry Rafferty		98	How's It Gonna Be Third Eye Blind
75	The Homecoming Hagood Hardy		86	Human Human League
98	Homeless Love Inc.		99	Human Being Seal
79	Honesty Billy Joel		96	Human Beings Van Halen
97	Honey Mariah Carey		83	Human Nature Michael Jackson
98	Hooch Everything		95	Human Nature Madonna
96	Hook Blues Traveler		83	Human Race Red Rider
93	Hope Of Deliverance Paul McCartney		83	Human Touch Rick Springfield
93	Hopelessly Rick Astley		92	Human Touch/Better Days Bruce Springsteen
78	Hopelessly Devoted To You Olivia Newton-John			
			93	Human Wheels John Mellencamp
78	Hot Blooded Foreigner		92	Humpin' Around Bobby Brown
78	Hot Child In The City Nick Gilder		90	Humpty Dance Digital Underground
92	Hot Fun In The Summertime Beach Boys		88	Hungry Eyes Eric Carmen
			80	Hungry Heart Bruce Springsteen
83	Hot Girls In Love Loverboy		83	Hungry Like The Wolf Duran Duran
84	Hot Hot Hot Arrow		76	Hurt Elvis Presley
88	Hot In The City Billy Idol		82	Hurt So Good John Cougar

90	Hurting Kind Robert Plant	76	I Do I Do I Do I Do ABBA
80	Hurts So Bad Linda Ronstadt	76	I Don't Believe In Miracles C.B. Victoria
98	Hurts To Love You Philosopher Kings		
75	The Hustle Van McCoy & The Soul City Symphony	93	I Don't Care Shakespear's Sister
		98	I Don't Ever Want To See You Again Uncle Sam
84	Hyperactive Thomas Dolby		
97	Hypnotize Notorious B.I.G.	90	I Don't Have The Heart James Ingram
87	Hypnotize Me Wang Chung	91	I Don't Know Anybody Else Black Box
88	Hysteria Def Leppard		
		79	I Don't Like Mondays Boomtown Rats
		88	I Don't Mind At All Bourgeois Tagg
		81	I Don't Need You Kenny Rogers
91	I Adore Mi Amor Color Me Badd	96	I Don't Need Your Love Angelina
81	I Ain't Gonna Stand For It Stevie Wonder	91	I Don't Wanna Cry Mariah Carey
		83	I Don't Wanna Dance Eddy Grant
97	I Ain't Mad At Cha 2 Pac	77	I Don't Wanna Forget You Denise McCann
90	I Am A Wild Party Kim Mitchell		
86	I Am By Your Side Corey Hart	88	I Don't Wanna Go On With You Like That Elton John
91	I Am Here Grapes Of Wrath		
95	I Am So Ordinary Paula Cole	88	I Don't Wanna Live Without Your Love Chicago
89	I Beg Your Pardon Kon Kan		
82	I Believe Chilliwack	97	I Don't Want To Toni Braxton
93	I Believe Bon Jovi	93	I Don't Want To Fight Tina Turner
95	I Believe Blessid Union Of Souls	88	I Don't Want To Live Without You Foreigner
95	I Believe Happy Clappers		
97	I Believe I Can Fly R. Kelly	98	I Don't Want To Miss A Thing Aerosmith
97	I Believe In You And Me Whitney Houston		
		96	I Don't Want To Think About It Wild Strawberries
75	(I Believe) There's Nothing Stronger Than Our Love Paul Anka		
		97	I Don't Want To Wait Paula Cole
84	I Can Dream About You Dan Hartman	88	I Don't Want Your Love Duran Duran
96	I Can Hear You Carolyn Arends	99	I Drive Myself Crazy 'N Sync
95	I Can Love You Like That All-4-One	89	I Drove All Night Cyndi Lauper
94	I Can See Cleary Now Jimmy Cliff	92	I Drove All Night Roy Orbison
99	I Can't Foxy Brown	84	I Feel For You Chaka Khan
92	I Can't Dance Genesis	77	I Feel Love Donna Summer
82	I Can't Go For That Daryl Hall & John Oates	89	I Feel The Earth Move Martika
		93	I Feel You Depeche Mode
84	I Can't Hold Back Survivor	97	I Fell In Love Rockell
91	I Can't Make You Love Me Bonnie Raitt	96	I Finally Found Someone Bryan Adams & Barbra Streisand
81	I Can't Stand It Eric Clapton		
79	I Can't Stand It No More Peter Frampton	88	I Found Someone Cher
		98	I Get Lonely Janet
78	I Can't Stand The Rain Eruption	88	I Get Weak Belinda Carlisle
98	I Can't Take The Heartbreak Killer Bunnies	95	I Go Blind Hootie & The Blowfish
		90	I Go To Extremes Billy Joel
80	I Can't Tell You Why Eagles	95	I Got A Girl Tripping Daisy
86	I Can't Wait Nu Shooz	93	I Got A Man Positive K
91	I Can't Wait Another Minute Hi-Five	97	I Got ID Pearl Jam
90	I Come Off Young M.C.	80	I Got You Split Enz
95	I Could Fall In Love Selena	85	I Got You Babe UB40 with Chrissie Hynde
88	I Could Never Take The Place Of Your Man Prince		
		76	I Got Your Love Stratavarious
99	I Could Not Ask For More Edwin McCain	84	I Guess That's Why They Call It Blues Elton John
96	I Cry Bass Is Base	94	I Had A Dream Carol Medina
86	I Didn't Mean To Turn You On Robert Palmer	88	I Hate Myself For Loving You Joan Jett & The Heartbreakers
90	I Didn't Want To Need You Heart	95	I Hate You Prince
83	I Do J. Geils Band	93	I Have Nothing Whitney Houston
98	I Do Lisa Loeb	87	I Heard A Rumour Bananarama

Year	Song	Artist
84	I Just Called To Say I Love You	Stevie Wonder
87	I Just Can't Stop Loving You	Michael Jackson
79	I Just Fall In Love Again	Anne Murray
78	I Just Wanna Stop	Gino Vannelli
77	I Just Want To Be Your Everything	Andy Gibb
87	(I Just) Died In Your Arms	Cutting Crew
82	I Keep Forgettin'	Michael McDonald
87	I Knew You Were Waiting (For Me)	Aretha Franklin/George Michael
95	I Know	Dionne Farris
98	I Know Where It's At	All Saints
98	I Know You	Jann Arden
88	I Know You're Out There Somewhere	Moody Blues
77	I Like Dreamin'	Kenny Nolan
89	I Like It	Dino
97	I Like It	Blackout Allstars
91	I Like The Way (The Kissing Game)	Hi-Five
94	I Like To Move It	Reel 2 Real
95	I Live My Life For You	Firehouse
81	I Love A Rainy Night	Eddie Rabbitt
76	I Love Music	O'Jays
94	I Love Music	Rozalla
82	I Love Rock N' Roll	Joan Jett & The Heartbreakers
78	I Love The Night Life	Alicia Bridges
76	I Love To Love	Tina Charles
81	I Love You	Climax Blues Band
91	I Love You	Vanilla Ice
96	I Love You Always Forever	Donna Lewis
93	I Love You Period	Dan Baird
92	I Love Your Smile	Shanice
86	I Miss You	Klymaxx
92	I Miss You	Joe Public
81	I Missed Again	Phil Collins
92	I Missed The Bus	Kris Kross
76	I Need A Harbour	Tom Middleton
88	I Need A Man	Eurythmics
76	I Need To Be In Love	Carpenters
96	I Need Your Love Tonight	Crewz Control
77	I Never Cry	Alice Cooper
75	I Only Have Eyes For You	Art Garfunkel
76	I Only Want To Be With You	Bay City Rollers
89	I Only Want To Be With You	Samantha Fox
80	I Pledge My Love	Peaches & Herb
82	I Ran (So Far Away)	A Flock Of Seagulls
89	I Remember Holding You	Boys Club
90	I Remember You	Skid Row
91	I Rhyme The World In 80 Days	Kish
88	I Saw Him Standing There	Tiffany
91	I Saw Red	Warrant
95	I Saw You Dancing	Yaki-Da
97	I Say A Little Prayer	Diana King
88	I Should Be So Lucky	Kylie Minogue
99	I Still Believe	Mariah Carey
84	I Still Can't Get Over Loving You	Ray Parker Jr.
87	I Still Haven't Found What I'm Looking For	U2
99	I Still Love You	Next
88	I Surrender	Samantha Fox
94	I Swear	All-4-One
90	I Think I Can Beat Mike Tyson	D.J. Jazzy Jeff & The Fresh Prince
90	I Think I Love You Too Much	Jeff Healey Band
87	I Think We're Alone Now	Tiffany
91	I Touch Myself	Divinyls
95	I Wanna B With U	Fun Factory
86	I Wanna Be A Cowboy	Boys Don't Cry
90	I Wanna Be Rich	Calloway
97	I Wanna Be There	Blessid Union Of Souls
87	I Wanna Dance With Somebody (Who Loves Me)	Whitney Houston
77	I Wanna Get Next To You	Rose Royce
91	(I Wanna Give You) Devotion	Nomad
89	I Wanna Have Some Fun	Samantha Fox
92	I Wanna Love You	Jade
92	I Wanna Make Love To You	Rythm Syndicate
91	I Wanna Sex You Up	Color Me Badd
84	I Want A New Drug	Huey Lewis & The News
89	I Want It All	Queen
99	I Want It That Way	Backstreet Boys
88	I Want To Be Your Man	Roger
92	I Want To Believe	Sass Jordan
84	I Want To Break Free	Queen
96	I Want To Come Over	Melissa Etheridge
85	I Want To Know What Love Is	Foreigner
95	I Want U	Rosie Gaines
94	I Want You	Juliet Roberts
97	I Want You	Savage Garden
84	I Want You Back	Sherry Kean
91	I Want You Back	West End Girls
98	I Want You Back	Mel B. featuring Missy "Misdemeanor" Eliott
98	I Want You Back	'N Sync
79	I Want You To Want Me (live)	Cheap Trick
80	I Want You Tonight	Pablo Cruise
79	I Want Your Love	Chic
87	I Want Your Sex	George Michael
79	I Was Made For Dancin'	Leif Garrett
79	I Was Made For Loving You	Kiss
90	I Was Made For You	Guys Next Door

78	I Was Only Joking Rod Stewart	98	I'll Be There For You The Moffatts
87	I Will Rock & Hyde	95	I'll Be There For You/You're All I Need (To Get By) Method Man featuring Mary J. Blige
93	I Will Always Love You Whitney Houston		
93	I Will Always Love You Sarah Washington	90	I'll Be Your Everything Tommy Page
		90	I'll Be Your Shelter Taylor Dayne
92	I Will Be Here For You Michael W. Smith	92	I'll Get By Eddie Money
		94	I'll Make Love To You Boyz II Men
87	I Will Be There Glass Tiger	97	I'll Never Break Your Heart Backstreet Boys
98	I Will Come To You Hanson		
92	I Will Remember You Amy Grant	93	I'll Never Get Over You (Getting Over Me) Expose
95	I Will Remember You Sarah McLachlan		
		79	I'll Never Love This Way Again Dionne Warwick
99	I Will Remember You (live version) Sarah McLachlan		
		94	I'll Remember Madonna
78	I Will Still Love You Stonebolt	92	I'll Respect You Debbie Johnson
79	I Will Survive Gloria Gaynor	90	I'll See You In My Dreams Giant
98	I Will Wait Hootie & The Blowfish	93	I'll Sleep When I'm Dead Bon Jovi
77	I Wish Stevie Wonder	94	I'll Stand By You The Pretenders
94	I Wish Gabrielle	94	I'll Take You There General Public
95	I Wish Skee-Lo	83	I'll Tumble 4 Ya Culture Club
88	I Wish I Had A Girl Henry Lee Summer	84	I'll Wait Van Halen
		97	I'm Afraid of Americans David Bowie
80	I Wish I Was 18 Again George Burns	80	I'm Alive Electric Light Orchestra
90	I Wish It Would Rain Down Phil Collins	80	I'm Alright Kenny Loggins
		87	I'm An Adult Now Pursuit Of Happiness
92	I Wish The Phone Would Ring Expose		
		92	I'm Crying Shanice
95	I Wish You Well Tom Cochrane	76	I'm Easy Ron Nigrini
89	I Won't Back Down Tom Petty	93	I'm Every Woman Whitney Houston
83	I Won't Hold You Back Toto	84	I'm Free Kenny Loggins
84	I Won't Stand In Your Way Stray Cats	93	I'm Free Jon Secada
98	I Wonder Tom Cochrane	85	I'm Goin' Down Bruce Springsteen
91	I Wonder Why Curtis Stigers	93	I'm Gonna Be (500 Miles) Proclaimers
85	I Would Die 4 U Prince & The Revolution	93	I'm Gonna Get You Bizarre Inc.
		78	I'm Gonna Take Care Of Everything Rubicon
94	I Wouldn't Normally Do This Kind Of Thing Pet Shop Boys		
		85	I'm Gonna Tear Your Playhouse Down Paul Young
76	I Write The Songs Barry Manilow		
92	I'd Die Without You PM Dawn	94	I'm In The Mood CeCe Peniston
93	I'd Do Anything For Love (But I Won't Do That) Meat Loaf	77	I'm In You Peter Frampton
		98	I'm Not A Player Big Punisher
94	I'd Give Anything Gerald Levert	75	I'm Not In Love 10cc
95	I'd Lie For You (And That's The Truth) Meat Loaf	91	I'm Not In Love Will To Power
		75	I'm Not Lisa Jessi Colter
76	I'd Really Love To See You Tonight England Dan & John Ford Coley	93	I'm Not Your Lover Jann Arden
		75	I'm On Fire 5000 Volts
93	I'll Always Be There Roch Voisine	85	I'm On Fire Bruce Springsteen
88	I'll Always Love You Taylor Dayne	77	I'm Ready Hometown Band
96	I'll Be Alright M.T.S.	98	I'm Ready Bryan Adams
91	I'll Be By Your Side Stevie B	77	I'm Scared Burton Cummings
76	I'll Be Good To You Brothers Johnson	95	I'm Shattered Barney Bentall
89	I'll Be Loving You (Forever) New Kids On The Block	84	I'm So Excited Pointer Sisters
		96	I'm So Happy I Can't Stop Crying Sting
97	I'll Be Missing You Puff Daddy & Faith Evans (featuring 112)		
		93	I'm So Into You SWV
86	I'll Be Over You Toto	75	I'm Sorry John Denver
91	I'll Be There Escape Club	97	I'm Still In Love With You New Edition
92	I'll Be There Mariah Carey	88	I'm Still Searching Glass Tiger
89	I'll Be There For You Bon Jovi	83	I'm Still Standing Elton John
96	I'll Be There For You The Rembrandts	79	I'm The Man Joe Jackson

92	I'm The One You Need Jody Watley	94	If You Go Jon Secada
93	I'm The Only One Melissa Etheridge	92	If You Go Away NKOTB
92	I'm Too Sexy Right Said Fred	99	If You Had My Love Jennifer Lopez
99	I'm Your Angel R. Kelly & Celine Dion	76	If You Know What I Mean Neil Diamond
90	I'm Your Baby Tonight Whitney Houston	86	If You Leave OMD
77	I'm Your Boogie Man KC & The Sunshine Band	76	If You Leave Me Now Chicago
		98	If You Leave Me Now Stevie B
86	I'm Your Man Wham!	95	If You Love Me Brownstone
87	I've Been In Love Before Cutting Crew	85	If You Love Somebody, Set Them Free Sting
91	I've Been Thinking About You Londonbeat	91	If You Needed Somebody Bad Company
81	I've Done Everything For You Rick Springfield	96	If Your Girl Only Knew Aaliyah
		82	I.G.Y. (What A Wonderful World) Donald Fagen
99	I've Dreamed Of You Barbra Streisand		
83	I've Got A Rock N' Roll Heart Eric Clapton	89	Iko Iko Belle Stars
		78	Imaginary Lover Atlanta Rhythm Section
77	I've Got Love On My Mind Natalie Cole		
		98	Imagination Tamia
88	(I've Had) The Time Of My Life Bill Medley/Jennifer Warnes	97	The Impression That I Get Mighty Mighty Bosstones
97	I've Just Seen A Face Holly Cole	90	Impulsive Wilson Phillips
82	I've Never Been To Me Charlene	83	In A Big Country Big Country
90	Ice Ice Baby Vanilla Ice	97	In A Dream Rockell
91	Iesha Another Bad Creation	88	In God's Country U2
93	If Janet Jackson	97	In My Bed Dru Hill
89	If A Tree Falls Bruce Cockburn	95	In My Dreams Darkness
84	If Ever You're In My Arms Again Peabo Bryson	89	In My Eyes Stevie B
		85	In My House Mary Jane Girls
97	If He Should Break Your Heart Journey	90	In The 21st Century Men Without Hats
		81	In The Air Tonight Phil Collins
78	If I Can't Have You Yvonne Elliman	78	In The Bush Musique
93	If I Could Regina Belle	92	In The Closet Michael Jackson
98	If I Could Joee	93	In The Heart Of A Woman Billy Ray Cyrus
89	If I Could Turn Back Time Cher		
93	If I Ever Fall In Love Shai	95	In The House Of Stone And Light Martin Page
93	If I Ever Lose My Faith In You Sting		
93	If I Had A $1,000,000 Barenaked Ladies	93	In The Meantime The Waltons
		96	In The Meantime Spacehog
93	If I Had No Loot Tony! Toni! Tone!	79	In The Navy Village People
94	If I Only Knew Tom Jones	93	In The Still Of The Nite (I'll Remember) Boyz II Men
96	If I Ruled The World Nas		
95	If I Wanted To Melissa Etheridge	93	In These Arms Bon Jovi
86	If I Was Midge Ure	87	In Too Deep Genesis
96	If I Were You k.d. lang	86	In Your Eyes Peter Gabriel
96	If It Makes You Happy Sheryl Crow	89	In Your Room Bangles
86	If She Knew What She Wants Bangles	88	In Your Soul Corey Hart
		82	Industrial Disease Dire Straits
90	(If There Was) Any Other Way Celine Dion	84	Infatuation Rod Stewart
		93	Informer Snow
84	If This Is It Huey Lewis & The News	80	Innocence Harlequin
90	If Wishes Came True Sweet Sensation	84	An Innocent Man Billy Joel
		93	Insane In The Brain Cypress Hill
92	If You Asked Me To Celine Dion	95	Insensitive Jann Arden
93	If You Believe In Me April Wine	90	Inside My Heart The Box
97	If You Could Only See Tonic	90	Inside Out Crash Vegas
98	If You Could Read My Mind Stars On 54	92	Inside That I Cried Ce Ce Peniston
		97	Insomnia Faithless
89	If You Don't Know Me By Now Simply Red	79	Instant Replay Dan Hartman
		98	Intergalactic Beastie Boys

94	**Interstate Love Song** Stone Temple Pilots	77	**It's Ecstasy When You Lay Down** Barry White
91	**Into The Fire** Sarah McLachlan	93	**It's Gonna Be A Lovely Day** S.O.U.L. System
92	**Into The Fire** Alias	80	**It's Hard To Be Humble** Mac Davis
76	**Into The Mystic** Jackson Hawke	97	**It's In Your Eyes** Phil Collins
80	**Into The Night** Benny Mardones	97	**It's Just Another...** Mighty Dub Kats
98	**Into You** 3 Deep	89	**(It's Just) The Way That You Love Me** Paula Abdul
85	**Invincible** Pat Benatar	98	**It's Like That** Run DMC Vs. Jason Nevins
85	**Invisible** Alison Moyet		
83	**Invisible Hands** Kim Carnes	84	**It's My Life** Talk Talk
97	**Invisible Man** 98°	92	**It's My Life** Dr. Alban
86	**Invisible Touch** Genesis	98	**It's My Life** Sash!
94	**Invitation** Lost & Profound	89	**It's No Crime** Babyface
98	**Iris** Goo Goo Dolls	97	**It's No Good** Depeche Mode
92	**Iron Lion Zion** Bob Marley And The Wailers	89	**It's Not Enough** Starship
		87	**It's Not Over ('Til It's Over)** Starship
96	**Ironic** Alanis Morissette	99	**It's Not Right But It's Okay** Whitney Houston
93	**Irresistible** Cathy Dennis		
86	**Is It Love?** Mr. Mister	76	**It's OK** Beach Boys
79	**Is She Really Going Out With Him?** Joe Jackson	93	**It's On** Naughty By Nature
		85	**It's Only Love** Bryan Adams/Tina Turner
86	**Is That It?** Katrina & The Waves		
83	**Is There Something I Should Know** Duran Duran	92	**It's Probably Me** Sting & Eric Clapton
		82	**It's Raining Again** Supertramp
88	**Is This Love** Whitesnake	77	**It's Sad To Belong** England Dan & John Ford Coley
93	**Is Your Mama Gonna Miss Ya** Bryan Adams		
		78	**It's So Easy** Linda Ronstadt
75	**Island Girl** Elton John	92	**It's So Hard To Say Goodbye To Yesterday** Boyz II Men
83	**Islands In The Stream** Kenny Rogers & Dolly Parton		
		80	**It's Still Rock And Roll To Me** Billy Joel
77	**Isn't It Time** The Babys		
91	**It Ain't Over Til It's Over** Lenny Kravitz	78	**It's The Same Old Song** KC & The Sunshine Band
77	**It Always Happens This Way** Toulouse		
		99	**It's The Things You Do** Five
97	**It Could Happen To You** Blue Rodeo	98	**It's Up To You** The Tuesdays
87	**It Doesn't Have To Be This Way** Blow Monkeys		

J

89	**It Doesn't Matter** Coleman Wilde	
85	**It Hurts To Be In Love** Gino Vannelli	
83	**It Might Be You** Stephen Bishop	82	**Jack & Diane** John Cougar
90	**It Must Have Been Love** Roxette	78	**Jack And Jill** Raydio
91	**It Never Rains (In Southern California)** Tony! Toni! Tone!	75	**Jackie Blue** Ozark Mountain Daredevils
75	**It Only Takes A Minute** Tavares	89	**Jackie Brown** John Cougar Mellencamp
93	**It Only Takes A Minute** Take That		
88	**It Would Take A Strong Strong Man** Rick Astley	99	**Jackie's Strength** Tori Amos
		87	**Jacob's Ladder** Huey Lewis & The News
78	**It's A Heartache** Bonnie Tyler		
84	**It's A Miracle** Culture Club	92	**Jam** Michael Jackson
83	**It's A Mistake** Men At Work	85	**Jamie** Ray Parker Jr.
87	**It's A Sin** Pet Shop Boys	80	**Jane** Jefferson Starship
98	**It's All About Me** Mya	94	**Jane** Barenaked Ladies
98	**It's All Been Done** Barenaked Ladies	90	**Janie's Got A Gun** Aerosmith
96	**It's All Coming Back To Me Now** Celine Dion	97	**Janie, Don't Take Your Love...** Jon Bon Jovi
94	**It's All Good** Hammer	80	**Janine** Trooper
77	**It's Almost Like A Song** Ronnie Milsap	95	**J.A.R.** Green Day
		90	**Jazzie's Groove** Soul II Soul
86	**It's Alright (Baby's Coming Back)** Eurythmics	96	**Jealousy** Natalie Merchant
		77	**Jeans On** David Dundas
97	**It's Alright, It's OK** Leah Andreone	97	**Jellyhead** Crush

83	**Jeopardy** Greg Kihn		77	**Just Remember I Love You** Firefall
96	**Jerk** Kim Stockword		92	**Just Take My Heart** Mr. Big
90	**Jerk Out** The Time		98	**Just The Two Of Us** Will Smith
80	**Jesse** Carly Simon		91	**Just The Way It Is Baby** The Remembrandts
81	**Jessie's Girl** Rick Springfield		78	**Just The Way You Are** Billy Joel
92	**Jesus He Knows Me** Genesis		77	**Just To Be Close To You** Commodores
96	**Jesus To A Child** George Michael		87	**Just To See Her** Smokey Robinson
77	**Jet Airliner** Steve Miller Band		79	**Just When I Needed You Most** Randy Vanwarmer
75	**Jive Talkin'** Bee Gees		92	**Justified And Ancient** KLF featuring Tammy Wynette
84	**Joanna** Kool & The Gang		90	**Justify My Love** Madonna
90	**Joey** Concrete Blonde			
86	**Johnny Come Home** Fine Young Cannibals			

K

99	**Joining You** Alanis Morissette		84	**Karma Chameleon** Culture Club
78	**Josie** Steely Dan		99	**Keep A Lid On Things** Crash Test Dummies
89	**Joy & Pain** Rob Base & D.J. E-Z Rock		91	**Keep Coming Back** Richard Marx
91	**Joyride** Roxette		83	**(Keep Feeling) Fascination** Human League
99	**Judgement Day** Method Man		77	**Keep It Comin' Love** KC & The Sunshine Band
82	**Juke Box Hero** Foreigner		92	**Keep It Coming** C&C Music Factory
84	**Jump** Van Halen		90	**Keep It Together** Madonna
92	**Jump** Kris Kross		81	**Keep On Lovin' You** REO Speedwagon
84	**Jump (For My Love)** Pointer Sisters		89	**Keep On Movin'** Soul II Soul
92	**Jump Around** House Of Pain		92	**Keep On Walkin'** Ce Ce Peniston
99	**Jump Around (Jason Nevins remixes)** House Of Pain		75	**Keep Our Love Alive** Pat Dahlquist
98	**Jump Jive And Wail** Brian Setzer Orchestra		96	**Keep Pushin'** Borish Dlugosch
93	**Jump They Say** David Bowie		94	**Keep Talking** Pink Floyd
98	**Jumper** Third Eye Blind		93	**Keep The Faith** Bon Jovi
86	**Jumpin' Jack Flash** Aretha Franklin		82	**Keep The Fire Burnin'** REO Speedwagon
77	**Jungle Love** Steve Miller Band		87	**Keep Your Hands To Yourself** Georgia Satellites
85	**Jungle Love** The Time		82	**Key Largo** Bertie Higgins
94	**Jurassic Park** "Weird Al" Yankovic		96	**Key West Intermezzo (I Saw Your First)** John Mellencamp
85	**Just A Gigolo/I Ain't Got Nobody** David Lee Roth		80	**The Kid Is Hot Tonite** Loverboy
96	**Just A Girl** No Doubt		90	**Kid N' Play** Funhouse
77	**Just A Song Before I Go** Crosby, Stills & Nash		93	**Killer/Papa Was A Rolling Stone** George Michael
92	**Just A Touch Of Love** C&C Music Factory		96	**Killing Me Softly** Fugees
91	**Just Another Day** Keven Jordan		77	**Killing Of Georgie** Rod Stewart
92	**Just Another Day** Jon Secada		98	**Kind & Generous** Natalie Merchant
97	**Just Another Day** John Mellencamp		86	**King For A Day** Thompson Twins
91	**Just Another Dream** Cathy Dennis		77	**The King Is Gone** Ronnie McDowell
85	**Just Another Night** Mick Jagger		97	**King Nothing** Metallica
85	**Just As I Am** Air Supply		96	**King Of New Orleans** Better Than Ezra
94	**Just Before Mary Goes** Universal Honey		83	**King Of Pain** The Police
81	**Just Between You And Me** April Wine		91	**King Of The Hill** Roger McGuinn
96	**Just Between You And Me** DC Talk		90	**King Of Wishful Thinking** Go West
90	**Just Came Back** Colin James		86	**Kiss** Prince
99	**Just Don't Give A F***** Eminem		89	**Kiss** Art Of Noise/Tom Jones
92	**Just For Tonight** Vanessa Williams		76	**Kiss And Say Goodbye** Manhattans
94	**Just Keep Me Movin'** k.d. lang		95	**Kiss From A Rose** Seal
94	**Just Kickin' It** Xscape		87	**Kiss Him Goodbye** The Nylons
88	**Just Like Paradise** David Lee Roth			
91	**Just Like You** Robbie Nevil			
80	**(Just Like) Starting Over** John Lennon			
98	**Just My Luck** V.I.P.			
87	**Just One Night** Triumph			

83	**Kiss In The Dark** Strange Advance	83	**Lawyers In Love** Jackson Browne
99	**Kiss Me** Sixpence None The Richer	78	**Lay Down Sally** Eric Clapton
88	**Kiss Me Deadly** Lita Ford	85	**Lay Your Hands On Me** Thompson Twins
91	**Kiss Me You Fool** Northern Pikes	89	**Lay Your Hands On Me** Bon Jovi
93	**Kiss Of Life** Sade	93	**Layla** Eric Clapton
81	**Kiss On My List** Daryl Hall & John Oates	76	**Lazy Love** New City Jam Band
83	**Kiss The Bride** Elton John	78	**Le Blues Du Business Man** Claude Dubois
98	**Kiss The Rain** Billie Myers	78	**Le Freak** Chic
87	**Kiss You (When It's Dangerous)** Eight Seconds	79	**Lead Me On** Maxine Nightingale
78	**Kiss You All Over** Exile	90	**Lead Me On** Boulevard
89	**Kisses On The Wind** Neneh Cherry	82	**Leader Of The Band** Dan Fogelberg
89	**Kissing A Fool** George Michael	87	**Lean On Me** Club Nouveau
97	**Kissing Rain** Roch Voisine	91	**Learning To Fly** Tom Petty & The Heartbreakers
79	**Knock On Wood** Amii Stewart	82	**Leather And Lace** Stevie Nicks (With Don Henley)
90	**Knocked Out** Paula Abdul	89	**Leave A Light On** Belinda Carlisle
91	**Knockin' Boots** Candyman	96	**Leave It Alone** Moist
93	**Knockin' Da Boots** H-Town	95	**Leave Virginia Alone** Rod Stewart
90	**Knockin' On Heaven's Door** Guns N' Roses	94	**Leaving Las Vegas** Sheryl Crow
94	**Know By Now** Robert Palmer	99	**Leaving On A Jet Plane** Chantal Kreviazuk
77	**Knowing Me, Knowing You** ABBA	97	**Legend Of A Cowgirl** Imani Cappola
76	**Knowing You Knowing When** Suzanne Stevens	84	**Legs** ZZ Top
88	**Kokomo** Beach Boys	93	**Lemon** U2
86	**Kyrie** Mr. Mister	97	**Lemon Tree** Fool's Garden
		87	**Lessons In Love** Level 42

L

		76	**Let 'Em In** Paul McCartney & Wings
87	**La Bamba** Los Lobos	95	**Let Her Cry** Hootie & The Blowfish
87	**La Isla Bonita** Madonna	76	**Let Her In** John Travolta
80	**Ladies Night** Kool & The Gang	96	**Let It Flow** Toni Braxton
79	**Lady** Little River Band	94	**Let It Go** Prince
80	**Lady** Kenny Rogers	95	**Let It Rain** East 17
81	**Lady (You Bring Me Up)** Commodores	96	**Let It Rain** Amanda Marshall
75	**Lady Blue** Leon Russell	96	**Let It Slide** Charlene Smith
76	**Lady Bump** Penny McLean	95	**Let Me Be The One** Blessid Union Of Soul
86	**The Lady In Red** Chris DeBurgh	97	**Let Me Clear My Throat** D.J. Kool
98	**Lady Marmalade** All Saints	90	**Let Me Go** Melissa Etheridge
86	**L'Affaire Dumoutier** The Box	80	**Let My Love Open The Door** Pete Townshend
92	**Laid So Low (Tears Roll Down)** Tears For Fears	84	**Let The Music Play** Shannon
90	**Lambada** Kaoma	78	**Let The Song Last Forever** Dan Hill
85	**Lamp At Midnight** Corey Hart	92	**Let This Housebeat Drop** Ya Kid K
94	**Land** Crash Vegas/Hothouse Flowers/ Daniel Lanois/Midnight Oil/Tragically Hip	90	**Let Your Backbone Slide** Maestro Fresh-Wes
86	**Land Of 1,000 Dances** The Wrestlers	76	**Let Your Love Flow** Bellamy Brothers
87	**Land Of Confusion** Genesis	96	**Let Your Soul Be Your Pilot** Sting
78	**Last Dance** Donna Summer	78	**Let's All Chant** Michael Zager Band
75	**The Last Farewell** Roger Whittaker	83	**Let's Dance** David Bowie
99	**Last Kiss** Pearl Jam	76	**Let's Do It Again** Staple Sisters
96	**Last Night** Az Yet	97	**Let's Get Down** Tony! Toni! Tone!
97	**Last Night On Earth** U2	92	**Let's Get Rocked** Def Leppard
87	**Last Of The Red Hot Fools** The Jitters	79	**Let's Go** The Cars
92	**The Last Song** Elton John	87	**Let's Go** Wang Chung
79	**The Last Time I Felt Like This** Johnny Mathis/Jane Olivor	86	**Let's Go All The Way** Sly Fox
91	**The Last To Know** Celine Dion	84	**Let's Go Crazy** Prince & The Revolution
80	**Late In The Evening** Paul Simon		
99	**Lately** Divine		

84	**Let's Hear It For The Boy** Deniece Williams	79	**A Little More Love** Olivia Newton-John
96	**Let's Make A Night To Remember** Bryan Adams	83	**Little Red Corvette** Prince
84	**Let's Stay Together** Tina Turner	90	**Little Salvation** Luba
91	**Let's Talk About Sex** Salt-N-Pepa	96	**Little Sins** Wendy Lands
90	**Let's Try It Again** New Kids On The Block	99	**A Little Sumthin' Sumthin'** Kayle
87	**Let's Wait Awhile** Janet Jackson	97	**Little Wonder** David Bowie
87	**Let's Work** Mick Jagger	92	**Live And Learn** Joe Public
90	**Letter Back** Zappacosta	92	**Live And Let Die** Guns N' Roses
92	**A Letter To Elise** The Cure	92	**Live For Lovin' You** Gloria Estefan
82	**Letting Go** Straight Lines	85	**Live Is Life** Opus
76	**Liars** Ian Thomas	86	**Live To Tell** Madonna
90	**Licence To Chill** Billy Ocean	99	**Livin' La Vida Loca** Ricky Martin
95	**Lick It** Roula	87	**Livin' On A Prayer** Bon Jovi
93	**Lick U Up** H-Town	93	**Livin' On The Edge** Aerosmith
77	**Lido Shuffle** Boz Scaggs	77	**Livin' Thing** Electric Light Orchestra
96	**Lie To Me** Bon Jovi	87	**Living Daylights** A-Ha
97	**Lie To Me** Jonny Lang	87	**Living In A Box** Living In A Box
83	**Lies** Thompson Twins	81	**Living In A Fantasy** Leo Sayer
91	**Lies** EMF	86	**Living In America** James Brown
96	**Lies To Me** 54.40	94	**Living In Danger** Ace Of Base
94	**Life (Everybody Needs Somebody To Love)** Haddaway	81	**Living Inside Myself** Gino Vannelli
86	**Life In A Northern Town** Dream Academy	77	**Living Next Door To Alice** Smokie
95	**Life In A Nutshell** Barenaked Ladies	89	**The Living Years** Mike & The Mechanics
98	**Life In Mono** Mono	92	**Locked In The Trunk Of A Car** Tragically Hip
77	**Life In The Fast Lane** Eagles	88	**The Locomotion** Kylie Minogue
91	**Life Is A Highway** Tom Cochrane	79	**The Logical Song** Supertramp
78	**Life's Been Good** Joe Walsh	98	**Lollipop (Candyman)** Aqua
86	**Life's What You Make It** Talk Talk	98	**London Rain** Heather Nova
92	**Lift Me Up** Howard Jones	77	**Lonely Boy** Andrew Gold
95	**Lightning Crashes** Live	76	**Lonely Night** Captain & Tennille
84	**Lights Out** Peter Wolf	85	**Lonely Ol' Night** John Cougar Mellencamp
89	**Like A Prayer** Madonna	79	**Lonesome Loser** Little River Band
86	**Like A Rock** Bob Seger	97	**A Long December** Counting Crows
95	**Like A Rolling Stone** Rolling Stones	80	**The Long Run** Eagles
85	**Like A Surgeon** "Weird Al" Yankovic	77	**Long Time** Boston
85	**Like A Virgin** Madonna	96	**Long Way Down** Goo Goo Dolls
96	**Like A Woman** Tony Rich Project	80	**Longer** Dan Fogelberg
81	**Limelight** Rush	84	**The Longest Time** Billy Joel
94	**Linger** The Cranberries	89	**The Look** Roxette
96	**A List Of Things** Damhnait Doyle	99	**Look At Me** Geri Halliwell
94	**Listen For The Laugh** Bruce Cockburn	89	**Look Away** Chicago
75	**Listen To What The Man Said** Paul McCartney & Wings	93	**Look Me In The Eye** Vivienne Williams
89	**Listen To Your Heart** Roxette	82	**The Look Of Love** ABC
93	**Little Bird** Annie Lennox	80	**Look What You've Done To Me** Boz Scaggs
76	**A Little Bit More** Dr. Hook	98	**Lookin' At Me** Mase
97	**Little Bit Of Ecstasy** Jocelyn Enriquez	80	**Lookin' For Love** Johnny Lee
91	**Little Bones** Tragically Hip	88	**Lookin' Out For Number One** Honeymoon Suite
81	**A Little In Love** Cliff Richard	87	**Looking For A New Love** Jody Watley
80	**Little Jeannie** Elton John	81	**Looking For Clues** Robert Palmer
92	**Little Lack Of Love** World On Edge	96	**Looking For It** Jann Arden
87	**Little Lies** Fleetwood Mac	76	**Looking Out For #1** Bachman-Turner Overdrive
90	**A Little Love** Corey Hart	93	**Looking Through Patient Eyes** PM Dawn
79	**A Little Lovin'** The Raes	77	**Looks Like We Made It** Barry Manilow
92	**Little Miss Can't Be Wrong** Spin Doctors	76	**Lorelei** Styx

94	**Loser** Beck	78	**Love Is Thicker Than Water** Andy Gibb
91	**Losing My Religion** R.E.M.	99	**Love Lift Me** Amanda Marshall
87	**Lost In Emotion** Lisa Lisa & Cult Jam With Full Force	85	**Love Light In Flight** Stevie Wonder
80	**Lost In Love** Air Supply	99	**Love Like This** Faith Evans
88	**Lost In You** Rod Stewart	76	**Love Machine** Miracles
89	**Lost In Your Eyes** Debbie Gibson	89	**Love Makes No Promises** Candi
93	**Lost In Your Eyes** Jeff Healey Band	77	**Love Me** Yvonne Elliman
92	**Lost Together** Blue Rodeo	98	**Love Me** 112 featuring Mase
94	**Lost Without You** Roch Voisine	92	**Love Me All Up** Stacy Earl
77	**Lost Without Your Love** Bread	82	**Love Me Tomorrow** Chicago
79	**Lotta Love** Nicolette Larson	92	**Love Monkey #9** Bootsauce
96	**Loungin'** L.L. Cool J	91	**Love Of A Lifetime** Firehouse
90	**Love And Affection** Nelson	76	**Love Of My Life** Gino Vannelli
91	**Love And Understanding** Cher	91	**Love On A Rooftop** Desmond Child
91	**Love At First Sight** Styx	80	**Love On The Rocks** Neil Diamond
88	**Love Becomes Electric** Strange Advance	82	**Love Plus One** Haircut One Hundred
88	**Love Bites** Def Leppard	87	**Love Power** Dionne Warwick/Jeffrey Osborne
86	**A Love Bizarre** Sheila E.	76	**Love Really Hurts Without You** Billy Ocean
93	**Love Can Move Mountains** Celine Dion	87	**Love Removal Machine** The Cult
88	**Love Changes (Everything)** Climie Fisher	76	**Love Rollercoaster** Ohio Players
88	**Love Changes Everything** Honeymoon Suite	89	**Love Shack** The B-52s
		94	**Love Sneakin' Up On You** Bonnie Raitt
90	**Love Child** Sweet Sensation	76	**Love So Right** Bee Gees
96	**Love Don't Live Here Anymore** Madonna	84	**Love Somebody** Rick Springfield
		76	**Love Song** Elton John
93	**Love Don't Live Here Anymore** Sven Gali	89	**Love Song** The Cure
		99	**Love Song** Sky
97	**Love Fool** The Cardigans	80	**Love Stinks** J. Geils Band
93	**Love For Love** Robin S	79	**Love Takes Time** Orleans
97	**Love Gets Me Every Time** Shania Twain	90	**Love Takes Time** Mariah Carey
		77	**Love Theme From "A Star Is Born" (Evergreen)** Barbra Streisand
76	**Love Hangover** Diana Ross		
76	**Love Hurts** Jim Capaldi	85	**Love Theme From "St. Elmo's Fire"** David Foster
76	**Love Hurts** Nazareth		
89	**Love In An Elevator** Aerosmith	76	**Love To Love You Baby** Donna Summer
76	**Love In The Shadows** Neil Sedaka		
89	**Love Is** Alannah Myles	86	**Love Touch** Rod Stewart
93	**Love Is** Vanessa Williams & Brian McKnight	93	**Love U More** Sunscreem
		97	**Love U More** Sunscreem
83	**Love Is A Battlefield** Pat Benatar	92	**Love Vibe** Lisa Lougheed
90	**Love Is A Fire** Donny Osmond	86	**Love Will Conquer All** Lionel Richie
83	**Love Is A Stranger** Eurythmics	78	**Love Will Find A Way** Pablo Cruise
91	**Love Is A Wonderful Thing** Michael Bolton	87	**Love Will Find A Way** Yes
		95	**Love Will Keep Us Alive** Eagles
76	**Love Is Alive** Gary Wright	75	**Love Will Keep Us Together** Captain & Tennille
94	**Love Is All Around** Wet Wet Wet		
82	**Love Is Alright Tonite** Rick Springfield	90	**Love Will Lead You Back** Taylor Dayne
87	**Love Is Fire** Parachute Club		
78	**Love Is In The Air** Martin Stevens	91	**Love Will Never Do (Without You)** Janet Jackson
78	**Love Is In The Air** John Paul Young		
78	**Love Is Like Oxygen** Sweet	88	**Love Will Save The Day** Whitney Houston
92	**Love Is On The Way** Saigon Kick		
96	**Love Is Paradise** First Base	96	**Love Won't Find Us Here** Mae Moore
94	**Love Is Strong** Rolling Stones	96	**Love You All** 54-40
76	**Love Is The Drug** Roxy Music	92	**Love You By Heart** Lisa Lougheed
91	**Love Is The Subject** Odds	87	**Love You Down** Ready For The World
		97	**Love You Down** Inoj

79	Love You Inside Out Bee Gees		84	Major Tom (Coming Home) Peter Schilling
91	Love You Till It Hurts Chrissy Steele		82	Make A Move On Me Olivia Newton-John
86	Love Zone Billy Ocean		92	Make It Happen Mariah Carey
82	Love's Been A Little Bit Hard On Me Juice Newton		98	Make It Hot Nicole
91	Love...Thy Will Be Done Martika		88	Make It Real The Jets
89	The Lover In Me Sheena Easton		96	Make It Up As You Go Hemingway Corner
90	Lover Of Mine Alannah Myles		76	Make It Up To Me In Love Odia Coates
85	Loverboy Billy Ocean		92	Make Love Like A Man Def Leppard
85	Lovergirl Teena Marie		85	(Make Me Do) Anything You Want Helix
84	Lovers In A Dangerous Time Bruce Cockburn		88	Make Me Lose Control Eric Carmen
85	Lovin' Every Minute Of It Loverboy		92	Make You A Believer Sass Jordan
76	Lovin' You Baby Wednesday		79	Makin' It David Naughton
79	Lovin', Touchin', Squeezin' Journey		83	Makin' It Work Doug & The Slugs
94	Loving Me Is Not A Sin Mitsou		76	Makin' Our Dreams Come True Cyndi Greco
95	Low Life Bryan Adams		83	Making Love Out Of Nothing At All Air Supply
75	Low Rider War		80	Making Plans For Nigel XTC
76	Lowdown Boz Scaggs		83	Mama Genesis
92	LSI (Love, Sex, Intelligence) The Shamen		79	Mama Can't Buy You Love Elton John
94	Lucas With The Lid Off Lucas		92	Mama I'm Coming Home Ozzy Osbourne
77	Lucille Kenny Rogers		78	Mama Let Him Play Doucette
85	Lucky In Love Mick Jagger		76	Mama Mia ABBA
96	Lucky Love Ace Of Base		91	Mama Said Knock You Out L.L. Cool J
94	Lucky One Amy Grant		84	Mama Weer All Crazee Now Quiet Riot
84	Lucky Star Madonna		88	Man In The Mirror Michael Jackson
87	Luka Suzanne Vega		93	Man On A Mission Hemingway Corner
97	Lull Smashing Pumpkins		93	Man On The Moon R.E.M.
98	Lullaby Shawn Mullins		95	The Man Who Sold The World Nirvana
95	Lump Presidents Of The United States Of America		87	Mandolin Rain Bruce Hornsby & The Range
97	Lunchbox Marilyn Manson		82	Maneater Daryl Hall & John Oates
98	Luv Me, Luv Me Shaggy featuring Janet		83	Maniac Michael Sembello
75	Lyin' Eyes Eagles		86	Manic Monday Bangles
90	Lyin' To Myself David Cassidy		97	March of the Pigs Nine Inch Nails

M

			77	Margaritaville Jimmy Buffet
78	Ma Baker Boney M		92	Maria TKA
95	Macarena Los Del Mar		92	Martika's Kitchen Martika
96	Macarena (Bayside Boys Remix) Los Del Rio		94	Mary Jane's Last Dance Tom Petty And The Heartbreakers
78	MacArthur Park Donna Summer		79	Mary's Boy Child Boney M
92	Machine Gun Warrant		87	Mary's Prayer Danny Wilson
78	Macho Man Village People		92	Masterpiece Atlantic Starr
86	Mad About You Belinda Carlisle		85	Material Girl Madonna
92	Mad Mad World Tom Cochrane		86	A Matter Of Trust Billy Joel
93	Mad Money The Mozz		77	Maybe I'm Amazed Paul McCartney & Wings
85	Madam Butterfly Malcolm McLaren		94	Maybe Love Will Change Your Mind Stevie Nicks
95	Made In England Elton John		77	Maybe Tomorrow Hagood Hardy
75	Magic Pilot		78	Maybe Your Heart Christopher Ward
80	Magic Olivia Newton-John		98	MDFMK KMFDM
84	Magic The Cars			
96	Magic Carpet Ride Mighty Dub Cats			
92	The Magic Friend 2 Unlimited			
81	Magic Power Triumph			
78	Magnet And Steel Walter Egan			
79	The Main Event/Fight Barbra Streisand			

91	**Mea Culpa** Enigma	92	**Missing You Now** Michael Bolton
81	**Medley** Stars On 45	96	**Mission Impossible** Adam Clayton
84	**Meet Me In The Middle** The Arrows	86	**Missionary Man** Eurythmics
94	**(Meet) The Flintstones** The B.C. 52's	85	**Mistake No. 3** Culture Club
84	**Melody** Boys Brigade	78	**Mr. Blue Sky** Electric Light Orchestra
91	**Melt In Your Mouth** Candyman	75	**Mr. Jaws** Dickie Goodman
95	**Memories** Netzwerk	94	**Mr. Jones** Counting Crows
92	**Memory Lane** One 2 One	92	**Mr. Loverman** Shabba Ranks
97	**The Memory Remains** Metallica	95	**Mr. Personality** Gillette
97	**Men In Black** Will Smith	83	**Mr. Roboto** Styx
95	**Mental Picture** Jon Secada	85	**Mr. Telephone Man** New Edition
90	**Mentirosa** Mellow Man Ace	93	**Mr. Vain** Culture Beat
88	**Mercedes Boy** Pebbles	93	**Mr. Wendal** Arrested Development
91	**Mercy Mercy Me (The Ecology)/ I Want You** Robert Palmer	76	**Misty Blue** Dorothy Moore
96	**Merkinball** Pearl Jam	80	**Misunderstanding** Genesis
80	**Message In A Bottle** The Police	89	**Mixed Emotions** Rolling Stones
93	**Metal Mickey** Suede	93	**Mmm Mmm Mmm Mmm...** Crash Test Dummies
85	**Method Of Modern Love** Daryl Hall & John Oates	97	**MMMBop** Hanson
83	**Mexican Radio** Wall Of Voodoo	97	**Mo Money, Mo Problems** Notorious B.I.G.
99	**Miami** Will Smith	94	**Moanie** Bootsauce
85	**Miami Vice Theme** Jan Hammer	81	**Modern Girl** Sheena Easton
83	**Mickey** Toni Basil	83	**Modern Love** David Bowie
84	**Middle Of The Road** The Pretenders	86	**Modern Woman** Billy Joel
75	**Midnight Blue** Melissa Manchester	85	**Mona With The Children** Doug Cameron
83	**Midnight Blue** Louise Tucker	80	**Money** The Flying Lizards
87	**Midnight Blue** Lou Gramm	85	**Money Changes Everything** Cyndi Lauper
97	**Midnight In A Perfect World** DJ Shadow	92	**Money Don't Matter 2 Night** Prince & The New Power Generation
97	**Midnight In Chelsea** Jon Bon Jovi	85	**Money For Nothing** Dire Straits
79	**Midnight Wind** John Stewart	76	**Money Honey** Bay City Rollers
99	**Milennium** Robbie Williams	98	**Money, Power & Respect** The Lox
96	**Mint Car** The Cure	91	**Moneytalks** AC/DC
79	**Minute By Minute** Doobie Brothers	88	**Monkey** George Michael
90	**Miracle** Jon Bon Jovi	87	**Montego Bay** Amazulu
91	**Miracle** Whitney Houston	87	**Mony Mony** Billy Idol
75	**Miracles** Jefferson Starship	77	**Moody Blue** Elvis Presley
95	**Miracles** Cartouche	88	**Moonbeam** Men Without Hats
94	**Miracles Happen** Lost & Profound	87	**Moonlight Desires** Gowan
83	**Mirror Man** Human League	76	**Moonlight Feels Right** Starbuck
95	**Misery** Soul Asylum	93	**More And More** Captain Hollywood Project
95	**Mishale** Andru Donalds	76	**More More More** Andrea True Connection
85	**Misled** Kool & The Gang	76	**More Than A Feeling** Boston
94	**Misled** Celine Dion	80	**More Than I Can Say** Leo Sayer
84	**Miss Me Blind** Culture Club	97	**More Than This** 10,000 Maniacs
93	**Miss My Love** Sheree Jeacocke	91	**More Than Words** Extreme
97	**Miss Sarajevo** Passengers	90	**More Than Words Can Say** Alias
81	**Miss Sun** Boz Scaggs	94	**The More You Ignore Me, The Closer I Get** Morrissey
78	**Miss You** Rolling Stones	75	**Morning Beautiful** Tony Orlando & Dawn
94	**Miss You In A Heartbeat** Def Leppard	93	**Morning Papers** Prince & The New Power Generation
89	**Miss You Like Crazy** Natalie Cole	81	**Morning Train (Nine To Five)** Sheena Easton
98	**Miss You Like Crazy** The Moffatts		
89	**Miss You Much** Janet Jackson		
96	**Missing** Everything But The Girl		
84	**Missing You** John Waite		
85	**Missing You** Diana Ross		
89	**Missing You** Chris Deburgh		
96	**Missing You** Brandy/Tamia/Gladys Knight/Chaka Khan		
96	**Missing You** Tina Turner		

94	**The Most Beautiful Girl In The World** Prince	93	**My Temptation** Vivienne Williams
91	**The Motown Song** Rod Stewart	91	**My Town** Glass Tiger
91	**Motownphilly** Boyz II Men	77	**My Way** Elvis Presley
96	**Mouth** Merill Bainbridge	98	**My Way** Usher
92	**Move Any Mountain** The Shamen	77	**My Wheels Won't Turn** Bachman-Turner Overdrive
86	**Move Away** Culture Club	92	**My World** Another Bad Creation
92	**Move This** Technotronic featuring Ya Kid K	92	**Mysterious Ways** U2
95	**Move This Night** Earthtones		
94	**Movin' On Up** M People		# N
78	**Movin' Out** Billy Joel	77	**Nadia's Theme** Devorzon & Botkin
98	**The Mummers' Dance** Loreena McKennitt	96	**Naked** Goo Goo Dolls
		96	**Name** Goo Goo Dolls
95	**Murder Incorporated** Bruce Springsteen	78	**Name Of The Game** ABBA
		99	**Nas Is Like** Nas
79	**Music Box Dancer** Frank Mills	86	**Nasty** Janet Jackson
98	**Music Sounds Better With You** Stardust	88	**Naughty Girls (Need Love Too)** Samantha Fox
76	**Muskrat Love** Captain & Tennille	88	**Need You Tonight** INXS
97	**My Addiction** Dayna Manning	94	**Neon Moonlight** Rosco Martinez
98	**My All** Mariah Carey	85	**Neutron Dance** Pointer Sisters
78	**My Angel Baby** Toby Beau	85	**Never** Heart
77	**My Best Friend's Wife** Paul Anka	93	**Never A Time** Genesis
89	**My Brave Face** Paul McCartney	80	**Never Be The Same** Christopher Cross
91	**My Definition Of A Boombastic Bass Line** Dream Warriors	91	**Never Change My Mind** Acosta Russell
98	**My Father's Eyes** Eric Clapton	85	**Never Ending Story** Limahl
98	**My Favorite Mistake** Sheryl Crow	98	**Never Ever** All Saints
98	**My Favourite Game** The Cardigans	88	**Never Give Up** Blvd
95	**My Friends** Red Hot Chili Peppers	76	**Never Gonna Fall In Love Again** Eric Carmen
81	**My Girl (Gone, Gone, Gone)** Chilliwack	99	**Never Gonna Give Up** 3 Deep
77	**My Heart Belongs To Me** Barbra Streisand	88	**Never Gonna Give You Up** Rick Astley
89	**My Heart Can't Tell Me No** Rod Stewart	83	**Never Gonna Let You Go** Sergio Mendes
98	**My Heart Will Go On** Celine Dion	77	**Never Had A Lady Before** Burton Cummings
86	**My Hometown** Bruce Springsteen	97	**Never Leave Me Alone** Nate Dogg
79	**My Life** Billy Joel	94	**Never Let You Go** NKOTB
75	**My Little Town** Simon & Garfunkel	99	**Never Never** D-Cru
90	**My Love Is A Fire** Donny Osmond	83	**Never Said I Loved You** Payola$ & Carol Pope
95	**My Love Is For Real** Paula Abdul	85	**Never Surrender** Corey Hart
97	**My Love Is For Real** Strike	88	**Never Tear Us Apart** INXS
97	**My Love Is The Shhh!** Somethin' For The People	88	**Never Thought** Dan Hill
92	**My Lovin' (You're Never Gonna Get It)** En Vogue	94	**New Age Girl** Deadeye Dick
		84	**New Girl Now** Honeymoon Suite
90	**My My My** Johnny Gill	77	**New Kid In Town** Eagles
99	**My Name Is** Eminem	84	**New Moon On Monday** Duran Duran
91	**My Name Is Not Susan** Whitney Houston	88	**New Sensation** INXS
92	**My Name Is Prince** Prince & The New Power Generation	84	**New Song** Howard Jones
		82	**New World Man** Rush
84	**My Oh My** Slade	94	**Newborn Friend** Seal
77	**My Own Way To Rock** Burton Cummings	87	**The Next Time I Fall** Peter Cetera/Amy Grant
89	**My Prerogative** Bobby Brown	98	**Nice & Slow** Usher
79	**My Sharona** The Knack	92	**Nice To Luv You** 54.40
91	**My Side Of The Bed** Susanna Hoffs	98	**Nick Shape CD** Backstreet Boys
88	**My Song** Glass Tiger	78	**Night Fever** Bee Gees

94	Night In My Veins The Pretenders	99	Nobody's Supposed To Be Here Deborah Cox
77	Night Moves Bob Seger	95	Not Enough Van Halen
81	The Night Owls Little River Band	92	Not Enough Time INXS
80	Night To Remember Prism	85	Not In Love Platinum Blonde
88	Nightmare On My Street D.J. Jazzy Jeff & The Fresh Prince	91	Not Like Kissin' You West End Girls
77	Nights Are Forever England Dan & John Ford Coley	97	Not Tonight Lil Kim
		93	Nothin' 'Bout Me Sting
75	Nights On Broadway Bee Gees	86	Nothin' At All Heart
85	Nightshift Commodores	93	Nothin' My Love Can't Fix Joey Lawrence
86	Nikita Elton John		
81	9 To 5 Dolly Parton	92	Nothing Broken But My Heart Celine Dion
85	19 Paul Hardcastle		
83	1999 Prince	90	Nothing Compares 2 U Sinead O'Connor
96	1979 Smashing Pumpkins		
80	99 Toto	87	Nothing Could Stand In Your Way Zappacosta
98	Ninety Nine John Forte		
84	99 Luftballons Nena	92	Nothing Else Matters Metallica
92	92 Days Of Rain Corey Hart	99	Nothing Really Matters Madonna
93	No Apologies Alanis	87	Nothing's Gonna Change My Love For You Glenn Medeiros
76	No Charge John Gilbert		
92	No Crossover EPMD	87	Nothing's Gonna Stop Me Now Samantha Fox
96	No Diggity Blackstreet		
94	No Excuses Alice In Chains	87	Nothing's Gonna Stop Us Now Starship
93	No Limit 2 Unlimited		
91	No Matter What George Lamond	87	Notorious Duran Duran
99	No Mercy Khaleel	87	Notorious Loverboy
93	No Mistakes Patty Smyth	92	November Rain Guns N' Roses
95	No More "I Love You's" Annie Lennox	94	Now And Forever Richard Marx
90	No More Lies Michel'le	86	Now And Forever (You And Me) Anne Murray
84	No More Lonely Nights Paul McCartney		
		98	Now That I Found You Terri Clark
79	No More Tears Donna Summer/ Barbra Streisand	91	Now That We Found Love Heavy D & The Boyz
91	No More Tears Ozzy Osbourne	96	Nowhere To Go Melissa Etheridge
90	No Myth Michael Penn	92	Nu Nu Lidell Townsell
86	No One Is To Blame Howard Jones	93	Numb U2
93	No Ordinary Love Sade	97	Numb Holly McNarland
99	No Pigeons Sporty Thievz	97	Number One Alexia
93	No Rain Blind Melon	97	#1 Crush Garbage
92	No Regrets Tom Cochrane	79	No. 1 Dee Jay Goody Goody
81	No Reply At All Genesis	93	N.Y.C. Charles & Eddie
99	No Scrubs TLC		
93	No Sexx With My Sister MCJ & Cool G		
91	No Sign Of Rain Keven Jordan	95	O Siem Susan Aglukark
91	No Son Of Mine Genesis	76	Ob La Di Ob La Da The Beatles
89	No Souvenirs Melissa Etheridge	85	Obsession Animotion
98	No Surprises Radiohead	90	The Obvious Child Paul Simon
97	No Tengo Dinero Los Umbrellos	95	Ode To My Family The Cranberries
96	No Woman No Cry Fugees	80	Off The Wall Michael Jackson
98	No, No, No Destiny's Child	93	Oh Carolina Shaggy
79	Nobody Doucette	90	Oh Girl Paul Young
82	Nobody Sylvia	81	Oh No Commodores
97	Nobody Keith Sweat	78	Oh Pretty Lady Trooper
77	Nobody Does It Better Carly Simon	85	Oh Sheila Ready For The World
96	Nobody Knows Tony Rich Project	96	Oh Shelly Barney Bentall
84	Nobody Told Me John Lennon	84	Oh Sherrie Steve Perry
81	Nobody Wins Elton John	96	Oh Virginia Blessid Union Of Souls
87	Nobody's Fool Cinderella	96	The Old Apartment Barenaked Ladies
88	Nobody's Fool Kenny Loggins	75	Old Days Chicago
		83	Old Emotions Spoons

96	Old Man & Me (When I Get To Heaven) Hootie & The Blowfish	88	One Step Up Bruce Springsteen
85	The Old Man Down The Road John Fogerty	96	One Sweet Day Mariah Carey/Boyz II Men
76	Old Time Movie Lisa Hartt Band	81	The One That You Love Air Supply
83	Old Time Rock N' Roll Bob Seger	83	One Thing Leads To Another The Fixx
98	Omobolasire Prozzäk	93	One Track Mind TBTBT
97	On & On Erykah Badu	79	One Way Or Another Blondie
98	On A Day Like Today Bryan Adams	98	One Week Barenaked Ladies
77	On And On Stephen Bishop	82	The One You Love Glenn Frey
95	On And On Crash Vegas	88	1-2-3 Gloria Estefan & Miami Sound Machine
94	On Bended Knee Boyz II Men	95	1-2-3 (Train With Me) Playahitty
86	On My Own Patti Labelle/Michael McDonald	96	1,2,3,4 (Sumpin' New) Coolio
97	On My Own Peach Union	92	1-4-All-4-1 East Coast Family
89	On Our Own Bobby Brown	93	Only Anthrax
84	On The Dark Side John Cafferty & The Beaver Brown Band	96	Only Happy When It Rains Garbage
		87	Only In My Dreams Debbie Gibson
80	On The Radio Donna Summer	96	Only Love (The Ballad Of Sleeping Beauty) Sophie B. Hawkins
89	Once Bitten, Twice Shy Great White		
92	Once In A Lifetime Love & Sas	76	Only Love Is Real Carole King
77	Once In A Long Time Christopher Ward	76	Only Sixteen Dr. Hook
		78	Only The Good Die Young Billy Joel
89	One Bee Gees	82	Only The Lonely The Motels
92	The One Elton John	91	Only The Lonely World On Edge
92	One U2	85	Only The Young Journey
97	One U2	96	The Only Thing That Looks Good On Me Is You Bryan Adams
96	One & One Robert Miles		
91	The One And Only Chesney Hawkes	82	Only Time Will Tell Asia
90	One And Only Man Stevie Winwood	95	Only Wanna Be With You Hootie & The Blowfish
96	One By One Cher		
88	One Good Woman Peter Cetera	98	Only When I Lose Myself Depeche Mode
97	One Headlight The Wallflowers		
86	One Hit (To The Body) Rolling Stones	84	Only When You Leave Spandau Ballet
94	100% Pure Love Crystal Waters	75	Only Women Bleed Alice Cooper
91	100 Watt Bulb Infidels	75	Only Yesterday Carpenters
87	The One I Love R.E.M.	84	Only You Flying Pickets
93	One Last Cry Brian McKnight	96	Only You 112
93	One Last Kiss Sofia Shinas	93	Oochigeas Roch Voisine
85	One Lonely Night REO Speedwagon	97	Ooh Aah...Just A Little Bit Gina G
94	One Love Nas	79	Ooh Baby Baby Linda Ronstadt
88	One Moment In Time Whitney Houston	93	Ooh Child Dino
		90	Ooh La La Perfect Gentlemen
95	One More Chance Notorious B.I.G.	93	Ooh, Whatcha Gonna Do Run-D.M.C.
95	One More Moment Julie Masse	90	Ooops Up Snap!
85	One More Night Phil Collins	82	Open Arms Journey
97	One More Time Real McCoy	94	Open Up Your Heart Premier
88	One More Try George Michael	97	Open Your Eyes Ivan
89	One More Try Brighton Rock	87	Open Your Heart Madonna
91	One More Try Timmy T	75	Operator Manhattan Transfer
96	One More Try Kristine W.	76	Ophelia The Band
97	One More Try Real McCoy	91	O.P.P. Naughty By Nature
85	One Night In Bangkok Murray Head	86	Opportunities (Let's Make Lots Of Money) Pet Shop Boys
94	One Night In Heaven M People		
85	One Of The Living Tina Turner	90	Opposites Attract Paula Abdul
75	One Of These Nights Eagles	98	Ordinary Day Great Big Sea
96	One Of Us Joan Osborne	87	Ordinary People The Box
83	One On One Daryl Hall & John Oates	93	Ordinary World Duran Duran
81	One Step Ahead Split Enz	84	Original Sin INXS
86	One Step Closer To You Gavin Christopher	89	Orinoco Flow Enya
		83	The Other Guy Little River Band

90	The Other Side Aerosmith		84	Penny Lover Lionel Richie
82	The Other Woman Ray Parker Jr.		85	People Are People Depeche Mode
95	Ou Eee Ou DFS		91	People Are Still Having Sex LaTour
77	Ou Sont Les Femmes Patrick Juvet		92	People Everyday Arrested Development
83	Our House Madness		98	Perfect Smashing Pumpkins
82	Our Lips Are Sealed Go-Gos		97	Perfect Drug Nine Inch Nails
78	Our Love Natalie Cole		86	Perfect Way Scritti Politti
79	(Our Love) Don't Throw It All Away Andy Gibb		88	Perfect World Huey Lewis & The News
93	Our World Our Times Alannah Myles		90	Personal Jesus Depeche Mode
93	Out Of My Head Junkhouse		76	Peter And Lou Valdy
99	Out Of My Head Fastball		86	Peter Gunn Art Of Noise
97	Out Of My Mind Duran Duran		79	Peter Piper Frank Mills
95	Out Of Tears Rolling Stones		97	Phenomenon L.L. Cool J
88	Out Of The Blue Debbie Gibson		75	Philadelphia Freedom Elton John
84	Out Of Touch Daryl Hall & John Oates		77	Photo Album Kristine
76	Over My Head Fleetwood Mac		83	Photograph Def Leppard
96	Over Now Alice In Chains		93	Photograph Of Mary Trey Lorenz
83	Overkill Men At Work		81	Physical Olivia Newton-John
84	Owner Of A Lonely Heart Yes		98	Picture Me Leaving You Tru-G'z
			97	Picture Of You Boyzone
	P		99	Pictures Boomtang Boys
83	Pale Shelter Tears For Fears		91	Piece Of My Heart Tara Kemp
76	Paloma Blanca George Baker Selection		98	Pig X-Mas Song Pig
			79	Pilot Ian Thomas
88	Pamela Toto		80	Pilot Of The Airwaves Charlie Dore
84	Panama Van Halen		75	Pinball Wizard Elton John
86	Papa Don't Preach Madonna		88	Pink Cadillac Natalie Cole
92	Paper Doll PM Dawn		93	Pink Cashmere Prince
87	Paper In Fire John Cougar Mellencamp		93	Pink Cookies L.L. Cool J
82	Paperlate Genesis		84	Pink Houses John Cougar Mellencamp
88	Paradise Sade		95	Pipe Dreamz Yakoo Boyz
78	Paradise By The Dashboard Light Meat Loaf		91	Place In This World Michael W. Smith
			92	Plastic Alanis
89	Paradise City Guns N' Roses		93	Plastic PM Dawn
99	Paradox 666		76	Play That Funky Music Wild Cherry
86	Paranoimia Art Of Noise		90	Play That Funky Music Vanilla Ice
88	Parents Just Don't Understand D.J. Jazzy Jeff & The Fresh Prince		95	Player's Anthem Junior M.A.F.I.A.
			99	Player's Holiday T.W.D.Y.
85	Part Time Lover Stevie Wonder		76	Playing In The Band Stampeders
86	Party All The Time Eddie Murphy		96	Please Elton John
98	Party Continues JD		97	Please U2
89	Partyman Prince		80	Please Don't Go KC & The Sunshine Band
90	The Pass Rush			
83	Pass The Dutchie Musical Youth		92	Please Don't Go Boyz II Men
81	Passion Rod Stewart		92	Please Don't Go KWS
91	P.A.S.S.I.O.N. Rythm Syndicate		97	Please Don't Go No Mercy
96	Paste Pluto		93	Please Forgive Me Bryan Adams
89	Patience Guns N' Roses		75	Please Mr. Please Olivia Newton-John
86	Patio Latterns Kim Mitchell		97	Please/Popheart Live E.P. U2
93	Paying The Price Of Love Bee Gees		97	Plus Belles Chansons D'Amour Jean Errat
90	Peace In Our Time Eddie Money			
77	Peace Of Mind Boston		93	Plush Stone Temple Pilots
92	Peace Of Mind One 2 One		98	Poets Tragically Hip
96	Peace On Earth/Little Drummer Boy David Bowie & Bing Crosby		86	Point Of No Return Nu Shooz
			87	Point Of No Return Expose
98	Peace On Earth/Little Drummer Boy David Bowie & Bing Crosby		90	Poison Bell Biv Devoe
			90	Poison Alice Cooper
96	Peaches Presidents Of The United States Of America		97	Poison Prodigy
			83	Poison Arrow ABC
78	Peg Steely Dan			

90	**Policy Of Truth** Depeche Mode	88	**Prove Your Love** Taylor Dayne
84	**The Politics Of Dancing** Re-Flex	89	**Pump Up The Jam** Technotronic featuring Felly
97	**Pony** Ginuwine		
78	**Poor Poor Pitiful Me** Linda Ronstadt	88	**Pump Up The Volume** M.A.R.R.S.
88	**Pop Goes The World** Men Without Hats	94	**Pure** West End Girls
		84	**Purple Rain** Prince & The Revolution
79	**Pop Muzik** M	94	**Push** Moist
89	**Pop Singer** John Cougar Mellencamp	97	**Push** Matchbox 20
90	**Possession** Bad English	99	**Push** Sky
93	**Possession** Sarah McLachlan	88	**Push It** Salt-N-Pepa
88	**Pour Some Sugar On Me** Def Leppard	89	**Put A Little Love In Your Heart** Annie Lennox/Al Green
90	**The Power** Snap!	78	**Put Your Head On My Shoulder** Leif Garrett
90	**Power Jam** Chill Rob G		
98	**The Power Of Good-bye** Madonna	83	**Putting On The Ritz** Taco
85	**The Power Of Love** Frankie Goes To Hollywood	83	**P.Y.T. (Pretty Young Thing)** Michael Jackson

Q

85	**Power Of Love** Huey Lewis & The News		
86	**The Power Of Love** Jennifer Rush	93	**Quality Time** Hi-Five
91	**Power Of Love** Deee-Lite	77	**Que Sera Sera** The Raes
94	**The Power Of Love** Celine Dion	81	**Queen Of Hearts** Juice Newton
91	**Power Of Love/Love Power** Luther Vandross	83	**Queen Of The Broken Hearts** Loverboy
91	**Power Windows** Billy Falcon	94	**Queen Of The Night** Whitney Houston
91	**Powerdrive** Longfellow	75	**Quick Change Artist** Bachman-Turner Overdrive
95	**Practice What You Preach** Barry White		
99	**Praise You** Fatboy Slim	97	**Quit Playing Games (With My Heart)** Backstreet Boys
90	**Pray** MC Hammer		

R

94	**Prayer For The Dying** Seal		
90	**Praying For Time** George Michael		
97	**Precious Declaration** Collective Soul	93	**R U Sexin' Me** West End Girls
93	**Pressing Lips** Pursuit Of Happiness	77	**Race Among The Ruins** Gordon Lightfoot
82	**Pressure** Billy Joel		
93	**Pressure Us** Sunscreem	90	**Radar Love** Oh Well
90	**Pretending** Eric Clapton	84	**Radio Ga Ga** Queen
99	**Pretty Fly (For A White Guy)** The Offspring	88	**Rag Doll** Aerosmith
		87	**Rain** Michael Breen
96	**Pretty Noose** Soundgarden	87	**The Rain** Oran "Juice" Jones
82	**Pretty Woman** Van Halen	93	**Rain** Madonna
90	**Price Of Love** Bad English	92	**Rain Down On Me** Blue Rodeo
84	**Pride (In The Name Of Love)** U2	94	**Rain King** Counting Crows
92	**Pride (In The Name Of Love)** Clivilles & Cole	78	**Raise A Little Hell** Trooper
		99	**Rally 'N'** Jully Black
91	**Primal Scream** Mötley Crüe	80	**Rapper's Delight** Sugarhill Gang
92	**Princess** Devon	81	**Rapture** Blondie
90	**Principal's Office** Young M.C.	85	**Raspberry Beret** Prince
85	**Private Dancer** Tina Turner	99	**Raspberry Swirl** Tori Amos
81	**Private Eyes** Daryl Hall & John Oates	79	**Rasputin** Boney M
95	**Private Fantasy** Lia	88	**Rave On** John Cougar Mellencamp
90	**Private Symphony** Maestro Fresh-Wes	98	**Ray Of Light** Madonna
		96	**Reach** Gloria Estefan
96	**Professional Widow** Tori Amos	84	**Read 'Em And Weep** Barry Manilow
91	**The Promise Of A New Day** Paula Abdul	90	**Ready Or Not** After 7
		96	**Ready To Go** Republica
79	**Promises** Eric Clapton	78	**Ready To Take A Chance** Barry Manilow
99	**Promises** The Cranberries		
96	**Promises Broken** Soul Asylum	80	**Real Love** Doobie Brothers
83	**Promises, Promises** Naked Eyes	89	**Real Love** Jody Watley
78	**Prove It All Night** Bruce Springsteen	91	**The Real Love** Bob Seger

92	Real Love Mary J. Blige		91	Right Here Right Now Jesus Jones
96	Real Love The Beatles		89	Right Here Waiting Richard Marx
91	Real Real Real Jesus Jones		91	Right Here, Right Now Jesus Jones
96	Real Stuff Colin James		93	The Right Kind Of Love Jeremy Jordan
94	The Real Thing 2 Unlimited			
93	Real World Alanis		97	Right On OMC
98	Real World Matchbox 20		87	Right On Track Breakfast Club
81	Really Wanna Know You Gary Wright		87	The Right Thing Simply Red
93	Reason To Believe Rod Stewart		96	The Right Time The Corrs
84	Rebel Yell Billy Idol		77	Right Time Of The Night Jennifer Warnes
95	Red Light Special TLC			
84	Red Red Wine UB40		79	Ring My Bell Anita Ward
84	The Reflex Duran Duran		83	Rio Duran Duran
80	Refugee Tom Petty & The Heartbreakers		79	Rise Herb Alpert
			83	Rise Up Parachute Club
93	Regret New Order		93	The River Of Dreams Billy Joel
84	Relax Frankie Goes To Hollywood		78	Rivers Of Babylon Boney M
90	Release Me Wilson Phillips		90	Roam The B-52's
92	Remedy Black Crowes		94	Rock & Roll Dreams Come Through Meat Loaf
80	Remember Aerosmith			
92	Remember The Time Michael Jackson		85	Rock & Roll Girls John Fogerty
			76	Rock & Roll Music Beach Boys
78	Reminiscing Little River Band		90	Rock And A Hard Place Rolling Stones
79	Renegade Styx			
91	Rescue Me Madonna		76	Rock And Roll All Nite Kiss
92	Rescued (By The Arms Of Love) Glass Tiger		78	Rock And Roll Cowboys Cooper Brothers
87	Respect Yourself Bruce Willis		78	Rock And Roll Is A Vicious Game April Wine
92	Rest In Peace Extreme			
92	Restless Heart Peter Cetera		95	Rock And Roll Is Dead Lenny Kravitz
97	Resurrection Moist		86	R.O.C.K. In The U.S.A. John Cougar Mellencamp
93	Return Of The Crazy One Digital Underground			
			84	Rock It Herbie Hancock
97	Return Of The Mack Mark Morrison		80	Rock Lobster The B-52s
94	Return To Innocence Enigma		86	Rock Me Amadeus Falco
79	Reunited Peaches & Herb		84	Rock Me Tonight Billy Squier
92	Revolution Arrested Development		76	Rock N' Me Steve Miller
76	Rhiannon Fleetwood Mac		89	Rock N' Roll Duty Kim Mitchell
75	Rhinestone Cowboy Glen Campbell		79	Rock N' Roll Fantasy Bad Company
92	Rhythm Is A Dancer Snap!		83	Rock N' Roll Is King Electric Light Orchestra
87	Rhythm Is Gonna Get You Gloria Estefan & Miami Sound Machine			
			76	Rock N' Roll Love Letter Bay City Rollers
90	Rhythm Nation Janet Jackson			
97	Rhythm Of Love DJ Company		83	Rock Of Ages Def Leppard
91	Rhythm Of My Heart Rod Stewart		88	Rock Of Life Rick Springfield
85	Rhythm Of The Night DeBarge		89	Rock On Michael Damian
91	The Rhythm Of Your Love Glass Tiger		95	Rock Steady Bonnie Raitt
			83	Rock The Casbah The Clash
77	Rich Girl Daryl Hall & John Oates		82	Rock This Town Stray Cats
91	Rico Sauve Gerardo		89	Rock Wit'cha Bobby Brown
80	Ride Like The Wind Christopher Cross		80	Rock With You Michael Jackson
91	Ride The Wind Poison		84	Rock You Helix
95	Ridiculous Thoughts The Cranberries		84	Rock You Like A Hurricane Scorpions
76	Right Back Where We Started From Maxine Nightingale		98	Rockafeller Skank Fatboy Slim
			89	Rocket Def Leppard
77	Right Before Your Eyes Ian Thomas		88	Rocket 2 U The Jets
94	Right Beside You Sophie B. Hawkins		90	Rocket To My Heart Paul Janz
90	The Right Combination Seiko And Donnie Wahlberg		75	The Rockford Files Mike Post
			85	Rockin' At Midnight The Honeydrippers
78	Right Down The Line Gerry Rafferty			
93	Right Here/Human Nature SWV		75	Rockin' Chair Gwen McCrae

90	Rockin' Over The Beat Technotronic
89	Rocklandwonderland Kim Mitchell
94	Rocks Primal Scream
75	Rocky Austin Roberts
79	Rolene Moon Martin
92	Roll The Bones Rush
95	Roll To Me Del Amitri
88	Roll With It Steve Winwood
84	Romancing The Stone Eddy Grant
91	Romantic Karyn White
90	Romeo Dino
98	Romeo & Juliet Sylk-E-Fyne featuring Chili
92	Romeo And Juliet Stacy Earl
80	Romeo's Tune Steve Forbert
89	Roni Bobby Brown
90	Room At The Top Adam Ant
89	Room To Move Animotion
89	Room's On Fire Stevie Nicks
88	Rooty Toot Toot John Cougar Mellencamp
82	Rosanna Toto
80	The Rose Bette Midler
75	Round And Round Octavian
84	Round And Round Ratt
88	Round And Round Frozen Ghost
94	Round Here Counting Crows
78	Round Round We Go Trooper
98	Roxanne '97 Sting & The Police
76	Roxy Roller Sweeney Todd
90	Rub You The Right Way Johnny Gill
93	Rubberband Girl Kate Bush
77	Rubberband Man Spinners
77	Ruby Baby Wednesday
97	Rumble In Jungle Fugees
86	Rumors Timex Social Club
93	Rump Shaker Wreckx-N-Effect
99	Run Collective Soul
95	Run Around Blues Traveler
75	Run Joey Run David Geddes
84	Run Runaway Slade
84	Run To You Bryan Adams
93	Run To You Whitney Houston
93	Run To You Rage
78	Runaround Sue Leif Garrett
78	Runaway Jefferson Starship
92	Runaway Deee-Lite
95	Runaway The Corrs
95	Runaway Janet Jackson
95	Runaway Real McCoy
93	Runaway Love En Vogue
93	Runaway Train Soul Asylum
84	Runner Manfred Mann
97	Runnin' 2 Pac
91	Running Back To You Vanessa Williams
89	Running Down A Dream Tom Petty
87	Running In The Family Level 42
78	Running On Empty Jackson Browne
85	Running Up That Hill Kate Bush
84	Running With The Night Lionel Richie

| 88 | Rush Hour Jane Wiedlin |
| 91 | Rush Rush Paula Abdul |

S

89	Sacred Emotion Donny Osmond
90	Sacrifice Elton John
92	Sad But True Metallica
96	Sad Caper Hootie & The Blowfish
79	Sad Eyes Robert John
84	Sad Songs (Say So Much) Elton John
91	Sadeness Part 1 Enigma
93	Safe Rumble
83	The Safety Dance Men Without Hats
93	Said I Loved You...But I Lied Michael Bolton
79	Sail On Commodores
80	Sailing Christopher Cross
97	Saint Orbital
85	St. Elmo's Fire (Man In Motion) John Parr
98	Saint Of Me Rolling Stones
96	Salvation The Cranberries
77	Sam Olivia Newton-John
86	Sanctify Yourself Simple Minds
77	Santa Maria Trooper
96	Santa Monica (Watch The World Die) Everclear
80	Sara Fleetwood Mac
86	Sara Starship
76	Sara Smile Daryl Hall & John Oates
89	Satisfied Richard Marx
95	Satisfied Odds
76	Saturday Night Bay City Rollers
95	Saturday Night Whigfield
81	Sausalito Summernight Diesel
85	Save A Prayer Duran Duran
90	Save Me Fleetwood Mac
91	Save Some Love Keedy
92	Save The Best For Last Vanessa Williams
98	Save Tonight Eagle Eye Cherry
76	Save Your Kisses For Me Brotherhood Of Man
91	Saved By Love Rik Emmett
88	Savin' Myself Eria Fachin
76	Saving All My Love Charity Brown
85	Saving All My Love For You Whitney Houston
93	Saving Forever For You Shanice
90	Say A Prayer Breathe
81	Say Goodbye To Hollywood Billy Joel
80	Say Hello April Wine
98	Say It Voices Of Theory
83	Say It Isn't So Daryl Hall & John Oates
86	Say It, Say It E.G. Daily
84	Say Say Say Paul McCartney/Michael Jackson
97	Say What You Want Texas
76	Say You Love Me Shirley Eikhard
88	Say You Will Foreigner
93	Say You Will Gogh Van Go

92	Say You'll Be Mine West End Girls	90	7 O'Clock London Quireboys
97	Say You'll Be There Spice Girls	94	7 Seconds Youssou N'Dour/Neneh Cherry
77	Say You'll Stay Until Tomorrow Tom Jones	87	Seven Wonders Fleetwood Mac
86	Say You, Say Me Lionel Richie	98	Sex & Candy Marcy Playground
97	Say...If You Feel Alright Crystal Waters	83	Sex (I'm A...) Berlin (U.S.A.)
		86	Sex As A Weapon Pat Benatar
96	Scary Kisses Voice Of The Beehive	91	Sex With Love Lee Aaron
95	Scatman (Ski-Ba-Bop-Ba-Dop-Bop) Scatman John	84	Sexcrime (Nineteen Eighty-Four) Eurythmics
84	Scatterlings Of Africa Juluka	93	Sexual Goddess
95	Scream Michael Jackson & Janet Jackson	96	Sexual Healing Max-A-Million
		83	Sexual Healing Marvin Gaye
87	Se La Lionel Richie	80	Sexy Eyes Dr. Hook
85	Sea Of Love The Honeydrippers	95	Sexy Girl Snow
85	The Search Is Over Survivor	92	Sexy MF Prince & The New Power Generation
98	Searchin' My Soul Vonda Shepard		
77	Seaside Woman Suzy And The Red Stripes	81	Shaddap You Face Joe Dolce
		78	Shadow Dancing Andy Gibb
88	Seasons Change Expose	79	Shadows In The Moonlight Anne Murray
89	Second Chance 38 Special		
98	Second Round K.O. Canibus	82	Shadows Of The Night Pat Benatar
86	Secret OMD	79	Shake It Ian Matthews
94	Secret Madonna	82	Shake It Up The Cars
95	Secret Garden Bruce Springsteen	87	Shake You Down Gregory Abbott
97	Secret Garden Bruce Springsteen	79	Shake Your Body (Down To The Ground) Jacksons
86	Secret Lovers Atlantic Starr		
89	Secret Rendezvous Karyn White	76	Shake Your Booty KC & The Sunshine Band
86	Secret Separation The Fixx		
80	The Seduction (Love Theme) James Last Band	79	Shake Your Groove Thing Peaches & Herb
91	See The Lights Simple Minds	88	Shake Your Love Debbie Gibson
97	See The People Soul Attorneys	87	Shakedown Bob Seger
84	Self Control Laura Branigan	78	Shame Evelyn "Champagne" King
97	Semi-Charmed Life Third Eye Blind	85	Shame The Motels
77	Send In The Clowns Judy Collins	95	Shame Zhane
93	Send Me A Lover Taylor Dayne	83	Shame On The Moon Bob Seger
84	Send Me An Angel Real Life	93	Shamrocks & Shenanigans House Of Pain
91	Send Me An Angel Scorpions		
79	Send One Your Love Stevie Wonder	76	Shannon Henry Gross
90	Sending All My Love Linear	79	Sharing The Night Together Dr. Hook
94	Sending My Love Zhane	88	Shattered Dreams Johnny Hates Jazz
91	Sensitivity Ralph Tresvant	90	She Ain't Pretty Northern Pikes
95	Sentimental Deborah Cox	90	She Ain't Worth It Glenn Medeiros
78	Sentimental Lady Bob Welch	79	She Believes In Me Kenny Rogers
85	Sentimental Street Night Ranger	83	She Blinded Me With Science Thomas Dolby
92	Senza Una Donna (Without A Woman) Zucchero		
		84	She Bop Cyndi Lauper
85	Separate Lives Phil Collins/Marilyn Martin	77	She Did It Eric Carmen
		89	She Drives Me Crazy Fine Young Cannibals
83	Separate Ways Journey		
79	September Earth, Wind & Fire	84	She Got The Radio Corey Hart
80	September Morn Neil Diamond	95	She Picked On Me Roch Voisine
94	Serious Sheree Jeacocke	86	She Sells Sanctuary The Cult
93	Sesame's Treat Smart E's	91	She Talks To Angels Black Crowes
91	Set Adrift On Memory Bliss PM Dawn	89	She Wants To Dance With Me Rick Astley
91	Set The Night To Music Roberta Flack/Maxi Priest	83	She Works Hard For The Money Donna Summer
96	Set U Free Planet Soul	83	She's A Beauty The Tubes
93	7 Prince & The New Power Generation	91	She's A Flirt Kish

95	She's A River Simple Minds	77	Signed, Sealed, Delivered Peter Frampton
78	She's Always A Woman Billy Joel	91	Signs Tesla
76	She's Gone Daryl Hall & John Oates	99	Silence Delerium
88	She's Having A Baby Dave Wakeling	91	Silent Lucidity Queensryche
88	She's Like The Wind Patrick Swayze	86	Silent Running Mike & The Mechanics
84	She's Mine Steve Perry	99	Silly Ho TLC
90	She's My Baby Traveling Wilburys	76	Silly Love Songs Paul McCartney & Wings
95	She's Not In Love Kim Stockwood		
80	She's Out Of My Life Michael Jackson	94	Silver Moist
92	She's Playing Hard To Get Hi-Five	93	Simple Life Elton John
83	(She's) Sexy & 17 Stray Cats	88	Simply Irresistible Robert Palmer
80	She's So Cold Rolling Stones	79	Since I Don't Have You Art Garfunkel
99	She's So High Tal Bachman	94	Since I Don't Have You Guns N' Roses
89	She's So Young Pursuit Of Happiness		
84	She's Trouble Musical Youth	98	Since When 54-40
97	Shed A Light Roch Voisine	93	Sinful Wishes Kon Kan
91	Shelter Me Cinderella	76	Sing A Song Earth, Wind & Fire
83	Sheriff The Tenants	92	Sinking Like A Sunset Tom Cochrane
77	Sherry Keane Brothers	77	Sir Duke Stevie Wonder
94	Shine Collective Soul	84	Sister Christian Night Ranger
79	Shine A Little Love Electric Light Orchestra	75	Sister Golden Hair America
		85	Sisters Are Doin' It For Themselves Eurythmics and Aretha Franklin
75	Shining Star Earth, Wind & Fire		
80	Shining Star Manhattans	90	Sittin' In The Lap Of Luxury Louie Louie
91	Shining Star INXS		
91	Shiny Happy People R.E.M.	77	(Sittin' On) The Dock Of The Bay Pagliaro
79	Ships Barry Manilow		
91	Shock Rock BB Jerome & The Bang Gang	88	(Sittin' On) The Dock Of The Bay Michael Bolton
82	Shock The Monkey Peter Gabriel	96	Sittin' Up In My Room Brandy
96	Shoebox Barenaked Ladies	83	Sitting At The Wheel Moody Blues
93	Shoop Salt-N-Pepa	90	Sitting In The Lap Of Luxury Louie Louie
91	The Shoop Shoop Song (It's In His Kiss) Cher		
		97	Sitting On The Top Of The World Amanda Marshall
76	Shop Around Captain & Tennille		
95	Short Dick Man 20 Fingers	85	Situation Critical Platinum Blonde
78	Short People Randy Newman	91	Six Minutes Of Pleasure L.L. Cool J
82	Should I Do It Pointer Sisters	82	Six Months In A Leaky Boat Split Enz
87	Should've Known Better Richard Marx	96	6th Avenue Heartache The Wallflowers
85	Shout Tears For Fears	82	'65 Love Affair Paul Davis
76	Shout It Out Loud Kiss	87	Skeletons Stevie Wonder
94	Shout Out Loud Roch Voisine	94	Skip To My Lu Lisa Lisa
98	Show Me D-Cru featuring Golden Child	75	Sky High Jigsaw
93	Show Me Love Robin S	94	The Sky Is Falling Junkhouse
98	Show Me Love Robyn	98	Sky's The Limit Majik
76	Show Me The Way Peter Frampton	98	Sky's The Limit Notorious B.I.G.
91	Show Me The Way Styx	86	Sledgehammer Peter Gabriel
92	Show Me The Way West End Girls	85	Sleeping Bag ZZ Top
76	Showdown Electric Light Orchestra	94	Sleeping In My Car Roxette
96	Shut Up (And Sleep With Me) Sin With Sebastian	93	Sleeping Satellite Tasmin Archer
		96	Sleepy Maggie Ashley MacIsaac
83	Shy Boy (Don't It Make You Feel Good) Bananarama	99	Slide Goo Goo Dolls
		97	Slip N' Slide Tia
95	Shy Guy Diana King	78	Slip Sliding Away Paul Simon
94	The Sign Ace Of Base	93	Slow & Sexy Shabba Ranks
87	Sign 'O' The Times Prince	77	Slow Dancin' Don't Turn Me On Addrissi Brothers
83	Sign Of The Times Mens Room		
88	Sign Your Name Terence Trent D'Arby	77	(Slow Dancin') Swayin' To The Music Johnny Rivers

81	**Slow Hand** Pointer Sisters	91	**Someday** Mariah Carey
92	**Slow Motion** Color Me Badd	92	**Someday** Concrete Blonde
91	**Slowly Slipping Away** Harem Scarem	99	**Someday** Sugar Ray
97	**Smack My Bitch Up** Prodigy	95	**Someday I'll Be Saturday Night** Bon Jovi
86	**Small Town** John Cougar Mellencamp		
85	**Smalltown Boy** Bronski Beat	97	**Someone** SWV
92	**Smells Like Nirvana** "Weird Al" Yankovic	82	**Someone Could Lose A Heart Tonight** Eddie Rabbitt
92	**Smells Like Teen Spirit** Nirvana	75	**Someone Saved My Life Tonight** Elton John
99	**Smile** Vitamin C		
77	**Smoke From A Distant Fire** The Sanford/Townsend Band	92	**Someone To Hold** Trey Lorenz
		95	**Someone To Love** Jon B./Babyface
85	**Smokin' In The Boys Room** Mötley Crüe	96	**Someone Who's Cool** Odds
		95	**Something 4 Da Honeyz** Montell Jordan
91	**Smooth As Silk** MCJ & Cool G		
85	**Smooth Operator** Sade	97	**Something About The Way You Look Tonight** Elton John
89	**So Alive** Love & Rockets		
84	**So Bad** Paul McCartney	86	**Something About You** Level 42
95	**So Blind** Alan Frew	95	**Something For The Pain/Lie To Me** Bon Jovi
90	**So Close** Daryl Hall & John Oates		
88	**So Emotional** Whitney Houston	91	**Something Go Me Started** Simply Red
86	**So Far Away** Dire Straits		
96	**So Far Away** Rod Stewart	90	**Something Happened On The Way To Heaven** Phil Collins
76	**So Glad You're A Woman** Neon Philharmonic		
		93	**Something In Common** Bobby Brown/Whitney Houston
90	**So Hard** Sass Jordan		
90	**So Hard** Pet Shop Boys	80	**Something On My Mind** Teenage Head
96	**So Hard** Voice Of The Beehive		
77	**So Into You** Atlanta Rhythm Section	87	**Something Real (Inside Me/Inside You)** Mr. Mister
98	**So Into You** Tamia		
90	**So Listen** MCJ & Cool G	87	**Something So Strong** Crowded House
94	**So Much In Love** All-4-One		
96	**So Much To Say** Dave Matthews Band	90	**Something To Believe In** Poison
99	**So Pure** Alanis Morissette	88	**Something To Live For** Barney Bentall & The Legendary Hearts
97	**So They Say** Soul Attorneys		
96	**Soaked** The Killjoys	91	**Something To Talk About** Bonnie Raitt
98	**Sock It 2 Me** Missy "Misdemeanor" Elliott	94	**Something's Always Wrong** Toad The Wet Sprocket
89	**Soldier Of Love** Donny Osmond	93	**Something's Going On** UNV
85	**Solid** Ashford & Simpson	99	**Sometimes** Britney Spears
94	**Solid Ground** Ginger	92	**Sometimes Love Just Ain't Enough** Patty Smyth with Don Henley
75	**Solitaire** Carpenters		
83	**Solitaire** Laura Branigan	90	**Sometimes She Cries** Warrant
84	**Some Guys Have All The Luck** Rod Stewart	77	**Sometimes When We Touch** Dan Hill
		94	**Somewhere** Shanice
83	**Some Kind Of Friend** Barry Manilow	76	**Somewhere In The Night** Helen Reddy
98	**Some Kinda Wonderful** Sky		
85	**Some Like It Hot** Power Station	87	**Somewhere Out There** Linda Ronstadt/James Ingram
85	**Some Things Are Better Left Unsaid** Daryl Hall & John Oates		
		98	**Song For Mama** Boyz II Men
85	**Somebody** Bryan Adams	86	**Song In My Head** M+M
86	**Somebody Somewhere** Platinum Blonde	92	**Song Instead Of A Kiss** Alannah Myles
77	**Somebody To Love** Queen	87	**Songbird** Kenny G
93	**Somebody To Love** George Michael and Queen	93	**Sonny Say You Will** Alannah Myles
		75	**Sorry Seems To Be The Hardest Word** Elton John
82	**Somebody's Baby** Jackson Browne		
95	**Somebody's Cryin'** Chris Isaak	75	**S.O.S.** ABBA
81	**Somebody's Knockin'** Terri Gibbs	86	**Soul City** Partland Brothers
84	**Somebody's Watching Me** Rockwell	85	**Soul Kiss** Olivia Newton-John
86	**Someday** Glass Tiger	79	**Soul Man** Blues Brothers

93	**Soul To Squeeze** Red Hot Chili Peppers	92	**Stay** Shakespear's Sister
94	**Souls Road** Lawrence Gowan	94	**Stay** Eternal
97	**The Sound Of...** Jann Arden	98	**Stay** Sash!
95	**Sour Times** Portishead	94	**Stay (Faraway, So Close)** U2
77	**Southern Nights** Glen Campbell	94	**Stay (I Missed You)** Lisa Loeb And Nine Stories
89	**Sowing The Seeds Of Love** Tears For Fears	87	**Stay The Night** Benjamin Orr
98	**Space Lord** Monster Magnet	99	**Stay The Same** Joey McIntyre
93	**A Space Shady** RuPaul	87	**Stay With Me** Tu
96	**Spaceman** Babylon Zoo	84	**Stay With Me Tonight** Jeffrey Osborne
98	**Spaceman** Bif	78	**Stayin' Alive** Bee Gees
77	**Spaceship Superstar** Prism	96	**Stayin' Alive** N-Trance
85	**Spanish Eddie** Laura Branigan	88	**Staying Together** Debbie Gibson
98	**Spark** Tori Amos	80	**Steal Away** Robbie Dupree
80	**Special Lady** Ray, Goodman & Brown	99	**Steal My Sunshine** Len
91	**Spending My Time** Roxette	93	**Steam** Peter Gabriel
97	**Spice Up Your Life** Spice Girls	90	**Steamy Windows** Tina Turner
96	**Spiderwebs** No Doubt	92	**Steel Bars** Michael Bolton
86	**Spies Like Us** Paul McCartney	81	**Step By Step** Eddie Rabbitt
97	**Spin Spin Sugar** Sneaker Pimps	90	**Step By Step** New Kids On The Block
90	**Spin That Wheel** Hi Tek 3 featuring Ya Kid K	97	**Step By Step** Whitney Houston
86	**Spirit In The Sky** Doctor And The Medics	93	**Step It Up** Stereo MCs
		91	**Step On** Happy Mondays
80	**The Spirit Of Radio** Rush	82	**Steppin' Out** Joe Jackson
82	**Spirits In The Material World** The Police	98	**Stick To Your Vision** Maestro
		79	**Still** Commodores
88	**Spot You In A Coalmine** Corey Hart	91	**Still Beating** World On Edge
76	**Springtime Mama** Henry Gross	89	**Still Cruisin'** Beach Boys
95	**Square Dance Song (I Wanna Go Higher)** BKS featuring Ashley MacIsaac	90	**Still Got This Thing** Alannah Myles
		82	**Still In The Game** Steve Winwood
		76	**Still The One** Orleans
76	**Squeeze Box** The Who	78	**Still The Same** Bob Seger
99	**Squeeze Toy** Boomtang Boys	79	**Stillsane** Carolyne Mas
86	**Stages** ZZ Top	89	**Stop** Sam Brown
89	**Stand** R.E.M.	98	**Stop** Spice Girls
90	**Stand** Paul Janz	99	**Stop & Panic** Cirrus
93	**Stand** Poison	81	**Stop Draggin' My Heart Around** Stevie Nicks (with Tom Petty & The Heartbreakers)
83	**Stand Back** Stevie Nicks		
87	**Stand By Me** Ben E. King		
98	**Stand By Me** 4 The Cause	77	**Stop I Don't Need No Symphony** Alma Faye Brooks
92	**Stand By My Woman** Lenny Kravitz		
93	**Stand By Your Man** L.L. Cool J	93	**Stop The World** Extreme
76	**Stand Tall** Burton Cummings	85	**Storm Before The Calm** Luba
93	**Stand Up** Def Leppard	83	**Straight From The Heart** Bryan Adams
96	**Standing Outside A Broken Phone Booth With Money In My Hand** Primitive Radio Gods	78	**Straight On** Heart
		91	**Straight To Your Heart** Bad English
		89	**Straight Up** Paula Abdul
91	**Standing Push & Fall** World On Edge	90	**Stranded** Heart
77	**Star Wars Theme/Cantina Band** Meco	95	**Strange Currencies** R.E.M.
		99	**Strange Disease** Prozzäk
97	**Staring At The Sun** U2	76	**Strange Magic** Electric Light Orchestra
92	**Stars** Simply Red	79	**Strange Way** Firefall
81	**Start Me Up** Rolling Stones	83	**Stranger In My House** Ronnie Milsap
92	**Start Me Up** Salt-N-Pepa	85	**Stranger In Town** Toto
82	**Start Tellin' The Truth** Toronto	89	**Stranger Than Paradise** Sass Jordan
84	**State Of Shock** Jacksons	94	**The Strangest Party** INXS
93	**State Of The Heart** West End Girls	77	**Strawberry Letter 23** Brothers Johnson
91	**State Of The World** Janet Jackson		
78	**Stay** Jackson Browne	83	**Stray Cat Strut** Stray Cats

97	**Street Dreams** Nas		Dummies
91	**Street Of Dreams** Nia Peeples	93	**Supermodel (You Better Work)** RuPaul
94	**Streets Of Philadelphia** Bruce Springsteen	93	**Supernatural** John James
84	**Strike** Eddie Schwartz	88	**Superstitious** Europe
91	**Strike It Up** Black Box	89	**Superwoman** Karyn White
81	**The Stroke** Billy Squier	99	**Suprize Packidge** Mix Master Mike
95	**Stroke You Up** Changing Faces	87	**Surfin' Bird** Pee Wee Herman
90	**Strokin'** Clarence Carter	89	**Surrender To Me** Ann Wilson/Robin Zander
95	**Strong Enough** Sheryl Crow	98	**Surrounded** Chantal Kreviazuk
99	**Strong Enough** Cher	86	**Suspicious Minds** Fine Young Cannibals
84	**Strut** Sheena Easton	85	**Sussudio** Phil Collins
84	**Stuck On You** Lionel Richie	97	**Swallowed** Bush X
86	**Stuck With You** Huey Lewis & The News	75	**Swearin' To God** Frankie Valli
79	**Stumblin' In** Suzi Quatro & Chris Norman	93	**Sweat (A La La La La Long)** Inner Circle
96	**Stupid Girl** Garbage	92	**The Sweater** Meryn Cadell
88	**Stutter Rap** Morris Minor & The Majors	88	**Sweet Child O' Mine** Guns N' Roses
92	**Success Has Made A Failure Of Our Home** Sinead O'Connor	99	**Sweet Child O' Mine** Sheryl Crow
99	**Sucks To Be You** Prozzäk	82	**Sweet Dreams** Air Supply
85	**Suddenly** Billy Ocean	94	**Sweet Dreams** La Bouche
83	**Suddenly Last Summer** The Motels	96	**Sweet Dreams** La Bouche
98	**Sugar Cane** Space Monkeys	83	**Sweet Dreams (Are Made Of This)** Eurythmics
77	**Sugar Daddy** Patsy Gallant	92	**Sweet Emotion** Aerosmith
97	**Sugar Is Sweeter** C.J. Bolland	86	**Sweet Freedom** Michael McDonald
92	**Sugar Sugar** DJ Les & Kool Kat	76	**Sweet Love** Commodores
85	**Sugar Walls** Sheena Easton	86	**Sweet Love** Anita Baker
95	**Sugarhill** AZ	78	**Sweet Misery** Teaze
90	**Suicide Blonde** INXS	94	**Sweet Sensual Love** Big Mountain
81	**Sukiyaki** A Taste Of Honey	87	**Sweet Sixteen** Billy Idol
95	**Sukiyaki** 4 P.M.	98	**Sweet Surrender** Sarah McLachlan
79	**Sultans Of Swing** Dire Straits	78	**Sweet Sweet Smile** Carpenters
76	**Summer** War	78	**Sweet Talkin' Women** Electric Light Orchestra
95	**The Summer Is Magic** Playahitty	76	**Sweet Thing** Rufus
99	**Summer Girls** LFO	93	**Sweet Thing** Mary J. Blige
76	**Summer Love** Craig Ruhnke	93	**Sweet Thing** Mick Jagger
79	**Summer Night City** ABBA	95	**The Sweetest Days** Vanessa Williams
78	**Summer Nights** John Travolta & Olivia Newton-John	86	**The Sweetest Taboo** Sade
85	**Summer Of '69** Bryan Adams	98	**Sweetest Thing** U2
90	**Summer Rain** Belinda Carlisle	81	**Sweetheart** Frankie And The Knockouts
98	**Summerlong** Emm Gryner	84	**Swept Away** Diana Ross
91	**Summertime** DJ Jazzy Jeff & The Fresh Prince	94	**Swimming In Your Ocean** Crash Test Dummies
86	**The Sun Always Shines On TV** A-Ha	89	**Swing The Mood** Jive Bunny & The Mastermixers
86	**Sun City** Artists United Against Apartheid	78	**Swingtown** Steve Miller
90	**Sun Comes Up, It's Tuesday Morning** Cowboy Junkies	95	**Sympathy For The Devil** Guns N' Roses
94	**Sun's Gonna Rise** Sass Jordan	83	**Synchronicity II** The Police
93	**Sunday Morning** Earth, Wind & Fire		
97	**Sunday Morning** No Doubt		
77	**Sunflowers** Glen Campbell		
84	**Sunglasses At Night** Corey Hart		
97	**Sunny Came Home** Shawn Colvin		**T**
98	**Sunshine** Jay-Z	96	**Taffy** Lisa Loeb
84	**Sunshine Reggae** Laid Back	82	**Tainted Love** Soft Cell
97	**Superbadgirls** Ivan	95	**Take A Bow** Madonna
91	**Superman's Song** Crash Test	78	**Take A Chance On Me** ABBA
		95	**Take Control** BKS

82	**Take It Away** Paul McCartney	96	**Tell Me** Dru Hill
94	**Take It Back** Pink Floyd	96	**Tell Me** Groove Theory
86	**Take It Easy** Andy Taylor	97	**Tell Me** Corey Hart
82	**Take It Easy On Me** Little River Band	98	**Tell Me** Billie Myers
76	**Take It Like A Man** Bachman-Turner Overdrive	99	**Tell Me It's Real** K-Ci & JoJo
81	**Take It On The Run** REO Speedwagon	90	**Tell Me Something** Indecent Obsession
76	**Take It Or Leave It** Moxy	95	**Tell Me What I Think** Spirit Of The West
76	**Take It To The Limit** Eagles	93	**Tell Me What You Dream** Restless Heart
78	**Take Me Away** Prism	92	**Tell Me What You Want Me To Do** Tevin Campbell
87	**Take Me Home Tonight** Eddie Money	95	**Tell Me When** Human League
75	**Take Me In Your Arms** Charity Brown	90	**Tell Me Why** Expose
75	**Take Me In Your Arms** Doobie Brothers	95	**Tell Me You Love Me** Carol Medina
99	**Take Me There** Blackstreet & Mya	84	**Tell No Lies** Spoons
83	**Take Me To Heart** Quarterflash	89	**Tell Somebody** Sass Jordan
96	**Take Me To Your Leader** Newsboys	90	**Temptation** The Box
86	**Take My Breath Away** Berlin	91	**Temptation** Corina
81	**Take Off** Bob & Doug McKenzie	99	**Tender** Blur
85	**Take On Me** A-Ha	86	**Tender Love** Force M.D.'S
90	**Take One Away** Burton Cummings	85	**Tenderness** General Public
79	**Take The Long Way Home** Supertramp	92	**Tennessee** Arrested Development
76	**Take The Money And Run** Steve Miller Band	92	**Tequila** ALT & The Lost Civilization
		98	**Tequila Sunrise** Cypress Hill
92	**Take This Heart** Richard Marx	96	**Test For Echo** Rush
92	**Take Time** Chris Walker	96	**Tha Crossroads** Bone Thugs N' Harmony
97	**Takes A Little Time** Amy Grant	75	**Thank God I'm A Country Boy** John Denver
76	**Takin' It To The Streets** Doobie Brothers	76	**Thank God I'm A Country Boy** Glen Campbell
87	**Talk Dirty To Me** Poison	98	**Thank U** Alanis Morissette
86	**Talk To Me** Stevie Nicks	95	**Thank You** Boyz II Men
87	**Talk To Me** Chico DeBarge	78	**Thank You For Being A Friend** Andrew Gold
97	**Talk To Me** Wild Orchid		
93	**Talkin' About Love** BKS	99	**That Don't Impress Me Much** Shania Twain
84	**Talking In Your Sleep** The Romantics		
88	**Tall Cool One** Robert Plant	82	**That Girl** Stevie Wonder
89	**Tango** Dalbello	96	**That Girl** Maxi Priest
86	**Tarzan Boy** Baltimora	96	**That Thing You Do** The Wonders
77	**Tattoo Man** Denise McCann	84	**That Was Then But This Is Now** ABC
84	**Teacher Teacher** 38 Special	86	**That Was Then, This Is Now** The Monkees
89	**Tear Drops** Womack & Womack		
76	**Tear The Roof Off The Sucker** Parliament	85	**That Was Yesterday** Foreigner
		76	**That'll Be The Day** Linda Ronstadt
98	**Tearin' Up My Heart** 'N Sync	84	**That's All** Genesis
85	**Tears Are Not Enough** Northern Lights	91	**That's Freedom** John Farnham
		90	**That's Life** Sue Medley
92	**Tears In Heaven** Eric Clapton	77	**That's Rock N' Roll** Shaun Cassidy
83	**Tears On Your Anorak** The Drivers	89	**That's The Way** Katrina & The Waves
87	**Teenland** Northern Pikes	75	**That's The Way I Like It** KC & The Sunshine Band
83	**Telefone (Long Distance Love Affair)** Sheena Easton		
		98	**That's The Way I Like It** Backstreet Boys
77	**Telephone Line** Electric Light Orchestra		
		91	**That's The Way Love Goes** Young M.C.
77	**Telephone Man** Meri Wilson		
83	**Tell Her About It** Billy Joel	93	**That's The Way Love Goes** Janet Jackson
97	**Tell Him** Barbra Streisand & Celine Dion		
81	**Tell It Like It Is** Heart		
88	**Tell It To My Heart** Taylor Dayne		

86	That's What Friends Are For Dionne & Friends	95	This Rod Stewart
93	That's What Love Can Do Boy Krazy	95	This Ain't A Love Song Bon Jovi
88	That's What Love Is All About Michael Bolton	90	This Beat Is Technotronic Technotronic
91	That's What Love Is For Amy Grant	95	This Cowboy Song Sting
78	Theme From "Close Encounters" Meco	91	This House Tracie Spencer
		95	This House Is Not A Home The Rembrandts
78	Theme From "Close Encounters" John Williams	95	This Is A Call Foo Fighters
81	Theme From "Greatest American Hero" Joey Scarbury	97	This Is For The Lover In You Babyface
77	Theme From "Rocky" - Gonna Fly Now Bill Conti	95	This Is How We Do It Montell Jordan
		98	This Is How We Party S.O.A.P.
76	Theme From "SWAT" Rhythm Heritage	80	This Is It Kenny Loggins
		85	This Is Not America David Bowie/Pat Metheny Group
76	Theme From "SWAT" THP Orchestra	91	This Is Ponderous 2nu
76	Theme From Mahogany (Do You Know Where You're Going To) Diana Ross	90	This Is The Right Time Lisa Stansfield
		96	This Is The Stuff Carolyn Arends
		87	This Is The Time Billy Joel
96	Theme From Mission: Impossible Adam Clayton/Larry Mullen	96	This Is Your Night Amber
		81	This Little Girl Gary "U.S." Bonds
84	There Goes My Baby Donna Summer	76	This Masquerade George Benson
85	There Must Be An Angel (Playing With My Heart) Eurythmics	87	This Mourning Chalk Circle
		90	This Old Heart Of Mine Rod Stewart
86	There Was A Time One To One	90	This One's For The Children New Kids On The Block
92	There Will Never Be Another Tonight Bryan Adams		
		76	This One's For You Barry Manilow
86	There'll Be Sad Songs (To Make You Cry) Billy Ocean	77	This Song George Harrison
		83	This Time Bryan Adams
76	(There's A) Kind Of Hush Carpenters	99	This Time Around Michael Fredo
88	There's The Girl Heart	89	This Time I Know It's For Real Donna Summer
96	These Are The Days Soul Attorneys		
99	These Are The Times Dru Hill	91	This Time Make It Funky Tracie Spencer
86	These Dreams Heart		
84	They Don't Know Tracey Ullman	92	This Used To Be My Playground Madonna
90	Thieves In The Temple Prince		
86	Thin Red Line Glass Tiger	75	This Will Be Natalie Cole
85	Things Can Only Get Better Howard Jones	87	Thorn In My Side Eurythmics
		92	Thought I Died And Gone To Heaven Bryan Adams
97	Things Just Ain't The Same Deborah Cox		
		98	3 am Matchbox 20
91	Things That Make You Go Hmmmm... C&C Music Factory featuring Freedom Williams	91	3 AM Eternal The KLF
		80	3 Dressed Up As A 9 Trooper
		78	Three Times A Lady Commodores
77	The Things We Do For Love 10cc	84	Thriller Michael Jackson
84	Think Of Laura Christopher Cross	89	Through The Storm Aretha Franklin/Elton John
95	Think Of You Whigfield		
94	Think Twice Celine Dion	83	Through The Years Tim Finn
88	Thinkin' About The Years Haywire	95	Throw Your Set In The Air Cypress Hill
99	Thinkin' About You 2 Rude featuring Latoya & Miranda		
		86	Throwing It All Away Genesis
92	Thinkin' Back Color Me Badd	94	Throwing It All Away Realworld
98	Thinking Of You Hanson	77	Thunder In My Heart Leo Sayer
97	Third Of June Corey Hart	78	Thunder Island Jay Ferguson
75	Third Rate Romance Amazing Rhythm Aces	90	Thunderstruck AC/DC
		85	Ti Amo Laura Branigan
80	Third-Time Lucky Foghat	96	Ti Amo Paul London
81	Thirsty Ears Powder Blues	90	Tic Tac Toe Kyper
97	Thirty-Three Smashing Pumpkins	97	Tic Tic Tac Cappricho featuring Chilli
98	32 Flavors Alana Davis	97	Tic Tic Tac Fruit De La Passion

90	**Tick Tock** Vaughan Brothers	80	**Too Bad** Doug & The Slugs
81	**The Tide Is High** Blondie	98	**Too Close** Next
91	**Til I Am Myself Again** Blue Rodeo	92	**Too Funky** George Michael
95	**Til I Hear It From You** Gin Blossoms	80	**Too Hot** Kool & The Gang
90	**Til The Fever Breaks** The Jitters	91	**Too Hot** Alanis
97	**Til You Love Somebody** Amy Sky	85	**Too Late For Goodbyes** Julian Lennon
81	**Time** Alan Parsons Project		
96	**Time** Hootie & The Blowfish	90	**Too Late To Say Goodbye** Richard Marx
83	**Time (Clock Of The Heart)** Culture Club		
		97	**Too Late, Too Soon/Amandolo** Jon Secada
84	**Time After Time** Cyndi Lauper		
98	**Time After Time** Inoj	82	**Too Many Times** Mental As Anything
93	**Time And Chance** Color Me Badd	91	**Too Many Walls** Cathy Dennis
90	**Time For Letting Go** Jude Cole	90	**Too Much** Bros
90	**The Time Of Day** Gino Vannelli	96	**Too Much** Dave Matthews Band
98	**Time Of Your Life (Good Riddance)** Green Day	98	**Too Much** Spice Girls
		79	**Too Much Heaven** Bee Gees
81	**Time Out Of Mind** Steely Dan	93	**Too Much Information** Duran Duran
78	**Time Passages** Al Stewart	96	**Too Much Love Will Kill You** Queen
91	**Time, Love And Tenderness** Michael Bolton	92	**Too Much Passion** Smithereens
		81	**Too Much Time On My Hands** Styx
77	**Timeless Love** Burton Cummings	78	**Too Much, Too Little, Too Late** Johnny Mathis/Deniece Williams
76	**Times Of Your Life** Paul Anka		
80	**Tired Of Toein' The Line** Rocky Burnette	83	**Too Shy** Kajagoogoo
		78	**Took The Last Train** David Gates
92	**TLC** Linear	93	**Top O' The Morning To Ya** House Of Pain
84	**To All The Girls I've Loved Before** Julio Iglesias & Willie Nelson		
		91	**Top Of The World** Van Halen
87	**To Be A Lover** Billy Idol	98	**Top Of The World** Brandy featuring Mase
92	**To Be With You** Mr. Big		
86	**To Live And Die In L.A.** Wang Chung	98	**Torn** Natalie Imbruglia
93	**To Love Somebody** Michael Bolton	77	**Torn Between Two Lovers** Mary MacGregor
97	**To Love You More** Celine Dion		
97	**To Make You Feel My Love** Billy Joel	84	**Torture** Jacksons
97	**To The Moon And Back** Savage Garden	83	**Total Eclipse Of The Heart** Bonnie Tyler
		95	**Total Eclipse Of The Heart** Nicki French
97	**Today** Smashing Pumpkins		
76	**Today's The Day** America	80	**Touch And Go** The Cars
87	**Together (The New Wedding Song)** Joey Gregorash	98	**Touch It** Monifah
		91	**Touch Me (All Night Long)** Cathy Dennis
98	**Together Again** Janet		
88	**Together Forever** Rick Astley	87	**Touch Me (I Want Your Body)** Samantha Fox
85	**Tokyo Rose** Idle Eyes		
90	**Tom's Diner** DNA featuring Suzanne Vega	87	**Touch Of Grey** Grateful Dead
		94	**Touch Of Your Hand** Glass Tiger
88	**Tomcat Prowl** Doug & The Slugs	85	**Tough All Over** John Cafferty & The Beaver Brown Band
97	**Tomorrow** James		
85	**Tonight** David Bowie	89	**Toy Soldiers** Martika
90	**Tonight** New Kids On The Block	79	**Tragedy** Bee Gees
82	**Tonight I'm Yours (Don't Hurt Me)** Rod Stewart	75	**Train** Shooter
		80	**Train In Vain** The Clash
75	**Tonight Is A Wonderful Time** April Wine	81	**Treat Me Right** Pat Benatar
		93	**Tribal Dance** 2 Unlimited
86	**Tonight She Comes** The Cars	78	**Tried To Love** Peter Frampton
96	**Tonight Tonight** Smashing Pumpkins	96	**Trippin' On A Hole** Stone Temple Pilots
76	**Tonight's The Night (Gonna Be Alright)** Rod Stewart		
		81	**Trouble** Lindsey Buckingham
83	**Tonight, I Celebrate My Love** Peabo Bryson & Roberta Flack	95	**Trouble** Shampoo
		83	**True** Spandau Ballet
87	**Tonight, Tonight, Tonight** Genesis	86	**True Blue** Madonna
96	**Tonite's The Night** Kris Kross		

90	True Blue Love Lou Gramm		78	Two Out Of Three Ain't Bad Meat Loaf
86	True Colors Cyndi Lauper		86	Two People Tina Turner
88	True Love Glenn Frey		93	Two Princes Spin Doctors
93	Truganini Midnight Oil		93	Two Steps Behind Def Leppard
82	Truly Lionel Richie		92	2001 Melissa Etheridge
98	Truly, Madly, Deeply Savage Garden		90	Two To Make It Right Seduction
97	Trust Me (This Is Love) Amanda Marshall		84	Two Tribes Frankie Goes To Hollywood
91	Trust Yourself Blue Rodeo		86	Typical Male Tina Turner
93	The Truth Banned In The UK			
95	Truth Untold Odds			

U

87	Try Blue Rodeo	
76	Tryin' To Get The Feeling Again Barry Manilow	90 U Can't Touch This MC Hammer
81	Tryin' To Live My Life Without You Bob Seger	87 U Got The Look Prince
		97 Uh La La La Alexia
77	Tryin' To Love Two William Bell	92 Uhh Ahh Boyz II Men
95	Tryin' To Tell Ya Andru Donalds	91 Unbelievable EMF
97	Tubthumping Chumbawamba	97 Unbreak My Heart Toni Braxton
96	Tucker's Town Hootie & The Blowfish	78 Unchained Melody Elvis Presley
88	Tunnel Of Love Bruce Springsteen	91 Unchained Melody Righteous Brothers
98	Turn Back Time Aqua	80 Under My Thumb Streetheart
98	Turn It Up/Fire It Up Busta Rhymes	82 Under Pressure Queen & David Bowie
81	Turn Me Loose Loverboy	
97	Turn My Head Live	92 Under The Bridge Red Hot Chili Peppers
76	Turn The Beat Around Vicki Sue Robinson	
		94 Under The Same Sun Scorpions
95	Turn The Beat Around Gloria Estefan	89 Under Your Spell Candi
99	Turn The Lights On Big Sugar	77 Undercover Angel Alan O'Day
78	Turn To Stone Electric Light Orchestra	84 Undercover Of The Night Rolling Stones
82	Turn Your Love Around George Benson	
		85 Understanding Bob Seger
99	Turn-a-round Phatts And Small	94 Understanding Xscape
90	Turtle Power Partners In Kryme	91 Unforgettable Natalie Cole
75	Tush ZZ Top	92 The Unforgiven Metallica
79	Tusk Fleetwood Mac	98 Uninvited Alanis Morissette
99	12 Years Old Kim Stockwood	84 Union Of The Snake Duran Duran
87	20th Century Boy Chalk Circle	90 Unison Celine Dion
96	Twenty Foreplay Janet Jackson	95 Unloved Jann Arden
83	Twenty Questions Tictoc	99 Unpretty TLC
86	25 Or 6 To 4 Chicago	99 Unsent Alanis Morissette
93	29 Palms Robert Plant	90 Unskinny Bop Poison
80	Twilight Zone Manhattan Transfer	94 Until I Fall Away Gin Blossoms
83	Twilight Zone Golden Earring	96 Until It Sleeps Metallica
92	Twilight Zone 2 Unlimited	95 Until The End Of Time Foreigner
88	The Twist Fat Boys	99 Until You Loved Me The Moffatts
94	Twist & Shout Chaka Demus & Pliers	92 Until Your Love Comes Back Around RTZ
86	Twist And Shout The Beatles	
89	Twist In My Sobriety Tanita Tikaram	97 Up Jumps Da Boogie Timbaland & Magoo
84	Twist Of Fate Olivia Newton-John	
96	Twisted Keith Sweat	97 Up To No Good Porn Kings
92	Twister Northern Pikes	82 Up Where We Belong Joe Cocker And Jennifer Warnes
83	Twisting By The Pool Dire Straits	
97	2 Become 1 Spice Girls	80 Upside Down Diana Ross
76	Two For The Show Trooper	96 Upside Down Groove Club
90	Two Girls In Love The Pursuit Of Happiness	77 Uptown Festival Shalamar
		83 Uptown Girl Billy Joel
87	2 Good 2 Be Enough Corey Hart	81 Urgent Foreigner
89	Two Hearts Phil Collins	78 Use Ta Be My Girl O'Jays
91	2 Legit 2 Quit Hammer	
86	Two Of Hearts Stacey Q	

V

82	Vacation Go-Gos		87	**Walking Down Your Street** Bangles
97	Vai Vai Vai Fruit De La Passion		91	**Walking In Memphis** Marc Cohn
88	Valerie Steve Winwood		93	**Walking In My Shoes** Depeche Mode
88	The Valley Road Bruce Hornsby & The Range		75	**Walking In Rhythm** Blackbyrds
			92	**Walking On Broken Glass** Annie Lennox
84	Valotte Julian Lennon		85	**Walking On Sunshine** Katrina & The Waves
87	Vanna Pick Me A Letter Doctor Dave			
94	Vasoline Stone Temple Pilots		96	**Walls** Tom Petty
86	Venus Bananarama		80	**The Wanderer** Donna Summer
75	Venus And Mars Rock Show Paul McCartney & Wings		83	**Wanna Be Startin' Something** Michael Jackson
92	Vibeology Paula Abdul		97	**Wannabe** Spice Girls
87	Victory Kool & The Gang		93	**Wannagirl** Jeremy Jordan
83	Video Kids Prototype		87	**Wanted Dead Or Alive** Bon Jovi
80	Video Killed The Radio Star Buggles		86	**War** Bruce Springsteen
86	Vienna Calling Falco		84	**The War Song** Culture Club
85	A View To A Kill Duran Duran		92	**Warm It Up** Kris Kross
90	Vision Of Love Mariah Carey		84	**The Warrior** Scandal feat. Patty Smyth
98	Viva Forever Spice Girls		90	**Was It Nothing At All** Michael Damian
92	Viva Las Vegas ZZ Top		98	**Was It Something I Didn't Say** 98°
90	Vogue Madonna		91	**Wash The Rain** World On Edge
81	The Voice Moody Blues		91	**Wash Your Face In My Sink** Dream Warriors
80	Voices Cheap Trick			
85	Voices Carry 'Til Tuesday		92	**Washed Away** Tom Cochrane
75	Volare Al Martino		81	**Wasn't That A Party** The Rovers
97	Voodoo People Prodigy		75	**Wasted Days And Wasted Nights** Freddy Fender
88	Voodoo Thing Colin James		82	**Wasted On The Way** Crosby, Stills & Nash
85	Vox Humana Kenny Loggins			
82	Voyeur Kim Carnes		96	**Watch Over You** Hemingway Corner
			81	**Watching The Wheels** John Lennon

W

			96	**Watching The World Go By** Maxi Priest
88	Wait White Lion		93	**Water From The Moon** Celine Dion
81	The Waiting Tom Petty & The Heartbreakers		95	**Water Runs Dry** Boyz II Men
			95	**Waterfalls** TLC
81	Waiting For A Girl Like You Foreigner		95	**Watermark** Mae Moore
89	Waiting For A Star To Fall Boy Meets Girl		98	**The Way** Fastball
			77	**Way Down** Elvis Presley
91	Waiting For Love Alias		92	**The Way I Feel About You** Karyn White
91	Waiting For The Day George Michael			
99	Waiting For The Tide Melanie Doane		78	**The Way I Feel Tonight** Bay City Rollers
96	Waiting For Tonight Tom Petty			
96	Waiting For Wednesday Lisa Loeb		75	**The Way I Want To Touch You** Captain & Tennille
82	Waiting On A Friend Rolling Stones			
84	Wake Me Up Before You Go Go Wham!		87	**The Way It Is** Bruce Hornsby & The Range
75	Walk Away From Love David Ruffin		94	**The Way She Loves Me** Richard Marx
87	Walk Like An Egyptian Bangles		75	**The Way We Were/Try To Remember** Gladys Knight
85	Walk Of Life Dire Straits			
93	Walk On The Water Toad The Wet Sprocket		78	**The Way You Do The Things You Do** Rita Coolidge
88	Walk On Water Eddie Money		90	**The Way You Do The Things You Do** UB40
78	Walk Right Back Anne Murray			
89	Walk The Dinosaur Was (Not Was)		88	**The Way You Make Me Feel** Michael Jackson
77	Walk This Way Aerosmith			
86	Walk This Way Run-D.M.C.		93	**The Ways Of The Wind** PM Dawn
91	Walkaway Alanis		94	**We All Need** Realworld
97	Walkin' On The Sun Smash Mouth		79	**We All Need Love** Domenic Troiano
89	Walking Away Information Society		79	**We Are Family** Sister Sledge

78	We Are The Champions Queen	88	What A Wonderful World Louis Armstrong
85	We Are The World USA for Africa		
87	We Are What We Are The Other Ones	85	What About Love Heart
85	We Belong Pat Benatar	84	What About Me? Kenny Rogers/Kim Carnes/James Ingram
86	We Built This City Starship		
90	We Can't Go Wrong Cover Girls	91	What About Now Robbie Robertson
89	We Didn't Start The Fire Billy Joel	92	What About Your Friends TLC
86	We Don't Have To Take Our Clothes Off Jermaine Stewart	92	What Becomes Of The Broken Hearted Paul Young
85	We Don't Need Another Hero Tina Turner	91	What Comes Naturally Sheena Easton
80	We Don't Talk Anymore Cliff Richard	86	What Does It Take Honeymoon Suite
92	We Got A Love Thang Ce Ce Peniston	92	What God Wants (Part 1) Roger Waters
82	We Got The Beat Go-Gos		
77	We Just Disagree Dave Mason	88	What Have I Done To Deserve This Pet Shop Boys/Dusty Springfield
99	We Like To Party Vengaboys		
80	We Live For Love Pat Benatar	86	What Have You Done For Me Lately Janet Jackson
85	We Run Strange Advance		
97	We Trying To Stay Alive Wyclef Jean	89	What I Am Edie Brickell & The New Bohemians
83	We Two Little River Band		
94	We Wait And We Wonder Phil Collins	93	What If I Came Knocking John Mellencamp
92	We Will Rock You Warrant		
87	We'll Be Together Sting	93	What Is Love Haddaway
78	We'll Never Have To Say Goodbye England Dan & John Ford Coley	90	What It Takes Aerosmith
		99	What It's Like Everlast
77	We're All Alone Rita Coolidge	81	What Kind Of Fool Barbra Streisand & Barry Gibb
77	We're Here For A Good Time Trooper		
84	We're Not Gonna Take It Twisted Sister	82	What Kind Of Love Is This Streetheart
98	We're Not Making Love No More Dru Hill	90	What Kind Of Man Would I Be Chicago
97	We've Got It Goin' On Backstreet Boys	75	What The Hell I Got Michel Pagliaro
		98	What Would Happen Meredith Brooks
83	We've Got Tonight Kenny Rogers & Sheena Easton	96	What Would It Take Anne Murray
		95	What Would You Say Dave Matthews Band
79	We've Got Tonite Bob Seger		
93	Weak SWV	89	What You Don't Know Expose
79	Weekend Wet Willie	87	What You Get Is What You See Tina Turner
77	Weekend In New England Barry Manilow		
		86	What You Need INXS
98	Weird Hanson	98	What You Want Mase
76	Welcome Back John Sebastian	93	What You Won't Do For Love Go West
87	Welcome To The Boomtown David & David		
		87	What's Going On Cyndi Lauper
89	Welcome To The Jungle Guns N' Roses	99	What's It Gonna Be?! Busta Rhymes featuring Janet
85	Welcome To The Pleasure Dome Frankie Goes To Hollywood	84	What's Love Got To Do With It Tina Turner
90	Welcome To The Real World Jane Child	97	What's Love Got To Do With It Warren G
78	Werewolves In London Warren Zevon	88	What's On Your Mind (Pure Energy) Information Society
86	West End Girls Pet Shop Boys		
98	Westside TQ	99	What's So Different Ginuwine
76	Wham Bam Silver	94	What's The Frequency, Kenneth? R.E.M.
75	What A Diff'rence A Day Makes Esther Phillips		
		93	What's Up 4 Non Blondes
79	What A Fool Believes Doobie Brothers	93	What's Up Doc Fu-Shnickens
		96	What's Up With That ZZ Top
78	(What A) Wonderful World Art Garfunkel With James Taylor And Paul Simon	78	What's Your Name Lynyrd Skynyrd
		89	Whatcha Do To My Body Lee Aaron

82	**Whatcha Gonna Do (When I'm Gone)** Chilliwack	88	**Where Do Broken Hearts Go** Whitney Houston
77	**Whatcha Gonna Do?** Pablo Cruise	96	**Where Do We Go From Here** Deborah Cox
92	**Whatcha Need** Bootsauce		
97	**Whatever** En Vogue	96	**Where Do You Go** No Mercy
77	**Whatever Goes Around** Mighty Pope	91	**Where Does My Heart Beat Now** Celine Dion
96	**Whatever You Need** Damhnait Doyle		
94	**Whatta Man** Salt-N-Pepa	97	**Where Have All The Cowboys Gone** Paula Cole
90	**When A Heart Breaks** Rik Emmett		
88	**When A Man Loves A Woman** Luba	99	**Where My Girl's At** 702
91	**When A Man Loves A Woman** Michael Bolton	96	**Where The River Flows** Collective Soul
94	**When Can I See You** Babyface	87	**Where The Streets Have No Name** U2
84	**When Doves Cry** Prince		
95	**When I Come Around** Green Day	91	**Where The Streets Have No Name** Pet Shop Boys
90	**When I Dream Of You** Tommy Page		
93	**When I Fall In Love** Celine Dion	92	**Where You Goin' Now** Damn Yankees
92	**When I Look Into Your Eyes** Firehouse		
		97	**Where's The Love** Hanson
89	**When I Looked At Him** Expose	83	**Wherever I Lay My Hat (That's My Home)** Paul Young
77	**When I Need You** Leo Sayer		
89	**When I See You Smile** Bad English	90	**Wherever You Run** Regatta
86	**When I Think Of You** Janet Jackson	90	**While My Guitar Gently Weeps** Jeff Healey Band
90	**When I'm Back On My Feet Again** Michael Bolton		
		81	**While You See A Chance** Steve Winwood
97	**When I'm Up (I Can't Get Down)** Great Big Sea		
		95	**Whiney Whiney** Willi One Blood
83	**When I'm With You** Sheriff	80	**Whip It** Devo
89	**When I'm With You** Sheriff	94	**Whipped** Jon Secada
88	**When It's Love** Van Halen	83	**Whirly Girl** Oxo
82	**When It's Over** Loverboy	84	**Whisper To A Scream (Birds Fly)** Icicle Works
95	**When Love And Hate Collide** Def Leppard		
		84	**White Horse** Laid Back
93	**When She Cries** Restless Heart	80	**White Hot** Red Rider
87	**When Smokey Sings** ABC	90	**White Hot** Tom Cochrane & Red Rider
90	**When Something Is Wrong With My Baby** Linda Ronstadt	95	**White Lines** Duran Duran
		92	**White Men Can't Jump** Riff
89	**When The Children Cry** White Lion	83	**White Wedding** Billy Idol
86	**When The Going Gets Tough, The Tough Get Going** Billy Ocean	95	**A Whiter Shade Of Pale** Annie Lennox
		98	**Who Am I** Beenie Man
98	**When The Lights Go Out** Five	78	**Who Are You** The Who
90	**When The Night Comes** Joe Cocker	82	**Who Can It Be Now?** Men At Work
92	**When The Stars Fall** Sue Medley	99	**Who Dat** JT Money
94	**(When There's) Time For Love** Lawrence Gowan	96	**Who Do U Love** Deborah Cox
		99	**Who Do You Love** Love Inc.
94	**When We Dance** Sting	93	**Who Is It** Michael Jackson
88	**When We Kiss** Bardeux	83	**Who Knows How To Make Love Stay** Doug & The Slugs
88	**When We Was Fab** George Harrison		
75	**When Will I Be Loved** Linda Ronstadt	75	**Who Loves You** Four Seasons
99	**When You Believe** Mariah Carey & Whitney Houston	84	**Who Wears These Shoes** Elton John
		96	**Who Will Save Your Soul** Jewel
93	**When You Gonna Learn** Jamiroquoi	87	**Who Will You Run To** Heart
96	**When You Love A Woman** Journey	96	**Who You Are** Pearl Jam
96	**When You're Gone** The Cranberries	81	**Who's Crying Now** Journey
99	**When You're Gone** Bryan Adams & Melanie R.	93	**Who's Gonna Ride Your Wild Horses** U2
79	**When You're In Love With A Beautiful Woman** Dr. Hook	97	**Who's Gonna Ride Your Wild Horses** U2
78	**Whenever I Call You "Friend"** Kenny Loggins	85	**Who's Holding Donna Now** DeBarge
		86	**Who's Johnny** El DeBarge
92	**Whenever I May Roam** Metallica	87	**Who's That Girl** Madonna

84	Who's That Girl? Eurythmics	76	With Your Love Jefferson Starship
93	Who's The Man House Of Pain	98	Without Expression John Mellencamp
85	Who's Zoomin' Who Aretha Franklin	92	Without Love Infidels
93	A Whole New World Peabo Bryson & Regina Belle	97	Without Love Donna Lewis
76	The Whole World's Goin' April Wine	87	Without You U2
93	Whoot, There It Is 95 South	90	Without You Mötley Crüe
92	Why Annie Lennox	94	Without You Mariah Carey
96	Why Bass Is Base	81	Woman John Lennon
86	Why Can't This Be Love Van Halen	90	Woman In Chains Tears For Fears
75	Why Can't We Be Friends War	80	Woman In Love Barbra Streisand
82	Why Do Fools Fall In Love Diana Ross	94	The Woman In Me Heart
99	Why Don't You Get A Job The Offspring	81	A Woman Needs Love Ray Parker & Raydio
83	Why Me? Irene Cara	90	Woman's Work Sheree
93	Why Must We Wait Until Tonight? Tina Turner	93	Won't Give Up My Music Lisa Lougheed
91	Wicked Game Chris Isaak	96	Wonder Natalie Merchant
97	Wide Awake In America U2	95	Wonderdrug Jann Arden
94	Wide Load One	95	Wonderful Adam Ant
93	Wide River Steve Miller	78	Wonderful Tonight Eric Clapton
90	Wiggle It 2 In A Room	96	Wonderwall Oasis
84	The Wild Boys Duran Duran	88	A Word In Spanish Elton John
87	Wild Horses Gino Vannelli	84	The Word Is Out Jermaine Stewart
94	Wild Night John Mellencamp	87	Word Up Cameo
89	Wild Thing Tone Loc	86	Words Get In The Way Miami Sound Machine
88	Wild Wild West Escape Club	96	Work It Out Def Leppard
99	Wild Wild West Will Smith	92	Work To Do Vanessa Williams
89	Wild World Maxi Priest	82	Working For The Weekend Loverboy
93	Wild World Mr. Big	80	Working My Way Back To You Spinners
75	Wildfire Michael Muprhy	93	World New Order
92	Wildside Marky Mark	96	The World I Know Collective Soul
93	Will You Be There Michael Jackson	94	The World Is Yours Nas
94	Will You Be There (In The Morning) Heart	90	The World Just Keeps On Turning Candi & The Backbeats
92	Will You Marry Me? Paula Abdul	92	World Love Lisa Lougheed
93	Will You Remember Me? Jann Arden	97	The World Tonight Paul McCartney
87	Will You Still Love Me? Chicago	87	Wot's It To Ya Robbie Nevil
89	Wind Beneath My Wings Bette Midler	92	Would I Lie To You Charles & Eddie
82	Wind Him Up Saga	85	Would I Lie To You? Eurythmics
92	Wind Me Up Paul Janz	99	Would You...? Touch & Go
91	Wind Of Change Scorpions	84	Wouldn't It Be Good Nik Kershaw
81	Winner Takes It All ABBA	76	Wow! Andre Gagnon
76	Winners & Losers Hamilton, Joe Frank & Reynolds	84	Wrapped Around Your Finger The Police
81	Winning Santana	76	The Wreck Of The Edmund Fitzgerald Gordon Lightfoot
87	Wipe Out Fat Boys	99	Written In The Stars Elton John & LeAnn Rimes
79	Wish I Could Fly Kinks	94	Written On Ya Kitten Naughty By Nature
83	Wishing A Flock Of Seagulls	96	Wrong Everything But The Girl
98	Wishing I Was There Natalie Imbruglia		
92	Wishing On A Star Cover Girls		
98	Wishing That Jann Arden		
88	Wishing Well Terence Trent D'Arby		
98	Wishlist Pearl Jam		
78	With A Little Luck Paul McCartney & Wings		
90	With Every Beat Of My Heart Taylor Dayne		
80	With You I'm Born Again Billy Preston/ Syreeta		

80	Xanadu Olivia Newton-John	

77	Year Of The Cat Al Stewart	
80	Yes I'm Ready Teri Desario & K.C.	

77	Yesterday's Hero Bay City Rollers	94	You Got Me Floatin' PM Dawn
82	Yesterday's Songs Neil Diamond	95	You Got Me Rocking Rolling Stones
79	YMCA Village People	95	You Gotta Be Des'ree
91	Yo Baby Yo Tarzan Dan And The John James Jungle Posse	92	You Gotta Believe Marky Mark
94	Yolanda Reality	91	You Gotta Love Someone Elton John
75	You George Harrison	87	(You Gotta) Fight For Your Right (To Party!) Beastie Boys
78	You Rita Coolidge	87	You Keep Me Hangin' On Kim Wilde
78	You & I Rick James	86	You Know I Love You...Don't You? Howard Jones
95	You & I JK	96	You Learn Alanis Morissette
77	You And Me Alice Cooper	94	You Let Your Heart Go Too Fast Spin Doctors
83	You Are Lionel Richie	92	You Lied To Me Cathy Dennis
99	You Are Everything Dru Hill	77	You Light Up My Life Debby Boone
85	You Are My Lady Freddie Jackson	85	You Look Marvelous Billy Crystal
95	You Are Not Alone Michael Jackson	95	You Lose And You Gain John Bottomley
76	You Are The Woman Firefall	77	You Made Me Believe In Magic Bay City Rollers
78	You Belong To Me Carly Simon	78	You Make Lovin' Fun Fleetwood Mac
85	You Belong To The City Glenn Frey	77	You Make Me Feel Like Dancing Leo Sayer
94	You Better Wait Steve Perry	97	You Make Me Mad Odds
81	You Better You Bet The Who	97	You Make Me Wanna... Usher
93	You Bring On The Sun Londonbeat	75	You Make Me Want To Be Dan Hill
86	You Can Call Me Al Paul Simon	81	You Make My Dreams Daryl Hall & John Oates
82	You Can Do Magic America	80	You May Be Right Billy Joel
96	You Can Make History (Young Again) Elton John	91	You May Be Right Grapes Of Wrath
79	You Can't Change That Raydio	94	You Mean The World To Me Toni Braxton
76	You Can't Dance Jackson Hawke	84	You Might Think The Cars
90	You Can't Deny It Lisa Stansfield	96	You Must Love Me Madonna
84	You Can't Get What You Want Joe Jackson	78	You Needed Me Anne Murray
83	You Can't Hurry Love Phil Collins	78	You Never Done It Like That Captain & Tennille
91	You Could Be Mine Guns N' Roses	96	You Never Done It Like That Carol Medina
82	You Could Have Been With Me Sheena Easton	95	You Oughta Know Alanis Morissette
79	You Decorated My Life Kenny Rogers	78	You Really Got Me Needing You Peter Pringle
78	You Don't Bring Me Flowers Barbra Streisand/Neil Diamond	81	You Saved My Soul Burton Cummings
77	You Don't Have To Be A Star Marilyn McCoo & Bill Davis Jr.	76	You Sexy Thing Hot Chocolate
91	You Don't Have To Go Home Tonight The Triplets	76	You Should Be Dancing Bee Gees
92	You Don't Have To Remind Me Sass Jordan	82	You Should Hear How She Talks About You Melissa Manchester
95	You Don't Know (Where My Lips Have Been) Carol Medina	92	You Showed Me Salt-N-Pepa
95	You Don't Know How It Feels Tom Petty	85	You Spin Me Round (Like A Record) Dead Or Alive
99	You Don't Know Me Armand Van Helden	99	You Stepped On My Life Philosopher Kings
92	You Don't Love Me "Weird Al" Yankovic	96	You Still Touch Me Sting
99	You Get What You Give New Radicals	84	You Take Me Up Thompson Twins
85	You Give Good Love Whitney Houston	79	You Take My Breath Away Rex Smith
87	You Give Love A Bad Name Bon Jovi	79	You Took The Words Meat Loaf
89	You Got It Roy Orbison	95	You Used To Love Me Faith
89	You Got It (The Right Stuff) New Kids On The Block	94	You Want This Janet Jackson
87	You Got It All The Jets	97	You Were Meant For Me Jewel
82	You Got Lucky Tom Petty	77	You Won't Dance With Me April Wine
99	You Got Me Roots feat. Erykah Badu	98	You Won't Forget Me La Bouche

97	You Won't Remember This Kim Stockwood	94	Zombie The Cranberries
92	You Won't See Me Cry Wilson Phillips	95	Zombie A.D.A.M.
80	You'll Accomp'ny Me Bob Seger	98	Zoot Suit Riot Cherry Poppin' Daddies

- 97 You Won't Remember This Kim Stockwood
- 92 You Won't See Me Cry Wilson Phillips
- 80 You'll Accomp'ny Me Bob Seger
- 76 You'll Never Find Another Love Like Mine Lou Rawls
- 96 You'll See Madonna
- 86 You're A Friend Of Mine Clarence Clemons/Jackson Browne
- 98 You're A Superstar Love Inc.
- 85 (You're A) Strange Animal Gowan
- 90 You're Amazing Robert Palmer
- 91 You're In Love Wilson Phillips
- 78 You're In My Heart (The Final Acclaim) Rod Stewart
- 96 You're Makin' Me High Toni Braxton
- 76 You're My Best Friend Queen
- 77 You're My World Helen Reddy
- 97 You're Not Alone Olive
- 85 You're Only Human (Second Wind) Billy Joel
- 79 You're Only Lonely J.D. Souther
- 92 You're So Tempting Acosta Russell
- 98 You're Still The One Shania Twain
- 85 You're The Inspiration Chicago
- 96 You're The One SWV
- 78 You're The One That I Want John Travolta & Olivia Newton-John
- 85 You're The Only Love Paul Hyde/The Payolas
- 80 You're The Only Woman (You & I) Ambrosia
- 87 You're The Voice John Farnham
- 87 You're What I Look For Glass Tiger
- 99 You've Got A Way Shania Twain
- 93 You've Got To Know Boomers
- 76 Young Blood Bad Company
- 76 Young Hearts Run Free Candi Staton
- 84 Young Thing, Wild Dreams (Rock Me) Tom Cochrane & Red Rider
- 81 Young Turks Rod Stewart
- 98 Young, Sad & Blue Lysette Titi
- 90 Your Baby Never Looked Good In Blue Expose
- 77 Your Backyard Burton Cummings
- 82 Your Daddy Don't Know Toronto
- 98 Your Life Is Now John Mellencamp
- 95 Your Little Secret Melissa Etheridge
- 86 Your Love The Outfield
- 77 Your Love Gets Me Around Ronney Abramson
- 77 (Your Love Has Lifted Me) Higher And Higher Rita Coolidge
- 95 Your Loving Arms Billie Ray Martin
- 89 Your Mama Don't Dance Poison
- 78 Your Smiling Face James Taylor
- 86 Your Wildest Dreams Moody Blues
- 96 Your Wildest Dreams Tom Cochrane
- 97 Your Woman White Town

Z

FACTS & FIGURES
A collection of chart achievements and records.

TOP 100 SINGLES   1975-1999

#	TITLE	ARTIST	YR	#1	WK
1.	Something About The Way You Look Tonight/ Candle In The Wind 1997	Elton John	97	45	97+
2.	The Boy Is Mine	Brandy & Monica	98	15	46
3.	I'll Be Missing You	Puff Daddy & Faith Evans (featuring 112)	97	13	38
4.	Goodbye	Spice Girls	98	13	33+
5.	The Power Of Love	Celine Dion	94	12	70
6.	Said I Loved You...But I Lied	Michael Bolton	93	12	47
7.	You Light Up My Life	Debby Boone	77	12	46
8.	Pop Muzik	M	79	12	32
9.	Fantasy	Mariah Carey	95	12	28
10.	(Everything I Do) I Do It For You	Bryan Adams	91	12	22
11.	Faith	George Michael	87	12	20
12.	I Just Called To Say I Love You	Stevie Wonder	84	11	30
13.	End Of The Road	Boyz II Men	92	11	23
14.	Have You Ever Really Loved A Woman?	Bryan Adams	95	10	38
15.	Stayin' Alive	Bee Gees	78	10	26
16.	God Bless The Child	Shania Twain	96	9	59
17.	Secret	Madonna	94	9	46
18.	Can You Feel The Love Tonight	Elton John	94	9	45
19.	Macarena	Los Del Mar	95	9	31
20.	Never Surrender	Corey Hart	85	9	23
21.	Stayin' Alive	N-Trance	96	9	22
22.	Islands In The Stream	Kenny Rogers & Dolly Parton	83	9	22
23.	Can't Nobody Hold Me Down	Puff Daddy	97	8	39
24.	The Lady In Red	Chris DeBurgh	86	8	28
25.	Le Freak	Chic	78	8	24
26.	Rapper's Delight	Sugarhill Gang	80	8	22
27.	Da Ya Think I'm Sexy	Rod Stewart	79	8	22
28.	Key West Intermezzo	John Mellencamp	96	8	18
29.	Can't Help Falling In Love	UB40	93	8	17
30.	Old Man & Me (When I Get To Heaven)	Hootie & The Blowfish	96	8	16
31.	Black Or White	Michael Jackson	91	8	14
32.	Always	Bon Jovi	95	7	49
33.	Where Do You Go?	No Mercy	96	7	34
34.	Sukiyaki	4 P.M.	95	7	34
35.	La Bamba	Los Lobos	87	7	24
36.	Live Is Life	Opus	85	7	24
37.	Part Time Lover	Stevie Wonder	85	7	23
38.	Billie Jean	Michael Jackson	83	7	20
39.	Karma Chameleon	Culture Club	84	7	20
40.	Tonight's The Night (Gonna Be Alright)	Rod Stewart	76	7	20
41.	Touch Me (I Want Your Body)	Samantha Fox	87	7	18
42.	I Love Rock N' Roll	Joan Jett & The Heartbreakers	82	7	17
43.	(Just Like) Starting Over	John Lennon	80	7	15
44.	Funkytown	Lipps Inc	80	7	13
45.	When You Love A Woman	Journey	96	7	12
46.	That's The Way Love Goes	Janet Jackson	93	6	38
47.	Don't Cry For Me Argentina	Madonna	97	6	32
48.	I'll Make Love To You	Boyz II Men	94	6	30

TOP 100 SINGLES   1975-1999

#	TITLE	ARTIST	YR	#1	WK
49.	Heart Of Glass	Blondie	79	6	28
50.	Star Wars Theme/Cantina Band	Meco	77	6	28
51.	Grease	Frankie Valli	78	6	28
52.	You're The One That I Want	John Travolta & Olivia Newton-John	78	6	26
53.	Girls Just Wanna Have Fun	Cyndi Lauper	84	6	24
54.	Love Theme From "A Star Is Born" (Evergreen)	Barbra Streisand	77	6	23
55.	Flashdance...What A Feelin'	Irene Cara	83	6	22
56.	Easy Lover	Phillip Bailey/Phil Collins	85	6	21
57.	Papa Don't Preach	Madonna	86	6	21
58.	Opposites Attract	Paula Abdul	90	6	20
59.	I Wanna Dance With Somebody (Who Loves Me)	Whitney Houston	87	6	19
60.	This Used To Be My Playground	Madonna	92	6	19
61.	Call Me	Blondie	80	6	17
62.	Justified And Ancient	KLF featuring Tammy Wynette	92	6	17
63.	Don't Go Breaking My Heart	Elton John/Kiki Dee	76	6	17
64.	Eye Of The Tiger	Survivor	82	6	16
65.	Life Is A Highway	Tom Cochrane	91	6	16
66.	Young Turks	Rod Stewart	81	6	14
67.	Jump	Kris Kross	92	6	14
68.	Gonna Make You Sweat	C&C Music Factory featuring Freedom Williams	91	6	12
69.	Wiggle It	2 In A Room	90	6	11
70.	Last Kiss	Pearl Jam	99	6	7+
71.	If You Go	Jon Secada	94	5	40
72.	I'll Be There For You/You're All I Need (To Get By)	Method Man featuring Mary J. Blige	95	5	37
73.	Groovy Kind Of Love	Phil Collins	88	5	25
74.	Another Brick In The Wall	Pink Floyd	80	5	23
75.	Every Breath You Take	The Police	83	5	23
76.	Straight Up	Paula Abdul	89	5	22
77.	Get Outta My Dreams, Get Into My Car	Billy Ocean	88	5	21
78.	Mickey	Toni Basil	83	5	21
79.	Hip Hop Hooray	Naughty By Nature	93	5	20
80.	Live To Tell	Madonna	86	5	20
81.	Buffalo Stance	Neneh Cherry	89	5	19
82.	Electric Avenue	Eddy Grant	83	5	18
83.	Ghostbusters	Ray Parker Jr.	84	5	18
84.	Release Me	Wilson Phillips	90	5	18
85.	All Around The World	Lisa Stansfield	90	5	17
86.	Joyride	Roxette	91	5	16
87.	Centerfold	J. Geils Band	82	5	16
88.	Afternoon Delight	Starland Vocal Band	76	5	15
89.	Jack & Diane	John Cougar	82	5	14
90.	Ebony & Ivory	Paul McCartney (with Stevie Wonder)	82	5	14
91.	Bad Blood	Neil Sedaka	75	5	14
92.	Bette Davis Eyes	Kim Carnes	81	5	13
93.	Morning Train (Nine To Five)	Sheena Easton	81	5	12
94.	Woman	John Lennon	81	5	11

TOP 100 SINGLES   1975-1999

	TITLE	ARTIST	YR	#1	WK
95.	Boogie Oogie Oogie	A Taste Of Honey	78	4	30
96.	Please Forgive Me	Bryan Adams	93	4	29
97.	Night Fever	Bee Gees	78	4	28
98.	Three Times A Lady	Commodores	78	4	28
99.	Nikita	Elton John	86	4	25
100.	Babe	Styx	79	4	24

Codes
YR: the year the single reached the #1 position
#1: the number of weeks the single stayed in the #1 position
WK: the number of weeks on the chart
+: still on the SoundScan singles chart as of July 18, 1999

Methodology
Ranked according to weeks at #1. Ties are broken by weeks in the top 40 and then weeks in the top 10.

SINGLES WITH MOST WEEKS IN THE TOP 40

WK	TITLE	ARTIST
97 +	Something About The Way You.../Candle In The Wind 1997	Elton John
85	Quit Playing Games (With My Heart)	Backstreet Boys
70	The Power Of Love	Celine Dion
60	God Bless The Child	Shania Twain
59	Any Time, Any Place	Janet Jackson
53	Get Down (You're The One For Me)	Backstreet Boys
53	Wild Night	John Mellencamp
52	Streets Of Philadelphia	Bruce Springsteen
51	Perfect Drug	Nine Inch Nails
49	Breathe	Prodigy
49	Always	Bon Jovi
47	The Boy Is Mine	Brandy & Monica
47	Said I Loved You...But I Lied	Michael Bolton
47	Do You Wanna Get Funky	C&C Music Factory
46	Mo Money, Mo Problems	Notorious B.I.G.
46	Secret	Madonna
45	Can You Feel The Love Tonight	Elton John
45	Insane In The Brain	Cypress Hill
45	All That She Wants	Ace Of Base
42	How Do I Live	LeAnn Rimes
44 +	Paradox	666
42	Misled	Celine Dion
41	Who Am I	Beenie Man
41	Dreamlover	Mariah Carey
40	If You Go	Jon Secada
40	Go On Move '94	Reel 2 Real
40	Someday I'll Be Saturday Night	Bon Jovi
40	Just Kickin' It	Xscape
40	Endless Love	Luther Vandross/Mariah Carey

TOP 100 ARTISTS   1975-1999

1. Madonna
2. Elton John
3. Rod Stewart
4. Michael Jackson
5. Janet Jackson
6. Mariah Carey
7. Bryan Adams
8. Prince
9. John Cougar Mellencamp
10. U2
11. Phil Collins
12. Celine Dion
13. Billy Joel
14. Whitney Houston
15. Paul McCartney
16. George Michael
17. Bon Jovi
18. Bee Gees
19. Rolling Stones
20. Daryl Hall & John Oates
21. Duran Duran
22. Michael Bolton
23. Donna Summer
24. Paula Abdul
25. Roxette
26. Lionel Richie
27. David Bowie
28. Backstreet Boys
29. Bruce Springsteen
30. Def Leppard
31. Olivia Newton-John
32. Boyz II Men
33. Aerosmith
34. Heart
35. Alanis Morissette
36. Stevie Wonder
37. Corey Hart
38. Queen
39. Fleetwood Mac
40. Electric Light Orchestra
41. Genesis
42. New Kids On The Block
43. Kenny Rogers
44. Tina Turner
45. Gloria Estefan
46. Chicago
47. Sting
48. Barbra Streisand
49. Tom Cochrane
50. Foreigner
51. Richard Marx
52. INXS
53. Huey Lewis & The News
54. Pet Shop Boys
55. ABBA
56. Eagles
57. Bob Seger
58. Cyndi Lauper
59. Culture Club
60. Pat Benatar
61. Barry Manilow
62. Eurythmics
63. Eric Clapton
64. Billy Ocean
65. Police
66. Glass Tiger
67. R.E.M.
68. Air Supply
69. Billy Idol
70. Styx
71. Commodores
72. Blondie
73. Tears For Fears
74. KC & The Sunshine Band
75. Sheena Easton
76. Shania Twain
77. Tom Petty & The Heartbreakers
78. Jefferson Starship/Starship
79. Bobby Brown
80. Amy Grant
81. Depeche Mode
82. Captain & Tennille
83. Linda Ronstadt
84. Notorious B.I.G.
85. Guns N' Roses
86. Puff Daddy
87. Metallica
88. Melissa Etheridge
89. Diana Ross
90. Sheryl Crow
91. Spice Girls
92. Rick Astley
93. Pointer Sisters
94. Taylor Dayne
95. Bay City Rollers
96. Barenaked Ladies
97. C&C Music Factory
98. Burton Cummings
99. Mase
100. The Cranberries

TOP 100 ARTISTS   1975-1999

Methodology
Ranked according to a point system. Points are awarded to all of the artist's charted singles (including all "airplay chart only" hits) based on peak position attained. Total number of weeks in the top 40 as well as total number of weeks at #1 are added. All points are summed for each artist.

When a chart single performed by two or more solo artists is being considered, such as "All For Love" by Bryan Adams/Rod Stewart/Sting, each artist is awarded the full point value tabulated for the record. Duos or groups, such as Daryl Hall & John Oates or New Kids On The Block, are considered regular recording acts and therefore, points are not awarded to each individual member.

ARTIST ACHIEVEMENTS

Most weeks at number one

	Artist	Weeks
1.	Elton John	76
2.	Madonna	48
3.	Stevie Wonder	28
4.	Bryan Adams	27
5.	Puff Daddy	21
6.	Rod Stewart	21
7.	Paula Abdul	20
8.	Mariah Carey	20
9.	Phil Collins	20
10.	Blondie	19
11.	Michael Jackson	19
12.	Bee Gees	18
13.	Boyz II Men	17
14.	Brandy	15
15.	John Mellencamp	15
16.	Monica	15
17.	George Michael	14
18.	Celine Dion	13
19.	Faith Evans	13
20.	112	13
21.	Spice Girls	13

Most discs at number one

	Artist	Hits
1.	Madonna	13
2.	Elton John	9
3.	Phil Collins	6
4.	Paula Abdul	5
5.	Mariah Carey	5
6.	Michael Jackson	5
7.	Stevie Wonder	5
8.	Bryan Adams	4
9.	Blondie	4
10.	Janet Jackson	4
11.	Paul McCartney/Wings	4
12.	Milli Vanilli	4
13.	Rick Astley	3
14.	Bee Gees	3
15.	Heart	3
16.	Cyndi Lauper	3
17.	John Cougar Mellencamp	3
18.	George Michael	3
19.	Roxette	3
20.	Rod Stewart	3
21.	Barbra Streisand	3

Top artists without a #1 single

	Artist	Top 100 Pos.
1.	Duran Duran	21
2.	Def Leppard	30
3.	Aerosmith	33
4.	Electric Light Orchestra	40
5.	Genesis	41
6.	Sting	47
7.	Huey Lewis & The News	53
8.	ABBA	55

Top groups and duos

	Artist	Top 100 Pos.
1.	U2	10
2.	Bon Jovi	17
3.	Bee Gees	18
4.	Rolling Stones	19
5.	Daryl Hall & John Oates	20
6.	Duran Duran	21
7.	Roxette	25
8.	Backstreet Boys	28

ARTISTS ACHIEVEMENTS

Most weeks in the top 40

	Artist	Weeks
1.	Madonna	710
2.	Elton John	596
3.	Mariah Carey	429
4.	Michael Jackson	387
5.	Rod Stewart	380
6.	Janet Jackson	370
7.	Bryan Adams	369
8.	Celine Dion	344
9.	Bon Jovi	319
10.	John Cougar Mellencamp	313
11.	U2	313
12.	Backstreet Boys	310
13.	Prince	292
14.	Billy Joel	275
15.	Bee Gees	239
16.	Phil Collins	237
17.	Paul McCartney	231
18.	Whitney Houston	224
19.	George Michael	222
20.	Michael Bolton	216
21.	Donna Summer	216
22.	Bruce Springsteen	209
23.	Lionel Richie	206
24.	Def Leppard	200
25.	Boyz II Men	194
26.	Roxette	194
27.	Duran Duran	194
28.	Daryl Hall & John Oates	189
29.	David Bowie	176
30.	Rolling Stones	174
31.	Olivia Newton-John	171
32.	Heart	171
33.	Gloria Estefan	170
34.	New Kids On The Block	166
35.	Fleetwood Mac	159
36.	Notorious B.I.G.	155
37.	Paula Abdul	154
38.	Stevie Wonder	150
39.	Queen	147
40.	Electric Light Orchestra	147
41.	Huey Lewis & The News	147
42.	Chicago	146
43.	Eurythmics	146
44.	Sting	145
45.	Foreigner	144
46.	Kenny Rogers	141
47.	C&C Music Factory	141
48.	Tina Turner	140

Most top 40 hits

	Artist	Hits
1.	Elton John	45
2.	Madonna	43
3.	Bryan Adams	31
4.	Prince	31
5.	Rod Stewart	31
6.	Janet Jackson	29
7.	Michael Jackson	27
8.	U2	27
9.	Billy Joel	26
10.	John Cougar Mellencamp	26
11.	Whitney Houston	26
12.	Celine Dion	22
13.	Mariah Carey	22
14.	Paul McCartney	22
15.	Aerosmith	21
16.	Bruce Springsteen	21
17.	Phil Collins	21
18.	Rolling Stones	20
19.	Corey Hart	18
20.	Daryl Hall & John Oates	18
21.	David Bowie	18
22.	Duran Duran	18
23.	Alanis Morissette	17
24.	Bon Jovi	17
25.	Def Leppard	17
26.	Genesis	17
27.	George Michael	17
28.	Heart	17
29.	Tom Cochrane	17
30.	Bee Gees	16
31.	Bob Seger	16
32.	Michael Bolton	16
33.	Sting	16
34.	Tina Turner	16
35.	Chicago	15
36.	Electric Light Orchestra	15
37.	Fleetwood Mac	15
38.	Gloria Estefan	15
39.	Lionel Richie	15
40.	Olivia Newton-John	15
41.	Queen	15
42.	Richard Marx	15
43.	Boyz II Men	14
44.	Donna Summer	14
45.	INXS	14
46.	New Kids On The Block	14
47.	ABBA	13
48.	Barry Manilow	13

The Number One Hits

Date   **Title** Artist   Weeks

1975

Steede Report begins compiling a singles chart on May 31, 1975. The first singles chart is published on June 14, 1975. From this point on, *Steede Report* charts are used.

Date	Title / Artist	Weeks
05/31/75	**Pinball Wizard** Elton John	2
06/14/75	**Sister Golden Hair** America	2
06/28/75	**Love Will Keep Us Together** Captain & Tennille	4
07/26/75	**Listen To What The Man Said** Paul McCartney & Wings	2
08/09/75	**The Hustle** Van McCoy	1
08/16/75	**Jive Talkin'** Bee Gees	4
09/13/75	**Rhinestone Cowboy** Glen Campbell	2
09/27/75	**Get Down Tonight** K.C. & The Sunshine Band	1
10/04/75	**Ballroom Blitz** Sweet	2
10/18/75	**Fame** David Bowie	1
10/25/75	**Bad Blood** Neil Sedaka	5
11/29/75	**Island Girl** Elton John	4
12/27/75	**That's The Way I Like It** K.C. & The Sunshine Band	3

1976

Date	Title / Artist	Weeks
01/17/76	**Saturday Night** Bay City Rollers	1
01/24/76	**I Write The Songs** Barry Manilow	1
01/31/76	**Convoy** C.W. McCall	2
02/14/76	**You Sexy Thing** Hot Chocolate	1
02/21/76	**50 Ways To Leave Your Lover** Paul Simon	3
03/13/76	**All By Myself** Eric Carmen	3
04/03/76	**Dream Weaver** Gary Wright	1
04/10/76	**December 1963 (Oh What A Night)** Four Seasons	2
04/24/76	**Right Back Where We Started From** Maxine Nightingale	1
05/01/76	**Boogie Fever** Sylvers	4
05/29/76	**Shannon** Henry Gross	1
06/05/76	**Silly Love Songs** Wings	3
06/26/76	**Get Up And Boogie (That's Right)** Silver Convention	1
07/03/76	**Love Hangover** Diana Ross	1
07/10/76	**Afternoon Delight** Starland Vocal Band	5
08/14/76	**Don't Go Breaking My Heart** Elton John & Kiki Dee	6
09/25/76	**You'll Never Find Another Love Like Mine** Lou Rawls	1
10/02/76	**Play That Funky Music** Wild Cherry	2
10/16/76	**Disco Duck** Rick Dees And His Casts Of Idiots	3
11/06/76	**If You Leave Me Now** Chicago	3
11/27/76	**Beth** Kiss	1
12/04/76	**Tonight's The Night (Gonna Be Alright)** Rod Stewart	7

The Number One Hits

Date   **Title** Artist   Weeks

1977

Date	Title / Artist	Weeks
01/22/77	**You Make Me Feel Like Dancing** Leo Sayer	2
02/05/77	**Hot Line** Sylvers	1
02/12/77	**Blinded By The Light** Manfred Mann's Earth Band	4
03/12/77	**New Kid In Town** Eagles	1
03/19/77	**Love Theme From "A Star Is Born" (Evergreen)** Barbra Streisand	6
04/30/77	**Don't Give Up On Us** David Soul	2
05/14/77	**Hotel California** Eagles	2
05/28/77	**When I Need You** Leo Sayer	3
06/18/77	**Sir Duke** Stevie Wonder	2
07/02/77	**Dreams** Fleetwood Mac	2
07/16/77	**Undercover Angel** Alan O'Day	3
08/06/77	**Da Doo Ron Ron** Shaun Cassidy	1
08/13/77	**I'm In You** Peter Frampton	1

From this point on, the Canadian Recording Industry Association charts are used.

Date	Title / Artist	Weeks
08/24/77	**Da Doo Ron Ron** Shaun Cassidy	2
09/07/77	**I Just Want To Be Your Everything** Andy Gibb	4
10/05/77	**Star Wars Theme/Cantina Band** Meco	6
11/16/77	**You Light Up My Life** Debby Boone	12

1978

Date	Title / Artist	Weeks
02/08/78	**Short People** Randy Newman	2
02/22/78	**Stayin' Alive** Bee Gees	10
05/03/78	**Night Fever** Bee Gees	4
05/31/78	**You're The One That I Want** John Travolta/Olivia Newton-John	2
06/14/78	**It's A Heartache** Bonnie Tyler	2
06/28/78	**You're The One That I Want** John Travolta/Olivia Newton-John	2
07/12/78	**It's A Heartache** Bonnie Tyler	2
07/26/78	**You're The One That I Want** John Travolta/Olivia Newton-John	2
08/09/78	**Grease** Frankie Valli	4
09/06/78	**Three Times A Lady** Commodores	2
09/20/78	**Grease** Frankie Valli	2
10/04/78	**Three Times A Lady** Commodores	2
10/18/78	**Kiss You All Over** Exile	4
11/15/78	**Boogie Oogie Oogie** A Taste Of Honey	2
11/29/78	**MacArthur Park** Donna Summer	2
12/13/78	**You Don't Bring Me Flowers** Barbra Streisand/Neil Diamond	2
12/27/78	**Le Freak** Chic	8

The Number One Hits

Date   **Title** Artist   Weeks

1979

Date	Title Artist	Weeks
02/21/79	**Da Ya Think I'm Sexy** Rod Stewart	8
04/18/79	**In The Navy** Village People *	2
05/02/79	**Heart Of Glass** Blondie	6
06/13/79	**Reunited** Peaches & Herb	2
06/27/79	**Hot Stuff** Donna Summer	2
07/11/79	**You Take My Breath Away** Rex Smith	2
07/25/79	**Ring My Bell** Anita Ward	4
08/22/79	**Born To Be Alive** Patrick Hernandez	2
09/05/79	**I Was Made For Lovin' You** Kiss	2
09/19/79	**My Sharona** The Knack	2
10/03/79	**Pop Muzik** M	10
12/12/79	**Babe** Styx	4

1980

Date	Title Artist	Weeks
01/09/80	**Pop Muzik** M	2
01/23/80	**Rapper's Delight** Sugarhill Gang	8
03/19/80	**Another Brick In The Wall** Pink Floyd	6
04/30/80	**Call Me** Blondie	4
05/28/80	**Funkytown** Lipps Inc.	6
07/09/80	**It's Still Rock And Roll To Me** Billy Joel	1
07/16/80	**Funkytown** Lipps Inc.	2

From this point on, the Canadian Broadcasting Corporation charts are used.

Date	Title Artist	Weeks
09/13/80	**Emotional Rescue** Rolling Stones	1
09/20/80	**All Out Of Love** Air Supply	4
10/18/80	**Another One Bites The Dust** Queen	4
11/15/80	**Woman In Love** Barbra Streisand	4
12/13/80	**(Just Like) Starting Over** John Lennon	7

1981

Date	Title Artist	Weeks
01/31/81	**The Tide Is High** Blondie	4
02/28/81	**Woman** John Lennon	5
04/04/81	**Rapture** Blondie	3
04/25/81	**Morning Train (9 To 5)** Sheena Easton	5
05/30/81	**Bette Davis Eyes** Kim Carnes	5
07/04/81	**Medley** Stars On 45	3
07/25/81	**The One That You Love** Air Supply	2
08/08/81	**Gemini Dream** Moody Blues	4
09/05/81	**Urgent** Foreigner	1
09/12/81	**Endless Love** Diana Ross & Lionel Richie	4
10/10/81	**Start Me Up** Rolling Stones	4
11/07/81	**Private Eyes** Daryl Hall & John Oates	1

The Number One Hits

Date	Title Artist	Weeks
11/14/81	**Every Little Thing She Does Is Magic** The Police	1
11/21/81	**My Girl (Gone, Gone, Gone)** Chilliwack	3
12/12/81	**Young Turks** Rod Stewart	6

1982

Date	Title Artist	Weeks
01/23/82	**Centerfold** J. Geils Band	5
02/27/82	**Tainted Love** Soft Cell	3
03/20/82	**I Love Rock N' Roll** Joan Jett & The Blackhearts	7
05/08/82	**Don't You Want Me** Human League	1
05/15/82	**Don't Talk To Strangers** Rick Springfield	2
05/29/82	**Ebony & Ivory** Paul McCartney with Stevie Wonder	5
07/03/82	**Rosanna** Toto	2
07/17/82	**Hurts So Good** John Cougar	1
07/24/82	**Abracadabra** The Steve Miller Band	2
08/07/82	**Eye Of The Tiger** Survivor	6
09/18/82	**Jack & Diane** John Cougar	5
10/23/82	**Downunder** Men At Work	3
11/13/82	**New World Man** Rush	1
11/20/82	**Look Of Love** ABC	1
11/27/82	**Up Where We Belong** Joe Cocker & Jennifer Warnes	2
12/11/82	**It's Raining Again** Supertramp	2
12/25/82	**Maneater** Daryl Hall & John Oates	3

1983

The Record begins publishing a singles chart on January 17, 1983. From this point on, *The Record* charts are used.

Date	Title Artist	Weeks
01/17/83	**Dirty Laundry** Don Henley	1
01/24/83	**Mickey** Toni Basil	5
02/28/83	**Pass The Dutchie** Musical Youth	1
03/07/83	**Do You Really Want To Hurt Me** Culture Club	3
03/28/83	**Billie Jean** Michael Jackson	7
05/16/83	**Beat It** Michael Jackson	2
05/30/83	**Flashdance...What A Feelin'** Irene Cara	6
07/11/83	**Electric Avenue** Eddy Grant	5
08/15/83	**Every Breath You Take** The Police	5
09/19/83	**Maniac** Michael Sembello	2
10/03/83	**Sweet Dreams (Are Made Of This)** Eurythmics	1
10/10/83	**Maniac** Michael Sembello	1
10/17/83	**Sweet Dreams (Are Made Of This)** Eurythmics	2
10/31/83	**True** Spandau Ballet	2
11/14/83	**Islands In The Stream** Kenny Rogers/Dolly Parton	9

The Number One Hits

Date   Title Artist   Weeks

1984

Date	Title / Artist	Weeks
01/16/84	**Say Say Say** Paul McCartney & Michael Jackson	1
01/23/84	**Major Tom (Coming Home)** Peter Schilling	1
01/30/84	**Karma Chameleon** Culture Club	7
03/19/84	**99 Luftballons** Nena	2
04/02/84	**Girls Just Wanna Have Fun** Cyndi Lauper	6
05/14/84	**Against All Odds (Take A Look At Me Now)** Phil Collins	3
06/04/84	**To All The Girls I've Loved Before** Julio Iglesias & Willie Nelson	3
06/25/84	**Time After Time** Cyndi Lauper	3
07/16/84	**Let's Hear It For The Boy** Deniece Williams	1
07/23/84	**Self Control** Laura Branigan	3
08/13/84	**When Doves Cry** Prince	2
08/27/84	**Ghostbusters** Ray Parker, Jr.	5
10/01/84	**What's Love Got To Do With It** Tina Turner	1
10/08/84	**Missing You** John Waite	3
10/29/84	**I Just Called To Say I Love You** Stevie Wonder	11

1985

Date	Title / Artist	Weeks
01/14/85	**Do They Know It's Christmas?** Band Aid *	1
01/21/85	**Like A Virgin** Madonna	3
02/11/85	**Easy Lover** Phillip Bailey/Phil Collins	6
03/25/85	**I Want To Know What Love Is** Foreigner	2
04/08/85	**Shout** Tears For Fears	2
04/22/85	**One Night In Bangkok** Murray Head	1
04/29/85	**Tears Are Not Enough** Northern Lights	2
05/13/85	**Shout** Tears For Fears	2
05/27/85	**Tears Are Not Enough** Northern Lights	2
06/10/85	**Everybody Wants To Rule The World** Tears For Fears	2
06/24/85	**Sussudio** Phil Collins	2
07/08/85	**Never Surrender** Corey Hart	7
08/26/85	**Everytime You Go Away** Paul Young	1
09/02/85	**Never Surrender** Corey Hart	2
09/16/85	**We Don't Need Another Hero** Tina Turner	4
10/14/85	**Part Time Lover** Stevie Wonder	3
11/04/85	**Money For Nothing** Dire Straits	2
11/18/85	**Part Time Lover** Stevie Wonder	4
12/16/85	**Separate Lives** Phil Collins & Marilyn Martin	1
12/23/85	**Live Is Life** Opus	7

1986

Date	Title / Artist	Weeks
02/10/86	**Say You, Say Me** Lionel Richie	2
02/24/86	**That's What Friends Are For** Dionne & Friends	3
03/17/86	**Conga** Miami Sound Machine	2
03/31/86	**How Will I Know** Whitney Houston	2

The Number One Hits

Date | Title Artist | Weeks

Date	Title Artist	Weeks
04/14/86	**Nikita** Elton John	4
05/12/86	**Don't Forget Me (When I'm Gone)** Glass Tiger	2
05/26/86	**Let's Go All The Way** Sly Fox	1
06/02/86	**West End Girls** Pet Shop Boys	2
06/16/86	**Live To Tell** Madonna	5
07/21/86	**Sledgehammer** Peter Gabriel	4
08/18/86	**Papa Don't Preach** Madonna	6
09/29/86	**Glory Of Love** Peter Cetera	1
10/06/86	**Venus** Bananarama	2
10/20/86	**Take My Breath Away** Berlin	3
11/10/86	**Spirit In The Sky** Dr. And The Medics	2
11/24/86	**True Colors** Cyndi Lauper	1
12/01/86	**Amanda** Boston	1
12/08/86	**The Lady In Red** Chris DeBurgh	8

1987

Date	Title Artist	Weeks
02/02/87	**Everybody Have Fun Tonight** Wang Chung	1
02/09/87	**Walk Like An Egyptian** Bangles	3
03/02/87	**Touch Me (I Want Your Body)** Samantha Fox	7
04/20/87	**The Final Countdown** Europe	1
04/27/87	**Nothing's Gonna Stop Us Now** Starship	3
05/18/87	**Lean On Me** Club Nouveau	3
06/08/87	**(I Just) Died In Your Arms** Cutting Crew	1
06/15/87	**La Isla Bonita** Madonna	1
06/22/87	**(I Just) Died In Your Arms** Cutting Crew	1
06/29/87	**I Wanna Dance With Somebody (Who Loves Me)** Whitney Houston	2
07/13/87	**You Keep Me Hangin' On** Kim Wilde	2
07/27/87	**I Wanna Dance With Somebody (Who Loves Me)** Whitney Houston	4
08/24/87	**Alone** Heart	2
09/07/87	**Who's That Girl** Madonna	2
09/21/87	**La Bamba** Los Lobos	7
11/09/87	**Bad** Michael Jackson	1
11/16/87	**Paper In Fire** John Cougar Mellencamp	1
11/23/87	**Mony Mony** Billy Idol	1
11/30/87	**Faith** George Michael	12

1988

Date	Title Artist	Weeks
02/22/88	**Pop Goes The World** Men Without Hats	1
02/29/88	**Pump Up The Volume** M/A/R/R/S	3
03/21/88	**Never Gonna Give You Up** Rick Astley	3
04/11/88	**Pump Up The Volume** M/A/R/R/S	1
04/18/88	**Never Gonna Give You Up** Rick Astley	1
04/25/88	**Get Outta My Dreams, Get Into My Car** Billy Ocean	5

The Number One Hits

Date	Title Artist	Weeks
05/30/88	**Always On My Mind** Pet Shop Boys	4
06/27/88	**Beds Are Burning** Midnight Oil	2
07/11/88	**Together Forever** Rick Astley	3
08/01/88	**Foolish Beat** Debbie Gibson	1
08/08/88	**Roll With It** Steve Winwood	3
08/29/88	**I Don't Wanna Go On With You Like That** Elton John	3
09/19/88	**Simply Irresistible** Robert Palmer	3
10/10/88	**Better Be Home Soon** Crowded House	2
10/24/88	**Don't Worry, Be Happy** Bobby McFerrin	4
11/21/88	**Groovy Kind Of Love** Phil Collins	5
12/26/88	**The Locomotion** Kylie Minogue	4

1989

Date	Title Artist	Weeks
01/23/89	**Baby, I Love Your Way/Freebird Medley** Will To Power	2
02/06/89	**Waiting For A Star To Fall** Boy Meets Girl	1
02/13/89	**Two Hearts** Phil Collins	2
02/27/89	**She Wants To Dance With Me** Rick Astley	3
03/20/89	**You Got It** Roy Orbison	1
03/27/89	**Straight Up** Paula Abdul	5
05/01/89	**She Drives Me Crazy** Fine Young Cannibals	2
05/15/89	**Like A Prayer** Madonna	1
05/22/89	**Girl You Know It's True** Milli Vanilli	1
05/29/89	**Like A Prayer** Madonna	2
06/12/89	**The Look** Roxette	1
06/19/89	**Forever Your Girl** Paula Abdul	3
07/10/89	**Buffalo Stance** Neneh Cherry	5
08/14/89	**Baby Don't Forget My Number** Milli Vanilli	1
08/21/89	**Batdance** Prince	2
09/04/89	**On Our Own** Bobby Brown	4
10/02/89	**Right Here Waiting** Richard Marx	2
10/16/89	**Cold Hearted** Paula Abdul	2
10/30/89	**Miss You Much** Janet Jackson	1
11/06/89	**Girl I'm Gonna Miss You** Milli Vanilli	1
11/13/89	**Miss You Much** Janet Jackson	1
11/20/89	**Listen To Your Heart** Roxette	2
12/04/89	**Bust A Move** Young M.C.	1
12/11/89	**Blame It On The Rain** Milli Vanilli	2
12/25/89	**Swing The Mood** Jive Bunny & The Mastermixers	4

1990

Date	Title Artist	Weeks
01/22/90	**Blame It On The Rain** Milli Vanilli	2
02/05/90	**Back To Life** Soul II Soul	3
02/26/90	**Opposites Attract** Paula Abdul	6
04/09/90	**Let Your Backbone Slide** Maestro Fresh-Wes	1
04/16/90	**All Around The World** Lisa Stansfield	5

The Number One Hits

Date	Title Artist	Weeks
05/21/90	**Vogue** Madonna	3
06/11/90	**All I Wanna Do Is Make Love To You** Heart	2
06/25/90	**Step By Step** New Kids On The Block	1
07/02/90	**U Can't Touch This** M.C. Hammer	3
07/23/90	**Step By Step** New Kids On The Block	3
08/13/90	**Bird On A Wire** The Neville Brothers	2
08/27/90	**Unskinny Bop** Poison	1
09/03/90	**Vision Of Love** Mariah Carey	1
09/10/90	**Release Me** Wilson Phillips	2
09/24/90	**Unskinny Bop** Poison	1
10/01/90	**Vision Of Love** Mariah Carey	1
10/08/90	**Unskinny Bop** Poison	1
10/15/90	**Release Me** Wilson Phillips	3
11/05/90	**Suicide Blonde** INXS	2
11/19/90	**Praying For Time** George Michael	1
11/26/90	**Something To Believe In** Poison	2
12/10/90	**Stranded** Heart	1
12/17/90	**Love Takes Time** Mariah Carey	1
12/24/90	**Wiggle It** 2 In A Room	6

1991

Date	Title Artist	Weeks
02/04/91	**Gonna Make You Sweat** C&C Music Factory	6
03/18/91	**Sadeness Part 1** Enigma	3
04/08/91	**I've Been Thinking About You** Londonbeat	4
05/06/91	**Joyride** Roxette	5
06/10/91	**More Than Words** Extreme	2
06/24/91	**Not Like Kissing You** West End Girls	1
07/01/91	**Rush Rush** Paula Abdul	4
07/29/91	**(Everything I Do) I Do It For You** Bryan Adams	12
10/21/91	**Enter Sandman** Metallica	2
11/04/91	**Life Is A Highway** Tom Cochrane	6
12/16/91	**Black Or White** Michael Jackson	8

1992

Date	Title Artist	Weeks
02/10/92	**Finally** Ce Ce Peniston	2
02/24/92	**I'm Too Sexy** Right Said Fred	3
03/16/92	**Don't Let The Sun Go Down On Me** George Michael & Elton John	1
03/23/92	**Justified And Ancient** The KLF featuring Tammy Wynette	6
05/04/92	**Save The Best For Last** Vanessa Williams	2
05/18/92	**Tears In Heaven** Eric Clapton	1
05/25/92	**Jump** Kris Kross	6
07/06/92	**I'll Be There** Mariah Carey	2
07/20/92	**Achy Breaky Heart** Billy Ray Cyrus	4
08/17/92	**This Used To Be My Playground** Madonna	6

The Number One Hits

Date	Title Artist	Weeks
09/28/92	**Humpin' Around** Bobby Brown	2
10/12/92	**End Of The Road** Boyz II Men	1
10/19/92	**Please Don't Go** KWS	3
11/09/92	**End Of The Road** Boyz II Men	10

1993

Date	Title Artist	Weeks
01/18/93	**How Do You Talk To An Angel** The Heights	2
02/01/93	**Deeper And Deeper** Madonna	2
02/15/93	**Flex** Mad Cobra	3
03/08/93	**Hip Hop Hooray** Naughty By Nature	2
03/22/93	**Informer** Snow	2
04/05/93	**Hip Hop Hooray** Naughty By Nature	3
04/26/93	**Cats In The Cradle** Ugly Kid Joe	4
05/24/93	**No Limit** 2 Unlimited	1
05/31/93	**That's The Way Love Goes** Janet Jackson	6
07/12/93	**Can't Help Falling In Love** UB40	8
09/06/93	**Oh Carolina** Shaggy	2
09/20/93	**Rain** Madonna	1
09/27/93	**If I Had No Loot** Tony! Toni! Tone!	2
10/11/93	**If** Janet Jackson	1
10/18/93	**Dreamlover** Mariah Carey	1
10/25/93	**Whoot, There It Is** 95 South	1
11/01/93	**Dreamlover** Mariah Carey	2
11/15/93	**Soul To Squeeze** Red Hot Chili Peppers	1
11/22/93	**Please Forgive Me** Bryan Adams	4
12/20/93	**Said I Loved You...But I Lied** Michael Bolton	12

1994

Date	Title Artist	Weeks
03/14/94	**The Power Of Love** Celine Dion	7
05/02/94	**Streets Of Philadelphia** Bruce Springsteen	1
05/09/94	**The Power Of Love** Celine Dion	3
05/30/94	**Streets Of Philadelphia** Bruce Springsteen	2
06/13/94	**The Power Of Love** Celine Dion	2
06/27/94	**If You Go** Jon Secada	5
08/01/94	**Can You Feel The Love Tonight** Elton John *	9
10/03/94	**I'll Make Love To You** Boyz II Men	5
11/07/94	**Secret** Madonna	2
11/21/94	**I'll Make Love To You** Boyz II Men	1
11/28/94	**Secret** Madonna	7

1995

Date	Title Artist	Weeks
01/16/95	**Always** Bon Jovi	7
03/06/95	**Sukiyaki** 4 P.M.	7
04/24/95	**Take A Bow** Madonna	1

The Number One Hits

Date	Title Artist	Weeks
05/01/95	**Have You Ever Really Loved A Woman?** Bryan Adams	10
07/10/95	**This Is How We Do It** Montell Jordan	2
07/24/95	**Macarena** Los Del Mar	9
09/25/95	**I'll Be There For You/You're All I Need To Get By** Method Man featuring Mary J. Blige	5
10/30/95	**Fantasy** Mariah Carey	1
11/06/95	**Runaway** Janet Jackson	2
11/20/95	**Fantasy** Mariah Carey	11

1996

02/05/96	**Stayin' Alive** N-Trance	9

The Record discontinues its Retail Singles chart. From this point on, *The Record*'s Hit Parade charts are used.

04/08/96	**Follow You Down** Gin Blossoms	4
05/06/96	**Because You Loved Me** Celine Dion	1
05/13/96	**Old Man & Me** Hootie & The Blowfish	8
07/08/96	**Ahead By A Century** Tragically Hip	1
07/15/96	**Give Me One Reason** Tracy Chapman	1
07/22/96	**The Only Thing That Looks Good On Me Is You** Bryan Adams	1
07/29/96	**You Learn** Alanis Morissette	3
08/19/96	**Change The World** Eric Clapton	3
09/09/96	**Key West Intermezzo (I Saw You First)** John Mellencamp	8

SoundScan begins compiling a top 200 singles chart on October 20, 1996. From this point on, the SoundScan singles charts are used.

10/20/96	**Where Do You Go?** No Mercy	7
12/08/96	**God Bless The Child** Shania Twain *	9

1997

02/09/97	**Discotheque** U2 *	1
02/16/97	**Don't Cry For Me Argentina** Madonna *	6
03/30/97	**I Want You** Savage Garden	4
04/27/97	**Can't Nobody Hold Me Down** Puff Daddy	8
06/22/97	**I'll Be Missing You** Puff Daddy & Faith Evans (feat. 112) *	13
09/21/97	**Candle In The Wind 1997/Something About The Way You Look Tonight** Elton John *	35

1998

05/24/98	**The Boy Is Mine** Brandy & Monica *	15
09/06/98	**Candle In The Wind 1997/Something About The Way You Look Tonight** Elton John	7

The Number One Hits

Date	Title Artist	Weeks
10/25/98	**Sweetest Thing** U2 *	1
11/01/98	**Thank U** Alanis Morissette	1
11/08/98	**Candle In The Wind 1997/Something About The Way You Look Tonight** Elton John	3
11/29/98	**...Baby One More Time** Britney Spears	2
12/13/98	**Goodbye** Spice Girls *	13

1999

Date	Title Artist	Weeks
03/14/99	**The Animal Song** Savage Garden *	3
04/04/99	**Squeeze Toy** Boomtang Boys *	4
05/02/99	**I Want It That Way** Backstreet Boys *	3
05/23/99	**Livin' La Vida Loca** Ricky Martin	3
06/13/99	**Last Kiss** Pearl Jam *	6
07/25/99	**The Day The World Went Away** Nine Inch Nails *	1+

Codes
Date: Date record first reached the #1 position
Weeks: Number of weeks record stayed at the #1 position
+: Still at #1 on the SoundScan singles chart as of July 25, 1999
*: Debuted in the top 40 at #1